MARRIAGE, FAMILY, AND RELATIONSHIPS

A CROSS-CULTURAL ENCYCLOPEDIA

ENCYCLOPEDIAS OF THE HUMAN EXPERIENCE

David Levinson, Series Editor

Marriage, Family, and Relationships

A Cross-Cultural Encyclopedia

Gwen J. Broude

ABC-CLIO
Santa Barbara, California
Denver, Colorado
Oxford, England

Library of Congress Cataloging-in-Publication Data

Broude, Gwen J.
    Marriage, family, and relationships : a cross-cultural
encyclopedia / Gwen J. Broude.
        p.   cm. — (Encyclopedias of the human experience)
    Includes bibliographical references and index.
        1. Marriage—Cross-cultural studies—Encyclopedias.
    2. Family—Cross-cultural studies—Encyclopedias. 3. Kinship—
    Cross-cultural studies—Encyclopedias. I. Title. II. Series.
    GN480.B76 1994   306.8'03—dc20   94-38979

ISBN 0-87436-736-0 (alk. paper)

01 00 99 98 97 96 95 94   10 9 8 7 6 5 4 3 2 1 (hc)

ABC-CLIO, Inc.
130 Cremona Drive, P.O. Box 1911
Santa Barbara, California 93116-1911

This book is printed on acid-free paper ⊗.
Manufactured in the United States of America

To John W. M. Whiting

and

To Kenneth R. Livingston and Nicholas B. Livingston

CONTENTS

Preface, xi

ADOLESCENT MALE-FEMALE INTERACTION, 3
AFFECTION BETWEEN THE SEXES, 4
AFFECTION, SAME-SEX DISPLAY OF, 6
AGE-GRADES, 8
AGE-SETS, 9
ALTRUISM, 13
ASSOCIATIONS, 19
ATTACHMENT, PRIMARY, 24
ATTRACTIVENESS, 29
AVOIDANCE RELATIONSHIPS, 32

BETROTHAL, 37
BOASTING, 38
BRIDE CAPTURE, 39
BRIDE PRICE, 40
BRIDE SERVICE, 43

CHAPERONS, 47
CHILD BETROTHAL, 48
CONCUBINAGE, 49
CONTINENCE AS A VIRTUE, 51

COURTSHIP, 52
CUCKOLDRY, 56

DEFERENCE OF WIFE TO HUSBAND, 61
DEFLORATION CUSTOMS, 63
DESCENT RULES AND GROUPS, 64
DIFFERENTIAL REPRODUCTIVE SUCCESS, 71
DIVORCE, 73
DOUBLE STANDARD IN SEXUAL BEHAVIOR, 82
DOWRY, 87

ELDERLY, 89
ELOPEMENT, 95
ENDOGAMY, 97
EXOGAMY, 99

FAMILY, 101
FAMILY LIFE, 104
FAMILY SLEEPING ARRANGEMENTS, 108
FATHERS ATTENDING BIRTHS, 110
FEMALE SECLUSION, 111
FICTIVE KIN, 114
FITNESS, 115

CONTENTS

FOREPLAY, 116
FRIENDSHIPS, ADULT, 117

GIFT EXCHANGE, 121

HOUSEHOLD, 123
HUMAN RELATIONSHIPS, EVOLUTION OF, 127
HUSBAND-WIFE EATING ARRANGEMENTS, 132
HUSBAND-WIFE JOINT WORK ACTIVITIES, 133
HUSBAND-WIFE LEISURE, 137
HUSBAND-WIFE RELATIONSHIPS, 138
HUSBAND-WIFE SLEEPING ARRANGEMENTS, 142
HYPERGAMY, 144

IMPOTENCE, 147
INCEST TABOO, 148

JEALOUSY BETWEEN CO-WIVES, 153
JEALOUSY BETWEEN MALES AND FEMALES, 155
JOKING RELATIONSHIPS, 158

KIN SELECTION, 161
KINSHIP, 164
KINSHIP TERMINOLOGY, 169

LEVIRATE, 173
LOVE MAGIC, 175

MALE-FEMALE HOSTILITY, 177
MALE-FEMALE INTERACTION, 179
MALE-FEMALE STATUS, RELATIVE, 182
MALE SEXUAL AGGRESSION, 187
MARRIAGE, 189
MARRIAGE, ARRANGED, 192
MARRIAGE, COUSIN, 196
MARRIAGE, TRIAL, 198
MARRIAGE AGE, 199
MARRIAGE CEREMONIES, 201
MARRIAGE FLEXIBILITY, 205
MARRIAGE FORMS, 206
MARRIAGE PARTNERS, CRITERIA FOR CHOOSING, 214
MARRIAGE PARTNERS, SELECTION OF, 219
MEN'S HOUSES, 222

MENSTRUAL TABOOS, 224
MODESTY, 227

NATURAL SELECTION, 231
NEWLYWEDS, 235

PARENTS-IN-LAW, 241
PREGNANCY, PREMARITAL, 243
PROMISCUITY, 245
PROSTITUTION, 246

RAPE, 251
REPRODUCTIVE STRATEGIES, 255
RESIDENCE RULES, 260
RESPECT RELATIONSHIPS, 263
ROMANTIC LOVE, 265

SEGREGATION OF CHILDREN FROM PARENTS, 269
SEGREGATION OF SEXES IN CHILDHOOD, 271
SEX, ATTITUDES TOWARD, 273
SEX, EXTRAMARITAL, 275
SEX, FREQUENCY OF, 278
SEX, INITIATIVE IN, 279
SEX, PREMARITAL, 281
SEX, TALK ABOUT, 285
SEX, TECHNIQUES FOR INITIATING, 287
SEX TABOO, POSTPARTUM, 290
SEX TABOOS, 291
SEX TRAINING IN CHILDHOOD, 293
SEXUAL BEHAVIOR, SAME-SEX, 296
SEXUAL PARTNERS, FIRST, 300
SEXUAL RECEPTIVITY, 301
SEXUAL RELATIONS, PATTERNS OF, 303
SEXUAL RELATIONS, PRIVACY IN, 304
SEXUAL SELECTION, 308
SLEEP-CRAWLING, 310
SORORATE, 311
SPOUSE BEATING, 312

TRANSVESTISM, 317

VIRGINITY, 321

Wedding Night, 327
Widow Remarriage, 328
Widower Remarriage, 333
Wife Sharing, 334
Woman Exchange, 336

Bibliography, 339

Illustration Credits, 353

Index, 355

Humans are profoundly social beings. This is so much the case that marriage seems to lengthen a person's life, a clear indication of the importance of social relationships, not just in our daily lives but also to our chances of staying alive. Contact with the living plays such a crucial role in our well-being that the health and life-span of people living alone is enhanced by providing them with a pet for companionship. The social nature of humans also becomes quite clear when we look at the effects of the absence of human contact. Hurdles to one's ability to form relationships are associated with certain forms of mental illness. For example, a key characteristic of autistic children is their inability to become attached to their caretakers. Similarly, schizophrenics are marked by their inability to connect with others. Human infants who are deprived of contact with a caretaker fail to thrive, and the longer they are deprived the more profound and enduring the effects. The same is true for nonhuman primates, rat pups, and other immature animals, indicating just how fundamental social relationships are for all social species. Deprivation of caretakers affects an infant's nervous system and other biological systems, underscoring the degree to which social animals, including human beings, need and expect social interaction in order to develop and function normally.

Because all humans are members of a social species, people in all cultures share the fundamental need to be with other people. But the similarities regarding the nature of human relationships across cultures do not stop here. Rather, the details of relationships from one culture to the next sound quite alike in a multitude of important ways. Thus, for example, we find the same types of relationships appearing over and over around the globe. Mothers and fathers form special attachments to their children and children to their parents. Mothers and not fathers are primarily responsible for the day-to-day care of babies and young children. People form friendships, usually with other people of the same sex and social status. Everywhere around the world, women and men marry, and every culture has rules that limit the choice of a spouse. Human beings everywhere live in families composed of relatives. When people need help, they are very likely to enlist the aid of kin, and people are more likely to help their kin than nonkin. Human beings across cultures also have similar emotional responses to other people. Boys and girls form romantic attachments the world over, even if feeling or expressing romantic love is not customarily condoned in the society in which they live. Where cultural rules prohibit marriage based on love, couples often elope, and the lure of romance is so well recognized even in cultures that condemn it that elopement is accepted as an escape hatch for star-crossed couples. Men and women the world over become jealous when their partners are unfaithful, and the reaction of husbands to infidelity tends to be more extreme than that of wives. Elderly people are respected to the degree that they remain in possession of goods, skills, or knowledge of value to other members of their community. A man usually avoids marrying a woman who is known as promiscuous, and a woman rarely marries a man whose status is lower than her own.

Cultures also differ in the way in which some aspects of human relationships are expressed. For example, in some cultures an individual's attachment to his or her parents is expected to remain primary for a lifetime, even after marriage, while in other cultures the husband-wife bond is expected to overshadow childhood affection and loyalty to parents. In some cultures boys and girls are expected to engage in premarital sex and to choose their own spouses, while in others premarital sex is condemned and marriages are arranged by third parties. In some cultures men and women live largely separate lives, while in other cultures the sexes mingle freely. In some cultures women are politically, economically, or socially inferior to men, while in others the relative status of the sexes approaches equality. Some societies have rules that require punishment for women who engage in extramarital affairs but ignore the sexual affairs of husbands, while in other societies the rules call for both men and women to be punished. Clearly then, some human relationships are played out in noticeably different ways in different societies around the world.

This volume covers major topics relevant to human relationships from a cross-cultural perspective. Some of these topics have to do with the basis of human relationships: processes such as altruism, attachment, kin selection, and romantic love. Others are general categories of relationships, such as marriage, family, sexual behavior, and kin groups. Still others apply to specific relationships, such as avoidance, extramarital sex, or trial marriage. And last are customs that have to do with the formation or playing out of relationships, such as attractiveness, betrothal, love magic, and spouse beating. Thus, while I cover a wide range of major topics, I also describe many other beliefs and customs specific to only a few cultures or, sometimes, only a single culture.

How do we make sense of all this patterning and diversity in the expression of human relationships around the world? Perhaps the most fruitful approach—from the perspective of understanding patterning in human relationships—is to begin with the premise that all human beings are born "blank slates" who come equipped with a set of predispositions to experience and behave in certain ways, and that these predispositions are reflected in the similarities we see across cultures. In this view, human relationships are alike across cultures because inborn human predispositions are similar regardless of where a person happens to be born.

The idea that humans and other species come equipped with a set of predispositions is consistent with the principles set forth in Charles Darwin's theory of evolution by natural selection. The evolutionary perspective suggests that particular physical characteristics, behavioral profiles, and related or underlying psychological mechanisms appear in a given species today because they were advantageous to the survival of members of the species in the past. In particular, they directly or indirectly helped individuals possessing them to increase the representation of their genes in the gene pool of the species. What kind of traits would have this effect? Individuals who are more successful than their neighbors in surviving to maturity, reproducing, and helping their biological kin to survive and reproduce will increase the representation of their genes in the gene pool of their species. To the extent that these traits are genetically grounded, they will appear more and more regularly down through the generations. Some will become components of what we call human nature.

The evolutionary process takes place very, very slowly. Thus, the traits that typify humans today evolved in an environment very different from the one in which most people live at present. This is because the agricultural and industrial societies in which most people now live are very recent developments—the former in existence for a few thousand years and the latter for only a few hundred years. Archaeologists remind us that for some 99 percent of the time that humans have existed as a distinct species (about 4 to 5 million years) we lived as hunter-gatherers or foragers (as they are sometimes now called.) This is the context in which traits of modern human beings have evolved because this is the context in which the human species was required to survive, reproduce, and help its kin for most of its existence as human beings. Of course, our species is still evolving, and we no longer live as hunter-gatherers, but we have not yet had time to shed the traits that made us successful in the past but are no longer useful in our current lifestyles. Thus, from the evolutionary perspective, we are still hunter-gatherers in many important ways.

What traits would have promoted the survival and reproduction of an individual and what traits would have inclined a person to promote the survival and reproductive efforts of kin in a hunter-gatherer world? Archaeologists and anthropologists tell us that our ancestors probably lived in small groups composed of relatives. A division of labor probably existed, with a woman gathering vegetables and fruit for herself, her mate, and her children and a man hunting for himself and his relatives and protecting the camp from predators and human antagonists. Females would have been responsible for childrearing, as they were the providers of nourishment and baby care is inconsistent with the requirements of hunting.

Even this sketchy description of the hunter-gatherer past allows us to make some predictions about the forms of relationship that would prove useful to our ancestors. For instance, imagine two men who lived in the remote past. One sought the company of other people of his kind while the other preferred to be alone. Who would be more likely to survive and reproduce? The sociable man would have the protection of the people with whom he interacted. He would have other people to help him and to share with him, and he would eventually find a woman to have children with. His mate would provide him with fruit and vegetables, and probably with firewood and water as well, and care for his children, while he would supply meat, hides, and other raw materials and provide protection. If he preferred to live with relatives rather than strangers, he would be in a position to help and be helped by those whom he would favor and who would favor him over strangers. The loner, by contrast, would have to fend for himself when faced by a predator or hostile human being. There would be no one to help him if he were hurt or hungry. His chances of finding a mate would be minimal. As a loner, he would have little opportunity to help or be helped by relatives.

Clearly, the sociable man would have a far greater chance of promoting the representation of his genes in the gene pool of his kind, and this begins to explain why we are such a profoundly social species. Those of our ancestors who sought the company of others were far more likely to survive and reproduce. They would also have had far more opportunities to cooperate and reciprocally assist relatives. We can also see why a tendency to form a long-term attachment with someone of the opposite sex, which we experience as romantic love and marriage, would have promoted survival and reproduction. Similarly, the special relationships that exist between parents and children would increase a mother's and father's willingness to care for a helpless infant. And individuals who formed friendships would have partners to depend on in times of need. Thus, the kinds of relationships people form the world over are just the sorts of relationships that would have been useful to our hunter-gatherer ancestors. Thus, from the evolutionary perspective, we can view those relationships or patterns of relationship that repeat across cultures as a legacy from our hunter-gatherer past. And we also need to remember that, while we are no longer hunter-gatherers, many of those same relationships and behavioral patterns continue to help individuals to promote the representation of their genes in the gene pool of today.

While the evolutionary perspective gives us a framework for understanding the similarities in relationships around the world, what about the variation that is superimposed on this regularity? First, we need to understand that these variations are not arbitrary. Rather, they seem to be responses, or adaptations, to other features of the culture or environment in which they are found. For example, for much of human history most people have lived in large families composed of relatives we would call parents, children, brothers, sisters, grandparents, aunts, uncles, and cousins. However, since the time of the industrial revolution (which actually affected different regions of the world at different times) more and more people have been living in small families composed mainly of only parents and children. These are called nuclear families. In cultures composed mainly of these nuclear families, people and families move about fairly often, and they earn their living working outside the home. This division of labor and mobility provides constraints that outweigh the human propensity to favor living with large numbers of kin for protection and support. If cross-cultural regularities reflect pan-human predispositions, then cross-cultural differences reflect the pan-human tendency to tailor behavior and customs to circumstances. Both the regularities and differences represent practical solutions to the problems that people face as they attempt to take good care of themselves, their children, and their kin.

MARRIAGE, FAMILY, AND RELATIONSHIPS

A CROSS-CULTURAL ENCYCLOPEDIA

to increase the likelihood that the warnings will be honored. These examples illustrate the extreme cultural differences regarding the extent to which boys and girls are permitted to interact. In a sample of 57 societies, 28 percent are characterized by extreme segregation of the sexes at adolescence. An additional 21 percent segregate adolescent boys and girls to some degree. The remaining 51 percent do not separate the sexes at puberty.

Cultural customs concerning the segregation of boys and girls may be related to cultural attitudes about pregnancy and about sexual relations between males and females who are not married to each other. In some societies that separate the sexes at adolescence there is also an emphasis on practicing contraception. Thus, an overall concern about containing reproduction shows up both in the practice of birth control and in attempts to limit the access of reproductively mature males and females to one another. In cultures where boys and girls freely interact they are likely to engage in sexual activity.

In Oceania, the connection between unrestricted boy-girl interaction and sexual activity is reflected in Marshallese philosophy, which assumes that the only motivation a man would have for talking to a woman would be to solicit sexual intercourse. The Marshallese, therefore, forbid males to touch or converse with females in public. Similarly, in New Guinea, once a Kwoma boy is given a small netted bag by his mother and betel-chewing apparatus by his father, he is considered to be a little man. From this time on, boys and girls avoid one another. Once a Kwoma boy leaves childhood, he will be criticized if he so much as stares at a girl, as such behavior indicates sexual interest. A boy, therefore, looks at the ground or sits or stands with his back to a woman if one should be in his vicinity. A male can talk to a female, but must never look at the woman to whom he is speaking.

Where boys and girls are allowed free contact, one or the other sex also tends to live

ADOLESCENT MALE-FEMALE INTERACTION

In the Caribbean, when Carib boys and girls reached adolescence they led active and unconstrained social lives. At sprees, adults made up sexually suggestive songs and told off-color jokes, all of which served to encourage adolescents to be sexually adventurous. Unmarried boys and girls inevitably ended up sleeping together at these social events and, indeed, their elders tried to make these encounters between the young people as easy as possible to arrange. A young man who was visiting another settlement was often provided with an unmarried girl he could try to seduce, and adolescent boys would attend sprees at as many settlements as possible in order to meet girls. The boys were aided by their fathers, who helped to organize such trips so that their sons could "sow their wild oats." Among the Havasupai of the southwestern United States, by contrast, contact between boys and girls is frowned upon, and girls are warned to stay at a respectable distance from both related and unrelated males. They are regularly overseen by female relatives apart from the parental home. A number of cultures segregate adolescents from their families, increasing the opportunity for sexual contact. For example, in the Sudan, at puberty a Nuba girl moves into a hut that she shares with five to eight other girls. Here the adolescents are visited by lovers and fiancees without any interference from parents or other adults. Marriageable Chagga girls of Tanzania sleep in a separate house that has been built for them by their fathers. Boys and girls play games and hold dances in these dormitories. In the Philippines, Ifugao boys and girls sleep in houses for the unmarried beginning as young as four years of age. Only boys stay in the males' dwelling, but the girls' dormitory can house females of all ages, as well as males. When the boys reach adolescence, they begin to visit the girls' dormitory, where much sexual activity occurs.

———

Barton, R. F. (1919) *Ifugao Law.*

Gutmann, Bruno. (1926) *Das Recht der Dschagga* [Chagga law].

———. (1932) *Die Stammeslehren der Dschagga* [The tribal teachings of the Chagga], vol. 1.

Kramer, Augustin, and Hans Nevermann. (1938) *Ralik-Ratak (Marshall Islands).*

Textor, Robert B. (1967) *A Cross-Cultural Summary.*

Whiting, John W. M. (1941) *Becoming a Kwoma: Teaching and Learning in a New Guinea Tribe.*

AFFECTION BETWEEN THE SEXES

For anyone who has walked through a park or down a street or been to a movie or mall in a Western city, the sight of couples walking hand in hand or perhaps stopping to embrace or kiss is unremarkable. But the public display of affection between people who are sexually involved, including husbands and wives, is not common across cultures and, indeed, rules of etiquette usually require that lovers and spouses maintain an appropriate reserve with each other when other people are around. Of a worldwide sample of 37 societies, 86 percent regard public shows of intimacy between husband and wife as improper or worse. In the Philippines, a special chant is sung at a Badjau wedding ceremony to prevent the bride and groom from laughing, which is thought to be an unsuitable public demonstration of a romantic attachment. Among the Havasupai of the southwestern United States, husbands and wives refrain from showing interest in each other when other people are around, as that would be showing off. The Chiricahua of the southwestern United States feel that kissing and other such displays of attachment are too personal to be indulged in publicly by adults, including spouses. In Argentina, a Mataco husband and wife are publicly distant in each other's company, and a wife will barely acknowledge the departure of a husband who is taking a trip nor will she publicly greet him with any enthusiasm when he returns.

Only 14 percent of the 37 cultures for which information is available allow spouses to openly display mutual affection. But this freedom of emotional expression is sometimes limited. In Chile, Mapuche couples are permitted to be openly affectionate early on in their marriage, but later the relationship must appear more reserved. The same is true in Brazil among Trumai spouses, who embrace and engage in mild sex play in front of other people when first married, but not later. In a few cultures spouses are free to be publicly affectionate for the duration of their marriage. For example, as night falls in Brazil, each Nambicuara family gathers around its own fire and married couples can be seen fighting playfully and cuddling as camp members talk, sing, or dance.

There appears to be an overall tendency across cultures to allow unmarried or young married couples greater leeway in the open expression of affection than is permitted to established married partners. However, attitudes regarding the demonstration of affection in public between unmarried couples are also restrictive in some cultures. Among the Balinese of Indonesia, lovers do not even appear in public together. A man is prohibited from touching a woman in public. Nor can the garments of men and women touch, even when not being worn. When a relationship is relatively new, Havasupai boys and girls go to great lengths to avoid one another, with each feigning indifference toward the other. In other societies, unmarried couples are permitted to engage in intimate displays in front of other people. In the United States, Hidatsa couples carry on courtships in public and are publicly affectionate. Among the Huichol of Mexico, boys and girls may be seen kissing and touching each other.

Rules regarding the public display of affection between sexually involved partners are not related to more general attitudes toward public or private demonstrations of physical intimacy. In Canada, for instance, while Slave husbands and wives avoid any open demonstrations of intimacy, there is much physical contact in the form of wrestling, jostling, and so on among children of the same sex. Adolescents will also playfully attack the genitals of others of their own gender. The Balinese, who avoid any public displays of intimacy between people who might be sexually involved, engage in open physical intimacy between parents and their children or grandparents and their grandchildren. And in private, sexual partners are physically demonstrative, sniffing and stroking each other and rubbing cheek to cheek. The intolerance of public displays of affection across cultures between men and women who are or may be sexual partners

seems to reflect a sense of the unseemliness of open demonstrations of behaviors that have a sexual overtone. Where physical contact between sexual partners is formalized and stripped of sexual significance, it may be tolerated in a society that otherwise condemns such open displays of intimacy. For instance, in the Amazon, Cubeo spouses refrain from any spontaneous intimate contact in public. But a wife will paint her husband's face, delouse him, and pick insect bite scabs from his skin. As these acts are defined by Cubeo society as nonsexual, they are not seen as improper. Most people around the world appear to think that sexual intimacy ought to be private and that the flaunting of one's sexuality is in bad taste.

See also AFFECTION, SAME-SEX DISPLAY OF.

Belo, Jane. (1935) "A Study of Customs Pertaining to Twins in Bali." *Tijdschrift voor Indische Taal- Land- en Volkenkunde* 75: 484–549.

———. (1936) "The Balinese Temper." *Character and Personality* 4: 120–146.

———. (1936) "Study of a Balinese Family." *American Anthropologist* 38: 12–31.

———. (1949) "Bali: Rangda and Barong." J. J. Augustin, 10: 59.

———. (1953) *Bali: Temple Festival.*

Covarrubias, Miguel. (1938) *Island of Bali.*

Faron, Louis C. (1956) "Araucanian Patri-Organization and the Omaha System." *American Anthropologist* 58: 435–456.

———. (1961) *Mapuche Social Structure: Institutional Reintegration in a Patrilineal Society of Central Chile.*

———. (1964) *Hawks of the Sun: Mapuche Morality and Its Ritual Attributes.*

Fock, Niels. (1963) "Mataco Marriage." *Folk* 5: 91–101.

Levi-Strauss, Claude. (1945) *La Vie Familiale et Sociale des Indiens Nambikwara* [Family and social life of the Nambikwara Indians].

———. (1945) "The Social and Psychological Aspect of Chieftainship in a Primitive Tribe: The Nambikuara of Northwestern Mato Grosso." New York Academy of Sciences *Transactions*, series 2, 7: 16–32.

———. (1948) "The Nambicuara." In *Handbook of South American Indians*, vol. 3, edited by Julian H. Steward, 361–369.

Lumholtz, Carl. (1902) *Unknown Mexico: A Record of Five Years' Exploration of the Western Sierra Madre: In the Tierra Caliente of Tepic and Jalisco; and among the Tarascos of Michoacan.*

Murphy, Robert F., and Buell Quain. (1955) *The Trumai Indians of Central Brazil.*

Opler, Morris Edward. (1946) "Chiricahua Apache Material Relating to Sorcery." *Primitive Man.*

Smithson, Carma Lee. (1959) *The Havasupai Woman.*

———. (1964) *Havasupai Religion and Mythology.*

AFFECTION, SAME-SEX DISPLAY OF

In the animal kingdom, physical contact serves as an important way of consolidating relationships and communicating intentions between individuals. Human beings also display their feelings for one other by touching, hugging, kissing, hand-holding and the like, underscoring our solid connections with the rest of the world's creatures. In the human case, cultural notions of propriety determine the kinds of other people toward whom an individual may or may not be physically demonstrative. Relationships between members of the same sex are affected by such cultural attitudes.

For example, while physical contact reflecting a friendship between two boys may be frowned upon in some western societies, such male-male displays of affection are commonplace in some societies around the world. In New Ireland, Lesu boys walk arm in arm, or perhaps one boy will put his arm around the shoulder of the other. Among the Trobrianders of New Guinea, male friends hug each other, walk about together arm in arm, and sleep with each other on the same couch. There are also cultures that approve of physical contact between males but find it unseemly in females. In Brazil, Aweikoma men sleep together, sometimes in pairs and sometimes in groups of three or four, arms and legs entwined. Women in this society do not display this kind of physical affection toward each other. Sometimes, both sexes enjoy equal freedom in the display of same-sex physical affection. In Alaska, Kaska boys wrestle with each other and one boy may sneak up on another and hug him from behind. Girls hold hands, sit close to each other, wrestle, and hug. Same-sex pairs among the Balinese of Indonesia embrace each other, publicly snuggle up with one another for a nap, and hold hands.

Cultural norms may also permit same-sex physical contact for men or women at one age but not at others. For instance, an Aweikoma man of between 10 and perhaps 40 years of age is *kelu* and enjoys a friendly physical relationship with his fellow hunters as the men lie about together caressing one another. But the man over 40 years of age is *choi*. He has now grown old and no longer indulges in this kind of relationship with his hunting companions. In other cases, physical demonstrations between members of the same sex are only likely to occur in specific contexts. During certain social events, Cayapa boys and men of Brazil will lie on the floor together with arms around each other or hold hands while reclining in a hammock. But this display of affection between males occurs only at fiestas, where alcoholic drinks are plentiful. Sometimes, a society will accept physical contact between males or between females but not between members of the opposite sex. Trobriand men sleep together, hug each other, and walk with arms entwined. Adolescents of the same sex, boys and girls alike, hold hands. But members of the opposite sex do not hand-hold; it is considered improper to do so in general and it is absolutely prohibited for males and females for whom any sexual relationship would be considered incestuous. Kwoma males of New Guinea will hug and pat one another and rub each other's cheeks with lime gourds when reunited after a long separation. Boys and adolescents also play games that include sexually suggestive physical contact. But between the sexes, touching is only permitted when people are old and related to one another.

Indeed, prohibitions against open displays of physical affection target couples whose relationship is or might become sexual in a number of cultures around the world. Acceptance of same-sex physical contact may reflect a culture's tolerance of such behavior when it has no sexual overtones. Same-sex physical contact of the sort described here does not imply sexual intent on the part of the participants. Nor do cultural attitudes about same-sex physical relationships tell anything about patterns of male-male or female-female sexual contact. Same-sex displays of physical affection are just that—displays of affection.

See also AFFECTION BETWEEN THE SEXES.

Altschuler, Milton. (1971) "Cayapa Personality and Sexual Motivation." In *Human Sexual Behavior: Variations in the Ethnographic Spectrum,* edited by Donald S. Marshall and Robert E. Suggs, 38–58.

Veiled Bedouin women in Egypt greet each other.

Covarrubias, Miguel. (1938) *Island of Bali.*

Gladwin, Thomas, and Seymour Sarason. (1953) *Truk: Man in Paradise.*

Henry, Jules. (1941) *The Jungle People: A Kaingang Tribe of the Highlands of Brazil.*

Honigmann, John J. (1949) *Culture and Ethos of Kaska Society.*

Malinowski, Bronislaw. (1929) *The Sexual Life of Savages in North-western Melanesia: An Ethnographic Account of Courtship, Marriage and Family Life among the Natives of the Trobriand Islands, British New Guinea.*

Powdermaker, Hortense. (1933) *Life in Lesu: The Study of a Melanesian Society in New Ireland.*

Turnbull, Colin M. (1965) *Wayward Servants: The Two Worlds of the African Pygmies.*

Whiting, John W. M. (1941) *Becoming a Kwoma: Teaching and Learning in a New Guinea Tribe.*

AGE-GRADES

All cultures around the world draw distinctions between people on the basis of age. At a minimum, a society will recognize differences between immature, mature, and elderly people. Americans commonly distinguish between infants, toddlers, school children, adolescents, young adults, middle-aged adults, and senior citizens. In many African cultures, males are classified into the categories of newly born infants, children on the lap, uninitiated boys, initiated bachelors, married men, elders, and retired elders. When cultures classify individuals into categories on the basis of age, each category forms an age-grade. People who are roughly the same chronological age are then members of the same age-grade.

All societies attach certain expectations to individuals in a particular age-grade. These may be only relatively vague assumptions about the kinds of behaviors that people in a certain age-grade will display. For instance, Westerners expect toddlers to be active and strong-willed, and parents anticipate the "terrible two's" with some anxiety. Similarly, individuals in the adolescent age-grade are expected to be somewhat rebellious against their parents and other authority figures. It is also assumed that adolescents will be confused about their identities and emotionally unstable. These profiles, however, are only predictions about how people in a given age-grade will behave. They are not prescriptions for behavior. In some societies, by contrast, age-grades are associated with sets of specific behavioral requirements so that a person who belongs to a particular age-grade is more or less obliged to conform to the behavioral profile identified with his or her age classification. These profiles include lists of responsibilities and privileges as well as expectations regarding how individuals belonging to a given age-grade will be viewed and treated by other members of society. The content of these profiles differs widely across cultures, but graduation through the age-grades typically brings with it increasing authority, with the elderly being treated with the greatest respect. Age-grading in which specific grades are associated with detailed rights and duties is especially common in African societies.

The Tiriki of Kenya recognize four age-grades for males, and each age-grade is identified with a specific set of duties to which all men belonging to the age-grade must attend. The warriors form the youngest recognized age-grade. A man is recruited into this age-grade once he has undergone the initiation rites required for all Tiriki males. Men who belong to the warriors' age-grade function as the active army for their country. A man's reputation for the remainder of his life will depend upon how he comports himself as a warrior, with demonstrations of courage and leadership earning a man great respect. Men who are graduated to the age-grade of elder warriors perform a number of administrative tasks. A member of the elder warriors age-grade may serve as chairman at meetings called to sort out the property claims of heirs of a deceased individual. Elder warriors also act as go-betweens when vital information needs to be communicated to elders of different subtribes. Men belonging to the age-grade of judicial elders serve as negotiators when there are disputes between members of the community. Any major disruption or complaint brought by the head of a household is handled by members of this age-grade. Thus, for instance, a judicial elder may settle a disagreement about bride-price payments. Accusations of assault are also heard by the judicial elders. Finally, the ritual elders supervise the religious life of the society. They oversee the rituals for household shrines and initiation rites. Ritual elders are also in charge of the semiannual community supplications and conduct the religious ceremonies associated with meetings about inheritance. Ritual elders are also believed to have magical powers. They expel or neutralize witches and punish anyone who has committed a serious crime with death by sorcery. The ritual elders also foretell the future when members of the community are embarking upon an important endeavor. For instance, members of the warrior age-grade will go to the ritual elders for advice when they are about to go on a raid and will postpone an attack if the elders foresee a bad result.

Age-grades are less well delineated for females than for males in many cultures that have age-grades. While prescriptions for behavior may be minutely detailed by age for males in a given culture, the behavioral expectations for females may be less formally specified in the same society. This is probably attributable to the fact that women are more typically preoccupied with domestic and child-rearing activities and therefore have little time left over to fulfill other kinds of obligations. However, in many cultures a woman's status, as well as the constraints that are placed on her behavior, alter significantly once she is past the age of childbearing. She may then be incorporated into the age-grading system. For instance, among some African societies, an older woman will often become an elder and participate in deliberations along with male members of this age-grade. Among the African Lunda, old men and women are both members of the highest age-grades and participate in all the affairs of the community.

In societies that exploit age-grades in order to assign rights and responsibilities to members of the community, individuals of roughly the same chronological age pass through the age-grades together. For example, a group of Tiriki males is initially recruited into the warriors age-grade together. The same group then progresses through the age-grades, finally arriving at the age-grade of ritual elders. A group of individuals who travel together through the age-grades described by their culture are known as an age-set.

See also AGE-SETS.

Haviland, William A. (1987) *Cultural Anthropology,* 5th ed.

Lebeuf, Annie M. D. (1963) "The Role of Women in the Political Organization of African Societies." In *Women of Tropical Africa,* edited by Denise Paulme.

AGE-SETS

Age forms the basis for recruitment into socially constructed groups in a number of societies around the world. Cultures everywhere classify people according to age, distinguishing at a minimum between the immature, mature, and elderly. Americans commonly distinguish between infants, toddlers, school children, adolescents, young adults, middle-aged adults, and senior citizens. Other societies recognize other chronological stages. Each of these categories of people forms an age-grade. Societies that exploit age as the criterion of group membership superimpose a system of age-sets onto the age-grade structure. That is to say, a group of individuals who are roughly the same age progress through the age-grades together. Such a group is an age-set. In cultures that have age-grades, everyone travels through a number of age-grades over a lifetime. In cultures that use age as a basis for the formation of groups, the people with whom an individual makes the trip comprise the age-set. Age-grades occur around the world but are especially common in east Africa. Males are more commonly grouped into age-sets than are females, although female age-sets also occur in some cultures.

In some societies, entrance into an age-grade and graduation through succeeding grades is automatic. The person does not have to do a thing beyond being the right age. In other societies, the individual is required to undergo some kind of initiation ritual in order to gain entrance into an age-grade. However, in societies that have age-grades, everyone is installed into an age-set along with the other people in his age-grade. That is, there is no choice about becoming an initiate. In this sense, membership in an age-set is practically guaranteed and automatic. Initiation as the strategy for gaining membership in an age-set is common in east Africa.

The Nuer of the Sudan are a society whose males are aggregated into age-sets. A male is initiated into his age-set when he is about 16 years of age. The initiation includes an operation during which the boy's forehead is deeply incised with lines. Each of the boys who are being recruited into their age-set first goes to an age-mate of his father to receive the ceremonial

Kenyan Masai warriors dance at initiation ceremony.

blessing. All of the boys then set off to the house of the surgeon. Usually, from four to twelve boys are initiated at one time. They then belong to the same age-set for life. An age-set will include males spanning some ten years in age because the operation is not performed continually. Rather, after some seven years during which groups of boys are regularly initiated, the surgeon will stop performing the operation for perhaps four years. Males whose foreheads are decorated with the characteristic lines are recognized as adults by the Nuer, so the initiation not only entitles the boy to membership in his age-set but also marks his transition from non-adult to adult status. Among the Nuer, each age-set is named, and males from different villages who are roughly the same age know the names of each other's age-sets. As a result, any male can immediately affiliate himself with the age-set that is equivalent to his own when he travels to another community.

In many societies that have age-sets, initiation includes a circumcision operation for males and, less frequently, a clitoridectomy, or cutting of the clitoris, for females. In Kenya, a Gusii boy is graduated from the status of little boy, or *omoisia,* to *omomura,* which means circumcised man or warrior, once he has undergone circumcision. Once a year, a number of boys are circumcised together at the same ceremony. Each boy novice chooses a sponsor the day before the operation. Novices shave their heads and then a number of initiates sleep in the hut of an already initiated boy, who will take them to the circumcision operation the next day. During the night, the initiated boys try to scare the novices with grizzly stories about the painful operation that they are about to undergo. The novices rise very early the next morning and walk about two miles to the house of the circumciser, arriving there before sunrise. They will continue to be badgered by the older boys along the way. The initiated boy, in front of an audience of his real and classificatory brothers and unrelated women,

stands with his back to a tree, arms above his head. The initiated boys and men aim clubs and spears at the head of the novice and scream that they will kill him if he moves or acts as if he is in pain. When the operation is completed, the boy joins his other circumcised age-mates. Groups of two or three boys are then led into newly built huts where they will remain secluded for a number of weeks. During this time, the newly circumcised boys are restricted from doing certain things, and they continue to be harassed in a variety of ways. But the seclusion is, on balance, enjoyable. When the period of seclusion is over, the boys are washed, blessed, and anointed a number of times and several feasts are thrown. The father of each boy rubs white earth on his son's forehead and promises to respect him, that is, to stop beating him for bad behavior. He also demands respect in return. After the initiation, a boy takes on the responsibilities of an adult. Gusii boys are usually eager to be initiated because they are looking forward to becoming big men and working away from home or going to high school. While uninitiated boys are afraid of being left behind in the status of little boy by braver age-mates, they are also likely to be frightened of the operation itself and the hazing that accompanies it. Nevertheless, boys will typically lobby to be initiated on their own and without prompting or pressure from adults.

Gusii girls also undergo initiation, including clitoridectomy. The initiation of Gusii girls takes place a few weeks before that of the boys. Girls are also eager to undergo initiation because they wish to become *enyaroka,* a circumcised thing, or *omoiseke,* an unmarried girl, thus leaving behind the status of *egesagane,* meaning little girl. Gusii girls who are being initiated in a given year do not necessarily have the clitoridectomy on the same day. The girls who are planning to undergo the operation on a given day leave the house before dawn with their mothers, naked except for a shawl about the shoulders. The girls all travel together to the house of the woman who will perform the operation. A girl who is about to undergo the procedure sits on a stone. Her back is supported by a woman who is squatting behind her. The girl's arms are pinned down and her hands are held over her eyes to prevent her from moving or seeing the operation. Afterwards, the girls are taken back home, while the women who lead them dance, sing obscene songs, and carry on along the way. Each girl remains squatting behind a bush or building near her mother's house for a few hours, after which she begins a seclusion at home for about a month. The seclusion is pleasant for the girl, who is visited on occasion by groups of initiated girls. There is singing and sexually suggestive dancing, but no hazing. At the end of seclusion the girl is smeared with butterfat, decorated with beads given by all of the community women, and called *omoriakari*, or bride. Once she has been initiated, the girl's behavior changes. She does work that is appropriate for a woman and shows considerable interest in appearing well dressed and groomed. Girls who have been initiated in the same year form close relationships, working and going to the market together until they are married.

Age-sets are exploited by societies to get various kinds of work accomplished. Once they were initiated, Zulu males of South Africa marched off as a group to the king's village to become the active army of the nation. Each age-set becomes a unit in a regiment of up to several thousand men. After a decade or so, the men were discharged and permitted to go home and get married. There is a retirement ceremony after which the men become elders. The age-set of elders may contain men ranging from 25 to 60 years in age. This age-set is also expected to take on a new set of responsibilities. The elders are the chief producers of agricultural goods and the owners of the herds. They are also in charge of governmental functions. Eventually, the elder age-set retires from active participation in community activities, formally handing over

power to the age-sets that have more recently left the army. The retired men are said to "become ancestors." Even in retirement, however, the men oversee the supernatural welfare of members of the community. In West Africa, age-sets often function as a labor force. Among the Igbo of Nigeria, the elders might determine that the community needs a new shrine or some refurbishing done on the marketplace. They will then summon three or four age-sets, each of which consists of some 20 to 30 men. Age-sets may also assist a person who has a grievance against his or her own relatives. This happens in a number of societies that have strong kin groups and in which, therefore, individuals require some protection from unreasonable treatment by kin. For instance, among the Tiv of Nigeria, a person's age-set will protect him when one of his kinsmen attempts to bewitch him. The victimized man may even go to live with an age-mate until the danger is past.

Age-sets also serve to draw members together emotionally. Among the Shavante of Brazil, for example, boys are segregated into age-grades. Boys belonging to the same age-grade have lived together in the same bachelor's hut, been initiated together, and gotten married in a joint ceremony. Their common experiences at once bind them together and separate them from older and younger age-grades whose lives have been characterized by a different set of experiences. Similarly, Igbo boys of Nigeria who have been initiated together belong to the same age-grade, and each grade can be observed sitting together at the weekly market, drinking, chatting, entertaining their friends, and talking about their common interests. In Kenya, Kikuyu males who have been circumcised together form a named age-grade. Men belonging to the same age-grade are like blood brothers, demonstrating deep loyalty and devotion to one another, and a man will lend his wife to a visiting age-mate. Age-grades participate in competitive dancing exhibitions when they meet each other. Although females also belong to age-sets, the role of the age-set tends not to be as vital in their lives. For instance, among the Shavante, girls and women as well as males belong to age-grades, but they tend to engage in communal activities such as food gathering or swimming with other females from their own household as opposed to members of their age-grades.

In societies that have age-sets, some kind of accommodation must be made so that younger age-sets can eventually replace the older age-set as the group with maximum power and status. The age-set in power does not necessarily retire gracefully. For example, among the Karimojong of East Africa, age-sets are also grouped into generation-sets. A generation-set is made up of five consecutive age-sets, each composed of men who belong to a younger age-grade than those in the next age-set. A generation-set thus spans some 25 to 30 years. Two generation-sets will be active at any one time. The senior generation-set will be composed of all five of its age-sets, and its membership will be older than that of the junior generation-set, which will still be adding age-sets at the lower end as males become old enough to be incorporated into its youngest age-sets. The senior generation-set is the seat of authority in the society, performing judicial, religious, and governmental functions, while men in the junior generation-set take on the roles of warriors and policemen. As the junior generation-set is completed, it will begin to lobby to take on the status and roles of the current senior generation-set. The senior men will finally submit to a ceremony that graduates the junior generation-set to senior status and converts the seniors to the status of retired generation-set. But the older men do not hand over power easily. Rather, they resist the transfer until it becomes unrealistic to retain authority because membership in the older age-sets in their generation-set has begun to dwindle.

See also AGE-GRADES.

Bohannan, Paul. (1963) *Social Anthropology.*

Ember, Carol R. and Melvin Ember. (1988) *Anthropology.* 5th ed.

Green, M. M. (1947) *Ibo Village Affairs.*

Haviland, William A., (1987) *Cultural Anthropology,* 5th ed.

Kenyatta, Jomo. (1961) *Facing Mount Kenya: The Tribal Life of the Gikuyu.*

LeVine, Robert A., and Barbara B. LeVine. (1966) *Nyansongo: A Gusii Community in Kenya.*

Maybury-Lewis, David. (1967) *Akwe-Shavante Society.*

Middleton, John. (1953) *The Central Tribes of the Northeastern Bantu: The Kikuyu, Including Embu, Meru, Mbere, Chuka, Mbiwi, Tharaka, and the Kamba of Kenya.*

ALTRUISM An individual has behaved altruistically if his or her actions benefit someone else and also represent a genuine cost to himself or herself. Every day, people behave in ways considered altruistic. People help other people in times of danger, provide others with food, aid the sick or wounded as well as the very young, and share both tools and knowledge. But while these acts look like authentic instances of altruism, the evolutionary perspective leads us to believe that human beings and other animals are not characteristically altruistic toward other members of their species. The prediction is in part the result of logical deduction. Imagine two people who are neighbors. One has a tendency to sacrifice himself for the benefit of other people, while the second does not. From the evolutionary perspective, the key issue is who is more likely to survive and to produce more surviving offspring? The prediction is that the non-altruistic individual will have a better chance of doing both. This is because he is exposing himself to less danger and reserving more of his resources for his own use and the use of his spouse and children. If the tendency to behave altruistically is in any way a product of human evolution, then individuals behaving altruistically will become less numerous in the population with the passage of time. Sooner or later, most people left will be those who are unlikely to sacrifice their own welfare for the good of another person.

If human beings and other species are not genuinely altruistic, then how do we account for the multitude of acts that individuals perform daily for the benefit of other people? The evolutionary perspective does not deny that people and other animals regularly behave in ways that benefit others. But these acts of supposed sacrifice may look less altruistic if they are inspected more closely. Many acts of sacrifice are likely to benefit the benefactor in the long run. For one thing, altruistic behavior also tends to be directed toward special kinds of people. The conclusion is that what looks like altruism on the surface is often ultimately self-interest.

People's behavior is characterized more by exchange of favors than it is by altruism. For instance, among the Gururumba of New Guinea, the exchange of goods and services constitutes a central activity of daily life. Some exchanges are between individuals and take the form of barter. On other occasions, groups of people, ranging in size from two to several thousand, participate in formal, public exchanges of food or prestige items. Typically, one group is obligated to the other for some past favor so that the exchange is in fact a repayment of the obligation. Individuals are likely to engage in some sort of exchange on an average of two times a week. Exchanges

also take place on a variety of formal occasions, or life-cycle transitions; for instance, at births, naming ceremonies, nose piercings, the first wearing of hair decorations by a young girl, a boy's first successful hunt, a girl's first menstruation, male initiation, the rejection of a marriage offer, betrothal, the completions of a betrothed girl's first month in her future husband's village and the planting of her first garden, the first meal that a new wife serves her husband, a pregnancy, the first crop in a new garden, the productive completion of a trading venture, and preparation for and actual death. Often an event will be accompanied by a series of exchanges. For instance, a male initiation rite consists of a number of discrete ritual and taboo periods occurring over a time span of ten to twelve months, and each period is the occasion of a gift exchange. Exchanges also occur in the context of such activities as house-building, clearing land for cultivation, and farming activities. Villagers and lineage mates are expected to help each other with tasks of this sort, and while the Gururumba say that no repayment is required for this kind of cooperation, gifts of food and small presents such as salt or sugarcane are always presented to the helper by the person who has benefitted. Entire villages, sibs, or phratries will also join together to give gifts to some other group in exchange for a favor, for help in a war, or for shelter and protection if the group has been driven from its land by an enemy, for instance. Or an exchange may be made as a way of making peace between groups who have been adversaries.

The Gururumba pattern features the mechanics of exchange. A single individual or a group of individuals bestow some resource or perform some work for someone else, but in the expectation that the favor will be returned. So the exchange, in a sense, is a wash. However, a closer examination of exchanges of this sort shows that, in such reciprocal give-and-take interactions, givers eventually get more back than the investment was originally worth to them. Further, this is true of both givers. If I do you a good turn now and you return the favor later, both of us profit. This is also predicted by the evolutionary perspective, as it would be a waste of time and resources to help out another person in return for no net benefit. Both parties to a reciprocal interaction can benefit from the exchange when the cost that one incurs by doing the other a favor is less than the benefit that the favor confers to the latter person. Evolution predicts, then, that individuals will only enter into reciprocal interactions when the costs that they incur are less than the benefits conferred on the other individual and when givers ultimately get back more than they paid. This dynamic is known as reciprocal altruism. And indeed, helping, in our own and other species, does tend to occur only in situations where the helper eventually nets a gain of one kind or another.

Hard-Core Altruism

There are two categories of individuals toward whom altruism is characteristically directed. The first are kin, and the helping of kin is called hard-core altruism. In the case of this kind of helping, the returns to the helper are not necessarily concrete. Rather, the benefit lies in the fact that relatives share genes, so that helping someone who is a blood relative is in essence helping some of one's own genes to survive in future generations. The act is still self-interested. The benefit, however, is not in the form of goods or service. It is in the form of increased fitness, that is, increased representation of one's own genes in the future gene pool. The Ilongot culture of the Philippines revolves around the notion that standards of behavior are regulated by *beya,* or knowledge, of kin ties. Relatives hunt communally, help each other to meet bride-price payments, and aid one another with subsistence activities. Kin visit each other and share medicinal skill, offer food, provide care, and collaborate on work activities. One sister will bring rice

to another because "we must all feed our children." In return, the sister's children frequently help their aunt hoe, pound rice, or chase the birds away from the crops. Similarly, an uncle will ask his nephew to help him out because a brother's son "really is my child." And much of the cooperative work characterizing Ilongot life involves the recruitment to the work force of a child with whose parents a person reckons kin ties. The importance of relatedness in predicting helping behavior is also demonstrated in the context of the gifting of food. Food sharing is very common across societies, and cultures typically specify in detail who is required to give what to whom and in what order. Among the Mundurucu of Brazil, when a man brings home meat from a hunting expedition, he hands it over to his wife or to his closest woman relative if he is a bachelor. The meat is then cut up and distributed among village families. But if the take has been modest, then the woman will only share it with a single household, usually the one in which her closest relatives are living. In many cultures around the world, kin networks form the basis for domestic, economic, religious, and political life, which means that hard-core altruism is frequently at the heart of human activity.

While the evolutionary perspective predicts that individuals will tend to be altruistic toward kin without material reward, people are still expected to act ultimately to promote their own concrete interests, and this also occurs in the context of hard-core altruism. A person is prone to be sensitive to kin who take advantage of the generosity of others. Among the Ilongot, it is considered somewhat crude to haggle over perceived imbalances in helping and sharing between kin. And small inequities are overlooked in favor of long-term harmonious relationships between relatives. But individuals remain vigilant with regard to possible cheating on the part of kin, so that one person may complain that her relative owes her a new pig in return for the one that was sacrificed to cure an illness contracted by the relative's son. Or another person might threaten to sue for damages done to his rice fields when a relative's carabao tramples on his crops once too often. In Samoa, a relative is a person to whom one is obligated in many ways and who owes one many favors in return. A relative is required to provide food, clothing, shelter, and aid in a feud, and someone who refuses a relation some resource or service will be labelled as stingy and lacking in human kindness. But anyone who sacrifices for a relative remembers the value of the gift or act and asks for a reciprocal benefit as soon as possible. The benefactor will go to visit the house of his relative and remain there all day, finally specifying what he wishes in return for the favor when night approaches and it is time to leave. Similarly, a Kwoma child in New Guinea can ask his maternal uncle for food whenever he wishes, and the uncle is obliged to comply. But the child thereby incurs a debt, and must pay a substantial amount of shell-money to his uncle at a later date.

Reciprocal Altruism

People also help other people who are not relatives. In this case, a concrete benefit is expected in return. This kind of helping is called softcore, or reciprocal, altruism. This kind of altruism will begin to play a dominant role in the activities of people when kin groups become spatially fragmented and individuals interact more with unrelated people than with kin. This is the case, for example, in industrial societies where people are mobile, moving away from the communities into which they were born, and moving away from their relations besides. In many cultures, people acquire goods and services by way of channels of patterned exchange. In one version of exchange, resources and services flow from person to person, with no expectation of an immediate return. Nevertheless, giving and receiving balance out in the long run so that no one comes out losing. Among the !Kung of

southern Africa, property is individually owned, but most possessions are sooner or later given away. A person also receives gifts, however, so that goods are being transferred on a regular basis. Where reciprocal altruism is characteristic of social interactions, any particular person is likely to have a small number of select partners with whom he or she regularly makes exchanges. While gift-giving is universal among the !Kung, any particular individual will exchange property with only a handful of partners. Such relationships may be lifelong and are sometimes inherited by the partners' children. Gift-giving is more or less formal, and everyone keeps a running tab of who gave what to whom and when. Balanced exchange operates on the expectation that a favor will be returned in kind within a limited time frame.

Balanced exchange of services is very common across cultures without a money system. Often individuals will gather together to form work parties, with everyone in the group helping a particular individual to get some task done. Later on, this person will participate in a work party for the benefit of one of the other members. In Liberia, the Kpelle work party illustrates this principle. A *kuu*, or cooperative work group, will involve from six to forty individuals. The members of the group work each other's farms. The owner of the land on which the group is working provides food and sometimes music. Among the Mundurucu, a wife who is engaged in subsistence activities is helped by all of the other village women. For example, while a single woman would be able to manufacture farinha, one of the important staple foods for the Mundurucu, she would have to work for many days just to make 20 pounds. But the time that it takes to produce the farinha is greatly reduced when all of the women pitch in. This also allows the community to share a single farinha-making facility, including a single oven, set of pans, and trough. If the work were not done collaboratively, each woman would need to own her own apparatus, a financial impossibility for people in this culture. These kinds of exchange also operate in the arena of kin relationships. But generalized exchange is more characteristic between close kin, while balanced exchange prevails more frequently between more distantly related kin. This is consistent with what we might expect from an evolutionary point of view. Close relatives have more at stake in providing for each other's welfare. Therefore, there is a greater tolerance for delayed reciprocity between people who are close kin. The more distantly related a giver is to a receiver, the more concerned the benefactor will be about the good intentions of the partner. Therefore, a return on the giver's investment is required without undue delay.

Spouses, while they are the originators of families of related people, are not usually related themselves. Nevertheless, across cultures the husband-wife relationship is very frequently characterized by a division of labor so that each partner is, in essence, helping the other as both contribute to the overall welfare of the family. Among the Andaman Islanders, marriage implies certain economic obligations owed by one partner to the other. A wife is expected to supply firewood and water. She also provides vegetable foods and cooks meals. The husband contributes meat to the family diet. In Ghana, Ashanti wives are expected to remain faithful to their spouses, to see to the affairs of the household, and to do some farming. In turn, husbands are required to provide their wives with food, housing, and clothing, to care for them when they are ill, and to satisfy them sexually. They must also provide their wives with money for household expenses on a regular basis and present their spouses with gifts of jewelry, cloth, and the like at seasonal celebrations. If a man wishes to take a new wife, he is obligated to obtain the permission of his current spouse. He is also responsible for his wife's debts. The habitual failure of either spouse to fulfill any of these duties can be cited by the other as grounds for divorce.

Husband-wife cooperation, then, can be viewed as an instance of soft-core altruism. In fact, marriage arrangements themselves are very frequently occasions for reciprocal exchange, and are consciously viewed as such by the concerned parties. In most societies around the world, a groom or his family presents the relatives of the bride with a bride price at marriage. These substantial gifts of goods or money are understood to be compensation to the bride's family for loss of a valuable household member. Bride price is also seen as a payment for a woman's reproductive potential. The idea that marriage arrangements are a kind of reciprocal altruism is supported by the fact that, if a marriage is dissolved, the groom often demands repayment of the bride price, unless the termination of the marriage was a result of wrongdoing on his part. Often, the bride price is only partially repaid if the couple has been married for some time or if children have been produced. Among the Gusii of Kenya, the amount of the reimbursement is contingent upon the number of children that have been born, so that the more children a woman provides to the husband, the less bride-price repayment he will receive upon divorce. Further, across bride-price societies, the amount of the payment tends to be consistent with the desirability of the bride. In some societies, men acquire wives by exchanging women so that, for example, each man will wed the sister of the other. Here again, marriage arrangements follow the pattern of reciprocal altruism. However, a woman is exchanged for a woman instead of for goods. Further, if one of the marriages is terminated, there is sometimes a requirement that the other also be dissolved. Both parties to the marriage arrangement expect to receive satisfaction for their investments.

Sometimes, in the case of reciprocal altruism, exchanges between individuals are not equal. That is, one individual receives some good or service that is more valuable than what he has given. At Christmas, for instance, parents give children gifts that are more costly than the presents that children give to their parents. This apparent disparity, however, is also predicted by evolutionary theory. Calculations about costs and benefits in reciprocal exchanges consider not the value of the good or service itself, but rather the cost that the gift represents to the giver and the benefit that it bestows on the receiver. An expensive gift may cost a parent relatively little in comparison with his or her total resources, but may be very valuable from the child's perspective. Similarly, from the child's point of view, an inexpensive gift presented to a parent may represent a large proportion of the child's monetary reserves. Inequalities of exchange tend to reflect imbalances in the statuses of the two individuals, which lead to differences in the relative costs and benefits to each person associated with the exchange.

Reciprocal altruism is more likely to exist in certain kinds of social groups. Where people are sedentary, where there is ample opportunity for regular face-to-face interaction, and where there are many circumstances in which one individual will genuinely benefit from some help, reciprocal altruism is likely to flourish. Some people have argued that the relative lack of helping behavior found in industrial societies, and especially in large urban settings, is a result of the lack of opportunity that communities of this sort provide for establishing and maintaining reciprocal exchange partnerships.

Altruistic relationships ultimately depend upon equity for their success. Each partner is making a leap of faith that the other will be true to the contract of equitable payment for a received favor. However, partners are vulnerable because the recipient of a favor may cheat the benefactor by failing to reciprocate or by reciprocating but paying less than the value of the favor. However, various aspects of what might be called human nature help to sustain relationships based on reciprocal altruism. The gut-level sense of fairness that characterizes human beings may help the recipient of an altruistic act to overcome the impulse to cheat. Similarly, a sense of fairness may underwrite the motivation of benefactors to see that they are equitably repaid. The moral outrage that people experience when they are cheated may play a similar role. Feelings of gratitude may also serve to keep people honest, as will the sense of guilt that plagues human beings when they have deceived another person. The psychological makeup of human beings may be tailored in part to make reciprocal altruism work smoothly in much of daily life in cultures around the world.

See also KIN SELECTION.

Amoo, J. W. A. (1946) "The Effect of Western Influence on Akan Marriage." *Africa* 16: 228–237.

Basedow, Herbert. (1925) *The Australian Aboriginal.*

Ember, Carol R., and Melvin Ember. (1988) *Anthropology.* 5th ed.

Fortes, Meyer. (1950) "Kinship and Marriage among the Ashanti." In *African Systems of Kinship and Marriage,* edited by A. R. Radcliffe-Brown and Daryll Forde, 252–284.

LeVine, Robert A., and Barbara B. LeVine. (1966) *Nyansongo: A Gusii Community in Kenya.*

Mead, Margaret. (1928) *Coming of Age in Samoa: A Psychological Study of Primitive Youth for Western Civilization.*

Newman, Philip L. (1965) *Knowing the Gururumba.*

Radcliffe-Brown, Alfred R. (1922) *The Andaman Islanders: A Study in Social Anthropology.*

Rosaldo, Michelle Z. (1980) *Knowledge and Passion: Ilongot Notions of Self and Social Life.*

Shostak, Marjorie. (1981) *Nisa: The Life and Words of a !Kung Woman.*

Trivers, Robert L. (1985) *Social Evolution.*

Whiting, John W. M. (1941) *Becoming a Kwoma: Teaching and Learning in a New Guinea Tribe.*

ASSOCIATIONS

All human beings are related to other people by blood or marriage and all human societies exploit these relationships by aggregating relatives into kin groups of one kind or another. Kin groups, then, perform a wide range of functions across cultures and may be implicated in the domestic, economic, political, and religious lives of the members of a culture. But kin groups are limited with regard to what they can ultimately accomplish. A kin group can be enormous, with individuals tracing relatedness to thousands of other people. But if the group becomes too unwieldy, it is no longer able to perform its functions efficiently. Groups depending upon relatedness by blood or marriage can only operate as the sole basis of organization of people and activities in small societies without complicated structures. In larger and more complex societies, kin groups exist alongside other kinds of groups whose membership depends upon something other than relatedness. Such ancillary groups occur in most cultures and are commonly referred to as societies or associations. An association is a kind of group organized on some basis other than kinship or territory. Associations exist for a wide range of purposes and have various kinds of membership. However, it is true of all associations that they have some sort of formal structure, that their members share some common trait, interest or purpose, and that membership is restricted.

Associations differ from each other, on the other hand, in their mode of recruitment and their purpose. For many associations, membership is determined by the age or sex of an individual, and in some of these groups individuals who fit the criterion are automatically recruited into the groups. Thus, membership is mandatory in this kind of association. Groups with nonvoluntary membership are more common in societies lacking class stratification. This is probably because the egalitarian nature of these cultures means that there are fewer differences between people to get in the way of their participating in the same activities and working toward the same goals. Many other kinds of associations the world over are voluntary. That is, individuals decide to found or join some particular group of their own volition. When people associate voluntarily in this way, it is generally to achieve some goal in which they are all interested. Associations based upon voluntary membership are found in all kinds of societies but are more common in cultures with class stratification, probably because individual interests in societies of this sort become specialized. This means that universal recruitment into a group is no longer practical. It also means that people with particular concerns will find it useful to band together in a group of people with the same interests.

In a number of societies around the world, associations are formed on the basis of age. These cultures begin by grouping people into age-based classes, or age-grades. For instance, infant, toddler, school child, adolescent, adult, and senior citizen are age-grades in American culture, and individuals who fit the chronological profile for a particular label belong to the same age-grade. Where age is exploited as a basis for group membership, people who travel together through the age-grades form an age-set. Each age-grade is usually associated with a particular set of rights and responsibilities. As an age-set is graduated through the age-grades, its members sequentially take on the roles regarded as appropriate for each age-grade. The Tiriki of Kenya provide an example of a society that uses age as a way of aggregating people. The culture recognizes seven age-sets. Each age-set is composed of men who were initiated over a period of 15 years. An age-set passes through four age-grades. As each new age-set is graduated to a higher age-grade, the age-set occupying that age-grade itself moves on to the next age-grade. Age-grades are associated with particular sets of duties. The youngest is the warriors age-grade. Men in this age-grade have the job of guarding the country. They "hold the land." The elder warriors age-grade follows. The duties of the elder warriors are less prestigious than are those of members of the younger warriors age-grade. They are essentially in training for the administrative duties that they will shoulder when they graduate to the next age-grade of judicial elders. It is the judicial elders who settle local disputes. The final age-grade, the ritual eldership, oversees various aspects of religious life. Ritual elders are also assumed to have magical powers. Cultures that have age-sets may integrate males and females into the same groups, or a culture may have separate age-sets for each sex. In some societies, only one sex is formed into age-sets. Membership in age-sets is automatic in the sense that an individual who is the right age, and—where it matters—the right sex, will become a member of the appropriate age-grade. Membership is also involuntary. Where age-sets exist, members of the culture are not given a choice about joining an age-set.

A number of societies have exclusively male or female associations that are not based on the principle of age-grades. Membership is also automatic in that a person need only be a particular sex to gain admittance and that membership is universal. If the society has a male-based association, then all males of a particular status belong. Similarly, if there is a female-based association, then all females of a certain class belong. All-male groups are more common than are all-female groups, with the exception of societies in West Africa, where female associations are very popular. Some societies have same-sex associations for males and females. When this happens, the male association often plays a greater role in the lives of its members than does the female association in a woman's life. In general, men's associations help to consolidate male power and cohesion. As men's associations cross-cut kin ties, they allow males to come together as a group without being pressured by the loyalties and constraints enjoined upon them by the kin group. Industrialized societies also have single-sex associations. Victorian England, for instance, was famous for its all-male clubs. These associations, however, are voluntary, making them very different from those in non-Western societies, where membership is not voluntary.

The Pacific island Palauans provide an example of how men's and women's associations operate. Traditionally, every Palauan belonged to a club. Membership was determined by age and sex. The men's clubs had their own houses, where a man might spend a good deal of his time, sleeping, working, engaging in business and leisure activities there. Women's clubs were not associated with their own houses, but women were permitted to use a men's house when they required a meeting place. Similarly, after they are tattooed, Samoan boys join an organization to which all the young men and older untitled men of the village belong. The group entertains visitors and supervises the social activities of the village. Unmarried women and wives of untitled men join a similar organization.

In some African cultures, women's associations confer considerable power to their members. Ijaw women in Nigeria can belong to any of seven women's groups. For example, a married woman, once she has begun to engage in marketing and trading, is required to become a member of the woman's association in her husband's patrilineage. She will be forced to pay a fine if she misses or shows up late to a meeting. Ijaw women belonging to a particular association will sometimes draw up a set of rules for the proper behavior of their members and punish anyone who flaunts these regulations. Ijaw associations may also settle disputes and punish wrongdoers. Among the Ube, Gere, and Wobe on the Ivory Coast, the village head is required to consult the head of the association of female initiates on matters of agriculture. In West Africa, among the Mende, the *Nyayei* and *Humoi* societies take care of the mentally ill and oversee activities promoting the fertility of the soil. Women who are members of these societies employ methods that help to increase people's self-esteem, and they are frequently asked for advice by the chiefs. The female leaders of these associations have hereditary titles and their status is so high in their communities that outsiders from the West have sometimes assumed that they were the chiefs of the society. Another influential kind of same-sex association found in Africa binds women together for the purpose of promoting the marketing activities of its members. Yoruba women in Nigeria have associations of this sort, some representing producers, some sellers, and some buyers of market goods. The leaders of these associations are often important people and are consulted by the political authorities. In a number of African cultures, women's associations are so influential that women in these cultures are in some ways more powerful than the men.

In some African societies, women form their own political councils. In Nigeria, each Igbo village has its own women's council, the members of each group maintaining connections with those of the others. A council is headed by an elected official. The women's councils plan the schedules for agricultural activities, oversee the protection of the crops, regulate ceremonies associated with the agricultural cycle, and look after the interests of women more generally. The Igbo women's councils have the power to punish anyone who violates the policies of the council.

In many societies, people become members of groups on the basis of criteria other than kinship, age, or sex. Such groups, which are variously called voluntary associations or common interest groups, share features in common with age-sets and same-sex groups. First, the functions of common interest groups can be performed by age-sets or by all-male or all-female associations and, indeed, in some cultures they are. Second, membership in common interest or voluntary associations is not always voluntary. That is, it is sometimes the case that such associations are able to coerce people to join. What distinguishes these associations from age-sets or single-sex groups is that recruitment is based upon some purpose or goal that is shared by members. It is the fact that a group of people have some interest in common and not the fact of their age or sex that motivates the founding of the association. The range of shared interests that underwrite the establishment of such associations is enormous. For instance, voluntary associations may be concerned with economic pursuits, political activity, recreation, or military endeavors. Associations also exist for the preservation of the language, history, religious tradition, songs, or beliefs of a culture.

Guilds in which tradesmen or craft people join together for their mutual protection and benefit are prime examples of common interest groups. They were prevalent in the Middle Ages in the West but also appear in other places, including in West Africa. For example, among the Yoruba, the production of crafts was traditionally in the hands of particular lineages. But as new crafts—for instance, the manufacture of bicycles, furniture, tailored clothing, and so on—began to be introduced in the early twentieth century, craft guilds became popular. Membership is voluntary. Usually, a craftsman invites a number of other people who do the same kind of work to his shop to talk about their mutual interests, and they decide among themselves to found an association. The Yoruba guild performs the same kinds of functions that are discharged by guilds more generally. In the first place, the guild plays a central role in the training of craftsmen. In the case of the Yoruba, when a boy reaches the age of 16, he is apprenticed to a guild member for a small fee paid by the boy's father. After his training, if he is successful at setting himself up as a master, he becomes a regular guild member himself. Otherwise, he will become a journeyman, working for another craftsman for wages. Guilds also act to standardize fees and wages. Among the Yoruba, the price charged for the training of an apprentice and the salary paid to a journeyman are both fixed by the guild. Guilds also set standards for the quality of the products that are produced by their members and settle disputes between masters and apprentices.

In a number of societies, people come together voluntarily for the purpose of forming what is essentially a credit union. These groups provide reciprocal aid and financial backing to their members. Where they exist, credit groups are often voluntary associations. The Igbo form *mikiri*, or voluntary associations, whose members contribute funds for the use of all. *Mikiri* include up to 50 members of either or both sexes. Some of these associations merely serve as a credit association for members, but other *mikiri* also function as social societies, meeting monthly to attend to business and also to eat and drink and converse together.

Many societies have military associations that function as common interest groups. The American Legion is an example of such a group. Wherever they exist, military associations exalt the activities of war and promote a sense of camaraderie among the members. Recruitment is based upon an individual's participation as a warrior or soldier. The Cheyenne of the U.S. Plains permitted any boy or man who had been

Political and military associations form in many cultures. These men are from different ethnic groups in Inner Mongolia and came together on 25 July 1966 to demonstrate against U.S. involvement in the Vietnam War.

to war to join its military associations. There were a number of these societies, each having different songs, dances, and dress.

Associations that begin as voluntary organizations can eventually gain so much power that they are able to force individuals to become members. Indeed, this happened among Yoruba craft guilds. Every individual who practiced a craft for which there was a guild was compelled by guild members to join the association and pay the required dues. A person who refused to join could have his tools confiscated and might even be deported by the local government. This is reminiscent of American labor unions, which also began as voluntary organizations. But individuals who do not wish to become union members cannot work in a union shop.

In a number of cultures, individuals join together to form secret societies. Membership is restricted in these associations and the nature of the activities in which the members engage is kept secret from nonmembers. The North American Omaha established a number of secret and social societies, each of which was composed of members sharing some role or attribute in common. Warriors formed the membership of one society, chiefs of another, and leading members of the tribe still another. A number of societies included men and women who have had special dreams or visions. Omaha men may have belonged to one of three feasting societies, and dancing societies may have recruited either or both sexes. Similarly, some Pomo men and women of California were members of secret societies. Women were strictly excluded from the ghost house except in very special circumstances. Indeed, the activities that transpired in the ghost house have the goal of frightening the women and persuading them to submit to male domination.

The *Poro* is a secret society that exists in a number of West African societies, including the Kpelle, Mende, and Temne. All males are eligible to belong to the society, but membership is contingent upon a man's undergoing a set of arduous physical ordeals. Candidates for membership are secluded for a period of time, traditionally three to four years but now considerably shorter, in a "bush school." Here, the initiate undergoes severe psychological indoctrination and is taught to take on a new Poro identity. The Poro society acts in part as a regulator of social behavior. Its power to persuade people to act in accordance with its dictates stems from the fear that the society instills. The Poro is associated with the spirits of the dead, who are very powerful as conduits to the supernatural. The Poro is also believed to own medicines that can cause disaster in the world if the rules of the Poro are disobeyed. Because these characteristics of the Poro are shrouded in secrecy, they become potent influences on people's behavior. Secret societies in other cultures also function to support the authority of political leaders and to uphold social norms. They all owe their power to the dread that secrecy evokes in those who do not belong to the society.

See also AGE-SETS; AGE-GRADES.

Barnett, H. G. (1949) *Palauan Society: A Study of Contemporary Native Life in the Palau Islands.*

Bohannan, Paul. (1963) *Social Anthropology.*

Ember, Carol R., and Melvin Ember. (1988) *Anthropology.* 5th ed.

Fletcher, Alice C., and Francis La Flesche. (1911) *The Omaha Tribe.* Twenty-seventh Annual Report of the Bureau of American Ethnology, 1905–1906.

Green, M. M. (1947) *Ibo Village Affairs.*

Haviland, William A. (1987) *Cultural Anthropology.* 5th ed.

Lebeuf, Annie M. D. (1963) "The Role of Women in the Political Organization of African Societies." In *Women of Tropical Africa,* edited by Denise Paulme.

Leith-Ross, Sylvia. (1939) *African Women.*

LeVine, Robert A., and Barbara B. LeVine. (1966) *Nyansongo: A Gusii Community in Kenya.*

Loeb, Edwin M. (1926) *Pomo Folkways.*

Murdock, George Peter. (1936) *Our Primitive Contemporaries.*

ATTACHMENT, PRIMARY

Human beings form a variety of attachments in the course of a lifetime. Some of these relationships turn out to be more central for an individual than do others. It is also the case that different societies emphasize the primacy of different kinds of interpersonal attachments, so that we can speak of the typical focus of affectionate bonds for most people in a particular culture. These are the individual's primary attachments. The deepest attachments are very often between people who are married or related to each other. But this is not always true. In some cultures, the expectation is that the strongest bond will be between two people who call each other friend, and indeed a person in such a society tends to make the most profound of emotional commitments to a chum. Individuals across cultures also differ regarding the extent to which an important childhood attachment remains strong for life or wanes in favor of other bonds, and patterns of continuity and discontinuity of attachment have far-reaching implications for the nature of the relationship between a husband and wife and between in-laws, especially when a person is compelled to leave home at marriage and move to the household or community of the spouse.

Marital Attachment

In contemporary Western society, the expectation is that the primary emotional commitment of a married person will be to a spouse and children. This view also appears in a number of other cultures. For example, a North American Omaha husband most deeply cherishes his wife so that, in the words of one Omaha widower, "no one is so near, no one can ever be so dear as a wife; when she dies, her husband's joy dies with her." And for the Iban of Malaysia, the relationship between a husband and wife should be closer than the bond between brothers. This expectation is borne out in Iban living arrangements. A newly married Iban couple can go to live with the parents of either the bride or groom, and a household, at one time or another, may include three generations of related families. When brothers remain in the natal household, however, the ties between siblings and those between husband and wife tend to conflict, in which case a spouse's loyalties remain with the partner. The extended family then breaks up and each individual family sets up a household of its own.

Cultures that elevate the marital bond to a privileged place in the life of the adult often recognize the potential for conflicts between an individual's loyalty to spouse and relatives and have customs that support the husband-wife bond, even if this weakens the attachment to other relatives. For instance, among the Khalka Mongols, a wife cannot make any informal visits to her family home for three years. She may only see her parents if they come to visit her in her husband's camp. The bride, as a result, is isolated from the people who have formerly been most important to her and is more likely to turn to her husband for emotional fulfillment.

Nonmarital Attachments

While the relationship between spouses is viewed as primary in some societies, many people the world over direct their primary affection and loyalty not to a mate, but to some other relative. Often, the marital bond is tenuous as a result. In many of these cultures, an adult retains a strong attachment to the mother. Among the Bemba of Zambia, a couple often moves in with the family of the bride after marriage. For a Bemba woman, the closest tie is with her mother, and the bond is sufficiently strong that a girl will on occasion refuse to leave her own community to go to live with her husband if he wishes to make his home in his own village. Similarly, a Hadza woman in Tanzania retains a strong attachment to her mother even after she is married, and a wife who must choose between going with her husband to his family's camp for an extended period of time or remaining with her mother will almost always opt to stay with her mother. If a man insists upon his wife's moving to his camp permanently, he risks seeing his marriage dissolve. For a Truk girl in Oceania, the most important person in her life is also her mother. But married Truk women are required to move away from home after marriage. Married women, as a result, visit their mothers when they can, for a month each year if they live far away and for frequent, informal visits if the distance between them is not so great. Mothers offer their daughters comfort, aid, and advice.

The tie between mother and son is also very strong in many cultures around the world. Among the Chagga of Tanzania, the mother-son relationship is primary, especially as a woman grows older and her life begins to center around her son. She sees to his needs and depends upon him to look out for her well-being, and the youngest son sees it as his primary responsibility to care for his mother, especially as it is unlikely that her husband can take equal responsibility for the welfare of all of his wives. If a woman goes back to her own family, her husband cannot deny her the youngest son, who will inherit his mother's banana grove when she dies. In the United States, a Hidatsa man traditionally retained a very strong attachment to his mother even after he was married. As a new groom, he visited his mother whenever he liked and it was at his mother's lodge that he gave feasts for his friends or relatives. A married man often ate at his mother's and never stayed in his

Attachment between husband and wife is important in primary cultures, as with this Siberian Nanai couple who when young worked alongside each other on fishing teams.

own house if his wife was absent, as it was considered improper for a man to remain alone in his lodgings with only his parents-in-law. A husband kept his own possessions at his mother's home and the younger members of her household looked after his horses. A son was expected to look after his mother's welfare even if he had married and moved away.

Where a husband typically moves in with the wife's family after marriage, he is likely to remain close to his mother and other kin. Among the Timbira in Brazil, where individuals trace descent only through the mother's line (matrilocal residence), a man's attachment to his mother's household tends to be stronger than is his newer alliance with his wife's family. A husband tries to spend a part of each day with his mother and, if his wife comes along, the mother will prepare a meal for the couple. After an official meeting of the council, a man will visit his mother's house, where a female relative will serve a meal already prepared and waiting for him. Only after he has eaten and consulted with his relatives about family matters will he go home to his wife. After an extended trip, he first stops at his sister's house, where he is fed and greeted by kinswomen. A Timbira man also leaves some of his own possessions at his mother's house.

The pattern of matrilocal residence coupled with a lifelong attachment to his natal household often creates a conflict of affection and commitment for a husband. Navajo men in Arizona retain loyalties to two families. On the one hand, the Navajo husband lives with his wife's relatives and participates in the activities of the household in which he resides. But he is also obliged to participate in the ceremonial and economic life of the family into which he was born. Navajo men often return to the households of their mothers and sisters for long and frequent visits, and the brother-sister relationship in this society is characterized by strong affection. Frequently, the demands of the two families collide, with the result that the Navajo husband may find himself torn between conflicting loyalties and obligations. Similarly, Navajo women are more likely to be affected by the advice of their own brothers or uncles than by that of their husbands, and a wife will more frequently take the side of her parents than of her husband in a family dispute. In the final analysis, Navajo men and women tend to think of themselves as belonging to the families into which they were born even after they have established new households at marriage. And of all the relationships that a Navajo individual enjoys, the most unambiguously positive attachment throughout life is the attachment to the mother. Among the matrilocal Chiricahua Apache in Arizona, a husband's re-

lationship with his wife's kin is less warm and more strained than is his connection to his own family. He owes economic assistance to his wife's family but he is also expected to observe customs of avoidance and restraint toward some of his in-laws. His attachment to his own kin is more familiar and intimate and he tries to maintain these bonds at least until his first child has been born and he feels more secure in his new household. Similarly, in traditional North American Creek society, a husband who moved in with his wife at the time of their marriage may have returned to his childhood home or alternated among the households of his own relatives when he got old, but he would never take the same liberty with the relatives of his wife. The word *home* was reserved for the households of his own female relatives and was not used to refer to the dwelling he shared with his wife, even if he had built it.

Sibling Attachments

Sometimes, it is a sibling bond that takes priority in the lives of most individuals in a given culture. The Pacific island Palauans expect a woman to direct her primary loyalty toward her brother, and men will in fact appeal to their sisters for favors that they would ask of no one else. Similarly, a woman will depend upon her brother instead of her husband for support and sympathy. Often, the interests of siblings clash with those of their respective spouses, in which case brothers and sisters will always side with their siblings. Additionally, the relationships between sisters are strong among Palauans. Among the West Punjabi in South Asia, the brother-sister relationship is primary, and a brother is said to come first in a woman's thoughts. Brothers protect their sisters, and the two share confidences with one another. A sister takes her brother's part in disputes between the boy and his parents, and she will also see to it that he is served his favorite meals. When a brother dies, it is his sister who grieves the most. A woman also remains attached to her mother for life and a married daughter goes back to her mother's home for family celebrations and the births of her children. An Ashanti (in Ghana) husband's strongest ties are to the women in his own family, and a man will trust his sister and not his wife when it comes to important matters. A husband confides in his sister about financial and legal affairs and concerns relating to his marriage or children. It is a man's sister who supervises his valuable property and his sister or mother on whom he depends to take charge of his catch on a fishing expedition. Similarly, an Ashanti wife puts her faith in her bother and not her husband in times of crisis, and it is common for a wife to continue to live with her own kin for a number of years after she is married, cooking and also sleeping there when she is not sleeping with her husband. A brother is connected to a woman by blood and can be counted on to protect her in times of need. The Comanche of the United States Plains view the brother-brother relationship as among the most intimate in a person's life, and it is said that a brother is more important to a man than is his wife. One brother will lend another his wife, and jealousy between brothers is disapproved. And among the Siriono of South America, the strongest lifetime attachment is between siblings of the same sex and roughly the same age. Brothers share secrets with brothers and sisters with sisters, while the spouse is left ignorant of these confidences. The closest companion and friend of the Siriono adult is the brother for a man and the sister for a woman.

Kin Group Attachment

Some cultures make an overarching distinction between a person's kin and the kin of the spouse, and decree that spouses direct their principal loyalties toward and attachment to their own kin groups. This is the case among the Ifugao of the Philippines, for whom marriage represents a strengthening of the tie between the two kin groups from which the spouses originate. If a quarrel arises between the groups, divorces are likely to occur because blood ties are always considered to be stronger than the bonds of marriage. Even after marriage, a Brazilian Mundurucu man's primary loyalties are to his own family, and a wife's to hers. A man does not initially feel any strong attachment to his wife's household. As a result, he has no compelling reason to stay with his wife if the two are having difficulties, and marriages are in fact brittle in the early years until spouses develop a more abiding affection for each other. Among the Murngin of Australia, a man's own brothers or his father's brothers and mother's sisters are his best friends. Male cross-cousins also form very close attachments, and one cousin will always solicit the other for help when he gets himself into a difficult situation. A Murngin wife is always viewed as belonging to her own clan even after her husband's group has adopted her. A society may sometimes attempt to derail any potential defections on the part of a member of the kin group.

In societies where wives live with the husband's family, women may still retain strong ties to their own kin. A Somali wife remains attached to her family emotionally and legally and she and her relatives exchange visits often. She is viewed as a member of the lineage of her natal family and her brothers and other kin are still concerned about her welfare even though she has married and moved away. Similarly, a Suku woman in Zaire remains a member of her own lineage after marriage. Whatever wealth she manages to accumulate goes to her kin, and her affections remain so much with her own family that, if she falls ill, she wishes to be cared for by her relatives instead of her husband's. Even after she is married, a Bhil woman of India remains attached to her own family. A few months after her wedding, a young bride is fetched by her father or older brother and brought back home for a short visit. Her mother or older sister-in-law ask her whether she is being treated well in her new home. If she has any complaints, one of her female relatives relates them to her husband when he comes to pick her up and take her back to his household. When a married daughter returns home to see her family, everyone is overjoyed. These visits are frequent and long, especially during the first years of her marriage, and sometimes an unhappy wife will run away to her own relatives, insisting that she is being mistreated by her spouse. Hausa women in Nigeria also remain strongly attached to their own kin after marriage, and the high divorce rate and overall instability of Hausa marriages are attributed to this abiding attachment.

Sometimes, cultural tradition demands that spouses abandon any attachments to their own relatives and transfer their primary fidelity to the kin groups of the spouse. In the opinion of the Igbo, a woman's first loyalty is to her husband's village. In keeping with this belief, a wife does not return to her natal home to have her children, nor is a child supposed to be taken for a visit to the village of its maternal grandparents until it is able to walk. In spite of these cultural expectations, husbands and wives often find the pull of the affection that they feel for their own kin groups to be powerful. In Indonesia, for example, when an Alorese woman marries, her allegiance belongs, in principle, to her husband's village and kin group. However, her own relatives still expect her to remain loyal to them and, indeed, her ties to her family remain strong after her marriage. When she is pregnant, it is her brother and, to a lesser degree, her sisters and mother who see to her material needs, not her husband. The emotional dislocation experienced by a newly married person who is expected to disavow family ties is appreciated by some societies, who try to smooth the adjustment. Beginning several days after her wedding, a Japanese bride makes a number of scheduled trips back home to see her own family. The visits are viewed as a respite from the stress of living with her new husband's family.

In a number of societies, a person feels most attached and owes the greatest loyalty not to a spouse or relative, but to a friend. Orokaiva boys in New Guinea who have been secluded together during their initiation rites become *naname* to each other, and over the years men acquire more *naname* among other communities. The relationship between *naname* is a special one that transcends all other obligations, even to the degree that a man's loyalty to his *naname* is viewed as stronger than that to his family and kin.

Barnett, H. G. (1949) *Palauan Society: A Study of Contemporary Native Life in the Palau Islands.*

Barton, R. F. (1938) *Philippine Pagans: The Autobiographies of Three Ifugaos.*

Beardsley, Richard K., John W. Hall, and Robert E. Ward. (1972) *Village Japan.*

Bowers, Alfred W. (1950) *Mandan Social and Ceremonial Organization.*

Christensen, James. (1954) *Double Descent among the Fanti.*

Dorsey, J. Owen. (1884) *Omaha Sociology.* Third Annual Report of the Bureau of American Ethnology, 1881–1882.

DuBois, Cora. (1944) *The People of Alor: A Social Psychological Study of an East Indian Island.*

Dundas, Charles. (1924) *Kilimanjaro and Its People: A History of the Wachagga, Their Laws, Customs, and Legends, Together with Some Account of the Highest Mountain in Africa.*

Dyk, Walter. (1951) "Notes and Illustrations of Navaho Sexual Behavior." In *Psychoanalysis and Culture,* edited by George B. Wilbur and Warner Muensterberger.

Eglar, Zekiye Suleyman. (1960) *A Punjabi Village in Pakistan.*

Ffoulkes, Arthur. (1908) "The Fanti Family System." *African Society Journal* 7: 394–409.

Fletcher, Alice C., and Francis La Flesche. (1911) *The Omaha Tribe.* Twenty-seventh Annual Report of the Bureau of American Ethnology, 1905–1906.

Fortes, Meyer. (1936) "Ritual Festivals and Social Cohesion in the Hinterland of the Gold Coast." *American Anthropologist* 38: 590–604.

———. (1949) *The Web of Kinship among the Tallensi: The Second Part of an Analysis of the Social Structure of a Trans-Volta Tribe.*

Freeman, John D. (1958) "The Family System of the Iban of Borneo." In *The Developmental Cycle in Domestic Groups,* edited by Jack Goody, 15–52.

Fuchs, Stephen. (1942) "The Marriage Rites of the Bhils in the Nimar District, C.P." *Man in India* 22: 105–139.

Gladwin, Thomas. (1948) "Comanche Kin Behavior." *American Anthropologist* 50: 73–94.

Gray, Robert F., and P. H. Gulliver. (1964) *The Family Estate in Africa.*

Green, M. M. (1947) *Ibo Village Affairs.*

Holmberg, Allen R. (1950) *Nomads of the Long Bow.* Smithsonian Institution. Institute of Social Anthropology 10.

Leighton, Dorothea, and Clyde Kluckhohn. (1969) *Children of the People: The Navaho Individual and His Development.*

Lewis, I. M. (1962) *Marriage and the Family in Northern Somaliland.*

Murphy, Robert F. (1960) *Headhunter's Heritage: Social and Economic Change among the Mundurucu Indians.*

Naik, T. B. (1956) *The Bhils: A Study.*

Nimuendaju, Curt. (1946) "The Eastern Timbira." University of California Publications in *American Archaeology and Ethnology* 41.

Opler, Morris Edward. (1941) *An Apache Life-Way: The Economic, Social and Religious Institutions of the Chiricahua Indians.*

Raum, O. F. (1940) *Chaga Childhood: A Description of Indigenous Education in an East African Tribe.*

Reay, Marie. (1953–54) "Social Control amongst the Orokaiva." *Oceania* 24: 110–118.

Richards, Audrey I. (1940) *Bemba Marriage and Present Economic Conditions.* Rhodes-Livingstone Papers 4.

Smith, Mary F. (1954) *The Baba of Karo: A Woman of the Muslim Hausa.*

Stirling, A. Paul. (1957) "Land, Marriage, and the Law in Turkish Villages." *International Social Science Bulletin* 9: 21–33.

———. (1965) *Turkish Village.*

Swanton, John. (1924–1925) *Social Organization and Social Usages of the Indians of the Creek Confederacy.* U.S. Bureau of American Ethnology, Annual Report 42.

Venieminov, Ivan Evsieevich Popov. (1840) *Zapiski ob Ostravakh Unalashkinskago Otdiela* [Notes on the islands of the Unalaska district], vols. 2–3.

Vreeland, Herbert H. (1953) *Mongol Community and Kinship Structure.*

Warner, W. Lloyd. (1937) *A Black Civilization: A Social Study of an Australian Tribe.*

Whiting, Beatrice B. (1950) *Paiute Sorcery.* Viking Fund Publications in Anthropology 15.

Wilbur, Donald N. (1964) *Pakistan: Its People, Its Society, Its Culture.*

Woodburn, J. (1964) *The Social Organization of the Hadza of North Tanzania.* Unpublished dissertation, Cambridge University.

ATTRACTIVENESS

Cultures vary widely regarding the particular traits that make for a beautiful woman or a handsome man. Not uncommonly, physical features that are preferred

A woman of Khevsur, Georgia, who displays Khevsur ideals of beauty. In most cultures, female attractiveness matters more than does male attractiveness.

in one culture will be regarded as unattractive in another. Gusii men of Kenya are attracted by small-breasted women, while the Alorese men of Indonesia like large breasts, and the Azande men of Zaire find long, pendulous breasts most appealing. Gusii men prefer girls with small eyes and narrow mouths, and a space between the front teeth is also preferred. Kwakiutl (United States), Lenge (Mozambique), and Tongan (western Polynesia) males like a woman with small ankles. In other cultures, women are regarded as more or less attractive based upon the length, texture, or color of hair or the shape of the ears.

Beyond the cross-cultural variation in criteria of attractiveness, a number of regularities appear in how people across cultures regard physical appearance. A plump woman is considered more attractive than a thin one in many societies around the world. Among the Goajiro of Colombia, the best wife is tall and buxom, and the Chiricahua of the southwestern United States and Pukapukans of Oceania, among others, prefer a plump body shape. Most cultures around the world, including the Chuckchee in Siberia, Hopi in Arizona, and Siriono in South America, also find a broad pelvis and wide hips more pleasing than their opposites. So are regular facial features preferred across cultures. Further, there is a set of characteristics that people around the world regard as unattractive. A poor complexion and disfigurements of the face or body are considered unappealing, as is filthiness in a person. A Gusii groom who finds on his wedding night that his new bride is scarred or deformed may even send her home. Siuai women in Oceania prefer men with hair free of lice and clean loin cloths, and men like women who are clean and good-smelling. Interestingly, physical attractiveness matters more in a woman than in a man in most societies. Men, by contrast, are more likely to be judged on the basis of their physical skills, wealth, and social standing.

Why are certain characteristics regularly associated with attractiveness across cultures? Physical attractiveness plays an important role in the choice of sexual partners across cultures. A woman's physical appearance is a consideration in the selection of a wife in many societies around the globe. Some of the universal indices of physical attractiveness, such as clear skin and a full figure, also reflect the health of an individual. Others, like wide hips and pelvis, are likely to make child-bearing less risky. Those traits that are commonly viewed as unattractive are also reflections of possible ill-health. Thus, cultures vary about the degree of attractiveness of reproductively inconsequential physical traits, but traits that are more useful in conveying information about the potential reproductive success of an individual tend to be noticed and similarly assessed by societies around the world. The discrepancy regarding the importance of physical appearance in men and women can be explained in the same way. The physical condition of a woman is more important to reproductive success than is the physical status of a man. It is the woman who is required to carry a fetus for nine months and then nurse an infant for some months or years. Evidence demonstrates that physically healthy women are more successful in bearing and nursing babies than are women who are not in good physical condition. Indeed, if the percentage of fat to body weight for a woman dips below a critical level, she will become infertile even if she has already attained sexual maturity. In societies where a woman's physical stamina matters to her ability to perform subsistence activities, this too can become a criterion of attractiveness. For instance, the Kwoma of New Guinea think of a woman who can carry a heavy load as attractive, and the Chuckchee say that a woman is beautiful if her body is strong. The focus on a man's social position, physical skills, and wealth instead of his physical appearance is consistent with this interpretation of evaluations of attractiveness:

while a man's physical condition is relatively unimportant to his ability to inseminate a female, his ability to provide resources for a child and family matter very much to reproductive success. Men have a tendency to concentrate on those characteristics of a woman that matter to her future as a successful mother, and women tend to concentrate on those traits in a man that will make him a good provider for her and her children.

Even when the same trait is regarded as attractive in one culture and unattractive in another, these contradictory views can do the same work. For instance, some cultures that regard fatness in a woman as appealing also have problems with food scarcity. Extra weight is an asset in these societies, such as the Chuckchee, because women who are overweight have nutritional reserves upon which to fall back in lean times. By contrast, in cultures where there is an abundance of food and obesity is a real threat to good health, slimness is sometimes seen as preferable. Similarly, in America the absence of a suntan was viewed as beautiful when it indicated that a person was well-off and did not need to work out in the sun. By contrast, sunburns became an index of attractiveness when they indicated that a person was wealthy enough to take vacations from work and sunbathe. This is not just an idiosyncrasy of Western culture. For example, among the Goajiro, light skin is an indication that a woman is able to take care of herself by staying out of the sun, and light-skinned women are thought of as beautiful.

See also MARRIAGE PARTNERS, CRITERIA FOR CHOOSING; NATURAL SELECTION; SEXUAL SELECTION.

Bogoras, Waldemar. (1904–1909) *The Chukchee.*

———. (1929) "Siberian Cousins of the Eskimo." *Asia* 29: 316–322, 334—337.

Ford, Clellan S., and Frank A. Beach. (1951) *Patterns of Sexual Behavior.*

Frayser, Suzanne G. (1985) *Varieties of Sexual Experience.*

Gutierrez de Pineda, Virginia. (1950) *Social Organization in La Guajira.*

LeVine, Robert A., and Barbara B. LeVine. (1966) *Nyansongo: A Gusii Community in Kenya.*

Oliver, Douglas. (1955) *A Solomon Island Society: Kinship and Leadership among the Siuai of Bougainville.*

Opler, Morris Edward. (1941) *An Apache Life-Way: The Economic, Social and Religious Institutions of the Chiricahua Indians.*

Whiting, John W. M. (1941) *Becoming a Kwoma: Teaching and Learning in a New Guinea Tribe.*

AVOIDANCE RELATIONSHIPS

A number of societies around the world require some relatives to avoid each other on a day-to-day basis. Avoidance customs can target different kinds of behaviors in different cultures. Individuals may be prevented from eating together, sleeping in the same house, talking to each other directly or when no one else is around, having eye contact, touching each other, and so on.

Avoidance customs are most commonly attached to the relationship between a man and his wife's mother. These avoidances take a variety of forms. Among the Gros Ventre of the United States, it is taboo for a husband and his wife's mother to speak to or look at each other or to be in the same tent together. A Ganda man in Uganda and his mother-in-law must not hold hands, pass each other in a doorway, look at each other directly, eat together, or speak together alone. When a Miskito husband in Central America is at home, his mother-in-law stays in her own room, which is separated from the rest of the house to allow the two to avoid each other more easily.

Second in frequency are rules of avoidance between a woman and her husband's father. In Oceania, a Manus wife must avoid her father-in-law, and a Manus house is partitioned into separate compartments by mats hanging from the ceiling to make it easier for a woman and her husband's father to respect this requirement. A daughter-in-law can never raise her voice for fear that her father-in-law might hear her. She is prohibited from entering his section of the house when he is there. And she must cover her face if she cannot actually run away whenever her husband's father appears.

The brother-sister relationship is the third most frequent target of avoidance. Among the Papago of the southwestern United States, the brother-sister relationship is mildly respectful. Opposite-sex siblings would never think of staying alone in the same house at night or being seen out with each other. Samoan brothers and sisters are prohibited from touching each other, talking informally together, sitting or eating in each other's presence, dancing on the same floor, or remaining in one another's presence except in a crowd or at home. In Tanzania, a Chagga brother is not allowed to sleep in his sister's house. When he visits her, he must sit on the floor and he may not reach across her bed for any purpose. A brother cannot use obscene language in his sister's presence, nor can anyone else who is in the company of a brother and sister. The same rules apply to girls in connection with their brothers, and opposite-sex siblings are very shy in all of their dealings with each other. Gros Ventre brothers and sisters may not look at or speak to each other unless it cannot be avoided, but they must help each other out when asked. Same-sex siblings, by contrast, are on friendly terms.

Other kin avoidance customs also occur in societies around the world. For instance, avoidance rules may apply to brothers. In New Guinea, Kimam brothers would be ashamed to touch each other and, therefore, never sit together. Neither do they eat with each other, and a brother will use a go-between instead of talking to his sibling directly. Avoidance customs may target the father-daughter relationship. In Alaska, Kaska girls begin to feel shy in front of their fathers as they become physically mature. From then on, fathers and daughters begin to avoid each other, and this continues after the girl is married. In some cultures, it is the parents and the eldest child who must avoid each other. This is the case among the Hausa of Nigeria, where, as a result, a firstborn child is adopted by relatives. Parents and their eldest child strictly avoid each other in public and a parent may not look directly at a firstborn or use the child's name. By contrast, mothers and fathers enjoy a playful relationship with the last-born child. Avoidance behavior is expected between spouse in a number of societies. Among the Manus, a betrothed couple is required to strictly avoid each other, and this constraint on their relationship remains in force for the early years of marriage. A husband and wife may not use each other's personal names, and spouses who have no children must avoid each other in public. Nor do they eat together until they have had two or three children. A man may not be light or playful with his wife, nor may a married couple engage in informal conversation. Among the Chiricahua of the American Southwest, all relatives of the opposite sex are supposed to be somewhat reserved in each other's presence. This overall expectation includes brothers and sisters, and many families erect an extra shelter to which a boy can retreat if his sister is alone in the main dwelling, as the two should not be found alone in a house together.

Avoidance rules may also be extended to classificatory kin, that is, to people whom one calls by the same kin term even though one is not related to them all in the same way. Trukese brothers and sisters begin to be restrained with each other once they have reached puberty. They avoid making any references to sex or excretion when in one another's company, and other people must also watch what they say when a brother and sister are present. A similar degree of reserve is practiced by classificatory siblings, that is, people who call themselves brothers and sisters. The relationship between real and classificatory brothers also changes as males attain physical maturity. Younger boys must treat their elder male siblings with respect and avoid off-color humor.

When a culture requires avoidance behavior between a particular category of kin, the avoidance is often extended in a predictable way to other kin relationships. For instance, if a man is compelled to avoid his sister, he must often also avoid his female cousins. A man who avoids his mother-in-law also tends to avoid some of his wife's other relatives. Similarly, when a woman avoids her father-in-law, she is also likely to avoid some of her husband's other kin. As a consequence of this tendency to extend avoidance customs, a society that invokes any avoidance rules is likely to insist upon avoidance behaviors for a large number of kin categories.

Sometimes avoidance is expected between pairs of individuals whose relationship is also circumscribed by other kinds of prohibitions. Among the !Kung Bushmen of southern Africa, certain categories of individuals are permitted to make sexual jokes with each other. Other classes of people are prohibited from alluding to sex in front of each other. Individuals who cannot joke with each other must also avoid sitting near one another or near each other's family fire and should not let their genitals touch the same place. Members of the nuclear family are exempted from the sitting taboo even though they avoid sexual joking in each other's presence. More generally, cultures that prescribe joking between some

kinds of kin tend also to prescribe avoidance behavior between other categories of kin.

Cultures establish avoidance rules to control relationships that have the potential to be disruptive, so the rules may act to contain conflict. Avoidance customs applied to a husband and his mother-in-law in matrilocal societies are consistent with this idea, and such avoidance rules are in fact common in societies where a man moves in with the family of his spouse. Matrilocality may promote conflict between a man and his wife's mother because men in these societies are often defined as outsiders, subordinate in status and power to the wife's kin. In a matrilocal society, it is often the mother-in-law who oversees household affairs, and an in-marrying man is likely to have trouble adjusting to his new role and position in his wife's family's house or village. Avoidance rules, therefore, minimize the contact between a new husband and the woman who has authority over him. The North American Cheyenne illustrate this principle. In this culture, a husband moved into his wife's camp and contributed to the economic functioning of his spouse's family. In the beginning, the son-in-law was likely to view himself as an intruder in his wife's community. During this time, he and his wife's mother avoided each other completely. The avoidance restrictions, however, may have been cancelled when the husband and his mother-in-law exchanged gifts publicly and tensions diminished between them. Avoidance rules may also serve to minimize sexual intercourse between individuals who are prohibited from engaging in sex according to the norms of the culture. In New Ireland, a Lesu brother and sister are friendly and helpful toward one another, and they often give each other gifts and do each other favors as adults. But a semi-avoidance relationship is also enjoined upon them and, as a consequence, brothers and sisters will rarely converse with each other or direct any intimate gestures to one another. The aim of this policy, according to the Lesu, is to guarantee that a brother and sister will have no sexual contact.

———————

Conzemius, Eduard. (1932) *Ethnographical Survey of the Miskito and Sumu Indians of Honduras and Nicaragua.*

Gladwin, Thomas, and Seymour Sarason. (1953) *Truk: Man in Paradise.*

Gutmann, Bruno. (1926) *Das Recht der Dschagga* [Chagga law].

Honigmann, John J. (1949) *Culture and Ethos of Kaska Society.*

Kroeber, A. L. (1908) *Ethnology of the Gros Ventre.* Anthropological Papers of the American Museum of Natural History 1.

Levinson, David, and Martin Malone. (1980) *Toward Explaining Human Culture.*

Marshall, Lorna. (1959) "Marriage among the !Kung Bushmen." *Africa* 29: 335–364.

Mead, Margaret. (1930) *Growing Up in New Guinea: A Comparative Study of Primitive Education.*

Murdock, George Peter. (1936) *Our Primitive Contemporaries.*

Opler, Morris Edward. (1941) *An Apache Life-Way: The Economic, Social and Religious Institutions of the Chiricahua Indians.*

Powdermaker, Hortense. (1933) *Life in Lesu: The Study of a Melanesian Society in New Ireland.*

Serpenti, I. M. (1965) *Cultivators in the Swamps.*

Smith, Mary F. (1954) *The Baba of Karo: A Woman of the Muslim Hausa.*

Stephens, William N. (1963) *The Family in Cross-Cultural Perspective.*

Stephens, William N., and Roy G. D'Andrade. (1962) "Kin-Avoidance." In *The Oedipus Complex: Cross-Cultural Evidence,* by William Stephens, 124–150.

Underhill, Ruth M. (1936) *The Autobiography of a Papago Woman.*

———. (1939) *Social Organization of the Papago Indians.*

ment be broken. But the boy and girl do take the proposed arrangement seriously and will only resist an eventual marriage if they dislike one another intensely. By contrast, betrothals in many Asian cultures are almost as binding as is a marriage itself. In India, a promise between two people to marry is so serious that, if the boy dies before the marriage can take place, the girl is treated as a widow and is compelled to remain unmarried for the remainder of her life.

Betrothals sometimes function as a sort of down payment for a bride. The groom or his family may present the bride or her family with gifts, sometimes in partial payment of the bride price, the remainder of which will be turned over at the marriage itself. The betrothal may be accompanied by a ceremony, often at the bride's home. In Sri Lanka, the prospective groom and his male kin march together in their best clothing to the house of the bride-to-be, where they are greeted by the girl and her kin. A formal document specifying that the couple is now betrothed is read and an astrologer determines when the wedding preparations and the ceremony itself can safely be conducted. The boy and girl give each other rings and half of the bride price is paid to the bride's family. After the betrothal has been finalized, plans for the marriage proper begin. In cultures where betrothals characterize the marriage arrangements of a culture, the betrothal itself may be said to emphasize the contractual aspect of the marriage, while the wedding itself focuses on the consummation of the marriage.

See also CHILD BETROTHAL; MARRIAGE, ARRANGED.

BETROTHAL A male and female are betrothed when a commitment to marry has been made on their behalf. The two people themselves may take the initiative in promising to marry one another, or the commitment may be made by third parties, as happens in arranged marriages. Betrothals may take place when the prospective spouses are grown or almost grown and are ready to enter into a marriage. But in a number of societies, children are betrothed in infancy, or even before they are born. The marriage may follow quickly after the betrothal has taken place, or, as is usually the case when children are promised to each other, the betrothal may precede the actual marriage by years.

Societies differ in the degree to which betrothals are considered binding. Among the Kwoma in New Guinea, a marriage may be arranged by the parents of a boy or girl, usually at puberty, although children may be promised to each other in infancy. The betrothal can be broken, as the parents of the would-be bride and groom exchange gifts of roughly equal value, making neither side a loser should the agree-

Ember, Carol R., and Melvin Ember. (1988) *Anthropology*. 5th ed.

Mace, David, and Vera Mace. (1960) *Marriage: East and West.*

Whiting, John W. M. (1941) *Becoming a Kwoma: Teaching and Learning in a New Guinea Tribe.*

———. (1970) *Kwoma Journal.*

BOASTING

A Navajo male who has engaged in sexual intercourse with a girl is circumspect about the episode. Men in this culture seldom talk to each other about women, and any reference that a relative or friend makes to an affair in which a boy is involved is likely to embarrass him greatly. Whereas both men and women among the Truk in Oceania actively aspire to have many sexual partners, any blatant boasting about one's victories is not approved. By contrast, Trumai boys in Brazil are proud of their sexual exploits and boast about their successes, and one man who wishes to insult another might accuse him of being impotent. This inclination to brag about one's sexual experiences is typical of males in many cultures around the world. Among Vietnamese villagers, men sit around in groups drinking and attempting to enhance their reputations by boasting about all of their girlfriends. Similarly, when they are drinking, Kaska boys in Alaska will brag to each other about the number of girls with whom they have had sexual intercourse in a single night and the number of orgasms they are capable of experiencing. Kwoma boys of New Guinea will boast about their sexual conquests to other males whom they know well, and a young man who is particularly successful with the girls is admired by his peers. Boys are encouraged to pursue active sex lives when they see how sexual conquests enhance the reputations of other males. At evening dances in New Guinea, a courageous Kapauku boy may grab a girl's breasts if the torches go out. Even if he is slapped and knocked to the floor by the other girls in retaliation, the chance to boast about his exploits to the other boys will make it all worthwhile. And during a war, Crow men of the United States practiced the custom of "naming of married women." Each man in turn took a piece of buffalo meat and recited: "I shall bring a horse for so-and-so," and called out the name of some other man's wife with whom he had slept. These declarations had to be truthful, as the outcome of the battle depended upon the honesty of the boasts. Similarly, Gusii grooms in Kenya compare with each other the number of times that they were able to have sexual intercourse on their wedding night. If a bride is unable to walk the next day, the new husband is considered to be a "real man" who can boast of his successes, especially if he was able to make the girl cry.

In cultures where boasting over sexual exploits is common, and perhaps expected, both premarital and extramarital sex are very frequent among males. By contrast, extramarital sex is condemned for wives, so there is a double standard regarding attitudes toward sexual activity for men and women outside of marriage. Men who boast about their sexual activities also tend to be aggressive in their sexual advances toward females.

Boasting is also characteristic of men who display a variety of aggressive behaviors. Thus, in cultures where boasting is typical, males tend to seek out military glory and to be generally belligerent. This profile of male behavior is often found in societies where fathers play a minimal role in childrearing and where, therefore, boys are raised primarily by the mother and other women. Some social scientists believe that boys who grow up in this kind of environment develop some insecurities about their identities as men and then exhibit excessively masculine behaviors as a way of compensating for this uncertainty about themselves as males. However, this same portrait of boasting, pugnacity, and so on is also typical of men who have grown up in households that fail to discipline aggressive behavior in boys. These are households in which male influence is absent. So the tendency of men to boast and to otherwise demonstrate aggressive behavior may be a result of child rearing strategies that do not penalize aggression in boys.

Broude, Gwen J. (1990) "Protest Masculinity: A Further Look at the Causes and the Concept." *Ethos* 18: 103–122.

Coughlin, Richard. (1965) "Pregnancy and Childbirth in Vietnam." In *Southeast Asian Customs,* edited by Donn V. Hart.

Gladwin, Thomas, and Seymour Sarason. (1953) *Truk: Man in Paradise.*

Honigmann, John J. (1949) *Culture and Ethos of Kaska Society.*

Leighton, Dorothea, and Clyde Kluckhohn. (1969) *Children of the People: The Navaho Individual and His Development.*

LeVine, Robert A., and Barbara B. LeVine. (1966) *Nyansongo: A Gusii Community in Kenya.*

Lowie, Robert. (1912) *Social Life of the Crow Indians.*

———. (1935) *The Crow Indians.*

Murphy, Robert F., and Buell Quain. (1955) *The Trumai Indians of Central Brazil.*

Pospisil, Leopold. (1958) *The Kapauku Papuans and Their Law.* Yale University Publications in Anthropology 54.

Whiting, John W. M. (1941) *Becoming a Kwoma: Teaching and Learning in a New Guinea Tribe.*

BRIDE CAPTURE

Across cultures, when a couple is married, it is usually with the approval of the bride herself or of her parents or kin group. But in some societies, a man may acquire a wife without obtaining the permission of the parties whose authorization is ordinarily required. Instead, the bride is forcibly abducted and married against the wishes of her kin or of the woman herself. This custom is referred to as bride capture or bride theft. Where it occurs, bride capture is infrequent and not the typical way of obtaining a wife.

Men will go to the trouble of stealing a wife for a number of reasons. Men will sometimes resort to bride theft when they cannot afford to marry in the traditional way. For instance, when some kind of monetary or other material payment is required from the bride's or groom's family at the time of marriage, bride theft begins to show up as a strategy for obtaining a bride. Bride capture is sometimes practiced as an alternate form of marriage for this reason among the rural Amhara of Ethiopia. The custom is preferred when the kin of a bride and groom cannot afford a "civil" wedding and are unable to provide the cattle that a couple normally receives when married.

A couple may also resort to bride theft when they wish to marry but are afraid that their families will disapprove of and try to block their marriage. When a Wogeo man and woman in New Guinea want to marry but are afraid that the match will not be approved by the woman's parents, the prospective groom may adopt a plan to have her kidnapped by a group of men. The man will later send a message to his bride's family to explain what he has done.

Sometimes, parents arrange for a daughter to be married to someone whom she dislikes. Bride capture then becomes the woman's way of sabotaging the match to which her elders have committed her. In Indonesia, Balinese marriages are often arranged by the parents of a couple. But if the girl has become attached to someone else instead, she may have her suitor kidnap her and marry her secretly. If the female's father is satisfied with his new son-in-law, no payment will be required of the young man. But if the father disapproves of the marriage, the groom must make a payment as compensation for the anger that his father-in-law feels.

A man will also sometimes depend upon bride theft to obtain a wife when he has his heart set on a particular woman but does not believe that he can win her by customary means. A Bhil man in India who has taken a fancy to some girl but who fears rejection from her parents or from the young woman herself may kidnap her. The man might take the woman to some secret place, where the two would stay for as long as it took to win the parents over to the match. Abduction is a criminal offense, but men frequently resort to the practice in spite of the possible repercussions. And when the parents of a woman or the woman herself resist a proposal of marriage, a Santal man in India sometimes resorts to marriage by capture. If the bride is willing to remain with her kidnapper, then the union is recognized as a genuine marriage. The girl's family receives double the normal bride price.

Sometimes, bride theft is reserved to men of a particular rank within the larger society. Among the various forms of marriage traditionally recognized by Hindus was *rakshasa,* or marriage by capture. A girl's relatives were first killed and then the girl herself was taken by force and married. *Rakshasa* was sanctioned only for members of the warrior caste.

In some cultures, the prospective groom only puts on a show of stealing a wife. The groom's family battles with the relatives of the bride until the girl is finally carried off by her suitor. This kind of mock bride capture is reminiscent of other practices in a number of cultures in which relatives of the marrying couple stage fights or insult contests with one another as part of the wedding ceremony.

Ayres, Barbara. (1974) "Bride Theft and Raiding for Wives in Cross-Cultural Perspective." *Anthropological Quarterly* 71: 138–252.

Belo, Jane. (1936) "Study of Balinese Family." *American Anthropologist* 38: 12–31.

Covarrubias, Miguel. (1937) *Island of Bali.*

Culshaw, W. J. (1949) *Tribal Heritage: A Study of the Santals.*

Ember, Carol R., and Melvin Ember. (1988) *Anthropology.* 5th ed.

Gamble, David P. (1949) *Contributions to a Socio-economic Survey of the Gambia.*

———. (1957) *The Wolof of Senegambia, Together with Notes on the Lebu and the Serer.*

Levinson, David, and Martin J. Malone. (1980) *Toward Explaining Human Culture.*

Mace, David, and Vera Mace. (1960) *Marriage: East and West.*

Messing, Simon D. (1957) *The Highland-Plateau Amhara of Ethiopia.*

Nath, Y. V. S. (1960) *Bhils of Ratanmal: An Analysis of the Social Structure of a Western Indian Community.*

BRIDE PRICE In most non-Western cultures around the world, some kind of transfer of money or goods occurs between the families of the bride and groom. The most common form of transfer is from the husband's family to that of the wife. In a sample of 565 societies, 47 percent are characterized by this kind of transaction, that is, by bride price or bride wealth.

Bride price, when it is customary in a culture, is almost always substantial. Payment of bride price provides the bride's family with the resources to furnish one of their sons with a wife. In this sense, bride price performs a function similar to the custom by which two families exchange women as wives for their sons.

Among the Subanum of the Philippines, the bride price is equivalent to the annual salary of

Payment of bride price occurs on Rossel Island as in most other cultures in which the bride moves to live near or with her husband's family.

the prospective husband a number of times over. In addition to this steep payment, the groom is expected to work on behalf of his wife's family for from three to five years. Bride-price payments can be dragged out for decades.

Livestock and food are common goods offered as part of the bride-price payment. But many other kinds of goods can serve as payment of bride price across cultures. The Arapesh of New Guinea include shell money and rings as part of the bride wealth payment. The Cheyenne of the U.S. Plains gave horses, and to food and money payments the Manus add pots and dog's teeth. The Somali present spears, shields, and, in the past, slaves to the father of the bride.

The value of the bride price may vary from marriage to marriage within the same culture.

Among the East European Abkhaz, the size of the payment is determined by the personal characteristics of the bride—for instance, her status as a virgin or nonvirgin, and, more importantly, her family's social class. Similarly, among the Swazi of East Africa, a girl's social status determines the size of the bride price. A princess may attract a payment of 15 or more head of cattle, while commoners bring perhaps 10 head. A hard-working Kapauku girl of New Guinea always attracts a larger bride price than does a widow or a woman who is ugly or known to be lazy. Age also influences the value of the bride price. The older the bride, the smaller the bride price. Azande women of Zaire do most of the work in any household and are, therefore, viewed symbolically as a kind of wealth in the eyes of their kin. So the bride price that is paid to a girl's family is a recognition of her value to her kin as well as a first installment of gifts given from time to time to the bride's family. If a bride proves to be barren, lazy, or irritable, the subsequent presents received by her family will not be as valuable as they would have been had she proven to be more satisfactory as a wife.

The payment of the bride price confers rights upon a husband. For instance, the Ashanti of Ghana allow unmarried couples to cohabit as if married, and this connection is treated as if it were in fact a proper marriage. But if the woman has an affair, no adultery compensation can be claimed by her housemate. Once the bride price is paid, however, a man can demand sexual exclusivity of his wife and acquires legal rights to any children born for the duration of the marriage. Payment of the bride price also entitles him to his spouse's household services. Among the Bambara of West Africa, a husband is entitled to expect proper behavior from his wife in return for bride price. If a husband is unhappy with his spouse's behavior, he will report this to her home community, the members of which will work to rectify matters for fear of otherwise having to return the bride price. The idea that bride wealth payments confer rights on the husband is highlighted by the case of the Bambara. Bambara marriages usually entail the payment of a bride price by the groom's community to that of the bride, and the girl is then considered to be ceded to her husband and his people. On occasion, however, a man may wish to forge an alliance with some individual who lives in another community. In this case, he may give the prospective ally a girl from his own community, along with a dowry. As the husband has not paid a bride price, he is required to treat his wife extremely well unless he wishes her to be repossessed by her community. Divorce customs also reflect the connection between bride price and a husband's rights to a woman. In Colombia, if a Goajiro wife fails to adequately perform the household chores, her spouse may not only divorce her but also demand repayment of the bride price. However, a portion of the original payment remains with the wife's family as compensation for the sexual services enjoyed by the husband while the couple was married. Similarly, if a Chagga wife in Tanzania leaves an abusive husband, the bride price is not returned. But if a wife does not fulfill her obligations to her spouse, he can return her to her parents and demand repayment of whatever expenses he has incurred during his marriage. The family of an Azande bride receives valuable spears periodically from the husband's family during the course of the marriage, but all of the spears revert to the man's kin if the marriage is dissolved. More generally, the bride wealth payment is forfeited if the husband does not fulfill his responsibilities. If the wife is at fault when a marriage fails, then her family is required to return part or all of the bride price.

The bride price can also serve as compensation from the husband's family in return for the wife's production of children. If a Balinese woman of Indonesia fails to provide her spouse with offspring, he can divorce her and also repossess the bride price that was paid at their marriage. An infertile woman may choose instead to propose that her husband recruit a second wife who will produce children. A Chagga husband whose wife cannot have children is not required to pay the balance of the bride price although he may still present his father-in-law with a gift of food as a sign of respect. When his wife dies, he will also give a bull in payment for the work she did while she was alive.

Bride price tends to make marriages more stable because the family of the bride cannot or does not wish to return the valuable goods or money given at marriage. Among the Kapauku, wealthier men are expected to pay a greater bride price than are less well-off men. The more valuable the bride price, the more stable is the marriage, as the bride price must be returned to the husband in the event of a divorce and the wife's kin are likely to have trouble accumulating a return payment of high value. A woman's relatives, therefore, attempt to induce her to stay married. Divorce is very rare among rich Kazak couples of central Asia because of the arguments that are likely to arise over the apportionment of the large bride price that the husband paid. Marriages among the less well-off are easier to terminate.

The custom of bride price tends to be found in particular kinds of societies. Thus, cultures that expect a groom or his family to make bride wealth payments are also likely to be patrilocal and patrilineal, with authority resting with the relatives of the male head of household. Bride-price societies also tend to have class stratification, individual property rights, and rules for inheritance in which wealth is passed down through the male line. Finally, where bride price is the norm, premarital sex for girls is likely to be punished and is, in fact, uncommon.

Comaroff, J., ed. (1980) *The Meaning of Marriage Payments.*

Covarrubias, Miguel. (1937) *Island of Bali.*

Ember, Carol R., and Melvin Ember. (1988) *Anthropology.* 5th ed.

Fortes, Meyer. (1947) "Ashanti Survey, 1945–46: An Experiment in Social Research." *Geographical Journal* 110: 149–179.

———. (1949) "Time and Social Structure: An Ashanti Case Study." In *Social Structure: Studies Presented to A. R. Radcliffe-Brown,* edited by Meyer Fortes.

———. (1950) "Kinship and Marriage among the Ashanti." In *African Systems of Kinship and Marriage,* edited by A. R. Radcliffe-Brown and Daryll Forde, 252–284.

Goody, J., and S. T. Tambiah. (1973) *Bridewealth and Dowry.*

Gutierrez de Pineda, Virginia. (1950) *Social Organization in La Guajira.*

Hudson, Alfred E. (1938) *Kazak Social Structure.*

Luzbetak, Louis J. (1951) *Marriage and the Family in Caucasia: A Contribution to the Study of North Caucasian Ethnology and Customary Law.*

Mace, David, and Vera Mace. (1960) *Marriage: East and West.*

Monteil, Charles Victor. (1924) *The Bambara of Segou and Kaarta: An Historical, Ethnographical and Literary Study of a People of the French Sudan.*

Murdock, George Peter. (1949) *Social Structure.*

Pospisil, Leopold. (1958) *The Kapauku Papuans and Their Law.* Yale University Publications in Anthropology 54.

———. (1959–60) "The Kapauku Papuans and Their Kinship Organization." *Oceania* 30.

Raum, O. F. (1940) *Chaga Childhood: A Description of Indigenous Education in an East African Tribe.*

Schlippe, Pierre de. (1956) *Shifting Cultivation in Africa: The Zande System of Agriculture.*

Stephens, William N. (1963) *The Family in Cross-Cultural Perspective.*

Textor, Robert B. (1967) *A Cross-Cultural Summary.*

BRIDE SERVICE

Bride service is the custom whereby a man does some kind of work for his in-laws in return for being permitted to marry their daughter. Fourteen percent of a sample of 565 societies expect a man to labor on behalf of his wife's family as part of the marriage contract. Thus, bride service is much less common than bride price.

In some societies, a man is required to do bride service for no more than a few months. In others, his term of service may last for a number of years. Bride service can mean moving in with the bride's family and being treated more or less like a servant, as is the case among the Muria of India, Chuckchee of Siberia, and Lepcha of Tibet. Or a man may only be asked to do certain chores. For instance, a Siriono groom in South America is expected to hunt for his wife's family, and in Mexico a Tepoztlan husband carries wood and water for his in-laws. Sometimes a prospective groom may choose bride service as one of a number of possible ways of paying for his bride. Among the Muria and Chuckchee, a groom can decide whether he prefers to pay bride price or do bride service. In some societies, a man is required both to pay bride price and to do bride service. Sometimes bride service serves as a substitute for bride price when a groom, for instance, is unable to make bride-price payments or if he can then pay less than is normally required.

In bride service cultures, parents can exploit the custom as a way of making a match between their child and a preferred partner. A Kaska male in Alaska is required to work for his father-in-law for a period of time as part of the marriage agreement, and a man will sometimes attempt to arrange a marriage between his daughter and an unattached male by inviting the boy to trap for him for one winter, thus allowing the two young people to get to know each other. If the match is successful, then the boy's trapping activities are counted as bride service. In cultures where a boy does bride service before he marries his prospective wife, bride service can allow the couple to become better acquainted. It also serves as an opportunity for the girl's parents to make sure that their daughter's prospective husband will be a responsible and good worker. Where bride service is performed before the marriage takes place, the girl's parents may try to make the most of their chance to benefit from the free labor of their prospective son-in-law. For example, in Mexico, Popoluca fathers are some-

times tempted to prolong the visits that suitors make for as long as possible, as the boy not only provides the older man with desirable commodities but also frees him from the burden of gathering wood himself. Would-be fathers-in-law, however, are reluctant to ask a boy to do too much work, as this might incline the couple to elope.

Bride service tends to be found in societies where individuals do not typically accumulate material resources and therefore have no wealth to use for bride-price payments. A man's labor then becomes the expected form of payment to his bride's family in return for his wife. For instance, nomadic hunters, who are required to carry their belongings with them wherever they go, acquire a minimum of goods. Among nomads, therefore, a man may move in with his in-laws and hunt for them for a time. A prospective North Alaskan Eskimo groom traditionally caught a seal for his future in-laws as fulfillment of his bride-price obligation once he and his bride-to-be had become officially engaged. More generally, bride service is more likely to be found in societies whose subsistence base is characterized by food gathering or horticulture rather than by more advanced food production strategies, again because the former produce little wealth. In keeping with this pattern, bride service is also more typical where people live in small communities where class stratification tends to be absent. Bride-service societies do not usually have cities, and money is not in general use.

Bogoras, Waldemar. (1904–1909) *The Chuckchee.*

———. (1929) "Siberian Cousins of the Eskimo." *Asia* 29: 316–322, 334–337.

Ember, Carol R., and Melvin Ember. (1988) *Anthropology* 5th ed.

Foster, George M. (1959) "The Coyotepec Molde and Some Associated Problems of the Potter's Wheel." *Southwestern Journal of Anthropology* 15: 53–63.

Honigmann, John J. (1946) *Ethnography and Acculturation of the Fort Nelson Slave.*

———. (1949) *Culture and Ethos of Kaska Society.*

Stephens, William N. (1963) *The Family in Cross-Cultural Perspective.*

Textor, Robert B. (1967) *A Cross-Cultural Summary.*

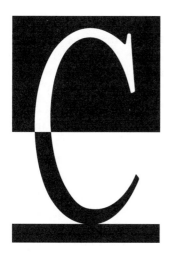

approve of sexual relations for unmarried girls. The constant presence of a companion for a girl is meant to minimize the chances that a sexual encounter can occur or be planned. In societies where distinctions between people are made on the basis of wealth or status, it is often the case that only girls from upper class families are chaperoned. This is because interested adults are especially likely to care about the company that their unmarried daughters keep when pregnancies or passions can get in the way of good marriages. In Indonesia, the Balinese girl of lower caste has many opportunities to meet and carry on affairs with boys, but higher caste girls are accompanied by chaperons and have far fewer opportunities to get to know any males.

Chaperonage is meant to keep boys and girls from becoming intimately involved. But young people are often able to circumvent the chaperon. It is expected that Burmese youth will be attended by chaperons whenever they are out in public, but they frequently manage to meet and size up members of the opposite sex at feasts and other gatherings without interference. Where chaperonage does occur, it is directed toward girls in particular. Perhaps this is because other societies agree with the Chiricahua, who say that you can warn a boy about getting a bad reputation, but "you can't keep a boy back."

CHAPERONS Whereas boys and girls are permitted to mingle freely in some cultures, other societies greatly restrict contact between males and unmarried females. One way of attempting to see that these restrictions are honored is to institute some mechanism of surveillance of young people. The chaperon is one such mechanism. A chaperon accompanies a young girl in public, keeping a sharp eye out for any behaviors on the part of her charge that might violate the prohibitions against intimate encounters between males and unmarried girls. The chaperon is often an older kinswoman. In the southwestern United States, a Havasupai girl was watched closely by a female relative when in public and was warned against any close contact with males. When a Chiricahua girl of the southwestern United States attends a dance, an older relative comes along. Sometimes, the girl is asked to take care of a younger child so that she will be too busy to become involved with any boys. In some cultures, all girls require chaperons in public. Such societies are likely to dis-

Brant, Charles. (1951) "Burmese Kinship and the Lifecycle: An Outline." *Southwestern Journal of Anthropology* 7: 437–454.

———. (1954) *Tadagale: A Burmese Village in 1950.*

Covarrubias, Miguel. (1937) *Island of Bali.*

Opler, Morris Edward. (1941) *An Apache Life-Way: The Economic, Social and Religious Institutions of the Chiricahua Indians.*

Smithson, Carma Lee. (1959) *The Havasupai Woman.*

CHILD BETROTHAL

In a number of cultures around the world, an individual's fate as a married person may be sealed long before the prospective spouse is old enough to take on the role of husband or wife or to even appreciate what it means to be married. Tiwi parents in Australia may promise a daughter's hand in marriage at the time of her birth, and sometimes an expectant mother and father will pledge their as-yet-unborn baby to be the wife of a particular man provided that the infant is a girl. Among the Amahuaca of Peru, sets of parents may strike a deal in which the children of one family will marry those of the other once they are grown. Among the Aleut of Alaska, parents also arrange marriages while the future spouses are still children, and the matches are taken so seriously that, if a male dies before he is able to marry the girl to whom he has been promised, she is likely to take on the status of widow and remain unmarried for the remainder of her life. An Aleut boy whose betrothed dies, however, does have the right to take another wife. The custom of promising an infant or child in marriage is child betrothal. Betrothing children is attractive to parents because it solves a variety of problems encountered by parents who want to make the best marriages for their children. The custom also serves to cement social ties between friends, families, and communities.

In a number of cultures, a parent will arrange a marriage for a son or daughter while the child is still quite young in order to maximize the chances of acquiring the most desirable spouse possible for the youngster. Rural Chinese parents betrothed their children at six or seven years of age so that they could choose from a wide range of potential partners before eligible mates were co-opted by other families. Similarly, Jivaro men of Ecuador try to arrange for future marriages to young girls because of the great demand for wives in this culture. The transaction is fa-cilitated by the fact that marriage partners are often related, sometimes closely, and live in the same community. A girl may be promised as a wife when she is five to ten years old, and some are betrothed shortly after birth.

Among the Nambicuara of Brazil, the chiefs and shamans tend to reserve the pretty young girls for themselves. Parents, therefore, often betroth their sons to girls while the two are still children so that the boy will not find himself unable to marry later on for lack of an available woman. Adults will also resort to child betrothal to prevent a child's own sentiments from interfering with the plans of the parents. Kimam children of New Guinea are usually betrothed before they reach puberty. In this way, the commitment is made before the prospective bride and groom are old enough to have formed attachments on their own. In some societies, child betrothal is viewed as an effective way to increase the chances that a marriage will be successful. Nyakyusa parents in Tanzania betroth their daughters long before puberty. A girl will then frequently visit her future husband, cleaning his house and cooking and fetching water for him. Adults believe that in this way the prospective bride will gradually become used to the man she is to marry. In Siberia, the Chuckchee custom of child betrothal seems to support this belief that marriages that are planned early are likely to be good marriages. The Chuckchee sometimes arrange marriages between kin. In these cases, the prospective bride and groom are betrothed at an early age, even in infancy. The marriage ceremony is performed and the youngsters grow up together, playing with each other when they are young and then herding together as they get older. Couples married in this way are often extremely close, and when one partner finally dies, the other may die soon after or, sometimes, commit suicide.

Child betrothal can also be the vehicle for consolidating relationships between families. In Indonesia, the Balinese have a caste structure, and social class is an important distinguishing feature between people. Sometimes the head of one high-caste family will betroth his baby daughter to the young son of another prominent household so that the two families can be united. The marriage then takes place as soon as the girl comes of age to prevent the possibility that the boy or girl will fall in love with some other person and resist the match made by their parents. Chuckchee families who enjoy a close relationship may decide to cement their relationship through marriage. One family may promise a child in marriage to the other, or a betrothal may be arranged even before the birth of a child. Sometimes, two individuals will arrange a marriage between their children as a symbol of their relationship. And two Kazak men in central Asia who have a close friendship might promise to marry their unborn children to each other.

Where marriages between cross-cousins are regarded as especially desirable, brothers and sisters may promise their children to each other. For instance, Trumai parents in Brazil arrange marriages between cousins while the prospective bride and groom are still infants. But these betrothals do not regularly end in marriage, in part because one or another promised partner sometimes dies before a union can take place and in part because, once they are grown, betrothed individuals often find spouses by alternative courtship practices and fail to carry out the plans of their parents. Infant betrothals between cross-cousins are often viewed as tentative arrangements rather than as iron-clad contracts. Betrothals arranged between children are broken without prejudice in other cultures as well. A Nyakyusa couple may agree not to marry after all even if the boy and girl have begun to sleep together once she reaches puberty. Similarly, among the Ainu of Japan, where child betrothal is a respected custom, either prospective spouse could refuse to go through with a marriage arranged by their parents.

Batchelor, John. (1927) *Ainu Life and Lore: Echoes of a Departing Race.*

Bogoras, Waldermar. (1904–1909) *The Chuckchee.*

Covarrubias, Miguel. (1937) *Island of Bali.*

DuBois, Cora. (1944) *The People of Alor: A Social Psychological Study of an East Indian Island.*

Fei, Hsiao-Tung. (1939) *Peasant Life in China: A Field Study of Country Life in the Yangtze Valley.*

Hart, C. W. M., and Arnold R. Pilling. (1960) *The Tiwi of North Australia.*

Hudson, Alfred E. (1938) *Kazak Social Structure.*

Karsten, Raphael. (1967) *The Toba Indians of the Bolivian Gran Chaco.*

Levi-Strauss, Claude. (1948) *La Vie Familiale et Sociale des Indiens Nambikwara* [Family and social life of the Nambikwara Indians.]

Murphy, Robert F., and Buell Quain. (1955) *The Trumai Indians of Central Brazil.*

Serpenti, I. M. (1965) *Cultivators in the Swamps.*

Venieminov, Ivan Evsieevich Popov. (1840) *Zapiski ob Ostravakh Unalashkinskago Otdiela* [Notes on the islands of the Unalaska district], vols. 2–3.

Wilson, Monica. (1957) *Rituals of Kinship among the Nyakyusa.*

CONCUBINAGE

A concubine is a woman who lives with a man and engages in sexual relations with him but who is not recognized as his wife according to the customs of their culture. Concubinage has been a recognized and accepted institution in a number of societies around the world.

In some cultures, women were forced to become concubines. For example, a Babylonian man could claim only one woman as his wife, who was accorded a social position equal to his own. But husbands were also permitted to keep concubines, and men regularly recruited their female slaves for that purpose. Quiche men of Guatemala also kept slaves as concubines on some occasions—for instance, when a wife had been forced to marry a man against her will and refused to allow him conjugal rights. Sometimes a woman voluntarily takes on the role of concubine because it nets her some advantage. A Kikuyu widow of Kenya may marry her deceased husband's brother. But if she prefers, she may also go to live with another man in concubinage. Some widows will also attempt to have sons with this man. If they are successful, the children belong to the dead husband.

While concubines do not enjoy the rights or status of legal wives, their role may provide them a certain kind of security in some cultures. In China, a concubine had a well-defined status in the home of her consort and was not regarded as in any way unsavory. The women and her children often had their own rooms in the home of the husband and their needs were adequately met. On the other hand, because the concubine had no hold over the husband, her position was secure only so long as the man to whom she was connected wished to retain her.

Men take concubines for a number of reasons. In some societies, women who find the sexual demands of their husbands too onerous persuade them to turn to a concubine. Men sometimes keep concubines for economic purposes. Many Lakher men of south Asia have perhaps two or three concubines in addition to a wife. These women help with work in the house and fields. Lakher women who become concubines are of low status, and the custom of attaining a concubine allows a man to have access to a woman without paying the bride price needed for an upper-class bride. Nor is such a

woman accorded the same rights as a legal wife. Concubines can also serve as substitutes for a legal spouse. Korean widowers are permitted to take concubines after having mourned their deceased wives for one and a half years. Concubines are also introduced into a household to serve as a sexual partner for a man when his wife is pregnant and, therefore, sexually unavailable. In some cultures, concubines are kept by men of high social status. In traditional Chinese culture, a woman of good family who married a high-ranking husband would provide her spouse with concubines as part of the dowry payment. The concubines might be overseen by ladies of the court, or the wife herself might take on the job of overseeing her husband's concubines. Sometimes the husband was required to ask his wife's permission to have sexual intercourse with one of his concubines on any given night.

In some cultures where individuals are distinguished by social rank, men are allowed to maintain legal wives and also concubines. In some Muslim cultures, harems are an option for privileged men. Concubines are kept in separate quarters for the exclusive pleasure of a particular man, with no one else permitted access to the women in the harem.

Bunzel, Ruth. (1952) *Chichicastenango: A Guatemalan Village.*

Dickemann, Mildred. (1981) "Paternal Confidence and Dowry Competition: A Biocultural Analysis of Purdah." In *Natural Selection and Social Behavior,* edited by Richard D. Alexander and Donald W. Tinkle.

Hewes, Gordon W., and Ching Hong Kim. (1950) *Korean Kinship Behavior and Structure.* Unpublished manuscript, Human Relations Area Files (New Haven, CT).

Kenyatta, Jomo. (1961) *Facing Mount Kenya: The Tribal Life of the Gikuyu.*

Mace, David, and Vera Mace. (1960) *Marriage: East and West.*

Parry, N. E. (1932) *The Lakhers.*

Saggs, H. W. F. (1962) *The Greatness That Was Babylon: A Survey of the Ancient Civilization of the Tigris-Euphrates Valley.*

CONJUGAL VIOLENCE

See Spouse Beating.

CONTINENCE AS A VIRTUE

Most human beings who have attained physical maturity are highly motivated to engage in sexual intercourse. The process of natural selection has resulted in this pan-human interest in sex and, indeed, any society whose members were not so motivated would soon disappear from the face of the earth. Nevertheless, cultures that value unrestricted heterosexual activity are in the minority. Most societies believe that people should abstain from sexual intercourse on at least some occasions. Thus, in a sample of 70 cultures around the world, only 17.1 percent customarily allow men and women to engage in sex whenever they wish to do so. The remaining 82.9 percent impose constraints of some kind on sexual intercourse. When an individual refrains from having sexual relations, the person is said to be practicing continence.

Customs that regulate sexual activity are connected to beliefs that too much sex is unhealthy or debilitating or that the effects of sexual activity interfere with other important human pursuits. The Yapese of Oceania claim that over-frequent sexual activity incapacitates men or makes them ill. Indeed, some Yapese legends tell of the eventual death of men who have indulged in too much sex. For the Yapese, excess sexual activity refers to anything over two to three times per month. The Kimam of New Guinea avoid sexual intercourse when ceremonial crops are being planted or harvested and after a child has been born. A man who is making a drum should also abstain from sexual activity, as the drum is associated with men and will have an inferior sound if its maker has had anything to do with women. Sex is also thought to interfere with activities that require physical strength so that, for instance, a man who is defeated in a wrestling match may be accused of having slept with his wife on the previous night. The Konso of Ethiopia believe that too much sexual intercourse saps a man's strength, interfering with his ability to do heavy work in the fields or to fight in a war. Therefore, men should not engage in sexual intercourse too often, and a father will admonish a newly married son who is sleeping too frequently with his bride. Konso males sleep in the men's houses to avoid being too weakened by overindulging their sexual appetites. The !Kung of southern Africa similarly worry that too much sexual activity interferes with a man's hunting ability when he is actually pursuing game, and his hunting power even when he is not actively hunting. One !Kung man will accuse another of knowing women instead of hunting or of being unable to leave his wife long enough to hunt. Jivaro men of Ecuador avoid sexual intercourse on many occasions, including after a death, after an enemy has been killed, when making poison arrows or other weapons, after planting narcotics, and when preparing a feast.

Attitudes about continence are related to other ideas about sexual behavior across cultures. Societies that approve of frequent sex and that place no value on abstinence are also more likely to allow extramarital liaisons on the part of wives. These are also societies that have a single standard in their attitudes about extramarital sexual activity, so that extramarital affairs are either accepted or condemned equally for both husband and wife. By contrast, where continence is emphasized, extramarital sex on the part of wives is more liable to be condemned and the double standard is more likely to prevail. Attitudes about continence are also connected to ideas about the acceptability of homosexuality. Where abstinence is not valued, homosexuality tends to be tolerated, while homosexual behavior is likely to be condemned where continence is an important feature of sexual conduct.

Many cultures have also instituted taboos on sexual intercourse with women who are menstruating or who are nursing infants. Continence is associated with female physiological processes in some way in 54 percent of societies, while 20 percent of these cultures restrict sexual intercourse in connection with economic activities, and 16 percent prohibit sex in conjunction with religious events. Military pursuits require sexual abstinence in 5 percent of the cultures.

Although it is common for societies to prohibit sex at certain times and for various reasons, many of the same cultures also promote sexual activity at least in moderation. The Kaska of Alaska believe that restraint in sexual activity promotes long life and good luck. But too much abstinence is considered dangerous, causing a man to "worry about girls" and perhaps to "lose his brains" and go insane. Men, therefore, should get married. A woman should also ideally have a sexual partner. The idea of a woman remaining a virgin for life is unthinkable to the Kaska, in part because girls are expected to want to have sexual intercourse and in part because the men themselves would never let a woman go without sexual experience for very long. The Chiricahua of the southwestern United States think that sexual intercourse two or three times per week is all right for married people. According to one Chiricahua informant, "Once a week won't hurt a man, I guess." But if sexual overindulgence is looked upon with disapproval, so is abstinence scorned. For the Chiricahua too, moderation is the key.

See also MENSTRUAL TABOOS; SEX TABOO, POST-PARTUM; SEX TABOOS.

Ford, Clellan S., and Frank A. Beach. (1951) *Patterns of Sexual Behavior.*

Frayser, Suzanne G. (1985) *Varieties of Sexual Experience.*

Hallpike, C. R. (1972) *The Konso of Ethiopia.*

Honigmann, John J. (1949) *Culture and Ethos of Kaska Society.*

Hunt, E. E., David M. Schneider, Nathaniel R. Kidder, and William D. Stevens. (1949) *The Micronesians of Yap and Their Depopulation.*

Karsten, Rafael. (1935) *The Head-Hunters Of Western Amazonas: The Life and Culture of the Jibaro Indians of Eastern Ecuador and Peru.*

Marshall, Lorna. (1959) "Marriage among the !Kung Bushmen." *Africa* 29: 335–364.

Opler, Morris Edward. (1941) *An Apache Life-Way: The Economic, Social and Religious Institutions of the Chiricahua Indians.*

Serpenti, I. M. (1965) *Cultivators in the Swamps.*

COURTSHIP

Whereas most men and women across cultures get married, the manner by which matches are made differs from society to society. Broadly speaking, we can distinguish between unions that are arranged by third parties—for instance, the families of the prospective bride and groom—and unions in which the partners themselves determine that they wish to marry. When marriages are prearranged by individuals other than the spouses, any preliminary interactions are between the people who are taking care of the marriage negotiations; in some cases the couple never even sees one another until the wedding ceremony. But where people are free to choose their own spouses, some kind of courtship typically occurs. During this time, couples get to know each other and to discover whether or not they wish to make the formal commitment of marriage.

In some cultures, courtships are conducted publicly, and young people transform both work and leisure schedules into courting opportunities. When a Lakher boy of south Asia wishes to win a girl over, he will arrange to spend the day with her. The two will help each other do their chores and will share tobacco and nicotine-water. The boy will then come to sleep that night in the girl's house. If she is interested in her suitor, the girl will move her bed closer to his, and he will understand that she regards him favorably. A boy may also try to advance his cause during a mixed-sex drinking party. He may put his arms around the girl and fondle her. If she seems not to mind, his approaches will become more intimate, and if she still does not object, the two will go to the girl's house. A Rwala youth might spend all of his time with his girlfriend, helping her to water the camels, fetch water, and strike and pitch the tent. In the evening, they might meet in a tent vacated for the purpose by some helpful campmate and stay there all night.

In other cultures, courtship takes place in the night, sometimes because there is no chance to conduct love affairs during the day and sometimes because of the importance attached to discretion in matters of courting. Among the Iban of Malaysia, males and females have little opportunity for private encounters in the daytime, so courtship occurs at night, when everyone has gone to sleep. Daughters sleep apart from their parents, making it relatively easy for a boy to creep up to the side of the bed of a girl in whom he is interested. He wakes her and offers her some betel nut to chew. If the girl wishes to discourage the boy, she will ask him to light the lamp or to blow on the fire. This is understood to be a rejection, and he will leave. But if the girl is pleased to have this particular boy visit, she will put the treat in her mouth, and the two will plan future meetings while they share the betel nut. If the girl's parents approve of her suitor, the couple continues to rendezvous for a number of weeks, remaining together for most of each night. They are unlikely, however, to engage in sexual intercourse during these visits. The girl will be given some gift—for instance, a necklace, ring, or handkerchief—by her suitor as a sign of his commitment to her, and the two are understood to be betrothed. When a couple has decided to get married, the boy tells his parents of their plans, and his relatives and friends then visit the prospective bride's parents to obtain their approval of the marriage. This meeting is usually a formality, as a girl's parents would never let things get to this point if they did not like the boy. Instead, they would prevent him from seeing the girl alone, and the relationship would be effectively ended. Lamet males also wait until evening to do their courting. Couples chat in front of the girl's house as night approaches and the suitor may serenade the girl. If his advances are accepted, the two may creep into the girl's house together after everyone else is asleep and settle down in the girl's bed, which is in the girl's sleeping quarters, apart from her parents. If the couple decides to marry, this night courtship will continue for some time, during which the two can live together openly. So, too, does a Paiute boy of the southwestern United States do his courting at night. He goes to the girl's house and sits at her feet as she sleeps. If the girl wishes to turn down his invitation, she will get up and go to lie by her mother. Or her mother may disapprove of the boy, in which case she will stoke the fire and embarrass him into leaving. But if her parents approve, they will encourage their daughter to sleep with the boy.

If his advances are not rejected, the suitor will continue to visit the girl until she sleeps with him. When the boy stays for breakfast, the marriage is said to be consummated. Among the Cayapa of Brazil, nighttime courting is preceded by a set of ritualized behaviors on the part of the boy that serve to announce to the community that he is interested in a particular girl. The would-be suitor refrains from engaging in any work or participating in any social interactions and sits for an entire day without speaking to anyone, even if provoked. After everyone has gone to sleep, he goes to visit his sweetheart, singing love songs as he approaches her house. The girl may be willing to sneak away from home and spend some time with him elsewhere, or the two might spend some of the night together under the girl's mosquito net. These visits will continue for a while if the couple is serious. Once they have decided to marry, they get the permission of their parents.

Sometimes, courtship is preceded by a set of actions by which a young person formally states his intentions. When a Tepoztlan boy of Mexico wishes to court a girl, he sends her a letter in which he declares his love for her. These are stilted and elaborately worded, often copied from an etiquette book by the boy or, if he cannot write, by a literate friend. Boys send such letters before they have actually talked to or even met the girl, and a hopeful suitor may send a number of unsigned messages before he gets up the nerve to identify himself. If the girl does not reject him, the boy arranges to meet her and a more personal courtship begins. Truk girls of Oceania are expected to resist the initial advances of suitors, so courtship typically begins with a boy's attempts to persuade a girl to meet him. Usually, a go-between will deliver a letter proclaiming the young man's great love for the girl and the great suffering that it is causing him. It is proper for the girl to ignore the first few letters, but if she likes the boy a rendezvous will eventually be arranged.

Courtships may or may not include the expectation of physical intimacy. Among the Mapuche of Chile, it is taken for granted that courting couples will engage in sexual intercourse, and the word for courtship also means sexual activity. Some girls will dawdle on the way home from school or linger by the stream while doing chores in order to meet boys, and couples often engage in sexual intercourse during these meetings. Similarly, when a Nicobarese man of the Asiatic islands talks about courting a girl, his words literally mean that he has had sexual intercourse with her. In other societies, a couple is expected to refrain from having sexual relations while courting. Even though a Mbundu boy and girl of Angola may live together and sleep in the same hut while courting, it is understood that no sexual intimacies will take place. If the boy tries to seduce his girlfriend, her parents will force him to sleep in their kitchen for a designated period of time, during which time he will not be permitted to see their daughter.

A courtship may sometimes turn into a trial marriage, that is, a relationship between a couple that is more than courting but also more tentative than a permanent marriage. For instance, among the Mbundu, a girl and boy may live together in the hut that the young man has built for himself. They are not supposed to have sexual intercourse. Rather, the goal of the custom is to allow prospective partners in marriage to come to know each other before they make a formal commitment.

Courting may begin at what is a very early age by western standards. Among the Otoro Nuba in the Sudan, boys and girls get to know each other at the dances and ceremonies that are attended by a number of different communities. Or they may become acquainted while working out on the farms. Boys begin looking for marriage partners by 13 to 15 years of age, and they focus in particular on girls who are about 8 to 12 years old. Once two youngsters become interested in each other, the boy will visit the girl in her hut in the evening, where they may have a pleasant talk or engage in some sexual experimentation. At public celebrations, a couple may go off into the bushes for a while. If the boy then reappears with a painted mark on his chest, the other youngsters will tease him about his activities with his girlfriend. If the relationship progresses into something serious, the boy will ask the girl whether he may speak to her parents about marriage.

Courting is typical not only of human beings but also of other species. In other animals, it is almost always the male who courts the female, attempting by various means to persuade her to mate. The evolutionary perspective makes sense of this male bias in courting by reminding us that, where males court females, it is the latter who invest the most in the couple's offspring. Thus, the female has the most to lose by mating foolishly and needs to be convinced that the male who wins her over would be a good bet as the father of her offspring. Where two parents are required for optimal care of the young, as, for instance, in the case of many birds, the female should also require evidence that her prospective mate will stay around to participate in the rearing of the young. Thus, given the relative risk to females of a poor mating decision, a female should be choosy regarding the males with whom she will mate and a male should have to work to convince the female that he is a good choice. This accounts for the tendency for males to court females in animal species.

It is the males who court the females in our own species as well. This is not surprising, as women invest more than men in offspring and require or want the help of a mate for the rearing of their young children. Various features of human courtship suggest that courting is partly an attempt by males to win over females. For instance, it is customary in many cultures for courting boys and men to give gifts to their sweethearts. Thonga boys of Mozambique live in their own huts and girls live in theirs, so courtships in this society are easy to conduct. A boy will visit his girlfriend at night, bringing her gifts in order to persuade her to have intercourse, and the boy may, indeed, be invited to stay all night. Or a hopeful Thonga boy will present a girl with a large cotton print, called *gangisa ntombi,* or make a girl choose one, in an attempt to make her feel more warmly toward him.

In some cultures, female choice shows up explicitly in courtship customs, as it is the girl who singles out a boy as a potential sweetheart and not vice versa. The boy's role is to wait passively to be chosen by a girl or to try to convince a girl he likes to choose him. Among the Mataco of Argentina, an initiated girl is considered ready for marriage, and girls who have undergone their initiation rites carry on a series of love affairs as they search for husbands. A girl surveys the available young men during the nightly dances, approaching a boy of her choice, and leaving with him after the dance, usually taking him to her parents' house. A boy who is interested in attracting a girl will paint his face with a specific pattern to designate his availability. A girl who wishes to pursue a relationship with such a boy will soon appear with the same design painted on her face. A boy is effectively compelled to accept a girl who responds to his advertisement for fear of otherwise incurring the anger of her family. Once a boy has been chosen as a suitor, he will serenade her. The couple will demonstrate their affection by leaving fingernail wounds on one another's cheeks. The marks are taken to express the strong attachment that the two feel for each other. The girl will then bring her suitor home at night and it is then said that the two have "begun to be married."

Among the Chagga of Tanzania, a girl who wishes to invite a particular boy to become her lover will roast him a mbo-banana. As he is about to remove the fruit from the fire, she blows ashes into the boy's face and tells him that she loves him and that he is the only boy she is willing to marry. Or a girl might cut a boy's right arm, saying: "I desire you and I cause you this wound and I make you taboo." She then licks the blood from the boy's arm, declaring: "This is the way I love you." The wounding of the young man is understood to be a binding alliance and marks him so that other girls will know that he is already committed. Once they have been initiated at puberty, Thonga boys may participate in the *gangisa*, or the choosing of a lover. A boy attempts to persuade a girl he likes to pick him to be her boyfriend, and young males can be seen dancing around a group of girls and crying: "Choose me! Choose me!" And a Comanche boy of the southwestern United States who liked a particular girl and hoped to attract her in return lingered in some place where she was likely to appear and approached her when she finally showed up, waiting for some indication that she was interested in him. If she gave him such a sign, the two made plans to meet later, or they may have loitered together if no one else was around. If the girl did not wish to become involved with the boy, she indicated this to him through her behavior, and he went away humiliated.

The difference in male versus female investment in offspring is also consistent with another feature of human courtship. In particular, girls and boys tend to interpret the meaning of a courtship differently. The pattern is illustrated by the Mapuche of Chile. Among Mapuche males, love affairs are understood to be ends in themselves. Mapuche girls, by contrast, view courtships as overtures to marriage. Boys know this, and regularly lead their girlfriends to believe that marriage is in the offing, but these commitments are broken again and again, and love affairs, as a consequence, tend to be rocky. In other words, females tend to regard courtship as a step toward the establishment of a secure setting for raising children. Males, on the other hand, tend to view it as an opportunity for producing offspring without further committing themselves to the care of mother and child.

See also NATURAL SELECTION; REPRODUCTIVE STRATEGIES; SEXUAL SELECTION.

Barrett, S. A. (1925) *The Cayapa Indians of Ecuador.*

Childs, Gladwyn M. (1949) *Umbundu Kinship and Character.*

Fock, Niels. (1963) "Mataco Marriage." *Folk* 5: 91–101.

Gillin, John. (1936) *The Barama River Caribs of British Guiana.* Papers of the Peabody Museum of American Archaeology and Ethnology, Harvard University, 14(2).

Gladwin, Thomas, and Seymour Sarason. (1953) *Truk: Man in Paradise.*

Gutmann, Bruno. (1926) *Das Recht der Dschagga* [Chagga law].

———. (1932) *Die Stammeslehren der Dschagga* [The tribal teachings of the Chagga], vol. 1.

Izikowitz, Karl Gustav. (1951) *Lamet: Hill Peasants in French Indochina.*

Junod, Henri A. (1927) *The Life of a South African Tribe,* vol. 1.

Parry, N. E. (1932) *The Lakhers.*

Raswan, Carl R. (1947) *Black Tents of Arabia.*

Stephens, William N. (1963) *The Family in Cross-Cultural Perspective.*

Titiev, Mischa. (1951) *Araucanian Culture in Transition.*

Wallace, Ernest, and E. Adamson Hoebel. (1952) *The Comanches: Lords of the South Plains.*

Whiting, Beatrice B. (1950) *Paiute Sorcery.* Viking Fund Publications in Anthropology 15.

CUCKOLDRY If a man's wife is unfaithful, the husband is referred to as a cuckold. People interested in the biological bases of behavior predict that males in our own and other species should be especially sensitive to the possibility of being cuckolded. In particular, cuckoldry is dangerous to males who cohabit with a specific female and who contribute to the raising of their young.

Men who invest in their children will worry about the sexual behavior of the women with whom they live because a female who has sex with other men may produce an infant who is not the offspring of her mate. The male, however, will have no way of knowing that this infant is not his own. As he is expected to help his mate to raise all of her children, he will be contributing his valuable time and energy to the rearing of children who have been fathered by someone else. He is contributing to the fitness of another male instead of to his own.

Fitness is a concept introduced by Charles Darwin. Darwin pointed out that individuals who succeed in producing more viable offspring than other members of their species are also contributing a greater proportion of their own genes to the gene pool of their kind. This means that whichever of their traits are influenced by their genetic heritage will be better represented in the gene pool. An individual's contribution to the gene pool is referred to as his fitness. The more successful an individual is in making such a contribution, the greater his Darwinian fitness. Darwin also suggested that the behavior of human beings and other animals is geared to maximize fitness. In other words, the activities of all creatures are directly or indirectly in the service of producing more viable offspring of one's own than are produced by other members of one's species. This is because behavior that is less likely to result in the creation of offspring will not be perpetuated in succeeding generations. It will die with its less fit owner. Across generations, the tendency will be for fitness-enhancing behavior to prevail.

Given this notion of Darwinian fitness and its relationship to behavior, it becomes easier to see why males might be concerned about the possibility of being cuckolded. A male whose mate has brought home someone else's offspring will be helping to increase the contribution of the other male to the gene pool of his species. This is not in his own best Darwinian interest. A male ought to be devoting his resources to maximizing the proportion of his own genes in the gene pool instead. Since behavior patterns are designed to serve fitness, the behavioral profile of males is assumed to include a special sensitivity to the possibility of being cuckolded. Indeed, male indifference to the sexual activities of a mate ought to die out because individuals exhibiting this indifference are likely to be raising fewer of their own offspring. Thus, the trait of indifference will not be well represented in succeeding generations.

Male behavioral repertoires ought also to include strategies for reducing the chances that their mates will be unfaithful. And across cultures we do find men behaving in ways designed to keep their wives faithful. In some societies, men keep a close eye on their wives. Tallensi husbands of Ghana do not like their wives to go off on long trips to visit their parents, even when the couple has been married for some years. While his spouse is away, the husband will be plagued by suspicions concerning her activities. Tallensi men believe in the natural fickleness of women, so that their vigilance over their wives becomes an even more pressing strategy for instituting sexual exclusivity. Other men cope with possible infidelity by spying on their spouses. In Colombia, the Goajiro husband watches his wife closely when she is around other men in an attempt to catch her out should she be cheating on him. The practice in some cultures of sequestering women also serves as a strategy for enforcing faithfulness. The Rajput woman of India carries out her daily chores in an enclosed courtyard adjacent to her dwelling. Her companions are other women and young children. When she wishes to go visiting, she travels by the walkways built on the roofs of Rajput houses and used only by women. Apartments within dwellings are also segregated by sex. The net result of living arrangements of this sort is that women have little opportunity to mingle with men and, therefore, no chance to conduct affairs outside of marriage. A husband will sometimes keep his wife at his side at all times, as was the case with a Chiricahua man of the American Southwest, who forced his wife to accompany him on winter hunting trips despite the bitterly cold weather.

Sometimes the persistent suspicion that a man displays concerning his wife's behavior is enough to reduce the chances that another man will risk an affair with a married woman. Yahgan husbands of Tierra del Fuego were so chronically jealous that other men were extremely careful in their demeanor when dealing with another's wife. More generally, men across cultures tend to be described as more jealous about the fidelity of their spouses than are women, and this difference may reflect the important reproductive significance of the unfaithfulness of a spouse for men as opposed to women. So does the double standard concerning extramarital sex reflect this vulnerability of men to cuckoldry. Women are far more likely to be severely punished for carrying on affairs outside marriage than are men, and there are no known societies where adultery in a wife is punished less severely than is adultery in a husband.

The sensitivity with which men respond to infidelity in their mates is highlighted by the fact that fights between men across cultures are often over women. The most common reason for poisoning an enemy among the Tiv of Nigeria is a disagreement over a woman. Among the Yahgan, most murders are the result of adultery. Much of the violence practiced by the Gheg of Albania stems from women's sexual peccadillos. And among the !Kung of southern Africa, poison arrows constitute a chronic threat to life and limb, and fights over women are the most usual reason for men to use them.

The Goajiro husband, forever suspicious of his wife, surveys his newborn infant's physical features hoping to determine whether the child bears any resemblance to some other man with whom his wife may have been involved. In America, the resemblance of a new infant to its father is given more attention than is its physical similarity to its mother. What is more, it tends to be the mother herself who points out the likeness. These examples are reminders of the threat that cuckoldry presents for males in our own and other species.

Whereas males are expected to be concerned about the possibility of being cuckolded themselves, Darwin's ideas about fitness also suggest that one man will be eager to cuckold another. If a man is successful at seducing another man's wife, the unknowing husband may end up raising the offspring of his wife's lover. The cuckolded husband, as a result, is contributing to another men's fitness, to the detriment of his own. The high fitness payoff for committing adultery with a married women is appreciated by the Lakher of south Asia. A Lakher man whose wife has been unfaithful is disgraced, and the stigma accompanies him when his spirit arrives in the next world. Indeed, the shame is so great that his wife's lover must provide the "cloth to wear on the head" with which the spirit of the humiliated husband covers his face upon arrival in the world of the dead. The spirit of the seducer of a married woman, by contrast, wears a white cock's feather in its hair and is much admired by the other dead spirits. When a seducer of another man's wife dies, his relatives place white cock feathers on his memorial post.

See also NATURAL SELECTION; REPRODUCTIVE STRATEGIES; SEX, EXTRAMARITAL; SEXUAL SELECTION.

Daly, Margo, and Martin Wilson. (1983) *Sex, Evolution, and Behavior.*

Durham, M. E. (1928) *Some Tribal Origins, Laws and Customs of the Balkans.*

East, Rupert. (1939) *Akiga's Story: The Tiv Tribe as Seen by One of Its Members.*

Fortes, Meyer. (1938) *Social and Psychological Aspects of Education in Taleland.*

———. (1945) *The Dynamics of Clanship among the Tallensi: Being the First Part of an Analysis of the Social Structure of a Trans-Volta Tribe.*

———. (1949) *The Web of Kinship among the Tallensi: The Second Part of an Analysis of the Social Structure of a Trans-Volta Tribe.*

Gusinde, Martin. (1937) *The Yahgan: The Life and Thought of the Water Nomads of Cape Horn.*

Gutierrez de Pineda, Virginia. (1950) *Social Organization in La Guajira.*

Marshall, Lorna. (1959) "Marriage among the !Kung Bushmen." *Africa* 29: 335–364.

Minturn, Leigh, and John T. Hitchcock. (1966) *The Rajputs of Khalapur, India.*

Opler, Morris Edward. (1941) *An Apache Life-Way: The Economic, Social and Religious Institutions of the Chiricahua Indians.*

Parry, N. E. (1932) *The Lakhers.*

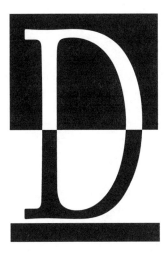

husbands are the first to be served at a meal and the first to take a bath. They also have a special seat near the fire. Among the Chuckchee of Siberia, the choicest food is given to the husband, while a wife eats what is left behind. And a traditional Rajput wife in India crouches on the floor with her sari over her face when her husband is present. While contact with Western culture is ending public displays of deference, such customs still exist in some cultures.

In some cultures, deference is required from wives more for the sake of appearance than because wives are in fact subordinate to their spouses. The pattern is illustrated by the Somali, who expect wives to be properly submissive to their husbands in public regardless of the actual balance of power characterizing their relationship. Thus, a bride should remove her husband's sandals on their wedding night and in the first weeks of their marriage. Somali wives cook for their husbands but eat separately. And when a husband and wife are out together in public the woman walks behind her spouse as an outward sign of deference.

In a number of societies where wives are expected to be deferential to their spouses, women tend in fact to have influence over their husbands, and sometimes the influence is considerable. Even in cultures where deference behavior accurately reflects the power relationship between spouses for most couples, some wives turn out to be dominant over their husbands in important ways. For instance, a Javanese wife owes her husband formal deference, but practically speaking she has most of the control and makes most of the decisions related to household matters. An especially tough-minded man may win himself a status equal to that of his wife. The marriage in which the husband is actually dominant over his spouse is very unusual. Similarly, a Mende woman of West Africa is expected to defer to her husband and should strive to obey and satisfy her spouse in all matters. Tradition dictates that a wife approach her husband on

DEFERENCE OF WIFE TO HUSBAND Deference customs refer to culturally prescribed patterns of behavior exhibited by one person toward another and understood to signify inequality in the statuses of the two individuals. The deferent person is formally acknowledging that the other individual is the more dominant, superior, privileged, or powerful of the pair. Deference can be communicated in a variety of ways, including bowing, kneeling, or standing in the presence of or walking behind the superior person, speaking in a low voice, remaining silent, or using special language when with the more powerful individual, and reserving a seat of honor or the choicest food for the revered person at meals. Wives are expected to exhibit one or another kind of deference behavior toward husbands in a number of cultures around the world. Deference of husbands toward wives, by contrast, is rare. Thus, for example, a traditional Ganda wife of Uganda was required to wash her husband's feet every night. A rural Ukrainian wife always walks behind her spouse in public and always enters the house after him. Japanese bended knee and that women walk behind their husbands in public. But in domestic matters, the wife is not subordinate to her spouse. Similarly, a Tuareg husband of the Sahara is supreme outside the household, but a wife nevertheless enjoys considerable autonomy. She owns her own property and, as she is not responsible for any household expenses, she can amass considerable wealth relative to her husband, whose resources are likely to remain the same or even diminish over the course of their marriage. Indeed, newly married couples live with the wife's family for the first year so that the husband's authority over his wife can be held in check while the spouses consolidate their relationship. Burmese girls learn in early childhood to regard any man with the utmost respect, and a female is expected to defer to the judgment of males in all matters. Nevertheless, a Burmese husband is likely to confer with his wife regarding both public and private affairs and will frequently be guided by her opinion. The Nambicuara of Brazil publicly speak about women with condescension. But when they are alone, a husband listens to his wife's problems, takes her desires into account, and asks for her assistance on a regular basis. And while a rural Egyptian husband is the head of the household, making the important decisions and taking responsibility for the actions of his wife, the woman is often the supervisor of the crops, money, and legal documents.

Sometimes, however, deference behavior is a genuine reflection of the imbalance of power between spouses. A Gandan wife is subordinate to her husband both formally and in practice. She plans household activities around his schedule, making meals when it is convenient for him, visiting only with his permission, and staying away from home only as long as he permits. Wives who do not obey their husbands can expect a beating. Except in rare cases, a North American Gros Ventre wife is required to remain with her husband even when she believes that she has grievances against him. If his ne-

glect of his spouse is obvious and extreme, her relatives may allow her to stay with them for a time, but she becomes a free woman only if he fails to send for her. Men have tremendous power over their spouses, but Gros Ventre women say that this authority of husband over wife makes "good wives of many women." Even if a Havasupai husband in the southwestern United States is excessively abusive toward his wife, the community makes no effort to come to her aid. The dominance of husbands over their wives is viewed as normal and proper and the use of force to persuade a wife to defer to her spouse is supported by public opinion. The relationship between Mapuche spouses of Chile is harmonious and affectionate, and husbands are helpful and thoughtful partners. But it is the man who dominates the marriage, and the wife is likely to give in when spouses quarrel. According to Korean custom, a wife's relationship to her husband is only slightly higher than that of a slave. Her job is to provide her spouse with children, supervise his household, and meet his sexual needs. Husbands are not viewed as having similar obligations toward their wives. In South Asia, a West Punjabi wife must always submit to her husband's authority. Further, when the couple lives with the husband's family, she is also dominated by the more senior women of the household.

In a handful of cultures, husbands behave toward their wives in ways that are normally thought to reflect deference. Among the Brno of Czechoslovakia, a wife is seated before her husband at meals, and she begins eating first. In Hungary, a Dragaletvsy wife rides the donkey while her husband follows on foot, dust flying in his face. And among the Madrid aristocrats, a wife walks to the right of her husband, which is considered to be the honored position. A man holds his wife's chair while she seats herself, and stands when she enters the room. Wives, further, are seated first and served first at dinner. All of these behaviors, when directed toward a husband by a wife, are viewed as signs of the woman's inferior status. But when directed by men toward women, these same behaviors remind us of the code of chivalry originating in the Middle Ages. The gestures are familiar to Westerners, who recognize them as examples of traditional etiquette in interactions between men and women. They are interpreted in this context, however, not as a statement of the man's inferior status, but rather as good manners. Thus, the meaning of the actions that are taken to signify deference may depend upon the sexes of the actor and the target.

Ammar, Hamed. (1954) *Growing Up in an Egyptian Village.*

Dallet, Charles. (1874) *A History of the Church in Korea.*

Flannery, Regina. (1953) *The Gros Ventre of Montana,* pt. 1.

Geertz, Hildred. (1961) *The Javanese Family.*

Hilger, M. Inez. (1957) *Araucanian Child Life and Its Cultural Background.*

Levi-Strauss, Claude. (1948) *Family and Social Life of the Nambikwara Indians.*

Lewis, I. M. (1962) *Marriage and the Family in Northern Somaliland.*

Lhote, Henri. (1944) *The Hoggar Tuareg.*

Little, K. L. (1951) *The Mende of Sierra Leone: A West African People in Transition.*

Scott, James George. (1910) *The Burman, His Life and Notions.*

Smithson, Carma Lee. (1959) *The Havasupai Woman.*

Stephens, William N. (1963) *The Family in Cross-Cultural Perspective.*

Wilber, Donald N. (1964) *Pakistan: Its People, Its Society, Its Culture.*

DEFLORATION CUSTOMS

Defloration refers to the breaking of a female's hymen. The hymen is a fold of mucous membrane covering the opening to the vagina. The hymen is generally intact in virgins but is punctured when any object is inserted deeply enough into the vaginal canal. In many cultures, defloration occurs without any official interest or notice and happens naturally when a girl has sexual intercourse for the first time. Other societies, however, have instituted customary ways of achieving defloration in girls before they engage in sexual relations.

Defloration techniques vary with respect to who performs the procedure and how the rupture of the hymen is accomplished. Among the Cubeo of the Amazon, a girl is digitally deflowered in private at around eight years of age by an old, sexually inactive man who belongs to her sib. The man inserts three fingers into her vagina and then announces that she is a woman. The Cubeo make defloration a requirement for girls at this early age for fear that intercourse will be painful and childbirth difficult if her hymen is still intact when she begins to menstruate. The Cubeo do not publicly acknowledge how defloration takes place. Rather, they claim that girls are deflowered by the moon, who has coitus with her and causes her first menstrual period. In India, Toda girls are also deflowered before puberty in a ceremony called "mantle over he puts." A man comes to the girl's village and lies down with her for a few minutes under a mantle covering the pair. Two weeks later, another man from a clan other than that of the girl has sexual intercourse with her. It is very important that the defloration take place before puberty. A woman might never live down the disgrace if her hymen remained intact beyond this time and she might have trouble finding a man who was willing to marry her. In central Africa, a Mbuti girl is officially deflowered by her boyfriend. The girl remains in a hut surrounded by armed women and the boy must fight the whips and missiles aimed at him as he attempts to make his way into the hut. If the boy successfully gains entrance, he pays the price of one ax and then spends the night with his girlfriend, during which time defloration takes place. The challenge that boyfriends undergo is now ritualized, but in former times the fighting was in earnest and people were liable to be killed. Palauan girls are deflowered by their mothers at adolescence, after which a wad of leaves is inserted into the vagina and left there for some months. During this time intercourse is prohibited, but girls are then tutored about sex and encouraged to become sexually active. Among the Marshallese in Oceania, a girl is deflowered by the chief during her puberty ceremony if she is still a virgin. In Australia, an Aranda girl is deflowered as part of the wedding ceremony. Certain of her male relatives take the girl to the bush, puncture her hymen with a stone knife, have intercourse with her, dress her in the customary way, and take her back to her husband-to-be. In some societies, girls customarily deflower themselves before beginning their sex lives. In Zaire, Nkundo girls perform a procedure called "opening the way" in which they gradually enlarge the vaginal opening by inserting larger and larger plant shoots into the vagina. Sometimes a group of girls will carry out the procedure together if they all intend to have sexual relations in the near future. A Pukapuka girl in Oceania breaks her own hymen with her finger before her first sexual experience to save the boy the trouble.

While the condition of the hymen is not always an accurate index of a girl's sexual history, most cultures equate an intact hymen with virginity. In societies where virginity before marriage is valued, therefore, relatives of the bride and groom and sometimes members of the larger community are likely to take an intense interest in the state of a girl's hymen on her marriage night and await indications that

it was the husband who deflowered his new bride.

See also VIRGINITY.

Barnett, H. G. (1949) *Palauan Society: A Study of Contemporary Native Life in the Palau Islands.*

Beaglehole, Ernest, and Pearl Beaglehole. (1941) "Pangai: Village in Tonga." *Polynesian Society* 2(4): 3–145.

Erdland, August. (1914) *The Marshall Islanders: Life and Customs, Thought, and Religion of a South Seas People.*

Goldman, Irving. (1963) *The Cubeo: Indians of the Northwest Amazon.*

Hulsaert, Gustave. (1928) *Marriage among the Nkundu.*

Murdock, George Peter. (1934) *Our Primitive Contemporaries.*

Rivers, W. H. R. (1906) *The Todas.*

Turnbull, Colin M. (1965) *The Mbuti Pygmies: An Ethnographic Survey.* Anthropological Papers of the Museum of Natural History 50, pt. 3.

DESCENT RULES AND GROUPS

In many societies, a person's life is profoundly influenced by kinship. Networks of relatives can affect whom a person marries, how politics are structured, who inherits what from whom, whom and how people worship, and how economic and domestic life are structured. Just how kinship intrudes into the individual's life depends upon how a society exploits the biological basis of kinship. Different cultures view biological connectedness, and therefore make use of kinship, in different ways.

While people everywhere are related to kin by the same genetic principles, most societies choose to emphasize only some kinds of genetic connections as important in reckoning kin ties. What is more, different cultures stress different kin ties. Rules specifying which relatives count as kin and which do not are called descent rules. Descent rules identify a set of people who are said to be related to one another through a chain of parent-child connections by common descent from a real or mythical ancestor. It is the way in which the tracing of these connections is accomplished that characterizes a particular rule of descent and that makes one descent rule different from another. Individuals who are reckoned as descending from a single ancestor form a descent group.

Unilineal Descent

One way of deciding the membership of a descent group is to let the sex of the parent through whom descent is traced be the principle of assignment. This is the most common strategy for determining descent group membership. Descent is patrilineal if it is traced through the male parent, or the father, and matrilineal if it is traced through the female parent, or the mother. In the case of patrilineal descent, the descent group consists of males and females whose fathers belong to the group. Brothers and sisters, therefore, belong to the same descent group. But a female's children do not belong to her descent group. Rather, they belong to their father's group. A matrilineal descent group, by contrast, consists of all males and females whose mothers belong to the group. Again, brothers and sisters belong to the same descent group. But a male's children do not belong to his descent group. Rather, they belong to the group of their mother. Where descent is traced through only one parent, people still recognize their connections to those relatives who belong to another lineage. Thus, according to the principle of complemen-

tary filiation, people in cultures that reckon descent through the father still acknowledge and make use of their relatedness to the mother and her kin, while in matrilineal societies relatedness to the father and his kin is similarly recognized and exploited.

In some societies, descent is traced exclusively through one or the other sex for all individuals and for all purposes. When descent is traced only through the father or only through the mother in a particular society, the result is unilineal, or one line, descent. But sometimes, rules for reckoning descent differ for different individuals or for different purposes so that in some cases descent is traced through the father and in others it is traced through the mother. When descent is reckoned patrilineally for some people and matrilineally for others, the resulting system is called ambilineal descent. The Samoans employ ambilineal descent rules. Thus, an individual may trace descent through either parent and the parent, in turn, may do the same. While a person may in theory belong to any or all of the groups to which he or she can claim a relationship, most people belong to only one descent group. This is the group on whose land he or she lives. A person will, nevertheless, take a part in the activities of several of the groups to which he or she can claim membership. While a Samoan can belong to several kin groups simultaneously, this is not the case in all ambilineal cultures. Often, membership in only one group is allowed. In other ambilineal descent societies, descent may be traced through males for females and through females for males. This is called alternating descent. In parallel descent the opposite is the case, so that a male reckons descent through his father to a line of males, while a female traces descent through her mother to a line of females. In double descent, by contrast, kin group membership is assigned patrilineally for some purposes and matrilineally for others. Ambilineal and double descent systems are not common strategies for tracing descent. The Yako

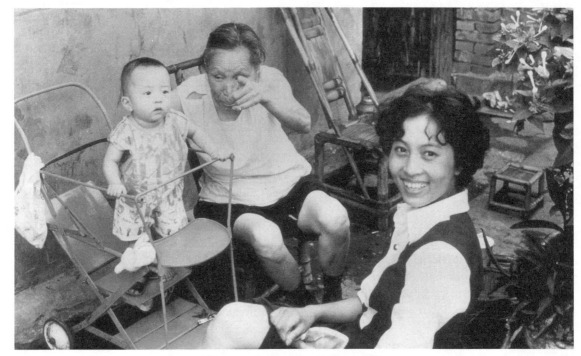

Three generations of a Chinese family.

of eastern Nigeria illustrate how double descent works. In this society, an individual's patrilineal descent group oversees political and land-holding functions. The same individual's matrilineage is in charge of inheritance of movable property. Priests are also sponsored by the matrilineage. As these functionaries act as a check on the political pursuits of the partilineage, the two descent groups create a balance of power in the Yako society.

There are a number of kinds of unilineal descent groups that reappear with regularity across cultures. Where descent is traced to a common ancestor through known links, the resulting descent group is a lineage. When descent is reckoned through the father, the descent group is a patrilineage, whereas a matrilineage traces descent through the mother. Lineages are often named for the common founder. When a group of relatives believe that they are descended from a common ancestor but cannot trace the links

back to the founder, or when the ancestor is in fact unknown, the resulting group is called a clan or sib. Patriclans reckon descent patrilineally and matriclans trace descent matrilineally. Clans may also take on identifying names, often of an animal or plant. Sometimes, a group of clans claim a relationship to each other, although the lines of descent are not known. Such a grouping of clans is called a phratry. Finally, when an entire society divides itself into two unilineal descent groups, but where the descent links are unknown, each resulting group is known as a moiety. Societies often have more than one kind of descent group. When this happens, individuals can belong to more than one descent group. Multiple descent groups exist; however, they really just nest inside each other. Thus, for example, if a society has both lineages and clans, a particular lineage is simply a smaller unit of the clan, with the latter claiming to trace its origins beyond the founder of the lineage. The term *clan* has also sometimes been used to designate another kind of kin group known as a compromise group. A compromise group is a group of individuals connected both by kin and by residence. When used to specify a compromise kin group, a clan is a group of individuals who reckon descent on a unilinear basis, share a common residence, and perceive themselves to be a cohesive social unit. This meaning of the word clan is clearly different from the meaning that focuses strictly on descent rules.

Bilateral Descent

An individual who belongs to a unilineal descent group traces descent along a line reaching back to an original ancestor, or founder, and into the future to all of the founder's descendants. As a result, unilineal descent groups are said to be vertically biased. Descent groups of this sort also emphasize relatedness with some relatives while ignoring relationships of equivalent biological significance with other relatives. For instance, a man who traces descent patrilineally acknowledges a connection to his father and father's parents but not to his mother and mother's parents, even though his biological relationship to the two sets of relatives is identical. By contrast, bilateral, or two-sided, descent rules reckon relatedness through both the mother and the father. The vertical dimension of a bilateral descent group is underplayed, with relatedness being traced back only as far as memory permits or custom dictates. Thus, bilateral descent groups do not recognize a common ancestor. In contrast with unilineal systems, bilateral descent rules focus on horizontal relatedness. That is, a bilateral system emphasizes connections between kin reaching outward from close to more distant relatives within the same generation.

Unilineal and bilateral descent groups are also different in another important way. In particular, unilineal descent rules produce nonoverlapping groups. Each individual belongs to one and only one descent group. Viewed from a different angle, each unilineal descent group has a distinct and unique identity and membership. In the case of bilateral descent, by contrast, no two individuals, with the exception of siblings, belong to the identical descent group because different people have different fathers and mothers and, therefore, trace descent through different people. Thus, an individual's own descent group is different from that of his or her cousins, and even parents and their children perceive themselves as belonging to somewhat different descent groups. This also means that bilateral descent rules result in overlapping groups. Thus, there are no distinct boundaries between groups. The differences between unilineal and bilateral descent groups lie in the point of origin for the assignment of membership in each kind of group. Because unilineal descent groups originate with a particular founder, the group really has an identity of its own, independent of the personnel. Thus, while any unilineal group can be described, at any point in time, as being composed of a particular set of descendants of the original ancestor, unilineal descent groups are corporate groups in the same way that a business is a corporation. IBM's existence as an entity does not depend upon the particular personnel who happen to work with the company at any point in time. By contrast, bilateral descent groups are ego-centered. I am the point of origin for reckoning membership in my bilateral descent group, my cousin is the point of origin for determining the membership of his descent group, and you are the point of origin for the tracing of yours. As a result, while the membership of unilineal descent groups is unambiguous, the membership of a bilateral group is indeterminate.

In societies with bilateral descent, the group of relatives that the individual traces through the father and mother compose the person's kin universe. Within that universe, the individual's close relatives are his or her kindred. An individual's

DESCENT RULES AND GROUPS

Ambilineal Descent

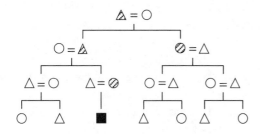

Bilateral Descent

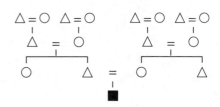

Matrilineal Descent

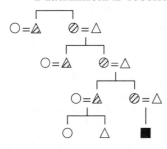

Patrilineal Descent

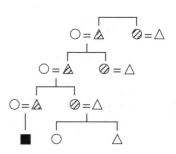

KEY TO SYMBOLS

△ Male   = Marriage
○ Female   ∣ Descent
■ Ego   ⊓ Siblingship
△,⊘ Kin of Ego

---

kindred have no identity as a group apart from the fact that they are psychologically important to the person who thinks of them all as close relations. And the same person belongs to a number of different and overlapping kindred. Thus, for example, you are a member of your mother's kindred, your maternal cousin's kindred, and your paternal aunt's kindred. None of these kindred, however, is identical, and you are probably a less central member in some of these kindred than you are in others. A person's kindred is not a group that maintains stability across time and circumstance. Thus, the ambiguity associated with bilateral descent groups more generally also infects these smaller groups of kindred. Any Westerner who has planned a family affair is familiar with one kind of effect that the ambiguity of bilateral descent groups and kindred have upon its members. Because the composition of these groups extends horizontally to include less and less closely related kin, who counts as a member of the group and who does not differs for different purposes. The group of relatives who are invited to a family reunion is likely to differ to some degree from the group invited to a daughter's wedding or to Thanksgiving dinner. By contrast, in societies with unilineal descent, the kin group is composed of the same individuals across settings and occasions.

Functions of Descent Groups

Because they are overlapping and vague, bilateral descent group membership and identity are not really suited to take on roles that require group stability and permanence. These characteristics of bilateral descent also make it hard for individuals to commit themselves and pledge their loyalties to a single, particular descent group. Rather, conflicts of interest which inevitably crop up between descent groups become conflicts of interest for the individuals belonging simultaneously to these groups. By contrast, unilineal descent groups, because they do consist of unambiguous, nonoverlapping membership, can and do act on behalf of the individual in many vital spheres of life. One of these is the domain of politics. For example, the lineage is the source of the individual's legal, or political, status in some African societies. Among the Tiv of Nigeria, a person's lineage membership decides his or her political allegiance, and a Tiv will say: "Mba Duku is my country and my patrilineage," where country is both a place and a political entity. More generally, lineages often function as governments, with heads of lineages settling disputes among lineage members, allocating land rights, and waging war.

Unilineal descent groups also perform economic functions. The lineage, clan, or other unilineal group may own land, shrines, houses, money, personal names, songs, canoes, and the like. Ceremonial and social events may be sponsored by the group. The members of a descent group are sometimes bound by the obligation to help one another, support poor members, or pay an individual's debts. Property is also frequently inherited through the lineage.

Religious activities are often centered in the unilineal descent group. In part, this is because a descent group sometimes reveres a unique set of supernatural beings, who are often the ancestors of the group. For instance, the Tallensi of Ghana believe that their dead ancestors oversee and influence the lives of descent group members. If the ancestors are angry, they can bring misfortune to their living descendants and if pleased, they can bring good luck. In other societies, each descent group makes its own unique contribution to the religious life of the larger society. Among the Hopi of the American Southwest, all of the clans take part in each religious festival, with each clan sponsoring at least one festival a year. It is the totality of activity among all of the clans that finally gives meaning to Hopi religious life. Across cultures, descent groups may also observe their own taboos and participate in their own religious ceremonies. Descent groups also frequently have their own myths, including a story of the group's origins.

Unilineal descent groups also have a role in regulating marriage. Thus, it is frequently the case that individuals who belong to the same unilineal descent group cannot marry. The group, therefore, is exogamous. On occasion, marriage within a unilineal group is favored. Exogamous marriage rules can pertain to any unilineal descent group. For instance, among the Kapauku of New Guinea, marriage is prohibited between persons belonging to the same patrilineage or patriclan. But members of the same patriphratry can marry each other.

Where a culture has a number of different kinds of descent groups, each group may take on a distinct set of functions. Thus, for instance, among the Haida of the United States, who have matrisibs, matrimoieties, and compromise kin groups (clans), marriage is regulated by the moiety, through exogamous rules of mate choice. The moiety is also the group that channels the ceremonial exchange of property. One moiety, for example, will throw a potlatch for the other moiety. The sib, by contrast, is the owner of intangible property—for instance, personal names, ceremonial titles, and rights to songs and ceremonies. The sib also regulates inheritance and ceremonial life. The clan, finally, is the basic political unit. Each clan is independent of all others, has its own chief, and holds all property rights in land.

Whereas rules of descent only dictate the manner in which individuals reckon relatedness, different descent rules tend to co-occur with other features of social life. Thus, societies that have patrilineal descent groups of some sort often look like each other in other ways. For instance, people from patrilineal societies tend to live in fixed settlements. Towns or cities are likely to be present. Food is usually produced, and not procured by gathering, hunting, or similar pursuits. Patrilineal societies will frequently place a high value on the personal ownership of property, which will be passed down through the male line. Marriage is generally accompanied in patrilineal societies by the payment of substantial goods or money to the bride's family by the lineage of the groom. When descent is traced through males, a bride and groom rarely live with or near the bride's family. Rather, they move in with or live in proximity to the new husband's natal household. Finally, domestic and political authority is vested in males.

The profile of a matrilineal society is in some ways the reverse of the patrilineal picture. Societies that trace descent through the female tend not to have cities or towns. Property is passed down through the female line. Economic transactions are token or absent at marriage. Perhaps a small bride price will be paid by the groom's family. Or the two sets of relatives might exchange gifts. A bride and groom will not live with or near the groom's natal household. Rather, the couple will move in with or live near the family of the bride, or they might move into the household or community of the husband's mother's brother. Power, however, is still vested in males, in this case in the male members of the matrilineage. Thus, in matrilineal societies, the mother's brother is usu-

ally the head of the household and the disciplinarian of his sister's children.

A number of people have proposed that different rules of descent are identified with different points in evolutionary time. According to this view, matrilineal descent is the original form, followed by patrilineal descent. Descent rules that emphasize relatedness of the individual to the relatives of both parents is then seen as the most modern form of descent reckoning. If this speculation about evolutionary sequencing is correct, then we might expect matrilineality to be prevalent in contemporary societies that most closely follow the ways of life of our remote ancestors, societies that make a living by hunting and gathering. However, matrilineality is virtually absent in these cultures. Rather, we find matrilineal descent rules predominantly in agricultural societies. Hunter-gatherer societies, by contrast, tend overwhelmingly to trace descent through both parents. These observations tend to undermine the speculation that matrilineality is the original form of descent.

Patrilineal descent rules occur in 40 percent of a sample of 185 cultures around the world. An additional 37 percent of these cultures have bilateral descent. Matrilineal descent rules appear in 14 percent of the 185 societies, while double descent occurs in 5 percent and ambilineal descent in the remaining 4 percent of these cultures.

Bohannan, Paul. (1963) *Social Anthropology.*

Bohannan, Paul, and John Middleton, eds. (1968) *Marriage, Family, and Residence.*

Buchler, Ira. (1980) "The Organization of Social Life: The Perspective of Kinship Studies." In *People in Culture,* edited by Ino Rossi, 314–398.

Ember, Carol R., and Melvin Ember. (1988) *Anthropology,* 5th ed.

Ember, Melvin, and Carol R. Ember. (1983)

Marriage, Family, and Kinship: Comparative Studies of Social Organization.

Fox, Robin. (1967) *Kinship and Marriage: An Anthropological Perspective.*

Haviland, William A. (1987) *Cultural Anthropology,* 5th ed.

Murdock, George Peter. (1949) *Social Structure.*

Murdock, George P., and Suzanne F. Wilson. (1970) "Settlement Patterns and Community Organization: Cross-Cultural Codes 3." *Ethnology* 9: 302–330.

Pasternak, B. (1976) *Introduction to Kinship and Social Organization.*

Schusky, Ernest L. (1974) *Variation in Kinship.*

Stephens, William N. (1963) *The Family in Cross-Cultural Perspective.*

Textor, Robert B. (1967) *A Cross-Cultural Summary.*

DIFFERENTIAL REPRODUCTIVE SUCCESS

Darwin's theory of evolution by natural selection proposes that genetically mediated traits are typical of members of a species today because these very characteristics gave ancestors an advantage in meeting the challenges of survival and reproduction in the past. Thus, for example, in an environment inhabited by predators, an animal who is alert to movements in the brush or on the horizon is more likely to survive and leave offspring than the animal who is oblivious to its surroundings. Our own species is believed to have evolved in an environment in which predators flourished, and human beings exhibit characteristics that would have been useful as safeguards against the dangers of predation. For example, in restaurants, most people prefer to sit in booths and not at tables, thus keeping their backs covered and themselves partially concealed from the eyes of potential enemies. Similarly, when people are eating or reading at a lunch counter, they periodically look up and scan the scene although they are unaware of doing so. So the human species has a set of built-in traits that are adaptations to a predator-rich environment. While the kinds of predators about which our ancestors had to worry no longer threaten today's world, by far the greater proportion of our existence as a species took place in an environment in which predators did pose a threat, and evolutionary theory reminds us that it is to this environment that our current traits are adapted.

Traits are characteristic of a species today because they contributed to the survival or reproduction of our ancestors. It is the assumption that these traits are in part genetically transmitted that allows evolutionary theory to make this claim. Otherwise, an advantageous trait would not be passed down from parent to child even if it did contribute to the parent's successful survival or reproduction. What is more, traits that typify a species as a whole do so because those individuals who exhibited these characteristics in the past left *more* surviving offspring than those who did not. Thus, it is the differential reproductive success of individuals exhibiting certain traits that accounts for the proliferation of those traits across generations. Differential reproductive success refers to differences between individuals of a species in the number of offspring that they produce who then go on to survive and to successfully reproduce in turn. In any given species, some individuals leave more surviving and reproducing offspring than others, while some leave none at all. It is the fact that individuals differ both with respect to their heritable traits and their reproductive success that accounts for genetically mediated species-wide characteristics.

How much of an effect can differential reproductive success really have on the prevalence of a trait in a population? Imagine two individuals, A and B. A has six offspring, each of whom also produces six offspring, and so on down through the generations. By contrast, B has five offspring, each of whom produces five offspring, and so on across generations. This difference of one child per reproducing individual represents a difference in reproductive success of about 17 percent. If individual A has a variant Ta of a given trait, and individual B has variant Tb of that trait, then in 24 generations the frequency with which Tb occurs will be one percent of its original frequency. If traits Ta and Tb were initially represented in equal proportion in the population, then in 24 generations only 1 percent of the population will exhibit Tb. If the relative number of surviving offspring produced by different individuals is less than 17 percent, then it will take longer for this kind of change to occur. If differential reproductive success is more extreme, then changes in the frequency with which a trait will occur will take less time. For human beings, it is estimated that in the case of a trait that costs an individual a 1 percent disadvantage in reproductive success compared with individuals lacking the trait, it takes approximately 10,000 years for that trait to decrease from a 99 percent to less than 1 percent representation in the population.

Differential reproductive success refers to the differences among individuals in the number of *surviving* offspring that are produced. It is critical from the perspective of evolution that individuals try to produce a maximum number of surviving offspring because offspring must themselves live long enough to reproduce in order to pass down the heritable traits of their parents. This requirement that offspring must not only be born but also survive places constraints on individuals regarding what strategies they will employ in order to maximize their reproductive success, and members of different species will adopt different strategies toward this end. One way of characterizing different reproductive strategies is to draw a distinction between r-strategists and k-strategists. R-strategists produce many offspring, investing relatively little time and energy in each. The development of infants is rapid, reproduction occurs early, life is short, and many offspring die. By contrast, the k-strategist produces fewer offspring and invests considerable time and energy in the rearing of each one. Mortality is lower and development slow, and the life span of k-strategists is relatively long. Why should some species be characterized by an r-strategy of reproduction and others by a k-strategy? The differences in reproductive strategy are associated with differences in environmental factors. In particular, r-strategists live in habitats where there are repeated periods of rapid population growth. Resources are abundant while the population remains low and competition between members of a species is, therefore, lax. In these circumstances, individuals who adopt an r-strategy may end up leaving a number of viable offspring who will themselves reproduce. K-strategists live in environments that are more or less at their population limits. Competition between species members is intense. K-strategists, therefore, spend considerable resources in order to raise a small number of individual offspring who will be able to compete successfully and survive in a crowded and challenging world. Human beings are k-strategists. The growth of the human population has been slower than that of virtually any other species, except for the elephant, at least until the introduction of agriculture 10,000 years ago.

In the case of the human species, natural selection has opted for a reproductive strategy that favors a high investment in a small number of offspring. Nevertheless, differential reproductive success is characteristic of our species, so that some individuals produce more surviving offspring than others even while adopting a k-strategy. As with other species, the disparity in reproductive success can be and is greater for males than for females. One of the strategies that males can employ for producing more offspring than other males of the species is to engage in sexual intercourse outside of marriage. Thus, a man who has two children with his wife can increase his reproductive success by one-third by producing just one child outside of his marriage. His reproductive success will increase more dramatically if he marries more than one woman and has the same number of children with both wives. In this case, his reproductive success doubles. In fact, in 69 percent of a sample of 55 cultures, extramarital sex on the part of husbands is universal or at least common. And polygyny, the marriage of a man to more than one woman, has been practiced in 81 percent of a sample of 238 cultures. The effectiveness of polygyny as a strategy for maximizing surviving offspring relative to other men is reflected in the fact that, while polygyny is the ideal in the majority of cultures, it is practiced in fact by a minority of men. Does polygyny really inflate a man's reproductive success? Anecdotal evidence demonstrates the effects of polygyny on reproductive success. Among the Shavante of Brazil, 16 of 37 men in one community had multiple wives at the time that the anthropologist reporting these numbers was visiting the society. The chief had five wives, which was more than the remaining polygynists. He had 23 surviving offspring, making up 25 percent of the living children in that generation. In the Amazon, among the Yanomamo, the most reproductively successful man had 43 children. His father had 14 children, 143 grandchildren, 335 great-grandchildren, and 401 great-great-grandchildren.

Differential reproductive success is less extreme among females in our own and other species, in part because females cannot increase the number of offspring they have by increasing the number of partners with whom they have intercourse. Thus, the average number of living children for Shavante women was seven, with little difference among the women. Among the Shavante, the most reproductively successful

woman had 14 living children. Because female reproduction is limited, not only is the difference in reproductive success across women relatively small, but also the disparity in reproductive success between the most successful woman and the most successful man can be extremely large. The fact that the number of sexual partners that a person has affects male but not female reproductive success is consistent with the fact that males have more premarital and extramarital sexual partners than females across cultures.

See also MARRIAGE FORMS; NATURAL SELECTION; REPRODUCTIVE STRATEGIES; SEX, EXTRAMARITAL; SEX, PREMARITAL.

Broude, Gwen J., and Sarah J. Greene. (1976) "Cross-Cultural Codes on Twenty Sexual Attitudes and Practices." *Ethnology* 15: 409–429.

Daly, Martin, and Margo Wilson. (1983) *Sex, Evolution, and Behavior.*

Ember, Carol R., and Melvin Ember. (1988) *Anthropology.* 5th ed.

Symons, Donald. (1979) *The Evolution of Human Sexuality.*

Trivers, Robert L. (1985) *Social Evolution.*

DIVORCE

In every known society, virtually all men and women marry. However, marriages are not always successful by the standards of the society or the marriage partners. Most cultures, therefore, permit couples to divorce. The Garo of India expect marriages to last until the death of a spouse, but partners are also expected to be compatible, so that divorce is considered to be appropriate if a husband and wife do not get along. Almost half of all Javanese marriages end in divorce, especially those that have been arranged by the parents of the husband and wife. Many men and women marry and divorce two or three times before they finally form a permanent relationship, and some never settle down but, rather, continue to make and break marriage commitments. First marriages among the Tallensi of Ghana may sometimes be of short duration, and brides tend to behave as if these unions were trial marriages. In fact, many of these relationships continue for only a few weeks, ending before the requisite gifts have been exchanged between families, or the bride price paid. They are viewed as marriages nevertheless, in part because many such unions do last.

While the Tanala of Madagascar recognize a number of legitimate grounds for divorce, and while the village council is required to grant a divorce to a woman whose husband has behaved badly, it is considered bad form for a wife to try to end her marriage, and a wife who makes the attempt will be criticized by the council and compared to a crowing hen. Disputes between spouses in which the husband is at fault are often resolved when the man publicly apologizes to his wife for his behavior. When a Cuna spouse in Panama wishes to end a marriage, the husband gathers up his belongings and leaves, returning to his mother's home or going to live with another relative. The marriage can be salvaged if the husband is persuaded by his spouse or her father to return or if he decides to come back to his wife of his own accord, and a man who is not entirely committed to a divorce may leave some of his things behind when he departs from his house. Otherwise, if the husband remains away for some months, then the couple is divorced. Of a sample of 88 societies around the world, only about 4 percent prohibit divorce. Societies differ regarding the ease with which a divorce can be obtained. Men can easily divorce their spouses without grounds in 67 percent and women in 47.7 percent of the sample of 88 cultures. Divorce without grounds is more difficult

than is divorce with grounds for males in 21.6 percent and for women in 37.5 percent of these cultures. Divorce is possible only with legitimate grounds for males in 8 percent and for females in 10.2 percent of the sample. Attitudes toward divorce also vary across cultures. The dissolution of marriages is expected or at least accepted without disapproval in 17.9 percent of 67 societies. In an additional 25.4 percent, divorce is accepted without stigma but it is mildly disapproved, so that, for example, attempts may be made on the part of other people to reconcile the couple. In 17.9 percent of the 67 cultures, divorce is approved if the reasons for the termination of the marriage are considered justified, but otherwise it is disapproved. Divorce is disapproved and a stigma is attached to the termination of a marriage in 16.4 percent of the sample. In the final 22.4 percent, divorce early on in a marriage is treated more or less lightly, but divorce once a couple has been married for a while or after children have been born is disapproved. Cultures also differ regarding the prevalence of divorce. It is universal or nearly universal in 8.5 percent of 94 cultures, common in 37.2 percent, occasional in 11.7 percent, and rare or absent in 29.8 percent. Divorce is frequent in the first years of marriage bur rare thereafter in 11.7 percent of the sample of 94 societies.

Grounds for Divorce

Societies recognize a wide variety of grounds for divorce. Marriage is recognized everywhere as the legitimate context for reproduction, so it is not surprising that couples who fail to have any children are permitted to divorce in cultures around the world. Divorce of a barren wife is common across cultures. Among the Abkhaz, a husband might divorce a wife who had no children by the time she was 30 years old or who produced no children for five years in a row. Among the Cayapa of Brazil, a man may divorce a woman who is barren and also if she has an unusual number of stillbirths. If a couple does not produce children, the wife may suggest that her husband try to impregnate another woman. If this second match is also barren, then the source of the infertility of the married pair will be assumed to be the husband, in which case the wife may divorce him and remarry. Sometimes, a married couple will find other means of having a family while staying together. In a number of cultures, a wife may obtain a divorce if her spouse is impotent or sterile. In Ghana, Ashanti women can divorce an impotent or sterile husband. A Chagga woman of Tanzania will divorce an impotent husband. Otherwise, she will be scorned because she has no children. Sometimes, however, if his wife agrees, the husband will allow her to attempt to produce offspring with his brother, although this is done discreetly so the husband can avoid being publicly humiliated by his circumstances. The intimate association between marriage and children is also reflected in the prohibition of divorce if a couple has begun a family. Among the Chagga, either spouse can divorce the other in the event of childlessness, but divorce is considered immoral once a couple has children.

Many cultures also allow divorce if one of the spouses does not fulfill the understood roles and responsibilities of married life. Typically, the failure to perform normal household chores counts as a breach of the marriage contract and, therefore, grounds for divorce. Abkhaz men may divorce a wife for laziness. An Ainu wife in Japan who allows fuel supplies to become depleted or fails to keep the pot filled with vegetables can be divorced. When a Goajiro wife in Colombia neglects her domestic responsibilities, her husband will not only divorce her but also demand repayment of the cattle that he paid as bride price when they were married, as well as any new cattle born since then. In societies where wives are expected to be deferent toward their husbands or in-laws, brazen behavior can lead to divorce. Abkhaz and Ainu wives who

are disrespectful toward their husbands may be divorced. An Ashanti husband can divorce a wife who habitually insults her own parents. Similarly, a woman can divorce a husband who chronically insults her kin. Husbands who fail to perform their proper roles can also be divorced. An Aztec husband who failed to support his wife or educate his children could be divorced. If a Chagga husband neglects his wife, especially while she is pregnant or if she is the mother of a young infant, his wife is entitled to divorce him.

Ill treatment or desertion of a spouse is also grounds for divorce in a number of cultures. Abkhaz wives can divorce their husbands for cruelty and keep the marriage payment. An Ashanti woman whose husband has remained away for at least three years without providing for her well-being in his absence can be divorced.

Infidelity is a very common reason for divorce. Divorces can result also from the chronic bad disposition of a spouse. Ashanti men can divorce their wives for quarrelsomeness. If a partner becomes incapacitated, this can lead to divorce in some cultures. Chronic illness on the part of a man is sufficient grounds for divorce among the Burmese. A woman can also divorce a man who becomes crippled after marriage or who is incapacitated by old age. One spouse can sometimes obtain a divorce on the grounds that the other spouse engages in dangerous, pathological, or antisocial behavior. An Ashanti husband can divorce a wife who practices witchcraft. Either spouse can obtain a divorce from a spouse who is a notorious thief. The practice of witchcraft is a legitimate reason for divorce among the Kikuyu of Kenya. Couples may also divorce on emotional grounds. An Ainu husband and wife may divorce for lack of love or incompatibility. A Burmese husband can divorce a wife who does not love him.

Sometimes marriages are dissolved because of trouble between a spouse and his or her in-laws, or because of divided loyalties for a spouse versus a relative. Among the Chinese, a mother-in-law can repudiate a daughter-in-law with whom she cannot get along, even if her son resists the separation. The wife may try to convince her husband to come to her defense, or she may threaten to commit suicide and thereby win a reconciliation. In Siberia, Chuckchee marriages are often terminated because the husband's mother cannot tolerate her daughter-in-law. Wives can be sent home because of conflicts with the husband's mother while the marriage is still new, but once a couple has been married for a year or so, a family who returned the bride to her parents would be looked upon askance. The bride's family can also terminate a marriage if they are unhappy with her husband, and such power remains in the hands of the bride's relatives for five or six years after she has been married, even if a number of children have been born. Ashanti couples frequently divorce even after many years of marriage, very commonly because one partner is torn between the loyalty felt for the spouse and that felt for his or her siblings.

Divorce can also result from strains associated with plural marriages. Among the Muria Gond of India, a senior wife may divorce her husband because she dislikes a junior wife, or the elder wife may worry a younger one into leaving. In Madagascar, a Tanala husband who spends a day with one co-wife when he is required to spend it with the other gives the neglected wife legitimate grounds for divorce.

Custody of Children

When a couple divorces, decisions need to be made concerning the disposition of any children produced during the marriage. The solutions to this problem vary considerably across cultures. When an Abkhaz couple divorces, the children always remain with the father. A nursing infant may stay with its mother until it is two years old, at which time the child goes to live with the father's family. Because divorce is relatively common among the Abkhaz, one household may contain youngsters belonging to as many as four or more mothers. Among the Badjau of the Philippines, a separated couple divide the children between husband and wife unless one spouse wishes to relinquish custody, in which case the other parent keeps them all. Kaska children in Alaska stay with the mother unless a youngster prefers to stay with his father and can take care of himself. Shavante children in Brazil remain with whichever parent has been left, unless a deserting mother still has infants, in which case they go with her. In the event of divorce, a Thai wife retains the first, third, and fifth children. A Hadza couple in Tanzania are considered married only as long as the two live together on a regular basis. If a husband leaves his house for more than a few weeks, the Hadza say that "his house has died." Under these circumstances, the man no longer has rights over the woman or any children they share. If her husband then returns, it is up to the woman to take him back or turn him away. The importance of the presence of children in affecting customs of divorce is illustrated by the Chagga of Tanzania. In this culture, in which children always remain with their father in the event of a divorce, a wife who divorces her husband can rescind her decision and go back to him, an option many women choose in order to be with their children. Childless women cannot return to their husbands, nor can a man who divorces his wife go back to her again.

Distribution of Property

Divorce also means that a couple must determine how to distribute property. Among the Badjau, a couple's possessions are evenly divided between them if both spouses wish to be divorced. The woman keeps all household property while the husband retains the boat and fishing gear. Arrangements for the division of property among the Burmese depend upon the reasons a partner gives for wishing a divorce. A spouse who asks for a divorce on grounds that are not considered entirely legitimate will suffer a greater financial loss than will a spouse whose reasons for wanting a divorce are judged as more sound. If a Khmer couple in Indochina divorces, the dowry is returned to the woman, but the husband retains two-thirds of the property that has been amassed during the marriage and the wife retains one-third. A Tanala wife can divorce her husband with or without reason. If she has what is viewed as a legitimate grievance, she will be granted a divorce by the village council and will receive one-third of her spouse's property. If she has no culturally accepted explanation for her wish to terminate her marriage, she can still end her marriage by returning home to her family, but she forfeits claims to any of her husband's resources.

Factors Stabilizing Marriage

Often, when a couple voice their desire to divorce, other people will attempt to negotiate a reconciliation. Divorce is both relatively easy and frequent among the Badjau, but before granting the separation the headman sends the disputing couple home for a few weeks to reconsider the decision to divorce. Similarly, divorce is common among the Huron of Ontario, but relatives and friends try to reconcile a couple who have been married for a long time but who are having problems. Before any children have been born, Iban couples in Malaysia divorce frequently and for frivolous reasons. But once a husband and wife have begun a family, friends and relatives will try hard to persuade couples entertaining the idea of divorce to stay together for the sake of the children. Sometimes they are successful. In Tierra del Fuego, Yahgan relatives try hard to reconcile a husband and wife who are thinking of divorcing, not only because security is most easily found in marriage but also because the

reputations of the divorced woman and her family suffer if the breakup was her fault.

In a majority of societies around the world, the groom or his family make a substantial payment to the family of the bride when a couple gets married. When a couple gets divorced, the disposition of this bride-price payment becomes an issue. The longevity of the marriage, the presence or absence of children, or the location of fault in the divorce may all affect decisions about who retains the bride price. If a Badjau couple divorces soon after the wedding, the bride price is given back to the groom. However, if the marriage has lasted for a number of years, the bride's family is unlikely to return the bride price even though the husband may demand it. A Kapauku husband in New Guinea can divorce his wife for any reason or for no reason at all, but unless he terminates his marriage for grounds recognized by the society, he forfeits the bride price that he paid upon his marriage.

Bride-price payments at marriage can help to stabilize the husband-wife relationship. Among the Alorese of Indonesia, the longer a couple has been married, the more complicated will be the financial agreements between the families of the spouses if there is a divorce. Further, as the bride price received by the bride's family is usually more valuable than the dowry that the new wife brings with her, the wife's kin will be in debt to the husband's relatives should a divorce occur. Sometimes a woman's family cannot or does not wish to repay the bride price, so a wife who wishes to be free of her husband may be locked into her marriage unless she can find another man who is willing to marry her and repay the bride price to her current husband. Kikuyu marriages are harder to dissolve when the couple has been together for a while, because the bride price has already been spent or the goats given in partial payment for the wife have died.

Other obstacles to divorce also tend to keep couples married across cultures. In Brazil, Shavante marriages tend to be exceptionally stable, perhaps because the divorcing spouse is required to leave the community in which the couple has lived as husband and wife. A husband need not in any case divorce a wife with whom he is not pleased in order to marry again. And women do not want to pay the price of moving away in order to terminate their marriages unless they have relatives who will also leave with them.

Remarriage

How does a person's status as a divorcee affect his or her chances of remarrying? A divorce does not harm the reputation of a Badjau man or woman, and people usually remarry soon after separating from a former spouse. However, other members of the community regard a person who has gone through a series of marriages and divorces with suspicion. Among the Chiricahua of the American Southwest, a divorced man is likely to remarry soon. If a divorced woman fails to remarry quickly, her reputation suffers. Huron divorcees remarry quickly, even if they already have children. In China, if a Lolo couple divorces, the wife cannot remarry while her former husband remains alive. Among the Mongols, public opinion makes it hard for a divorced mother to remarry if she was to blame for the termination of her former marriage, but remarriage is possible if the divorce was a result of her husband's misbehavior. A Quiche woman of Guatemala can divorce her husband for any reason, but wives do not treat their marriages lightly, as a man looking for a spouse does not consider a divorcee an ideal marriage partner. A divorced Abkhaz man or woman can marry again if former obligations regarding the bride price have been met. A divorced husband and wife who wish to remarry each other can do so only if there has been an intervening marriage and divorce.

Factors Affecting Divorce

While couples may divorce at any time in the course of married life, new marriages are especially vulnerable across cultures, in part because the beginning months and years of their relationship are still a testing ground for the couple and in part because there are usually no children yet to complicate divorce arrangements. Divorce is pandemic among the Aweikoma of Brazil during the early years of marriage, and people typically marry and divorce once or twice before they settle into a stable relationship. But by the time they have had three children, couples remain together. The first year of marriage is particularly difficult for Egyptian couples, in part because of the perpetual criticism that the families of the bride and groom level at each other. Thus, the new husband's family may find fault with the bride's jewelry or the manner in which the groom's pigeons are cooked, and the new wife's relatives may belittle the husband's ability to provide for his spouse. Therefore, if a couple divorces, this is most likely to happen early on in the marriage.

In some cultures either males or females have the exclusive right of divorce. In other cultures, either spouse can terminate a marriage, although one may be more inclined than the other to let things ride. When the right of divorce is denied to one of the partners, it is still possible for the spouse to provoke the partner to ask for a divorce. Divorce is an option for both husbands and wives among the Kiribati of the Pacific islands. A man who wishes to be separated from his spouse just throws her out of his house, while a wife simply returns to her parents if she wishes to end her marriage. A Navajo spouse need only leave the partner to effect a divorce, and only a minority of men and women remain married to the same person for life. It is not uncommon to find Navajo men who have been married to seven women in a row. In Australia, an Aranda husband may easily divorce his wife; a woman, by contrast, cannot divorce her husband, but can only run away. In West Africa, a Fon marriage may be dissolved by a wife but not by a husband. A man who wishes a divorce, however, can goad his wife into leaving him by neglecting her to the point that she is no longer willing to live with him. A Fon couple can also be coerced into divorcing even though the husband and wife themselves do not wish to be separated. This may occur, for example, if the wife's father and her husband have a disagreement and the woman's family compels her to return home as a result. Among the polygynous Ganda of Uganda, a husband who is unhappy with a spouse can simply neglect her, directing his attention to his other wives. A Ganda husband, therefore, does not usually divorce a wife unless she is barren. Ganda women cannot initiate divorces, but they can goad their husbands into setting them free by running away repeatedly, and wives do avail themselves of this strategy, so that, where they occur, divorces are usually at the instigation of the wife and not the husband.

In the United States, a Gros Ventre wife was rarely allowed to obtain a separation from her husband. A woman who tried to return to her own family was likely to be sent back along with a present to the husband as a gesture of goodwill. A wife who was openly and excessively neglected might be allowed to leave him for a while and live with her family. She would be considered free to remarry if he did not send for her. It is the man who formally obtains a divorce among the Javanese, but wives who wish to end a marriage are usually good at getting a husband's cooperation, although if a husband does not want to grant his spouse a divorce, it becomes more difficult for her to terminate her marriage. Under these circumstances, she must demonstrate that her spouse has failed to live up to the promises he made to her at the time of their marriage. A Kwoma woman in New Guinea can divorce her husband simply by going home to her parents. A husband cannot divorce his wife; rather, he must irritate her sufficiently that she

will leave him. Sometimes divorce is easier for one spouse than for another. Among the Cayapa of Brazil, divorce is easier for a man than for a woman. A husband who wishes to end his marriage simply tells his wife to leave. A Lozi husband in Zambia who wishes to divorce his wife can simply send her home. A woman who wishes a divorce must sue for it and prove that her spouse has rejected her as his wife.

While a Kapauku husband of New Guinea can divorce his spouse at his whim, divorce for a wife is harder, as, in the eyes of the Kapauku, her mate has paid for her. Women, therefore, often obtain separations from their husbands by more indirect means. A wife may run away with another man or hide in the woods while her relatives attempt to come to some understanding with her spouse. A wife whose husband is arbitrarily cruel or who does not properly support her and her children is entitled to a divorce. A Quiche wife can end her marriage simply by returning to her family. By contrast, a Quiche husband who wishes to be rid of his wife must make her life with him sufficiently difficult that she will want to leave, as he cannot otherwise turn her out of his house, especially if there are children.

In some cultures, divorce is easy for both spouses. A Cayapa husband or wife who wishes a divorce simply leaves, taking along his or her personal property. A woman who does not want a divorce cannot impede a husband who wishes to end their marriage. If a man resists his wife's intentions to divorce, he can try to restrain her forcibly, but a woman can usually get away from her husband and seek refuge in the home of her parents. Among the Garo of India, both a husband and a wife can terminate a marriage. A man who wishes a divorce will just leave and a woman who wishes to be rid of her husband can turn him out of the house. The separation is publicly formalized and the spouse who wants the divorce pays a compensation to the other partner. An Iban spouse in Malaysia who wishes a divorce simply announces that he or she has had a bad dream or ill omen and both partners become free agents. Among the Marshallese in Oceania, marriages between young people are brittle and easily ended, and most young husbands and wives marry with the expectation that they will separate at the first sign of marital discord or unfaithfulness. Sometimes, even though divorce customs are officially equivalent for husbands and wives, attitudes toward one divorcing spouse are harsher than those toward the other. Among the Montagnais of Canada, a marriage can be terminated with equal ease by a husband or wife; the spouse simply leaves the partner. But public opinion responds more harshly to a wife who abandons her husband than to a husband who leaves his wife.

Within any given society, divorce customs may also differ depending on a couple's social status. For instance, divorce is officially impossible among upper-class Botswanan Tswana couples, largely because there is no way of canceling the obligations that the families of the husband and wife owe each other by virtue of the payment of bride price. By contrast, divorce is easy and frequent when partners are from the lower classes, as there were no complicated financial arrangements at the marriage that need to be undone in the event of divorce.

Altschuler, Milton. (1964) *The Cayapa: A Study in Legal Behavior.*

Ammar, Hamed. (1954) *Growing Up in an Egyptian Village.*

Basedow, Herbert. (1925) *The Australian Aboriginal.*

Batchelor, John. (1927) *Ainu Life and Lore: Echoes of a Departing Race.*

Bennett, Wendell C., and Robert M. Zingg. (1935) *The Tarahumara: An Indian Tribe of Northern Mexico.*

Bogoras, Waldemar. (1904–1909) *The Chuckchee.*

Broude, Gwen J. (1983) "Male-Female Relationships in Cross-Cultural Perspective: A Study of Sex and Intimacy." *Behavior Science Research* 18: 154–181.

Broude, Gwen J., and Sarah J. Greene. (1976) "Cross-Cultural Codes on Twenty Sexual Attitudes and Practices." *Ethnology* 15: 409–429.

———. (1983) "Cross-Cultural Codes on Husband-Wife Relationships." *Ethnology* 22: 263–280.

Bunzel, Ruth. (1952) *Chichicastenango: A Guatemalan Village.*

Burling, Robbins. (1963) *Rengsanggri: Family and Kinship in a Garo Village.*

Cagnolo, C. (1933) *The Akikuyu: Their Customs, Traditions, and Folklore.*

Covarrubias, Miguel. (1937) *Island of Bali.*

De Smidt, Leon Sylvester. (1948) *Among the San Blas Indians of Panama, Giving a Description of Their Manners, Customs and Beliefs.*

DuBois, Cora. (1944) *The People of Alor: A Social Psychological Study of an East Indian Island.*

Dundas, Charles. (1924) *Kilimanjaro and Its People: A History of the Wachagga, Their Laws, Customs, and Legends, Together with Some Account of the Highest Mountain in Africa.*

Elmendorf, W. W. (1960) "The Structure of Twana Culture." *Washington State University Research Studies, Monograph Supplement 2.*

Elwin, Verrier. (1947) *The Muria and Their Ghotul.*

Erdland, August. (1914) *The Marshall Islanders: Life and Customs, Thought, and Religion of a South Seas People.*

Fei, Hsiao-Tung. (1939) *Peasant Life in China: A Field Study of Country Life in the Yangtze Valley.*

Ffoulkes, Arthur. (1908) "The Fanti Family System." *African Society Journal* 7: 394–409.

Flannery, Regina. (1953) *The Gros Ventres of Montana*, pt. 1.

Fortes, Meyer. (1945) *The Dynamics of Clanship among the Tallensi: Being the First Part of an Analysis of the Social Structure of a Trans-Volta Tribe.*

———. (1949) *The Web of Kinship among the Tallensi: The Second Part of an Analysis of the Social Structure of a Trans-Volta Tribe.*

———. (1950) "Kinship and Marriage among the Ashanti." In *African Systems of Kinship and Marriage,* edited by A. R. Radcliffe-Brown and Daryll Forde, 252–284.

Geertz, Hildred. (1961) *The Javanese Family.*

Gillin, John. (1936) *The Barama River Caribs of British Guiana.* Papers of the Peabody Museum of American Archaeology and Ethnology, Harvard University, 14(2).

Gomes, Edwin H. (1911) *Seventeen Years among the Sea Dyaks of Borneo: A Record of Intimate Association with the Natives of the Bornean Jungles.*

Grimble, A. (1921) "From Birth to Death in the Gilbert Islands." *Journal of the Royal Anthropological Institute* 5l: 25–54.

Gusinde, Martin. (1937) *The Yahagan: The Life and Thought of the Water Nomads of Cape Horn.*

Gutierrez de Pineda, Virginia. (1950) *Social Organization in La Guajira.*

Henry, Jules. (1941) *The Jungle People: A Kaingang Tribe of the Highlands of Brazil.*

Herskovitz, Melville J. (1938) *Dahomey: An Ancient West African Kingdom.*

Honigmann, John J. (1949) *Culture and Ethos of Kaska Society.*

Karsten, Rafael. (1935) *The Head-Hunters of Western Amazonas: The Life and Culture of the Jibaro Indians of Eastern Ecuador and Peru.*

Kenyatta, Jomo. (1961) *Facing Mount Kenya: The Tribal Life of the Gikuyu.*

Kluckhohn, Clyde, and Dorthea Cross Leighton. (1947) *Children of the People.*

Lin, Yueh-hwa. (1961) *The Lolo of Liang Shan.*

Linton, Ralph. (1933) *The Tanala: A Hill Tribe of Madagascar.*

Lips, Julius E. (1947) "Naskapi Law (Lake St. John and Lake Mistassini Bands): Law and Order in a Hunting Society." *American Philosophical Society Transactions* 37(4): 379–492.

Luzbetak, Louis J. (1951) *Marriage and the Family in Caucasia: A Contribution to the Study of North Caucasian Ethnology and Customary Law.*

Manoukian, Madeline. (1950) *Akan and Ga-Adange Peoples of the Gold Coast.*

Maybury-Lewis, David. (1967) *Akwe-Shavante Society.*

Opler, Morris Edward. (1941) *An Apache Life-Way: The Economic, Social and Religious Institutions of the Chiricahua Indians.*

Pospisil, Leopold. (1958) *Kapauku Papuans and Their Law.* Yale University Publications in Anthropology 54.

Roscoe, John. (1911) *The Baganda: An Account of Their Native Customs and Beliefs.*

Roth, H. Ling. (1892) "The Natives of Borneo." *Anthropological Institute of Great Britain and Ireland* 21: 110–137; 22: 22–64.

Schapera, I. (1930) *The Khoisan Peoples of South Africa.*

Scott, James George. (1910) *The Burman: His Life and Notions.*

Spoehr, Alexander. (1949) *Majuro: A Village in the Marshall Islands.*

Steinberg, David J. (1959) *Cambodia: Its People, Its Society, Its Culture.*

Venieminov, Ivan Evsieevich Popov. (1840) *Notes on the Islands of the Unalaska District*, vols. 2–3.

Vreeland, Herbert H. (1953) *Mongol Community and Kinship Structure.*

Whiting, John W. M. (1941) *Becoming a Kwoma: Teaching and Learning in a New Guinea Tribe.*

Woodburn, J. (1964) *The Social Organization of the Hadza of North Tanzania.* Unpublished dissertation, Cambridge University.

Young, Ernest. (1898) *The Kingdom of the Yellow Robe: Being Sketches of the Domestic and Religious Rites and Ceremonies of the Siamese.*

Zingg, R. M. (1938) *The Huichols.* University of Denver Contributions to Anthropology.

DOUBLE STANDARD IN SEXUAL BEHAVIOR

Rules regarding sexual behavior vary widely across cultures. In some societies premarital sex is approved or at least accepted, while in others it is harshly condemned. In some cultures extramarital affairs are tolerated, but in others violations of sexual exclusivity between spouses are swiftly and severely punished. Overlying these differences in sex norms is a striking regularity regarding how cultures attempt to control sexual activity. The world over the sexual behavior of females tends to be more restricted than is that of males, both before and after marriage. The different regulation of the sexual activities of girls and women versus boys and men is what is meant by the double standard.

The double standard is readily apparent in the patterning of premarital sex norms across cultures. Of 98 societies, 87 percent either permit or restrict the premarital sexual behavior of both girls and boys. In the remaining 13 percent, boys are free to experiment sexually before marriage, but girls are not. In no society are girls accorded more sexual freedom than boys. In

Oceania, the Marshallese have adopted a permissive single standard regarding the sexual behavior of unmarried individuals. They are indifferent regarding virginity in brides, and every girl has already had sexual relations by the time she reaches puberty. Marshallese boys try to have coitus with every available girl. The Azande of Zaire and Lepcha of Tibet both believe that premarital sex is required for the attainment of physical maturity in adolescents and condone sexual activity for all of their young people. The restrictive single standard also operates in a number of cultures around the world. Chagga adults in Tanzania attempt to persuade both girls and boys to refrain from engaging in premarital sex. If a girl proves not to be a virgin at marriage, her father must forfeit a goat for purification and the girl can only become a junior wife. Boys are told that they will become sterile if they father a child before marriage, and that the crops of the entire community will deteriorate, the herds will diminish, and the udders of the cattle will dry up. In the past, if a Havasupai girl of the American Southwest were caught having sexual relations before marriage, her father might shoot her lover and would certainly provoke a fight with him. Now, he is more likely to shoot one of the boyfriend's horses or do some other damage to the boy's property. For their part, boys are told that sexual relations interfere with their growth and sap their strength and that they had best, therefore, avoid sex. The double standard is illustrated by the moral code of the Ingalik of Alaska, who prescribe chastity for girls until they are married. But any male who does not exploit a chance to engage in sexual relations is thought abnormal. In Madagascar, Tanala girls are expected to remain virgins until marriage, but boys are not. Indeed, a boy who did not have sexual experience before he was married would be admitting that he was impotent and would have trouble attracting a wife. It is assumed that unmarried boys will seek out older or married women as sex partners. In West

Africa, Fon girls are supervised closely once they reach puberty and are warned of what will happen if they are not virgins at marriage. But adolescent boys are permitted to indulge their sexual impulses with older women or prostitutes.

The double standard becomes more pronounced for married men and women. Of 116 societies, 11.2 percent permit both husbands and wives to engage in extramarital sex. An additional 23.3 percent condemn and punish affairs outside of marriage equally harshly for both spouses. The remaining 65.5 percent of the 116 cultures punish any extramarital sexual activities on the part of wives more severely than they do that of husbands. In some cases, affairs are permitted for husbands but not for wives while in others, infidelity is not approved for either sex but is punished more severely in women than in men. In no society are extramarital sex norms more lenient for wives than for husbands. The permissive single standard is again reflected in the attitudes of the Lepcha, who are publicly indifferent regarding the extramarital sexual activity of either spouse, a husband objecting only to his wife's having sexual intercourse with another man in his presence. Further, married people are openly teased about past affairs. Lesu husbands and wives in New Ireland both carry on affairs outside of marriage, and a married person who avoids extramarital sexual relationships is regarded as suspect. Each time a Lesu wife meets a lover, he gives her a string of *tsera,* which she then presents to her husband. The Garo of India exemplify the restrictive single standard. In this society, an extramarital affair on the part of either spouse is an infringement of the rights of the other. A husband or wife whose spouse has been unfaithful will demand a fine of 30 rupees from the spouse's lover.

The double standard in extramarital sex norms is played out in a variety of ways across cultures. Extramarital sex is punished in a wife but not in a husband in 43.1 percent of 116 societies. Among the Abkhaz, an adulterous wife

can be divorced, mutilated, or put to death, and the bride price paid to her family at marriage must be returned to the husband. Infidelity in a husband, by contrast, cannot be punished by a wife. In Uganda, if a Gandan husband engages in extramarital affairs, this is not considered to be an infringement of the wife's rights. To their spouses' intrigues women respond: "We know what men are." The common sentiment is that a reasonable woman will not make a fuss if her husband strays and ought to aid his efforts if he happens to be attracted to a friend of his wife. If, on the other hand, a Gandan wife is unfaithful, this is seen as a breach of the husband's rights. In the past, the injured husband might assault his wife for the offense of adultery. In the past in the United States, a Gros Ventre husband not only had a right to punish his adulterous wife, he was virtually required to do so if he wished to save face. A man who forgave an unfaithful wife would be ridiculed by and lose the respect of his community, although some husbands who were especially attached to their wives were willing to run this risk and overlook a spouse's misconduct. A wronged husband could kill his adulterous wife, and some women met this fate on their husbands' mere suspicion of infidelity. A husband might also cut off his unfaithful wife's hair, nose, or ears and then abandon her to her relatives. By contrast, a Gros Ventre wife had no formal recourse in response to her husband's infidelity and, in fact, girls were admonished to expect and allow their husbands to carry on affairs outside of marriage. A wife whose husband was unfaithful might try to make his life miserable to pay him back for the pain he caused her, and a man might get a bad name if he ran around with too many women, but it was nevertheless expected that brave young husbands would try to have as many extramarital affairs as they could.

In 22.4 percent of the 116 societies, extramarital sex is condemned for both spouses, but the affairs of wives are punished more severely, sometimes dramatically so, than that of husbands. A Wogeo wife of New Guinea who commits adultery will be sharply chastised and beaten, and perhaps turned out of her home. She will go to live with her relatives for a while. The couple will eventually reconcile when the husband accepts a special dish of his favorite food prepared and sent to him by his wife. An unfaithful husband can expect a less serious and less disruptive response from his wife, who can reprimand him and perhaps leave home. Within a week, the husband will give his wife a present as a way of making up, and things will return to normal. Infidelity in a Sherpa husband in Nepal is punished by a fine; adultery by a wife costs twice the amount. In the American Southwest, a wronged Chiricahua husband could beat his wife, cut off her nose so that she would no longer attract other men, or kill her. A wife whose husband had an affair could reprimand him and complain to her own kin, or perhaps, if she was very angry, send him away. But women did not usually make any response to their husbands' infidelities. A wife who took drastic action against her husband would have a very hard time finding another man to marry her in the future.

Even when the single standard officially applies to the extramarital sexual activities of spouses, men may enjoy greater freedom in the pursuit of affairs outside of marriage than do their wives. The Javanese assume that each spouse has the right to expect fidelity of the other. Each is continuously on the watch in case the other is carrying on an affair. Nevertheless, actual infidelity is less frequent for wives than it is for husbands, and women are likely to put up with the dalliances of their husbands because men are thought to be naturally irresponsible. A man who commits adultery is *nakal,* or naughty, the same label used to describe mischievous children. Among the Ifugao of the Philippines, husbands and wives are formally required to pay the same fine for committing adultery, but the wife is much more likely to be punished for infidelity, while husbands frequently engage in extramarital sex with impunity. Ifugao women do not like to initiate proceedings against unfaithful husbands and would prefer to be kept ignorant of a spouse's extramarital affairs. Thus, the official differences that are reflected in the treatment of unfaithful wives and husbands in extramarital sex norms across cultures are inflated by informal understandings in many societies that allow husbands but not wives to philander.

These patterns regarding norms of sexual behavior across cultures reveal a number of interesting trends. First, the double standard is always more indulgent regarding the sexual conduct of males as opposed to females. Second, the discrepancy in attitudes regarding the sexual behavior of males and females is less pronounced for unmarried than for married people. Finally, the double standard is much more likely to target extramarital than premarital sex. This difference can be traced to the notable tendency for societies to restrict the sexual conduct of women more after they are married than when they are single. Thus, 44.7 percent of 141 societies at least tolerate premarital sex in unmarried girls, and an additional 17 percent try to dissuade single girls from engaging in sex but do not punish transgressors. In contrast, only 13 percent of 112 societies approve of extramarital sex for wives. The rest condemn such behavior and are likely to punish it, often severely.

The bias of the double standard always targeting the sexual behavior of females can be traced to the fact that a girl's sexual activities can have far-reaching consequences. The fundamental problem, of course, is that sexually active girls can become pregnant. Premarital pregnancies can be very disruptive to the girl and her kin, to the father and his kin, and to society at large. The illegitimate child also sometimes suffers. In some cultures, it is difficult to assign a social identity or provide a home and family to a child whose mother is unmarried. It is in the interest of these societies to try to minimize the number of girls who become pregnant before they are married.

Across cultures, the premarital sexual history of a girl is also taken as an indicator of how she is likely to conduct herself sexually once she is a wife. Men worry that girls who have been sexually active before marriage will be unfaithful wives. There are reasons why males should wish their wives to be sexually loyal, and a girl who gives a prospective husband cause to doubt her sexual fidelity will have trouble attracting a worthy spouse. Restrictions on the sexual activity of single girls, then, act to preserve the reputations of future wives whose families wish them to make the best possible matches.

The issue of why fidelity in a wife is so important to men the world over has to do with whether or not a man can be certain that his spouse's children are also his own. Obviously, a woman is always sure that she is the mother of the infant to whom she has given birth, but a husband always runs the risk of raising a child who has been fathered by another man. Charles Darwin pointed out that members of our own and other species exhibit many behaviors that result in the production of the greatest possible number of surviving offspring. Individuals who produce more viable offspring than others of their kind make a larger relative contribution to the gene pool of their species. Thus, they have greater reproductive success than other individuals. This means that those of their traits that are genetically influenced will be better represented in succeeding generations. A husband who is unconcerned with the sexual behavior of his wife may be helping another man's reproductive success, to the detriment of his own. Darwin observed that males across species are very sensitive about infidelity in a mate because the genetically influenced behavior of males in the past who did not display this concern are no longer importantly represented in the gene pool. The extramarital sexual activities of husbands can have some negative effects upon a wife. A husband who philanders is investing time and may be investing valuable resources in someone other than his own spouse and her children, and this is harmful to a woman's reproductive success as it places the future of her youngsters in jeopardy. But ultimately, infidelity in a wife can be much more devastating to a man than is the unfaithfulness of a husband to his wife.

How effective is the double standard in restraining the sexual behavior of wives? Restrictive extramarital sex norms for women do not reliably transform women into faithful spouses. In the majority of societies that condemn extramarital sex for married women, many or most wives are still conducting affairs outside of marriage. Why would women risk public disapproval and potentially severe punishment to carry on an extramarital affair? A woman who is able to attract a lover who is in some way superior to her husband may help out her own reproductive success in a number of ways. If she becomes pregnant, her child may display favorable genetically influenced traits inherited from the father. If the man is wealthy or powerful and she benefits in some way from his high status, then she may be able to transfer the advantages accruing from the high status of her lover to her children. If the man is willing to marry her, then she can swap her adequate husband for a better one.

The double standard of extramarital sex is associated with a number of other customs and behavioral patterns across cultures. Where the double standard prevails, rules regarding premarital sex for girls are restrictive, reflecting the general tendency for some cultures to wish to rein in the sexual behavior of females in general. Homosexuality is also condemned in societies with the double standard. Where rules regarding extramarital sex are more restrictive for wives than for husbands, men and women tend to do different kinds of work, and special houses where men eat, sleep, and spend their leisure time tend to be present. Thus, cultures that wish to restrict the sexual behavior of wives may be attempting to minimize the opportunities that a woman will have to meet a man by segregating the sexes on a daily basis. Finally, where the double standard prevails, men tend to be more likely to boast to their peers about their sexual and other exploits. Perhaps where social norms make married women more inaccessible to other males, the man who manages to circumvent the rules and attract or seduce someone else's wife wishes to brag about his successes.

See also BRIDE PRICE; CUCKOLDRY; DIFFERENTIAL REPRODUCTIVE SUCCESS; PREGNANCY, PREMARITAL; REPRODUCTIVE STRATEGIES; SEX, EXTRAMARITAL; SEX, PREMARITAL; SEXUAL SELECTION; VIRGINITY.

Broude, Gwen J. (1975) *A Cross-Cultural Study of Some Sexual Attitudes and Practices.* Unpublished dissertation, Harvard University.

———. (1980) "Extramarital Sex Norms in Cross-Cultural Perspective." *Behavior Science Research* 13: 181–218; 15: 409–429.

———. (1981) "Cultural Management of Sexuality." In *Handbook of Human Development,* edited by Robert Munroe, Ruth Munroe and Beatrice B. Whiting.

Broude, Gwen J., and Sarah J. Greene. (1976) "Cross-Cultural Codes on Twenty Sexual Attitudes and Practices." *Ethnology* 15: 409–429.

Burling, Robbins. (1963) *Rengsanggri: Family and Kinship in a Garo Village.*

Dundas, Charles. (1924) *Kilimanjaro and Its People: A History of the Wachagga, Their Laws, Customs, and Legends, Together with Some Account of the Highest Mountain in Africa.*

Evans-Pritchard, Edward Evan. (1971) *The Azande: History and Political Institutions.*

Flannery, Regina. (1953) *The Gros Ventres of Montana,* pt. 1.

Fürer-Haimendorf, Christoph von. (1948) "The Raj Gonds of Adilabad." In *The Raj Gonds of Adilabad,* 1–21.

Geertz, Clifford. (1959) "Form and Variation in Balinese Village Structure." *American Anthropologist* 61: 991–1012.

Gorer, Geoffrey. (1938) *Himalayan Village: An Account of the Lepchas of Sikkim.*

Gutmann, Bruno. (1932) *Die Stammeslehren der Dschagga* [The tribal teachings of the Chagga], vol. 1.

Herskovitz, Melville J. (1938) *Dahomey: An Ancient West African Kingdom.*

Linton, Ralph. (1933) *The Tanala: A Hill Tribe of Madagascar.*

Luzbetak, Louis J. (1951) *Marriage and the Family in Caucasia: A Contribution to the Study of North Caucasian Ethnology and Customary Law.*

Mair, Lucy P. (1965) *An African People in the Twentieth Century.*

Marshall, Lorna. (1959) "Marriage among the !Kung Bushmen." *Africa* 29: 335–364.

Opler, Morris Edward. (1941) *An Apache Life-Way: The Economic, Social and Religious Institutions of the Chiricahua Indians.*

Osgood, Cornelius. (1958) *Ingalik Social Culture.* Yale University Publications in Anthropology 55.

Powdermaker, Hortense. (1933) *Life in Lesu: The Study of a Melanesian Society in New Ireland.*

Raum, O. F. (1940) *Chaga Childhood: A Description of Indigenous Education in an East African Tribe.*

Spier, Leslie. (1928) *Havasupai Ethnography.* Anthropological Papers of the Museum of Natural History 29.

DOWRY

The custom whereby the bride's family transfers goods to the groom or his relatives at the time of marriage is known as dowry. Dowry is present in only 3 percent of a sample of 1,267 cultures. It is found in highly stratified, complex societies, and is largely confined to Asia and Europe. In cultures where the custom of dowry exists, it tends to be confined to people belonging to the upper classes. Further, women generally make relatively small contributions to the subsistence economy in dowry cultures. For example, when a Rajput couple in India is married, the bride's relatives present a number of gifts to the groom. Members of his family also receive presents, although these are somewhat less valuable, as do their servants. Gifts include expensive jewelry, kitchen items, bed linens, and clothing. The total cost of the presents that a female's family must give away at her marriage is quite high, and her parents will have begun to accumulate these articles while their daughter is just a baby.

The custom of dowry is extremely rare. More common is the practice of bride price, whereby a groom's family presents goods or money to the family of the prospective bride. Evolutionary perspective offers one explanation as to why it occurs in some societies. Across species, females make a greater investment than do males in the reproductive process. First, their gametes are more biologically expensive to produce. If fertilization is internal, then the female also contributes considerable time and energy to the development of the fetus. In the case of mammals, the mother must also feed and otherwise care for her infants. As a result, it costs a male very little to mate with a female, while for a female mating is very costly. This inequality leads to the prediction that males ought to compete with each other for females because females are bringing more to the shared reproductive effort than are males. In the case of human beings, the relative popularity of bride price is thus interpreted as the man's attempt to make himself more attractive to the woman of his choice in a market where other men are also interested in obtaining her as a sexual partner. By contrast, the custom of dowry should be rare because females, as the sex that invests more in reproduction, do not characteristically need to court males by offering them material rewards for mating. If this reasoning about relative investments in reproduction and their relationship to property exchanges at marriage is correct, then why does the custom of dowry occur at all? This dilemma may be resolved by considering the kinds of societies that have the dowry as a feature of marriage. The fact that dowries are present in cultures with class stratification suggests that a girl's family may be trying to exchange goods for a high-status husband, who will be able to provide more in the way of resources for the girl and her children than will other, less well-placed men. Thus, where class distinctions exist in a culture, competition between females for the most powerful and wealthy males may begin to emerge. For example, in India the upper classes marry by dowry while the lower classes marry by bride price. Further, the relatively small contribution that women make to the subsistence economy in dowry societies decreases their value relative to that of females who are important in subsistence activities. This serves to inflate the value of males in comparison with that of females. Finally, because marriage is always monogamous in dowry cultures, a husband's resources will not be spread across a number of wives and children as happens in polygynous families. Thus, a girl's parents can be more assured of getting what they are paying for if they exchange valuables for a high-status male as a husband for their daughter.

Comaroff, J., ed. (1980) *The Meaning of Marriage Payments.*

Daly, Martin, and Margo Wilson. (1983) *Sex, Evolution, and Behavior.*

Gaulin, Steven, and James Boster. (1990) "Dowry as Female Competition." *American Anthropologist* 92(4): 994–1005.

Goody, J., and S. T. Tambiah. (1973) *Bridewealth and Dowry.*

Minturn, Leigh, and John T. Hitchcock. (1966) *The Rajputs of Khalapur, India.*

Schlegel, Alice, and Rohn Eloul. (1987) "A New Coding of Marriage Transactions." *Behavior Science Research* 21: 118–140.

van den Berghe, Pierre L. (1979) *Human Family Systems.*

Economic Arrangements at Marriage

See BRIDE PRICE; BRIDE SERVICE; DOWRY; GIFT EXCHANGE.

Elderly

In Western society, the elderly represent a special category of persons. On the one hand, older people hold some of the most powerful and prestigious positions and perform some of the most important roles in society. On the other hand, the aged often present special problems to themselves and to other people. Old people may have outlived family and friends and find that they are now alone and lonely. They may be failing in health and no longer able to perform their usual work or take care of themselves. The problem then arises as to who should be responsible for the old person. The story of the elderly mirrors these themes from one society to the next. Old people are some of the most and least powerful individuals across cultures. They may be the supervisors of younger people or may need supervision themselves. And everywhere the question of how to support the more helpless and decrepit aged requires the attention of their kin and the community.

In Western cultures an individual is often said to be old when he or she has arrived at a particular chronological age. But in nonliterate cultures, people do not record or remember exact birth dates and, therefore, have no way of calculating an individual's precise chronological age. Cultures that have no way of determining absolute age nevertheless have a number of ways of judging how old a person is likely to be. For instance, relative age may be used as a yardstick. If one person was born before another person, then the first is older than the second. Thus, comparative age may help in determining who is old and who is not. In some societies, individuals who were born at roughly the same time are recruited into groups based upon age. A group of people travels through the age-grades, arriving ultimately at the age-grade of old people. Age-grading, then, can also provide an estimation of an individual's age and a signpost marking the person's arrival at old age. Thus, chronological age may support concepts regarding who is old even in societies that do not keep track of birthdays. There are, however, other criteria that figure importantly in the assignment of individuals to the category of the aged. Prominent among these are the person's physical condition and the roles that the individual plays. The two are closely related, of course. A person who begins to deteriorate physically may no longer be able to perform the kinds of tasks that a younger person can handle. As a result, physical signs of aging can become signs that an individual will have to abandon certain roles.

In traditional cultures around the world, it is unusual for people to live to a ripe old age. For example, in 1894 about 4.5 percent of Bontoc Igorot men in the Philippines and 5.3 percent of the women lived to be older than 50. A Bontoc woman is said to be in "her prime" when she is 23. By the time she is 30, she is "getting old," and she is old in fact before she turns 45. Similarly, 7.2 percent of Omaha Native American men and 8.2 percent of the women survived beyond 55 years of age in 1884. The Andamanese rarely live beyond 60 years and the Arawak of British Guiana usually die before they reach 50. Mongolian women are wrinkled and old by the time they are 40. A Chuckchee of Siberia is likely to die before the age of 40, and a man who lives to be 60 will be very decrepit. According to estimates, perhaps 3 percent of individuals in traditional societies reach the age of 60. Thus, what chronologically counts as aged in one society may not in another.

The status and fate of the elderly differ in important ways across cultures, but the factors that determine the fortune of older people are similar from one place to the next. For instance, if an old person has resources of some kind to compensate for failing powers, he or she is more likely to find old age a satisfactory or even satisfying time of life. Often the ownership of property is influential in making the life of an older person relatively secure. In traditional Hopi culture in northern Arizona, elderly people retained their property rights, bartering them in exchange for care and support in their old age. Old people who had property were better cared for than those who did not and received superior treatment even in death, as the relatives who took responsibility for their burial got a greater share of the deceased person's possessions. Among the Chuckchee, an old father, even if he is feeble or mentally incompetent, is treated very well because he is the owner of the family's herd. As women are far less likely to be in control of property than are men, this insurance against hard-

ship in old age is biased in favor of males across cultures.

Where elderly people possess knowledge or skills that are valued by other members of their society, they are able to trade on them in order to procure the necessities, and even the luxuries, of life. Among the Crow of the Plains, elderly storytellers were paid with a feast. Old Navajo men were paid for their magic songs, charms, and so on, and young men who wished to be taught magic by the elderly practitioners gave their turos large gifts in return. In California, an old Yokuts woman who performed the services of a midwife received most of a fat animal in payment. Because of their accumulated knowledge and experience, old people in many cultures are accorded the respected roles of priest, medicine man, magician, seer, and the like. The music and ritual of the Omaha were handed down by the elderly "for only the old men knew the songs perfectly." And it was the Hopi elders who knew the legends, rituals, and traditions of war and hunting. Elderly men also frequently take on or continue in political leadership roles. Sometimes age alone is the qualifying characteristic for positions of authority. Often, it is the special expertise and wide knowledge of the old person that qualifies him for such roles. Older people also act as the judges in many societies, arbitrating disputes, handing out punishments, and seeing to it that the traditions of their cultures are respected and followed.

In many societies around the world, the elderly are accorded a considerable degree of respect. But this is usually because of some specific quality of the old person. Thus, elderly people in various cultures are respected for their knowledge, skill, wealth, experience, power, and the like. Andamanese children are taught to respect old people, in part because older men have more experience than other members of society. Arunta men in Australia are respected in their old age because they are thought to be able to cause illness. Among the Polar Eskimo, aged men were respected because they knew magic and could understand hidden things and could, therefore, protect members of their community from famine. Old Labrador Eskimo women were accorded great respect because they could interpret dreams and old men were treated with deference as healers. Elderly Iroquois women in New York were politically powerful and landowners as well. They were powerful enough to stop any war of which they did not approve, and were highly respected. Hopi old people commanded respect as long as they retained their property and positions of leadership. But old persons who no longer had any power or importance were liable to be neglected by their families and even abused by the younger children. In general, then, respect is accorded to an old person to the extent that there is something tangible about the individual that earns respect. Even in the same society, more capable, powerful, knowledgeable, or skillful elderly people may be treated with great deference at the same time that more enfeebled and useless old people do not attract respect. In some societies an old person is revered regardless of personal qualities, but this is the exception and not the rule.

The lives of older people may also be improved because they are not required to observe taboos that do apply to younger people. On the northwest coast of the United States, Kwakiutl women, once they were past their reproductive years, could become members of secret societies. Omaha women were allowed to sit with their legs stretched out as a privilege of age, although younger women and girls were expected to adopt a dignified and modest position when seated. Among the Kiwai Papuans only old men were allowed to grow beards. And elderly Samoan brother-sister pairs were no longer required to feel ashamed in each other's presence.

Status differences between men and women also tend to disappear in old age. Among the Mundurucu in Brazil, the status of women is inferior to that of men, with males dominating the political and religious offices. Women are expected to be retiring and demure, and while in mixed-sex groups, the men will sit on chairs while the women will sit on the floor in the background. However, these constraints no longer apply to a woman past child-bearing age. An old woman can sit wherever she pleases, and men will scurry to make room for her. She can talk on any topic that interests her, and interrupt the conversation of men if she wishes. She will give her opinion on community matters and her views will be respected. Yanomamo society is also characterized by a pervasive bias toward males. Female infanticide is more common than is male infanticide. Little girls are incorporated into the work force earlier than their male counterparts, and women are delegated work that is considered too menial for men. A wife is expected to obey the commands of her husband, and women are quick to do so in order to avoid the battering that a tardy response will provoke. But a woman comes to be respected when she is old and has adult children to care for her and treat her well. Elderly women become important in intervillage politics and warfare because they can travel from village to village without being bothered by raiders. As a result, they act as messengers and sometimes recover the bodies of the dead.

Across societies, all capable individuals are expected to contribute to the subsistence economy. Participation in subsistence tasks typically begins in childhood, as soon as youngsters can be recruited to do the kinds of chores required in their particular culture. Thus, from a very young age, and throughout life, people earn their keep. Elderly men and women, then, face a problem when their diminished capacities prevent them from continuing to take part in subsistence tasks. They must now find different ways of making themselves valuable or else trust to the generosity and good will of other people to keep them alive. Sometimes old people can earn their keep by doing chores that require less fortitude than the normal subsistence activities. Old

Gypsy elder in the Ukraine sharing his experiences with children of the community. In many cultures elders are the repository of important information for future generations.

Labrador Eskimo women who could no longer do strenuous work stayed indoors making straw hats and baskets and tending the family's clothes. A woman who cared for the boots of members of her household might receive a few biscuits as payment. Old Ainu men in Japan carved pegs and skewers that were then given to other members of the camp. Old people may find their status diminished as they are recruited to perform new kinds of tasks in place of their old activities. An elderly Pomo man who was a warrior or hunter in his prime might have found himself being bossed around by the women of the household as he helped them pick fruit, make bread, thresh grain, and the like. When old people cannot perform any useful function, they sometimes become a real burden to their relatives and communities. For example, one Khoi family in South Africa abandoned an old grandmother because she could no longer carry home meat from the hunt or fetch firewood or tote her grandchildren on her back. Among the !Xhosa, also in South Africa, old people will be fed as long as they can do some kind of work. But when they are too feeble to perform any function, they may be left to starve.

Because in most societies around the world people are expected to earn their keep, elderly often continue to work even when they have become relatively incapacitated. Enfeebled Hopi men would care for their herds even when they were nearly blind. When they were no longer able to tend their cattle, they would devote themselves to their fields and orchards, lying down on the ground to rest for a while when they were too tired to go on. A man who could no longer farm would knit, spin, card wool, or make sandals, and frail old crones continued to spin when they could no longer see or walk. Among the South American Inca, no one was allowed to "eat the bread of idleness" if there was any task that he or she could do. Thus, old people who could no longer perform other work would act as scarecrows to scare birds and rodents away from the fields, or old blind people might pick seeds out of the cotton and maize.

When older people can no longer provide for themselves, relatives or members of the society at large may take on the burden of keeping the elderly individual alive. Thus, for example, every Creek was part of a clan, and members of any given clan were likely to be found scattered among many villages. As clan members were required to provide food and clothing for each other, even old people could count on being provided for when they were unable to fend for themselves. Among the Navajo, an old person could be assured of having enough to eat as long as any of his many relatives had food to give him and he could get to their houses to accept it. An elderly Semang in Malaysia is cared for by his children when he can no longer provide for himself, and a child will even carry a parent on his back when he moves from one campsite to another. Crow cultural rules required children and other relatives to provide an old person with the very best food there was to offer. Among the Lengua, elderly people are fed at the expense of the entire community as long as there is enough food to go around. And among the Chuckchee, an old person who has no kin will be cared for by herders who can afford the extra burden. Sometimes an older person can depend upon the repayment of old debts as a way of keeping himself fed. Among the Kiwai Papuans, a man who gives a boy gifts can expect to receive presents on a regular basis in return, even though many years may have elapsed since the original gifts were bestowed. And sometimes older people are able to exploit food taboos in order to feed themselves. Thus, in many cultures, certain categories of individuals are prohibited from eating particular foods, but elderly people are often exempt from these rules. For example, old Polar Eskimo men and women who had given birth to more than five children had eggs, the internal organs of animals, and small animals (such as young seals, hares, and grouse) at their disposal, as no one else was permitted to eat these foods. Similarly, among the Crow, only old people ate entrails and marrow bones. And in California, only an old Pomo man or woman was permitted to eat a lark. While it is true that elderly people in many cultures manage to stay fed even when they cannot provide for themselves, the old and infirm do not always fare so well. Among the Witoto of the Amazon, elderly people had to forage for themselves since a person who can no longer engage in any useful activities is no longer thought to have a life worth living. And an elderly Navajo who could not travel to the home of a relative to ask for food might starve to death.

In many cultures, old people have greater power and prerogatives than those who are not yet old. Old men may have greater wealth, domestic authority, political power, or access to women. Old women often attain greater freedom, prestige, and influence than younger females, whose lives are often far more restricted. In farming communities, older men are often the owners of the land, making younger men dependent upon them for its use and, ultimately, its transfer. In herding communities, elderly men often own the livestock. In societies that require transfers of wealth from the groom's to the bride's family at marriage, young males frequently depend upon older ones in meeting the bride-price payments. And it is often the older men in the bride's family who receive the marriage gifts, adding to their power base. In these cultures, conflict between the old and the young is likely to be pronounced. Some of the most serious strains are between older and younger family members. Especially in societies where power and property are vested in male relatives, the relationship between a father and son may be tense. In these cultures, sons are dependent on their fathers economically, which means that the younger man is beholden to his father for his livelihood and even his ability to marry. When a married couple moves into the household of the

new husband, a grown son is also under his father's thumb as regards his domestic life. Often a father will try to retain his power in the household for as long as he can, while his sons wait impatiently for the older man to hand over the reins. In the Indian village of Gaon, a man, although full grown and married, is still expected to wait on his father and obey him in all matters, relegating the son to something like the status of servant. In some societies, a son, even if he does not live in his father's house, is still expected to work for him. Among the Anlo Ewe of southern Ghana, a married man establishes his own household near to his father's and at a place of the older man's choosing and works a parcel of land that his father has given him to use. The son is expected to weed, sow, and hoe for his father. In some societies, it is the mother's brother who retains power over a nephew. In these cultures, tensions tend to occur between uncle and nephew, while the father-son relationship is more harmonious. In societies where a man owes payments to or is required to work for his father-in-law, the relationship between the two may be strained. Among the Kpelle of Liberia, bride-price payments are drawn out for many years, during which time a husband remains obligated to his wife's father. Kpelle fathers-in-law, therefore, feel justified in asking for financial assistance from the daughter's husband any time they need it.

Similar kinds of tensions can erupt between old and young women across cultures. Age often means greater access to public life and sometimes also greater control over material resources, and older women are frequently able to wield power over younger members of their household. Strains between mothers and sons are not commonly reported, perhaps in part because women are rarely in control of the kinds of resources or in the kinds of positions of power that threaten sons. Similarly, the mother-daughter relationship is usually described as warm even when a daughter is living in her mother's household and therefore under her influence to some extent. Tensions between older and younger co-wives are more common. In some polygynous societies, co-wives are ranked by age, with the older and more senior wife having authority over the junior woman. The oldest wife in an Australian Tiwi household can assign chores to the remaining women and can tell them how to manage their own children. Younger wives may resent this kind of tyranny. The most common kind of tension is between a mother-in-law and her son's wife, especially where a woman moves in with her husband's family at marriage. Under these circumstances, a bride often finds herself in a position of subordination to her mother-in-law, whom she must obey and to whom she is often expected to show exaggerated respect. In contrast to her husband, who is surrounded by familiar relations, she is a stranger in someone else's stronghold. The young wife may find herself competing with her mother-in-law for her husband's affection. The younger woman may be impatiently waiting for the older one to die so that she can finally take control of her own life. In New Delhi, a wife remained in the house under the surveillance of her husband's mother. The mother-in-law's activities often allowed her to leave the house, but the younger woman stayed home doing household chores, often the more burdensome ones. A daughter-in-law served her husband's mother, massaging her legs or scrubbing her back when she bathed. A woman could find herself nursing an invalid mother-in-law for years.

Chagnon, Napoleon A. (1968) *Yanomamo: The Fierce People.*

Foner, Nancy. (1984) *Ages in Conflict.*

Glascock, Anthony. (1984) "Decrepitude and Death-Hastening: The Nature of Old Age in Third World Societies." *Studies in Third World Societies* 22: 43–67.

Levinson, David, and Martin J. Malone. (1980) *Toward Explaining Human Culture.*

Murphy, Yolanda, and Robert F. Murphy. (1985) *Women of the Forest.* 2d ed.

Simmons, Leo W. (1945) *The Role of the Aged in Primitive Society.*

Sokolovsky, Jay, ed. (1990) *Culture, Aging, and Society.*

ELOPEMENT

Customs surrounding the choice of a marriage partner vary considerably from culture to culture. Nevertheless, the majority of men and women living in any particular society manage to conform to whatever mate-choice practices are imposed upon them. From time to time, however, individuals find themselves at loggerheads with cultural rules that specify whom they should marry. In such cases, a couple may circumvent social conventions by eloping. Elopements provide an individual who cannot marry the partner of his or her choice through accepted avenues an alternative to secure the desired mate.

Elopement often serves as an escape hatch in societies where marriages are traditionally arranged by third parties. Sometimes a person does not wish to marry the partner to whom he or she has been promised. If there is some other potential mate the individual would rather marry, the two may try to circumvent the plans of the matchmakers by eloping. For example, romantic love does not usually figure prominently in the marriages of the Badjau, among whom marriages are arranged by the parents, but a couple who has fallen in love may take matters into their own hands by eloping.

In some cultures where marriages are not actually arranged by third parties, a match requires the approval of the parents or relatives of a potential bride or groom. Off the coast of New Guinea, a Trobriand marriage is not considered legal unless the girl's parents agree to her choice of spouse. When a couple cannot obtain the blessing of the prospective bride's parents, the two may elope to another village in an effort to soften opposition to the marriage. After they are married, the couple will stay indoors and refuse to eat, while the boy's father or uncle offers the girl's parents an expensive gift in an attempt to persuade them to accept the union. If the parents still object to the marriage, they will come to "pull the girl back." The boy's family and friends try to interfere with the rescue, in which case a fight is likely to erupt.

In some cultures, a man and woman may wish to marry but are prohibited from doing so for reasons of status, kinship, or the like. They may then resort to elopement. For instance, among the Aranda Aboriginals in Australia a man may run away with a girl of whom he is fond but who does not belong to the cohort from whom he is legally allowed to select a wife. Elopement may also serve as a means of circumventing other cultural restrictions. For example, a Lozi woman in West Africa cannot divorce a husband unless he has actually dismissed her as his wife, but some women will force a divorce by eloping with another man. After her lover has paid damages, the two are considered married.

Sometimes a man and woman will elope if the prospective husband is unable to fulfill the usual obligations associated with a conventional marriage. Thus, for example, a Kwoma couple may elope if the boy cannot pay the required bride price before the marriage.

When a couple elopes, sentiments are sometimes with the runaway couple. Thus, for instance, if a Havasupai girl wants to marry a boy of whom her parents disapprove, the couple might run away together. The community is sympathetic, and after the boy has given them a small gift the girl's parents are also likely to relent and sanction the marriage, although the new

bride's relatives may make a fuss. The Burmese conceive of daughters as belonging to their parents. A girl, therefore, is understood to require the consent of her father in order to marry. But if a boy and girl elope, once the couple has had two or three children or lived together for a number of years with the knowledge of the girl's parents, the marriage no longer needs to be approved by any third parties. Runaway marriages, therefore, are a popular refuge for couples whose parents oppose their choice of partner.

In some cases, some kind of compensation must be paid to the parents of the bride or groom before a marriage by elopement is regarded as legitimate. Traditionally in India, Muria Gond adolescents lived in *ghotuls,* or dorms, and conducted a series of sexual liaisons while they were single. Marriages, however, were arranged by parents, and former *ghotul* partners were not supposed to marry or to have anything to do with each other once one or the other was betrothed. While most young people were willing to abide by their parents' choices, once in a while a boy and girl who had been lovers in the *ghotul* and who were greatly attached to each other would elope. Parents usually reconciled themselves to these unions, but a compensation payment had to be made to the girl's parents or, if she was already engaged to be married, to her fiance.

Marriages by elopement are not always recognized by the couple's parents or community. The Aranda regard elopements with strong disapproval. If a couple runs away to be married, attempts will be made to apprehend the pair, in which case both partners will be beaten with sticks and clubs so severely that an offender may die of the injuries. Eloping couples may be so afraid of being punished that they will attempt to find a permanent home with another tribe instead of returning home to face the outrage of their own community. Without parental blessings, couples who have eloped are sometimes unable to make a go of the marriage. Unless an eloping Trobriand girl's parents are willing to acknowledge her marriage, the union is doomed to fail because a married couple depends upon the wife's family to provide them yearly with a generous supply of food, which will not be forthcoming without parental approval of the union. Without this support, a household inevitably disintegrates.

Sometimes parents who would otherwise object to the marriage of an eloping couple will reconcile themselves to the marriage for fear of the consequences of crossing their children. In Oceania, Trukese marriages require the consent of the families of both the bride and groom and the failure to obtain such approval is generally enough to quash any marital plans on the part of a couple. But sometimes a boy and girl persist in their desire to marry, in which case they may run away in an attempt to change the minds of their relatives. The fear that the pair will commit suicide by hanging themselves can have the effect of softening the resistance of their families even though an eloping couple does not explicitly threaten to take their own lives.

In some societies, elopement is an acknowledged alternative to more conventional ways of marrying. Among the Iban of Malaysia, it is acceptable for a couple to attempt to marry by elopement if a girl's family does not approve of the boy she loves, and elopements are essentially a culturally patterned custom. The boy and girl rendezvous at an available boat, the girl bringing a paddle with her, and the pair begin to row away from shore as fast as they can. If the couple is followed by the girl's family, the boy will begin a series of short excursions to the shore, each time leaving some valuable item, such as a gun or jar that he has brought for the purpose. The girl's relatives will retrieve these peace offerings. Finally, when he has no other goods to give, he will leave his sword. When the pair arrive at the boy's village, he will quickly set out food and drink with which to greet the girl's family when they appear. When his future in-laws finally return home, the boy and girl remain

together and the elopement comes to a successful conclusion.

See also MARRIAGE, ARRANGED.

Basedow, Herbert. (1925) *The Australian Aboriginal.*

Coon, Carleton Stevens. (1950) *The Mountains of Giants: A Racial and Cultural Study of the North Albanian Mountain Ghegs.*

Elwin, Verrier. (1947) *The Muria and Their Ghotul.*

Gladwin, Thomas, and Seymour Sarason. (1953) *Truk: Man in Paradise.*

Gluckman, Max. (1959) "Lozi of Brotseland in North-western Rhodesia." In *Seven Tribes of British Central Africa,* edited by Elizabeth Colson and Max Gluckman.

Malinowski, Bronislaw. (1922) *Argonauts of the Western Pacific: An Account of Native Enterprise and Adventure in Archipelagoes of Melanesian New Guinea.*

Nimmo, H. A. (1964) "Nomads of the Sulu Sea." Unpublished dissertation, University of Hawaii.

Roth, H. Ling. (1892) "The Natives of Borneo." *Anthropological Institute of Great Britain and Ireland* 21: 110–137; 22: 22–64.

Scott, James George. (1910) *The Burman, His Life and Notions.*

Spier, Leslie. (1928) *Havasupai Ethnography.* Anthropological Papers of the American Museum of Natural History 29.

Whiting, John W. M. (1970) *Kwoma Journal.*

ENDOGAMY

Endogamy refers to culturally imposed rules that require a member of the culture to marry within a particular social category. The category might be a lineage, clan, caste, class, village, tribe, and so on. Because the term *endogamy* does not consistently apply to any particular reference category across cultures, it is impossible to say whether a culture is endogamous without specifying the relevant social category. If the reference group is the nuclear family, then no society is endogamous because the universal taboo against sexual intercourse between parents and children or between siblings effectively prohibits marriage between members of the same family and thereby forces everyone to marry outside his or her nuclear family. However, if the group is a population of individuals who think of themselves as sharing a common identity, then endogamy is characteristic of virtually all societies the world over.

Generally speaking, endogamous marriage patterns are a product of both explicit or implicit rules and personal preference. Often, a man and woman simply end up marrying endogamously because they live near one another, are familiar and comfortable with each other, speak the same language, share the same customs, beliefs, and values, and so on. The pattern of people marrying others like themselves is called homogamy. With the exception of the modern industrial society, the human endogamous group has been quite small, including perhaps a few hundred or thousand individuals. People have traditionally chosen spouses from nearby villages or even from within the same community. Thus, human cultures have historically been characterized by a relatively high degree of inbreeding. The taboo against marrying a member of one's nuclear family coupled with the tendency to select a partner from a small local sedentary population means that human beings have characteristically struck a balance between radical inbreeding and extensive outbreeding. As individuals living in traditional communities are typically related to each other, ties of blood help to maintain the solidarity of the local group and harmony among its members. Members of the community generally appreciate that they are tied together not only by shared residence but also by blood. People living in endogamous local communities tend to feel a strong loyalty to their own local group and to view other groups as outsiders. In some cultures, parents also prefer endogamous marriages because the custom maximizes the chances of arranging appropriate matches between young people. The Ashanti of Africa prefer marriages between members of the same village or chiefdom because the character and kin of one proposed partner are known to the family of the other, allowing an informed decision to be made in arranging a match for one's child. Where individuals marry first cousins from the same village so that the marriage is characterized by both kin and community endogamy, the relationship does, in fact, tend to be stable.

When societies differentiate between people on the basis of caste or class, rules prohibiting or strongly disapproving marriage between individuals of different ranks begin to appear, and most stratified societies are endogamous in this sense. In India, a Hindu traditionally marries within his own caste. This caste endogamy has been a major factor in maintaining the caste system for several thousand years. The same kind of caste endogamy is found in some African cultures. For instance, among the Masai in Kenya a warrior will not marry an ironworker's daughter.

Ackerman, Charles. (1963) "Affiliations: Structural Determinants of Differential Divorce Rates." *American Journal of Sociology* 69: 13–20.

Ember, Carol R., and Melvin Ember. (1988) *Anthropology*, 5th ed.

Fortes, Meyer. (1947) "Ashanti Survey, 1945–46: An Experiment in Social Research." *Geographical Journal* 110: 149–179.

Haviland, William A. (1987) *Cultural Anthropology*, 5th ed.

Murdock, George P. (1949) *Social Structure.*

van den Berghe, Pierre L. (1979) *Human Family Systems.*

Exogamy refers to cultural rules that require a person to marry outside a particular social category. This category or social group may be an aggregate of relatives, such as a lineage or clan, or it may be a geographic locale, such as a community or village. Most commonly, however, rules of exogamy focus on kin groups, specifying that individuals bearing a kin-based relationship to each other of one kind or another cannot marry. All societies prohibit marriage between individuals belonging to some sort of group. Thus, all mate-choice customs respect exogamy. The difference between societies lies in the kind of group within which individuals may not marry.

Rules requiring people to marry outside a particular group may at first glance look like an extension of the incest taboo. This idea is supported by the observation that, just as the incest taboo prohibits sexual intercourse between parents and children or brother and sister, patterns of mate choice always exclude marriage between these individuals. But on closer examination, rules of exogamy do not restrict sexual activity between kin in a way that we would predict if their function was to prevent inbreeding. For example, cultures often prohibit marriage between distantly related people while permitting it between close kin. Further, it is marriage that is prohibited by rules of exogamy and not sexual activity itself, and in fact individuals who are prevented from marrying may often engage in sexual intercourse with impunity.

Exogamy has also been interpreted as a strategy for promoting the survival of cultures. In this view, rules enforcing marriage between members of different groups encourage alliances between those groups, thereby diminishing the chances of intergroup conflict and making each cohort stronger because each has a friend in the other. It has also been proposed that exogamy may increase harmony within a group by removing the possibility that within-group marriages will encourage conflicts between families of the bride and groom. But there is no good evidence that exogamy really does produce these effects across cultures.

Bohannan, Paul, and John Middleton, eds. (1968) *Marriage, Family, and Residence.*

Levinson, David, and Martin J. Malone. (1980) *Toward Explaining Human Culture.*

van den Berghe, Pierre L. (1979) *Human Family Systems.*

The term *family* has been used to refer to a variety of overlapping, but not identical, kinds of social units. Definitions have variously emphasized the biological, residential, or functional aspects of families. A well-known definition combines these components into a notion of the family as "a social group characterized by common residence, economic cooperation, and reproduction." A number of important questions have been asked about the nature of the family. These have included inquiries into the functions of the family and the forms that families take across cultures. It is hard to address these questions without deciding which definition of the family one has in mind. This is especially true in the case of what is probably the most well-publicized question about the family, that is, the issue of whether the family is universal, as the answer to this puzzle will naturally depend upon what is meant by family. One way of attacking the problem of how to think about families is to begin by simply describing the membership of different kinds of families. It then becomes possible to determine who makes up the family as a residential unit, a domestic unit, a reproductive unit, and so on in a given culture. In some cultures the same people will make up all of these units and in others they will not.

Across cultures, people collect into a number of recognizable and predictable kinds of groups that conform to the idea of family. The simplest form that appears in a variety of cultural settings is the *matrifocal family,* consisting of a woman and her children. The *nuclear family* consists of two parents and their children. A *polygynous family* is made up of a man, two or more wives, and their children. All of these families are comprised of some combination of parents and children. Many families, by contrast, include not only parents and offspring but also other relatives. A *stem family* consists of a nuclear family to which a small number of additional relatives—a widowed parent or an unmarried sibling, for instance—are attached. In stem families, there continues to be only one married couple. When a family includes two or more married couples, it becomes an *extended family.* An extended family can include married couples of the same generation—for instance, married brothers or married sisters and their children. Or it can include married people of different generations—for instance, one set of parents, their unmarried children, their married sons and daughters-in-law, and grandchildren.

These descriptions of families only provide information about how to name different groups of people when we wish to identify them as comprising a family in some way. They do not, in and of themselves, say anything about what families do, what kind of family is characteristic of a specific society, or whether there is anything universal about families the world over. We can begin to examine families in more detail by noting that human beings the world over need to successfully reproduce, socialize their children, and provide shelter and nourishment for themselves and their dependents. These jobs are viewed as the central functions of the family, and they are in fact all typically accomplished within the context of groups of relatives.

In Western societies, it is frequently the same members of kin who produce and rear children, live together, and act as the units of production and consumption. This, however, does not have to be true, and there are many societies around the world where it is not true. The Kapauku Papuans illustrate this point. The Kapaukus use the term *uwougu* to identify a residential unit. About a third of these units are made up of extended families, including a number of adult males and their wives and children, as well as some other relatives. The fact that the Papuans have a distinct word to name this unit suggests that it has significance to them as a unified group, so an *uwougu* is a family in a psychological sense for a member of Kapauku culture. The *uwougu*, however, is not strictly a residential unit. Rather, people comprising a single *uwougu* in reality live in a number of separate dwellings. Thus, all the males of the *uwougu* who are older than seven years sleep in the front half of the main house, while there is a separate single-room house for each woman and her children. As some Kapauku men have more than one wife (they are polygynous), this means that each co-wife has her own house. Each wife has a separate plot in her husband's garden and each woman works on her plot independently and is financially independent. The husband supervises all subsistence activities and does much of what is viewed as man's work in each of the gardens of his wives. A wife shares some of her produce with her husband, but the rest is reserved solely for herself and her own children. A man provides each wife with pork, game, salt, and other foods that he has produced, and he is also expected to contribute supplies to the other men in his household. The nuclear family bears the responsibility for the rearing of children. A child who misbehaves is punished by the father. Youngsters are also taught manners and work skills by their parents. Further, only a husband can discipline a woman once she is married.

The Kapauku illustrate the ambiguity of the term *family*. The family is matrifocal for women and children as regards residence. So is the consumption unit. For men, the consumption unit is the entire extended family, as each man depends upon his wives and the other men in his household for food supplies. When it comes to food production, each polygynous family works as a unit and is, therefore, the family in this context. On the other hand, each husband-wife-child unit—that is, each nuclear family—acts both as the reproductive and socialization unit. Given the complicated network of rights, obligations, and logistics among members of the Kapauku *uwougu*, there is no way of isolating any single group of relatives that perform all of the jobs viewed as the functions of human families. Rather, different aggregates of relatives perform different functions. It is possible, therefore, to say that there are a number of functional families for the typical Papuan, and this is also true for people in many other cultures around the world.

A basic question about the family is whether it is universal—that is, does it occur in all societies? The answer depends upon what we are really asking. One version of the question focuses on the nuclear family as the most elementary form and asks whether the mother-father-children unit universally performs the reproductive, residential, and economic functions required for the survival of the individual in any culture. People have attempted to discredit the idea that the nuclear family performs these functions the world over by finding exceptions to the claim. For instance, on the Israeli kibbutz, children live in independent children's houses from birth and are raised and educated by *metaplot*, or caretakers, who are unrelated to them. So in the kibbutz, the nuclear family does not perform the functions of the socialization or economic support of the young. However, over time many kibbutzim have shifted away from group child rearing to the nuclear family model and are no longer exceptions to the rule. Another frequently cited exception is the Nayar subcaste of South India. In the past, husbands did not contribute to the support of their wives, and it is not even clear that the Nayar had formal marriage, which is the foundation of any nuclear family. Again, however, the Nayar shifted to practicing marriage in the twentieth century, and family households became common. These and other counter-examples, however, do not represent the normal arrangement in any society. Rather, the putative exceptions to the universality of the nuclear family are also exceptions to the way in which the average person experiences family life. It has also been pointed out that, while some cultures emphasize the marital bond as the most important relationship in an individual's life, in other cultures the relationships with a person's own kin take priority. In the first kind of society, the nuclear family tends to perform the functions viewed as the province of the parent-child unit by those who claim that the nuclear family is universal. In the second kind of society, a parent's brothers, sisters, and other relatives play a larger role in the person's own life and that of the child than does the nuclear family unit. In these societies, then, the functions that have been ascribed to the nuclear family are really performed by a parent's kin.

This distinction presents a real challenge to the claim that the nuclear family is universal. It

Two San families in the Kalahari Desert set out to hunt and gather.

also reminds us about how human beings manage the tasks of survival and reproduction: When it comes to solving the problems of where to live and how to provide for oneself and one's children, people the world over rely on kin. They live with kin, give to and receive food from kin, depend on kin to help them raise their children, and go to kin when in need of help. This is not surprising in the context of human evolution. Any tendency to help one's relatives, if it has a genetic basis, will actually spread in the population and, therefore, will be characteristic of members of the human species as a whole. This is because relatives share genes in common. If my genes underwrite the tendency to aid my kin, then the very kin that I am helping are likely to have these same genes. The closer the relationship between us, the greater this likelihood becomes. Helping one's kin, then—which contributes to the chances of survival of the relative—also contributes to the survival of the genes that underwrite the impulse to help relatives. Scientists who attempt to explain behavior in the context of human evolution believe that the tendency to help kin has been passed down across generations in just this way and is now characteristic of human beings generally. If this is indeed true, then it makes sense for people to go to relatives for help in meeting life's challenges. Relatives are predisposed to do right by their kin. If we are willing to define the family as the people to whom one is related, then the idea that the family universally acts as a reproductive, economic, and residential unit makes sense. It is just that different constellations of relatives perform each of these functions within and across societies.

Bohannan, Paul. (1963) *Social Anthropology.*

Ember, Carol R., and Melvin Ember. (1988) *Anthropology,* 5th ed.

Ember, Melvin, and Carol R. Ember. (1983) *Marriage, Family, and Kinship: Comparative Studies of Social Organization.*

Levinson, David, and Martin J. Malone. (1980) *Toward Explaining Human Culture.*

Murdock, George Peter. (1949) *Social Structure.*

Pospisil, Leopold. (1964) *The Kapauku Papuans of West New Guinea.*

Stephens, William N. (1963) *The Family in Cross-Cultural Perspective.*

FAMILY LIFE

People in all cultures live in some kind of residential setting with members of their families. Everyone, therefore, has the opportunity to form a variety of relationships with the relatives with whom he or she lives. The nature of the relationships among family members, however, is not the same across all cultures. A major influence upon the degree of intimacy between relatives who live in the same house is the way in which members of a residential unit are dispersed in the dwelling itself.

In some societies, houses are configured so that all of the members of the family tend to congregate in a single room of the house or move freely through the living quarters, so that everyone who lives in the same dwelling has ample opportunity to interact on a regular basis. In India, Garo houses are like tremendous bamboo baskets balanced on posts. The building is long and narrow and is partitioned into two rooms. The family cooks, eats, and relaxes in the larger, centrally located room, and if a younger married couple lives in the household, they also sleep here along with their children. There is also a porch where the men and women sometimes work and where the young people congregate after a dance. This use of household space means that all members of the family spend time with each other each day. This is also true of the Siuai families in Oceania. The Siuai household conists of parents and their children, and each family inhabits a single house, which may be a single, one-floor room or a first floor with a high platform used for sleeping and storage. The house is the center of activity for family members beginning in the mid-afternoon, with much cooking, eating, playing, baby-tending, feeding of pigs, napping, and handiwork going on. Houses are grouped into small hamlets, and members of a particular hamlet are close relatives, so that a hamlet is actually a kind of extended family surrounding the more intimate nuclear household.

In many other cultures, different family members typically confine themselves to different sections of the house, so that interaction between some household members is limited. In Ecuador, a Jivaro house is partitioned into two sections, each with its own door. One-half of the dwelling is reserved for the men of the household, and it is here that unmarried males over seven years old eat, sleep, and stay when they are in the house. The women eat, sleep with their children, and perform their domestic tasks in the other section. A woman will only enter the men's half of the dwelling to serve beer or food to her husband or his guests. This same pattern of segregation between some family members often occurs in polygynous households when wives have separate dwellings. A polygynous Hausa household in Nigeria is a compound consisting of a cluster of huts and divided into two sections. The outside series of dwellings includes an entrance hut, where the men congregate with neighbors and friends and work at their crafts, and a separate house for adolescents that also serves as a guest house. The inner section of the compound also has an entrance hut opening onto the women's quarters. Each woman has her own house in this part of the compound, where she stores her personal property and where she and her children sleep. At night, in the company of the women, children hear folk tales, fables, and stories about historical events. Young-

sters are largely in the company of women and do not spend much time with their older brothers or fathers. Married sons have their own houses in the women's section but separated from the other huts by a mat fence.

Sometimes, the segregation of family members extends to the removal of youngsters to their own dwelling. The Kikuyu of Kenya traditionally preferred a household that consisted of two huts even when a marriage was monogamous. One hut was divided into sections, one for the husband and the other for his wife and children. The other hut was reserved for the husband's personal use, and it is here that a man entertained visitors. Strangers were not permitted to enter the wife's hut. In addition, there were bachelor huts where boys from several families slept.

Yards and courtyards often function as the center of activity for members of a family. This is true among the Ilocano of the Philippines, for whom the yard functions more or less as an extension of the house proper. It is shaded by trees or by an overhang, decorated with flowers and perhaps a bench, and regularly swept clean. Here is where the women of the household do most of their daily chores. Most of the men's nonfarming activities and much of the family's leisure pursuits take place in the yard as well. Children play in the yard, animals are fed here, infants are supervised and light tasks are performed, and guests at baptisms, marriages, feasts, dances, and birthdays gather in the yard.

Sometimes, the residential layout allows different groups of extended family members to interact for different kinds of activities. Often, members of individual nuclear families mix together for some kinds of activities but retain their separate identities for others. Mixtecans in Mexico live in extended-family households. Each household shares a compound, which consists of a large central patio surrounded by enclosed rooms that serve as the living quarters for individual nuclear-family units. Women keep each other company in the courtyard or visit a

A Guatemalan Native American woman grinding cornmeal. In most cultures women prepare food and serve meals

neighboring compound, and children play there together. But separate nuclear families sleep and eat in their own living quarters and each woman also has her own cooking house where she prepares meals for her own family. The !Kung of southern Africa live out-of-doors, using their tiny huts mainly for storage and sleeping. Camps are small, and huts are separated by only a few feet, with doors facing the center of the campsite. A single camp might be composed of perhaps six or seven huts. Thus, family life is really camp life, with members of an entire camp forming the household in a practical sense. On any day, the camp will include some men who have not gone hunting, women who have not gone gathering, older people who can no longer engage in subsistence activities, and children old enough to be willing to stay behind while their mothers are off gathering. But when the family reunites after the day's work, each family sits by its own fire in front of its own hut for the evening meal.

In cultures where a person is surrounded by kin living in nearby households, a person's own house does not necessarily define the limits of family and home. Thus, for instance, in Samoa, relatives live in close proximity, and a child who has some grievance against her residential family will simply pack up and move in with nearby kin. In this culture, the family is the neighborhood.

Household layout is only partially responsible for patterns of interactions among family members. Where some or all residents of a household spend much of their time away from home, family interaction is greatly influenced by the logistics of their daily schedules. In a typical Guianan Taira household, family members will see each other from time to time in the course of the day as parents go about their busy work routines. But it is only at dinner, which may not be served until eight o'clock in the summer, that the entire household gathers together. This is when plans are drawn up for the next day's work schedule and family matters are discussed. Simi-larly, each member of a Gusii household in Kenya can usually be found working close to home and, therefore, within shouting distance of everyone else, but the family does not spend much time together as a unit. Even at night when chores are done, a man will go in search of a house where a beer party is in progress. Meanwhile, his wife cooks dinner and eats with her children, leaving a portion for her husband to have when he returns home. If the entire family remains home for the evening, everyone goes to sleep soon after dinner is over.

Burling, Robbins. (1963) *Rengsanggri: Family and Kinship in a Garo Village.*

Cagnolo, C. (1933) *The Akikuyu: Their Customs, Traditions, and Folklore.*

Karsten, Rafael. (1935) *The Head-Hunters of Western Amazonas: The Life and Culture of the Jibaro Indians of Eastern Ecuador and Peru.*

LeVine, Robert A., and Barbara B. LeVine. (1966) *Nyansongo: A Gusii Community in Kenya.*

Maretzki, Thomas W., and Hatsumi Maretzki. (1966) *Taira: An Okinawan Village.*

Mead, Margaret. (1929) *Coming of Age in Samoa: A Psychological Study of Primitive Youth for Western Civilization.*

Nydeggar, William F., and Corinne Nydegger. (1966) *Tarong: An Ilocos Barrio in the Philippines.*

Oliver, Douglas. (1955) *A Solomon Island Society: Kinship and Leadership among the Siuai of Bougainville.*

Romney, Kimball, and Romaine Romney. (1966) *The Mixtecans of Juxtlahuaca, Mexico.*

Shostak, Marjorie. (1981) *Nisa: The Life and Words of a !Kung Woman.*

Smith, Mary F. (1954) *The Baba of Karo: A Woman of the Muslim Hausa.*

Smith, Michael G. (1955) *The Economy of Hausa Communities of Zaria.*

———. (1957) "Cooperation in Hausa Society." *Information* 11: 1–20.

Stirling, Matthew. (1938) *Historical and Ethnographical Material on the Jivaro Indians.*

FAMILY SLEEPING ARRANGEMENTS

Across cultures, people adopt widely different traditions regarding where members of a household may sleep. These customs influence the degree and kind of intimacy enjoyed between members of a family. In Nigeria, an Igbo family lives in a house consisting of a kitchen, a sleeping room with a shelf serving as the children's bed, and a veranda with mud couches. The husband and wife sleep on one of these mud couches. Children of both sexes sleep together in the sleeping room until they are nine or ten years old. The boys then sleep on one of the veranda couches opposite their parents. A woman who is menstruating, in her last month of pregnancy, or nursing sleeps in the inner sleeping room with the girls and small boys. Young unmarried Igbo men sleep in a "single house" consisting of a veranda and inner room, but a girl continues to stay in her parents' house until she marries and goes to live with her husband. In Indonesia, a Balinese married couple will sleep on the porch, each spouse on a separate couch. Babies sleep with their mothers, while small children will curl up with one of their parents or grandparents or may huddle together by themselves. Newlyweds and unmarried girls sleep in the inner rooms of the house, providing privacy for the married couple and protection for the single girl. And, in Ethiopia, Amhara men, women, and children all sleep together in a single room along with their mules, ponies, and other animals.

Sometimes nuclear families will sleep together but will be separated from other parent-child units living in the same household. A rural Chinese couple sleeps in the same bed along with any children younger than seven or eight years of age. An older child sleeps in a separate bed in the parents' room. If there are two married couples in the same house, the bedroom is divided in two by a wooden partition, providing a separate space for each nuclear family. Among the Eyak of Alaska, extended families live in large houses with boxlike rooms along the walls, each of which serves as sleeping quarters for a nuclear family.

In many cultures, males and females sleep in separate quarters. This is the case among the Muria Gond in India. A wife and her mature daughters sleep in the *angadi*, which also serves as the kitchen. The *agha* is the husband's room and serves as his living and sleeping quarters. Grown women, including a man's wife and older daughters, are strictly forbidden from sleeping in the *agha*, although young daughters may do so. A boy who is still too young to stay in the bachelor's house also sleeps in the *agha* with his father. A married son may live in a separate part of his father's or uncle's house if there is room; otherwise he will erect his own house as close to his father as possible. A Tuareg husband of the Sahara sleeps on one side of the tent with his sons and the wife sleeps on the other side with the daughters, although exceptions are sometimes made for married couples. Similarly in Ecuador, a Jivaro house is divided into two sections, each with its own entry. Grown boys and unmarried men sleep in one section, while the women and their children sleep in the other half of the house. Married men sleep in the women's section. The Burusho of India live in extended-family households, with a number of adults of each sex inhabiting the same residence. There is a large bench on either side of the common living room. Women sit by day and sleep by night on the minor bench while the major bench serves the same functions for the men of the household. Children sleep with the women.

In some societies, children only sleep with their parents when they are small. After that, they sleep in separate dwellings. These may be dormitories established especially for older unmarried boys and girls, or male children may go to sleep in the community's men's house. Among the Dorobo of Kenya, married couples and their children sleep in the same hut. Unmarried older boys, however, generally sleep in the warriors' hut, where they are visited by unmarried girls. Sudanese Shilluk boys sleep in the cattle byres once they reach adolescence. Unmarried girls sleep together in any house that happens to be empty.

While many societies segregate both boys and girls from their parents, it also frequently happens that only boys sleep away from home, while girls remain with their parents. A Lakher family of South Asia consists of an average of five individuals. If a married son has not yet established his own household, then as many as ten people may inhabit one house. The husband and wife sleep in the bed in the main room of their house, along with their smaller children. An older girl may sleep near her parents or near the hearth in the back room by herself. A bachelor is prohibited from sleeping in his parents' house, so a group of young unmarried men will spend the night in the house of a girlfriend. The girl places a wooden log near the hearth in the back room for the boys to use as a pillow and the bachelors huddle together under their blankets for the night. A Tallensi girl of Ghana may continue to sleep with her mother until she is close to adolescence, but a boy who sleeps with his mother past the age of seven or eight will be laughed at by his peers, and boys of this age begin to sleep with a grandparent or with the older boys in a separate room.

In some cultures, brothers and sisters are required to sleep in separate places once they have reached a certain age. Among the Trobrianders of New Guinea, an older boy must sleep in the bachelor's hut if there is a sister living in his parents' house. Truk brothers and sisters in Oceania are required to sleep at opposite ends of the house or in separate rooms once they reach puberty if the boy does not move out of the house altogether. Sometimes other family members are segregated for the purpose of sleeping. Not only do Igbo brothers and sisters stop sleeping in the same house once they have reached the age of eight, but a grown daughter will leave her mother's house on nights when her father sleeps there.

There are also cultures in which more or less everyone sleeps alone. In Zaire, each Azande individual has a separate hut in which to sleep. A small child will sleep with its mother. Among polygynous Azande families, each wife has a separate house and the husband visits each woman in turn. Among the Nyakyusa of Tanzania, polygynous husbands have their own houses, where boys go to sleep from the ages of six to eleven. A girl sleeps in her mother's hut until she is married.

In societies that have class stratification, sleeping arrangements are likely to be more elaborate for privileged families than for those on the lower end of the scale. Among upper-class Roman families, each married couple slept in a separate room. In less well-to-do families, there were no extra rooms available to serve as sleeping quarters for individual family members; instead, everyone slept in the same bed. The most desirable household arrangement for the Kazak of central Asia is one in which each nuclear family has its own separate dwelling, with married sons living next to their fathers, but many families cannot afford such luxurious living quarters, so a married son and his family often live in his father's house. The entire household then sleeps in the same room, with the head of the house and his wife sleeping on the left, his sons and their wives and children on the right, and guests and other inhabitants in the middle.

Baxter, P. T. W., and Audrey Butt. (1953) *The Azande, and Related Peoples of the Anglo-Egyptian Sudan and Belgian Congo.*

Belo, Jane. (1936) "Study of a Balinese Family." *American Anthropologist* 38: 12–31.

———. (1949) *Bali: Rangda and Barong.*

Birket-Smith, Kaj, and Frederica De Laguna. (1938) *The Eyak Indians of Copper River Delta, Alaska.*

Carcopino, Jerome. (1940) *Daily Life in Ancient Rome: The People and the City at the Height of the Empire.*

Fei, Hsiao-Tung. (1939) *Peasant Life in China: A Field Study of Country Life in the Yangtze Valley.*

Fortes, Meyer. (1936) "Ritual Festivals and Social Cohesion in the Hinterland of the Gold Coast." *American Anthropologist* 38: 590–604.

———. (1938) *Social and Psychological Aspects of Education in Taleland.*

Gladwin, Thomas, and Seymour Sarason. (1953) *Truk: Man in Paradise.*

Grigson, Wilfrid. (1949) *The Maria Gond of Bastar.*

Gunn, Harold D. (1956) *Pagan Peoples of the Central Area of Northern Nigeria.*

Henry, Jules. (1941) *The Jungle People: A Kaingang Tribe of the Highlands of Brazil.*

Hudson, Alfred E. (1938) *Kazak Social Structure.*

Huntingford, G. W. B. (1951) "The Social Organization of the Dorobo." *African Studies* 1: 183–200.

Huxley, M., and C. Capa. (1964) *Farewell to Eden.*

Jenness, Diamond. (1922) *The Life of the Copper Eskimos.*

Leith-Ross, Sylvia. (1939) *African Women.*

Lhote, Henri. (1944) *The Hoggar Tuareg.*

Lorimer, E. O. (1939) *Language Hunting in the Karakorum.*

Malinowski, Bronislaw. (1929) *Sexual Life of Savages in North-western Melanesia: An Ethnographic Account of Courtship, Marriage and Family Life among the Natives of the Trobriand Islands, British New Guinea.*

Parry, N. E. (1932) *The Lakhers.*

Rey, C. F. (1935) *The Real Abyssinia.*

Seligman, C. G., and B. Z. Seligman. (1932) *Pagan Tribes of the Nilotic Sudan.*

Stirling, Matthew. (1938) *Historical and Ethnographical Material on the Jivaro Indians.*

Wilson, Godfrey. (1936) "An Introduction to the Nyakyusa Society." *Bantu Studies* 10: 253–292.

FATHERS ATTENDING BIRTHS

There is no more universally shared experience in the lives of women than that of giving birth, but the details of how labor and delivery proceed differ enormously from one society to the next. Salient among those differences are cultural conventions regarding the role of the expectant father during the confinement of his wife. A father may be an important player in the drama of the birth of his children or he may be denied any part. The regular presence of husbands when their wives are giving birth is unusual across cultures. Of a worldwide sample of 74 societies, a father-to-be is generally in attendance at his wife's confinement in only 17.6 percent of the cases. The Ifugao of the Philippines are one such culture. During a long labor, the husband may kneel on the floor and support his wife as she assumes the proper position for delivering her infant. Husbands are permitted access to their wives during labor but are not in fact usually present in an additional 5.4 percent of the sample. A Badjau husband of the

Philippines will generally be present at the birth of his first child, but men whose wives have delivered a number of children go about their business while their wives are in labor as if the imminent appearance of a new child were a routine event. Husbands attend the births of their children in emergencies in an additional 5.4 percent of the 74 cultures and are prohibited from being with their wives but have special tasks associated with their infants' births in another 10.8 percent of the sample. If his wife's labor is difficult, a Mapuche husband of Chile will help with the delivery, perhaps by pressing down on his wife's abdomen to expedite the birth. Otherwise, he may be shooed from the house. In India, a Burusho woman is attended by her mother or some other experienced woman during labor, but her husband still has a role to play. He guards the door of the house to prevent any evil men or spirits from gaining access. In the remaining 60.8 percent of the societies, husbands do not participate in the births of their children. Thus, among the Mbundu of Angola, for instance, an expectant father will absent himself during his wife's labor. Otherwise, they believe, the infant would be ashamed to be born. A husband also avoids the birth scene because blood is potentially dangerous to him. This theme that the blood associated with birth is harmful to the expectant father is in keeping with the more general belief in many cultures that women, their blood, or their sexual activities with women are dangerous to men. Some societies that prohibit husbands from attending the births of their children also extend the taboo to men in general because female biological processes are believed to be hazardous to males. The strong tendency across cultures to exclude fathers-to-be and other men from the delivery room is also part of the more general cross-cultural convention that views birth as a woman's affair. Thus, when women are having babies, men are expected to make themselves scarce. In cultures where husbands do attend the births of their children, spouses are also likely to spend their leisure time together, suggesting that customs regarding the husband's attendance during his wife's confinement may reflect the closeness of the relationship between spouses more generally.

Barton, R. F. (1938) *Philippine Pagans: The Autobiographies of Three Ifugaos.*

Broude, Gwen J. (1981) *Cross-Cultural Study of Sex and Intimacy.* Paper presented at the 10th annual meetings of the Society for Cross-Cultural Research, Washington, DC.

Broude, Gwen J., and Sarah J. Greene. (1983) "Cross-Cultural Codes on Husband-Wife Relationships." *Ethnology* 22: 263–280.

Childs, Gladwyn M. (1949) *Umbundu Kinship and Character.*

Faron, Louis C. (1961) *Mapuche Social Structure: Institutional Reintegration in a Patrilineal Society of Central Chile.*

Lorimer, E. O. (1939) *Language Hunting in the Karakorum.*

Nimmo, H. A. (1964) "Nomads of the Sulu Sea." Unpublished dissertation, University of Hawaii.

FEMALE SECLUSION

In traditional Korean society, when an upper-class Korean woman reaches marriageable age, she is not permitted to see or speak to anyone but her closest relatives, and even these encounters are circumscribed by ceremony. She becomes even more isolated after marriage. She remains in her own rooms and must ask her husband's permission even to look out at the street. Women have been killed by their fathers or husbands, or have taken their own lives,

Western Egyptian Bedouin women wear veils in a man's presence.

merely because a stranger has brushed against them with his fingers. In Nigeria, traditional Hausa religious beliefs dictate complete seclusion for females. When she pays the required visits to her relatives and close friends, a woman ventures outside with an escort in the day or with or without a companion after dark. In some Islamic cultures girls must wear veils beginning at adolescence. Extra folds of material are also worn under their clothes to cover the shape of their breasts. Adolescent boys become embarrassed, even angry, if their mothers or sisters go outside at night or look out of a window without being adequately covered, even if no man is walking by. In a number of societies around the world, women are expected to live their lives largely out of the sight of men. Sometimes, as among the traditional Hausa and Koreans, females are physically separated from males. In some Islamic cultures, a woman may remain in the vicinity of a man, but only if she conceals herself so that the contours of her face and body cannot be observed.

The custom of secluding females is perhaps most closely identified with some Asian cultures. Chinese tradition viewed the dominance of women by men as a law of nature. In this view, females were incapable of taking care of themselves and therefore needed to be supervised by male guardians. Chinese men agreed that this was most effectively accomplished by locking females up. Women had their own quarters within the household, and the custom of foot binding, which crippled a woman for life, prevented her from leaving these rooms or moving around easily outside the home.

In India, the seclusion of females is known as *purdah,* which means "curtain." *Purdah* was originally a Muslim practice and was adopted by many Hindus, especially in the north. *Purdah* often involves shutting women away in crowded, stuffy rooms at the rear of the house. The women are prevented from participating in the activities of the outside world and barely catch a glimpse of life beyond the four walls surrounding them. This kind of extreme seclusion essentially becomes a status symbol in the eyes of some Hindu women, who see it as a cause for boasting that they have never seen the light of day. Among some Rajputs, a privileged warrior caste of India, women of child-bearing age are secluded in the courtyard, which is surrounded by mud walls. The women cannot see out of this space and no one can see in. It is here that a woman spends her days with her mother-in-law and sisters-in-law, tending the children and performing household tasks. Any chores that require leaving the courtyard must be done by boys or men. Women from different households can visit each other by walking along the alleys built on the rooftops of their attached houses. Men are not permitted in the courtyards or on the roofs. Millions of Indian women have been isolated from the outside world for their entire married lives, and at the end of the eighteenth century there were perhaps 40 million Indian women in *purdah*. It has been argued that *purdah* originated as a strategy for protecting women at a time when war between neighboring communities was chronic and females were liable to be harmed by hostile armies. More recently, men have continued to practice the custom because it adds to a man's social status.

If the seclusion of females is an ideal in some societies, it is by no means universally practiced in these cultures. This is because the isolation of females means that the women of the household can no longer contribute as much as they otherwise would to the economic and domestic welfare of the household. Someone else has to take up the slack, so female seclusion is expensive. For this reason, seclusion customs are usually reserved for the more established members of society. Thus, complete seclusion of wives is typical among the higher ranking Hausa, including wealthy merchants, aristocrats, and clerics, but lower-class women—for instance, the wives of butchers—are not characteristically required to follow *purdah* customs. Nor is *purdah* practiced by less well-off Indian households. It is a luxury that the poor cannot afford.

In a number of cultures, females do not lead lives completely isolated from males, but their contact with the opposite sex is severely constrained. In rural Haiti, adolescent girls are strictly supervised in an effort to prevent them from interacting with boys. They may not fetch wood or water or do other chores without taking a child along, and they are prohibited from ever going outside alone. Among the Kiribati, young, pretty wives are not allowed to appear at any public function. A girl is also prohibited from going out except in the company of her husband or mother-in-law. In the United States, Gros Ventre parents attempted to restrict the premarital sexual behavior of their daughters by sending the girls at seven or eight years of age to live with a grandmother, widowed aunt, or other solitary female relative. Besides spatially segregating girls from their male relatives, the adults also kept young females under close surveillance.

Women who are required to live in seclusion do not necessarily view their living arrangements as oppressive. This is reflected in the comments of one Indian woman, who observed: "We lead a quiet, peaceful, protected life within our own homes. And with men as they are, we should be miserable, terrified, outside."

Ammar, Hamed. (1954) *Growing Up in an Egyptian Village.*

Barton, R. F. (1946) "The Religion of the Ifugaos." *American Anthropologist* 48.

Flannery, Regina. (1953) *The Gros Ventre of Montana*, pt. 1.

Griffis, William. (1882) *Corea: The Hermit Nation.*

Grimble, A. (1921) "From Birth to Death in the Gilbert Islands." *Journal of the Royal Anthropological Institute* 51: 25–54.

Herskovitz, Melville J. (1937) *Life in a Haitian Valley.*

Mace, David, and Vera Mace. (1960) *Marriage East and West.*

Smith, Mary F. (1954) *The Baba of Karo: A Woman of the Muslim Hausa.*

Smith, Michael G. (1955) *The Economy of Hausa Communities of Zaria.*

Whiting, Beatrice B., ed. (1963) *Six Cultures: Studies of Child Rearing.*

FICTIVE KIN

In many cultures certain individuals who are not related to another person by either blood or marriage are nonetheless referred to by a kin term and treated as if they are kin. Such relations are called fictive kin, and the essence of such relationships is that they resemble the relationships between actual kin. Fictive kin include namesakes, blood brotherhood, godparenthood, coparenthood, and a variety of forms of fictive marriage.

Namesakes are persons who have the same name. Naming one person after another—usually a living or deceased ancestor—is quite common around the world. In these cases, of course, the namesakes are actual kin. In a smaller number of cultures individuals with the same name may be treated as kin equivalents, and in a few other cultures people with the same name stand in special relationships to one another that mirror or resemble kin relationships. In equivalent namesake situations, the namesake will be treated in the same way as the person after whom he has been named. For example, among the Hausa in Nigeria, if a person is the object of joking or avoidance relations by certain other kin, so too will be his namesake. In some small foraging societies, such as the !Kung in southern Africa and some Inuit cultures in North America, men with the same name will have a special relationship resembling brotherhood that requires them to assist one another. Such a custom was evidently helpful in the past when men travelling away from their community to hunt or trade needed to rely on members of other communities. Having a namesake in a community insured that assistance would be granted.

Many non-Western cultures influenced by Roman Catholicism have adopted and often elaborated the custom of godparenthood. In the village of Tepoztlán in southern Mexico, for example, the institution of *compadrazgo* is very important. *Compadrazgo* involves both godparent relations between godparents and godchildren and co-parent relationships between the parents and godparents. As in Spain, godparents are a backup set of parents who will assist in religious education, look after the child in various ways, and adopt him or her if the parents die. The co-parent relationship is one of reciprocal respect with rules requiring a certain degree of formality and the performance of certain reciprocal obligations, such as the payment of funeral expenses if one should die. The co-parent also plays an important social function, as a family might increase its social standing by engaging a higher class person as a godparent, or a man can create a social and political support network by having many godchildren.

Fictive marriages are unusual forms of marriage. They are rare across societies and are also rare in the societies where they occur. While they are socially defined as marriage, they deviate from typical marriages in the society in important ways. Adoptive marriage, found among some wealthy families in Asia, involves the husband of one of the daughters being adopted into the family as a son who then takes on his wife's family name and the responsibilities of the role. The motivation for such marriages is strong in wealthy families where there is no male heir, so the husband-son takes that role. In some West African cultures, various forms of surrogate marriage are used to produce children when the wife

is believed to be barren. In one form, a first wife may arrange for a second wife for her husband. If the second wife bears him children, they refer to the first wife as father, recognizing her role (usually carried out by a male father) in arranging the marriage. Another form of surrogate marriage is woman marriage, in which a barren wife marries another woman who then has sex with the first woman's husband. If a child results, it is considered the child of the first wife. Finally, the Nuer of the Sudan practice the custom of ghost marriage, in which the widow of a man who dies without an heir marries another man and has a child by him. The child is then considered to be the child of the deceased husband. These customs all serve to provide heirs to wealthy men and thereby keep his wealth in the family or kin group.

Alford, Richard D. (1988) *Naming and Identity: A Cross-Cultural Study of Personal Naming Practices.*

Hiebert, Paul G. (1976) *Cultural Anthropology.*

Lewis, Oscar. (1960) *Tepoztlán: Village in Mexico.*

FITNESS

Fitness refers to the proportionate representation of an organism's genes in the gene pool of its species relative to others of its kind. The greater the representation of an organism's genes compared to others of its species, the more fit the organism is said to be. Organisms with a smaller proportionate gene representation in the gene pool of their species are said to be less fit. Fitness, therefore, is a relative term.

A distinction can be made between two kinds of fitness. It was Charles Darwin who pointed out the connection between success in reproduction and fitness. Darwin began with the observation that individuals of the same species differ from each other and that these differences differentially affect an individual's chances of surviving and reproducing. Those individuals endowed with traits leading them to produce more offspring than others of their species have greater Darwinian fitness. Individuals who produce fewer offspring have less Darwinian fitness. Thus, one kind of fitness—Darwinian fitness—concentrates on comparisons in reproductive success across members of a species. Recently, biologist W. D. Hamilton has extended Darwin's insights. Hamilton noted that, while one way to increase the representation of one's own genes in the gene pool is to produce offspring, this is not the only way. Thus, organisms can also inflate their representation in the gene pool by increasing the reproductive success of other individuals to whom they are related. This is because relatives, by definition, share genes in common. The overall representation of an organism's genes in the gene pool as the product of its own reproductive success and its contribution to the reproductive success of kin is the individual's inclusive fitness. This fitness assessment includes a calculation of genes shared by the organism and its offspring and genes shared by the individual and kin whose survival it has aided. Thus, inclusive fitness is really a more comprehensive measure of fitness, with Darwinian fitness being just one component.

Trivers, Robert L. (1985) *Social Evolution*.

FOREPLAY Information regarding the details of sexual activity across cultures is hard to obtain because it is generally impossible to observe sexual behavior in progress and because people in many societies are unwilling to describe the intimate facts of their sex lives. Some descriptions of patterns of precoital activity, or foreplay, across cultures are available. Kissing and mouthing, stimulation of a woman's breasts, and manipulation of both male and female genitals are all found in at least some cultures around the world. The Badjau of the Philippines indulge in much fondling and kissing. A woman may loosen her sarong so that it can cover both her and her partner, who may exchange saliva with her and kiss her all over her body. Among the Trobrianders of New Guinea, precoital activity is also extended. Partners may caress each other, with bodies intertwined. They may rub nose to nose, mouth to mouth, and cheek to cheek and whisper loving words to each other. By contrast, the Lepcha of Tibet assume that the very thought that sexual intercourse is about to occur is enough to stimulate a couple, making any foreplay superfluous. The Truk of Oceania share a similar attitude and, indeed, a young girl will not allow her partner to see or touch her genitals but, rather, loosens her skirt sufficiently to allow intercourse to occur. Among the North American Saulteaux, kissing is not traditional, nor do men find a woman's breasts sexually arousing. Men do not handle the genitals of females, although the opposite may sometimes occur. Rather, the major focus of sexual activity for the Saulteaux is genital-genital contact. Of 39 societies for which there is information about foreplay, 53.8 percent typically engage in prolonged noncoital activity as a preliminary to sexual intercourse. A little over 10 percent of the cultures have some, but not extensive or elaborate, foreplay, while precoital activities are absent in the remaining 35.9 percent of cultures.

Patterns of foreplay coexist with other customs and attitudes across cultures. Societies that have more elaborate foreplay also allow males to choose their own marriage partners, whereas the choice of a wife tends to be left up to third parties in places where foreplay is not an important feature of sexual behavior. Where foreplay is present, extramarital affairs on the part of husbands are condemned, while sexual liaisons outside of marriage are more liable to be accepted for husbands where foreplay is absent. Thus, elaborate foreplay appears to be associated with marriages that are based upon personal choice and that require loyalty on the part of the man. Cultures that have more extensive foreplay are also more likely to accept or tolerate homosexuality, whereas the opposite is true where foreplay is minimal.

Ford, Clellan S., and Frank A. Beach (1951) *Patterns of Sexual Behavior.*

Gladwin, Thomas, and Seymour Sarason. (1953) *Truk: Man in Paradise.*

Gorer, Geoffrey. (1938) *Himalayan Village: An Account of the Lepchas of Sikkim.*

Hallowell, A. Irving. (1955) *Culture and Experience.*

Malinowski, Bronislaw. (1929) *The Sexual Life of Savages in North-Western Melanesia: An Ethnographic Account of Courtship, Marriage and Family Life among the Natives of the Trobriand Islands, British New Guinea.*

Nimmo, H. A. (1964) "Nomads of the Sulu Sea." Unpublished dissertation, University of Hawaii.

FRIENDSHIPS, ADULT

People are social animals. They depend upon the nurturing of other people from the beginning of life and remain healthier and happier throughout life in the company of others. An important source of human contact for the individual is the family. Families provide social, emotional, and economic support to their members. But people also form friendships. While friends can provide the same rewards as kin, unlike family ties, friendships are voluntary associations and can be based upon compatibility and liking. Friendships, as a consequence, contribute uniquely to the psychological well-being of human beings. Across cultures, friends tend to be of the same sex. We do not hear of societies in which the closest and most satisfying friendships are typically between males and females. The Nyakyusa of Tanzania capture this cross-cultural regularity when they say that *ukwangala,* the enjoyment of good company, of good conversation, and comfortable give-and-take, cannot occur between men and women. Similarly, the Siuai of Oceania cannot imagine why grown men and women would wish to spend time in each other's company unless for sexual intercourse. If a man and woman are seen alone together, it is assumed that they are about to engage in sex. Men and women, as a consequence, tend to stay away from each other.

The Kaska of Alaska highlight some of the features of friendship across cultures. Boys and girls form same-sex attachments beginning in late childhood and friendships remain important until an individual marries. Adolescents are almost never seen abroad without a same-sex companion. Friends display physical affection openly. Boys may lean on each other while resting and one boy may sneak up on a friend and hug him from behind. Girls hold hands, hug, wrestle, and sit with bodies touching. Friendships among Kaska youth may be temporary, but while the relationship lasts friends share both affection and confidences. It is as unusual to see young people of the opposite sex walking and talking together as it is common to see same-sex companions doing so.

Friendships in other cultures echo similar themes. In New Guinea, Trobriand males forge same-sex friendships that may last a lifetime and

Across many cultures, it is usual for people to socialize mainly with people of the same sex.

that provide emotional and concrete support to the partners. Friends choose one another on the basis of personal preference and communicate their affection for each other by close physical contact. Male friends hug one another, walk about with arms around each other, and sleep together. Trukese men of Oceania spend much of their time with their same-sex friends, doing their chores together or walking around holding hands during their leisure time. Friendships are important for both sexes among the North American Omaha, and companionships originating in childhood often last a lifetime. Chagga women of Tanzania have the greatest opportunity to get together with friends at the market. Here, gossip is exchanged and confidences are shared. Younger girls learn about married life as they listen in on the shared secrets of the more mature women.

Sometimes individuals who have become good friends may formalize their relationship.

Among the Kapauku of New Guinea, two people may declare themselves "best friends." Best friends are closer than brothers. They share their deepest secrets, tell each other their problems, and advise, reassure, and comfort each other. They eat, sleep, and sit together and visit one another. Each best friend helps the other during life crises. Among the Pawnee of the United States Plains, formally recognized friendships bind two young men or two young women together for their entire lives, with each friend sharing the happiness and sorrow of the other. Among the Pentecost of Oceania, ceremonial friends view one another as brothers and would never think of fighting or hurting each other. All Brazilian Shavante boys adopt one or two partners during their tenure in the bachelor's house. These partnerships are viewed by the society as formal connections in which the participants form economic partnership and pledge reciprocal assistance. Partners sleep next to each other in the bachelor's hut and dance next to one another at ceremonials.

While friendships are important to both sexes, there is a tendency for males to have greater freedom in the nature of their friendships and choice of friends across cultures. Aweikoma men of Brazil enjoy gathering together in groups, making blankets and chatting with each other away from the women. A wife may join a group of this sort if her husband happens to be there, but women do not congregate in groups of this sort. Rather, they visit with each other on a more individual basis. Among the Kaska, males have a wider variety of friendships than females, whose companions are either female relatives or girls who happen to live close by. More generally, girls and women are likely to make friends with other female kin or with neighbors, while males have more choice and a wider pool from which to choose.

Dorsey, George Amos, and James R. Murie. (1940) *Notes on Skidi Pawnee Society.*

Gladwin, Thomas, and Seymour Sarason. (1953) *Truk: Man in Paradise.*

Henry, Jules. (1941) *The Jungle People: A Kaingang Tribe of the Highlands of Brazil.*

Honigmann, John J. (1949) *Culture and Ethos of Kaska Society.*

Lane, R. B. (1965) "The Melanesians of South Pentecost." In *Gods, Ghosts, and Men in Melanesia,* edited by P. Lawrence and M. J. Meggitt, 250–279.

Malinowski, Bronislaw. (1929) *The Sexual Life of Savages in North-western Melanesia: An Ethnographic Account of Courtship, Marriage and Family Life among the Natives of the Trobriand Islands, British New Guinea.*

Maybury-Lewis, David. (1967) *Akwe-Shavante Society.*

Oliver, Douglas. (1955) *A Solomon Island Society: Kinship and Leadership among the Siuai of Bougainville.*

Pospisil, Leopold. (1958) *Kapauku Papuans and Their Law.* Yale University Publications in Anthropology 54.

Raum, O. F. (1940) *Chaga Childhood: A Description of Indigenous Education in an East African Tribe.*

Wilson, Monica. (1951) *Good Company.*

bride and groom. It is much more common for goods to flow in one direction at the time of a marriage, particularly from the groom's family to that of the bride. Cultures that do practice gift exchange tend to be characterized by communities of fewer than 200 people. Further, individuals in these cultures are likely to procure rather than produce their food, with hunting or gathering being typical subsistence activities. Where food is produced, it is by simple, as opposed to intensive, agriculture. The food supply in these cultures is also secure. Gift exchange is often found in societies with status or wealth distinctions. The requirement that families exchange property of roughly equal value increases the likelihood that they will also be of more or less equivalent status. Thus, gift exchange acts as a check against marriages between people of widely different rank in some cultures.

Comaroff, J., ed. (1980) *The Meaning of Marriage Payments.*

Ember, Carol R., and Melvin Ember. (1988) *Anthropology.* 5th ed.

Schlegel, Alice. (1991) "Status, Property, and the Value on Virginity." *American Ethnologist* 18(4): 719–734.

Stephens, William N. (1963) *The Family in Cross-Cultural Perspective.*

Textor, Robert B. (1967) *A Cross-Cultural Summary.*

Whiting, John W. M. (1941) *Becoming a Kwoma: Teaching and Learning in a New Guinea Tribe.*

GIFT EXCHANGE

In a small number of societies around the world, marriage is accompanied by the exchange of gifts of more or less equal value between the families of the bride and groom. Gift exchange occurs in 2 percent of a sample of 565 worldwide cultures. The Andaman Islanders are one of the few cultures that practices gift exchange. Once a girl and boy decide that they wish to be married, gifts of food and other goods begin to flow back and forth between the parents of the prospective couple by way of a go-between. The gift exchange stops when the boy and girl are finally married. The Kwoma of New Guinea sometimes betroth their children at a very young age, in which case the families of the two children send each other small presents at regular intervals over the years. And when well-to-do Samoans are married, the bride's relatives give hundreds of bark-cloth mats to the boy's family. In turn, the girl's kin will receive money amounting to as much as one thousand pounds in sterling from the groom's family. Gift exchange is quite rare as a way of transferring resources between the families of a

GROUP MARRIAGE

See MARRIAGE FORMS.

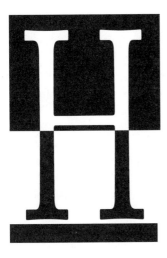

Across the world, people typically live in the company of other people who are their relatives or who are married to relatives. Which relations live with whom varies enormously from place to place. Household composition takes a number of predictable forms across cultures. For example, in the United States, a Haida girl moves in with her husband's family when she marries. A Haida household can consist of 30 individuals living under one roof, including the senior male and his wife or wives, his unmarried daughters and young sons, his married daughters and their husbands and children, a married younger brother with his wife and children, unmarried sons of his sister, a married nephew and his family, and perhaps a poor relative and a few slaves. Boys over ten years of age go to live with the mother's brother. This is a type of extended-family household. Another type is the polygynous household or compound, as found among the Otoro Nubians of the Sudan, where a husband sets up independent households for each wife and generally eats and sleeps with a different spouse each day. When a

husband or wife dies, the surviving spouse will go to live in a single hut near the home of a son or younger brother. A married daughter will go to live with her husband, and a son may build himself and his wife a hut near his father's house. On the other hand, the Nepalese Sherpa prefer households that are composed only of the nuclear family, although the youngest or an only child may be allowed to remain in the parents' home. This ideal is sufficiently strong that, if a newly married son or daughter cannot move into an independent household, the parental home is partitioned into two households, with separate entrances and stairways, until the bride and groom can set out on their own, but this accommodation is relatively rare.

A majority of societies around the world permit the marriage of one man to more than one woman at a time, with the result that at least some households are polygynous in many cultures around the world. Once a man has two or more wives, he faces the problem of how to house his family. Some polygynous families live in a single dwelling, an arrangement that is more likely if the co-wives are also sisters. In Mexico polygyny is common among Popoluca men, and co-wives who are sisters live in the same house. By contrast, if a Popoluca man's spouses are not siblings, as when one of the wives has been acquired through inheritance from a brother, it generally turns out better if the women live in separate dwellings. When co-wives share a house, arrangements may be made to provide each woman some breathing space. Among the Wogeo of New Guinea, where co-wives live in a single dwelling, each has her own section of the house and her own fireplace. This is where she sleeps and entertains. Wives are not supposed to invade each other's territory, although there are no physical barriers separating the domains of the women. In Tanzania, a Nyakyusa wife who does not have a hut of her own will be provided with a separate alcove in a larger hut, where she will cook over her own fire and eat with her own daughters. In many polygynous cultures, wives have their own dwellings. The goal of separating co-wives is to minimize the risk of jealousy and fighting between women.

When a wife has a house of her own, her children live with her. Such an arrangement is known as a mother-child or matrifocal household. If co-wives are provided with separate houses, the question arises as to where the husband will live. Sometimes a man will have his own dwelling, in which case he will visit each of his wives or entertain each in turn on his own turf. In Zaire, a Nkundo co-wife visits her husband in his own hut, and a man will spend an equal number of nights with each of his spouses. A husband will not usually see a wife in her own house if he has a hut of his own. In Suriname, a Saramaka husband builds a separate hut for each of his wives and one for himself to which he can retreat when he wishes to be relieved of the tribulations of married life. Sometimes his wives may be scattered among a number of villages. A woman conducts the routine affairs of everyday life in her own dwelling, where she lives with her children. Women are prohibited from entering a man's hut. In other cases, a husband will not have a dwelling of his own. Among the Khoi of southern Africa, a polygynous husband will share a hut with his first wife, while each other wife will have a hut for herself and her children.

The majority of people in cultures around the world live in extended-family households at one time or another. A residential unit is composed of an extended family if two or more married couples share a dwelling. Extended households are established when married sons or daughters and their spouses and children live in the parents' house or when married siblings and their families share a residence. Separate nuclear families may be accorded some privacy in a separate room or section of the common dwelling, or everyone may live in the house as a single family. Among the Pawnee of the United States Plains, up to ten related families lived in a single lodge measuring perhaps 40 feet in diameter. Each family had its own designated space along the wall of the dwelling, blocked off from other family spaces by willow mats. Children slept near the altar of the house, grandparents closest to the door, with parents and aunts and uncles in between. In the summer, everyone slept outside the lodge, either in separate family units or together as a single large extended family.

The single-family household is the typical residential unit in a relatively small number of societies around the world. However, as many non-Western cultures are drawn into the industrialized, urbanized world, household type often shifts to the single-family form. A model Thai family consists of a father, mother, and unmarried children, and children are expected to found their own households as soon as they are married. But because land is scarce, young married couples are sometimes forced to live and work with the parents of one spouse for a number of years until they can acquire enough money to buy their own land, animals, and farm equipment. Because the Thai believe that a person's primary loyalty is to a spouse and children, the Thai family is rarely expanded even to make room for an elderly parent or other relative. In Oceania, the Siuai household consists of parents and their children, and each family inhabits a single house, which may be a single, one-floor room or a first floor with a high platform used for sleeping and storage. Houses are grouped into small hamlets, and members of a particular hamlet are close relatives, so that a hamlet is actually a kind of extended family surrounding the more intimate nuclear household.

In many cultures, children, once they reach a certain age, move out of the parents' home. This is more common in the case of sons than of daughters. Boys may move into a house reserved for the use of men if such an establishment exists. Once they reached adolescence, Ingalik boys of Alaska lived, worked, and ate in the *kashim*, or men's house, chatting with each

Interior of a traditional Maritime Koryak house in Siberia.

other and telling stories after dinner. Other cultures provide dormitories for older children, who remain there until they marry. These dorms may be segregated by sex, or boys and girls may live together in the same house. In New Guinea, the Trobriand household includes a father, mother, and their small children, but adolescents and unmarried men and women live in small bachelor's houses, each of which houses perhaps two to six individuals. In some societies, young unmarried people set up their own independent neighborhoods, villages, or the like. Among the polygynous Murngin of Australia, a husband establishes a separate household with his wives. A girl lives with her parents until she marries and moves in with her husband and co-wives, if she is a junior spouse. Boys move into a different camp reserved for single men when they reach puberty. Children may also move out of the parental house and go to live with relatives.

Among the Bemba of Zambia, a child who is two or three years of age, and therefore weaned, will go to sleep in the hut of its grandparents, who may as a result have five or six youngsters underfoot. Slightly older girls may sleep in the house of a widow or of a married woman whose husband is away, while a boy will build himself a hut. Among the Hadza of Tanzania, housing accommodations are assigned on the basis of an individual's age and sex. A father and mother live in their own hut along with any children who are under five or six years old. Older boys and bachelors live in a separate hut, as do older girls and unmarried women. A younger child will often go to sleep in the maternal grandmother's hut.

While households are typically described as if they were still-frames, families in real life tend to change in composition across time. For example, while the ideal Siuai household is a nuclear family made up of a mother, father, and unmarried children, over time a house may be inhabited by a bachelor, a childless couple, a widowed person, or a husband and wife with their children and an elderly grandparent or two. While one type may be the ideal for a culture, actual practice will show much variation. In one Garo village in India, 27 households consisted only of a husband and wife and their children, 22 also contained some extra relatives, including married daughters and their spouses or widowed parents, 8 were polygynous households, and 3 houses were inhabited by widows living alone.

The form that a household takes is predictably related to other aspects of a culture. Most saliently, nuclear family households are found in the simplest and the most complex kinds of cultures. Both small hunting and gathering societies and large, industrialized societies tend to favor households comprised of a mother, father, and children. Extended families, by contrast, are found most typically in settled agricultural societies. Farming families may opt for extended-family households as a way to prevent the division of their land. When members of an agricultural family set up independent households, land tends to be divided among family members, with the result that farms become smaller and smaller across generations. The smaller the farm, the more difficult it becomes for a family to make a living. Extended families are also somewhat more common in societies where a single husband-wife pair cannot easily perform all of the necessary economic and domestic chores alone. For instance, a mother whose subsistence chores take her far from home cannot easily tend to her children, or a father who is often away at war cannot perform economic activities on behalf of his family. When a nuclear family cannot get all of the necessary work done, families will sometimes combine into a single household. Adults can then divide up the work load so that everyone's needs are adequately met.

Cultures that have a high degree of social stratification are also likely to have extended-family households.

Bohannan, Paul, and John Middleton, eds. (1968) *Marriage, Family, and Residence.*

Bowers, Alfred W. (1950) *Mandan Social and Ceremonial Organization.*

Burling, Robbins. (1963) *Rengsanggri: Family and Kinship in a Garo Village.*

Dorsey, George Amos, and James R. Murie. (1940) *Notes on Skidi Pawnee Society.*

Ember, Carol R., and Melvin Ember. (1988) *Anthropology,* 5th ed.

Foster, George M. (1942) *A Primitive Mexican Community.*

Fürer-Haimendorf, Christoph von. (1964) *The Sherpas of Nepal, Buddhist Highlanders.*

Hogbin, H. Ian. (1942–1943) "A New Guinea Infancy, from Conception to Weaning in Wogeo." *Oceania* 13: 285–309; 15: 324–352; 16: 185–209, 275–296.

Hulsaert, Gustave. (1928) *Marriage among the Nkundu.*

Kahn, Morton C. (1931) *Djuka: The Bush Negroes of Dutch Guiana.*

Lehman, F. Rudolf. (1951) "Notes on the Daily Life of the Nyakyusa." *Sociologus* 1: 138–148.

Levinson, David, and Martin J. Malone. (1980) *Toward Explaining Human Culture.*

Linton, Ralph. (1923) *Annual Ceremony of the Pawnee Medicine Men.*

Murdock, George Peter. (1934) *Our Primitive Contemporaries.*

Nadel, S. F. (1947) *The Nuba.*

Netting, R. M. C., E. R. Wilk, and E. J. Arnould, eds. (1984) *Households: Comparative and Historical Studies of the Domestic Group.*

Niblack, Albert F. (1890) *The Coast Indians of Southern Alaska and Northern British Columbia.* Annual Reports of the Board of Regents, Smithsonian Institute.

Oliver, Douglas. (1955) *A Solomon Island Society: Kinship and Leadership among the Siuai of Bougainville.*

Richards, Audrey. (1940) *Bemba Marriage and Present Economic Conditions.* Rhodes-Livingstone Papers 4.

Schapera, I. (1930) *The Khoisan Peoples of South Africa.*

Sharp, R. L., et al. (1954) *Siamese Village.* Bangkok.

Warner, W. Lloyd. (1937) *A Black Civilization: A Social Study of an Australian Tribe.*

Wilson, Godfrey. (1936) "An Introduction to Nyakyusa Society." *Bantu Studies* 10: 253–291.

Wilson, Monica. (1951) *Good Company.*

Woodburn, J. (1964) *The Social Organization of the Hadza of North Tanzania.* Unpublished dissertation, Cambridge University.

HUMAN RELATIONSHIPS, EVOLUTION OF

The patterning of human relationships as we see them played out across cultures today is the result of the long process of evolution by natural selection, taking us from our direct ancestors—who are thought to have appeared in Africa between three and five million years ago—to modern men and women. Human beings and their ancestors share ancestry with the modern apes (in fact, we share over 99 percent of our genetic material in common with chimpanzees). The divergence of human beings and apes from their common ancestor was the result of natural selection. Traits that were helpful in advancing the survival of individuals and the representation of their genes in succeeding generations were selected for and came to be better and better represented in the population. Apes became apes and people became people because differences in environmental pressures made somewhat different traits most useful for the ancestors of each group. Thus, contemporary patterns of human relationships are characteristic of our species today because they proved to be beneficial for the survival and reproduction of our ancestors in the environment in which they lived. So it is impossible to appreciate the significance of human relationships today without understanding their function in the world in which they evolved.

People who are interested in tracing the evolution of the human species focus on two physical traits that seem to have set the scene for evolving interpersonal relationships. These are bipedalism and increased brain size. Bipedalism, or upright walking on two feet, predated the growth of the brain—in fact, permitted it, as this novel way of locomoting allowed other physical and behavioral changes so that females could produce offspring whose brains could become larger and be fine-tuned by experience. Bipedalism may have been useful to our ancestors because walking on two legs frees the hands. Individuals who have the use of their hands are able to do a number of new things, for instance carrying food and other items, such as immature babies. They could use and make tools, allowing them to dig up food not previously accessible to them or to chop, crush, or grind food that was otherwise difficult to eat. Tools could also be used to kill predators or to hunt animals for food. The meat could then be cut up and brought elsewhere to be eaten in safety and shared with other individuals. No one knows exactly what selection pressure or pressures actually favored bipedalism in our ancestors, but any or all of these advantages might have figured into the story of the evolution of up-right walking.

Bipedalism and subsequent brain enlarge-ment seem to have been important in driving the evolution of the human species. These are physical divergences from ancestral forms, so they are relatively easy to document because physical traits remain over time as part of the archaeological record. But minds and behavior patterns do not fossilize, so anyone who is in-terested in reconstructing the evolution of hu-man relationships is forced to extrapolate from the physical remains to possible behavioral and psychological correlates of those remains. The extrapolations are not made up out of whole cloth. Knowing something about their physical traits, we can make educated guesses about the behavior and psychological makeup of our an-cestors by noting what kinds of physical traits go with what kinds of behavior and psychologi-cal profiles in other living animals. That is, we can infer about the behavioral and psychologi-cal functions that our own ancestral physical traits underwrote by noting the same kind of function in animals about whose behavior we do have direct information. We can also hypoth-esize about the behavior of our ancestors by ob-serving the behavior of our contemporary cousins, the nonhuman primates, especially the chimpanzees, since there is an overwhelmingly similar genetic connection between us and them. Finally, people who are interested in reconstruct-ing human behavioral and psychological origins look to contemporary hunter-gatherers for hints. This is because we assume that our evolution took place while we were hunter-gatherers and that a hunter-gatherer life will require similar kinds of adaptations regardless of when or where it exists. This is not to say that present-day hunter-gatherers are just like our remote ances-tors. Indeed, people who live in hunter-gath-erer societies have evolved for just as long and in just the same way as people from other kinds of cultures. Hunter-gatherers are, therefore, fully modern. But since the hunter-gatherer way of life is assumed to be a conservative one, changing little across time, we assume that behaviors dis-played by hunter-gatherers today tell us impor-tant things about the behavior of our ancestors.

As we attempt to trace the evolution of hu-man relationships, what are we attempting to account for? Human relationships are charac-terized by a number of features that seem to be shared by people across cultures:

1. Mothers form long-term bonds with their infants, who are too immature to care for themselves. This not only allows a helpless youngster to survive, but also permits young members of the species to learn from their mothers and any other individuals with whom they may be living. The enduring mother-infant bond also permits close and enduring relationships to develop between siblings.

2. Men and women in all cultures also form relatively long-term bonds that include sexual rights of each partner to the other and the expectation that the couple will produce children. Fatherhood is recognized and val-ued in all human societies.

3. Among couples, there is a universal division of labor by sex, with women always taking the primary responsibility for the caretaking of children and men taking the primary role as warriors. Both sexes are likely to contrib-ute to the subsistence of the family, with very predictable kinds of subsistence activities being performed by each sex across cultures. For instance, if the society depends upon hunting, it is the men who hunt. If a society depends upon gathering, it is almost always the women who do the gathering.

4. Males and females and their children are al-ways embedded in larger kin groups.

5. Human beings are fundamentally social creatures, who do not thrive physically or psychologically in isolation from others of their kind.

These features of human relationships themselves assume certain things about the capacities of the human being, including the ability to learn, to communicate complex information, and to remember all kinds of details and contingencies. These capacities, in turn, assume a large brain.

These human traits did not suddenly appear in our ancestors without prior warning. Rather, some version of many of these characteristics is also found in other primates, and many are exhibited by our closest nonhuman primate relatives. For example, chimpanzees are sociable animals that form long-term mother-child attachments as well as close sibling bonds and live in kin-based groups. Mothers share food with their infants and males will sometimes share meat with other members of the troop. Chimpanzees depend largely on plant and insect foods, but males occasionally hunt other animals, and when they do they are likely to cooperate with each other in stalking and capturing their prey. Chimpanzees are known to use and sometimes to make tools. They are intelligent, able to communicate a variety of emotions and kinds of information, and capable of relatively complex learning. There are also clear differences between chimpanzees and human beings. Chimpanzees eat where they find food and do not save provisions for later consumption. Males do not play any role in the lives of the infants they have fathered, nor do they provide food for females, except on rare occasions. Weaned animals are not habitually fed by anyone else and must, therefore, fend for themselves. And males and females do not form long-term sexual or domestic attachments. Even where chimpanzee and human behavioral and psychological profiles do overlap,

there are differences of degree between the species. For instance, while chimpanzees sometimes walk upright or use tools or communicate or learn, we do all of these and other things more and better than chimps. Thus, the evolutionary story of the human species needs to explain why the ancestors of our species diverged from those of the primates in such a way as to produce a human as opposed to some other profile.

Attempts to explain human evolution begin with a set of assumptions about the conditions underwriting our appearance as a group. It is assumed that our early ancestors emerged from the trees and out onto the flat savannas when environmental conditions made this move a necessary one. Therefore, they lived in an environment of fringe forest and open land. This new lifestyle would also have left them more vulnerable to predators, since animals on the prowl would more easily see an individual located on a flat landscape than in a forest or up a tree and since an individual on the ground is more easily pursued once sighted. It would also have provided an opportunity to take advantage of a wide variety of new foods.

How would these new conditions have influenced evolutionary processes to produce human ancestors? One theory proposes that the primary force behind human evolution was the advantage accruing to an individual who was able to throw rocks or sticks at the newly threatening predators. The small size and relative slowness of our ancestors compared with the animals that habitually would have pursued them made them vulnerable. But weapons would have given them an advantage. The value of weapons to fight off predators, in turn, favored bipedalism, as walking upright would free hands to make and use weapons. Bipedalism and the use of tools also would have allowed ancestors to hunt more efficiently. As females would have been handicapped by the presence of immature young, it would have been the males who took on the roles of protector and hunter. The introduction of hunting is then assumed to have had additional effects. The hunting of large animals is best accomplished in groups. Thus, once our ancestors began to hunt for a living, group living would have been favored. And while males took on the roles of hunting and protecting, females became the gatherers and caretakers. Thus, the division of labor by sex that we observe in every culture the world over is proposed to have had its origins in the emergence of the male hunter. The division of labor also creates relationships of interdependence between males and females in which males provide protection and the important nutriments derived from meat to females while females provide the important fruit and vegetable foodstuffs upon which men must depend when the hunt has been a failure. Additionally, both sexes are advancing the survival of their shared offspring. The advent of bipedalism would also require alterations in the patterning of human growth and relationships. Competent walking takes a relatively long time to emerge, and individuals who are physiologically adapted to walk are no longer able to cling to the mother as well as primate ancestors. So the walking adaptation, so useful to tool use and creation, also creates a need for a more enduring mother-infant bond.

Some scientists believe that the emphasis on protecting and hunting by men as the motivating force behind human evolution is overstated. In this view, the arms and shoulders of our early ancestors would not have permitted very effective throwing, so that the use of weapons to hunt or to neutralize predators would not have conferred much of an advantage. Nor would rocks and the like have been very effective against the large animals living during our early history. Thus, a rival theory of human origin proposes that the crucial push in the transition from the ancestral line to the human species was not hunting, but innovations in gathering. By adopting new technologies that increased the food supply produced by gathering, a female would be better able to feed herself and her offspring. The improvement of gathering skills by females becomes the driving force behind the evolution of the species according to this way of thinking. Further, this improvement is connected to a number of characteristics of a female and her offspring. The mother would need to be intelligent enough to invent new gathering technologies. For instance, she would need to appreciate what kinds of new tools would increase gathering efficiency. She would also need to be inclined to share what she had gathered with her offspring. The offspring most likely to survive to maturity would be those most able to learn and improve upon successful food-gathering techniques from their mothers. They would then share food with their own young. Thus, the traits of increased intelligence and of selective sharing with offspring would be favored by natural selection.

Further, as females began to share gathered food with their young, the investment made by a female in her offspring would be increased relative to that made by ancestral females. As maternal investment became more significant, females would become a more precious commodity relative to males. This is because the male contribution to the production of viable offspring, consisting only of the investment of sperm, would be minuscule by comparison. Males, therefore, would find themselves competing for females. As a result, females would be able to choose the males with whom they were willing to mate and reject males who did not meet the qualifications of an acceptable mate. What might females select for? One possibility is that females preferred males who had traits very similar to their own. Thus, sociable males with excellent manipulative skills would be more likely to effectively groom females and therefore to be chosen as sexual partners. Intelligent males would also be more successful at attracting intelligent, busy females. Males who were appropriately aggressive in the presence of predators, and therefore able to protect females and their young, would also be preferred, as would males who sometimes shared meat that they had captured or plant food that they had foraged. Thus, females might have had a hand in shaping the profile of protohuman males to mirror the female traits of intelligence, manual dexterity, and sociability, mingled with aggression directed at enemies.

The long mother-child relationship would have had other effects. Once mothers began to feed children with gathered food, the period of time available for infant immaturity would be increased. Children would have a longer time to observe and learn from their mothers. Because infants and immature young would remain with the mother for extended periods of time, sibling relationships would begin to become important. As siblings became adults and continued to associate with each other, larger groups would emerge, consisting, for instance, of a number of adult females with their offspring and even the offspring of their female offspring. Adult brothers and the sons of older females might also be incorporated into such groups. Thus, infants would be socialized within a group consisting of a variety of kin, with the mother-infant bond at the center of the group.

The primacy of the mother-infant relationship is guaranteed by the fact that it is only mothers who can give birth to infants and who can nurse them. Nevertheless, the cooperation of a male would certainly have increased the chances that an infant would survive to maturity. As other ideas about the origins of the human species remind us, males can supply females and young with meat and can protect them against predators. Thus, regardless of whether or not these contributions on the part of males were primary in motivating human evolution, they would have been important to our early ancestors. Once a male began to invest significant time and energy in feeding and protecting a female and her

young, he would have a stake in being assured that her offspring were also his. Thus, the joint contribution that a male and female made to the welfare of each other and their young would also lead to the formation of exclusive sexual relationships between the sexes, focusing especially upon the sexual fidelity of the female.

The evolution of the human species from prehuman ancestors also meant other changes in sexual behavior and relationships. For instance, the characteristic genital swelling that signals ovulation in other primates would no longer be as visible to males once females began to habitually walk upright, and the chemical odors normally given off by primate females to communicate information about sexual status would no longer act as effective signals because males could no longer easily smell the female genital region. These changes would leave males with considerably less information about female readiness for sexual contact. One possibility is that this left the initiative regarding when to engage in sexual intercourse in the hands of females, as there would no longer be any better or worse time for sexual relations from the perspective of the male. Thus, the loss of swelling and pheromone might have allowed protohuman females to exercise more mate choice than was possible for their ancestors. It might also mean that sexual relationships came to rely more on behavioral cues than on physical ones, significantly changing the nature of sexuality. Upright posture and the shift in the position of male and female genitals also favored face-to-face sexual intercourse, making the human pattern of copulation different from that of the typical primate pattern in which the male approaches the female from behind.

While no one knows the precise details regarding what factors motivated the evolution of the human species, scientists are relatively sure that upright posture and big brains were important to the story of our origin. Further, archaeological evidence indicates that the hunting-gathering way of life served as the canvas for the delineation of the human physiological, psychological, and behavioral profile. The broad strokes of this profile as it is played out in human beings today are very much consistent with the hunter-gatherer way of life, in spite of the fact that most of the people who live in today's world have adopted lifestyles that are dramatically different from the hunter-gatherer baseline. Thus, the task of tracing our origins is the task of attempting to determine *precisely* how and when and in what order pressures on our ancestors to become proficient hunter-gatherers caused us to become what we are today.

See also NATURAL SELECTION; REPRODUCTIVE STRATEGIES; SEXUAL SELECTION.

Daly, Martin, and Margo Wilson. (1983) *Sex, Evolution, and Behavior.*

Ember, Carol R., and Melvin Ember. (1988) *Anthropology.* 5th ed.

Ember, Melvin, and Carol R. Ember. (1983) *Marriage, Family, and Kinship: Comparative Studies of Social Organization.*

Frayser, Suzanne G. (1985) *Varieties of Sexual Experience.*

Tanner, Nancy M. (1981) *On Becoming Human.*

HUSBAND-WIFE EATING ARRANGEMENTS

Eating arrangements are among the features of married life that characterize the nature of the husband-wife relationship across cultures. Spouses may eat together, as is expected in Western cultures, or they may have their meals separately, as often occurs in dual-earner households, or a wife may serve her husband but refrain from eating with him, although she might keep him company until he has finished his meal.

In the southwestern United States, traditional Papago married couples share meals together, with husband and wife eating out of the same dish as a symbol of their intimate relationship. Among the Tanala of Madagascar, a polygynous society, a husband and all of his wives will eat together, with cooking duties rotating among co-wives. Igbo husband and wife and their children eat out of the same pot. If an Igbo man has more than one wife, each brings him a helping of food. He tastes and chooses from all of the offerings and eats with the wife whose meal he has selected, along with their children.

In many societies, men and women are prohibited from eating together, and this includes spouses. Neither a north African Songhai nor a Sudanese Teda wife will eat in the presence of her husband. Among the polygynous Katab of Nigeria, junior wives eat their meals on the porch of the senior wife's hut, while the husband eats elsewhere. In Oceania, Manus couples do not eat together until they have had two or three children or until they have been married for a number of years. Husbands may eat at the home of a sister while the sister's spouse removes himself from their company.

While married couples in many societies depart from the Western tradition of eating together, the habit of sharing meals is quite common across cultures. Husbands and wives eat together in 65 percent of a sample of 117 cultures around the world. However, in 35 percent of these societies, spouses eat apart. In 27 percent of these cultures, a wife may serve her husband his meal and possibly the two will chat with each other, but the woman will have her own meal elsewhere. In the remaining 73 percent, husbands and wives are often or always segregated during meals.

Eating arrangements tend to be consistently related to other kinds of everyday husband-wife interaction. Where spouses eat apart, they tend also to sleep and spend their leisure time apart. Societies with marital arrangements of this sort are likely to have special houses where men can retire to eat, sleep, gossip, and relax whenever they wish.

See also HUSBAND-WIFE RELATIONSHIPS.

Briggs, L. L. (1958) *The Living Races of the Saraha Desert.* Papers of the Peabody Museum, Harvard University, 28.

Broude, Gwen J., and Sarah J. Greene. (1983) "Cross-Cultural Codes on Husband-Wife Relationships." *Ethnology* 22: 263–280.

Green, M. M. (1947) *Ibo Village Affairs.*

Gunn, Harold D. (1956) *Pagan Peoples of the Central Area of Northern Nigeria.*

Linton, Ralph. (1933) *The Tanala: A Hill Tribe of Madagascar.*

Lumholtz, Carl. (1912) *New Trails in Mexico.*

Mead, Margaret. (1930) *Growing Up in New Guinea: A Comparative Study of Primitive Education.*

Murdock, George Peter. (1934) *Our Primitive Contemporaries.*

HUSBAND-WIFE JOINT WORK ACTIVITIES

In cultures around the world, husbands and wives take advantage of having two able-bodied adults in the household by dividing economic and domestic chores between them. Most typically, this means employing a "divide and conquer" strategy for getting tasks done. Husbands do one kind of work and wives another. This division of labor usually also separates spouses spatially for most of the day. Married partners may also specialize in different stages of the same overall activity. Or, less frequently, a husband and wife may work side by side at the same task.

Belauans divide and conquer. They make a living by fishing and farming, husbands doing the former and wives the latter. Indeed, women are said to be afraid of the ocean and are taught to be so from an early age. Men also grow tobacco and pepper vines. A Belau wife will make the clothing for her husband and children, while husbands concentrate on woodworking skills, making ornately carved canoes and elaborately constructed houses. In Mexico, Mixtecan husbands spend most of the day away in the fields. Wives, meanwhile, go to the market or prepare food and attend to other household chores. For a few days during the planting and harvesting season, a temporary shelter is built near the fields, and the entire family pitches in to help the father for a few days. This is the only notable exception to the segregation of chores and meagerness of contact that characterizes the daily routine of a married Mixtecan couple. Similarly, Navajo husbands in Arizona build the corrals and fences, do most of the farming, take care of the horses, cattle, and wagons, haul the water, and cut the firewood. Wives butcher mutton, cook, gather farm crops for meals, keep the house clean, and tend the children.

A husband and wife may also adopt an assembly-line strategy for getting work done. One spouse sees to one part of a job and the other focuses on another. Husband and wife may or may not perform these specializations in each other's presence. For example, Navajo wives weave while the men dress skin and make moccasins and clothing for the family. At the sheep dip, husbands take the adult animals through the vat while wives see to the lambs and kids. A husband will also build the family's house, while his wife plasters and chinks the dwelling. Similarly, Gururumba husbands of New Guinea break the soil for the gardens, put up the fence, and dig drainage ditches while wives prepare the

Indian women working in the building industry.
In most cultures, this sort of work would be done by men.

broken soil for planting and see to the weeding. The sugarcane, bananas, taro, and yams are the responsibility of husbands, while women tend the vegetables and sweet potatoes, an important daily food for the family. Men do the major portion of the work associated with building a house, and the women cut and carry the thatch. Food served at feasts is prepared by the men, but women do the daily cooking. It is also the job of the husband to kill, castrate, loan, trade, or give away the pigs. A wife feeds and cares for them.

In some societies, spouses cooperate in the same activities or perform different activities in each other's company. Among the Bhil of India, husbands and wives perform many chores together. A married couple will weed, manure, and harvest crops side by side. A wife may also visit her husband at the logging camp, cooking his meal for him and perhaps helping him in the manufacture of charcoal. A father will tend the children while his wife is preparing a meal. Most of the subsistence activities performed by the Taira of Guiana are performed by either sex. Husband and wife, along with children over 12 years old, trek to the forests together to cut lumber and carry it back to the village, selling it later for cash. A pregnant woman may continue to make a number of trips back and forth from forest to village until the day she delivers her baby. Both spouses also sow and seed the rice beds, and the whole family works together for many hours in the rice paddies. A husband and wife may also do the same kinds of work, but not as a team. For example, while most Gururumba work is sex-typed, either spouse may boil food for family meals or tend the fire.

In many societies, some tasks are done by both spouses and others are delegated by sex. Taira families lumber and work their rice paddies together, but only men fish and tend horses, while women do housework, tend pigs, and farm potatoes. The job of fetching water is also considered women's work, although boys sometimes help out.

Where there is a division of labor by sex, it is often considered inappropriate for men to do women's work and vice versa. Among the Bhil, a number of tasks are sex-typed, and an individual who violates these norms is the target of back-biting by other members of the community. A Navajo man would never be seen milking a goat, although many will cook or tend a baby even when there are women around to perform these tasks. In Siberia, a Chuckchee husband will rarely do women's work and, in fact, would not know how to perform the chores assigned to his wife. Men are ignorant of much of the vocabulary relating to house construction, household utensils, and the dressing of skins, all of which have to do with tasks that are the province of women. By contrast, when the Taira build houses, repair roads, erect fences or the like, the men are responsible for the construction work while the women carry materials and prepare meals for the work team, but if either sex happens to take on the job of the other, no one makes a fuss.

Men in many cultures have less flexibility in performing roles typically reserved for the opposite sex than do women. A Tepotzlan man in Mexico would not think of doing housework or tending small children. If his wife is ill, a husband will ask a female relative for help rather than take over his spouse's work, or he may hire someone to do his wife's chores, even if money is in short supply. The few men who are willing to do women's work are laughed at and considered odd. Women, by contrast, can perform chores normally viewed as the work of males with impunity, especially if they are widows. No widower or bachelor would be caught washing, ironing, or grinding corn for tortillas.

Wives also do more work than their husbands in many societies. A New Guinea Kiwai wife is expected to carry the heavy loads of food that she and her husband have gathered from their garden. A husband will not help unless they have an unusually long way to walk,

Women in India hauling water, an activity performed by women in most cultures.

and if he does help his wife on these occasions he does so with some embarrassment. Ifaluk wives in Micronesia always have tasks to get done, but their husbands sit around their canoe houses for hours doing nothing. And among the Alor of Indonesia, hard physical labor is only appropriate for women and young people, especially in the opinion of wealthier men, who spend their time sitting around, visiting, gossiping, and chewing areca.

While there are clear cross-cultural differences regarding the allocation of tasks to spouses, we also see very striking tendencies for men to be assigned some kinds of work and women others across societies. Metalworking, making weapons, hunting, boatbuilding, mining, woodworking, stoneworking, trapping, and herding are either universally or overwhelmingly assigned to males. Women usually or always grind grain, fetch water, cook, gather, make or repair cloth-

ing, preserve food, make pottery, and gather firewood. Why is one specific set of chores so consistently allocated to men and another to women the world over? Some people believe that sex-typed task assignment in part reflects male-female differences in physical strength and the ability to nurse infants. In this view, men monopolize the tasks that require the greatest physical exertion or the ones that are incompatible with child care, while women perform tasks that are commensurate with their strength limitations and that still allow them to tend infants and young children. Once a particular activity is assigned by sex, other related activities may also be monopolized by the same people for reasons of efficiency. For example, if men do the hunting they will also be assigned the making of the weapons used in the hunt. The kinds of chores monopolized by males and by females make this explanation attractive. Nevertheless, in some societies women do hunt and lift heavy loads, even when pregnant. And many mothers the world over recruit older members of their community or children to help with baby tending, freeing them to perform work that takes them from home. Thus, physical differences between the sexes may bias but do not absolutely determine the kinds of work that men and women do.

The allocation of tasks to husbands and wives appears to follow another consistent pattern across cultures. Men are more likely to be assigned work that is instrumental, which means that men's chores are of a practical sort. Women, by contrast, tend to be involved in work that is more expressive in nature. That is, females are typically in charge of those aspects of family life that contribute to the emotional well-being of household members.

Cross-cultural differences in the degree to which tasks are sex-typed are associated with other customs. Men and women are more likely to be assigned the same tasks in places where people choose their own marriage partners. Customs surrounding task delegation are also correlated with a number of sex norms. Thus, where men and women do different kinds of work, sex is regarded as dangerous, premarital sex norms for girls tend to be restrictive, and extramarital sex norms for husbands tend to be permissive. Patterns of actual sexual behavior, by contrast, are not predictably related to sex-typing in task assignment. Large distinctions between men's and women's work are also more likely to occur in societies that pressure boys to be aggressive and where men are expected to act aggressively.

Barnett, H. G. (1960) *Being a Palauan.*

Broude, Gwen J. (1990) "The Division of Labor by Sex and other Gender-Related Variables: An Exploratory Study." *Behavior Science Research* 24: 29–50.

Leighton, Dorothea, and Clyde Kluckhohn. (1969) *Children of the People: The Navaho Individual and His Development.*

Levinson, David, and Martin J. Malone. (1980) *Toward Explaining Human Culture.*

Maretzki, Thomas W., and Hatsumi Maretzki. (1966) *Taira: An Okinawan Village.*

Naik, T. B. (1956) *The Bhils: A Study.*

Nath, Y. V. S. (1960) *Bhils of Ratanmal: An Analysis of the Social Structure of a Western Indian Community.*

Newman, Philip L. (1965) *Knowing the Gururumba.*

Romney, Kimball, and Romaine Romney. (1966) *The Mixtecans of Juxtlahuaca, Mexico.*

Stephens, William N. (1963) *The Family in Cross-Cultural Perspective.*

HUSBAND-WIFE LEISURE

When they are not busy earning a living, attending to household chores, and meeting other responsibilities, married couples have the option of spending whatever free time remains to them in each other's company or pursuing independent activities. Whether married people spend their leisure time together or apart is influenced in part by the degree to which same-sex activities are emphasized in a society. In 53 percent of a worldwide sample of 104 cultures, spouses spend at least a significant portion of their spare time with members of their own sex. Sometimes, this amounts to more or less entire segregation of partners during leisure hours. This is the pattern among the Mbundu of Angola. Boys and men in this society spend much of their spare time in the men's house, which serves as a school, hotel, dining room, and recreation area. Women, for their part, congregate in the kitchens. Dances are very important in Mbundu social life and last two or four days each month, but here, too, men and women, including husbands and wives, are separated from each other, with males gathering on one side of the dance floor and females on the other. On other occasions, the men pass around a pipe while engaging in lengthy conversations, while the women sit quietly, perhaps smoking their own pipes, perhaps watching the men. In less extreme cases, husband and wife might go to a dance or to market together, but then break off into same-sex cliques.

In another 21 percent of the 104 cultures, couples usually remain together during their free hours, but often their activities take place within a larger group. For instance, married people might go to dances or sit around camp with their neighbors. In southern Africa, the !Kung live in intimate camps of around 25 people inhabiting an area of perhaps 20 feet in diameter. Their free time is typically spent out in the open where small groups gather together during the day to talk while doing chores or where they chat in family groups or visit at the fires of campmates at night.

In another 21 percent of the 104 societies, married people spend most of their spare time together at home but sometimes join a larger group of people, for example, visiting neighbors. The Kikuyu of Kenya enjoy family evenings at home and can regularly be found converging around the fire in the evenings and enjoying a pleasant chat while dinner is cooking. Husbands and wives also attend various ceremonies together during the year, as well as many dances that both men and women attend. A wife also helps her husband entertain guests, especially special visitors, in the husband's hut. In a small minority (5 percent) of the 104 societies, husbands and wives usually spend their free time together at home, either alone or with other members of the nuclear family. For instance, each Nambicuara family in Brazil gathers around its own fire in the evening, singing, dancing, or

chatting until things wind down and everyone falls asleep.

When husbands and wives spend their leisure time together, they tend to enjoy a close relationship in other ways. They are likely to eat together, and husbands can be expected to attend the births of their children. Societies where married partners are together during their spare time are also unlikely to have separate houses in which only men congregate. Where husbands and wives pursue independent activities during their leisure time, they also tend to eat apart. Husbands generally do not attend their children's births, and men's houses are likely to be present.

See also HUSBAND-WIFE RELATIONSHIPS.

Broude, Gwen J., and Sarah J. Greene. (1983) "Cross-Cultural Codes on Husband-Wife Relationships." *Ethnology* 22: 263–280.

Cagnolo, C. (1933) *The Akikuyu: Their Customs, Traditions, and Folklore.*

Childs, Gladwyn M. (1949) *Umbundu Kinship and Character.*

Kenyatta, Jomo. (1961) *Facing Mount Kenya: The Tribal Life of the Gikuyu.*

Levi-Strauss, Claude. (1948) *Family and Social Life of the Nambikwara Indians.*

Marshall, Lorna. (1959) "Marriage among the !Kung Bushmen." *Africa* 29: 335–364.

Oberg, Kalervo. (1953) *Indian Tribes of Northern Mato Grosso, Brazil.*

HUSBAND-WIFE RELATIONSHIPS The institution of marriage is found in all known human societies. However, there are enormous differences across cultures regarding the nature of the relationship between a husband and wife. Couples may live together or apart. They may sleep in the same or different beds. Meals may be shared or eaten separately. Married people may spend their leisure time in each other's company or not. One spouse may help and support the other during momentous events or remain detached. Marriages, moreover, tend to be consistent in their overall character. Husbands and wives who live together tend also to eat, sleep, and engage in leisure activities with each other. And expectant fathers in these marriages are likely to be present for the births of their children. Conversely, where spouses live apart they can generally be expected to eat, sleep, and spend their leisure time apart. In this case husbands do not usually attend the births of their infants. Thus, marriages within any particular culture can often be described as uniformly *intimate* or *aloof,* reflecting the degree to which a couple acts separately or as a unit in the pursuit of life's daily activities. In a sample of 73 societies from around the world, marriages in 56 percent of these cultures are typically intimate while in 44 percent they are usually aloof.

The Trobrianders of New Guinea illustrate the intimate marriage pattern. In this island society, husband and wife occupy their own hut along with their young children, while any adolescent or older children live in separate houses. They also eat and sleep together and spend most of their work and leisure time in each other's company, talking and joking freely. Spouses share household chores, including baby tending. Married people are devoted to one another, often give each other gifts, and remain close and valued companions, calling each other by the word *ubaygu,* "my friend." The Garo of India have predominantly intimate marriages. Families most generally consist of a nuclear family, although other relatives—including married daughters with their husbands, widowed parents, and so on—may also augment the household. The oldest married couple has a private sleeping room in the family house, while a larger front room serves as the living area where the family cooks, eats, and visits. Husbands and wives work side by side in the fields. While men and women tend to sit apart from each other during public events, spouses sit together, talking and laughing with each other, when alone or in the company of a few friends and neighbors. The relationship between Garo husband and wife is characterized by friendship, confidence, mutual need, and a joint sense of responsibility and understanding. Over the years, each partner becomes the most important person in the life of the other.

At the opposite extreme are marriages that are best described as aloof. The Rajputs of Khalapur, India illustrate this kind of husband-wife relationship. The Rajputs are a *purdah* society. In such cultures, women are secluded from public life. Rajput women spend most of their time in their houses or courtyards with other women and apart from men, including their husbands. It is here that women eat, cook, sleep, and care for their children. A woman who wishes to visit a neighbor must use the special roof corridors that connect houses to each other. That way, women are accorded some mobility but are still shielded from males. Men, when not working, sit talking and smoking with other male relatives and friends in the men's quarters, where husbands may also sleep. The daily separation between spouses is bolstered by an ethic that expects a son's attachment to his mother to be and remain the most important relationship in his life. As a result, the primary focus of a Rajput marriage is sexual and reproductive. Only after the death of her husband's mother, and after she has had children of her own, does a Rajput wife become a companion to her spouse. Marriages among the Kapauku of New Guinea also tend to be aloof. A number of related families typically inhabit the same house. The males sleep together in one room while each woman has a room with a hearth of her own in which to sleep with her children. If the number of women in a family is too large to be accommodated in a single house, then a small one-room dwelling for each woman is built near the main house. Men have breakfast and dinner in the common male sleeping room, but women eat in their own rooms with their youngsters. People have lunch in the fields, but here, again, men and women eat separately. A man may have his meal alone, while the women eat meals together, relaxing and enjoying themselves or providing each other with useful information. The exception to this general segregation of the sexes during meals occurs when a man has a coveted piece of meat. He may then share it in secret with his wife and children. Men and women, including husbands and wives, also tend to spend their leisure time separately. After they quit work in mid-afternoon, the men congregate around the houses, chatting about politics and other news. The women, meanwhile, work until late afternoon. If no special events are taking place in the evening, the men assemble in the common sleeping room and talk until they fall asleep. On day off, husbands may catch up on business chores or they may just sleep. Women, on the other hand, like to visit friends or relatives or spend time at the lake fishing, swimming, gossiping and eating with others of their sex. The Kapauku enjoy a number of kinds of special relationships. There is the bond of "special friend," a connection that is formalized in Kapauku society and one in which there is strong affection, trust, and sharing. Best friends share their problems and give each other advice. They tell each other their deepest secrets. They visit each other, eat and sleep together, and refer to each other's relatives as kin. Best friends are generally of the same sex and are said to be closer than brothers. There is often also a special relationship of affection between brothers and sisters. A brother may become jealous if his sister marries before he does

A Siberian Chuckchee husband and wife.

because her new relationship threatens his attachment to his sibling. The bond between opposite-sex siblings takes on some of the qualities of a husband-wife relationship and this can interfere with the performance of marital obligations. Thus, the Kapauku derive the kinds of satisfactions from attachments to friends or relatives that are provided by marriage in other cultures.

Some social scientists believe that aloof marriages occur in societies where men fear and wish to avoid sex and women. Such fear and avoidance is itself seen to be a result of mothering that is seductive and/or hostile. Ideas of this sort really propose a cross-generation cycle of events in which women of aloof marriages shower affection on their sons as substitutes for their spouses, but also exhibit hostility toward their male children as symbols of their aloof husbands. Boys who have experienced this kind of mothering then grow up to be distant husbands because of the attitude toward women engendered by their experiences with their mothers, and so the pattern is perpetuated. While these psychodynamic theories seem logical, they have not been tested using direct measures of mothering behavior or male attitudes toward sex or women and are not, therefore, supported by concrete evidence.

Patterns of marital intimacy and aloofness have been shown to be related to other features of a society. Nomadic societies almost always have intimate marriages, while aloof marriages are very likely to occur when the population is sedentary. Marriages are also more likely to be aloof when kin ties are an important component of community identity. By contrast, when community identity depends upon such things as shared religious, political or social values, or where communities are mainly defined by who happens to live nearby, marriages tend to be intimate. These trends indicate that intimate marriages are most likely to occur when people lack other sources of human connectedness. When people have a stable home base and a solid network of relatives surrounding them, marriage is no longer the major emotional and social resource. Rather, community and kin are. This is the case, for example, among the Rajputs and Garo, both of whom depend upon a stable network of relatives and friends for affection, companionship, and support.

Marriages tend to be consistent with respect to the degree to which spouses act separately or as a unit in their daily lives. But day-to-day intimacy and aloofness are not predictably related to other aspects of male-female interaction. For instance, marriages that have been contracted by the partners themselves may be characterized by close daily contact. But it is just as likely that an intimate marriage will have originally been arranged by a third party and, indeed, the partners may have been strangers before their wedding. Conversely, aloof marriages may have been arranged without any or much voice on the part of the prospective couple. But so may marriages be aloof when husband and wife have married by personal preference. Neither is the closeness of the marital relationship within a culture related to the frequency within which divorce occurs in the same society. This suggests that marital stability across cultures is not predicted by the degree to which marriages themselves are central or peripheral as sources of emotional and social support in people's lives.

Aloofness or intimacy of daily contact between spouses is related to certain attitudes about sex but not to others. Some societies regard all sexual activity as dangerous and there is modest evidence that these societies also have aloof marriages. Cultures in which husband and wife have frequent day-to-day contact believe that sex is never dangerous or that it is only dangerous to certain people or under some circumstances. Societies that are uninhibited in talking about sexual matters also tend to have intimate marriages, whereas aloof marriages are more likely to be found in cultures where talk about sex is thought to be shameful in all or least some contexts. On the other hand, patterns of intimacy and aloofness regarding daily contact between spouses is unrelated to ideas about the desirability or undesirability of frequent sexual activity. Nor are the rates of premarital or extramarital sex for males or females connected to daily contact between married partners. Neither impotence in males nor homosexuality is related to marital intimacy and aloofness. Patterns of daily marital contact are unrelated to whether or not males are rough in their sexual advances, force intercourse with their wives, make unsolicited sexual advances to women in general, or engage in rape. Finally, husband-wife intimacy and aloofness are related to the overall balance of power between men and women in a culture as regards leadership roles, tangible contributions to the well-being of others, and control or ownership of goods. The greater the range of things over which women have these kinds of power in a society, the more likely it is that marriages in that culture will be intimate. This connection between women's power and marital intimacy may reflect the tendency for women to prefer more enduring and intense opposite-sex relationships than men. Perhaps a more powerful woman is able to affect her relationship with her husband in a way that produces the kind of marital closeness that is more to her liking. Perhaps, also, when women do attain status in a society, the tendency to segregate the sexes is diminished, resulting in a higher degree of day-to-day contact between spouses.

See also FATHERS ATTENDING BIRTHS; HUSBAND-WIFE EATING ARRANGEMENTS; HUSBAND-WIFE LEISURE; HUSBAND-WIFE SLEEPING ARRANGEMENTS.

Broude, Gwen J. (1983) "Male-Female Relationships in Cross-Cultural Perspective: A Study of Sex and Intimacy." *Behavior Science Research* 18: 154–181.

———. (1983) "Roots: Some Correlates of Marital Intimacy and Aloofness." Paper presented at the 12th Annual Meetings of the Society for Cross-Cultural Research, Washington, DC.

———. (1986) "The relationship between Male-Female Roles and Marital Intimacy and Aloofness." Paper presented at the 15th Annual Meetings of the Society for Cross-Cultural Research, San Diego.

Burling, Robbins. (1963) *Rengsanggri: Family and Kinship in a Garo Village.*

Levinson, David, and Martin J. Malone. (1980) *Toward Explaining Human Culture.*

Malinowski, Bronislaw. (1929) *The Sexual Life of Savages in North-western Melanesia: An Ethnographic Account of Courtship, Marriage and Family Life among the Natives of the Trobriand Islands, British New Guinea.*

Minturn, Leigh, and John T. Hitchcock. (1966) *The Rajputs of Khalapur, India.*

Pospisil, Leopold. (1958) *The Kapauku Papuans and Their Law.* Yale University Publications in Anthropology 54.

———. (1959–1960) "The Kapauku Papuans and Their Kinship Organization." *Oceania* 30.

HUSBAND-WIFE SLEEPING ARRANGEMENTS

Husband-wife sleeping arrangements vary widely across cultures. Spouses may sleep next to each other or they may sleep in the same room without being in close proximity. Sometimes married partners sleep in different rooms or even in different houses altogether. A couple is overwhelmingly likely to sleep in the same room if their marriage is monogamous. When spouses do sleep in the same bed or room, they may be accorded privacy or they may share their beds or rooms with other people. These roommates may range from a couple's small infant to all of their prepubescent children to all members of the nuclear family below marriageable age. In 47 percent of a worldwide sample of 95 cultures, married people share their sleeping quarters with at least one other family member past infancy but not yet ready to marry. In the remaining 53 percent of these societies, other adults sleep with a married couple, either temporarily or permanently.

Married people may sleep separately for a variety of reasons. Where marriages are polygynous, it is common for each co-wife to have her own lodgings. The husband may have a house of his own or he may rotate between wives. In either case, wives will inevitably be sleeping alone at least some of the time. Separate husband-wife sleeping arrangements are also found in cultures with men's houses, that is, with special enclosures where males congregate during the day and/or night. In some societies, it is traditional for mothers to sleep with their infants. When this occurs, fathers may sleep elsewhere, resulting in separate husband-wife sleeping arrangements, at least until the infant is considered old enough to sleep elsewhere. Often, however, children in these cultures continue to sleep with their mothers for years. Finally, some societies segregate males and females as a general rule. In such cultures, husbands and wives may also sleep separately.

The Zuni of New Mexico provide an example of the extreme case in which husbands and wives sleep together and apart from other people. A married couple has a separate room apart from the rest of the family. Babies sleep with their parents, but strapped on a board that is then placed near the mother. Similarly in Oceania, a Pukapuka household sleeps in the same sleeping house and, if there is only one mosquito net, everyone will sleep together un-

der it. On the coast of Puget Sound, Twana arrange sleeping platforms along the wall of their winter homes. Each section of a platform is occupied by a particular family, with no separations between family sleeping spaces. In New Guinea, Kwoma families sleep together in the same room, but husband and wife never sleep in the same bed. Instead, each has a separate bark slab on which to sleep. The Kwoma insist that they would be ashamed to sleep with a spouse; it is a bad thing to do and would make important people angry.

The Ganda of Uganda represent the case of a polygynous society where each wife has her own house. These huts are built next to each other, while the husband has his own hut in front of those of his wives. The husband invites one of his spouses to sleep with him in his hut on any given night. In other polygynous societies arrangements for alternating between wives are more formal. The Gond of India have a separate living and sleeping room for the husband, and it is taboo for the wife, a grown daughter, or any other woman to sleep there. Young sons and daughters are allowed to sleep with the father in his quarters, but a wife and her grown daughters sleep in the kitchen. Finally, the Manus of Oceania represent an example of a society in which husbands and wives sleep separately by preference. Manus husbands and wives say that a house is good in which there are two children, one to sleep with his father on one side of the house and one to sleep with the mother on the other side.

Where husbands and wives sleep together, they also tend to eat and spend their leisure time together. Special houses where only men may gather are unlikely to be found in societies with this kind of sleeping arrangement. Where husbands and wives sleep apart, men's houses are typical and spouses usually eat and spend their spare time apart.

See also HUSBAND-WIFE RELATIONSHIPS.

Beaglehole, Ernest, and Pearl Beaglehole. (1938) *Ethnology of the Pukapuka.*

Broude, Gwen J., and Sarah J. Greene. (1983) "Cross-Cultural Codes on Husband-Wife Relationships." *Ethnology* 22: 263–280.

Donner, Kai. (1926) *Among the Samoyed in Siberia.*

Elmendorf, W. W. (1960) *The Structure of Twana Culture.*

Elwin, Verrier. (1943) *Muria Murder and Suicide.*

———. (1947) *The Muria and Their Ghotul.*

Grigson, Wilfred. (1949) *The Maria Gond of Bastar.*

Mair, Lucy P. (1965) *An African People in the Twentieth Century.*

Mead, Margaret. (1930) *Growing Up in New Guinea: A Comparative Study of Primitive Education.*

Murdock, George Peter. (1934) *Our Primitive Contemporaries.*

Roscoe, John. (1911) *The Baganda: An Account of Their Native Customs and Beliefs.*

Stevenson, Matilda Cox. (1901–1902) *The Zuni Indians.* Twenty-third Annual Report of the Bureau of American Ethnology, Smithsonian Institute.

Whiting, John W. M. (1941) *Becoming a Kwoma: Teaching and Learning in a New Guinea Tribe.*

HYPERGAMY

Hypergamy refers to the practice of marrying a spouse whose social status is higher than one's own. In cultures where marriages do occur between individuals of unequal status, it is usually the woman who "marries up." Much less common is the case in which a husband will come from a social class that is considered to be lower than that of his wife. For instance, in Indonesia, a Balinese man may marry any woman who comes from a social caste equal or inferior to his own, but no man may ever marry a woman from a higher social caste. In the past, if a Balinese male of lower status had sexual relations with a woman of the royal or priestly castes, both parties were liable to be put to death. In all likelihood, the woman would be stabbed by one of her disgraced relatives and the man would be stuffed into a sack and thrown into the ocean. Similarly, while marriages among the Kazak of central Asia are usually confined to people of the same social and economic status, a well-off man may marry a girl who is poor but attractive, but no instance of a poor man who married a rich woman was remembered. A high-status New Zealand Maori girl who wishes to marry a man from a lower class is likely to be confined in a hut until she abandons the troublesome attachment. Among the Santal of India, kin groups are ranked by higher or lower social status. Girls avoid marrying boys who belong to groups regarded as inferior in status, but a girl from a less desirable group finds it less difficult to acquire a husband from a more prestigious group. This discrepancy is accounted for in part by the fact that wives become members of the kin groups of their husbands, so that the status of a married woman is determined by that of her husband. Therefore, a woman who married a man of inferior status would lose prestige, while a union between a lower-status female and a higher-status male would benefit the woman while having no effect on the social rank of the man.

Where marriages between lower-status men and higher-status women are accepted, it is hard for the prospective husband to acquire the means of obtaining such a wife. For instance, every south Asian Lakher man is highly motivated to raise his status by marrying a woman from a class higher than his own, but such wives are hard to find, and it can take years to accumulate the high bride price required for such a match.

The strong bias in favor of marriages in which the wife may be lower on the status hierarchy than the husband, but not vice versa, is consistent with what natural selection tells us about patterns of mate choice. Natural selection reminds us that human young have the best chance of surviving if two parents cooperate in child rearing. In the environment in which human psychological and behavioral characteristics evolved, the cooperation entailed a division of labor in which women gathered vegetables for the family and gave birth to, nursed, and otherwise tended infants and small children, while men provided meat and protection from enemies and predators. The complementary nature of these child-care roles highlights the importance of the health and nurturing skills of the woman and the "breadwinning" skills of the man. As societies become more complex, differences in wealth and status begin to act as distinguishing features of members of a community. Social class then becomes a good indicator of how successfully a prospective husband might provide for a wife and children. Status matters less, however, as a measure of a woman's potential as a mother. Thus, a woman and her family are motivated to find a husband whose status is as high as possible, as more privileged men are likely to make better providers. Men are willing to marry lower-status wives because a lower-status woman can make as good a wife and mother as one of higher status. Indeed, a man may use his own wealth and position as a bargaining chip in return for a beautiful bride. By contrast, a woman who "marries down" is committing herself and her children to life with a man who may be less well able to provide for his family than would a higher-status man who would have been willing to marry her. Thus, patterns of hypergamy may reflect cross-cultural regularities in people's assessments of what factors are likely to contribute to their success as a spouse and parent.

See also MARRIAGE PARTNERS, CRITERIA FOR CHOOSING; NATURAL SELECTION; REPRODUCTIVE STRATEGIES; SEXUAL SELECTION.

Best, Elsdon. (1924) *The Maori.*

Covarrubias, Miguel. (1937) *Island of Bali.*

Datta-Majumder, Nabendu. (1956) *The Santal: A Study in Culture Change.*

Hudson, Alfred E. (1938) *Kazak Social Structure.*

Parry, N. E. (1932) *The Lakhers.*

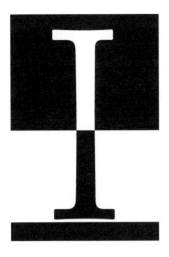

reported the result to a tribunal in charge of such matters. A husband may be granted up to 12 months to find a cure. If he fails, the two are divorced. A Lakher wife can also divorce her spouse for impotence, but the husband is first granted a grace period of perhaps a year during which he can offer sacrifices in an attempt to reverse his condition.

In some cultures, an impotent man has the option of becoming a transvestite. Among the Lango of Uganda, an impotent man may wear women's clothes, imitate menstruation, and become the wife of another man. The Lango believe that such men are under the power of the supernatural. They are not highly respected by other members of the community. Similarly, in Madagascar, an impotent Tanala man may become a *sarombavy*. Such men take on a female role and become another man's wife. They are accepted by their society and are said to display female characteristics from childhood.

The idea that impotence is a product of witchcraft is common across cultures in which men are susceptible to this condition. An Azande woman of Zaire whose solicitations are rebuffed may use witchcraft to render the man impotent. Sexual dysfunction is common among Azande men, who wear amulets in an attempt to insure potency. A Bedouin of the Middle East who wishes to render a man impotent can resort to witchcraft. This occurred in the case of a jealous wife who, with the help of a witch, caused her husband to be incapable of having sexual relations with his new spouse, who therefore left him, still a virgin. The witch can then reverse her magic, allowing the man to have intercourse with his original wife if the proper treatments are administered and payments made. Among the Amhara of Ethiopia, the *dabtara,* a church functionary, may be asked by a client to use magic to render a lover impotent with all other women.

Impotence is also attributed to other causes in other cultures. The Hausa of Nigeria believe

IMPOTENCE Because marriage is assumed to include sexual intimacy between spouses, societies are sensitive to the possibility that a man may not be able to perform sexually, a condition known as impotence. Some cultures actually insist that a new husband demonstrate his potency. In Kenya, Kikuyu brides must give evidence that their new husbands are able to have intercourse. If the groom proves to be impotent, the matter is taken to a council of the families of the couple and the marriage is annulled. Among some Turkish families, a woman observes through the keyhole while a couple are consummating their marriage in order to determine whether the groom can perform sexually. If he proves to be impotent, the bride's parents are immediately informed. Many societies also permit the termination of a marriage if the husband is sexually dysfunctional. In Suriname, impotence is common among Saramaka men beyond the age of 35 and is considered a sufficient reason for divorce. Among the Wolof of Senegal, a wife can divorce an impotent husband after the couple has spent a night together in a special room and that if mother's milk touches a male infant's genitals, he will become impotent later in life. According to the Gond of India, a man who has coitus with an insane woman will become impotent. In some societies, impotence is believed to be retribution for some unworthy action on the part of the afflicted man. The Fon of West Africa believe that any man who directly refuses a woman's marriage proposal, tries to divorce his wife, or denies paternity of a child, even though he knows himself to be the father, may be rendered impotent. A West African Bambara man, especially one who belongs to the Komo society, who has caused trouble for the society or one of its members may be made impotent by an official of the group. The victim must then collect a large number of grey lizards and have them sacrificed in his name to reverse the punishment. According to the Nyakyusa of Tanzania, a man who commits some misdeed will become paralyzed or impotent.

Dieterlen, Germaine. (1951) *An Essay on the Religion Bambara.*

Evans-Pritchard, Edward Evan. (1937) *Witchcraft, Oracles and Magic among the Azande.*

Ford, Clellan S., and Frank A. Beach. (1951) *Patterns of Sexual Behavior.*

Gamble, David P. (1957) *The Wolof of Senegambia, Together with Notes on the Lebu and the Serer.*

Grigson, Wilfred. (1949) *The Maria Gonds of Bastar.*

Herskovits, Melville. (1938) *Dahomey: An Ancient West African Kingdom.*

Kahn, Motron C. (1931) *Djuka: The Bush Negroes of Dutch Guiana.*

Kenyatta, Jomo. (1953) *Facing Mount Kenya: The Tribal Life of the Gikuyu.*

Makal, Mahmut. (1954) *A Village in Anatolia.*

Messing, Simon D. (1956) "Ethiopian Folktales Ascribed to the Late Nineteenth Century Amhara Wit." *Journal of American Folklore* 70: 69–72.

———. (1957) *The Highland-Plateau Amhara of Ethiopia.*

Murdock, George P. (1936) *Our Primitive Contemporaries.*

Parry, N. E. (1932) *The Lakhers.*

Raswan, Carl R. (1947) *Black Tents of Arabia.*

Smith, Mary F. (1954) *Baba of Karo: A Woman of the Muslim Hausa.*

Wilson, Godfrey. (1936) "An Introduction to Nyakyusa Society." *Bantu Studies* 10: 253–292.

INCEST TABOO The incest taboo refers to any cultural rule that prohibits some class of relatives from engaging in sexual relations. All known human societies have incest taboos forbidding sexual intercourse between parents and children and between brothers and sisters. In rare cases, people of special status are allowed to enter into intimate relationships with immediate kin. For example, the Azande of Zaire expect chiefs and their daughters to have sexual intercourse. Among the Thonga of Mozambique, a hunter is permitted to engage in sexual relations with his daughter before a hunt. And the royal Incas and ancient Egyptian and Hawaiian upper classes practiced brother-sister marriage. When unions of this sort are permitted, the goal is to preserve royal lineages or to keep wealth and property within a powerful family. However, where sexual license between members of the nuclear family exists, it is reserved for special cases and does not apply to the general populace.

Incest prohibitions also extend beyond the nuclear family in all societies, but cultures differ concerning which other relatives are covered by the extended taboo. A society may prohibit sexual intercourse with an aunt or uncle but allow relations between relatives who are more distantly connected. Usually, a greater range of kin relationships is covered by incest prohibitions, with many societies extending the taboo to at least one or more first cousins. Often, individuals who are not related but who refer to each other by kin terms may be prevented from becoming sexual partners. Neither is a society always consistent regarding who is and who is not covered by the extended taboo. Sexual relations may be prohibited with a mother's sister but not with a father's sister, or with some first cousins but not others. Or a taboo may apply to certain distant relatives but not to kin who are more closely related.

While all societies prohibit incest between some categories of relatives, the kinds and severity of punishment for violating the taboo differ from place to place. Offenders may be put to death, mutilated, made sterile, or banished from the community. Less severe forms of punishment include temporary disapproval or ostracism. Some cultures believe that any child produced from an incestuous relationship will be marked—by some kind of physical deformity, for instance. Children of such unions may even be put to death. In some societies, it is thought that an incestuous couple's entire kin group or community will be adversely affected—by crop failures or wholesale disease, for instance.

Social scientists have long wondered why societies prohibit sexual relations between at least some related individuals. Sigmund Freud's psychoanalytic theory tries to account for the incest taboo by constructing a story of its origins. Freud describes a hypothetical event in the lives of early human ancestors during which a group of brothers killed their father and engaged in sexual relations with their mother. To atone for the guilt they subsequently felt, the brothers erected the incest taboo and extended it to include an individual's entire kin group. The broth-

ers hoped that the taboo would protect subsequent generations from committing the same acts and suffering the same remorse that they had. The theme of incestuous longings for the mother on the part of the son reappears in Freud's theory of the Oedipal complex and its resolution. Freud proposes that, from roughly the ages of three to five years, the male child has a secret wish to take his father's place with his mother. But the fear that his father will castrate him as retribution for these feelings leads the boy to renounce his incestuous desires. Thus, the story of the ancestral brothers is replayed in the life history of every son. While often cited, Freud's theories of the incest taboo and Oedipal complex are not documented by archaeological or developmental evidence, nor does his origins theory account for the particular patterning of the extended incest taboo across cultures. The Freudian theory of the incest taboo is now viewed as unpersuasive.

The incest taboo has also been explained as a mechanism for maintaining harmony within the family. The taboo is said to prevent jealousy and conflict between kin and to protect the privacy and emotional well-being of family members. Where wives are viewed as the property of their spouses, the incest taboo is also proposed to deter men from the same family from fighting over ownership of women, as each man must look outside the family for a wife of his own. There are other postulated advantages to compelling men to seek wives outside the family. Where men marry women belonging to other kin groups, reciprocal bonds between different families can be formed. This is thought likely to reduce interfamily strife and to forge larger and stronger economic and political networks. These theories of the incest taboo are better able to account for variations in the patterning of the extended taboo across cultures. For instance, the patrilineal Tallensi of Ghana strongly condemn sexual relations with wives of the lineage men. In the matrilineal Ashanti, also of Ghana, it is sexual intimacy between brother and sister that is most strongly denounced. As it is the wives who perpetuate the lineage in patrilineal cultures and the sisters who do so in matrilineal societies, these patterns of prohibition are consistent with theories interpreting the incest taboo as a mechanism for protecting and strengthening the kin group.

Biologically-oriented theories of the incest taboo point to the deleterious genetic effects of inbreeding as the likely reason for the prohibition of sexual contact between relatives. Inbreeding is known to increase the likelihood of harmful recessive traits in offspring, including greater susceptibility to disease, slower growth, smaller size, reduced life span, and lowered fertility. Outbreeding leads to variation in the gene pool, which means that at least some of a parent's offspring may be able to survive in a variable environment. There is another advantage to outbreeding. If two relatives produce a child together, all of their genetic investment is in that one offspring. If the child dies, the entire genetic contribution to the gene pool that the two relatives have made for that mating is gone. However, if each of the same two relatives mates with a different person, their genetic investment will be divided between two offspring. If one child dies, some of the genes of the relative who has lost the child still remain in the survivor, as kin share genes with each other and, therefore, with each other's offspring. Thus, outbreeders avoid putting all of their genetic eggs in one basket.

Inbreeding is avoided in animals by a variety of methods. Among chimpanzees, young males will leave their home territory, and hence their kin, before they are sexually mature. By the time the males are old enough to mate, they are far away from their female kin and, therefore, cannot inbreed. Hamadryas baboon males capture young females from foreign groups; the females remain with their captors through adulthood, thus preventing mating between fathers and daughters. Male rhesus macaques seem to have a natural aversion to mating with their mothers. A mature male will mate with a female of the same age and status as his mother but will avoid copulation with the mother herself. A maturing female prairie dog will fail to come into estrus at the normal time if her father is around. These examples demonstrate that barriers to incest are sometimes a result of outside forces and sometimes a result of some mechanism within the animal.

The taboo itself is a deterrent to inbreeding in humans, but a number of mechanisms for inbreeding avoidance in human beings have been proposed that parallel those found in some animals. One theory claims that human beings have a natural aversion for mating with people to whom they are genetically related. The incest taboo is seen as a cultural reflection of this innately grounded sentiment. The childhood familiarity theory, by contrast, proposes that human beings are not sexually attracted to people with whom they have been raised. Therefore, once they are sexually mature, individuals will avoid sexual relations with any relatives who happen to have been a part of their childhood households. Taiwan marriage customs illustrate this avoidance. Among the Taiwanese, one form of marriage requires little girls to come to live in the households of their future husbands from a young age. Couples married in this way are less interested in each other sexually than are Taiwanese couples who have met and married in adulthood. They also have fewer children, higher divorce rates, and a greater likelihood of extramarital affairs.

Patterns of dating and marriage in Israeli kibbutzim tell a similar story. Here, peer groups are raised from birth in their own houses, away from their parents. Children in these groups form close attachments to each other, but when they reach adolescence, boys and girls raised in the same group show no romantic interest in each other, nor do they marry. There has been *no* report of a marriage between individuals who were raised from birth in the same peer group, despite the fact that adults encourage such marriages. The Taiwanese and kibbutz examples demonstrate that males and females who have been raised together may be psychologically inhibited from engaging in sexual relations. Since the people with whom a child is raised are usually his or her close kin, this familiarity effect results in avoidance of inbreeding. This suggests that human beings may have a natural inclination to respond to their social environments in just the right way for maximizing the likelihood of outbreeding. The tendency for adolescents to break away from their parents and insist on their autonomy is another example of a natural process that serves to distance kin from one another physically and/or emotionally and, therefore, to promote outbreeding.

The inbreeding hypothesis has been criticized for failing to explain the extended taboo. According to this argument, if incest prohibitions support the avoidance of inbreeding, then cultures should be uniform as to which relatives are targeted as sexually taboo and the taboo should be uniformly more severe for close kin and less severe for distant kin, but this is not the case. The inclusion of nonkin in the extended taboo is difficult to reconcile with inbreeding theory. Finally, it has been argued that the deleterious effects of inbreeding are impossible to detect, making it unlikely that a society would institute barriers to sexual relations between close kin. But evidence has suggested that variations in the extended taboo may be consistent with inbreeding theory after all. Variations in those targeted by the extended taboo have in some instances been found to be related to settlement patterns. For instance, marriage between first cousins is found in societies where the large population means that actual first cousin mating will be rare, while prohibitions against such marriages will occur where small populations would make them more likely. There is also evidence that the adverse effects of inbreeding show up with sufficient frequency to make their connection to mating between kin noticeable. The inbreeding theory of the incest taboo is supported by many kinds of data, but the incest taboo may also serve the functions proposed by other interpretations.

Bohannan, Paul, and John Middleton, eds. (1968) *Marriage, Family, and Residence.*

Durham, William H. (1991) *Coevolution, Genes, Culture, and Human Diversity.*

Ember, Melvin. (1975) "On the Origin and Extension of the Incest Taboo." *Behavior Science Research* 10: 249–281.

Ford, Clellan S., and Frank A. Beach. (1951) *Patterns of Sexual Behavior.*

Frayser, Suzanne G. (1985) *Varieties of Sexual Experience.*

Freud, Sigmund. (1950) *Totem and Taboo.* Originally published 1910.

Leavitt, Gregory C. (1989) "Disappearance of the Incest Taboo: A Cross-Cultural Test of General Evolutionary Hypotheses." *American Anthropologist* 91: 116–131.

Levinson, David, and Martin J. Malone. (1980) *Toward Explaining Human Culture.*

Murdock, George P. (1949) *Social Structure.*

Parker, Hilda, and Seymour Parker. (1986) "Father-Daughter Sexual Abuse: An Emerging Perspective." *American Journal of Orthopsychiatry* 56: 531–549.

Westermarck, Edward. (1922) *The History of Human Marriage.* Originally published 1897.

Wolf, Arthur P. (1994) *Sexual Attraction and Childhood Association: A Chinese Brief for Edward Westermarck.*

INTIMACY

See HUSBAND-WIFE RELATIONSHIPS.

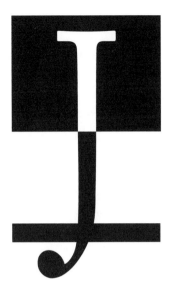

Jealousy between co-wives may focus on sexual envy. When a Suiai man sleeps with one co-wife, the other will pout for the entire following day. If he sleeps with the same wife two nights in a row, the other will not cook his meals the next day. "Since I am not good enough for you to sleep with," she might say, "then my food is not good enough for you to eat." She will send him to his other wife for his meals. However, sexual jealousy is not always the only, or even the major source of conflict between wives. Among the Aweikoma of Brazil, for example, sexual exclusivity is not valued, even within marriage. Nevertheless, a first wife may become jealous enough of a new co-wife that her chronic resentment toward the woman will drive her away, even if she has children. A senior wife will not herself leave because she is jealous of her husband's other spouse.

Sometimes one wife will envy the sexual attention another receives because of the further implications of sexual favoritism. Among the Siriono of South America there can be pronounced animosity between co-wives that stems from the fact that the wife with whom the husband sleeps most frequently also frequently receives the largest share of food. Therefore, women compete for the sexual attention of their spouse, and bitter confrontations can erupt from these rivalries. More generally, jealousy between co-wives is more pronounced in cultures where the welfare of a woman and her children is in the hands of the husband.

Aware of the potential disruption a new wife can bring to his household and the hurt feelings it can engender in the old spouse, a husband may try to present the arrival of a co-wife in the most favorable light possible. A Baiga man of India reminds his senior wife that she is the queen of his home, but notes that she has too many chores to do and needs help. If the household were to acquire another woman, the senior wife could wile away the time in the company of her friends while the junior wife saw to the housework. In

JEALOUSY BETWEEN CO-WIVES

According to a Hindu proverb, "A thousand moustaches can live together, but not four breasts." The saying alerts us to the potential conflicts between co-wives invited by the institution of polygyny. Jealousy and fighting between women who share a husband are common in cultures that permit polygyny. In Oceania, Siuai co-wives chronically battle with each other, and it is said that no polygynous family is tranquil. In one household with five co-wives, the quarreling was so pervasive and so disruptive that the family was unable to sleep at night. A husband in this society hesitates to interfere in his wives' battles for fear that one of the women will poison or practice witchcraft on him, and stories are told of wives who have murdered their husbands for favoring one wife or interfering in the women's disputes. The Siuai do not condemn this kind of destructive behavior in wives, as any man who takes more than one spouse is thought to be getting more or less what he deserves.

some cultures, men attempt to minimize the amount of conflict likely to exist between wives by marrying sisters. The frequent jealousy and rivalry that typically exists between Siriono co-wives is attenuated when a man weds two siblings.

Nevertheless, women in polygynous cultures often resist sharing their husbands. Among the Gusii of Kenya, a first wife will quarrel with a husband who wishes to marry another woman, and fighting among co-wives shows up frequently in Gusii folktales. The fact that Gusii husbands clearly favor new wives over old ones helps to explain the resistance that women show to polygyny. Co-wives compare such things as the material goods they receive from a shared husband, the number of children that each bears or loses, and the investment the father makes in each set of children, and the jealousy that chronically exists between Gusii co-wives is fueled by any imbalances. One woman may accuse another of witchcraft or attempted murder if some disaster, such as the illness of a child, befalls her.

In some societies, jealousy among polygynously married women is acted out according to specific cultural conventions. Among the Alor of Indonesia, this takes the form of a public quarrel between co-wives when a husband brings a new spouse into the household. In front of all of the other village women, the two wives hurl insults at each other, and the quarrel quickly escalates into a tugging, pulling, and hitting match in which both women have a number of allies recruited from the crowd of onlookers. The remaining women try to reconcile the wives but also get in some fighting of their own, so that all of the females in the community end up tussling on the ground for several hours while the men watch. This ritualized battle occurs even when a senior wife has coaxed her husband into acquiring a new wife. So does a Baiga woman cause a commotion when her husband marries a new wife, even if she approves of the match. At the ceremony, the senior wife laments that her spouse no longer loves her and will beat and starve her once the new woman is established in her household. All of the presents that her husband has bestowed upon his new wife already indicate his preference for her. The senior wife's friends then attempt to comfort and reason with her. The new wife will be a help around the household, and there is nothing that can be done about the situation; the woman is here to stay, so there is no point in being upset. The senior wife eventually allows her anger to dissipate. If her husband also brings her gifts, her feelings toward her new co-wife will soften even if she is genuinely jealous.

The depth of jealousy among co-wives will vary in a given society depending upon the temperament of the women themselves and the efforts made by the husband to smooth things over between his spouses. Thus, for example, while bitter dissention among co-wives is common among the Gusii, some polygynous women get along well. Sometimes this is because the husband has managed to create a good family climate and sometimes it is because the junior wife is inclined to be submissive to the older and more senior woman. Among the Murngin of Australia, polygynously married women often get along well, but some women remain jealous. When the husband of three co-wives wished to sleep with one of his more senior spouses, the youngest one would remain awake all night to keep an eye on the man, thus preventing him from going to the other woman. The two older wives, by contrast, lived together peaceably.

While dissention between co-wives is the cross-cultural norm, women in some societies find that it can be an advantage to have another wife in the household. Tanala women of Madagascar, for instance, band together with their co-wives to pressure a reluctant husband to do their bidding.

See also JEALOUSY BETWEEN MALES AND FE-
MALES.

Henry, Jules. (1941) *The Jungle People: A Kaingang Tribe of the Highlands of Brazil.*

Holmberg, Allan R. (1950) *Nomads of the Long Bow: The Siriono of Eastern Bolivia.*

Levinson, David. (1989) *Family Violence in Cross-Cultural Perspective.*

Levinson, David, and Martin J. Malone. (1980) *Toward Explaining Human Culture.*

Stephens, William N. (1963) *The Family in Cross-Cultural Perspective.*

JEALOUSY BETWEEN MALES AND FEMALES

Someone who displays envy and resentment toward a real rival or fear and suspicion of an imaginary or potential one is said to be jealous. Jealousy is associated with all kinds of human relationships, including those between males and females. Descriptions of jealousy as played out across cultures concentrate on the marital bond. From these portraits, we can conclude that concern on the part of one spouse about the loyalty of the other is very common the world over. Moreover, jealousy between married partners consistently focuses on sexual exclusivity. The jealous spouse wishes to be the only sexual interest in the life of the partner. This emphasis invites the speculation that human beings are especially sensitive to sexual betrayal and that the deepest passions between men and women are inseparable from sexual attraction and feelings of desirability.

Jealousy between married partners often provokes a violent physical response on the part of the injured party. The aggression can be directed at the offending spouse or at the intruder. The Nkundo of Zaire illustrate this kind of reaction. A husband whose wife has been unfaithful may beat and even kill her. If he catches her in the act, he may torture her. For her part, a jealous wife may verbally abuse her husband. She might also withhold food, drink, and sexual access and set fire to the dwelling in which her husband was unfaithful. A betrayed wife may also vent her anger on her husband's lover by physically injuring the woman. Nor will anyone blame her for her actions. In Oceania, the Marshallese wife will also attack her rival, and there is one reported case of a woman who tore a piece out of the cheek of her husband's lover. A Mataco husband in Argentina can beat a wife who has been unfaithful, and in former times he might have killed both his wife and her lover as revenge for their betrayal of him. A Mataco wife never cuts her fingernails, which may come in handy should another woman seduce her husband. A Tikopian wife in Oceania is likely to remain awake all night waiting for an errant husband. When he finally arrives home toward morning, hoping that she is asleep, he is greeted by blows to the back and legs with a stick and pinches that break skin. Affairs between married men and unmarried girls are accepted by the Tikopia, but the behavior of husbands is moderated by the jealousy of wives.

Sometimes, a jealous spouse will seek a divorce. Among the Chiricahua of the American Southwest, jealousy and the chronic bickering that it evokes are the underlying cause of divorces. Sometimes jealous spouses will communicate the depth of the emotional injury done to them by self-destructive behavior. For instance, Navajo husbands in Arizona will sometimes carry huge rocks, thus overexerting themselves and prompting people to say that he caused himself harm because he wished to die. Jealousy and quarrels between spouses are often given as the reason for suicides.

Jealousy can sometimes lead a spouse to be obsessively concerned with the fidelity of a partner. Some Goajiro husbands in Colombia are chronically jealous and suspicious of their wives' activities. Such a man may be driven to set traps or spy on all of his wife's activities in an attempt to determine the identity of a suspected lover. Among the Lozi of Zambia, a man who so much as walks with another man's wife or gives her some beer or snuff has committed adultery. As a result, men worry about helping their brothers' wives with gardening or other work for fear of being accused of sleeping with their sisters-in-law.

In some cultures, extramarital affairs are sanctioned and feelings of possessiveness between spouses are frowned upon. But cultural norms do not always coincide with individual emotions, and jealousy can get the best of a forsaken husband or wife in spite of formal disapproval of jealous feelings. The Paiute of the southwestern United States think that a husband should not depend too much on his wife, nor should he make a fuss if she leaves him for some other man. In reality, Paiute husbands whose wives are unfaithful may beat the offending spouse and fight with, and even kill, her lover. A case is reported of a husband and his wife's lover who dragged each other off their horses, tore off each other's clothes and jewelry, and pulled on each other's braids. Similarly, a wife may attack some other woman who has philandered with her husband. Mounds of hair were left on the ground after one jealous wife had picked a fight with a woman who had slept with her husband. Another wife tackled her husband's lover, fought her to the ground, banged her head against the floor, and hit her in the eyes. The Tallensi husband of Ghana is theoretically allowed to carry on affairs outside of his marriage,

but he does so only with great discretion for fear of incurring his wife's wrath. The Lepcha of Tibet are said to keep sex and emotion separate, and jealousy is not a prominent feature of their relationships, but blatant reminders of a wife's infidelity arouse the resentment of a Lepcha husband. A man who witnesses his brother and wife engaging in sex will object, saying something like, "Look here, you should not do that sort of thing with my wife while I'm about, and certainly not in my presence."

There are societies where most people are reported to experience little sexual jealousy. Among the Masai of Kenya, all men and women of a given age-set are permitted sexual access to each other. Masai husbands are said to be indifferent to the sexual activities of their wives, and any man who is the biological father of a wife's child is considered to be a special friend of the husband. The Sherpa of Nepal are said to devalue sexual exclusivity and will share a wife with a brother or a husband with a co-wife without signs of jealousy.

While there are many vivid examples of the aftermath of wifely jealousy across cultures, on the whole men tend to react more angrily and are more violently jealous than women. A Burmese man whose wife is unfaithful will probably exhibit great anger, beat her, and end the marriage. Cross-culturally, it appears that men react most strongly to suspected or actual affairs by their wives in cultures where marriage is considered very important, where sexual gratification is confined mainly to marriage, and where personal property is valued. A Burmese wife, by contrast, may show that she is upset if her husband has an affair, but her response will be far less extreme than that of a husband. Among the Ifugao of the Philippines, extramarital affairs are punishable by an equivalent fine for either husbands or wives, but in fact women are much more likely to pay the penalty for adultery than are men because husbands are more jealous than are wives. Ifugao women are willing to overlook the infidelities of their spouses as long as a husband is discreet. Wives may say to their spouses, "It would be all right for you to have a mistress if you could only do so without my hearing of it." Ifugao wives, on the other hand, are usually punished by their husbands for any infidelities, and are frequently divorced.

The difference in degree to which wives versus husbands will tolerate infidelity is consistent with biological facts and the evolutionary perspective. Women always know that the children they bear are their own. A man, by contrast, can never be sure that his wife's children are his biological offspring.

The evolutionary perspective reminds us that any human being or other animal tends to behave in ways that are likely to mean that the individual will leave a maximum number of surviving children. This is because individuals who have fewer of their own offspring will have a smaller proportion of their own genes represented in future generations. This means that their own genetically mediated traits will tend to die out. This will include whatever genes underlie their tendency not to have as many offspring as other individuals of their species. Because males can end up raising the offspring of another man if their wives are unfaithful, men are predicted to be more concerned about the sexual exclusivity of their spouses than are women. The display of jealousy across cultures indicates that this may, indeed, be the case.

See also CUCKOLDRY; JEALOUSY BETWEEN CO-WIVES; NATURAL SELECTION; REPRODUCTIVE STRATEGIES; SEXUAL SELECTION.

Barton, R. F. (1919) *Ifugao Law.*

Brant, Charles. (1954) *Tagdale: A Burmese Village in 1950.*

Daly, Margo, M. Wilson, and S. J. Weghorst. (1982) "Male Sexual Jealousy." *Ethology and Sociobiology* 3: 11–27.

Erdland, August. (1914) *The Marshall Islanders: Life and Customs, Thought and Religion of the South Seas People.*

Firth, Raymond. (1936) *We, the Tikopia: A Sociological Study of Kinship in Primitive Polynesia.*

Fock, Niels. (1963) "Mataco Marriage." *Folk* 5: 91–101.

Fortes, Meyer. (1945) *The Dynamics of Clanship among the Tallensi: Being the First Part of an Analysis of the Social Structure of a Trans-Volta Tribe.*

Fortes, Meyer. (1949) *The Web of Kinship among the Tallensi: The Second Part of an Analysis of the Social Structure of a Trans-Volta Tribe.*

Fürer-Haimendorf, Christoph von. (1948) "The Raj Gonds of Adilabad." In *The Raj Gonds of Adilabad,* 1–21.

Gluckman, Max. (1959) "Lozi of Brotseland in North-Western Rhodesia." In *Seven Tribes of British Central Africa,* edited by Elizabeth Colson and Max Gluckman.

Gutierrez de Pineda, Virginia. (1950) *Social Organization in La Guajira.*

Hulsaert, Gustave. (1928) *Marriage among the Nkundu.*

Hupka, Ralph B., and James M. Ryan. (1990) "The Cultural Contribution to Jealousy: Cross-Cultural Aggression in Sexual Jealousy Situations." *Behavior Science Research* 24: 51–72.

Leighton, Dorthea Cross, and Clyde Kluckhohn. (1947) *Children of the People: The Navaho Individual and His Development.*

Morris, John. (1938) *Living with Lepchas: A Book about the Sikkim Himalayas.*

Opler, Morris E. (1941) *An Apache Life-Way:*

The Economic, Social and Religious Institutions of the Chiricahua Indians.

Whiting, Beatrice B. (1950) *Paiute Sorcery.* Viking Ford Publications in Anthropology 15.

JOKING RELATIONSHIPS

Joking relationships are found in many cultures around the world and affect the nature of interaction between specified classes of people. Individuals who stand in a joking relationship with respect to one another are expected to exhibit particular kinds of verbal and physical behavior toward each other, including teasing, belittling, sexual innuendo, obscenity, touching, pushing, and so on. For example, when a Mundugumor of New Guinea encounters his father's sister during the course of the day, he slaps her on her back, comments that she is getting old and will in all likelihood soon be dead, and remarks on the ugliness of her nose ornament. He may also try to steal some areca-nut from her basket. A man will treat any women classified as his father's sisters in the same way. A Tarahumara man of Mexico tells lewd jokes to his brother's wife and tries to lift her skirt or pull off her clothes and touch her genitals. Among the North American Saulteaux, joking is not only allowed between cross-cousins of the opposite sex, it is required. As cross-cousins are bound to encounter each other every day in every camp, lewd interchanges are frequent at any social event. Each of these vignettes is an instance of a joking relationship in action. In cultures where they exist, joking relationships seem paradoxical because they are defined by the display of informal and even disrespectful behavior, but the expression of this behavior is mandatory. Thus, two people who have a joking relationship and who therefore insult each other, pinch each other's genitals, or physically abuse one another are exhibiting proper behavior and would, indeed, be out of order if they did not treat one another in this manner. By contrast, the same behavior directed toward someone with whom an individual does not enjoy a joking relationship is viewed by the culture as utterly inappropriate.

Joking relationships almost always target people who are related to each other by blood or marriage. Cross-cousins are very often singled out as people who are required to joke with each other. Manus cross-cousins in Oceania enjoy a familiar, playful relationship. A male can make sexual allusions to female cross-cousins that he cannot direct at his own wife and he can engage in innocent sex play with her, pulling her hair and touching her breasts. This free and easy interaction remains characteristic of cross-cousins for life, so that a middle-aged man will still tease and rough up his elderly, widowed cross-cousin.

Joking relationships also exist between many other kinds of relatives. In Arizona, a Navajo grandfather and grandson have a joking relationship. A grandfather can steal his grandson's clothes while the boy is in the sweathouse. Similarly, the boy puts pieces of cactus in his grandfather's moccasins. Among the Hopi of the southwestern United States, a man can sexually tease any male who calls him grandfather, and old men may be seen grabbing the penises of younger males and threatening to cut them off. As a boy grows older, he in turn can beat up the older man, roll him in the snow, throw him in a puddle, and threaten to sleep with his wife. Joking relationships also exist between nieces or nephews and their aunts or uncles. For example, if a Kiribati child asks his father's sister's husband for tobacco and is turned down, the youngster may knock the older man down and kick and hit him with impunity. The same kind of behavior is not permissible in the context of other relationships.

While joking relationships are predominantly confined to people who are related, joking can also be mandated between individuals who are not kin. Among the Chagga of Tanzania, the nature of the relationship between members of the opposite sex is determined in part by their relative ages. Young men from one age-grade will not allow girls of their own groups to be approached by boys from a younger age-grade, but a boy enjoys a joking relationship with girls in his own group.

In societies where patterned joking occurs, many different kinds of relationships may be characterized by joking. For instance, the Fon of West Africa require joking behavior between a variety of classes of individuals. A Fon woman may joke with any of her husband's brothers, one of whom she will marry if her spouse dies. Sisters-in-law also have a joking relationship. A Fon mother-in-law may joke with her son's wife, along with the wife's mother and grandmother, who also supervise the sexual activities of the couple when they are newly married. So does a son-in-law have a joking relationship with his wife's mother and grandmother. A daughter-in-law also jokes with her husband's father because he receives the cloth on which the couple consummated their marriage.

Joking relationships frequently occur between people who are potential marriage partners. Among the Navajo, individuals who are cross-cousins are permitted special license in their discussions of sexual matters, and conversations between men and women who are cross-cousins almost compulsively focus on sex. Similarly, Marshallese cross-cousins in Oceania are encouraged to marry, and sexual joking between them is taken as a matter of course. But the children of cross-cousins, who are viewed as classificatory sibs, are prohibited from joking about sex. The Lugbara of Uganda dramatize this connection between joking and the possibility of marriage between joking partners. A joking relationship is mandatory between a Lugbara man and his mother's brother as well as his mother's brother's wife. The latter is called

o'da, which, besides being a kin term, means "to joke." Joking partners are required to direct obscene, usually sexual, insults at one another when they meet. A man who does not joke sexually with his *o'da* will develop scabies as a punishment for failing to behave correctly toward his kin. The joking relationship between a man and his *o'da* is explained by the fact that, had he been born into his mother's lineage, he might have inherited his *o'da* as a wife. While joking relationships often occur between potential spouses, the opposite is sometimes also true. A Fon man may inherit his father's wives, but is explicitly prohibited from joking with them.

The connection between joking and the possibility of marriage between joking partners highlights the connection in many cultures between patterned, mandatory joking behavior and sex. Where sexual relations are potentially permissible between two people, joking between them is also often demanded. Conversely, where sexual relations between two individuals are prohibited, so is joking in some cultures. Thus, Fon girls are permitted to joke with their mothers, but a daughter does not joke with her father and boys may not refer to sexual matters with either parent because "talk of these things is insulting; children must not discuss what gave them their birth." And joking with a wife's father would "inform the father of what that man has done to his daughter." Therefore, it is forbidden.

Joking relationships tend to occur in societies that also require certain classes of individuals to avoid one another. Among the Fon, who have many kinds of joking relationships, a girl is not allowed to joke with her mother's sisters because they are the primary disciplinarians. When a daughter wishes to have a conversation about intimate matters with her mother, she will first say to her aunt: "Do not listen to the words I am going to say." It is also possible that joking helps to foster cooperation between individuals who are required to work in harmony but between whom conflict is likely.

Hallowell, A. Irving. (1955) *Culture and Experience.*

Herskovits, Melville J. (1938) *Dahomey: An Ancient West African Kingdom,* vol. 1.

Leighton, Dorothea, and Clyde Kluckhohn. (1969) *Children of the People: The Navaho Individual and His People.*

Levinson, David, and Martin J. Malone. (1980) *Toward Explaining Human Culture.*

Mead, Margaret. (1930) *Growing Up in New Guinea: A Comparative Study of Primitive Education.*

Middleton, John. (1965) *The Lugbara of Uganda.*

Raum, O. F. (1940) *Chaga Childhood: A Description of Indigenous Education in an East African Tribe.*

Serpenti, I. M. (1965) *Cultivators in the Swamps.*

Spoehr, Alexander. (1949) *Majuro: A Village in the Marshall Islands.*

Stephens, William N. (1963) *The Family in Cross-Cultural Perspective.*

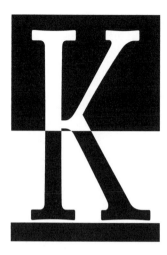

While the most obvious way of passing on genetically grounded traits is through the production of offspring, this is not the only way. It was biologist W. D. Hamilton who recognized that an organism could also contribute to the proliferation of its own genes by promoting the survival and reproduction of other organisms with whom it shares genes in common. Individuals share genes in common with relatives, or kin. Thus, Hamilton proposed that traits in human beings and other species that have been selected for incline them to help kin to survive and reproduce. This selection of traits that promote the well-being of kin is called kin selection. Acts that have the goal of helping relatives are examples of hard-core altruism. The joint insights of Darwin and Hamilton converge into what is known as neo-Darwinism.

Hamilton made another prediction about helping kin. In particular, he proposed that an individual is more or less likely to help a relative in direct proportion to the degree to which he shares genes with that relative. The sharing of genes is measured by a ratio called the coefficient of relatedness. Coefficients of relatedness compute the average degree of relatedness between kinds of relatives. Thus, for example, siblings share half of their genes in common and are thus related to each by $r = 1/2$. A child is related to a parent's sibling by an average of $r = 1/4$, and cousins are related to each other by an average of $r = 1/8$. Other kin relationships are described by other coefficients of relatedness. Thus, according to Hamilton's prediction, an organism is twice as likely to help a sibling as an aunt and four times as likely to help a sibling as a cousin. We can also compute the degree of relatedness of an organism to itself. Since any organism shares all of its own genes with itself, an organism is related to itself by $r = 1$. It may seem odd to be computing degrees of relatedness between an organism and itself, but the computation is important for kin selection theory.

KIN SELECTION   According to Darwin's theory of evolution by natural selection, members of a species are characterized by a particular set of traits today because these traits proved to be adaptive to the ancestors of these individuals in the past. In Darwinian terms, a trait is adaptive if it has either promoted the survival of the organism or if it has permitted the organism to reproduce. Darwin's theory is based upon the assumption that all traits have genetic grounding, although the genetic basis of most human behavior is highly complex and as yet not fully understood. An organism with traits that advance survival lives long enough to reproduce. If the same organism is also endowed with characteristics that result in reproduction, then these very traits are passed along to the organism's offspring. Traits that promote survival and reproduction and that are, therefore, advantageous to an individual, are said to be selected for. Traits that decrease the chances of survival or reproduction are disadvantageous to the individual and are said to be selected against. The process of selecting for and against traits is called natural selection.

Hamilton also predicted that an individual will only help a relative if the act of helping ultimately nets the helper an increase in the proportion of his or her genes that will be represented in the gene pool. How can the likelihood of such a net increase be calculated? The calculation takes a number of things into account. First, we need to know what the act of helping actually costs the helper. Costs refer to any decrease in a helper's reproductive success to which an act of helping contributes. We also need to determine how much the act of helping benefits the recipient. Benefits refer to an increase in a recipient's reproductive success to which a helper's behavior contributes. Finally, degrees of relatedness of the helper to self and to the recipient matter to the calculation. Let us take the most extreme case. I am placed in the position of being able to save the life of some relatives who are drowning in a leaky boat. However, I will lose my own life in the effort. The cost here will be all of my own genes that I share with myself. Since this is the ultimate sacrifice, we can measure the cost by allocating it a value of 1. If I succeed in saving my relative, then the benefit to him or her will be the ultimate benefit, so we can measure the benefit to my relative by also allocating it a value of 1. These benefits and costs would change if my relatives and I were to have any offspring in the future, so to keep calculations simple, let us assume that no one is having any more children. We also need to take into account the degree of relatedness of the helper and benefactor to the helper. This, it will be remembered, is represented in the coefficient of relatedness. I am related to my self by a coefficient of $r = 1$. Suppose that the drowning relative is my brother. I am related to him by a coefficient of $r = 1/2$. Will the act of saving my brother net me an increase in the representation of my genes in the gene pool? This is determined by multiplying the cost of help to me by the degree of my relatedness to myself and comparing it to the benefit of my help to my brother multi-

plied by the degree of my relatedness to him. The calculation is as follows:

Cost to me: $(1)(1) = 1$

Benefit to my brother: $(1)(1/2) = 1/2$

Compare cost to me of 1 to benefit to my brother of 1/2

If I save my brother, it will cost me twice what it will benefit him. So I should not try to save my brother.

What if a number of my relatives were drowning? Perhaps my brother and my three aunts have all gone out sailing. Now, the calculation is as follows:

Cost to me: $(1)(1) = 1$

Benefit to my brother: $(1)(1/2) = 1/2$

Benefit to my first aunt: $(1)(1/4) = 1/4$

Benefit to my second aunt: $(1)(1/4) = 1/4$

Benefit to my third aunt: $(1)(1/4) = 1/4$

Add all benefits to my relatives: $1/2 + 1/4 + 1/4 + 1/4 = 1\ 1/4$

Compare cost to me of 1 to benefit to my relatives of 1 1/4.

The cost to me of saving my brother and aunts is less than the accumulated benefits that they derive, so I should try to save my kin. Note that these calculations talk about comparing the costs to me of performing an act to the benefits accruing to the *recipient* of the help. But the benefits received by my relative are ultimately benefits accruing to me, because they represent the genes that my relatives and I share that will be preserved in the gene pool by my helping those relatives. Their gain is my gain from an evolutionary point of view. Thus, hard-core altruism is not really altruism at all, as helping will only occur when there is no sacrifice on the part of the helper in the long run. In fact, the helper will benefit in this case.

Ordinarily, the situations that invite an individual to help relatives are not so extreme. Life and death do not usually hinge on our decisions to help or not to help, but the calculations are, in principle, the same even when a person is only asked to share some food or pitch in on some task to aid a related individual. Suppose that my brother asks me to help him fix his roof. Say that the cost to me of doing so is X but, from my brother's perspective, the benefit is 3X. Thus, my cost is $(X)(1) = 1X$ and my brother's benefit is $(3X)(1/2) = 1.5X$. My brother benefits more than I sacrifice. Thus, I should help my brother. Notice that, in this example, when I do my relative a favor, the same act costs me less than it benefits him. It is this discrepancy between cost to the helper and benefit to the recipient of the very same act that explains why helping can happen as often as it does. This difference is what compensates for the fact that one is more related to oneself than to anyone else (except for the case of identical twins).

If organisms are endowed with traits that incline them to help kin, how do individuals know how to identify kin? And how does an individual know his or her degree of relatedness to a particular relative? In the case of human beings, we are told who our relatives are. But members of other species that do not have this easy access to knowledge about kinship also help their relatives, so there must be other sorts of indicators of relatedness that allow organisms to recognize their kin. And indeed, there are such nonlinguistic cues. Some organisms are able to tell that another individual is a relative because of certain auditory, visual, or odor cues. Or, in species where relatives are found in close physical proximity while nonrelatives live further away, an organism may simply help other organisms with whom it has grown up. Some species also distinguish between kin and nonkin based upon degrees of physical resemblance. This works because relatives tend to be more alike physically than are nonkin. And while human beings know

their relatives because they are provided with linguistic information, there is also considerable evidence that in our own species, many of these other cues are also available. Thus, a newborn human infant is able to recognize and display a preference for its mother's voice within three days of birth. An infant also soon knows the characteristic odor of its mother. And by four days of age, a baby recognizes and shows a preference for its mother's face. Similarly, mothers are very good at recognizing the cries and odors of their own babies. Family resemblance is also typical of the human species. Evidence demonstrates that strangers can match up mothers and their newborn babies on the basis of both visual facial resemblance and similarity of odor. Finally, children appear to learn that the people with whom they are raised should be treated differently from other people, even in the absence of any direct information from those around them. For instance, children of the opposite sex who are reared together are unlikely to become romantically involved even if they are not actually related to each other. It is as if there is an unlearned aversion to sexual impulses directed at people who are likely to be related. Once an organism has access to cues that distinguish between kin and nonkin, the same information can then be used to assess degree of relatedness. Thus, for example, strong physical resemblance can be taken to indicate that two individuals are closely related, while only moderate physical resemblance can be interpreted as reflecting only modest relatedness.

Kin selection theory proposes that across species organisms will, given the right cost-benefit consequences, help their relatives. Observations of the human interactions across cultures confirm this prediction for the human species. In many societies around the world, the kin group is the basic functional unit. People depend upon relatives instead of nonrelatives for their domestic, religious, economic, and political well-being. When people share resources or pitch in on a task or project, they preferentially do so with kin. When a person dies, it is kin who inherit what property is left behind. The human partiality toward kin is captured in the phrase, "Blood is thicker than water." Human beings and other animals also help nonkin. This is called soft-core altruism. This kind of helping has also been shown to benefit the helper ultimately. Thus, individuals are most likely to help nonrelated individuals who will help them in return at a later date.

Hamilton's theory of kin selection promotes an understanding of why it is that organisms, including human beings, are inclined to help kin. The theory also clears up some confusion about the workings of natural selection more generally. A common misconception about natural selection is that it works on an entire species. In this view, particular traits have been selected for because they have helped the species to survive. For instance, the common trait of warning other animals when a predator is near is explained in this way. Why do warning signals invite an explanation that focuses on what is good for the species? Animals give warning calls when something dangerous is occurring in their vicinity. Most characteristically, an animal gives an alarm call when a predator is nearby. Since warning signals of this sort attract attention to the caller, the behavior looks as if it is threatening the survival of the animal who is giving the warning. On the other hand, other animals who understand the significance of the call are helped because they can evade the predator. Thus, warning calls are viewed as having been selected for because they are good for the species, although harmful for the individual who exhibits the trait. Although this reasoning is very persuasive to many people, logic tells us that it must be wrong. Imagine two animals from the same species. One gives alarm calls when a predator is nearby and the other does not. Clearly, the animal who is most likely to survive and reproduce is the one who does not give calls. This means that alarm

calling will soon disappear from the repertoire of this species. By extension, any trait that is disadvantageous to an animal who manifests it but helpful to those who do not will soon die out entirely. How, then, do we explain alarm calling? An animal who gives a warning call is indeed likely to place itself at some risk. But evidence shows that the animal is also helping other organisms to whom it is related. This will include its offspring and also its relatives. For instance, certain squirrels will give warning calls when a predator appears and relatives are around but will not do so when there are no relatives in close proximity; further, the higher the density of relatives nearby, the more likely the squirrel is to call. This means that the animal, while it may be putting its own survival at risk, is helping its genes to be replicated in succeeding generations, including the genes that underwrite the tendency to give warning calls. The genes just happen to be in other animals.

See also ALTRUISM; NATURAL SELECTION.

Porter, Richard H. (1987) "Kin Recognition: Functions and Mediating Mechanisms." In *Sociobiology and Psychology,* edited by Charles Crawford, Martin Smith, and Dennis Krebs, 175–204.

Trivers, Robert L. (1985) *Social Evolution.*

Wolf, Arthur P. (1970) "Childhood Association and Sexual Attraction: A Further Test of the Westmarck Hypothesis." *American Anthropologist* 72: 503–515.

KINSHIP In all human cultures, people are connected to other people by blood or by marriage. Indeed, if we trace out these relationships for a single individual, we are soon entangled in a complex and enormous network of links from person to person. In places where people make a career of tracking these connections, everyone in an entire small society can claim some relationship to everyone else. In Oceania for instance, every Tikopian is able to specify a relationship of blood or marriage to every other Tikopian in a community of more than 1,200 people. The Tikopians say that "the whole land is a single body of kinsfolk." Relationships defined by blood or by marriage are objective facts of life. The recognition, interpretation, and exploitation of these relationships by cultures transform connections by blood and marriage into connections of kinship. Kinship refers to the social translation of genetically and sexually grounded relationships. Cultures cannot and do not recognize all genealogical relationships as kinship relations. All people have innumerable genealogical relatives of whom they are ignorant, and many individuals know of relatives who, nevertheless, play no role in their lives. Genealogical relationships that have no social significance, either because the individuals to whom they refer are unknown or because they are known but ignored, are not kinship relationships. Genealogical ties of which people customarily take notice are what constitute an individual's kin.

The web of relationships formed by connections of blood and marriage make up a person's kin network. Blood relationships are more formally known as consanguineal relationships, while relationships formed as a result of marriage are affinal relationships. Thus, a female is related consanguineally to her mother, daughter, and son, while she is related affinally to her husband. Affines also include all of a spouse's own biological relationships. Thus, a man's sister is an affinal relation of his wife. Finally, the spouses of a person's own consanguineal relatives are his or her affines. For instance, while one's father's sister is one's consanguineal relation, one's father's sister's husband, who is not related to one by blood, is one's affine. Genealogies describe the consanguineal and affinal relationships of individuals. It is possible to distinguish between consanguineal versus affinal relationships by inspecting a person's genealogy. Genealogies graphically depict networks of relationships between individuals. Males and females are distinguished by means of different symbols. On the genealogy in Figure 1, males are depicted by triangles and females by circles. A marital-sexual relationship between two people is signified by an equals sign (=) connecting the partners. Vertical lines from an equals sign indicate the children of a couple. Horizontal lines indicate sibling relationships. Thus, in Figure 1, 1 and 2 are husband and wife. They have a son, 4, and a daughter, 5, who are siblings to each other. When anthropologists attempt to describe a set of relationships from the point of view of a particular individual, they designate the target person as "ego." In Figure 1, "ego" is 4. The genealogy in Figure 1 depicts a number of kinds of relationships between ego and other individuals represented in the genealogy. Thus, for example, ego, or 4, is related consanguineally to 1, 2, 5, 8, 10, 12, 14, 15, 16, 17, 18, 19, 20, 21, and 22 and affinally to 3, 6, 7, 9, 11, and 13.

Genealogies can also be viewed as a set of connections that are established by the fact that people generally claim membership in two kinds of families. That is, most people the world over eventually belong to a family of orientation and a family of procreation. The family of orientation, or natal family, is the group into which a person is born, so that any individual is a son or daughter in a family of orientation. By contrast, the family of procreation is the family that a person creates by marrying and having children. Thus, an individual is either a husband and father or a wife and mother in his or her family of procreation. A spouse, however, is also a member of a family of orientation, and people in that family are members of both families of orientation and families of procreation. In short, if we trace the relationships on a genealogy, we will

GENEALOGICAL RELATIONSHIPS

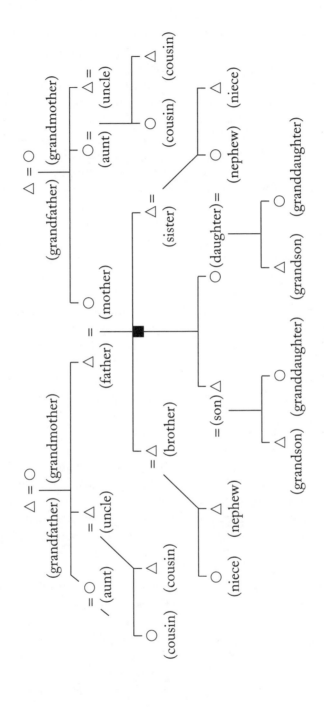

KEY TO SYMBOLS

△ Male   = Marriage
○ Female   - Descent
■ Ego   ⊓ Siblingship

see that the web of connections between and among individuals is produced by chains of consanguineal and affinal connections between many families, each of which is a family of orientation for some of its members and a family of procreation for others.

Consanguineal relationships may be of two kinds. Lineal relationships are blood connections that are exclusively vertical. By contrast, collateral relationships are horizontal blood relationships. It is possible to determine whether a connection between two individuals is lineal or collateral by tracing their relationship on a genealogy (see chart on facing page). If the chain of links between the two people contains no marriage symbol (=) but does contain a horizontal line, then the two are related collaterally. If the chain of links contains neither a marriage symbol nor a horizontal line but does contain at least one vertical line, then the relationship is lineal. Lineal relationships exist between people for whom the connections are only ones of "begetting" or "bearing," that is, if procreative links are the only links between them. Summarizing the variety of ways in which genealogical relationships are described, a female is both an affinal and a consanguineal relation. She is an affinal to her husband and his consanguines and to the spouses of any of her own consanguines. She is a consanguineal relation to her blood relatives. Some of these consanguineal relations are lineal and some are collateral. For instance, she is a lineal relation to her mother and her own daughter and a collateral relation to her brothers and sisters.

Kinship translates genealogical relationships into socially meaningful relationships. Central to this translation is the cultural assignment of behavioral expectations to certain categories of kin. In a number of cultures, particular classes of kin are required to avoid each other. For example, a Kiowa-Apache husband in the west-central United States cannot touch his mother-in-law, talk to her, look at her, say her name or remain alone with her in a tipi. The wife's mother avoids her son-in-law in the same way. In some cultures, particular categories of kin are expected to treat each other with a degree of formality or respect. Among the Fox of Iowa, a husband and his mother-in-law or a wife and her father-in-law are especially restrained in each other's presence. They will only address one another on matters of business. It does not occur to them to simply pass the time with each other in idle chatter. Sometimes, specific relatives are required to joke with each other, and often this joking is expected to be sexual. Among the Tarahumara of Mexico, a brother tells his sister-in-law obscene jokes, roughhouses with her, tries to pull off her clothes and touch her genitals, and so on. None of this behavior is generally approved, not even between spouses. Patterned kin behavior displays regularity across cultures. Thus, the relationship between a daughter's husband and wife's mother is overwhelmingly characterized by avoidance or respect, as is the relationship between a son's wife and a husband's father. Joking is virtually never permitted between these people. Similarly, patterned kin behavior between brother and sister emphasizes avoidance or respect. Sometimes, a degree of informality between opposite-sex siblings is permitted or expected, but nonsexual and sexual joking are almost never allowed. By contrast, joking is the predominant form of patterned kin behavior between a man and his sister-in-law and between cross-cousins.

Why is the patterning of behavior among kin so predictable across cultures? Rules mandating avoidance and respect characteristically exist for people between whom sexual relations are disapproved or prohibited. Thus, sexual intercourse between a man and his mother-in-law or a woman and her father-in-law is considered inappropriate across cultures, and so is joking that might evoke sexual feelings. Similarly, a brother and sister are prevented from engaging in sex across cultures, and neither do they joke with each other. On the other hand, many societies mandate marriage between a man and his sister-in-law if the woman's husband dies, and marriage between cross-cousins is preferred or even required in a number of societies. This means that men and their sisters-in-law, as well as cross-cousins, are potential sexual partners in many places around the world. The expectation that these kin will also joke with each other is consistent with the possibility that they may eventually marry.

Cultures also define a certain set of rights and obligations as mandatory between particular categories of kin. For instance, a Kwoma child in New Guinea is justified in taking whatever food he wants from his mother's brother. In return, the nephew must pay his uncle a substantial amount of shell money at a later date. Among the Samoans, any older kinsman is permitted to boss around a younger relation, even if the older relative is just a child. Expectations regarding appropriate behavior toward kin are often tagged onto the kin names that the culture employs. A limited number of different but orderly systems for naming kin occur across cultures. These systems classify different people under the same kin term. For instance, the kin terminology used in the United States labels both mother's mother and father's mother as "grandmother." Similarly, mother's sister, father's sister, mother's brother's wife, and father's brother's wife are all "aunt." It is characteristic of kinship systems that people who are called by the same kin name are treated similarly and expected to behave similarly. Thus, in American society, grandparents are reputed to spoil their grandchildren. Among the Ganda of Uganda, a husband avoids not only his wife's mother, whom he calls *muko*, but also all the other kinswomen he calls *muko*.

No human society is without a kinship system. That is to say, all cultures take the objective facts of genealogies and interpret and exploit them in the service of patterning interpersonal behavior, roles, privileges, and obligations. In nonindustrial societies, many of the vital pursuits of life are conducted in the context of kinship so that a person's economic, political, domestic, and spiritual well-being depend upon the behavior and the trustworthiness of relatives. And human beings the world over live with other people who are their consanguineal or affinal kin. This reliance upon kin as the individual's most basic interpersonal network is predictable in the context of evolutionary theory. As consanguineal kin share genes in common, it is in the interests of one relative to look out for the other. Kin-based solicitude, when it results in the increased likelihood that a relative will survive and reproduce, benefits not only the person who is helped but also the person who does the helping. This is because the helper is contributing to the survival of his or her own genes. Further, cultural prescriptions for regulating interpersonal behavior focus on consanguineal relatedness. That is, where kinship does play an important role in a society, guidelines for conducting life's affairs focus on rights and obligations between blood kin. Thus, the social patterning of interpersonal relationships is consistent with what is most likely to increase personal Darwinian fitness.

See also ALTRUISM; DESCENT RULES AND GROUPS; FAMILY; FITNESS; RESIDENCE RULES.

Bohannan, Paul. (1963) *Social Anthropology.*

Bohannan, Paul, and John Middleton, eds. (1968) *Marriage, Family, and Residence.*

Buchler, Ira R., and Henry A. Selby. (1968) *Kinship and Social Organization: An Introduction to Theory and Method.*

Ember, Carol R., and Melvin Ember. (1988) *Anthropology* 5th ed.

Ember, Melvin, and Carol R. Ember. (1983) *Marriage, Family, and Kinship: Comparative Studies of Social Organization.*

Fox, Robin. (1967) *Kinship and Marriage: An Anthropological Perspective.*

Haviland, William A. (1987) *Cultural Anthropology,* 5th ed..

Levinson, David, and Martin Malone. (1980) *Toward Explaining Human Culture.*

Murdock, George P. (1971) "Cross-Sex Patterns of Kin Behavior." *Ethnology* 10: 359–68.

Pasternak, B. (1976) *Introduction to Kinship and Social Organization.*

Stephens, William N. (1963) *The Family in Cross-Cultural Perspective.*

KINSHIP TERMINOLOGY

All human beings are related to other people by blood or marriage. These networks of relationship are called genealogies, and they are the same across cultures. Thus, every human being can trace a connection to a mother, father, mother's mother, mother's father, father's mother, father's father, father's sister and brother, mother's sister and brother, and so on. Cultures, however, interpret these genealogical ties by emphasizing some connections and underplaying others. Societies also affix labels, or kin terms, to various categories of relatives appearing in a genealogy. These labels then come to be associated with specific expectations about appropriate behavior. The result is a system of kinship—that is, a social translation of genealogies, complete with names for categories of relatives to which patterned roles, responsibilities, and privileges are attached.

Kinship systems, including kin terminology, are not uniform across cultures. Different societies employ different strategies for labeling kin and assigning behavioral expectations to people called by specific names. However, the variation in systems of kinship in general, and in kin terminology in particular, is limited and predictable. That is, we find a small number of repeating systems of kin labeling, or kinship terminology, across cultures.

While kinship terminology differs across cultures, most systems of kin naming use the same label for kin who are in fact related to the same individual in a somewhat different way. For instance, the terminological system used in the United States collapses mother's sister, father's sister, mother's brother's wife, and father's brother's wife into "aunt." This strategy of applying the same term to different kinds of kin produces what is called by anthropologists a classificatory kin term. People who are different from each other regarding the nature of their relatedness to a given individual are nevertheless labeled or classified in the same way by that individual. If societies did not employ classificatory terms to name kin, systems of kin terminology would not be different from one society to the next, except for the trivial detail of what each kin name sounded like in a particular language. It is the fact that kin terminology systems use classificatory terms, and thus treat different relatives as equivalent for the purposes of naming, that makes systems different. When systems do diverge, this is because they are packaging relatives under particular classificatory terms in different ways. Thus, while we collapse all the sisters of our parents and all the wives of our parents' brothers into "aunt" but distinguish between these people and "mother," other cultures collapse a person's mother and mother's sister into the same term. Thus, a particular system of kinship labeling makes some relatives terminologically equivalent and others terminologically distinct. The differences between systems are a result of the differences in kin who are terminologically lumped together and kin who are terminologically distinguished. This collapsing together of some kin and separating of others tends to reflect similarities and differences between kin. Where kin are named by the same term, they are likely to share roles, while kin who are named differently often practice dissimilar roles. Because of this, systems of kinship terminology tend to reflect features of a society's social structure, including what other kin people live with or near, descent rules, and family organization.

In all cultures around the world, kinship terminological systems rest on some combination of nine basic criteria in differentiating kin into different kinship categories. Five of the nine indicated here are used in the American terminological system: (1) generation; (2) lineality and collaterality, which indicate direct descent or absence of direct descent; (3) sex; (4) affinity, which indicates relation by blood versus marriage; (5) polarity, which means that kin refer to each other by different kin terms; (6) bifurcation, which means that a distinction is made on the basis of the sex of the person through whom the kin tie is established; (7) relative age of kin born in the same generation; (8) sex of the speaker; and (9) decedence, meaning whether or not the kin through whom the tie is established is alive or dead.

Terminological Systems

Six different systems of kinship terminology have been identified across cultures. Each lumps together and distinguishes between kin in a somewhat different way. Societies that are designated as employing the same kinship terminology use the same lumping and splitting strategy for naming relatives. Thus, the same kind of kin are named similarly and the same kind of kin are named differently, although the actual words that are used as labels for kin of course will differ if the languages of the cultures are different. Each system of kinship labeling is named after one of the societies that employs the system, but each system of course also reappears in many other cultures.

In the Omaha system of kinship terminology the same term is used to refer to father and father's brother. Another term refers to mother, mother's sister, and mother's brother's daughter. All of the males of the mother's patrilineage, regardless of generation, are collapsed under one name. Thus, mother's brother and mother's brother's son are called by the same term, and so is mother's father. Terminology for cousins depends upon sex of the cousin and the identity of the individuals through whom the cousin relationship is traced. A parallel cousin is traced through individuals of the same sex, so my parallel cousin is my mother's sister's child or my father's brother's child. A cross-cousin is traced through individuals of the opposite sex, so my cross-cousin is my mother's brother's child or my father's sister's child. Taking the two factors of sex and type of cousin, male parallel cousins are called by one term, which is the same name that is used for the brother. Female parallel cousins are collapsed under the same label that is also used for the sister.

Omaha kinship terminology is usually found in patrilineal societies, that is, in cultures that trace descent through the father. This means that a person belongs to the same descent group as his or her father and father's blood relatives and that all of these relatives think of themselves as belonging to one descent group. The fact that societies with the Omaha system trace descent through one parent may begin to explain why different terms are used for relatives on the father's and mother's side. The difference in terminology may reflect the difference in a person's affiliation with the father's versus the mother's kin. It is also true that members of the same descent group are bound together by networks of rights and privileges, and these will depend in part upon the age of a relative. The Omaha system is asymmetric when we compare terminology conventions for the mother's versus the father's side of the genealogy, and this asymmery is accounted for by the fact that the system makes a greater number of generational distinctions for kin traced through the father than it does for kin traced through the mother. It is possible that this difference is a result of the unique roles that members of the patrilineage play in each other's lives. For instance, members of the father's generation are likely to be authority figures in a person's life while members of a person's own generation will be companions and colleagues. The generational terminology distinctions may mirror these differences in behavioral expectations. By contrast, the behavioral expectations of mother's kin in a patrilineal society are not so clearly distinguished, and neither are the kin terms. Patrilineal societies are also usually patrilocal, which means that a married couple lives with or near the husband's natal household. This means that children of both sexes will be living near their father's relatives and that neither children nor married individuals will live with a concentrated group of mother's relatives. Thus, the day-to-day contact that a male will have with members of his father's kin for all of his life and that a female will have for some of hers may be facilitated by a clearer differentiation of father's kin on the basis of generation.

The Crow system of kinship terminology is the mirror image of the Omaha system. Thus, the merging and differentiating of relatives by name follow the same rules for the Omaha and Crow systems except for the fact that the Crow system collapses individuals across generations on the father's side but not on the mother's side of the genealogy. Thus, father, father's brother, and father's sister's son are all called by the same term. Mother and mother's sister are also referred to by the same label, but mother's brother's daughter is called by a different term. This reversal in kinship terminology parallels a difference in descent rules in societies using the Omaha versus the Crow systems. In particular,

Crow system societies are matrilineal. Thus, the greater degree of differentiation between relatives on the mother's side may reflect the fact that the interactions between members of the matrilineage are richer, more differentiated, and more frequent in these societies than are those between members of the father's relatives.

The Iroquois system of kinship terminology labels individuals in the parents' generation according to the same conventions used by the Omaha and Crow systems. Thus, the same term is used for father and father's brother and the same word is used for mother and mother's sister. However, the naming of cousins is handled differently in the Iroquois system. Thus, male cross-cousins, that is, mother's brother's sons and father's sister's sons, are referred to by the same term. Similarly, female cross-cousins, that is, mother's brother's daughters and father's sister's daughters, share a name. Parallel cousins are sometimes referred to by the same names used for brothers and sisters, but sometimes different terms are used. The Iroquois system is also used in unilineal societies, that is, societies that trace descent through only one parent, and we see this reflected again in the difference in terms for father's and mother's relatives.

The Sudanese system also differentiates between relatives on the father's and mother's side, but it also differentiates between *all* relatives, so that each person who bears a different kind of relationship to some individual will be labeled differently. For this reason the Sudanese system is also called the descriptive system of kinship terminology. Societies that employ the Sudanese system are patrilineal, and also tend to be relatively complex cultures that have class stratification, occupational specialization, and complicated political organization. Perhaps the interpersonal specialization associated with these cultures invites maximum distinctions among relatives as well.

The Hawaiian system of kinship terminology is the simplest of the systems. It makes no distinctions between relatives on the father's and mother's side. Nor does it distinguish between relatives of the same generation except on the basis of sex. Thus, all females in the mother's generation, including the mother, are called by one term. The same is true for all males of the father's generation. All males of the individual's own generation are referred to by the same label as the brother, and all females of a person's own generation are called by the same term as the sister. Societies that use the Hawaiian system do not tend to have unilineal descent systems. This may account for the absence of a distinction between the father's and mother's relatives. It is not clear why no distinctions other than sex are made within generations in this system.

Finally, the Eskimo system is the most familiar to people who live in the United States and other Western cultures. No distinctions are made between mother's relatives and father's relatives. All mother's sisters and father's sisters are called by the same term, which is different from the label for mother. And all mother's brothers and father's brothers are referred to by the same label, which is different from the word for father. All cousins are collapsed into the same term which is, however, different from the terms for brother and sister. Brothers and sisters are also named by distinct labels. One result of the Eskimo convention for naming is that members of the nuclear family do not share labels with any other relatives. Societies that employ the Eskimo system tend to trace descent through both parents. This may account for the lack of distinction between the mother's and father's relatives. Where descent is traced through both parents, those kin who are most closely related to an individual tend to be most important in his or her life, while more distantly related kin are less important. This may explain the unique naming for nuclear family members as well as the tendency to collapse more remote kin—for instance, aunts, uncles, and cousins—into shared labels.

While kin terminologies collapse different kinds of kin into the same label, individuals know the difference between relatives who are called by the same name. For example, a son who lives in a society that employs the Omaha system distinguishes between his mother and his aunt even though the two are called by the same name in the same way that an American user of the Eskimo system knows the difference between his mother's sister and his father's sister even though they are both called "aunt." This means that, if kin terms really do facilitate the tagging of relatives according to their expected roles and behaviors, this is a tagging that is only partial. It does not interfere with a person's ability to think of each relative as a unique individual.

Bohannan, Paul. (1963) *Social Anthropology.*

Buchler, Ira R., and Henry A. Selby. (1968) *Kinship and Social Organization: An Introduction to Theory and Method.*

Ember, Carol R., and Melvin Ember. (1988) *Anthropology,* 5th ed.

Fox, Robin. (1967) *Kinship and Marriage.*

Haviland, William A. (1987) *Cultural Anthropology,* 5th ed.

Hiebert, Paul G. (1976) *Cultural Anthropology.*

Kroeber, Alfred L. (1909) "Classificatory Systems of Relationship." *Journal of the Royal Anthropological Institute of Great Britain and Ireland* 39: 77–84.

Murdock, George P. (1949) *Social Structure.*

Pasternak, B. (1976) *Introduction to Kinship and Social Organization.*

Schusky, Ernest L. (1974) *Variation in Kinship.*

solves the problem of who will care for the woman now that her provider is gone. This is the case among the Lamet of Southeast Asia, who practice the levirate. The widow's brother-in-law is expected to marry his dead brother's wife and to see to her needs. If he does not wish to marry his sister-in-law, she still has the right to remain in his household and he is obliged to support her. Questions about the disposition of the dead father's children are also resolved by the marriage of a widow and her brother-in-law. Omaha men married the widows of their dead brothers in order to be able to take care of the children and keep them close to the dead husband's family. However, a man who mistrusted his own family for some reason and wished to protect his children counseled his wife not to remarry within his kin group if he should die. A surviving brother who disapproved of his dead brother's wife took charge of the children without marrying the widow. In North Africa, Riffian customs regarding widow remarriage underscore the role the levirate plays in guaranteeing the proper management of a dead man's children. A Riffian widow with no dependents returns to her parents' household when her husband dies, and is free to marry anyone she wishes while retaining rights to her inheritance from her spouse. But a woman who has unmarried children is required to marry one of her deceased husband's brothers unless he releases her from this obligation. Should she marry some other man, her children remain with her brother-in-law, although her husband's property remains with her.

The levirate also simplifies the disposal of the dead man's property. A Kimam widow in New Guinea commonly marries the brother of her deceased husband. The arrangement proves convenient because a woman's children are entitled to their father's gardens and the marriage of a widow and her husband's brother permits the property of the deceased man to be kept in the family.

LEVIRATE

The custom whereby a widow is expected to marry a brother of her deceased spouse is called the levirate. The levirate is the most common form of widow remarriage across cultures. In a survey of 185 societies, 69 percent require or prefer marriages between a widow and one of her brothers-in-law. In at least 22 percent of those cultures where the levirate is practiced, a widow can marry only the younger brother of her dead spouse. Customs requiring a man to marry the widow of his brother are understood to impose an obligation on both the woman and her brother-in-law. For instance, among the North American Omaha, a woman was viewed as having the right to expect such a remarriage, and if her husband's brother failed to marry her, the woman or her relatives might assault the man or his property.

The popularity of the levirate may be explained by the fact that it averts a variety of potential complications that are threatened by the death of a husband and father. Marriage between a widow and her deceased husband's brother

In some cultures, a widow is required to marry her husband's brother. In these societies there are no loopholes that would allow the woman some other option. But in a number of cultures, the levirate can be circumvented. In Nepal, a Sherpa widow and her husband's family are still bound by the duties and privileges of marriage, even though her spouse is no longer living, and a younger brother of the husband is supposed to marry the widow. But she can free herself of this obligation by paying a fee and participating in a special ceremony that sets her free. The deceased husband's family may not wish to accept the fee, but the widow can still marry any a man of her choice if she pays an adultery fine or her new spouse pays the "new husband" fine. Sometimes, a woman is required to marry her brother-in-law but need not remain with him permanently. In Suriname, a Saramaka widow is expected to marry her oldest brother-in-law, but as long as they remain together for a few months, she is free to leave him if she prefers not to remain his wife. Similarly, a Maori widow in New Zealand is required to marry her dead husband's brother, and if she marries another man instead, her husband's relatives might burn down his house and rob him of his possessions. A widow can, however, marry her spouse's brother and then leave him and remarry.

Where a widow does not marry her husband's brother, complications can occur if marriages customarily entail a bride price, that is, a transfer of money or property from the groom or his family to the wife or her family. In such societies, the levirate preserves the balance initiated by the original exchange of a woman for some kind of material compensation. If the widow were to leave her former husband's household, then the equity of the original arrangement would be compromised. Where, therefore, societies have bride-price customs but also make the levirate optional, the widow, her new husband, or her family is expected to compensate the dead spouse's family. For instance, if a Lamet widow wishes to marry someone else, her chosen husband must pay a bride price to her former husband's brother, as a wife is viewed as the property of her husband's household, and loss of such property requires compensation.

When there are no available brothers for a deceased husband's widow to marry, his family may make other arrangements. A rural Chinese widow is expected to marry any brother of her former spouse who is not already betrothed, but if there is no man in this category for her to marry, her mother-in-law will find her a new spouse, who will take the last name of the woman's first husband and will live in the dead man's house with his new wife. Any children produced from the marriage will be considered the offspring of the first husband. In other levirate cultures, a widow may marry another of her former husband's kinsmen if no brother-in-law is available for her to marry.

See also SORORATE; WIDOW REMARRIAGE; WIDOWER REMARRIAGE.

Barth, Fredrik. (1961) *Nomads of South Persia.*

Coon, Carleton S. (1931) *The Tribes of the Rif.* Harvard African Studies 9.

Dorsey, J. Owen. (1884) *Omaha Sociology.* Third Annual Report of the Bureau of American Ethnology, 1881–1882.

Dupire, Marguerite. (1963) "The Position of Women in a Pastoral Society." In *Women of Tropical Africa,* edited by Denise Paulme, 47–92.

Fei, Hsiao-tung. (1939) *Peasant Life in China: A Field Study of Country Life in the Yangtze Valley.*

Gillin, John. (1936) *The Barama River Caribs of British Guiana.* Papers of the Peabody Museum of American Archaeology and Ethnology, Harvard University, 14(2).

Hiroa, Te Rangi. (1949) *The Coming of the Maori.*

Izikowitz, Karl G. (1951) *Lamet: Hill Peasants in French Indochina.*

Kenyatta, Jomo. (1961) *Facing Mount Kenya: The Tribal Life of the Gikuyu.*

Murdock, George P. (1949) *Social Structure.*

Serpenti, I. M. (1965) *Cultivators in the Swamps.*

LOVE MAGIC

Love magic refers to a wide-ranging set of practices meant to affect the feelings and/or behavior of a desired person. These customs are common across cultures and are used for a variety of purposes. Love magic may be invoked to attract another person, to insure that a partner will remain faithful, to seek revenge on a loved one or pay back an interloper, or to bring about a reconciliation with an estranged lover. Of 90 societies, 72 percent practice love magic to attract or keep a partner while an additional 8 percent use magic to avenge a slight or infidelity. Only 20 percent do not use love magic. Men are much more likely to employ love magic than are women. People in love in many cultures use numerous types of love magic to make their wishes come true. In Colombia, when a Goajiro girl reaches puberty, she is given a charm to hang around her neck. She will wear this necklace while she remains in seclusion during her first menstrual period. The charm will make her attractive to men and will help her to win a husband who will pay a high price for her. In Indonesia, a Balinese man who wishes to attract a girl may steal her thoughts by thinking of her constantly and calling her mentally as he falls asleep. She will be so miserable that she will not be able to eat, sleep, or work until she succumbs to her suitor. Cuna husbands in Panama who wish to make up with their wives after a quarrel will take a potion to promote marital harmony. And, as a reversal, the Aymara of Peru employ charms and spells to repulse mates or lovers in whom they are not interested.

Human beings tend to resort to magical practices when they are faced with circumstances that are of great importance to them but over which they have little control. The use of magic serves to alleviate the anxiety that this kind of uncertainty evokes. Love and sex certainly count as events that are of great consequence to people but that can also create much anxiety. A hopeful lover always risks rejection and a real lover faces the possibility that a partner will be unfaithful, so love magic may serve to decrease the anxiety associated with forming and maintaining love relationships. This explanation of the function of love magic helps to make sense of other features of societies in which these strategies are used. Societies are more likely to have love magic when people limit the circumstances in which they are willing to talk about sex. Where love magic is present, sex is likely to be seen as bad, dangerous, or debilitating unless indulged in with moderation. Modesty for women is emphasized in societies with love magic. Premarital sex for girls is restricted and homosexuality is disapproved where love magic occurs. Finally, in cultures that employ love magic, sex socialization is severe. Each of these cultural attitudes reflects or can lead to concern about sexual relationships. So love magic appears to be especially prevalent in societies where anxiety about sex is likely to be especially high. Love magic customs may alleviate this anxiety.

Love magic may have another use beyond its ability to decrease the worry associated with finding and keeping a love partner. It may help the user to communicate his hopes and intentions to the targeted person in a way that is less threatening than is a direct declaration of love. Even though love magic is often supposed to be performed in secret, the person toward whom the magic is being directed is frequently aware of what is going on. If the target also believes in love magic, then she may give herself up to the relationship. She may also be flattered that someone would go to the trouble of employing love magic to win her favor, and this might increase the chances that the relationship will succeed, or she might simply feel obligated.

If love magic does act as a strategy for communicating interest and as a means of jumpstarting a relationship, then this would help to explain why the custom persists. If successful love relationships tend to follow the use of love magic, then to the casual observer it looks as if love magic works.

Covarrubias, Miguel. (1938) *Island of Bali.*

Gillin, John. (1936) *The Barama River Caribs of British Guiana.* Papers of the Peabody Museum of American Anthropology and Archaeology, Harvard University, 14(2).

Gutierrez de Pineda, Virginia. (1950) *Social Organization in La Guajira.*

Marshall, Donald Stanley. (1950) "Cuna Folk: A Conceptual Scheme Involving the Dynamic Factors of Culture, as Applied to the Cuna Indians of Darien." Unpublished manuscript, Harvard University.

Rosenblatt, Paul C. (1967) "Marital Residence and the Functions of Romantic Love." *Ethnology* 6: 471–480.

Shirley, Robert W., and A. Kimball Romney. (1962) "Love Magic and Socialization Anxiety: A Cross-Cultural Study." *American Anthropologist* 64: 1028–1031.

Titiev, Mischa. (1951) *Araucanian Culture in Transition.*

Tschopik, Harry, Jr. (1946) "The Aymara." In *Handbook of South American Indians,* edited by Julian H. Steward.

———. (1951) *The Aymara of Chucuito, Peru.*

In a number of cultures around the world, the relationship between the sexes is characterized by considerable hostility. For example, antagonism between spouses is commonplace in Manus marriages in Oceania. A husband and wife are required to avoid each other during the period of their betrothal, and continue to avoid each other in public and eat apart for a number of years after their marriage. Casual conversation and playfulness are alien to Manus spouses, nor are relationships characterized by cooperativeness, tenderness, or good feelings. Women view sexual intercourse as humiliating and experience pain from sexual relations at least until the birth of the first child. Both partners look forward to having children, saying that the house is good that has two youngsters, one to sleep with the husband and one to sleep with the wife. Rape is the ideal form of sexual activity for men.

Sexual antagonism is also conspicuous among the Azande of Zaire. Men constantly spy on their wives. A husband will try to keep his spouse within earshot whenever possible, and wives are treated like enemies. Their exclusion from the poison oracle reflects this sentiment. The poison oracle plays a pivotal role in Azande life. No endeavor is attempted unless the oracle has been consulted. Life crises, important legal disputes, collective ventures, and any activity that affects the welfare of a particular individual requires the authorization of the poison oracle. Banning women from any dealings with the poison oracle is a strategy by which men express sexual antagonism toward women.

Similarly, the relationship between the sexes is generally antagonistic among the Coniagui of Guinea. This hostility may be reduced in the case of a husband and wife, but the man does not show it for fear that his wife will see chinks in his emotional armor as signs of weakness and try to take advantage of him. The brittleness in the Coniagui marital relationship is mirrored in their living arrangements. Formerly, a woman moved in with her husband only after she had given birth to a number of children. Now she goes to live in her husband's house when she first becomes pregnant, but if the two quarrel the woman will promptly return to her own home and stay there until a reconciliation is achieved. In African societies more generally, the relationship between a husband and wife is characterized by mutual constraint that is liable, however, to erupt into combativeness when one or the other is provoked. At times of crisis, the normal aggressive banter between spouses turns into outright antagonism.

Where cross-sex antagonism occurs, it colors interactions between both husbands and wives and males and females in general. While the underlying sources of pervasive ill will between people of the opposite sex are not thoroughly understood, a number of patterns of cross-sex antagonism crop up across cultures. Thus, in societies where interactions between males and females are unfriendly, the status of women tends to be lower than that of men. Females are accorded fewer privileges than males and are expected to be submissive to members of the opposite sex. Further, in a number of cultures with male-female antagonism, men marry women from groups that are traditionally viewed as enemies. Cross-sex antagonism, then, may be a response to attitudes toward the relative status of the sexes and also to intimate association with adversaries.

In Brazil, Mundurucu tradition has it that the status of women is inferior to that of men, and this prejudice pervades the culture. Women, however, do not passively accept this judgment. As a result, relations between the sexes do not tend to be harmonious. Living arrangements are segregated by sex. Women and children live in their own dwellings, while husbands live in the men's house. Women say that a man only comes home for water and sex. Subsistence activities are performed cooperatively but also respect sexual segregation, so that men help other men and women help women. Various transgressions on the part of women are punished by gang rape. Further, a woman alone runs the risk of being sexually assaulted. As a result, women travel together, even to fetch water or wood or attend to light gardening chores, all of which are easily accomplished by a solitary female. Mundurucu women view gang rape as cruel and oppressive and resent men for committing rapes. They also resent males for retreating to the men's house instead of living at home, as is the habit of men in neighboring cultures. The division of labor by sex also antagonizes the women, who complain that men never help them with their chores. This irritates women because their work is often boring and tedious and a woman's workload is greater than that of a man. As a result, males can frequently be found relaxing in the men's house while the women are busy with their tasks. Sometimes, this resentment will erupt into open hostility, with a group of women challenging the men to get out of their hammocks and pitch in on the chores while the men ignore them. Women do not depend upon their husbands for

security because they assume that men cannot be trusted. Rather, a woman counts on the other female members of the household. Among the Sebei of Uganda, the overarching tone regarding interactions between unmarried males and females is antagonism, and sexual relationships have the flavor of a battle between the sexes. In part, this is because boys are willing to employ whatever means are required to obtain sexual intercourse with a girl. In fact, no act of coitus can be interpreted as rape unless more than one male is involved. For their part, girls use teasing, promises, and deceit in their contacts with boys, so that male-female interactions become a matter of sexual gamesmanship. When they are married, a husband and wife continue to mistrust each other. A husband is especially prone to worry about the motivations of his spouse because wives are in possession of magic that allows them to control their husbands. Men believe that women use techniques in order to usurp the power that men otherwise have over women in Sebei society. A wife is expected to be submissive to her husband, who can beat her as a matter of course. More generally, the marital relationship is characterized by manipulation of one spouse by the other, hostility, and deceit. Indeed, when her sons are mature and have established themselves, a woman is likely to leave her husband's household and live near one of her grown children.

Among the Gusii of Kenya, individuals belonging to the same clan are relatives and, therefore, cannot marry. As a result, marriage is always between members of different clans who are, in fact, enemies and have engaged in blood feuds in the past. Thus, the Gusii say, "Those whom we marry are those whom we fight," and a Gusii wife, when she marries and goes to live with her husband, feels like an intruder in an enemy camp. The cultural patterning of the wedding night pits the bride and groom against one another, with the girl resisting the boy's sexual advances, while the groom looks forward to the challenge of overcoming his new wife's reluctance. The bride may go so far as to use magic to make her husband sexually impotent. The boy, in turn, will eat bitter herbs and large quantities of coffee beans in order to increase his potency and, therefore, to win this contest of wills. The girl may refuse to get on the marriage bed, in which case a number of boys will take off her clothes and force her to lie down. The couple is then locked in a conflict in which the boy tries to force coitus while the girl tries to prevent him from doing so. The groom then tries to have sexual intercourse as many times as possible, the goal being to cause pain to the bride. The idea that sexual intercourse is a battle between husband and wife remains active through a couple's marriage and is symbolic of the more general hostility between spouses. Among the Mae Enga of New Guinea, relationships between males and females are actively hostile. This may in part reflect the fact that Mae Enga men in this culture also marry women from groups with whom they are chronically at war. Once they are five years old, boys begin to be warned about spending too much time with women. They are persuaded, instead, to join other males in the men's house. A 15-year-old boy will have joined the community's bachelor association, pledging not to have sexual intercourse with a woman or eat food from her hands. Boys who have joined the bachelor's association periodically go into seclusion for four days to be decontaminated from the influence of women. They refrain from eating pork because women take care of the pigs, and they are prohibited from looking at the ground while walking in the forest for fear of seeing a woman's footprints or pig feces. The bodies of the bachelors are washed and their dreams are interpreted. They are then safe for a while against the impurity of females.

Ember, Carol R., and Melvin Ember. (1988) *Anthropology*, 5th ed.

Evans-Pritchard, Edward Evan. (1971) *The Azande: History and Political Institutions.*

Gessain, Monique. (1960) "Coniagui Women." In *Women of Tropical Africa*, edited by Denise Paulme.

Goldschmidt, Walter. (1966) *The Culture and Behavior of the Sebei.*

LeVine, Robert A., and Barbara B. LeVine. (1966) *Nyansongo: A Gusii Community in Kenya.*

Mead, Margaret. (1931) *Growing Up in New Guinea: A Comparative Study of Primitive Education.*

Meggitt, M. J. (1964) "Male-Female Relationships in the Highlands of Australian New Guinea." *American Anthropologist* 66: 204–224.

Paulme, Denise. (1960) "Introduction." In *Women of Tropical Africa*, edited by Denise Paulme.

Sanday, Peggy R. (1981) *Female Power and Male Dominance.*

MALE-FEMALE INTERACTION

People the world over regularly engage in the same kinds of activities. They make a living, provide a home for themselves and their dependents, take part in the religious, political, and social life of their communities, and set aside some time for relaxing. There is variation, however, in the degree to which males and females pursue these activities in each other's company. In some cultures, one's sex is not typically important as a basis upon which to determine group membership, and the sexes mix freely most of the time. Often, however, males and females spend some time together and some apart. In other cultures, men and women live in largely separate worlds.

In the United States during the nineteenth century, the Comanche were a culture where men and women participated regularly in mixed-sex leisure activities. Neighbors wandered in and out of one another's tipis as the resident women performed their routine domestic chores and the men made weapons, discussed important matters, or simply relaxed or slept. Evenings were usually taken up with singing and storytelling, or boys and girls might collect around the fire for a dance while the rest of the camp members watched. Adults of both sexes participated in sports or gambling, and the whole camp marked both sad and happy events together.

In other societies, males and females are segregated much of the time. In south Asia, West Punjabi men and women generally congregate in same-sex groups during their leisure time. The men gossip, smoke, tell stories, exchange news, and play cards in guest houses, which serve as retreats for the men of the village as well as entertainment centers for male visitors, or they may visit the bazaars or coffeehouses. The lives of the village women are much more confined. They visit one another in the women's quarters or, accompanied by the girls and small boys, relax and gossip in the courtyard. Similarly, the men and women perform their religious duties separately, the males going to the mosque to pray and the women praying at home. When they are not working, Brazilian Shavante men can generally be found in the men's circle. Here, men gossip, make artifacts, and attend to whatever business needs doing. Young men gather in the bachelor's hut, which functions like a men's club and which women typically avoid, although they are not explicitly prohibited from entering. And every evening, when the older males are conducting the men's council, women are expected to stay away. Siriono men and women in South America participate in the same kinds of activities when they are not working, but they engage in these pastimes separately. For instance, dances are frequently held in the evenings, but people only dance in same-sex groups. Similarly, adults attend drinking parties whenever the ingredients for making beer are available, but when a man throws a beer party, he invites his male relatives, with women only waiting in the background to break up the fights that inevitably occur on such occasions. Women are only active participants in their own drinking feasts. Because Papago men of the southwestern United States fear contact with a menstruating woman, males and females are generally segregated into same-sex work and play groups, and even husbands and wives spend little time together during the day. In the evening, the men might be called together to smoke and make plans for future activities while the women remain sitting by their home fires and chatting about one thing or another.

In some societies, males and females are more or less strictly segregated in public, but not in the privacy of their homes. Among the Siuai of Oceania, men, women, and children mix freely for many hours at home, cooking, eating, playing, and tending to animals and babies together. But outside the home, there is a strict separation of males and females. During public ceremonies or fishing expeditions, men stay with other men and women with women. Among the Trumai of Brazil, a husband and wife spend much of their leisure time in each other's company when they are at home. A married couple may be found sitting in the shade of their house, the wife making or mending a hammock and the husband fashioning new arrows, or the two might make a brief gathering expedition or just pass the time together. In public, however, men and women lead largely separate lives. The men monopolize the log bench and fireplace located in the center of the plaza, where the social life of the Trumai is concentrated. Women are prohibited from approaching the log bench even when the men are absent. Thus, females cannot attend the ceremonials, wrestling matches, and other activities regularly taking place in the plaza, but can only watch the action as they sit in front of their own houses. Men also gather each evening from dusk until bedtime to smoke, gossip, and debate. Women are also barred from these nightly social meetings.

Similarly, in his own home, a New Ireland Lesu husband may be found tending the infants while his wife cooks dinner, or the family may be found around the fire in front of their house eating dinner together. But outside of the family, males and females almost always collect into same-sex groups and engage in same-sex activities. Women will go to visit female friends in another hamlet while the men congregate in the men's house or stroll about chatting together. Or a group of women may meet to gossip or cook while the men gather together to eat, fish, or converse. Most feasts are attended only by men. Dances are also performed by same-sex groups, and the women will rehearse their dance routines for months at one end of the village, with men practicing on their own at the other end. Again, Balinese families of Indonesia will spend the evening at home together when nothing is going on in the village to attract them out of doors. The wife may be found cooking meat by the fire and chatting with her husband, who is sitting on a raised platform near the hearth, and the children will be sitting nearby listening to the talk of the adults. But when out in public males and females remain segregated and are shocked to see men and women from other communities mingling at a show or bathing in each other's company. Thus, the men may collect in groups at a gate or in the street, talking and playing with their fighting cocks, or they may rehearse for an orchestral performance, attend a meeting, or drink palm beer together. The women, meanwhile, like to dress up in the evening and go visiting or take a walk.

Sometimes men and women will engage in joint activities at home only when no one else is around. A Bribri family of Central America will spend the evening together, with the women and older children squatting on low benches by their fire and the men relaxing in hammocks or repairing tools or arrows. Meanwhile, the older members of the household might tell stories to the group. By contrast, when visitors are being entertained the men monopolize the conversation, and if some of the guests are women, they will go off with the females of the household to chat by themselves.

In some societies, men and women exist in largely separate worlds with respect to their public and private lives. Among the rural Turks, the sexes do not normally engage in social activities together. Men prefer to spend their leisure time together and away from women, and a group of males will stay out in a snowstorm rather than retreat inside with their wives. Alternatively, all of the men may congregate at the house of the headman. No women are permitted inside the headman's establishment when men are visiting, including the headman's wife, who prepares food for the male guests before their arrival and then makes herself scarce. At feasts men collect together in a room in the host's house or in the field, while women, after serving food, retire. The sexes are also segregated in the mosque, with women sitting in the balcony where no one can see them or, more typically, staying home to pray. The same separation of sexes that characterizes public life also prevails at home. Different rooms are reserved for males and females in houses that can afford the luxury, and women entertain other females in their section of the house, while men entertain men in theirs. The men's room ideally has its own entrance and is thus independent of the rest of the house, so that male visitors will not have to enter the host's home. No man will call upon a friend who is passing the time inside his house with his wife and children.

Patterns of interaction between men and women can vary as a result of changing circumstances even in the same culture. In Tanzania, Hadza living arrangements are dictated by variations in ecological conditions across the year, and these variations, in turn, affect the degree to which males and females spend time together. During the dry season, when watering holes are scarce, people congregate in larger camps, and men and women spend most of their time in the company of their own sex. Women eat on their food-gathering excursions and then send the remaining food to the men when they return to camp. Men gather together daily to sing and dance together. These activities may last for several hours and exclude women. Men also spend a considerable amount of time gambling together apart from the camp's female population. During the monthly *epeme* dance, participants are segregated into same-sex groups, and women are not permitted to join the men. During the wet season, by contrast, when water holes are plentiful and camps are small, the sexes are more likely to spend time in each other's company. The men hunt close to camp and often return home to eat with their wives. Men and women sit together when engaged in their routine activities, and males participate in fewer of the dry-season activities that are reserved for men.

Belo, Jane. (1949) *Bali: Rangda and Barong.*

Eglar, Zekiye. (1960) *A Punjabi Village in Pakistan.*

Gladwin, Thomas. (1948) "Comanche Kin Behavior." *American Anthropologist* 50: 73–94.

Holmberg, Allan R. (1950) *Nomads of the Long Bow.* Washington, DC: Government Printing Office.

Maybury-Lewis, David. (1967) *Akwe-Shavante Society.*

Murphy, Robert F., and Buell Quain. (1955) *The Trumai Indians of Central Brazil.*

Oliver, Douglas. (1955) *A Solomon Island Society: Kinship and Leadership among the Siuai of Bougainville.*

Pierce, Joe E. (1964) *Life in a Turkish Village.*

Powdermaker, Hortense. (1933) *Life in Lesu: The Study of a Melanesian Society in New Ireland.*

Stirling, A. Paul. (1965) *Turkish Village.*

Stone, D. (1962) *The Talamancan Tribes of Costa Rica.* Papers of the Peabody Museum, Harvard University, 43.

Underhill, Ruth M. (1939) *Social Organization of the Papago Indians.*

Woodburn, J. (1964) *The Social Organization of the Hadza of North Tanzania.* Unpublished dissertation, Cambridge University.

MALE-FEMALE STATUS, RELATIVE

People from a variety of the behavioral and social sciences are interested in exploring cross-cultural variations in the relative status of men and women. Efforts to describe and explain status differences between the sexes, however, are hampered considerably because no one is sure about how to define or measure status. When we talk about relative status, we have in mind a variety of things, including differences in the degree to which one as opposed to another person or class of people has power, prestige, respect, control over resources or over other people, and access to valued commodities or attractive roles. Further, when we refer to status differences, we may mean formal statements about who enjoys higher and lower status or we may be referring to who in fact seems to enjoy or be excluded from the privileges of high status. We also tend to assume that status is a unitary phenomenon. That is, we think of a person as being high or low in status in a general kind of way. As soon as the notion of status is closely inspected, however, it becomes clear that the concept is fuzzier than we might initially suppose. To begin with, individuals may enjoy high status in one domain of life but low status in another. This means that there is really no such thing as just plain "status" in general and no way of talking about differences in male-female status. Rather, we need to focus on status differences between the sexes with regard to particular aspects of life. There are also significant discrepancies between a culture's stated view about who is higher than whom on the status hierarchy and actual on-the-ground differences in status, and it is not always easy to tell whether descriptions of cultures are referring to the former or the latter. Finally, it is sometimes hard to be sure what constitutes high or low status. For instance, when wives are put in charge of domestic activities, some people will automatically see this as a reflection of the woman's low status. But it is equally possible to argue that when a woman is given control of an entire household, she is occupying a position of high status. Because ideas about the meaning of status and methods for measuring it have not as yet been fine-tuned, knowledge about the nature and origins of status differences between the sexes is not extensive. But we do have some indications about how male-female status is patterned across cultures and about why particular patterns appear when they do.

While it is impossible to predict whether a woman will be accorded a high or low status in one sphere of life just by knowing her status in another sphere, it is still the case that, as a general rule and across domains, women occupy positions of lower status relative to men. Thus, societies are more likely than not to agree with the reindeer Chuckchee of Siberia, who say: "Being women, eat crumbs." Males are the exclusive or main participants in collective religious ceremonies and rituals in 55.8 percent of 73 societies. In none of these cultures are women the sole participants. Similarly, men are the exclusive political leaders in 87.8 percent of 74 cultures. In an additional 9.5 percent of the sample, females have some leadership roles but male leadership still predominates. Again, in none of

these societies are positions of political leadership reserved only for women. The statistics are similar in regard to leadership positions in kin groups. Males are the exclusive leaders in 83.9 percent of 64 societies and have more influence in an additional 9.7 percent. In only 6.4 percent are the roles of men and women more or less equal. Regarding the inheritance of property, males are preferred in 63.4 percent of 71 cultures. In 31 percent, both sexes have roughly equal rights of inheritance, while women are preferred in only 5.6 percent of the sample. Men own or control the use of houses exclusively or more often than women in 47.3 percent of 72 cultures. Women are more likely to own or control dwellings in only 18.1 percent of these societies. Women are prohibited from joining social gatherings in 69 percent of a sample of 48 societies. Wives are expected to show deference to their husbands in 65.5 percent of 84 cultures. And in 66.7 percent of 63 societies, there is an explicit assumption that husbands should dominate their wives, and they do.

How is the low status of females relative to that of males played out in particular cultures? The position of the Nyakyusa woman of Tanzania is very inferior to that of men. Women are expected to show respect and obedience to both fathers and husbands, and men assume that all females will be meekly compliant in their presence. It is only with her brother and his sons that a woman may assert herself at all. Further, women are excluded from participating in any aspect of public life. In the southwestern United States, Havasupai custom dictates that girls should be modest, shy, and retiring. A female is expected to be submissive to males in all matters, public and private. The status of Belau women is also inferior to that of men. A woman has no jurisdiction over her husband's money and no voice in government. She owns no property or any other substantial asset and it is her brother who has control over the fields. Women are excluded from dances or occasions when chiefs or

Japanese Ainu people. Note the women sitting behind the group of men.

other dignitaries are paying a visit, except when they serve the men or are required to entertain. Toda women of India are prohibited from participating in the political, religious, or magical activities of their society. They are not involved in the ceremonial life of the community and are required to leave the village when some ceremonies are being performed. There are also particular paths on which women must avoid walking. In New Guinea, Trobriand women cannot hold office, participate in tribal councils, or own land. In a number of cultures, the exclusion of women from roles that are accessible to men also means that females are excluded from full-fledged status as adults. Santal women of India are prohibited from participating in the worship of the deities and from eating the sacrificial meat. As these activities are required of any full-fledged member of Santal society, a woman is not viewed

as such and is excluded from the rites that entitle a person to perform the duties and enjoy the privileges of a Santal. Similarly, in the religious, judicial, and political spheres, Tallensi women of Ghana are viewed as minors.

Women are also commonly expected to show deference to men. A Ganda woman of Uganda must kneel down when greeting a man. A Rajput woman of India is required to crouch on the floor and pull her sari over her face when with her husband or another male who is older than her husband. A Ukraine wife remains at least a half step behind her spouse when they are strolling together and walks while he rides if there is only one animal available. In many societies across the world, women are required to kneel, crouch, bow, or walk behind their husbands or men in general. A female may be expected to stand while a man is seated or to kneel on the floor while he sits or to stand when her husband or some other male approaches. Often, women are expected to remain quietly and respectfully in the background while men are talking.

While women are generally accorded a lower status than are men across cultures and domains, females occupy a relatively high status in a variety of arenas in some societies. For example, in south Asia, Nicobarese husbands and wives are viewed as equal partners and all property is owned jointly. If a wife happens to be superior to her husband as a result of greater wealth, talent, knowledge, or the like, no objections are made because she outshines her spouse. Similarly, in Navajo society individual accomplishment is based more upon individual ability than upon sex. Men and women own property separately. Indeed, wives often have greater financial resources at their disposal than do their husbands, which tends to give them considerable power in the family in spite of the formal understanding that it is the most senior male who is the final decisionmaker in any household. Women are entitled to participate in most religious ceremonies and, in the past, a female who had distinguished herself in war might become a member of the tribal council and even advance to the status of chief. A Balinese woman of Indonesia controls her own possessions and income and the majority are economically independent, control domestic finances, and share responsibility for meeting household expenses with their spouses. Women participate in various priestly activities. Indeed, the two sexes are interchangeable with regard to most of life's endeavors, and married couples function as cohesive and complementary units. Navajo women are more likely than men to have their own dependable outside income. Many Navajo women have control of the family financial resources and this gives them an influential voice in family decision making.

In a majority of cultures, husbands are formally more powerful than their wives. For ex-

ample, a Ganda wife is expected to obey her husband and to plan household affairs to suit his needs. A wife cooks when her husband wishes to eat and does not prepare meals for herself when he is away. A woman cannot go visiting unless her husband gives her permission, and she can only stay away from home for the number of days agreed to by her spouse. However, in many societies wives wield much informal power even though it is the husband who is the formal head of household. Perhaps the balance of power between men and women begins to even out in domestic life because the vast proportion of household work is done by women, giving them the upper hand in how domestic matters are managed and how domestic resources are distributed. For instance, forceful Navajo women are often successful in vetoing the decisions of their spouses in spite of the stated presumption that the husband's word is final. Husbands, sons, and brothers often seek the advice of the female head of household and take her opinions seriously. A Khoi woman of southern Africa is subordinate to men in the public realm and is required to walk a few steps behind her husband in public as a sign of deference. In her own household, however, she is the master. She owns her own cattle, which her husband cannot sell, and he generally consults with her before he disposes of his own. She has absolute autonomy over domestic affairs and can even prohibit him from entering their hut if she chooses. Santal women are more or less barred from most social and religious activities and are not permitted to attend the important festivals that take place a few times each year. Nevertheless, a Santal wife is master when it comes to the affairs of her household.

Why are women accorded a lower status than men in so many domains and in so many societies? A number of researchers have proposed that women's status is closely connected to the role that females play in the subsistence economy of a society. According to this reasoning, those individuals who participate substantially in the subsistence economy in a culture will also come to have control over property, leading in turn to substantial political power. As men are typically in control of subsistence activities, the prediction is that male status is higher than that of females in most cultures. In spite of the intuitive appeal of this idea, the fact is that we cannot predict relative male-female status simply by knowing who contributes most to the subsistence economy. Recognizing this, some have gone on to propose that an important contribution to the subsistence economy on the part of a woman may be a necessary but not sufficient precursor of high female status, but we have no evidence that this is the case. Some people have been attracted by the idea that female status or submissiveness should be related to a culture's focus on male strength or aggression, but there is in fact no consistent relationship between attitudes about male strength or pugnacity and women's status.

However, women's status is associated with the complexity of a culture, so that status is lower in more complex societies than it is in simpler ones. So is female status predictably related to particular aspects of cultural complexity. Thus, low status is more likely in societies with intensive plow agriculture, complex political hierarchies, weaving, the individual ownership of property, and social stratification. Female power is also related to patterns of trading. Thus, women's power is the greatest where women are able to trade goods that are produced by both sexes and weakest where men trade items produced by both sexes. In societies where a person's descent is traced through females, a woman has most control over her own life where both husbands and brothers have equal authority over her. This may be because a woman in this kind of culture can play a brother and husband against each other, thereby canceling out to some extent the power that each has over her. By contrast, where either a husband or a brother has

most or all of the authority over females, the woman herself has less control over her own fate.

A number of theorists have proposed that, if men seem to hold a more privileged status than women in contemporary cultures, this was not always the case, and that early in the history of our species it was women who were in power. Thus we have claims of original matriarchal families and societies that were eventually displaced by the patriarchal pattern. This idea is not confined to social scientists in our culture. In a number of other societies, the origin myths passed down from generation to generation also tell a similar tale. Indeed, 9.2 percent of 93 cultures believe that the founders of their cultures were solely or most importantly female, while another 30.8 percent assign women a role equal to that of men in the founding of the society. Thus, for example, the Mundurucu of Brazil believe that it was the women who in the beginning discovered and controlled the men's house and the *karoko*, the musical instruments containing the ancestral spirits. However, the men took the *karoko* away from the women so that now women are prohibited from even seeing the *karoko*, and the men's house is the province of males. Women are now viewed as second-class citizens over whom males are dominant.

While Westerners tend to equate the lower status of females with notions of females as inferior, this association is not typically made across cultures. Thus, in spite of the pervasive tendency for women to occupy positions of low status, there is a clearly stated belief that women are inferior to men in only 29 percent of 93 societies around the world. Neither do women accept the idea of inferiority when it is a stated view in a given culture. Mundurucu men are clear in their opinions that women are inferior. Women resent the allegation. The prevalent segregation of the sexes alongside a pronounced antagonism between men and women in Mundurucu culture is the result. Men live in their world and women live in theirs, enjoying a camaraderie and exercising authority in their own sphere that is equivalent to that of the men in theirs.

Belo, Jane. (1949) *Bali: Rangda and Barong.*

Covarrubias, Miguel. (1938) *Island of Bali.*

Culshaw, W. J. (1949) *Tribal Heritage: A Study of the Santals.*

Datta-Majumder, Nabendu. (1956) *The Santal: A Study in Culture Change.*

Ember, Carol R., and David Levinson. (1991) "The Substantive Contributions of World-wide Cross-Cultural Studies Using Secondary Data." *Behavior Science Research* 25: 79–140.

Leighton, Dorothea, and Clyde Kluckhohn. (1969) *Children of the People: The Navaho Individual and His Development.*

Levinson, David, and Martin J. Malone. (1980) *Toward Explaining Human Culture.*

Mukhopadhyay, Carol C., and Patricia J. Higgins. (1988) "Anthropological Studies of Women's Status Revisited: 1977–1987." *Annual Review of Anthropology* 17: 461–495.

Murdock, George P. (1936) *Our Primitive Contemporaries.*

Reichard, Gladys A. (1928) *Social Life of the Navaho Indians.*

Rivers, W. H. R. (1906) *The Todas.*

Schapera, Isaac. (1930) *The Khoisan Peoples of South Africa: Bushmen and Hottentots.*

Spier, Leslie. (1928) *Havasupai Ethnography.* Anthropological Papers of the Museum of Natural History 29.

Stephens, William N. (1963) *The Family in Cross-Cultural Perspective.*

Whyte, Martin K. (1978) "Cross-Cultural Codes Dealing with Relative Status of Women." *Ethnology* 17: 211–237.

———. (1978) *The Status of Women in Preindustrial Society.*

Wilson, Monica. (1951) *Good Company.*

MALE SEXUAL AGGRESSION

In a number of cultures, male sexual overtures are typically physically aggressive. Sometimes, this roughness on the part of males is preferred by the women of a particular culture and sometimes it is not. Physical aggression is characteristic of male sexual advances in 37 percent of 65 societies around the world. In the remaining cultures, men's sexual interactions with women are not characteristically aggressive. In Alaska, when an Ingalik boy wishes to sleep with a particular girl, he puts his hand under her trousers. If she tries to run away, he may follow her and push her to the ground. Also in Alaska, Kaska adolescents are shy in front of members of the opposite sex, and it is hard for them to suggest verbally any sexual encounters. Boys, therefore, will often solicit intercourse by engaging in teasing and roughhousing or by touching a girl's genitals. In the Philippines, if an Ifugao wife resists her husband's sexual advances, he has a right to force her to have intercourse, although he cannot actually injure her. Among the Tuareg of the Sahara, a boy courts a girl by kissing and touching her.

Women typically like or even solicit physical aggressiveness on the part of men in 29 percent of the cultures in which this kind of sexual approach is characteristic. A North American Saulteaux boy who meets a girl along the trail will try to brush against and touch her. The girl will pretend to be embarrassed, but she does not move out of the boy's way very quickly, and in fact girls will linger on a private part of the trail hoping to be waylaid by some boy. The Siuai of Oceania view it as somewhat crude for a man to force a woman to have sexual intercourse, but a male will ambush a girl who is on her way home from her garden, toppling her as she tries to balance the heavy load that she is carrying. Girls do not typically display much resistance, and are often initiated into sex in this way. Cubeo women of the Amazon like to be physically overpowered before having sexual intercourse. Mbuti boys of central Africa will sometimes try to tear off a girl's bark cloth, but never does a male have sexual intercourse with an unwilling girl.

In 71 percent of the cultures where men characteristically employ physical aggression in their sexual overtures, these advances are not welcomed by women. Sudanese Otoro Nuban girls occasionally object when boys try to touch them in an intimate way. If a couple is not engaged, then the boy is required to stop. If they are betrothed, however, he can beat his fiancee until she stops resisting. He may not, however, force her to have intercourse if they are not actually married. Among the Trumai of Brazil, men like to touch women's buttocks as they pass by and often jokingly threaten rape. Women who have no men to protect them are in fact in danger of being raped. Because the possibility of rape is real, women become nervous whenever men begin to tease them and are chronically worried about their own safety. Lakher males of South Asia are permitted to touch an unmarried girl's breasts whether or not she objects. If a boy sneaks up on a sleeping girl and has intercourse with her without her knowledge, he is not considered to have committed any crime, and boys attempt this often with girls they think will not resist too much.

Physical aggressiveness is not a universal component of male sexual style. Murngin boys of Australia are often so shy about approaching females that a girl herself needs to invest a good deal of effort in persuading a boy to have intercourse. A Thai male does not touch a girl before they have been married. Any male who grabbed a girl's arm would be attacking her *kwon*, or soul-stuff. Even when he has been drinking a man will not become sexually aggressive with a woman. And while a Kwoma male of New Guinea will try to attract a female in whom he is interested, he will not make any overt physical advances toward her for fear of being accused of rape. In Ghana, Tallensi boys enjoy flirting with girls at dances, but it is considered unforgivable to seduce a girl.

Male sexual aggression is part of a larger profile of male-female interaction across cultures. Where males are sexually aggressive, husbands and wives eat apart and divorce is common. Thus, sexual aggression appears to be connected to a more general tendency for marriages to be aloof and brittle. Sexual aggression in males is also associated with low incidences of extramarital sex for females, so that an aggressive style of sexual interaction on the part of men seems to discourage women from engaging in sexual activity except as a marital duty. Males who are inclined toward sexual aggressiveness are also likely to boast about their sexual exploits.

See also BOASTING.

Barton, R. F. (1938) *Philippine Pagans: The Autobiographies of Three Ifugaos.*

Barton, R. F. (1946) "The Religion of the Ifugaos." *American Anthropologist* 48.

Blanguernon, Claude. (1955) *The Hoggar.*

Broude, Gwen J. (1983) "Male-Female Relationships in Cross-Cultural Perspective: A Study of Sex and Intimacy." *Behavior Science Research* 18: 154–181.

Dunning, R. W. (1959) *Social and Economic Change among the Northern Ojibwa.*

Fortes, Meyer. (1945) *The Dynamics of Clanship among the Tallensi: Being the First Part of an Analysis of the Social Structure of a Trans-Volta Tribe.*

———. (1949) *The Web of Kinship among the Tallensi: The Second Part of an Analysis of the Social Structure of a Trans-Volta Tribe.*

Goldman, Irving. (1963) *The Cubeo: Indians of the Northwest Amazon.*

Hallpike, C. R. (1972) *The Konso of Ethiopia.*

Honigmann, John J. (1949) *Culture and Ethos of Kaska Society.*

Murphy, Robert F., and Buell Quain. (1955) *The Trumai Indians of Central Brazil.*

Nadel, S. F. (1947) *The Nuba.*

Oliver, Douglas. (1955) *A Solomon Island Society: Kinship and Leadership among the Siuai of Bougainville.*

Osgood, Cornelius. (1958) *Ingalik Social Structure.* Yale University Publications in Anthropology 55.

Parry, N. E. (1932) *The Lakhers.*

Serpenti, I. M. (1965) *Cultivators in the Swamps.*

Turnbull, Colin M. (1965) *The Mbuti Pygmies: An Ethnographic Survey.* Anthropological Papers of the Museum of Natural History 50, pt. 3.

Warner, W. Lloyd. (1937) *A Black Civilization: A Social Study of an Australian Tribe.*

Whiting, John W. M. (1941) *Becoming a Kwoma: Teaching and Learning in a New Guinea Tribe.*

MARRIAGE

A man and woman are said to be married when they enter into a socially sanctioned relationship that is assumed by them and by their community to be relatively permanent. Married people are obligated to each other sexually and usually also form an interdependent economic and domestic unit. Men and women marry in all known human societies. The universal impulse on the part of males and females to form a long-term, publicly acknowledged bond may have its roots in the evolutionary history of our species. In the environment in which we are believed to have evolved, our ancestors faced a number of survival problems. Our diet consisted of both meat and fruit and vegetables. Members of any local group had to worry about nonhuman predators and hostile human groups. Further, human infants are born relatively helpless as compared with the young of many other species and need more or less constant supervision. Human infants are also built to be "continual feeders." The composition of human milk and the pattern of infant sucking parallel those of other species where infants stay in close proximity to their mothers and feed multiple times per hour. This picture of the human situation in our evolutionary past suggests to some scientists that the survival of adults and children would have been best served by a division of labor between a man and woman. Because she was the source of nutrition for the infants, the woman would bear the major responsibility for child care. She would also be able to gather fruits and vegetables for her family while her children were toted along. As her role as caretaker would make her less effective as a hunter or defender, these roles would fall to the men. Men and women who were inclined to become attached to and remain with each other, therefore, had a better chance of surviving and raising their children to maturity. The evolutionary story suggests that the tendency to marry is carved deeply into the human psyche and social order.

Meanings of Marriage

While all cultures regard married people as having sexual and economic rights in each other, beyond these shared core features the meaning of marriage is differently elaborated in different societies. In some cultures, marriages unite communities, kin groups, tribes, and/or other similar groups. Among the Ashanti of Ghana, marriage is regarded as a contract between not only the bride and groom but also the clans of the two marital partners. One clan provides one of its members to another clan for the purpose of perpetuating itself in the children produced. In Zaire, an Azande marriage binds the families of the bride and groom in a relationship that requires each to give help and support to the other. The obligations between families united by marriage are felt to be even greater than those between kin. The Bambara of West Africa also exploit marriage as a way of uniting families. A man who wishes to form an alliance with another family will arrange for his daughter to marry into that household. The marriage oath will specify that the members of the two families are obligated to assist each other. Among the Ifugao of the Philippines, a marriage between two people consolidates the tie between two kin groups, making them allies, especially after the couple has children. Consistent with this view of marriage, a formal disagreement between members of the kin groups can result in the divorce of two spouses who represent the groups. In Oceania, Marquesan chiefs arrange marriages between their children as a way of forging alliances between their tribes. In the past in West Africa, Mende marriages were viewed primarily as compacts between the relatives of the bride and groom. Similarly in Tanzania, Nyakuysa marriages were traditionally thought of as contracts between lineages, not just between the partners themselves, and this interpretation of the meaning of marriage was reflected in the betrothal customs of the society. Girls were betrothed as children, and if a man died before he could marry the girl who had been promised to him, she became the fiancee of his heir. Similarly, should a betrothed girl die before she married, her sister would take her place. Thus, the binding of lineages was what mattered. The union of particular partners was irrelevant. The fact that an Orokaivan marriage in New Guinea is understood to be a transaction between two

clans and not just two individuals is underscored by the fact that the bride price is paid to the girl's clan as a whole and not just to the girl's family.

Marriage is also the vehicle for obtaining children, and children are critical to the happiness of a married couple in some cultures and to the social status of people in others. Among the Wogeo of New Guinea, men marry in order to gain independence from their parents and to have someone to cook for them. Further, a man must be married in order to be socially recognized as a father. In Malaysia, Iban men similarly conceive of marriage as the means of acquiring children. Consistent with this view, when a husband and wife fail to produce children together, their friends typically try to persuade them to separate. Childless couples may, nevertheless, remain together, perhaps adopting a youngster, in spite of the pressure brought upon them to try their luck in other marriages.

The Kapauku of New Guinea also see marriage as the prerequisite for having children, and Kapauku men want to have as many offspring as possible. Men also wish to marry because a wife's work in the gardens and her oversight of the pigs make her a valuable economic asset. Marriage is valued for its economic returns in other cultures as well. Iban women see marriage as a way of obtaining a man to work for them, and wives whose husbands prove to be lazy are likely to seek a divorce, complaining that a woman whose spouse won't do his work might as well not be married at all. Marriage is also the vehicle for inflating one's position in some cultures. For instance, an Azande man of Zaire boosts his prestige and status both socially and legally by marrying.

In a number of societies, marriage is viewed as payment of a debt owed to one's culture or as the only way of becoming a fully integrated member of one's culture. For the Aztecs, marriage was a social responsibility, and boys in their early twenties and girls in late adolescence were expected to find spouses. In Indonesia, Balinese work, social, and religious life all depend for their smooth functioning upon an intact husband-wife unit. If a husband is working in the fields, his wife can stand in for him at the temple, or if the wife is required to be at home, he can substitute for her. It is, therefore, virtually inconceivable for a person to remain unmarried, as a person without a spouse cannot properly participate in all of the activities that make up Balinese existence. For the Tallensi of Ghana, marriage is of the utmost importance in the life of the individual. As in other societies, it is through marriage that a person can produce legitimate children and perpetuate and strengthen his or her lineage. But a Tallensi man or woman also depends upon marriage as the only means of enjoying a normal social life, and virtually all Tallensi, including those who are disabled, get married.

People in many cultures marry in order to attain personal fulfillment of one kind or another. For the Muria Gond of India, marriage is the means by which one acquires a home, partner, and children of one's own. Marriage symbolizes permanence and security. In comparison with life in the adolescent dorm, where young people carry on a series of romantic affairs and sexual activity is a salient feature of life, spouses focus less on the sexual aspect of their relationship and more on its domestic advantages. For Wogeo women, marriage means a home, economic security, and children.

See also HUMAN RELATIONS, EVOLUTION OF.

Amoo, J. W. A. (1946) "The Effect of Western Influence on Akan Marriage." *Africa* 16: 228–237.

Barton, R. F. (1919) *Ifugao Law.*

———. (1938) *Philippine Pagans: The Autobiographies of Three Ifugaos.*

Baxter, P. T. W., and Audrey Butt. (1953) *The Azande, and Related Peoples of the Anglo-Egyptian Sudan and Belgian Congo.*

Belo, Jane. (1936) "Study of a Balinese Family." *American Anthropologist* 38: 12–31.

Bohannan, Paul, and John Middleton, eds. (1968) *Marriage, Family, and Residence.*

Collier, J. F., ed. (1988) *Marriage and Inequality in Classless Societies.*

Elwin, Verrier. (1947) *The Muria and Their Ghotul.*

Ember, Carol R., and Melvin Ember. (1988) *Anthropology.* 5th ed.

Ember, Melvin, and Carol R. Ember. (1983) *Marriage, Family and Kinship: Comparative Studies of Social Organization.*

Evans-Pritchard, Edward Evan. (1971) *The Azande: History and Political Institutions.*

Fortes, Meyer. (1945) *The Dynamics of Clanship among the Tallensi: Being the First Part of an Analysis of the Social Structure of a Trans-Volta Tribe.*

———. (1949) *The Web of Kinship among the Tallensi: The Second Part of Analysis of the Social Structure of a Trans-Volta Tribe.*

Fox, Robin. (1967) *Kinship and Marriage.*

Gomes, Edwin H. (1911) *Seventeen Years among the Sea Dyaks of Borneo: A Record of Intimate Association with the Natives of the Bornean Jungles.*

Handy, Edward Smith Craighill. (1923) *The Native Culture of the Marquesas.*

Hogbin, H. Ian. (1944–1945) "Marriage in Wogeo, New Guinea." *Oceania* 15: 324–352.

Little, Kenneth L. (1951) *The Mende of Sierra Leone: A West African People in Transition.*

Murdock, George P. (1936) *Our Primitive Contemporaries.*

Paques, Viviana. (1954) *Les Bambara.*

Pasternak, B. (1976) *Introduction to Kinship and Social Organization.*

Pospisil, Leopold J. (1963) *Kapauku Papuan Economy.*

Williams, Francis E. (1930) *Orokaiva Society.*

Wilson, Monica. (1959) *Communal Rituals of the Nyakyusa.*

MARRIAGE, ARRANGED A marriage is considered to have been arranged when the match originates with someone other than the future spouses. Males marry women chosen for them by third parties in 29.3 percent of 157 societies, while ar-ranged marriages are an alternative to matches made by the partners themselves in another 17.8 percent. Of 161 cultures, 44.1 percent arrange marriages for girls, while in another 17.4 percent a husband is sometimes chosen for a girl by third parties. Where marriages are arranged, it can be the parents or relatives of the prospective couple, friends of the concerned families, or professional go-betweens who take the initiative in negotiating the marriage.

Even when marriages are arranged, there are wide differences across cultures regarding the extent to which the prospective bride and groom themselves have a say in the person they will marry. In many Asian cultures, the boy and girl traditionally had no say in the choice of a spouse. In China the heads of the families of the new husband and wife sign the marriage contract, but the signatures of the bride and groom themselves are not required. Javanese marriages are arranged by the parents of the couple and many Javanese do not meet their future spouses until their wedding day. A younger girl may not know the purpose of the visit that her would-be husband makes to her house as he looks her over, and brides are sometimes ignorant of the fact that they are to be married until a day or two before the wedding.

By contrast, in many societies with arranged marriages the preferences of the boy and girl do figure importantly in the parents' decisions about the choice of a partner for a son or daughter. Among the Burusho of India the parents of a boy and girl theoretically negotiate a marriage without consulting the young people themselves, but prospective brides and grooms have often played and worked together as children and know each other well, and their feelings are taken into account when matches are being made.

Sometimes a third party will first consult a prospective bride or groom before initiating any negotiations. Young people may also have the right of veto over a match made on their behalf. Among the Huron of Ontario, a boy's parents will often suggest a prospective spouse for their son. If the boy likes their choice, they will approach the girl's parents to obtain their approval of the match. The would-be groom's parents then provide the boy with a present to give to the girl and, if she takes the gift, the two spend a number of nights together. A girl is not, however, compelled to go through with the marriage at this stage in the courtship, and some may collect a number of gifts from boys they have eventually turned away. A Ganda boy in Uganda who likes a particular girl must ask her brother for permission to marry her. The brother will talk the match over with his paternal uncle, and inquiries will be made about the boy and his relatives. If the boy is acceptable, he and some of his relations visit the brother, bringing a pot of beer and the bride price. The girl can accept or reject a suitor. If she wishes to marry the boy, her uncle drinks some of the beer. A girl must marry a boy whose proposal she has accepted, unless the boy himself releases her from her promise.

In cultures where a child's sentiments are taken into account in the arrangement of marriages, parents may try to stack the cards in favor of their own choice of spouse for their son or daughter. Some Malaysian Iban parents try to arrange for the development of a relationship between a daughter and a boy of whom they approve. While the proposed bride and groom are still young, the parents invite the boy for a visit. They go out of their way to make his stay pleasant so that he may come to like the girl and think of her when he is old enough to marry.

Arranged marriages are preferred over matches initiated by the partners themselves for a variety of different reasons across societies. In a number of cultures, marriages are contracted in order to obtain some benefit for the neighborhood, lineage, tribe, or the like. Among the Bambara of West Africa, first marriages are arranged by the community in which a prospective bride or groom lives. A marriage takes place between members of different groups and is viewed by each community as an opportunity to make a lucrative deal for itself. The boy and girl, therefore, are not consulted, and an individual who resists the arrangements of the community will be harshly penalized. If a boy tries to take a wife without the approval of the community, the marriage will not be recognized as legal and the woman and her child will have no claims to legitimacy among their neighbors. If a woman resists entering into a marriage arranged for her by her community, the most brutal means will be employed to persuade her to give in, and if she has children they can be taken from her. Similarly in India, Garo parents arrange marriages between children, without consulting them and sometimes before the child is born, for the purpose of strengthening their lineage and, by extension, the tribe. It would be a disgrace for the bride and groom to see one another before they are married. These relationships are typically unstable, and girls thus married repeatedly run away from their husbands.

Marriages are arranged in some societies as a means of cementing or expressing close connections between families. Among the Chuckchee of Siberia, two friendly families may arrange a marriage between their respective members. Sometimes two children are promised to each other, or there may be a betrothal before one or both of the children are born. More usually, a woman from one family may be given in exchange for a woman from the other family.

Parents will sometimes take the initiative in choosing mates for their children in an attempt to protect the line of descent from being diluted by a foolish attachment on the part of a son or daughter. For the Bellacoola of the northwest coast of North America, marriage represents the context within which the family line is perpetuated. Therefore, parents take the responsibility of finding spouses for their children for fear that, if left to themselves, young people will make foolish choices. It is the parents of a boy who initiate marriage negotiations. They will attempt to arrange a match for him while he is still a child, seeking out a prospective wife whose lineage is as prestigious as their own. If they are able to find a girl whose father is an important chief, so much the better.

In class-stratified societies, arranged marriages are sometimes reserved for the upper classes or for important personages. Among the Wogeo of New Guinea, a headman or other influential individual may arrange a marriage for his son or daughter in order to insure that the child will make a proper match. Such arrangements are considered to be binding regardless of whether or not the prospective spouses themselves have been consulted. The bride and groom may separate after they are married if they find that they cannot live together.

Sometimes parents will choose spouses for their children because the young people are too shy to approach potential mates themselves. Some Cayapa boys in Brazil will propose marriage to a girl on their own, but many are too bashful to court someone on their own, in which case a marriage may be arranged by a boy's or girl's parents or a tribal official. Sometimes a boy's relatives decide that he is taking too long to get married. In these circumstances, they may take it upon themselves to find him a suitable girl. Once they have obtained the consent of the girl's parents, they will immediately take her to the home of their recalcitrant kinsman. If the young man resists the marriage, his relatives will attempt to persuade him to accept the girl. If he still refuses, she may be given to another man or returned to her own home if the young man refuses to marry her.

How do the prospective bride and groom respond to the idea of marrying a partner chosen by someone else? Muria Gond parents in India arrange marriages for their children, and while a boy or girl might not like a particular choice of prospective spouse, the general idea of arranged matches is not questioned by young people. In part this is because they care more about how the married state will affect their lives than about the particular person they marry. The attitude is reflected in the stability of Gond marriages, only 2.6 percent of which end in divorce. Where marriages are arranged there are sometimes avenues of recourse open to a boy or girl who cannot be reconciled to the choice of spouse made by a third party. Among the Kapauku of New Guinea, a girl is expected to marry the man of her father's choosing, and a girl who refuses is likely to be punished by her relatives in an attempt to persuade her to relent. But there are recognized ways by which a young woman can avoid marrying a man who is not to her liking. Some girls elope with another man, in which case the family of the new husband will try to smooth things over by offering a relatively valuable bride price to the new bride's parents. Or a girl might hide away until the man to whom she has been promised gives up on her and marries someone else. In this case, her

A Moldovan matchmaker. Matchmakers are common in cultures where wealth is exchanged between families as part of the marriage transaction.

friends, maternal kin, and sweetheart, should she have one, help to make her situation tolerable while she is in hiding. In Tibet, Lepcha parents usually arrange the marriages of their children and it sometimes happens that the spouses do not like one another. If there is no way of reconciling the boy and girl to the marriage, the wedding can be called off and the bride price returned, or other spouses can be found for the would-be bride and groom, usually the younger brother of the rejected boy and the younger sister of the girl. But in cultures where marriages are arranged, other cultural beliefs can serve to soften the attitude of boys and girls toward marrying partners not of their own choosing. The Chinese, for instance, say that a husband and wife are linked together by fate. One special man is made for one particular woman and the two are tied to one another by an invisible red string. When a match is made by parents, their choice is directed by fate. And an Indian woman does not think of herself as marrying a stranger. She has nurtured the idea of being married since she was a little girl so that when she marries, she is becoming the wife to a man who is the concrete manifestation of her dreams.

The fact that a woman's marriage has been arranged by her family and the kin of her husband can be to her benefit when it comes to the treatment that she can expect from her spouse. For instance, among the Aztec, the careful negotiations that preceded a marriage tended to translate any ill treatment of the woman by her spouse into a breach of the social contract between the two families. However, arranged marriages can also be unstable. Traditional Japanese marriages are orchestrated by a go-between at the request of the parents of a boy or girl. Once a tentative match has been agreed upon, the prospective bride and groom and their families get together so that the boy and girl can look one another over. The first year of marriage is regarded as a trial union, and marriages are not officially recorded during this time. These arranged marriages have a good chance of failing, as almost half of such relationships end in divorce.

Altschuler, Milton. (1971) "Cayapa Personality and Sexual Motivation." In *Human Sexual Behavior: Variations in the Ethnographic Spectrum,* edited by Donald S. Marshall and Robert C. Suggs, 38–58.

Bandelier, Adolph F. (1876–1879) *On the Social Organization and Mode of Government of the Ancient Mexicans.*

Beardsley, Richard K., John W. Hall, and Robert E. Ward. (1972) *Village Japan.*

Bogoras, Waldemar. (1904–1909) *The Chuckchee.*

Elwin, Verrier. (1947) *The Muria and Their Ghotul.*

Geertz, Hildred. (1961) *The Javanese Family.*

Goldman, Irving. (1963) *The Cubeo: Indians of the Northwest Amazon.*

Gorer, Geoffrey. (1938) *Himalayan Village: An Account of the Lepchas of Sikkim.*

Hogbin, H. Ian. (1934–1935) "The Father Chooses His Heir." *Oceania* 11: 1–39.

Lorimer, Emily O. (1939) *Language and Hunting in the Karakoram.*

Mace, David, and Vera Mace. (1959) *Marriage: East and West.*

McIlwraith, Thomas F. (1948) *The Bella Coola Indians.*

Monteil, Charles Victor. (1924) *The Bambara of Segou and Kaarta: An Historical, Ethnographical and Literary Study of a People of the French Sudan.*

Pospisil, Leopold J. (1958) *Kapauku Papuans and Their Law.*

Roscoe, John. (1911) *The Baganda: An Account of Their Native Customs and Beliefs.*

Roth, H. Ling. (1892) "The Natives of Borneo." *Anthropological Institute of Great Britain and Ireland* 21: 110–137; 22: 22–64.

Trigger, Bruce G. (1969) *The Huron: Farmers of the North*.

MARRIAGE, COUSIN

Marriage between cousins is either prescribed or preferred in 26 percent of a sample of 370 societies. Anthropologists distinguish between two kinds of cousin relationships. Cross-cousins are children of siblings of the opposite sex. You are my cross-cousin if you are my father's sister's child or my mother's brother's child. Children of siblings who are the same sex are parallel cousins. By far the more common type of cousin marriage is that between cross-cousins. Perhaps this is because cross-cousins necessarily belong to different kin groups, regardless of whether descent is traced through the father or the mother. Parallel-cousin marriage, by contrast, is very rare. This may be because a marriage between parallel cousins would be a union of two people from the same lineage. When parallel-cousin marriage occurs—among the Bedouin Arabs, for example—there may be exceptional pressures to consolidate ties within the kin group of the husband and wife. In cultures that permit cross-cousin marriages, variations exist regarding which cross-cousins may marry. In some societies, an individual may marry either a mother's brother's child or a father's sister's child. Other cultures allow only one of these options. When a Nambicuara girl of Brazil gets married, her new husband is frequently her mother's brother's son. Parents will often arrange a marriage between a son and his cousin while the two are still children in order to insure that the boy will have a wife once he is grown. Among the Siriono of South America, the preference for marriages between cross-cousins is reflected in the society's kinship terminology. A boy will call his mother's brother's daughter "potential spouse" and the same term is applied by a girl to her father's sister's son. If a first cross-cousin is unavailable as a spouse, an individual can then marry a second cross-cousin, a first cross-cousin once removed, or a classificatory cross-cousin. Marriages between unrelated people are also possible, but they are rare.

Cousin marriage may serve to consolidate ties between families. In the Amazon, Cubeo brothers and sisters remain close to one another in part by arranging marriages between their children. Such marriages are convenient for Cubeo boys, in part because there is little opportunity for courtship in this culture and in part because boys prefer to marry and move into communities where they already have connections. Marriage to a cousin means that a new husband will know many members of his wife's settlement because they will be his own kin whom he has visited with his own family over the years. The Tanala of Madagascar say that their ancestors approve of cross-cousin marriages because such connections keep their descendants together, but the fact that cross-cousin marriages also keep property within the family is also appreciated by the Tanala.

Other societies also recognize that marriages between cousins help to consolidate a family's wealth. Marriage to a mother's brother's daughter is preferred over all others among the Siuai of Oceania, and those to a father's sister's daughter are also desirable. Sometimes a girl is the daughter of both a boy's mother's brother and his father's sister, and marriages to such a cousin are considered to be the best possible kind of union. Cross-cousin marriages are viewed as convenient because they keep land and other resources from being divided up among different families as they pass down from generation to generation. For this reason, marriages between classificatory cousins, while still regarded positively, are looked upon less favorably than are those between real kin. As classificatory cousins are not related, marriages of this kind do not allow for consolidation of property through inheritance.

The Tuareg of the Sahara regard cross-cousin marriage as ideal and other kinds of marriage as undesirable. While they understand that such marriages between cross-cousins keep both people and livestock within the family, they also see other advantages in cousin marriage. Thus, because cross-cousins enjoy a joking relationship before they are married, the Tuareg believe that they have a better chance of forming a relationship that is relatively free of quarrels and other disruptions. Similarly, cousin marriage is recommended among the Wolof of Senegal because, they say, unions between relatives make for sturdier relationships. When married cousins disagree, the dispute can be arbitrated by kinsmen. And spouses who are related are less likely to behave badly toward one another in the first place because they are bound by kin ties. For the Wolof, marriages between distant relatives are superior to those between unrelated individuals, but the best match is between cross-cousins, ideally between a man and his mother's brother's daughter or, if this is impossible, his father's sister's daughter. Such marriages are thought to be especially stable because related spouses will conduct themselves in line with the interests of their mutual relations and will resist divorcing in order to avoid causing their families to quarrel. These examples reflect the popularity of the idea that cousin marriages are stable marriages in cultures that prefer this kind of union.

In many societies where cousin marriage is preferred, a couple will not be forced into a marriage if the boy and girl do not like each other. Among the Cubeo, a brother and sister may sometimes tentatively arrange for their children to be married. The cousins, however, have the final say regarding whether or not they will become husband and wife. The two young people are given an opportunity to look each other over when the boy and his family visit the girl's community. This process of mutual appraisal is conducted with caution. At first, the would-be spouses may ignore each other. The boy may flirt with other girls and his male peers may pretend to court the prospective bride. The young man's character and skills, however, are being assessed by the girl and her kin while she is being observed by her would-be husband and in-laws. Sometimes these mock flirtations with third parties turn into serious relationships and the cousins never marry each other. Similarly, while the Tanala prefer marriages between cross-cousins, such unions are not forced. However, if a pair of cross-cousins fails to marry in one generation, a marriage between their children is considered especially desirable.

In other societies, marriages between relatives are forbidden or looked upon with disfavor. For instance, there are no restrictions on the choice of marriage partner among the Yokuts of California, as long as prospective spouses are unrelated. Relatives who marry are not punished, but such unions are viewed with scorn and the social standing of the couple suffers.

Ames, David. (1953) *Plural Marriage among the Wolof in the Gambia.*

Gayton, Anna. (1948) *Yokuts and Western Mono Ethnography.*

Goldman, Irving. (1963) *The Cubeo: Indians of the Northwest Amazon.*

Holmberg, Allan R. (1950) *Nomads of the Long Bow.* Washington, DC: Government Printing Office.

Levinson, David, and Martin J. Malone. (1980) *Toward Explaining Human Culture.*

Levi-Strauss, Claude. (1948) *Family and Social Life of the Nambikwara Indians.*

Linton, Ralph. (1933) *The Tanala: A Hill Tribe of Madagascar.*

Nicolaisen, Johannes. (1963) *Ecology and Culture of the Pastoral Tuareg.*

Oliver, Douglas. (1955) *A Solomon Island Society: Kinship and Leadership among the Siuai of Bougainville.*

Textor, Robert B. (1967) *A Cross-Cultural Summary.*

MARRIAGE, ECONOMIC ARRANGEMENTS AT

See BRIDE PRICE; BRIDE SERVICE; DOWRY; GIFT EXCHANGE.

MARRIAGE, TRIAL

Men and women form many different kinds of attachments, each of which has a different meaning for both the partners themselves and society at large. Some relationships are recognized by the couple and the community as temporary. The pair may enjoy each other's company but there is no plan of a long-term commitment. Marriage, by contrast, is distinguished from other involvements precisely because the expectation is that the commitment between a husband and wife is more or less permanent and it is publicly recognized as such.

Between these two extremes is what is known as the trial marriage. In a number of societies, a man and woman are accorded the special status of being "experimentally" married. The couple engages in some or all of the activities normally considered appropriate to married partners and the arrangement is recognized by others as a test in anticipation of the real thing.

The Mataco of Argentina capture the essence of the trial marriage when they say that young people who have formed a special kind of attachment "have begun to be married." The couple shows all of the signs of being in love, and the girl invites the boy to spend the night with her at her parents' house. The Mataco custom also highlights one of the functions of trial marriages. Mataco parents exploit the trial marriage to try to influence the final choice of mate that a daughter makes. Whereas girls are likely to bring home a particular young man because he is sexually attractive and personally appealing, parents wish the mate choices of their children to be economically advantageous. The trial marriage gives parents an opportunity to look over a girl's choice and to try to affect her decision.

In Angola, the Mbundu version of the trial marriage suggests another benefit of allowing young people to play at being husband and wife. Mbundu youths must amass enough resources to be able to present gifts to a girl and her mother and to afford betrothal payments. If a young man then finds a girl he likes, he may get permission from her mother to take her home each night to the hut that he has built for himself at puberty. In this way, the pair can get to know each other before they make the more serious commitment of marriage. The couple is not expected to have sexual relations, and if the boy is caught trying to seduce the girl, he will have to sleep in her mother's house for a while so that he may be supervised.

The Ifugao of the Philippines distinguish between trial and contract marriages. The contract marriage conforms to the idea of the officially recognized union of a man and woman. When the Ifugao speak of trial marriages, by contrast, they have in mind the relationships that boys and girls form in the dormitories in which the young people sleep. Trial marriages among the Ifugao also provide an opportunity for two unmarried people to determine whether they are compatible. These relationships are close to courtships and always involve sexual intimacy. If a boy and girl find that they are suited to one another, each obtains parental permission to be married and a ceremonial meeting is called so that the boy may formally propose. Sometimes a trial marriage gives a couple the chance to get to know each other before the wedding when the decision that they will marry has been made by third parties. In Indonesia, the Bali custom of *gendak* allows two people whose marriage has been prearranged to live together before they are officially married. Their relationship is not yet legal, but the woman cannot be abandoned and any children that she might have are declared legitimate.

Trial marriage also often allows a man and woman to determine whether they will be able to have children together before they make a more permanent commitment. For the Albanians, the most critical goal of marriage is to produce sons. An engaged couple, therefore, lives together but is not formally married until the woman bears a son.

Barton, R. F. (1938) *Philippine Pagans: The Autobiographies of Three Ifugaos.*

———. (1946) "The Religion of the Ifugaos." *American Anthropologist* 48.

Childs, Gladwyn M. (1949) *Umbundu Kinship and Character.*

Covarrubias, Miguel. (1937) *Island of Bali.*

Durham, M. E. (1928) *Some Tribal Origins, Laws, and Customs of the Balkans.*

Fock, Niels. (1963) "Mataco Marriage." *Folk* 5: 91–101.

MARRIAGE AGE

Among the Siriono of South America, a girl may marry before she reaches puberty. The Murngin girl of Australia is likely to become a wife when her breasts first begin to develop and a boy might marry for the first time when his beard begins to appear. A Lepcha girl in Tibet is sometimes married at eight years of age, while boys are often wed when they are 12 years old. And in the Egyptian village of Silwa, a girl will frequently be a wife by the age of 12 or 13. Across cultures, married life begins at a relatively early age. Boys marry at 15 years of age or less in 10 percent of 58 societies. Another 42 percent marry between 16 and 19 years of age. Thirty-eight percent are married in their twenties, and 10 percent marry when they are 30 years or older. Girls marry when they are 15 years old or younger in 45 percent of 69 cultures. In another 51 percent of these societies, girls become wives at between 16 and 19 years of age. Two percent of women marry in their twenties and an additional 2 percent are wed at or after they are 30 years old.

Why do people tend to marry so early across cultures? In traditional societies, boys and girls have usually begun to do serious work well before they are physically mature. Girls are often cooking, weaving, gardening, and baby tending by the time they are seven or eight years of age, and sometimes when they are as young as three or four. Meanwhile, boys are farming, herding, and hunting well before they reach puberty. By adolescence, both sexes are proficient at the skills required of a married person, so marriage becomes a realistic option for these young people. Mothers and fathers often attempt to settle the marital fates of their children as soon as it is realistically possible. In South Asia, Punjabi parents start serious marriage negotiations when their sons are 17 or 18 and when their daughters are between 15 and 20 years old, and guardians who fail to marry a child at the proper age are thought to be neglecting their responsibilities, with their reputations suffering accordingly.

Marriage is delayed for men and women in a handful of societies around the world. The cause is typically economic. Among the residents of Inis Beag in Ireland, men usually marry at 36 years of age and women at 25, much later than the cross-cultural averages. In this culture, the typical father is reluctant to surrender his land and household to his sons, so young men have no way of supporting a family. Subanum men of the Philippines may delay marriage until they are able to accumulate the required bride price.

Across cultures, females tend to be married earlier than males. Boys are married later than girls in 85 percent of 45 cultures. In the remaining 15 percent, both sexes marry at roughly the same age. The differential in age of marriage for males and females is from one to five years in 78 percent of 37 societies and between six and ten years in another 16 percent. In the remaining 6 percent, the difference in age of marriage for males and females is over ten years.

Male-female differences in age of marriage are the result of a number of factors. In many cultures, parents wish to settle a daughter's marital fate early to avoid her doing anything that might damage her chances of attracting a suitable husband. People in a number of cultures also believe that early marriage makes a girl a better wife. Among the Amhara of Ethiopia, boys are married late in adolescence, but girls may become wives even before they are physically mature. Girls are also married off at an early age in part out of a desire to preserve their virginity. The Amhara also explain that a bride must be "tamed" by her husband, and the younger she is, the easier it is to tame her. The Gros Ventre of the United States betroth their prepubescent daughters to older, already married men on the view that a young girl will be more likely to become attached to the man that her elders choose for her and will, therefore, be a good wife to him. The practice is also viewed as a way of preventing girls from forming relationships with a variety of boys and ending up either in trouble or with a ruined reputation. The tendency for girls to marry earlier than boys may also be traced to the earlier onset of physical maturity in females. The fact that prospective husbands must often accumulate a hefty bride price before they marry may also explain the age discrepancies between brides and grooms in some societies. The custom of polygyny may also help to account for differences in marriage ages of males and females. Where men are permitted to have more than one wife at the same time, a shortage of women may result. The early marriage of girls relative to boys may help to alleviate this potential scarcity of available females. Age differentials between spouses may sometimes result from certain cultural prescriptions regarding who should marry whom. The Comanche of the U.S. Plains required marriages between certain categories of people that resulted in wide age discrepancies between husband and wife. For instance, if a spouse died, the surviving partner was expected to marry a sibling of the dead mate. If a widow was much younger than her brother-in-law or a widower was much older than his wife's sister, then a young woman would be marrying a much older man.

It is also the case that, as the age of marriage for men increases, so does the age discrepancy between males and females. Thus, men in general seem to prefer to marry young women, regardless of their own age. And young women are willing to marry older men. The opposite pattern is not common across cultures. Older women do not tend to marry younger men. How can this trend be explained? Evolutionary theory suggests that, when it comes to marriage, men and women are engaging in a kind of bartering. A female's most valuable resource is her youth and health, as the young and healthy wife offers a husband the greatest opportunity to produce a large family. Males are able to father children at any age once they have reached physical matuity, so youth in a spouse is not important from the point of view of a prospective wife. What does matter is the ability of the man to support his family and to see to it that the children get a good start in life. The older and more established man is more likely to be able to provide these benefits to his family. Hence, the tendency for a man to marry the youngest wife he can get and for a woman to find older men attractive.

See also NATURAL SELECTION; REPRODUCTIVE STRATEGIES; SEXUAL SELECTION.

Eglar, Zekiye. (1960) *A Punjabi Village in Pakistan.*

Elwin, Verrier. (1947) *The Muria and Their Ghotul.*

Flannery, Regina. (1953) *The Gros Ventre of Montana,* pt. 1.

Messing, Simon D. (1957) *The Highland-Plateau Amhara of Ethiopia.*

Stephens, William N. (1963) *The Family in Cross-Cultural Perspective.*

Wallace, Ernest, and Edward Adamson Hoebel. (1952) *The Comanches: Lords of the South Plains.*

MARRIAGE CEREMONIES	In all known societies, men and women publicly acknowledge their intention to begin their

lives together as a couple. They are then said to be married. In a few cultures, no further fuss is made beyond the simple declaration of the couple's new status. But in most societies, marriages are accompanied by some sort of celebration, including perhaps dressing up, eating, drinking, singing, and dancing. A society is more likely to have marriage ceremonies when there is a transfer of property from one family to the other or when spouses may bring inherited wealth to the marriage.

Sometimes wedding ceremonies are elaborate and expensive, involving multiple events and feasts. The initial round of gift-giving can begin an entire year before the actual wedding takes place, as when, in the United States, a Kwakiutl chief's daughter was married in the past. The prospective groom might have given his future father-in-law a gift of some 200 blankets to insure that his future bride was not promised to another man. The ceremony itself was attended by all of the people from the bride's and groom's tribes, who collected at the girl's village in canoes. The chief of each visiting and home tribe made speeches and perhaps another thousand blankets were presented by the groom's family to the bride's father. As each blanket was counted, the chiefs of the bride's clan said, "walk in with this," to remind the groom that he was walking into their home to take a daughter of their clan in exchange for the blankets. The groom sat in his canoe during this part of the ceremony. The celebration continued the next day, when the bride's father returned some blankets to the groom, who would give them away to the bride's kin at an elaborate celebration. The women were then invited to a feast by the wife of the groom's brother. This was the first time that the bride ate in her husband's house. The girl was fed by a woman who was considered to be a good wife. Once she had taken a bite, all of the other women ate and the wives of the chiefs made speeches.

A marriage ceremony can also be very simple. For instance, a couple from the Andaman Islands in the Indian Ocean are married when a man and woman embrace in front of the members of the community. This act symbolizes the affection that a husband and wife should feel for each other, as well as the new set of privileges and obligations that the couple owe to one

An Armenian couple opens the dancing by performing the first dance at their wedding celebration.

another. The ceremony also permits the community as a whole to acknowledge the new status of the man and woman as a married couple. Marriage ceremonies tend to be more elaborate when there is a considerable transfer of property between the families of the bride and groom. Where little or nothing of value is exchanged between the kin of the bride and groom, ceremonies are more likely to be simple or absent altogether.

In some societies, there are no formal celebrations marking the beginning of a marriage. The Hadza of Tanzania consider any couple who lives together as married. Thus, for instance, if a man goes to a woman's hut in the evening before other people have gone to sleep and then leaves again in the morning after other members of the household have awakened, the two are understood to be husband and wife. The marriage may also be acknowledged by way of a

ceremony, but this is not a requirement. Similarly, among the Siriono of South America, where cross-cousin marriage is preferred and common, there is no wedding ceremony. A boy and girl simply inform their parents of their intention to marry, and the boy moves his hammock from its usual spot near his own parents' sleeping place to a location near that of the parents of his bride.

In some societies, a couple follows other customs that serve to take the place of a marriage ceremony. In central Africa, a Mbuti marriage is not marked by any celebration, but when a Mbuti man marries, he must provide a female relative for one of the men in his new wife's family to marry, so that his own marriage is in fact marked by the exchange of women as well as gifts. The absence of a ceremony may reflect the fact that a couple is not considered married until the new wife becomes pregnant. The Trukes of Oceania marry without ceremony, but require the approval of the families of the pair if they are to be recognized as husband and wife.

Sometimes there is no formal ceremony to define the beginning of a marriage because the graduation to the married state is a gradual one. A Maori boy and girl in New Zealand who like each other might begin to live together. If they remain happy with their relationship, this arrangement comes to be accepted as a genuine marriage, first by the boy and girl themselves and later by their parents. The recognition of the relationship as a marriage makes the union legal. If the parents are not willing to approve the marriage, the couple can either separate or live elsewhere. Among the Bribri of Central America, marriages are usually arranged by the partners themselves, although the boy may ask permission of the girl's father once things have been settled between the young people themselves. The boy and girl initially go to live with the girl's parents for from eight days to one year

before moving in with the boy's family. The time spent within the bride's household serves as a trial marriage.

In a number of cultures, the marriage ceremony includes some kind of dramatized expression of hostility between the relatives of the bride and groom. At a Pukapuka wedding in Oceania, the kin of the bride and groom have contests in which each cohort insults the other, as well as the new husband and wife. Among the Hopi of the American Southwest, the female relatives of the bride and groom have mud-smearing and insult contests. And a Muria bride and groom in India put on a performance in which each beats the other. These ceremonial battles tend to be found in societies where the kin groups of the bride and groom are actual rivals or enemies and, in fact, men marry women from antagonistic groups in a number of cultures around the world.

Wedding ceremonies include some kind of religious or magical component in some cultures,

A traditional Hindu marriage ceremony. The couple is holding hands while the official pours ghee in the fire. An attendant holds sweets on a tray.

A Moldovan bride being dressed for the ceremony by her female relatives. In all cultures, women relatives assist the bride.

but this connection is not pervasive across societies. Hindu weddings are religious in character, and a Hopi couple will pray at the edge of the mesa during the wedding celebration. In Siberia, a Chuckchee bride and groom are sprinkled with reindeer blood—and in the Philippines, a Subanum couple with chicken blood—at their weddings. Noisemakers will be used to banish bad omens at an Iban wedding in Malaysia, and the Muria scare away demons at their marriage ceremonies.

Wedding ceremonies sometimes also include symbolic expressions of the married state. The union of a Hopi bride and groom is expressed in a ceremony in which the hair of bride and groom is washed in yucca suds and tied together. In Kenya, a Gusii husband expresses his ownership of his new bride by putting iron rings on her ankles. And the western custom of presenting a bride with a ring symbolizes the union of the hearts of the couple. The ring is placed on the fourth finger because that finger was believed to be the "string" from a woman's heart.

Batchelor, John. (1927) *Ainu Life and Lore: Echoes of a Departing Race.*

Beaglehole, Ernest, and Pearl Beaglehole. (1938) *Ethnology of the Pukapuka.*

Buck, Peter H. (1952) *The Coming of the Maori.*

Cipriani, Lidio. (1966) *The Andaman Islanders.*

Ember, Carol R., and Melvin Ember. (1988) *Anthropology,* 5th ed.

Gabb, William. (1876) *On the Indian Tribes and Languages of Costa Rica.* American Philosophical Society Proceedings 14.

Gladwin, Thomas, and Seymour B. Sarason. (1953) *Truk: Man in Paradise.*

Holmberg, Allan R. (1950) *Nomads of the Long Bow.* Washington, DC: Government Printing Office.

Levinson, David, and Martin J. Malone. (1980) *Toward Explaining Human Culture.*

Little, K. L. (1951) *The Mende of Sierra Leone.*

Malinowski, Bronislaw. (1922) *Argonauts of the Western Pacific: An Account of Native Enterprise and Adventure in Archipelagoes of Melanesian New Guinea.*

Putnam, Patrick. (1948) "The Pygmies of the Ituri Forest." In *A Reader in General Anthropology,* edited by Carleton S. Coon, 322–342.

Rosenblatt, P., and D. Unangst. (1974) "Marriage Ceremonies: An Exploratory Cross-Cultural Study." *Journal of Comparative Family Studies* 5: 41–56.

Stephens, William N. (1963) *The Family in Cross-Cultural Perspective.*

Stone, D. (1962) *The Talamancan Tribes of Costa Rica.* Papers of the Peabody Museum, Harvard University, 43.

Turnbull, Colin M. (1965) *The Mbuti Pygmies: An Ethnographic Survey.* Anthropological Papers of the Museum of Natural History 50, pt. 3.

Woodburn, J. (1964) *The Social Organization of the Hadza of North Tanzania.* Unpublished dissertation, Cambridge University.

Marriage Flexibility

In all known cultures, men and women who wish to regularize their relationship get married. Some societies, however, recognize different forms of marriage, each of which defines a somewhat different kind of connection between the married man and woman.

Sometimes variations in forms of marriage reflect different expectations about the permanence of the relationship. For instance, the Ifugao of the Philippines recognized two kinds of marriage. Trial marriages were really just sexual associations that are established between couples in the dormitories in which young people lived together. Contract marriages, by contrast, imply a formal and more permanent commitment between partners.

In some cases, differences in marriage type represent differences in status of the couple. Amhara couples in Ethiopia can marry in one of three ways. A small number of people—including, for instance, some of the nobility and all of the priesthood—have a *qurban,* or church marriage. More common is the kin-negotiated *semanya,* or "civil" union, presided over by the headman. The most frequent form is the *damaz,* or temporary marriage, in which a man makes a commitment to pay his wife periodic household wages. The social status of a *damaz* wife is usually lower than that of her husband, or she may be a woman whose kin do not own any land. Some *damaz* wives are divorcees who provide travelling men with nighttime accommodations. A man who has a *semanya* wife may transact a *damaz* marriage for the duration of a long journey so that his spouse will not have to travel with him. A prospective husband and wife have the least degree of personal freedom in choosing a mate in the church marriage and the greatest freedom in the temporary union. Civil marriages permit some individual selection of spouses, but the complicated arrangements that must take place between the kin of the couple constrain free choice considerably.

Variations in the form of marriage in a single culture may also imply differences in the degree of legality of the relationship. Two kinds of marriage are recognized in rural Haiti. In the first, known as *placage,* a couple simply lives together. By contrast, a church wedding entails a legalization of the union. A man and woman who have been married by *placage* can be divorced if the pair agree to separate. When a couple has been married legally, divorce becomes virtually impossible. People often settle for a *placage* marriage until they have the money to pay for a legal marriage. This can take some 10 or 15 years.

In many societies a couple resorts to an unconventional form of marriage when the more customary form is not economically feasible. For example, a Nyakyusa man of Tanzania ideally makes a match by negotiating with the father of the girl he wishes to marry. Sometimes the arrangements will be made while the girl is just a baby. The man will present the girl's father with one or two cows as a token of good faith. Additional cows are paid to the bride's father at the time of the marriage. Sometimes, however, a man wishes to marry a girl but cannot immediately pay the required cows to her father. In this case, he may run away with her, paying the cows later on in order to normalize the marriage. Similarly, the Yurok of California recognize two kinds of marriage. In the first and more respectable form, a groom pays the full bride price to his wife's family and takes his bride home to live with him. In the half-marriage, the new husband pays what bride price he can and works off the rest of the debt by laboring for his father-in-law. In this case, the couple lives with the wife's father and they are dependent upon him. Children produced from the marriage are owned by the wife's kin.

In general, the cultural recognition of different forms of marriage is an accommodation of the differences in the motives, status, resources, level of commitment, mode of mate choice, or goals of different marrying couples. This is captured in the list of traditional Hindu marriage forms. A man might marry a woman by forcibly capturing her and raping her, or by courting her and winning her heart. Marriage by bride price and marriage in return for a head or two of cattle were also recognized. Or, a daughter might be given to a student of the sacred Hindu writings or to a priest. Each of these marriages has a special name and is considered a different form of relationship between a husband and wife.

Barton, R. F. (1919) *Ifugao Law.*

Herskovits, Melville J. (1937) *Life in a Haitian Valley.*

Kroeber, Alfred L. (1925) *Handbook of the Indians of California.*

Mace, David, and Vera Mace. (1959) *Marriage: East and West.*

Messing, Simon D. (1957) *The Highland-Plateau Amhara of Ethiopia.*

Waterman, Thomas T., and Alfred Kroeber. (1934) *Yurok Marriages.*

Wilson, Godfrey. (1936) "An Introduction to Nyakyusa Society." *Bantu Studies* 10: 253–291.

MARRIAGE FORMS

Marriage is a cultural universal. This means that men and women in every known society publicly announce their intention to unite more or less permanently as a couple. In most Western societies, marriage is monogamous. In other words, a person is permitted to be married to only one other individual at a time. But in most other areas of the world, at least until recently, polygamy has been legally permissible. A culture is polygamous when either a man or a woman is legally allowed to be married to more than one spouse simultaneously. Polygamy can take two forms. Polygyny refers to the marriage of a man to more than one woman. Polyandry is the marriage of a woman to more than one man. Throughout human history, polygyny has been an acceptable form of marriage in most of the cultures around the world. By contrast, polyandry is very rare. Monogamy occurs in all cultures, but it has traditionally been the preferred form in only about 19 percent of 238 cultures. Polygyny is practiced in approximately 81 percent of these societies. A small handful of cultures allow marriage between a woman and more than one man. Whereas polygyny is permitted in a large majority of cultures, most marriages the world over are in fact monogamous. This is because most men are married to only one woman at a given time even when they have the legal option of taking more than one wife. The reasons for this discrepancy are practical. Thus, multiple wives often mean greater expenses for a man. Further, a first wife may resist her husband's desire to introduce a second woman into her household. Finally, co-wives often fight, or they may form a united front against their husband. In any case, the man's life becomes more difficult than it would be if he had only one wife. In spite of these complications, polygyny is the goal of virtually all men in cultures that allow it, and husbands in these societies are monogamous because they are prevented for some reason from acquiring extra wives.

Polygyny

In many cultures, polygyny is a mark of high status. This is true regardless of whether there are class distinctions in the society. For example, polygyny is practiced by older men among the Azande of Zaire and is a sign of their economic and political prestige relative to younger men. Aranda men of Australia may marry two or three women, and a man's wealth is judged by the number of wives he has. Further, the younger the wives the greater their value. In societies where class distinctions exist, the rich, the powerful, and the prestigious have multiple wives, and sometimes the right of polygyny is reserved for only certain classes of men. For instance, polygyny is prohibited to all but the highest ranking Trobrianders of New Guinea. And among the Tanala of Madagascar, chiefs have more wives than commoners do.

Polygyny, apart from issues of status, is an expensive proposition, so that many men are unable to obtain or support more than one wife. Nkundo men of Zaire are rarely monogamous by choice. Generally, a man will have only one wife because he is too poor to afford another. Similarly, while the Greenland Eskimos permitted polygyny, few men were good enough hunters to support more than one wife. Thus, only about 5 percent of Greenland Eskimo marriages were polygynous.

Polygyny can also create wealth for a man. Among the Siuai of Oceania, the ownership of pigs is important to a man's social and economic standing. Since women are necessary to the raising of pigs in this society, the more women there

Three-generation polygynous Kenyan Kikuyu family.

POLYGYNY/POLYANDRY

Polygyny

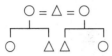

Sororal Polygyny

Polyandry

Fraternal Polyandry

KEY TO SYMBOLS

△ Male
○ Female
= Marriage
⊓ Siblingship

---

are in a household, the more pigs will be possessed by the head of the family. Polygynous men have more pigs than do men with only one spouse, and Siuai males often marry second and third wives for the purpose of increasing their pig herds. A Siuai man with multiple wives also obtains extra in-laws, and thus more collaborators in his various economic pursuits. And among the Azande ruling class, men prefer to acquire a number of wives because marriages help to forge alliances with other families, thereby enhancing the man's political power.

Polygynous wives may live together. More commonly, each has her own independent household, where she lives with her children. Co-wives are more likely to live together when they are also sisters, that is, when a husband practices sororal polygyny. In societies where wives are sisters in some cases and not in others, co-

wife residence will depend upon the relatedness of the women. Thus, for instance, Crow wives in North America lived in the same tipi if they were siblings, in different tipis if they were not. Where wives live in their own houses along with their children, it is customary for boys to move to a different dwelling somewhere around puberty. Thus, an already dispersed family, in which fathers live apart from their wives and children, becomes an even more fragmented one as a son grows up and leaves his mother, sisters, and younger brothers behind.

In polygynous families, the first wife (the senior wife) is typically accorded special status, which can include power over the other wives, privileges that the junior wives do not enjoy, and increased influence over the husband. In West Africa, the senior wife in a Bambara polygynous marriage is the manager of the household. She oversees the work and other activities of the remaining wives, distributes supplies, and in general takes on the role of a mother to the other women. Among the Chagga of Tanzania, the senior wife is her husband's closest confidant and it is she who arranges and consents to his next marriage. A betrothed young Banen girl in Cameroon is raised by the woman who is the senior wife in the household into which she will marry.

Men across cultures also characteristically make an effort to treat co-wives equally in certain matters. In many cultures, a husband will visit and sleep with each wife according to a strictly egalitarian schedule regardless of his personal preferences. Each wife is likely to be provided with equivalent economic resources, gifts, help, attention, and the like. For instance, in Western Polynesia, Tongan co-wives are provided with the same clothing for themselves and their children, as well as the same food. A husband divides his own personal belongings equally among the houses of his wives and spends an equal number of nights with each woman. A Tanala husband in Madagascar must sleep with each of his wives in turn, and if he spends a night with one wife when he should be with another, this constitutes adultery in the eyes of the community. Sometimes equality between co-wives includes the uniform sharing of duties. Thus, Tanala women divide farming and child-care chores so that one wife stays home on a given day to mind all of the children while the others work in the fields. Wives also take turns cooking for the entire polygynous household.

In many polygynous societies, co-wives run their own households independent of each other. For instance, each Tongan co-wife has her own hut, kitchen, field, and granary. Each woman is responsible only for her own field, and the food that she harvests is her own to distribute. One wife may help another at her own discretion, and women may do their housework together, look after each other's children, and the like, but this kind of cooperation is by no means required.

The elaborate rules followed by polygynous husbands to insure equal treatment of their co-wives are instituted in order to minimize the jealousy that often erupts between co-wives. But women in polygynous societies may also welcome the addition of another woman into their lives. Among the Bambara, an only wife is overworked and may urge her husband to bring another spouse into the household to help her with the chores. An Azande wife encourages her husband to marry again so that she will no longer be lonely.

Co-wives may also band together, supporting each other in opposition to their husband. Tongan wives, while they are often jealous and suspicious of each other, may also stick up for one another in quarrels with their husband or go off to drink beer together, leaving him at home to take care of himself. Tanala co-wives conduct extramarital affairs with each other's knowledge while still feeling secure that the husband will not find out. And if their husband attempts to force one woman to do something against her will, the other wives will gang up on him.

Since virtually all adults are married in most of the world's cultures, polygyny cannot work in a society unless there are more women of marriageable age than there are men. The surplus of potential wives has been explained as a consequence of more frequent warfare in polygynous societies. As it is virtually always men who wage war, men will be scarce relative to women in societies where there is a high rate of fighting. Some polygynous societies also create an excess of marriageable women by encouraging women to marry young and men to wait before marrying.

Polyandry

In contrast to polygyny, polyandry—the marriage of a woman to more than one man—is extremely rare and has only been reported as a regular marriage form in four societies: the Toda of India, Tibetans, Marquesans of Oceania, and Nayar of India. In cultures that allow a woman to have more than one husband, the mode of marriage is often fraternal polyandry. This means that co-husbands are often brothers. Among the Tibetans, a woman marries brothers. And when a Toda woman marries one man she is automatically also the wife of his brothers, including those who are as yet unborn. In some places, other marriage forms are predominant and polyandry is practiced occasionally. Pawnee boys of the U.S. Plains sometimes became the husband of an uncle's or older brother's wife. The arrangement was for the temporary convenience of adolescents and lasted perhaps three or four years.

Polyandrous marriage partners opt for one of a variety of living arrangements across cultures. Among the Lesu of New Ireland, both polygyny and polyandry sometimes occur, although monogamy is the most frequent form of marriage. When a woman has more than one husband, everyone eats together, the husbands with a bundle of *turo* between them and the wife sitting close by. All three spouses may also sleep in the same house, each in a separate bed with the woman between them. Sometimes, however, the junior husband will sleep in the men's house, or the wife may sleep with each man in turn. A Toda wife may have three or four husbands, living with each for a month in turn.

When a number of men are married to the same woman, co-husbands must deal with the fact that they are sharing one woman sexually. Sexual jealousy is not openly displayed between Toda or Marquesan husbands, but in these cultures the expression of such jealousy is consid-

Egyptian Bedouin co-wives prepare lunch.

ered to be in bad taste. The Toda also attempt to minimize the chances of direct sexual confrontations between co-husbands by requiring one husband to place a staff outside the door of the house to warn the other husbands away when he intends to have sexual relations with his wife. Among the Aweikoma of Brazil and the Lesu of New Ireland, where there are no sanctions against sexual possessiveness, men do sometimes exhibit jealousy toward co-husbands or potential co-husbands. It is possible, therefore, that polyandrous men are likely to feel possessive about their wives but will be less inclined to show this when cultures disapprove of the exhibition of sexual antagonism between men.

When a woman has more than one husband, questions arise about the paternity of the woman's children. Among the Toda, all of the wife's husbands are viewed as the fathers of all of her children. The Lepcha of Tibet assume that the first husband is the father of all of the children in a polyandrous marriage.

Where polyandry occurs, the reasons for the practice tend to be economic. A well-to-do or powerful Marquesan man might marry a woman who has a number of men already attached to her. These males would then become part of the new husband's household, providing it with more manpower. The more males in a household, the wealthier it is able to become. Thus, polyandry adds to the economic well-being of a man's family and allows him to accrue prestige as a result. Tibetans make a living by farming. However, poorer families do not have enough land to divide among all of the children while still allowing each new household to make a proper living. Thus, a number of sons marry one woman and work the farm as a cooperative unit. The land is then handed down to the next generation of sons, who also marry one woman and labor cooperatively. Richer Tibetan families do not practice polyandry, as men who are economically better off can afford to support a wife and children on their own. Well-to-do Tibetan men, then, are

monogamous, and some have more than one wife. A married Lepcha man may ask a brother to become a co-husband if he cannot do all of the farm work alone, either because the job is too demanding for him or because he is involved in other ventures that take him away from the fields.

Female infanticide exists in at least two of the cultures that permit polyandry. This means that there are more men than women in at least some polyandrous societies. The two practices are thus compatible, as the marriage of one woman to more than one man compensates for the relative excess of males in comparison with females.

Group Marriage

In discussions of marriage forms, references are sometimes made to group marriage, a joint marital bond between a number of men and a number of women. In fact, however, there are no unambiguous examples of group marriage. Rather, cases that are cited as the joint marriage of groups of men and women turn out to look more like instances of wife-borrowing or temporary variants on some other kind of marriage arrangement. For instance, the Chuckchee of Siberia are sometimes described as having practiced group marriage in former times with men participating in such an arrangement called "companions in wives." Each man has a right to the wives of his marriage companions. In reality, the men who form a group live in different camps, so that these are not so much group marriages as they are wife-lending compacts. Men living in the same camp are reluctant to become companions in marriage, although there are exceptions.

The Siriono of South America also pattern sexual access in a way that looks to some people like group marriage. A man is allowed to engage in sexual intercourse with his wife and also with women considered to be sisters, and a

Polyandrous wedding in Nepal with one wife and two husbands. Polyandry is very rare across cultures.

woman may have sexual relations with her husband and his real and classificatory brothers. But the relationship between spouses is clearly different from the connection between a husband and his sisters-in-law or a wife and her brothers-in-law. Thus, Siriono spouses publicly announce their change to married status, whereas there is no formalized relationship between individuals and their in-laws.

Group marriage is associated with polyandry among the Toda, where it sometimes happens that each man who shares a single wife also has a wife of his own. Sometimes several Toda men have several wives between them. And a well-off Marquesan household, which starts off as polyandrous, may add a wife or two to the household. In this case, all the men and women have sexual access to each other. Thus, we can find isolated instances of arrangements where a number of men have sexual access to a number of women, but no society sanctions group marriage as the preferred form of marriage and in no society is group marriage in fact a common practice.

Causes of Polygyny

Monogamy is the most common marriage form across cultures, but polygyny has been by far the preferred form of marriage. By contrast, polyandry, which is the opposite of polygyny, is extremely uncommon and is really a cultural curiosity more than a cultural variation. Why is this the case? Why do most societies idealize the marriage of one man to multiple wives and why do so few sanction unions between one woman and many men? The popularity of polygyny is consistent with predictions from the evolutionary perspective. In particular, this form of marriage has the potential to maximize the number of offspring that a man can produce and look after. This is because the reproductive success of a male depends upon the number of females to whom he has sexual access. A woman, by contrast, does not increase the number of children that she can have by having sexual intercourse with more men, and in fact there is evidence that the opposite is the case. So multiple spouses do not provide the benefit for women that they do for men from the point of view of reproductive success. This alone helps to explain the relative desirability of polygyny and rarity of polyandry. But the sexual sharing of a woman by a number of men is also detrimental to the reproductive success of the husbands, as each man is reducing his own chances of producing children, and, in the worst case, may produce none at all. Thus, polyandry labors under the twin burdens of adding little to a woman's reproductive success and substantially reducing that of a man. As it has little to recommend it to either husband or wife from an evolutionary point of view, it is little wonder that it is so uncommon.

The tendency for polyandrous wives to marry brothers may help to explain why men are willing to share a wife in the few cases where this does occur. When the two men who have sexual access to the same woman are related, all of the woman's offspring share at least some genes with each husband. Thus, a man who ends up decreasing the number of children he has still manages to have at least some of his own genes survive. If husbands were totally unrelated, then a man might spend his life married to a woman who never produced children who shared any of his genes. The practice of sororal polygyny can be explained in a similar fashion. Where women

who share a husband are sisters, any offspring that a man has with one of his wives is the niece or nephew of the remaining wives. Thus, the sacrifice that co-wives are making by sharing a man is partially returned by the production of children who share some of their genes.

It is also true that polygyny is not the only means by which a male can increase the number of children he has. The same result is produced by having sexual intercourse with a woman without marrying her, and the frequency of extramarital sex for men across cultures suggests that males do employ this strategy for maximizing their reproductive success. But the evolutionary perspective also suggests that human children have the best chance of surviving when they are cared for by two parents. Polygyny allows a man to have many children and to supervise and contribute to their rearing as their recognized father, thus maximizing the chances that they will survive to be parents themselves.

See also DIFFERENTIAL REPRODUCTIVE SUCCESS; JEALOUSY BETWEEN CO-WIVES; NATURAL SELECTION; REPRODUCTIVE STRATEGIES; SEXUAL SELECTION.

Basedow, Herbert. (1925) *The Australian Aboriginal.*

Bogoras, Waldemar. (1904–09) *The Chukchee.*

Bohannan, Paul, and John Middleton, eds. (1968) *Marriage, Family and Residence.*

Dorsey, George A., and James R. Murie. (1940) *Notes on Skidi Pawnee Society.*

Dugast, I. (1954) "Banen, Bafia, and Balom." In *Peoples of the Central Cameroons: Tikar,* edited by M. McCulloch, M. Littlewood, and I. Dugast, 134–153.

Dundas, Charles. (1924) *Kilimanjaro and Its People: A History of the Wachagga, Their Laws,*

Customs, and Legends, Together with Some Account of the Highest Mountain in Africa.

Ember, Carol R., and Melvin Ember. (1988) *Anthropology.* 5th ed.

Ember, Melvin, and Carol R. Ember. (1983) *Marriage, Family, and Kinship: Comparative Studies of Social Organization.*

Fox, Robin. (1967) *Kinship and Marriage.*

Hulstaert, Gustave. (1928) *Marriage among the Nkundu.*

Larken, P. M. (1930) "Impressions of the Azande." *Sudan Notes and Records* 13: 99–115.

Lehmann, F. Rudolf. (1951) "Notes on the Daily Life of the Nyakyusa." *Sociologus* 1: 138–148.

Levine, Nancy. (1988) *The Dynamics of Polyandry: Kinship, Domesticity, and Population in the Tibetan Border.*

Marshall, William E. (1873) *A Phrenologist among the Todas.*

Monteil, Charles V. (1924) *The Bambara of Segou and Kaarta: An Historical, Ethnographical and Literary Study of a People of the French Sudan.*

Murdock, George P. (1949) *Social Structure.*

Paques, Viviana. (1954) *The Bambara.*

Pasternak, B. (1976) *Introduction to Kinship and Social Organization.*

Schulze, Louis. (1891) "The Aborigines of the Upper and Middle Finke River." *Royal Society of South Australia, Transactions and Proceedings and Report* 14: 210–246.

Stephens, William N. (1963) *The Family in Cross-Cultural Perspective.*

Wilson, Godfrey. (1936) "An Introduction to Nyakyusa Society." *Bantu Studies* 10: 153–291.

Wilson, Monica. (1951) *Good Company.*

———. (1957) *Rituals of Kinship among the Nyakyusa.*

———. (1959) *Communal Rituals of the Nyakyusa.*

MARRIAGE PARTNERS, CRITERIA FOR CHOOSING

Across cultures, the suitability of an individual as a potential spouse is judged on the basis of characteristics likely to make the person a valuable and productive mate and an agreeable companion. In India, when a Bhil woman imagines the ideal husband, she pictures a hard-working, obedient man, thrifty and free of debt. The Bhil girl who is beautiful, industrious, shy, and dutiful toward her mother and father is considered to make the best wife. The reputation of the kin group of a prospective Bhil spouse is also important. A marriage is in part an alliance between families, and lineages known for honesty, thriftiness, and hospitality are preferred over those reputed to be lazy, miserly, dishonest, quarrelsome, or poor. In Brazil, Cayapa girls are taught how to keep themselves clean and make themselves pretty, and a Cayapa mother counsels her daughter to appear happy and pleasant around boys if she wishes to marry. Diligence, an equable temperament, and cooking skill are also important traits in a girl who wants to get and keep a husband. Japanese parents look for a daughter-in-law who is healthy, skilled in housework and farming, good-natured, and docile and a son-in-law who is healthy, hard-working, and likely to be successful as a provider. An Igbo parent in Nigeria searching for a prospective spouse for a child is interested in the health and social status of the candidate's family, including incidences of early death and twin births and number of divorces. Once a likely bride is found for a young man, she moves in with the boy's family. During her visit, the girl's behavior is observed by her prospective in-laws, who assess her social and domestic skills and disposition.

Among the qualities desired in a spouse, willingness and ability to work are the most greatly valued traits in a majority of cultures. Of 39 societies, 67 percent rate industry and skill in domestic and subsistence activities as of major importance in a husband or wife. In none of these societies are these traits thought to be of only minor significance. A Copper Eskimo woman of Alaska is interested in procuring a husband who will see to it that she is housed, fed, and clothed, and a Callinago woman in the Caribbean looks for a man who will be a good provider. Southern African !Kung parents want their children to marry into families that "are able to feed themselves" and whose members are not selfish, lazy, or thin. Industriousness and competence are equally valued traits in a prospective bride. Among the Burusho of India, if the woman in charge of the domestic affairs of her home fails to ration food resources from one harvest to the next, her family will go hungry for extended periods of time. Therefore, the woman who fails to manage household duties competently will be divorced and sent back to her parents. Among the Alor of Indonesia, the most valued attribute in a prospective bride is the willingness to work hard. And the rural Thai girl who is a competent planter of rice has no trouble attracting boys.

The wealth and social status of a potential spouse are also a major concern in many cultures. Of 37 worldwide societies, 57 percent view the family background and assets of a prospective mate as very important. For instance, an ideal Alorese husband should be rich. Similarly, Cayapa girls are admonished to avoid suitors who are poor. And in India, a Muria Gond boy who is looking for a first wife is advised to choose a woman who is known to work hard and who has her own property and who can, therefore, help him to advance himself and perhaps obtain a second wife. In Ethiopia, the Amhara boy's father is also interested in assessing the lineage of a prospective daughter-in-law, preferring that the bride come from Amhara stock. Among the Abkhaz, individuals can only marry within their own social class. And social rank is the most important criterion in mate choice among the

Javanese, with religious affiliation ranking second in importance.

In many societies, a prospective mate's character is taken very seriously. Of 34 societies, 53 percent regard qualities such as honesty, intelligence, loyalty, and obedience as very important in a spouse. Among the Javanese, marriages are arranged by the parents of a prospective spouse. Once a man's family has found an acceptable girl, the would-be groom and his family pay her a visit. This gives the man an opportunity to look over his potential wife. He is especially pleased with a woman who walks demurely and avoids looking about excessively, as this indicates that she may be willful and disobedient. Women who display these characteristics may be rejected by a man who is seeking a spouse. An Amhara boy will be warned by his father to pay attention to the character of the mother of a girl he is thinking of marrying, as the daughter will take after her.

Physical attractiveness in a potential mate is viewed as very important in a minority of cultures. Of 30 societies, only 37 percent are highly concerned about the looks of a prospective mate, while an additional 47 percent take attractiveness in a spouse to be moderately important. In Oceania, Marquesan men looking for a bride first consider a girl's sexual expertise and physical attractiveness, and these traits figure prominently in the social rank of a woman. The most attractive girls become the senior wives in prominent families. Similarly, beauty is a primary criterion in the choice of a bride among the Marshallese of Oceania. The Cubeo of the Amazon also care about large breasts, a strong back, and unblemished skin in a woman. Among the Goajiro of Colombia, physical appearance and mode of dress are important criteria in the choice of a marriage partner and a beautiful, well-dressed woman will attract a good bride price. The beauty of a woman also figures into the equation of mate choice among the Bambara of West Africa. A woman whose bosom is scarred or whose face has been disfigured by smallpox is less desirable than one with flawless skin.

While the physical appearance of a spouse is clearly important in some societies, the criteria for assessing beauty often reflect other attributes that are valued in a mate. For the Chuckchee of Siberia, the most important quality in a bride is physical strength and the capacity for work, and womanly beauty is defined first and foremost by bodily strength. Among the Kwoma of New Guinea, it is the large, strong woman who can carry a heavy load of vegetables or wood up the mountain that attracts the suggestive gestures and comments of the men.

In a number of societies, the appearance of an individual is of minor importance as a criterion for choosing a mate. Attractiveness in a husband or wife is not emphasized in 16 percent of 30 societies. In Alaska, a Copper Eskimo male looks for a woman who can prepare his meals and turn the caribou hides that he provides into clothing and tents. Physical appearance does not figure importantly into his choice of a bride. While unblemished skin in a woman is attractive to the Bambara male, a man who is looking for a wife is more concerned that a prospective bride is hardworking and a good cook and has a good head for business. Jivaro men in Ecuador look for a woman who is strong and can work hard. A man who chooses a wife on the basis of good looks is said to be foolish. The North American Kutenai man who is looking for a wife wants a good tanner and wood gatherer. A woman's physical appearance is of secondary importance. Neither does attractiveness matter in the choice of a wife among the Navajo of Arizona, unless a girl is extremely ugly, in which case it may be more difficult to find her a husband. Among the Vietnamese, good health and skill in housekeeping are more critical in the choice of a wife than are good looks. Wogeo boys of New Guinea are warned not to marry a girl who is lazy no matter how pretty

she may be. Even a girl with ringworm is better than a wife who is good to look at but who will not work. And among the Cubeo, physical endurance and the willingness to work are regarded as more vital qualities for a wife than is physical appeal. In fact, sexual attractiveness in a wife is considered to be a potential liability, as such women can cause dissension among male relatives, and a sullen woman is preferred to one who is lively.

Even where attractiveness in a spouse is valued, it is unlikely to be the major criterion motivating the choice of a spouse. An ideal Goajiro wife should be tall and full-bodied, with wide hips, small upright breasts, and, most importantly, firm flesh. Her skin should be light and she should dress well. Women know that good looks are important to attracting a husband who will pay a high bride price and to keeping a husband from straying, and women go to some lengths to try to maintain their physical appearance. But while beauty in a woman matters to a Goajiro man, other traits in a woman figure importantly in a man's choice of a spouse. A woman who wishes to marry well must be able to care for a husband and children. A man is also happy if his wife's kin are wealthy, as well-off relatives are likely to help in the support of a woman and her family once her husband has paid the bride price. Rich relatives will also provide a woman with a large dowry that the husband then administers, and they will present a number of gifts to his children. Even the interest in the physical attractiveness of a woman reflects a larger concern with other matters. Light skin is an indication that the woman is able to take care of herself by staying out of the sun. And dress is important because it is a reflection of a woman's social status.

In some societies, beauty is equated with cleanliness. Cleanliness is especially important among the Alorese of Indonesia, and adolescents begin to bathe and comb their hair more often when they become interested in finding a spouse. Siuai girls of Oceania prefer a man who is young, with clear skin and lice-free hair who bathes often and wears a clean loincloth. For their part, Siuai men avoid women who are unclean, disfigured, epileptic, or mentally deficient, although epileptics are acceptable as mistresses. By contrast, a clean, pleasant-smelling woman who sees to her appearance attracts men looking for potential marriage partners. The health of a potential spouse is emphasized in many societies. Before they enter into any marriage agreements for their sons, Amhara fathers of Ethiopia try to determine the health background of the girl's family, including any incidences of venereal disease, leprosy, or other conditions thought to be heritable by children.

Of all considerations that contribute to mate choice across cultures, the affections of the prospective bride and groom are most often discounted. In 40 percent of 33 societies, people believe that love is of only minor importance, while in 42 percent people think that it is very important that a marriage be based on love. Among the Burmese, romantic love based upon physical attraction and compatibility figure importantly in the choice of a spouse. And the Mbuti of central Africa believe that a "real" marriage is underwritten by mutual affection between spouses, as a husband and wife who care for each other will wish to have children, thus bringing stability to their relationship. A marriage without affection, by contrast, is "empty." Nor does romantic love figure prominently in the choice of marital partners among the Navajo. Rather, Navajo men say that one woman is as good as another as a wife as long as she is healthy and a good worker. Skilled weavers are especially desirable as wives. In Madagascar, Tanala marriages are typically based upon economic concerns. Men are satisfied if their wives are strong and hard-working, whereas a woman is content as long as her husband is industrious;

if he is rich, so much the better. When love does enter into the equation, it is generally confined to first marriages, and people think of romance as foolishness.

If the importance of love is underplayed in matchmaking in many cultures, people in many societies are concerned that a man and woman will be able to get along with each other once they are married. The Ainu of Japan emphasize the importance of compatibility between a husband and wife, and when parents arrange marriages for their children, the prospective bride moves in with the proposed husband and his family to determine whether the two get along well together. If not, the girl is sent back to her kin.

Men and women in American culture have different ideas about what qualities are important in a potential mate. Males tend to be inclined toward physical beauty, while females are more interested in the economic potential of a possible mate. The pattern may have some cross-cultural validity. For instance, Burmese males are initially attracted by a girl's physical appearance, but females are more interested in a man's intelligence, level of education, gentleness, and even-mindedness than in his looks.

It is also the case that parents and the society at large may view the goals of marriage and the criteria for choosing a spouse according to priorities that differ dramatically from what matters to the young people themselves. Among the Chiricahua of the American Southwest, older people think of marriage as an economic arrangement, but for Chiricahua boys and girls, romantic attachment looms large as a basis for mate choice, and people frequently point out some young man who, it is said, has married for love instead of stopping to consider whether a girl was a good worker. Mataco girls of Argentina take the initiative in choosing boyfriends, and a boy who is so chosen must accept the girl's advances if he wishes to save face and to avoid incurring the anger of the girl's parents. When a girl brings a boy home for the night, the couple is understood to be provisionally married. The relationship, however, is not considered to be permanently binding, especially because girls choose potential husbands largely on the basis of sexual attraction and similar qualities, while parents are more interested in seeing a daughter make an economically sound match.

See also ATTRACTIVENESS.

Batchelor, John. (1927) *Ainu Life and Lore: Echoes of a Departing Race.*

Beaglehole, Ernest, and Pearl Beaglehole. (1938) *Ethnology of Pukapuka.*

Beardsley, Richard K., John W. Hall, and Robert E. Ward. (1972) *Village Japan.*

Bogoras, Waldemar. (1904–1909) *The Chukchee.*

Dyott, George M. (1926) *On the Trail of the Unknown in the Wilds of Ecuador and the Amazon.*

Elwin, Verrier. (1947) *The Muria and Their Ghotul.*

Fock, Niels. (1963) "Mataco Marriage." *Folk* 5: 91–101.

Fuchs, Stephen. (1942) "The Marriage Rites of the Bhils in the Nimar District, C.P." *Man in India* 22: 105–139.

Geertz, Hildred. (1961) *The Javanese Family.*

Goldman, Irving. (1963) *The Cubeo: Indians of the Northwest Amazon.*

Graham, Walter. (1924) *Siam,* vol. 1–2.

Gutierrez de Pineda, Virginia. (1950) *Social Organization in La Guajira.*

Henry, Joseph. (1910) *The Soul of an African People. The Bambara, Their Psychic, Ethical, Religious and Social Life.*

Hickey, Gerald C. (1964) *Village in Vietnam.*

Hogbin, H. Ian. (1944–1945) "Marriage in Wogeo, New Guinea." *Oceania* 15: 324–352.

Jenness, Diamond. (1922) *The Life of the Copper Eskimos.*

Kramer, Augustin, and Hans Nevermann. (1938) *Ralik-Ratak (Marshall Islands).*

Leighton, Dorothea, and Clyde Kluckhohn. (1969) *Children of the People: The Navaho Individual and His Development.*

Linton, Ralph. (1933) *The Tanala: A Hill Tribe of Madagascar.*

Linton, Ralph. (1939) "Marquesan Culture." In *The Individual and His Society,* edited by Abram Kardiner, 138–196.

Lorimer, E. O. (1939) *Language Hunting in the Karakorum.*

Luzbetak, Louis J. (1951) *Marriage and the Family in Caucasia: A Contribution to the Study of North Caucasian Ethnology and Customary Law.*

Marshall, Lorna. (1959) "Marriage among the !Kung Bushmen." *Africa* 29: 335–364.

Messing, Simon D. (1957) *The Highland-Plateau Amhara of Ethiopia.*

Nash, M. (1965) *The Golden Road to Modernity.*

Nath, Y. V. S. (1960) *Bhils of Ratanmal: An Analysis of the Social Structure of a Western Indian Community.*

Oliver, Douglas. (1955) *A Solomon Island Society: Kinship and Leadership among the Siuai of Bougainville.*

Opler, Morris E. (1941) *An Apache Life-Way: The Economic, Social and Religious Institutions of the Chiricahua Indians.*

Raum, O. F. (1940) *Chaga Childhood: A Description of Indigenous Education in an East African Tribe.*

Taylor, Douglas M. (1938) *The Caribs of Dominica.*

———. (1946) "Kinship and Social Structure of the Island Carib." *Southwestern Journal of Anthropology* 2: 180–212.

Turnbull, Colin M. (1965) *The Mbuti Pygmies: An Ethnographic Survey.* Anthropological Papers of the Museum of Natural History 50, pt. 3.

Turney-High, Harry H. (1941) "Ethnography of the Kutenai." *American Anthropologist* 43(2) (Supplement).

Uchendu, Victor C. (1965) *The Igbo of Southeast Nigeria.*

Whiting, John W. M. (1941) *Becoming a Kwoma: Teaching and Learning in a New Guinea Tribe.*

MARRIAGE PARTNERS, SELECTION OF

In most traditional cultures around the world, it is expected that all men and women will marry. But social customs concerning the choice of mates vary widely. In some cultures, marriages are arranged by parents or matchmakers and the prospective bride and groom have no say at all. Sometimes the intended partners will not even meet each other until the day of the wedding. In some societies the opposite is true, and boys and girls may have virtual autonomy in deciding whom they will marry. In still other places, mate choice may be a matter of joint decision making between parent and child.

Wives are chosen by the parents of a boy in 29.3 percent in a sample of 157 societies around the world. In 44.1 percent of 161 cultures, a girl is expected to marry the man selected by her parents. Among the Abkhaz, a father can arrange a marriage for his child without consulting anyone. In fact, however, the opinions of the young people themselves, especially the boys, are taken into account. In Zaire, an Azande father can require his daughter to marry a man of his choosing, and has the right to punish a girl who refuses by isolating or chaining her. Usually, fathers permit a daughter to choose her own husband, unless the girl rejects all of her boyfriends as candidates for marriage. In this case, her father will force the issue. The community at large is severely critical of a recalcitrant girl, largely because a daughter who does not marry deprives her father of the bride price that her marriage would net him.

In a number of cultures, the prospective bride and groom get a greater hearing by the parents. Among the Cubeo of the Amazon, prospective marriage partners are tentatively chosen before the couple meets, but the boy and girl are then given an opportunity to assess each other during a visit that the young man and his family pay to the girl's home. If the boy is not pleased with the proposed bride, the visit will be terminated quickly, but if the girl is acceptable to him, his family will prolong their stay. The girl must also agree to the match, and one way that she communicates her interest in a boy is by running in his presence when she would normally walk. Or she may pinch or punch him as they pass each other. If the proposed union is initially agreeable to both parties, then the relationship will progress toward marriage. The girl may throw some manioc (tapioca) mash in the boy's face, and he will pretend to be angry and try to catch her. Perhaps she will then escape to her garden, where the boy will catch up and have sexual intercourse with her. The couple are then understood to be engaged.

In 17.8 percent of 157 cultures, marriages are sometimes arranged for a boy by his parents, while sometimes the boy himself may choose a spouse. The same pattern holds for the marriage of a girl in 17.4 percent of 161 societies. Among the Ashanti of Ghana, for instance, the feeling is that a father should provide a wife for his son. A boy may also choose his own spouse, but he would not dream of marrying a girl without the consent of his parents and, while their approval is not legally necessary, everyone agrees that it is indispensable before a couple can be married. Nor can a marriage take place unless the girl's father agrees, as it is his responsibility to make sure that a prospective groom can provide for his daughter. Similarly, among the Havasupai of the American Southwest, marriages can be arranged in one of two ways. Matches might be agreed upon by the families of the prospective bride and groom. The boy would also present a gift to the girl's parents before the engagement was finalized. Or a suitor might visit his girlfriend in her bed at night. A gift is then given to the girl's parents and permission to be married is obtained from the boy's parents later on in the courtship. Arranged marriages typically occur when the parents desire a particular match but the boy and girl do not know each other or when a boy is too shy to approach a girl on his own. When two young people already know each other or when a boy is confident that the girl of his choice will accept his advances, then on their own the boy and girl will make preliminary plans to be married.

A discontented spouse may resist an arranged marriage. A Guatemalan Quiche girl who has been married to a man she does not like may refuse to have sexual relations with her husband. Her spouse cannot force the matter, but he may divorce her. In the past, he might take a slave as a concubine to punish his recalcitrant wife as well as to meet his sexual needs. Parents in many cultures appreciate that marriages are more likely to fail if the spouses dislike one another, and for this reason the approval of the young people is often sought by their elders before a match is finalized. In the American Southwest, Chiricahua parents prefer that their children marry into a family of good standing, and a parent may try to persuade a son or daughter to agree to a particular match. But the Chiricahua also believe that a forced marriage is

fated to be an unsuccessful one, and are therefore sympathetic to the preferences of the young people themselves when it comes to choosing a spouse. A boy who likes a specific girl may try to find out whether she returns his feelings and, if she appears interested, he may ask his father or uncle to approach the girl's father with a marriage proposal. The girl, for her part, will have told her mother that she likes this particular boy.

Boys choose their own wives, perhaps then obtaining the approval of parents, in 49.7 percent of 157 societies. Girls have the same freedom to choose their own husbands in 36.1 of 161 cultures. Among the Iban of Malaysia, a boy who has had a marriage proposal accepted by the girl of his choice will give her a ring as a symbol of his commitment. He then obtains the approval of his parents who, if they consent to the match, in turn visit the girl's parents, taking a cup with them. If her parents agree to the marriage, they accept the cup as the final symbol of the arrangement and a decision is made regarding when the groom will fetch the girl. Among the Yukaghir of Siberia, an intermediary sent by a young man will attempt to obtain the consent of a girl's father for her hand in marriage, but in reality the boy is already certain of the outcome of the negotiations, as the two have already become intimate and have determined between themselves that they wish to marry.

Customs surrounding the choice of marriage partners may depend upon the age and marital history of a prospective bride or groom. For the Amhara of Ethiopia, the first marriage takes place when a boy is in his late teens, and a girl is married even before then, sometimes before she is physically mature. The parents of the couple have a good deal of influence regarding the arrangement of these marriages, many of which end in divorce. By contrast, individuals have much more freedom in the choice of spouses in subsequent marriages. Similarly, Azande men were traditionally responsible for providing their sons with a first wife, and the father of a son would negotiate directly with a man who had a daughter, usually while the children were still infants. Neither parent could make a move without first consulting oracles. But subsequent marriages are arranged by the prospective groom himself.

In some cultures, if a man wishes to marry a particular woman, he must provide the woman's household or community with a bride for one of its members in return. In central Africa, a Mbuti boy who falls in love with a certain girl is required to find a "sister" for a man in his sweetheart's family to marry. While the "sister" can in fact be any female relative, it is not always easy to find a girl who is willing to marry the man for whom his prospective in-laws wish to find a wife. Further, if one girl proves to be infertile, or if one of the couples divorces, then the remaining marriage is also terminated.

Across cultures, boys tend to have more freedom in the choice of marriage partners than do girls. When a Comanche boy of the U.S. Plains found a girl he wished to marry, he found a go-between who approached her brother, father, or guardian on his behalf, and a smart boy tried to strike up a friendship with a relative of the girl he desired to wed. The girl's feelings might or might not be consulted, but a Comanche female was required to marry any man who was preferred by her brother or father and a girl who resisted their choice might legally be killed by them. Among the Trobrianders of New Guinea, a couple is legally married when the woman moves in with the man and gifts are exchanged between them. If the woman's parents do not approve of the match, these arrangements become only an attempt to marry and not a genuine marriage. By contrast, a man may marry anyone he likes, the approval of his parents being irrelevant to his plans. The need for the consent of the woman's parents is consistent with the fact that the wife's family is required to provide a son-in-law with a large annual supply of food.

Customs for arranging marriages are consistently related to other aspects of sex and marriage across cultures. Where marriages are arranged for girls, consummation of the marriage is regarded as a special occasion, while the wedding night is not culturally recognized as special when the bride has had a say in the choice of her husband. Where choice of spouse is left up to the girl herself, extramarital sex for husbands tends to be condemned, while male infidelity is regarded more leniently where a girl's parents choose a spouse for her. Finally, in cultures where males select their own spouses, they are also more likely to engage in premarital sex, while premarital continence on the part of boys is more likely to occur where parents arrange marriages for their sons.

Bandelier, Adolph F. (1876–1879) *On the Social Organization and Mode of Government of the Ancient Mexicans.*

Broude, Gwen J. (1975) *A Cross-Cultural Study of Some Sexual Beliefs and Practices.* Unpublished dissertation, Harvard University.

Broude, Gwen J., and Sarah J. Greene. (1976) "Cross-Cultural Codes on Twenty Sexual Attitudes and Practices." *Ethnology* 15: 409–429.

———. (1983) "Cross-Cultural Codes on Husband-Wife Relationships." *Ethnology* 22: 263–280.

Bunzel, Ruth. (1952) *Chichicastenango: A Guatemalan Village.*

Evans-Pritchard, Edward Evan. (1971) *The Azande: History and Political Institutions.*

Fortes, Meyer. (1945) *The Dynamics of Clanship among the Tallensi: Being the First Part of an Analysis of the Social Structure of a Trans-Volta Tribe.*

———. (1949) *The Web of Kinship among the Tallensi: The Second Part of Analysis of the Social Structure of a Trans- Volta Tribe.*

Fürer-Haimendorf, Christoph von. (1948) "The Raj Gonds of Adilabad." In *The Raj Gonds of Adilabad*, 1–21.

Goldman, Irving. (1963) *The Cubeo: Indians of the Northwest Amazon*.

Howell, William. (1908–1910) "A Collection of Articles on the Sea Dyak." *Sarawak Gazette* 38–40.

Jochelson, W. (1926) *The Yukaghir and Yukaghirized Tungus*. Memoirs of the American Museum of Natural History 13.

Luzbetak, Louis J. (1951) *Marriage and the Family in Caucasia: A Contribution to the Study of North Caucasian Ethnology and Customary Law.*

Malinowski, Bronislaw. (1922) *Argonauts of the Western Pacific: An Account of Native Enterprise and Adventure in Archipelagoes of Melanesian New Guinea.*

Messing, Simon D. (1957) *The Highland Plateau Amhara of Ethiopia.*

Opler, Morris E. (1941) *An Apache Life-Way: The Economic, Social and Religious Institutions of the Chiricahua Indians.*

Smithson, Carma Lee. (1959) *The Havasupai Woman.*

Turnbull, Colin M. (1962) *The Forest People.*

———. (1965) *Wayward Servants: The Two Worlds of the African Pygmies.*

Wallace, Ernest, and Edward Adamson Hoebel. (1952) *The Comanches: Lords of the South Plains.*

MEN'S HOUSES

In a majority of societies around the world, people live with their families. They eat and sleep with relatives, and home is where their families live. In a large mi-nority of societies, however, a male does not think of his own household as his only home. Rather, boys and men also have some kind of communal dwelling to which they retire for the purpose of engaging in a variety of activities. Separate quarters to which males can retreat are found in 45 percent of a sample of 120 cultures around the world. There are differences in the extent to which these male sanctuaries monopolize the social life of men in a culture. In 29 percent of the societies that have men's houses, men only congregate in these establishments to gossip with each other in their spare time. Men in these cultures eat and sleep at home with their families. Thus, the West Punjabi of South Asia maintain guest houses for the use of any males who come to visit. The houses also serve as a refuge for the men of the village, who congregate in the houses to relax and gossip. Women do not visit the guest houses, although the village headman's female relatives may give female visitors a tour of the houses when the men are absent. In Southeast Asia, the Lamet community house functions primarily as meeting place for the men of the village, who gather there in the morning before work and then again after the day's work is finished to discuss the day's events.

In 38 of the societies that have houses exclusively for men, males not only meet to gossip and pass the time, but also eat or sleep in the house. A Yokuts community in California has a sweathouse where any male is welcome to relax or to sleep. Unmarried men often sleep in the sweathouse every night, and a married man may spend the night there after his wife has had a baby. Younger boys are also allowed to sleep in the sweathouse on occasion, especially if it is crowded at home. "Sweats" are frequently held twice a day, after which the men go for a swim. Men also often withdraw to the sweathouse to keep warm until it is time to have dinner. The Pomo of California construct sweathouses, which function as retreats from which females are more or less excluded. Men sleep and spend much of their leisure time in the sweathouse, and any matters discussed there are kept from the women.

In the final 33 percent of cultures that have men's houses, the dwelling serves more or less as the living quarters for the male population. For the traditional Alaskan Ingalik male, the *kashim* was the center of life. All unmarried males lived here from adolescence. They worked, bathed, and ate their evening meal in the *kashim* and gossiped and told stories together afterwards. Married men also may have spent the evening in the *kashim,* returning home only when they were ready to go to bed. Ceremonial activities also took place in the *kashim,* with all of the men from the nearest village attending. Mundurucu men of Brazil, whether single or married, live in the *eksa,* or men's house. A husband will provide his wife with supplies of food, which she then cooks and brings to her spouse in the *eksa.* Men eat their meals communally.

When men's houses are customary in a culture, women tend to avoid these establishments even when they are not specifically barred from joining the men. Lamet women are not permitted to sleep in the community houses and are rarely seen there, although they are not explicitly banned. A woman will come into the house when visitors from some other village are being entertained there. A Yokuts woman will only enter the sweathouse if no men are around. Or a group of women may sit outside the house listening to the singing of the men. But a female will immediately make herself scarce if a man is about to approach or exit the house. Young Shavante men of Brazil gather in the bachelor's hut, which functions like a men's club. Women do not usually enter the huts, even though they are not explicitly prevented from doing so.

In some instances, women will enter the men's house and may even participate in some of the activities that take place there. Females are permitted into the Pomo sweathouses when the men are gambling or when social events are held there. On such occasions, the men may gather around a group of singers while the women listen in. Sometimes an Ingalik woman may bring her husband and sons their meal at the *kashim* and then wait for the empty dish, lingering on occasion until her husband comes home with her. Women also participate in some *kashim* activities. They are sometimes present for ceremonies and sometimes share meals with the men. But the *kashim* does not play the kind of central role in the life of a woman that it does for men.

Often, however, the men's house is just that, a retreat for males, and females are not permitted on the premises. Siuai men of Oceania meet in the men's clubhouse to gossip, chew betel, feast, and play their slit gongs. Women are prohibited from joining or even watching the men's activities. Men, by contrast, can observe any female kin who happen to be engaged in similar pursuits. A Mundurucu woman of Brazil will only enter the men's house when there is an important reason for her to do so, and even then she is confined to the sleeping portion of the building. Access to the room in which the sacred trumpets are kept is absolutely prohibited.

Men's houses can also serve as a second home for men when they are temporarily barred from their own households. A Lamet male will sometimes eat in the community house and men who are about to go on a hunting expedition sleep there, as they are prohibited from staying at home with their wives.

Men's houses are often frequented by boys as well as grown men. Ingalik males move into the *kashim* as soon as they reach adolescence. All Mundurucu males spend most of their time in the men's house once they have reached puberty. Among the Mae Enga of New Guinea, a boy will go to live in the communal men's house at five years of age. And Yokuts boys will sleep in the sweathouse if it is crowded at home.

The presence or absence of men's houses is associated with a number of other aspects of male-female interaction. Where a culture provides some kind of house for the more or less exclusive use of men, there tends not to be a special honeymoon period for newlyweds. Societies with men's houses also tend to treat extramarital sexual affairs on the part of men more leniently than it does the same behavior on the part of women. Where no men's house exists, the honeymoon and single standard of extramarital sexual activity are more likely to prevail.

Barrett, Samuel A. (1916) "Pomo Buildings." In *Holmes Anniversary Volume, Anthropological Essays*, 1–17.

———. (1917) *Ceremonies of the Pomo Indians.*

———. (1926) *Pomo Folkways.*

Elgar, Zekiye. (1960) *A Punjabi Village in Pakistan.*

Ember, Carol R., and Melvin Ember. (1988) *Anthropology*, 5th ed.

Gayton, Anna. (1948) *Yokuts and Western Mono Ethnography.*

Izikowitz, Karl G. (1951) *Lamet: Hill Peasants in French Indochina.*

Kroeber, Alfred L. (1925) *Handbook of the Indians of California.*

Murphy, Robert F. (1960) *Headhunter's Heritage: Social and Economic Change among the Mundurucu Indians.*

Murphy, Yolanda, and Robert Murphy. (1985) *Women of the Forest.*

Oliver, Douglas. (1955) *A Solomon Island Society: Kinship and Leadership among the Siuai of Bougainville.*

Osgood, Cornelius. (1958) *Ingalik Social Structure.* Yale University Publications in Anthropology 55.

MENSTRUAL TABOOS

Some kind of restriction on the behavior of a menstruating woman is common across cultures. However, societies differ regarding the nature and severity of these constraints. In Tanzania, when a Nyakyusa woman is menstruating, her husband keeps his distance. If a man flouts this taboo, his legs may begin to hurt and become swollen. Or he may become very tired and unable to run with any speed. His body may also become red and his stomach painful. The Nyakyusa insist on the isolation of women during menstruation because they believe that menstruating women are filthy. In New Mexico, menstruating Zuni women isolate themselves in specially built menstrual houses, where they cook for themselves, eating on dishes reserved for menstruating women. Andamanese women are prohibited from having sexual relations or else their arms and legs will swell. And in New Guinea, a menstruating Wogeo woman should not have contact with another person. She should not touch her own skin with her fingernails, and she must also eat with a fork instead of her fingers for a few days. These are examples of menstrual taboos, that is, culturally patterned constraints on the activities of menstruating women.

Variations in menstrual taboos follow a predictable pattern. Thus, if particular taboos are viewed as ranging from more to less trivial, then any culture that imposes a taboo of a particular level of severity also imposes all the less severe taboos besides. In societies that explicitly restrict the activities of menstruating women, the least severe taboo is against sexual intercourse. Other of the less trivial taboos are against certain personal behaviors on the part of a woman. For instance, a female who is menstruating may be prohibited from eating certain foods, scratching herself, laughing loudly, and the like. Still more severe are rules prohibiting contact with anything belonging to males, especially implements such as bows or fishing equipment that are employed in subsistence, war, or ritual activities. Even more extreme are taboos prohibiting menstruating women from cooking for men. Finally, in some societies women are required to live in special huts while they are menstruating. Given the patterning of menstrual taboos across cultures, then, if women remain in menstrual huts during menstruation, they are also constrained by all of the remaining menstrual taboos. Similarly, where the most severe taboo in a culture prevents a woman from cooking for men while she is menstruating, other taboos also forbid her touching male property, engaging in certain personal behaviors, or having sexual intercourse, but she is not required to live in a menstrual hut. If the most restrictive taboo is upon touching male possessions, then a woman is prohibited from

exhibiting certain personal behaviors or engaging in sexual intercourse, but she can cook for men and does not retire to a hut when menstruating. Finally, in societies where the personal behavior of menstruating women is circumscribed, they are nevertheless permitted to touch men's possessions and cook for men and do not live in a separate hut. For example, a Manchu woman of China is considered impure while she is menstruating and is, therefore, dangerous to men and offensive to the spirits. A menstruating woman, as a result, must avoid walking over a man's clothes or a man himself while she is menstruating. Nor can she place her shoes in a place that has religious significance. She must burn incense around any person, place, or thing that she has polluted and wash herself and all of her garments when her menstrual period is over.

Lese girls in Zaire at celebration of first menstruation.

Nor should a menstruating woman engage in sexual relations for fear of causing a variety of illnesses. Thus, the most severe taboo imposed upon the Manchu female has to do with the prohibition against touching male possessions. She is also required to observe all of the less severe taboos.

Some social scientists believe that menstrual taboos are a manifestation of male fear of castration. In this view, where castration anxiety is intense, menstrual taboos will be severe. Menstrual taboos have also been explained as a male strategy to control women. Both of these interpretations of menstrual taboos depend upon assumptions about the psychological makeup of males that are not universally accepted. A related interpretation of menstrual taboos proposes that males are jealous of female reproductive functions and impose menstrual restrictions as a way of compensating for their envy by disparaging women. Since menstrual taboos are not universal, an explanation is required for why men in some cultures are more envious of a woman's ability to have a baby than are men in other societies. A final explanation for menstrual taboos suggests that these restrictions are more likely to occur in societies that emphasize male-female differences. In this view, the taboos serve to highlight and intensify these distinctions.

In Western societies, where women tend to have few children and do not nurse their babies, menstruation is a regular and familiar monthly occurrence. But where women have babies at regular intervals and then nurse their children, sometimes for years, menstruation is a much less usual event. This is because menstruation stops both during pregnancy and during nursing as a result of the influence of female hormones. It is also the case that bleeding, which is generally a sign of illness or injury, evokes anxiety on the part of human beings. It is possible, therefore, that taboos on menstruation simply reflect a response to the unusual circumstance of female bleeding. The fact that a number of cultures regard menstrual blood as dangerous is consistent with this view of menstrual taboos.

Some cultures place no explicit prohibitions on a menstruating woman. Among the Mbuti pygmies of central Africa, there are no formal prohibitions against having sexual relations while a woman is menstruating. A woman is obliged to inform her partner if she is having her period, however, so that he will be able to decide whether or not he wishes to sleep with her. In some societies, menstruation causes some embarrassment, but is not surrounded by explicit taboos. Siuai females of Oceania are embarrassed by menstrual blood and never refer directly to menstruation. Men also believe that the term *menstruation* is too strong a word to be used conversationally. If a man talks about menstruation in front of other males, they are ashamed and say that he must spend too much time with women since he knows as much as he does about such things. Women stay in their houses while they are menstruating and attempt to check the bleeding by applying heated leaves to the abdomen. Nevertheless, people are not hesitant about using euphemistic references to refer to menstruation, saying that a woman has "gone to the moon," for instance. A Manus girl of Oceania is taught to hide the fact that she is menstruating and men are unaware that women do menstruate every month, claiming that, if that is the case in other societies, then Manus females are different.

In one human culture, menstruation is imitated by adult males. Thus, a Wogeo man will occasionally cut and draw blood from the penis when he is engaging in any potentially dangerous activity. He is then said to be "menstruating" and is also required to observe the customs associated with menstruation.

Benedict, Ruth. (1934) *Patterns of Culture.*

Cipriani, Lidio. (1961) "Hygiene and Medical

Practices among the Onge (Little Andaman)." *Anthropos* 56: 481–500.

Ember, Carol R., and David Levinson. (1991) "The Substantive Contributions of Worldwide Cross-Cultural Studies Using Secondary Data." *Behavior Science Research* 25: 79–140.

Hogbin, H. Ian. (1970) *The Island of Menstruating Men: Religion in Wogeo, New Guinea.*

Levinson, David, and Martin J. Malone. (1980) *Toward Explaining Human Culture.*

Mead, Margaret. (1931) *Growing Up in New Guinea: A Comparative Study of Primitive Education.*

Oliver, Douglas. (1955) *A Solomon Island Society: Kinship and Leadership among the Siuai of Bougainville.*

Shirokogoroff, S. M. (1924) *Social Organization of the Manchus.*

Stephens, William N. (1962) *The Oedipal Complex: Cross-Cultural Evidence.*

Titiev, Mischa. (1951) *Araucanian Culture in Transition.*

Turnbull, Colin M. (1965) *The Mbuti Pygmies: An Ethnographic Survey.* Anthropological Papers of the Museum of Natural History 50, pt. 3.

Wilson, Godfrey. (1936) "An Introduction to Nyakyusa Society." *Bantu Studies* 10: 253–292.

MODESTY

Across the animal kingdom, physical appearance provides many cues to a creature's status, intentions, approachability, and so on. Human beings are no exception, and an important feature of self-presentation for members of our own species entails the desire to maintain a modest demeanor in the presence of others. An individual is modest to the extent that he or she conforms to cultural notions of what is proper. As it relates to physical appearance, modesty refers to ideas about what is and is not appropriate regarding the exposure of one's body.

Cultural ideas of what constitutes modest and immodest comportment differ enormously. Rural Irish couples are offended by nudity of any kind. Individuals always dress and undress in private, often under the bed covers, and wear their underwear during sexual relations. Even infants are covered in the presence of other people, including other babies. Manus men of Oceania avoid nudity in each other's presence, and by the time she is grown a woman has learned that the spirits will punish her if she so much as removes her skirt in front of another woman. Indeed, a woman will not allow her skirt to be loosened and her sexual organs inspected even on her death bed. In Arizona, Navajo adults are extremely modest in front of members of the same and the opposite sex. Men and women do not bathe together and a man who is about to take a bath will cover his genitals with his hand until he can no longer be seen inside the dark sweathouse. Women continue to wear their dresses while in labor, even if there are only other women present. Couples have sexual intercourse in the dark and with clothing on. People believe that if a man sees the genitals of a woman, he will be struck by lightning. Exposure of the sexual organs is shameful, embarrassing, and rare. The Chiricahua of the American Southwest similarly avoid nudity in front of any other adult. A man would be disgraced if he were seen unclothed by another male, and men wear loincloths even when swimming. People are also circumspect as well as modest about elimination and learn early on to avoid alluding directly to excretory functions. Finally, the Islamic tradition requires extreme modesty of Pakistani adults. Disrobing before another person is prohibited, and women must cover the entire body, to ankle, chin, and wrist. They must also wear a veil in public or cover their heads when not veiled.

In contrast to these cases, there are societies in which the covering of the body is not emphasized. In Australia, Aranda adults wear a variety of ornaments but no real garments. Women may wear strings of beads about the neck, some adornment on the forehead, and, on rare occasions, a small fur apron hanging from the waist. Men wear belts, arm bands, and a small tassel hanging about, but not concealing, the genitals. Trumai men and women of Brazil wear only a cord belt. Eastern cultures have tended to regard nudity with equanimity. Public bathing has been a tradition for hundreds of years and men and women retire to the baths at the end of the day to relax and chat. Nor are the Tikopia of Oceania shy about bathing or eliminating in full view of one another, and Pawnee adults of the Great Plains of North America bathed together, while men went about nude when in their lodges. Samoans traditionally wore girdles and skirts, but these were frequently shed in the presence of other people. The Kwoma of New Guinea go about naked. And Korean men and women may remove their clothing when they are fishing or working in the fields. The woman may slip on a jacket if someone walks by, but no one exhibits any embarrassment, and a girl who passes a naked man wading through the water will not even avert her eyes.

Whereas cultures differ regarding their ideas of what is appropriate dress, there is no connection between customs relating to the covering of the body and the value placed on modest comportment. The Shavante of Brazil illustrate the lack of necessary relationship between the amount of clothing worn by members of a society and attitudes toward modesty. Beginning in boyhood, Shavante males wear nothing but penis sheaths, which cover only the tip of the organ. But anyone, even a child, who is seen without his penis sheath is thought to be extremely immodest. Among the Kwoma, neither men nor women wear clothes, but a boy is trained from an early age not to look at a girl's genitals, and a youngster who fails to abide by this rule may be reprimanded or beaten. If a child is looking at her sexual organs, a woman will tell him that he has no right to do so because they are her private property. If a man stares at a woman's genitals, or is even suspected of trying to do so, her relatives will interpret the act as a sexual advance and insult or even threaten him. Men, therefore, avert their eyes in the presence of any girls or women other than a wife or lover. Siriono women of South America wear no clothing and many men also go entirely naked, while some others wear only a bark g-string wound about the waist. But males do not wish the glans of the penis to be exposed to others, and men are continually pulling at their foreskins to lengthen them and to provide coverage. And a woman always covers her sexual organs with her heel when sitting on the ground.

Cultural attitudes clearly differ regarding what parts of the body may be exposed by a modest person. One of the focuses of this variation is the female breast. While Western cultures have traditionally required women to cover the upper body in public, other societies permit exposure of the breasts even when the woman is expected to cover other parts of her body. By the age of three or four years, Kaska children in Alaska are warned to exhibit modest behavior in public and not to expose themselves in an indecent manner. People are extremely circumspect about excretory functions. No one refers directly to elimination and people are careful not to take notice if someone goes to the bush to eliminate. Females will make sure they are alone before attending to their bodily needs. But a Kaska woman will uncover her breasts in public when nursing as a matter of course. The !Kung of southern Africa display great modesty regarding the exposure of their genitals. A woman would never expose her buttocks in public, for instance. But a female does not cover her breasts.

The buttocks are associated with sex, the breasts with nursing.

Requirements regarding modest demeanor sometimes depend upon the company that the individual is keeping. The Lepcha of Tibet exhibit extreme modesty when in the presence of people toward whom they are required to show respect, parents-in-law and social superiors, for instance. Otherwise, people regard overmodesty of speech or behavior as childish and sometimes blame too much reserve on the part of a young couple as the source of marital problems.

In some cultures, immodest behavior on the part of an individual is regarded as a sexual invitation. This is the case, for instance, among the Lesu of China, where a woman may suggest sexual intercourse to a man by exposing her genitals. The association between immodesty and sexual solicitation is explicitly recognized among the Kwoma. Therefore, Kwoma girls are taught to sit with their legs close together and knees straightened. No Kwoma female will bend over when a man is present. A girl who displays her genitals in front of men gets a bad reputation and will have trouble attracting a good husband.

Perhaps it is this association between immodesty and sexual solicitation that explains the difference in rules regarding modesty for the two sexes. Societies frequently require females to wear more clothing and to behave more circumspectly than males, and this difference often begins in childhood. For instance, Kikuyu boys of Kenya do not typically wear much in the way of clothing. They may walk around completely naked in the village and perhaps throw a piece of goatskin around their shoulders when they are herding. Little girls, on the other hand, generally wear a small piece of material about the waist and covering their genitals, as well as a larger skin for the upper body. In Ethiopia, Konso men traditionally wear a blanket, which they drape about themselves like a toga. But when they are doing hard manual work, they strip naked for convenience. No one is bothered by the fact that these men are entirely naked. Women, on the other hand, wear skirts and their clothing masks any suggestion of feminine anatomy. This sex difference in modesty requirements begins early on. Boys walk around without trousers until they are as much as eight years old, but girls begin to wear skirts by the time they are crawling, if not earlier. Cuna boys of Panama may go about naked until puberty, but girls wear clothing by one year of age and sometimes sooner. A Thai girl, once she begins to wear clothing, is never seen undressed, and even when changing in private, she will wrap herself in her new garment before taking off the old one. Boys, however, will go swimming together naked, even after they have reached puberty. In fact, most cultures around the world expect women to remain clothed in front of other people and to eliminate in private. Of 48 societies, only 14.6 percent permit women to undress, eliminate, or bathe in front of members of the opposite sex. An additional 12.5 percent permit these activities in front of other women. Finally, a full 73 percent of the 48 societies insist that women undress, bathe, and eliminate in private. Changes in demands for modesty may also be noted differently by the society depending upon the sex of the individual. For instance, among the Saramaka of Suriname, both boys and girls first wear clothing at about ten years of age. But the occasion is cause for a ceremonial in the case of boys, while no official notice is taken of the girl's altered habits.

While in some societies children's dress habits anticipate the behaviors that will be expected of them in adulthood, child training does not always mimic adult modesty requirements. Manus adults are extremely reserved as regards nudity and will not be seen undressed even in front of another person of the same sex. But children go naked, and even when a little girl begins to wear a grass skirt at seven or eight years of age, she is apt to take it off in public and forget about it. Children only become embarrassed about nudity at puberty. So do Chiricahua adults of the American Southwest avoid nudity in front of other people, but their children wear little or no clothing, especially when the weather is warm. In Madagascar, Tanala men and women are careful to avoid exposing themselves, but Tanala children run around naked until they are four or five years old.

Attitudes toward modesty in women are predictably associated with other sexual attitudes and behaviors across cultures. Where modesty is not emphasized, talk about sex is permitted and uninhibited, premarital sex for males is common, and love magic is present. And societies that underplay modesty requirements for women tend to prohibit sexual intercourse between a husband and wife for a relatively long time after the birth of a baby.

Benedict, Ruth. (1952) *Thai Culture and Behavior.*

Broude, Gwen J. (1975) *A Cross-Cultural Study of Some Sexual Beliefs and Practices.* Unpublished dissertation, Harvard University.

Firth, Raymond. (1936) *We, the Tikopia: A Sociological Study of Kinship in Primitive Polynesia.*

Gorer, Geoffrey. (1938) *Himalayan Village: An Account of the Lepchas of Sikkim.*

Holmberg, Allan R. (1950) *Nomads of the Long Bow.* Washington, DC: Government Printing Office.

Honigmann, John J. (1949) *Culture and Ethos of Kaska Society.*

Kahn, Morton C. (1931) *Djuka: The Bush Negroes of Dutch Guiana.*

Kenyatta, Jomo. (1961) *Facing Mount Kenya: The Tribal Life of the Gikuyu.*

Leighton, Dorothea, and Clyde Kluckhohn. (1969) *Children of the People: The Navaho Individual and His Development.*

Lewis, I. M. (1962) *Marriage and the Family in Northern Somaliland.*

Marshall, Lorna. (1959) "Marriage among the !Kung Bushmen." *Africa* 29: 335–364.

Materi, Irma. (1949) *Irma and the Hermit: My Life in Korea.*

Maybury-Lewis, David. (1967) *Akwe-Shavante Society.*

Mead, Margaret. (1930) *Growing Up in New Guinea: A Comparative Study of Primitive Education.*

Messenger, John C. (1971) "Sex and Repression in an Irish Folk Community." In *Human Sexual Behavior,* edited by Donald S. Marshall and Robert C. Suggs, 3–37.

Murdock, George P. (1936) *Our Primitive Contemporaries.*

Murphy, Robert F., and Buell Quain. (1955) *The Trumai Indians of Central Brazil.*

Opler, Morris E. (1941) *An Apache Life-Way: The Economic, Social and Religious Institutions of the Chiricahua Indians.*

Powdermaker, Hortense. (1933) *Life in Lesu: The Study of a Melanesian Society in New Ireland.*

Slair, John B. (1897) *Old Samoa.*

Stout, David. (1948) "The Cuna." In *Handbook of South American Indians,* vol. 4, edited by Julian H. Steward, 257–268.

Whiting, John W. M. (1941) *Becoming a Kwoma: Teaching and Learning in a New Guinea Tribe.*

Wilber, Donald N. (1964) *Pakistan: Its People, Its Society, Its Culture.*

MONOGAMY

See MARRIAGE FORMS.

unfavorable counterparts are selected against. This process by which variations are unequally preserved across time is called natural selection. Nature, so to speak, selects from the variability in traits those characteristics that are most friendly to survival and reproduction. While we talk as if natural selection has a purpose, it is in fact a process without goals. Thus, natural selection occurs simply because traits resulting in longer survival and the production of more offspring have a greater likelihood of being passed on to succeeding generations. An organism's success at producing surviving offspring is an index of its Darwinian fitness. Thus, the more surviving offspring the organism leaves relative to other members of its species, the greater its fitness. Organisms that leave fewer surviving offspring are said to be less fit.

Natural selection does not work in a vacuum. Rather, it is a profoundly environment-driven process. That is, an advantageous trait promotes survival or reproduction in a particular environment. In another environment, the same trait may be less advantageous or even deleterious. This means that there are no good or bad traits independent of the context in which they operate. This fundamental Darwinian insight is often overlooked in discussions of evolution and fitness. The role of the environment in determining the usefulness of a trait for an organism is illustrated in a well-known example from the animal world. Before the industrial revolution, the cities of England were populated by moths, most of whose wings were light in color. Only a small minority of moths had dark wings. The predominance of light coloring in the moth population would lead an evolutionary theorist to suspect that a moth with light wings had a selective advantage over a dark-winged variant. And indeed, light-winged moths were better off in the world in which they lived. In particular, they were difficult for predator birds to see when they lit on the light bark of the birch trees that were found in England. After the industrial

NATURAL SELECTION

All species, including our own, have arrived at their current physical and behavioral status through the process of evolution by natural selection. The theory of natural selection is most closely associated with Charles Darwin, although Alfred Russell Wallace, a contemporary of Darwin's, independently reached similar conclusions about how species develop. Darwin's insights rest upon three related ideas. The first is that individuals of a given species are different from each other regarding the traits that they exhibit. This is the principle of variation. Second, certain variations of these traits are more capable of promoting the survival of the individual than are others. Finally, individuals also vary in their success at producing offspring. This is called differential reproductive success. To the extent that traits underwriting survival and reproductive success are inherited, favorable variations will become more and more common across generations while unfavorable variables will decrease in frequency. In Darwin's language, favorable variations are selected for, while their revolution, the bark of the birch trees began to be covered by soot and thus became much darker. Within a century, the proportion of light-winged to dark-winged moths in the cities reversed, and the darker variant predominated. The chronicle of the English moths is a story of environment-dependent selection. As long as tree bark was light, light-winged moths were eaten less often and were, therefore, more likely to survive and reproduce than were their more dark-winged counterparts. Therefore, the moth population became increasingly light. Moths with light coloring had a selected advantage, and that trait was selected for. As the tree bark became darker, dark-colored moths were eaten less frequently and were more likely to survive and reproduce. Dark coloring was now a selective advantage and the trait was selected for. Thus, the same trait in the same species was highly useful in one environmental context and highly harmful in other.

The example of the English moths also highlights another evolutionary principle. Evolution by natural selection is often a tremendously slow process, but given strong selective pressures, traits can be selected into or selected out of a population on a time scale that is instantaneous by geological standards. The population of moths changed from light to dark in a mere 100 years, less than an evolutionary blink of an eye. Thus, it is possible for evolution to produce rapid change. In the case of traits that are underwritten by multiple genes, selection is expected to take far longer to effect a change in the proportion of individuals who exhibit variants of a particular trait. Many human traits are of this kind, so evolution often operates at a snail's pace in the case of the human species.

The English moths remind us that environment is the real mover behind the process of evolution by natural selection. When we wish to understand a particular trait from an evolutionary perspective, we must always ask how the trait might have been adaptive in the environment in which it actually evolved. But the environment cannot be counted on to produce change rapidly when the genetic basis of a trait is complex. Thus, in the case of slow-changing traits, the environment that selected for a trait, and therefore the environment in which the trait was useful, is not necessarily the one in which the individual currently lives. There is often a long lag time between environmental pressures and decisive changes in the traits typifying a population. This is assumed to be the case for human beings. Thus, according to evolutionary theory, the traits that are characteristic of the human species today were adaptive and selected for in the environment in which we evolved. The best guess is that this was a savannah environment not unlike what we find in certain areas of Africa today. The savannah environment, further, is conducive to a way of life dependent upon hunting and gathering, and archaeological evidence points to the conclusion that during the time that traits now characteristic of the human species evolved, we were living as hunters and gatherers. So evolutionary explanations must locate current human traits as adaptations within a savannah, hunter-gatherer environment. This is our assumed EEA, or environment of evolutionary adaptedness.

It is impossible to know the details of a way of life of people who existed one or two million years ago. However, hunter-gatherer societies still exist in various parts of the world, and it is possible to use these societies as models for the ancestral way of life, especially because all contemporary hunter-gatherer people share some characteristics in common. Thus, among all hunter-gatherers around the world, there is a consistent division of labor, with men doing the hunting and women doing the gathering. Men always share their take with their immediate families and other members of their camp, while women share fruits and vegetables that they have foraged with their spouses and children and perhaps with other members of their household if they live in extended-family settings. Women

Charles Darwin (1809–1882), ca. 1875, who developed the theory of natural selection.

also have the greater responsibility in caring for infants and young children, while the job of protection is reserved for the males. Because these features of life are typical of hunter-gatherer groups in general, they are taken to be fundamental characteristics of the hunter-gatherer way of life. If this is true, then the lifestyle of our ancestors would also have been consistent with this description. The task then becomes one of explaining how traits characteristic of human beings today proved adaptive to this hunter-gatherer way of life.

Consider the human fondness for sweets. It might initially seem hard to explain this weakness as adaptive, and in fact it appears to be downright harmful. Thus, individuals who eat chocolate cookies and eclairs are likely to become overweight, to get cavities, and so on, none of which promotes survival and reproduction. In our environment of evolutionary adaptedness, however, to like sweet things was to like ripe fruit, an important dietary staple for individuals living back then. It was only with the introduction of refined sugar that an important adaptation became a liability. It is also important to remember that traits in our own as well as other species are still being selected for or selected against by the environment in which we live. That is to say, evolution has not stopped. This selection process is still in progress. Our species is adapted to the past savannah environment. And, as our collective sweet tooth warns us, traits that were advantageous to members of our species in the past can nowadays have the opposite effect. It is assumed that natural selection is currently weeding out such traits when science does not intervene to override their harmful biological consequences.

The effect of environment on the physical traits of human beings is illustrated by a consideration of body shape. The typical body shape of people differs in different climates. Thus, people who live in hot climates tend to be tall and thin. By contrast, a cold climate is associated with a shorter, rounder body build and shorter arms and legs. Why is this the case? The key to this puzzle lies in the differences in the ratio of weight to surface area of these two body types. A rounder shape produces less body surface for a given weight, while a lankier shape produces a greater body surface for the same weight. When an individual is hot, the body compensates by perspiring. The evaporation of the perspiration on the skin cools down the body. If you are living in a hot climate, you want more body surface to act as the vehicle for perspiration. The less the body surface to body weight, the less efficiently this system can function. Thus, long, thin body shape is selected for in hot climates and round, short body types are selected for in cold climates. The connection between body shape, temperature, and fitness was illustrated during World War II when a number of American soldiers died from heat stroke during basic training. It turned out that the victims were disproportionately overweight men. They had died when the weather was either hot or humid, two environmental conditions that make it especially difficult for the body to cool down.

Behavioral traits are also explained as adaptations to the evolutionary environments of organisms. For example, in societies around the world, males have a greater tendency than females to be aggressive, and there are physiological differences between the sexes that are known to underwrite this behavioral difference. The role of ancestral males as hunters and protectors would certainly be helped by this lower threshold for aggression. By contrast, a tendency to be aggressive would be antagonistic to the female role as caretaker of immature, and often irritating, infants and young children. A multitude of other behavioral dispositions having to do with human interpersonal relationships have also been explained as adaptations to our hunter-gatherer past. Can every trait exhibited by an organism be explained as a product of natural selection?

Some schools of evolution tend to be conservative in their application of evolutionary theory, claiming that only certain traits have been the targets of natural selection. In this view, other traits are the product of random genetic occurrences and have no selective advantage to members of a species. Other evolutionary thinkers disagree, claiming that every trait characteristic of a species has some direct or indirect bearing upon the survival and reproductive success of its members.

Daly, Martin, and Margo Wilson. (1983) *Sex, Evolution, and Behavior.*

Ember, Carol R., and Melvin Ember. (1988) *Anthropology.* 5th ed.

Trivers, Robert L. (1985) *Social Evolution.*

NEWLYWEDS

Most men and women the world over get married. The transition to the status of newlywed is, therefore, a virtually universal experience in the lives of human beings. The passage into married life can mean momentous changes in a person's sexual functioning, living arrangements, rights and responsibilities, attachments, and loyalties, all of which require large adjustments on the part of the bride and groom. Many cultures recognize that the shift to newlywed status is a special time requiring special management. This includes special treatment of the couple on their first night together and special arrangements designed to smooth their settling into their new roles.

In a number of societies, the bride and groom are accorded extra privacy during their early married life. The Rwala pitch a special tent for the use of the new bride and groom on their first night together. If a family is too poor to be able to afford a separate tent, a corner of the family tent is reserved for them. In New Ireland, a newlywed Lesu couple may go to live in the bride's mother's house for a few days if they do not as yet have a house of their own. The wife's parents will stay somewhere else until the husband has built a residence for himself and his bride. A Khalka Mongol couple lives in their own tent in the bride's camp for from ten days to a month. They then move permanently to the camp of the husband's family. And among the Nambicuara of Brazil, a newlywed couple spends their first night together in a hut of their own at a distance from the camp.

Sometimes a society allows a bride and groom some degree of privacy but also supervises the newlyweds' sexual activities. Newlywed Burusho couples in India sleep in a barn or outhouse during the early days of their marriage, and therefore enjoy some degree of privacy. However, the groom's mother stays with the couple in order to counsel them in proper sexual technique, and she will sleep between the boy and girl if the new bride is too fearful or too young to cope with the advances of her husband. Sometimes, the wedding night is celebrated by the entire community. In Suriname, Saramaka newlyweds are taken to their new hut and left there while the rest of the village dances and sings fertility songs outside all night. And sometimes the sexual behavior of the couple is treated as a source of humor. For example, Guatemalan Quiche newlyweds receive no special consideration on their first night as a married couple. They are accorded no privacy and their sexual activities become the focus of taunts in the morning.

When privacy is not accorded to a bride and groom in their first days of marriage, the couple may simply refrain from engaging in sexual intercourse. Although they have probably been sleeping together in the men's dormitory before their marriage, Trobriand newlyweds in New Guinea are shy about having sexual intercourse because they are now living with the parents of the bride or groom. The couple shares the same bed, but they are so embarrassed that they leave their clothes on while they sleep. As a result, the Trobriand bride and groom are likely to remain abstinent for the early days of their marriage. Among the Wogeo of New Guinea, propriety dictates that newlyweds sleep in different beds unless they have a room of their own. Otherwise, the bride stays in a corner of the family sleeping room while the groom continues to sleep in the men's house. In that case, the senior members of the family make sure that the couple get a chance to be by themselves for a few hours during the day.

Sometimes a society will disapprove if a bride and groom appear too eager to engage in sexual intercourse after they are married. The Lakher of South Asia consider it somewhat unseemly for a newly married couple to consummate their marriage too quickly, and a husband and wife who have a child too soon will be ridiculed by their neighbors. As a result, newlyweds wait for some weeks and perhaps as long as a year before they begin to sleep together. Until then, the bride sleeps in her husband's house while he stays elsewhere and courts his wife as if they were not married at all. Of 62 societies, 47 percent regard the wedding night as special and accord a couple some degree of privacy. The remaining 53 percent do not treat the wedding night as special and do not make special arrangements for a couple to be alone on their first night together as husband and wife.

Newlywed couples continue to be treated as special for some days or weeks after their marriage in a number of societies around the world. In 11.3 percent of 53 societies, a bride and groom are sent off on a honeymoon. A Somali groom receives a bridal house as a gift from the new wife's relatives. This is the hut in which the woman will live during her marriage. The couple is expected to seclude themselves in the house for seven days and to devote themselves to con-

summating their marriage. A Mexican Huichol newlywed couple is put together on a mat and a special ritual is performed. The bride's parents take away her clothes until the next morning. If the girl makes a fuss about being left with her husband, her mother will stay with the couple all night to stop her from running away. The couple is left alone for five days with the expectation that they will become comfortable and familiar with each other during this seclusion. Meanwhile, the parents wait for the bride to take food from the groom as the signal that she accepts the marriage. Among the Semang of Malaysia, a newly married couple goes off into the forest together for a few days after the wedding feast. There they construct a temporary dwelling for themselves, where they collect food, cook, eat, and make love. The bride and groom then return to the new wife's band, where they live for a year or two. For the East Pomo of California, the honeymoon serves as a couple's way of announcing their marriage. Thus, when they decide that they want to marry, a boy and girl retire into the bush and build themselves a small shelter there. The girl's mother searches for the couple, taking a number of days to find them if the marriage is acceptable. The bride and groom then come home with her.

In 51 percent of 53 societies, a new bride and groom are excused from some of the responsibilities of normal married life. Sometimes the goal is to allow the couple to spend some extra time together. Or this vacation from normal responsibilities may serve to smooth the newlyweds' transition into a new role or new family. In New Guinea, Orokaiva brides are excused from doing work for anywhere from three or four days to an entire month. Instead, the new wife sits on a platform in the village for some portion of each day and receives gifts. This is the ceremony of welcoming the bride. Similarly, the new Quiche wife is permitted to passively watch for two days while the members of her new family do their chores. This brief holiday allows her to become used to her new household. A newly married Pacific island Negri Sembilan couple spends the first few days of marriage making formal calls to kin. In the United States, Haida newlyweds visit the homes of each of the groom's sisters in rotation for the first months after their marriage and are extravagantly entertained. A newly married Javanese couple moves in with the bride's parents for a month, where they receive visitors but never leave the house. After the puberty ceremony, which also marks her marriage, the young Nyakyusa bride of Tanzania goes to her new husband's house escorted by two younger friends who stay with her for a number of days and nights.

Cultural expectations can also require that a newly married couple avoid each other for a designated period of time after marriage. A Kimam groom in New Guinea continues to sleep in the men's house for the two weeks following his marriage. His father then reminds him that he should begin to live with his bride. The new husband finally goes home to his parents' house, where his bride is staying, and, after eating with his family, spends the night with his wife. Grooms are expected to keep somewhat aloof from their brides for awhile after they are married. Similarly, Korean newlyweds are expected to be reserved in each other's presence for some time after their marriage. The wife is silent in her husband's presence, so that there is no conversation, no sharing of confidences, and no familiarity between the two. A newlywed Nama Hottentot couple in South Africa and Namibia spends part of their wedding night together in a hut erected for them near the house of the bride's parents. The groom then returns to his old house before morning, where he must remain for an entire day without seeing his bride. Only after three or four days are the new husband and wife permitted to be together on a regular basis.

In Nigeria, Hausa newlyweds participate in an extended post-marriage mock courtship. After the marriage ceremony, the new wife is given her own hut, where she stays with her girlfriends for a number of nights. The groom goes off with the men. After the couple has been married for a week, the new husband's friends begin on a nightly basis to attempt to push the groom into his bride's hut, but he runs away. Finally, after another week has passed, he goes into the girl's hut and sleeps there, but now she runs away. Her husband begins to send her gifts and eventually the two remain in the bride's hut together. The marriage is then said to have "taken." The wife continues to be excused from most of the usual household duties for three months, after which the couple settles down to a more normal married life. An Abkhaz bride lives in a small hut by herself for a number of months before she moves into her permanent household. Her husband visits her in secret. A newly married couple is prohibited from being seen together in public or before strangers. Nor may they appear together in front of the bride's or the groom's parents for their first year of marriage. This kind of reserve between a bride and groom is expected in 15 percent of 53 cultures.

Where does a newly married couple live once they settle down to the normal routine of daily life? In 36 percent of 121 cultures, a bride and groom will set up their own independent household. In Zaire, a prospective Suku husband builds a house for himself and his bride at some distance from his father's household, thus avoiding the embarrassment of having his parents witness any intimacies between the couple. By contrast, newlyweds will move in permanently with the parents of one or the other spouse in 34 percent of 121 societies. In Arizona, a Navajo bride and groom do not generally set up their own households. Instead, the couple moves in with the wife's family. A new husband and wife will initially move in with parents but will then move into a home of their own in 26 percent of 121 cases. If a Havasupai girl of the southwestern United States is serious about a particular suitor, the two will sleep together for a few nights. The boy will then come to live with the girl in her parents' house, perhaps until they have had one or two children, at which time the pair set up their own household. The boy plants, hunts, and collects wood for his in-laws. A Nkundo bride of Zaire moves into her new husband's house. After a few days, she begins to do household chores and cook meals under the watchful eye of her mother-in-law. When, after a few weeks, she has become familiar with the family routines, the new wife and her husband are provided with their own home. In the final 4 percent of these cultures, a couple will initially live apart for a time. A Tibetan Lepcha bride returns to her own home after her wedding, where she remains for two weeks. Her husband then comes for her and takes her to his parents' house for a week. They return together to the bride's home for a few days, after which they go back to the groom's home to stay.

While these rules describe cultural ideals, in reality a couple may have a choice of living arrangements, depending upon their unique circumstances. A newly married Thai couple generally moves in with the bride's parents for a period of time. As a result, a girl's parents must approve of her choice of husband before the pair can be married. If a boy has sufficient resources to set up an independent household immediately upon marrying, a couple may elope and thus avoid obtaining parental approval. In the southwestern United States, Paiute newlyweds initially live with the wife's family for the first few months of their marriage. The couple may then remain where they are, move in with the husband's family, or set up their own household near the relatives of either spouse, depending upon their personal preferences. Pomo newlyweds alternate between living with the bride's and groom's families until their first child is born. The couple then moves in permanently with one or another set of in-laws if the house is large enough. Otherwise, they set up an independent household.

What determines how the shift to the status of married person will be treated from one society to the next? Customs regarding the management of newlyweds are predictably related to other aspects of male-female relationships from one society to the next. Where spouses choose their own marriage partners, the wedding night is not regarded as special, nor are there other special accommodations made on behalf of a new couple during their first days of marriage. Nor are newlyweds treated as special in societies where husbands and wives eat together. Where special houses for the use of men are absent, there are no special newlywed customs. There is no honeymoon in societies where sexual aggressiveness in males is absent. And the wedding night is not regarded as special where extramarital affairs on the part of husbands are rare. Finally, if newlyweds get any special treatment at all, this distinctive handling tends to generalize across aspects of the newlyweds' life. For instance, if the wedding night is regarded as special, then a couple is also likely to have a honeymoon as well as a special routine in the first days of marriage.

Bergman, Sten. (1938) *In Korean Wilds and Villages.*

Broude, Gwen J. (1983) "Male-Female Relationships in Cross-Cultural Perspective: A Study of Sex and Intimacy." *Behavior Science Research* 18: 154–181.

Bunzel, Ruth. (1952) *Chichicastenango: A Guatemalan Village.*

Dyk, Walter. (1951) "Notes and Illustrations of Navaho Sexual Behavior." In *Psychoanalysis and Culture,* edited by George B. Wilbur and Warner Muensterberger.

Geertz, Hildred. (1961) *The Javanese Family.*

Gorer, Geoffrey. (1938) *Himalayan Village: An Account of the Lepchas of Sikkim.*

Gray, Robert F., and P. H. Gulliver. (1964) *The Family Estate in Africa.*

Hogbin, H. Ian. (1970) *The Island of Menstruating Men: Religion in Wogeo, New Guinea.*

Hulstaert, Gustave. (1928) *Marriage among the Nkundu.*

Kahn, Morton C. (1931) *Djuka: The Bush Negroes of Dutch Guiana.*

Levi-Strauss, Claude. (1948) *Family and Social Life of the Nambikwara Indians.*

Lewis, I. M. (1962) *Marriage and the Family in Northern Somaliland.*

Lips, Julius E. (1947) "Naskapi Law: Law and Order in a Hunting Society." *American Philosophical Society* 379(4): 379–492.

Loeb, Edwin M. (1926) *Pomo Folkways.*

Lorimer, E. O. (1939) *Language Hunting in the Karakorum.*

Luzbetak, Louis J. (1951) *Marriage and the Family in Caucasia: A Contribution to the Study of North Caucasian Ethnology and Customary Law.*

Malinowski, Bronislaw. (1929) *The Sexual Life of Savages in North-Western Melanesia: An Ethnographic Account of Courtship, Marriage and Family Life among the Natives of the Trobriand Islands, British New Guinea.*

Murdock, George P. (1936) *Our Primitive Contemporaries.*

Musil, Alois. (1928) *The Manner and Customs of the Rwala Bedouins.*

Parry, N. E. (1932) *The Lakhers.*

Powdermaker, Hortense. (1933) *Life in Lesu: The Study of a Melanesian Society in New Ireland.*

Schapera, Isaac. (1930) *The Khoisan Peoples of South Africa: Bushmen and Hottentots.*

Serpenti, I. M. (1965) *Cultivators in the Swamps.*

Smith, Michael G. (1954) *Baba of Karo: A Woman of the Muslim Hausa.*

Spier, Leslie. (1928) *Havasupai Ethnography.* Anthropological Papers of the American Museum of Natural History 29(3).

Swift, M. G. (1965) *Malay Peasant Society in Jeleb.*

Vreeland, Herbert H. (1953) *Mongol Community and Kinship Structure.*

Whiting, Beatrice B. (1950) *Paiute Sorcery.* Viking Fund Publications in Anthropology 15.

Williams, Francis E. (1930) *Orokaiva Society.*

Wilson, Monica. (1951) *Good Company.*

Young, Ernest. (1898) *The Kingdom of the Yellow Robe: Being Sketches of the Domestic and Religious Rites and Ceremonies of the Siamese.*

Zingg, Robert M. *The Huichols.* University of Denver Contributions to Anthropology 1.

her husband and in-laws. Among the Mossi of West Africa, avoidance customs between a husband and his in-laws are so extreme that a man cannot enter his wife's village. If a husband wishes to retrieve a wife who has paid a visit to her parents, he must wait for her under a tree outside the village boundaries (a particularly tardy wife might leave a spouse lingering there for a day or two). In the Sahara, the distance that must be maintained between a Tuareg husband and his in-laws is symbolized by the veil with which he covers the lower half of his face in the presence of his wife's parents. In Kenya, a Gusii man's relationship with his parents-in-law is always formal and deferential. They are prohibited from entering his house and must always be treated as honored guests.

In many societies, more than mere respect of her husband's mother is required of a wife. Extreme deference to her mother-in-law is also expected, and the life of a married woman may be constrained to a remarkable degree by the autocratic demands of her husband's mother. This is especially the case in the many cultures in which a wife moves into the household of her husband and his family. The typical Turk household is an extended family, with a husband and wife, their sons and daughters-in-law—along with their children—and unmarried daughters. When a Turkish woman marries, she goes to live with her husband, becoming a member of his extended-family household. In the early years of her marriage, the new wife is treated more or less like a servant and is ordered about at the whim of her husband's relations. A Chinese bride traditionally has been expected to be submissive to her in-laws, and her husband's mother supervises her household work. If she disobeys, her husband can beat her on behalf of his mother and a man will take his mother's side in any disagreement between her and his wife. At meals, the young wife is allocated the least important place at the table, if she appears there at all, and her husband treats her with indifference. A

PARENTS-IN-LAW In cultures around the world, the relationships between spouses and their parents-in-law are characterized by a greater or lesser degree of formality. In 90 percent of 84 cultures, a husband and his mother-in-law either actually avoid each other or else treat one another with a considerable amount of respect. These behaviors are often not simply recommended by the culture, they are positively required. In 80 percent of 66 cultures, the relationship between a woman and her husband's father is either avoidant or respectful. Joking about sex or sexual playfulness are entirely absent between mother-in-law and son-in-law and extremely rare between father-in-law and son-in-law. Among the Lugbara of Uganda, a newly wedded girl is expected to fear and respect not only her husband, but also his parents and brothers. She sits on the ground quietly in their presence and will not speak before they have spoken. She provides them with mats and stools when they enter the house and cooks for them, but eats separately. In the early years of her marriage, she thinks of her hut as the homestead of

Burundi mother-in-law in Zaire exercises considerable power over her daughter-in-law. A husband's mother has the right to assign tasks to her husband's wife and can, if she chooses, overload her with chores. A husband's mother can pressure her son into sending his wife back home, and she can even poison a daughter-in-law she dislikes. The Burundi say that a wife awaits the death of her mother-in-law so she can finally be the mistress of her own house. The best years of a woman's life come after she has herself become a mother-in-law and grandmother.

Where the mother-in-law exerts dictatorial power of this sort over her husband's wife, the situation of the daughter-in-law often gets better when she has had a baby. Upon the birth of her first child, the status of a Chinese wife begins to improve so that she becomes a more integrated member of her husband's household. The situation of a Turk wife improves if a new bride is brought into the house or when she has given birth to a son. And upon marrying, a wife's domestic workload then becomes equivalent to that of her husband's sisters.

In Brazil, a new Bororo wife of Brazil is entirely at the mercy of her mother-in-law, who continues to be in charge of her son's cows and does not turn over these rights to the younger woman until her daughter-in-law has given birth to her first child. It is not until she has had a baby that the daughter-in-law is given her own hut. She is then permitted access to the dowry that her parents have provided for her. She is also allowed to milk her husband's cows. This improvement in the status of the wife does not mean, however, that she and her mother-in-law become equals. Once she has had a number of children, a Bororo wife's relationship with her mother-in-law becomes somewhat more relaxed. She can eat in front of her husband's mother, and her demeanor is less timid in her mother-in-law's presence. But she is still required to use the polite form of address, is still forbidden to

speak in a loud voice or sing in front of her mother-in-law, and would be ashamed to spend a night with her husband in his mother's hut. Further, the two still avoid any physical contact. With the passage of years, a woman and her husband's mother begin to be able to show each other some affection, but this is done indirectly so that, for example, one might send the other a small present, using a child as a go-between.

In many cultures, women are also expected to be reserved in their interactions with their fathers-in-law. A Manus wife of Oceania never raises her voice in her own house for fear that her husband's father will hear her. She must not enter her father-in-law's section of the house when he is there. She must attempt to make a hasty retreat when her father-in-law appears on the scene, or at least cover her face in his presence. Further, even when relations between a wife and her husband's mother relax, a daughter-in-law may still be required to behave toward her husband's father with reserve. In the Sudan, a Fulani woman's interactions with her mother-in-law become somewhat more familiar with the passage of time, but a daughter-in-law continues to be respectful toward her husband's father and does not speak to him directly except under special circumstances. A Gusii bride of Kenya is told by her parents to be obedient to her parents-in-law because they have paid cattle for her, and in fact new wives are shy and submissive with their in-laws. When a girl first becomes pregnant, however, she begins to relax somewhat in the presence of her mother-in-law, and over the years the relationship becomes much more egalitarian and intimate. Her relationship with her father-in-law, by contrast, is still one of avoidance and respect, although she may not be as openly submissive as she was as a bride.

Sometimes, in a conflict between a woman and her mother-in-law, it is the wife who prevails. For instance, if a newlywed Irish couple moves in with the husband's parents, there is likely to be considerable conflict between the new wife and her mother-in-law. In this case, the new husband is expected to stand up for his bride's interests, and if the friction becomes too intense, the mother-in-law will have to move out.

Interactions between husbands or wives and their parents-in-law are so consistently surrounded by formality across cultures because these relationships have the potential to be highly disruptive to a family. When a son or daughter marries, a parent may view this new attachment as a threat to the emotional bonds between parent and child. A new spouse may also worry about the power of parents-in-law to disrupt his or her marriage. Thus, the marriage of a child means that relationships now become more complicated, with conflicts of affection and loyalty threatening to appear at any time. Thus, cultural conventions mandating formality between spouses and their in-laws may help to check potential discord and decrease the chances that conflicts between spouses and in-laws will get out of hand. It is also the case that sexual relations are generally prohibited between a man and his daughter-in-law or a woman and her son-in-law. So it may be that some of these customs of avoidance or respect between spouses and in-laws may support the ban on sexual intercourse between these individuals.

Albert, Ethel. (1963) "Women of Burundi: A Study of Social Values." In *Women of Tropical Africa,* edited by Denise Paulme, 179–216.

Arensberg, Conrad M., and Solon T. Kimball. (1940) *Family and Community in Ireland.*

Beardsley, Richard K., John W. Hall, and Robert E. Ward. (1959) *Village Japan.*

Dupire, Marguerite. (1963) "The Position of Women in a Pastoral Society." In *Women of Tropical Africa,* edited by Denise Paulme, 47–92.

Fei, Hsiao-Tung. (1939) *Peasant Life in China: A Field Study of Country Life in the Yangtze Valley.*

LeVine, Robert A., and Barbara B. LeVine. (1966) *Nyansongo: A Gusii Community in Kenya.*

Levinson, David, and Martin J. Malone. (1980) *Toward Explaining Human Culture.*

Middleton, John. (1965) *The Lugbara of Uganda.*

Murdock, George P. (1971) "Cross-Sex Patterns of Kin Behavior." *Ethnology* 10: 359–368.

PLURAL MARRIAGE

See MARRIAGE FORMS.

POLYANDRY

See MARRIAGE FORMS.

POLYGYNY

See MARRIAGE FORMS.

POSTPARTUM SEX TABOO

See SEX TABOO, POSTPARTUM.

PREGNANCY, PREMARITAL

If a girl becomes pregnant before she is married, her situation can cause problems for the girl herself, for her family, for the father of her baby, and for the child. In light of this, many cultures disapprove of premarital pregnancy and expect an unmarried pregnant girl to rectify or to pay for her mistake one way or another. Among the Kapauku of New Guinea, a girl who becomes pregnant before marriage is humiliated in front of her married peers. A girl who finds herself pregnant, therefore, either attempts to induce an abortion or tries to persuade the father to marry her. In the southwestern United States, if an unmarried Havasupai girl becomes pregnant, her reputation is damaged. She is "bad" and becomes the focus of wagging tongues for some time. Her child is called "everybody's baby." A girl who repeats the error loses even more prestige and will be mocked behind her back. If a Cuna girl of Panama is pregnant and unmarried, her hair will be cut off. In the past, she and her baby would have been killed.

The Rwala illustrate an important source of the disapproval of premarital pregnancy that reappears across cultures. Because the Rwala trace descent only through the father, the child of an unwed mother is not a member of the mother's lineage. Nor would the baby be a member of the father's clan, as a Rwala man does not acknowledge an illegitimate child as legally his. As a result, children of unwed mothers have no clan identity and would have no kin to depend upon for aid and protection. This is so unthinkable that when a pregnancy is detected, the relatives of the girl immediately try to induce a miscarriage. If this fails, attempts are made to persuade the father to marry the girl. Otherwise, she is likely to commit suicide or to run away. If a Rwalan girl does have a baby without being married, her kin will not take her in. Should a father discover that his daughter is pregnant, he will kill her. More generally, a child born to an unmarried girl presents problems in a society where a child belongs to his father's lineage and lives in the home or community of his father, since the irregularity of the child's birth often deprives him of membership in his

father's lineage and a place in his home. Where a child traces kinship through the mother and lives with or near the mother's relatives, it matters less if the father does not acknowledge paternity.

Premarital pregnancies also create complications in societies where a prospective husband or his family pays a bride price to a bride or her kin. Among the Kwoma of New Guinea, no man will pay the entire traditional bride price for a girl who has had a child before she was married. For this reason, the relatives of a pregnant girl will attempt to discover the identity of the father. If he is found out, he will be compelled to pay damages or else to marry her. The girl's family may resort to threats of violence or sorcery in an effort to persuade the man to comply. Similarly, the Mbundu of Angola require the father of an illegitimate child to pay a fine in compensation for the reduced value of the pregnant girl, who will no longer be a desirable match for a man seeking a bride.

Even when a premarital pregnancy does not disrupt residence, descent, or marriage customs in a particular culture, the girl who becomes pregnant before she is married often must face the disapproval of her family and neighbors. The Saami permit a child to live with the mother's kin. Further, kinship is traced through both the father and mother, so an illegitimate baby still has membership in a kin group. Nor is there any bride-price payment that would be jeopardized if a girl became pregnant before marriage. A pregnant girl might refuse to marry the father of her child, yet the infant will still have a home even in the absence of a father. Nevertheless, in spite of the fact that premarital pregnancies cause little social upheaval, the Saami disapprove of unwed motherhood. In Oceania, a Siuai child lives with his mother's brother and traces descent through his mother. Thus, a Siuai child whose mother is unmarried fits into society without difficulty and, indeed, such children are treated with special care by their relatives. But a

Siuai girl who becomes pregnant before marriage shames her brother and must pay him a fine to compensate him for his embarrassment. A Haitian girl brings a dowry to her marriage. Haitian husbands, therefore, acquire wealth when they marry rather than sacrificing it. Further, a child belongs to its mother's as well as its father's lineage in Haiti. The children of unmarried girls, therefore, do not cause any enormous complications for society, and indeed the girl's family takes care of such youngsters. But premarital pregnancies are considered to be shameful and unfortunate, and an unmarried girl who becomes pregnant will be badly beaten by her family.

There are some societies that do not disapprove of premarital pregnancy. The Sherpa of Nepal find it inconvenient for an unmarried girl to become pregnant, but there is no shame attached to her condition, nor are her chances of finding a suitable husband affected by her pregnancy. Among the Lepcha of Tibet, a premarital pregnancy creates no problems for the girl. On the contrary, the fact that she is obviously fertile makes her more attractive as a prospective wife. In the Caribbean, a Callinago couple will marry only after the woman has demonstrated her fertility, and many women will have had a number of children by different men before they finally settle down in marriage. Indeed, even when a society disapproves of premarital sex, exceptions are sometimes made for couples who are engaged to be married so that the future husband and wife can make sure that they are able to have children together.

Childs, Gladwyn M. (1949) *Umbundu Kinship and Character.*

Collinder, Bjorn. (1949) *The Lapps.*

Fürer-Haimendorf, Christoph von. (1964) *The Sherpas of Nepal: Buddhist Highlanders.*

Gorer, Geoffrey. (1938) *Himalayan Village: An Account of the Lepchas of Sikkim.*

Herskovitz, Melville. (1937) *Life in a Haitian Valley.*

Marshall, Donald S. (1950) "Cuna Folk: A Conceptual Scheme Involving the Dynamic Factors of Culture, as Applied to the Cuna Indians of Darien." Unpublished manuscript, Harvard University.

Pospisil, Leopold. (1958) *The Kapauku Papuans and Their Law.* Yale University Publications in Anthropology 54.

Raswan, Carl R. (1947) *Black Tents of Arabia.*

Spier, Leslie. (1928) *Havasupai Ethnography.* Anthropological Papers of the American Museum of Natural History 29.

Taylor, Douglas. (1938) *The Caribs of Dominica.*

———. (1946) "Kinship and Social Structure of the Island Carib." *Southwestern Journal of Anthropology* 2: 180–212.

Whiting, John W. M. (1941) *Becoming a Kwoma: Teaching and Learning in a New Guinea Tribe.*

PROMISCUITY

In many societies around the world, men and women have more than one sexual partner during the course of their lives. This variety may be tolerated and even approved by cultural standards. Nevertheless, even in societies where a liberal attitude toward sexual activity exists, people tend to distinguish between diversity and promiscuity. Promiscuity refers to a lack of discrimination in choice of sex partners. An individual who is promiscuous engages in sexual relations with any willing partner.

The Tanala of Madagascar illustrate this prejudice against promiscuity. The Tanala admire chastity in an unmarried person, but do not require it. A girl who is not a virgin will have no trouble finding a husband as long as she has not been too free in her sexual behavior. Promiscuity, however, is not only strongly disapproved, it is thought to result in sterility. The rural Vietnamese also value but do not insist upon virginity in girls. Wanton sexual behavior, by contrast, is not acceptable. The Suiai of Oceania assume that couples have slept together before marriage and do not value virginity in brides. But Suiai men are loath to marry a girl of easy virtue. In Oceania, Truk adolescents have a good deal of freedom in their sexual behavior, and are permitted and even expected to enter into a number of sexual liaisons. But even here, if it gets around that a young person pursues more than one relationship simultaneously, the news is likely to provoke a scandal. The Thonga of Mozambique also disapprove of a boy who involves himself sexually with more than one girl at a time. Among the Timbira of Brazil, a girl who has a habit of making and breaking engagements acquires a bad reputation and has trouble attracting any further serious marriage proposals.

Why is the promiscuous person regarded with suspicion, even in cultures that sanction some variety in sexual partners? Promiscuity may signal an inclination to divorce sex from affection and act as a warning to potential partners that an individual is unlikely to remain faithful to any one person. In New Guinea, a Kapauku man of means avoids marrying a girl who has run around with too many boys because he fears that her behavior will cause marital problems. Human beings tend to be especially sensitive to sexual infidelity, and much of the jealousy that spouses may feel revolves around a partner's real or imagined sexual transgressions. Cultures also exhibit special concern over female promiscuity, presumably because a man who marries a sexually undisciplined wife runs the risk that she will become pregnant with another man's child. A husband usually takes responsibility for the rearing of all of his wife's children. As a man has no way of knowing for certain which of his spouse's children are his own and which are not, husbands with promiscuous wives may end up rearing children that are not their own. Males ought to resist entangling themselves in any situation that might lead to their taking care of offspring that are not their own, since to do so decreases their reproductive fitness. Thus, the tendency to distrust promiscuity, especially in women, may serve to protect a man from marrying a woman who will not serve his own fitness interests.

See also JEALOUSY BETWEEN MALES AND FEMALES; REPRODUCTIVE STRATEGIES; SEXUAL SELECTION.

Gladwin, Thomas, and Seymour B. Sarason. (1953) *Truk: Man in Paradise.*

Hickey, Gerald C. (1964) *Village in Vietnam.*

Junod, Henri A. (1927) *The Life of a South African Tribe,* vol. 1.

Linton, Ralph. (1933) *The Tanala: A Hill Tribe of Madagascar.*

Nimuendaju, Curt. (1946) "The Eastern Timbira." University of California Publications in American Archaeology and Ethnology 41.

Oliver, Douglas. (1955) *A Solomon Island Society: Kinship and Leadership among the Siuai of Bougainville.*

Pospisil, Leopold. (1958) *The Kapauku Papuans and Their Law.* Yale University Publications in Anthropology 54.

PROSTITUTION

A prostitute is an individual who performs sexual acts with another person in return for some kind of compensation and without any personal attachment or attraction to the partner. Prostitution overwhelmingly involves women who provide sexual services to paying men, although male homosexual prostitution occurs in some societies. Prostitution is found in many cultures around the world and is reportedly absent in only 12 percent in a sample of 150 societies for which information about the custom is available.

Girls or women become prostitutes for a variety of reasons. Sometimes a girl or woman turns to prostitution because she is not married or marriageable. To be unmarried is a great handicap for women in many societies because females are often dependent upon men for their economic support, and it is expected that a grown woman will find a husband to take care of her, freeing her father and brothers from the responsibility. Widowed women have trouble or are actually prohibited from getting married in some cultures. Often, they become prostitutes in order to support themselves. The Pawnee of the United States Plains traditionally drove widows out of the tribe, with the result that they were compelled to set themselves up as prostitutes just beyond the village. Among the Marshallese of Oceania, it was taken for granted that a widow would be a prostitute. Women who have failed to produce children in a prior marriage or sexual relationship may also have trouble marrying. Among the Amhara of Ethiopia, some unattached women who were infertile when they were married take in travellers and provide them with food and shelter as well as sexual services. If such a woman becomes pregnant, she may increase her chances of finding a husband by proving that she is no longer barren. Women who have been adulterous may also be forced into prostitution. A Bororo husband of Brazil who has reason to believe that his wife has been unfaithful makes her available to the young men in the *bahito,* or men's house, and she is henceforth identified as a tribal prostitute. The woman stays in the men's quarters permanently. Unmarried girls who have a reputation for being pro-

miscuous will also have trouble finding a husband in some cultures. Indeed, their sexual conduct may be equated with prostitution. Aranda tribes in Australia often include one or more women whose sexual behavior is considered to be morally unacceptable by other members of the community. Such women are regarded as prostitutes and are scorned by their neighbors. In societies where a family is expected to give gifts of substantial value to the new bride or her husband on the marriage of a daughter, some girls may have trouble marrying because their relatives are too poor to scrape together the required dowry. They may then become prostitutes.

Sometimes a woman may be marriageable but may decide not to marry. Such women may support themselves through prostitution. Shilluk girls of the Sudan do not consider a man to be an appropriate candidate for marriage unless he owns cattle. When no such men present themselves as possible suitors, a woman may become a prostitute rather than marry. In many societies, a man can marry more than one wife. The first wife is the senior and often most privileged woman in the household. She usually has authority over the junior wives, who must do her bidding. In such societies, some women prefer to become prostitutes rather than take on the role of junior wife. Kikuyu girls of Kenya sometimes turn to prostitution rather than marry a polygynist when they cannot find a man who will marry them as senior wives. Sometimes a woman is able to marry, but prefers the life of a prostitute to the hard work required of wives. Bemba women of Zambia and Amhara women of Ethiopia who become prostitutes instead of marrying can earn enough to pay men to do what is normally considered women's work.

While prostitutes are strongly condemned in some societies, in others they are not regarded negatively and can sometimes even achieve a high-status position. Where prostitution is not disapproved, some women may become temporary prostitutes as a way of finding husbands, acquiring a dowry, gaining sexual expertise, or simply accumulating wealth or pocket money. Amhara "temporary wives" learn new sexual techniques from their clients and then teach them to other people in the community. Indeed, Amhara women who act in this role are accorded some small respect, and to be referred to as a prostitute is not insulting. A woman who finds a particular man attractive as a potential mate will attempt to prolong their relationship and may ultimately manage to become his wife. Ulad-Nail girls of Algeria use money earned from prostitution for their dowries. Goajiro girls of Colombia sometimes resort to prostitution to earn money for needed commodities in the summer, when resources become scarce. In former times, Haitian girls might become prostitutes after they had been abandoned by well-to-do men who had supported them for a time. Nowadays, a girl who is living with a young man who is unable to support her may supplement her income by secretly meeting other men.

In some cultures, females are recruited as prostitutes by other members of their community, who then reap the benefits of their activities. Sometimes a Belau chief will send all of the members of some girl's club to serve as prostitutes in another district. The women stay in the foreign village for some months and are then paid for their services. Some of the money goes to the women, who hand it over to their financial guardians. The chiefs of the village from which the women come are also handsomely paid. Villages typically form partnerships in which the women of each community are exchanged. Even married women are obliged to go along, and the leader of the club is heavily fined if anyone fails to join the expedition. On occasion, a polygynous man will marry secondary wives in order to turn them into prostitutes and then collect the rewards. Fang husbands of Cameroon and Trobriand husbands of New

Guinea sometimes prostitute their junior wives.

Sometimes prostitutes are spatially segregated from their communities. This separation may take place for a number of reasons. Women who pursue the occupation of prostitute may move to large towns or cities where there is a greater chance to build up a clientele. Cities also provide a degree of anonymity for women when prostitution is condemned. Sometimes women are forced to live apart by other members of their community. An Inca woman who became a prostitute was compelled to live alone in a rude hut out in a field. She was not allowed into the towns nor could she have anything to do with other women. Prostitutes may also be forced to alter their appearance in a way that will identify them as a prostitute to other people in their culture. In the United States, Creek women who had extramarital affairs were abandoned by their husbands to become prostitutes and were compelled to wear their hair short or to paint their faces.

The roots of the pattern of intercourse overwhelmingly bought by males from females can be traced to the unequal investment made by males and females in the production and rearing of offspring. The extremely small investment of sperm on the part of a male is enough to produce a viable offspring. Further, the more females a male impregnates, the greater the number of offspring he is likely to leave behind. As a result of these facts about male reproduction, males across species tend to be less discriminating in their sexual behavior. They are more willing to have sexual relations with any female to whom they can gain access, and the more females with whom they can have sexual relations, the better. This characteristic male pattern of sexual behavior is also mirrored in human male sexuality. Males seek more sexual intercourse more often with more partners than do females. Because females invest not only a relatively expensive egg but also nine months of pregnancy, a number of months or years in lactation, and a considerable part of a lifetime in the caretaking and socialization of a child, human females should be much more conservative in their sexual conduct, and indeed they are. This conservatism includes an unwillingness to engage in sexual intercourse indiscriminately. Females, therefore, are not likely to seek out sex for its own sake. This inequality in reproductive investment means that females have something that males want. Women are, therefore, able to barter sex for something else of concrete value. Sexual relations with a prostitute may also be especially attractive to males because they allow a man to engage in intercourse while avoiding the complications that other kinds of sexual relationships may introduce into his life. Prostitutes do not ask for emotional commitments or long-term involvements. And in cultures where premarital or extramarital sex are condemned, sexual intercourse with a prostitute does not involve the intrigue and risks associated with engaging in sex outside of marriage.

Prostitution is defined as the impersonal exchange of sex for some kind of concrete payment. Thus, a female who accepts gifts from a man in the context of a sexual relationship is not a prostitute by this definition. Nevertheless, across cultures, girls and women do receive, and even solicit, rewards of some sort from boys or men with whom they engage in sex, and sometimes a girl will not engage in sex unless she receives something concrete in return. In central Africa, Mbuti men pay a girl's parents to deflower or to have sexual intercourse with their daughter. A Thonga boy in Mozambique will bring his girlfriend gifts in an attempt to persuade her to have sexual intercourse. A Gond boy in India will give a comb that he has carved to a girl in whom he is interested.

In some societies, husbands will lend their wives to other men in return for gifts or services. A Mende husband in West Africa will sometimes allow another man to have sexual intercourse with his wife in return for help with subsistence activities. Among the Huron of Ontario, Kazak of central Asia, and Lesu of New Ireland, husbands lend their wives to other men in return for concrete aid or resources. Thus, one element of prostitution, the acceptance and even expectation of a concrete return for sex, is an accepted part of sexual negotiations between men and women across cultures. This is the case because females across species make a greater investment in offspring than males, and because their reproductive potential is more limited than is that of males. Females as sex partners are in essence a scarce commodity much in demand by males, so females can afford to trade sex for concrete rewards. But in species where two-parent care is important, females are also vulnerable when it comes to reproduction. This is because a male can impregnate a female and then abandon her to raise any resulting offspring on her own. As a way of minimizing this risk, women typically refuse sex to males who do not provide some evidence of their willingness to invest in mother and offspring. One way in which males can demonstrate their seriousness is by giving females concrete resources. Thus, the pervasive gift-giving by males of our own and other species in the context of courtship and sexual intercourse reflects both the nature of female sexuality as a scarce resource, and the female strategy of requiring some kind of insurance that a male with whom she has intercourse is in earnest and will not leave her should she become pregnant.

Barnett, H. G. (1949) *Palauan Society: A Study of Contemporary Native Life in the Palau Islands.*

Basedow, Herbert. (1925) *The Australian Aboriginal.*

Elwin, Verrier. (1947) *The Muria and Their Ghotul.*

Junod, Henri A. (1927) *The Life of a South African Tribe,* vol. 1.

Little, Kenneth L. (1951) *The Mende of Sierra Leone: A West African People in Transition.*

Messing, Simon D. (1957) *The Highland-Plateau Amhara of Ethiopia.*

Murdock, George P. (1936) *Our Primitive Contemporaries.*

Powdermaker, Hortense. (1933) *Life in Lesu: The Study of a Melanesian Society in New Ireland.*

Simpson, G. E. (1943) "Sexual and Familial Institutions in Northern Haiti." *American Anthropologist* 44: 655–674.

Symanski, Richard. (1981) *The Immoral Landscape: Female Prostitution in Western Societies.*

PURDAH

See FEMALE SECLUSION.

Rape is sexual intercourse physically forced on one person by another. Only rape by a man of a woman is reported across cultures. This definition includes both normative rape (rape that is condoned by society) and nonnormative rape (rape that is not condoned and is considered wrong or a crime). When both forms of rape are considered, rape is a cultural universal, although in some societies it is very rare. When only nonnormative rape is counted, rape can be considered present in about 50 percent of cultures.

Among the Cuna of Panama, rape is rare, perhaps because the punishment entails forcing a briar up the man's penis and leaving him to die. Rape is also virtually unheard of among the Siriono of South America, who believe that the supernatural punishes such acts with illness or even death. Similarly, in New Ireland, any Lesu woman can refuse sexual solicitations, and rape is unknown in this culture.

In contrast, rape is frequent among Trumai men of Brazil, who often attack unmarried strangers or older women who have no spouses or kin to protect them, and threats about rape are frequently made in jest. As a result, women are often nervous when they anticipate this kind of teasing, even when they know that the men are joking. In Alaska, an Ingalik woman is always in danger of being raped if a man comes upon her by surprise, and some men acquire a reputation for forcing themselves on women. If the woman is married, her husband is likely to beat the man if he can find him and, on occasion, an irate husband may kill his wife's attacker. Rape is also common among the Hidatsa of the United States. The rapist may be severely beaten by the girl's brothers, while the sisters of the offender may attempt to smooth things over by giving the girl's family a horse or some other gift. The reputation of a rapist is damaged because the Hidatsa view forcible sex as a cowardly act. Acts of rape are reported to be frequent among the Lepcha of Tibet, who do not disapprove of forced sex but, rather, regard it as humorous. Among the Manus of Oceania, men view rape as the ideal way to obtain sexual gratification. The Navajo of Arizona say that a woman is quite able to ward off any unwanted sexual advances, and women do protect themselves by grabbing the penis of their molester. Men are fearful of being dragged all the way home in this manner and may end up trying to placate the woman with a gift, such as a blanket or some beads. Women are sometimes plied with liquor and then gang-raped. These episodes are not condemned, but the woman may appropriate some property belonging to the men who attacked her as compensation for the rape.

Sometimes rape will be practiced in unusual circumstances, while remaining rare or absent in the normal life of a culture. For instance, the rape of women during wartime may be common among men who do not otherwise commit rape. Thus, while Siuai men of Oceania do not rape women in their own society, warriors did rape the women of their enemies during wartime.

RAPE

Similarly, all of the men taking part in the abduction of a woman from another tribe rape her on the spot, while any men who have stayed back at the village may rape her later. The woman is then given to one of the men as a wife. A kidnapped woman who is related to her captors will not be raped. In Tanzania, Hadza men who have a grudge against the members of another camp may attack the women of their antagonists without facing any repercussions. By contrast, other cultures, for example, the Chiricahua of the southwestern United States, disapprove of the rape of captive women.

In some cultures, a husband may force his wife to have sexual intercourse with impunity. Among the Tikopia of Oceania, a man sometimes acquires a wife by abducting her and marrying her against her will. Under these circumstances, the bride may be unwilling to have sexual relations with her new husband. The groom's brothers may then hold the woman down so the husband can consummate the marriage. In other societies, such as the Lesu, a wife cannot be forced to have sexual relations with her husband against her will.

Cultures also differ in their attitudes toward and responses to rape. Rape is mildly disapproved of in 21 percent and strongly disapproved of in 42 percent of 38 societies. In the remaining 37 percent, it is ignored, accepted, or ridiculed. The stronger the sentiments against rape, the harsher the punishment for men who commit rape. For the Abkhaz, the crime of rape is as serious as the crime of murder. A rapist may be killed, but if permitted to live, he is required to pay a heavy fine and to marry the girl he has attacked. A rapist is also put to death among the Hottentots of southern Africa. If a Rwala woman is raped, her relatives will also kill the guilty man. If the woman becomes pregnant, the baby, too, will be killed, as it would otherwise have no kin, making its position in the community ambiguous. The rapist's kin will also be re-

quired to pay a compensation for the injury done to the girl.

The Kwoma of New Guinea view rape as a sexual transgression and an act of violence. A boy who has raped a girl runs the risk of being killed by her relatives unless he can escape to his own village, where his kin will shield him. The girl's family may still use sorcery to punish the offender. In Kenya, a Kikuyu man who attempts to rape a girl is fined three goats. Rape is frequent among the Teda of the Sudan and is also punished by a fine.

The punishment for rape may also be tailored to fit the circumstances. If an Ifugao man of the Philippines commits a rape during the day, the fine is increased to compensate the greater shame that the woman feels at having been forced to have sexual relations at such an unseemly hour. The marital status of the raped woman also figures into the rapist's punishment in a number of places. Among the Ifugao, the rape of a married woman by an unmarried man is a serious crime, but the rape of a married woman by a married man is even more grave. In the first case, the man pays fines to both the woman and her kin and her husband and his kin. In the latter case, he must also pay his wife to compensate her for his adultery. The Kapauku of New Guinea view the rape of a married woman as both a moral and economic offense, as the husband has paid a bride price for his wife. A man who rapes a married woman is likely to be executed, although a husband may accept a large payment from the culprit instead. By contrast, the Chiricahua regard the rape of an unmarried woman as more serious than the rape of a married one. The family of a single girl will seek revenge against the attacker. A husband does, however, have the right to do anything he wishes to a man who has raped his wife. The rapist's relatives may attempt to offer a compensation payment as a way of smoothing things over. The Kikuyu regard rape as an offense against the girl's guardian. Therefore, the rape of either an unmarried or married woman is regarded as equally serious. So is the rape of a sexually inexperienced girl treated very seriously in some cultures. If a Babylonian man raped a virgin, the girl's father turned the rapist's wife into a prostitute and could force him to marry the victim. An attack on a girl who is engaged to be married is also regarded as a serious offense in some places. For instance, a Babylonian man who raped a betrothed girl was killed.

Rape is sometimes used as a means of punishing a woman for some misdeed. A Brazilian Caraja girl who intrudes on the secret activities of the men's cults is gang-raped. She thereafter lives the life of a wanton. The Mundurucu of Brazil do not disapprove of rape and use it as a punishment when a woman violates certain rules. For instance, if a wife has frequently been unfaithful to her husband or if an adolescent girl runs away from school, gang rape may be employed as a form of discipline. Men view gang rape as a source of amusement and will recount stories of rape in public, which makes any women who are present extremely anxious.

The line between consensual sexual intercourse and rape can blur in some situations across cultures. In many places around the world, a male may sneak sexual intercourse with a woman. The act is not strictly accomplished by force, as the girl does not resist. These instances of sexual intercourse are not always considered rape by the culture in which they occur. This is the case in Samoa, where a boy will sometimes be invited to visit a girl secretly in her house at night if she likes him, but is fearful of meeting him elsewhere. A boy who cannot attract a sweetheart may decide to creep into a girl's bed and have sexual intercourse with her without her permission, hoping that she will mistake him for someone she is expecting. Or a boy who has fought with his girlfriend may use the same trick to get her to sleep with him against her will. If the girl

makes a fuss, the boy will be pursued by all of the members of the household and, if caught, will be beaten and laughed at. No respectable girl will regard such a boy favorably as a suitor. The Lakher of South Asia do not view it as rape if a man successfully has intercourse with a girl while she is asleep, as stealth is employed instead of force in such cases. Indeed, a boy who succeeds in getting a girl in this way is thought to have been quite resourceful. Forcible sex, on the other hand, is viewed as shameful and is almost nonexistent. The Siuai of Oceania regard the use of force by men as improper, and rape is absent in this society. In fact, women are viewed by many men as the more aggressive gender. But a man may waylay a woman who is on her way home from her garden. Because such women typically have heavy loads of firewood and vegetables strapped to their backs, it is easy to push and hold them down. Men claim that women who walk home alone don't mind being ambushed and don't protest very hard.

Where females are expected to resist sexual advances by custom, the line between rape and coyness becomes fuzzy for the people involved. Among the Ifugao, a girl who accepted the sexual advances of a boy without resistance would cause a scandal. As a result, it is hard to know whether hesitation on the part of a girl is genuine or a matter of form. Thus, the Ifugao do not regard it as rape if a boy who has been sleeping regularly in the same house with a girl forces her to have sexual intercourse. Coercion by a boy who has not been staying in the girl's dormitory is considered rape.

Across cultures, males run the risk of being accused of rape when no rape has in fact occurred. Because Ifugao women are expected to resist the advances of a boy, a girl can claim that she has been raped after the fact even though she was a willing partner at the time. On occasion, a Kwoma girl may accuse a boy of trying to rape her if she is angry with him for some reason. A boy is therefore very careful not to make sexual advances toward a girl if he is unsure of her response.

Attitudes toward and frequency of rape are associated with a small number of other sexual norms and practices across cultures. Where rape is approved, accepted, or ridiculed, homosexuality is disapproved. Where extramarital sex on the part of husbands is absent or rare, rape is disapproved but present. Rape is particularly characteristic of cultures where men dominate women and where men often use physical force to control or punish women.

While people tend to regard rape as a purely human behavior, forced sex is present in other species. Thus, for example, rape is reported for some kinds of insects. Why do males in other species force females to have sex? Scorpionfly males typically court females by offering them a dead arthropod. While the female eats the gift, the male copulates with her. If a male cannot find a dead arthropod, he secretes a salivary mass and offers this to a potential mate instead. Females prefer to mate with males who have food to offer because they are then receiving something important to their survival in return for providing the male with an opportunity to reproduce. But when a male has nothing to offer a female, he may knock a female from the air as she flies by, hold onto her, and inseminate her by force. Females attempt to escape these abductions and are often successful, but sometimes the male gets his way. Why do scorpionfly males force sex on females of their species? Their behavior functions as a strategy for reproducing. It is also their least-preferred strategy, so that a scorpionfly will not rape a female if he has a gift to offer. Rape is his last resort. Human beings are not scorpionflies, but some men who rape also appear to have no other way of attracting a female. Thus, we may be seeing a common evolutionarily based reproductive strategy that kicks in for males across species when other ways of obtaining a mate are not available.

In many kinds of nesting birds—herons, albatrosses, gulls, and swallows, for example—males also force sex, but for another reason. Among these birds, both parents invest an enormous amount of time and effort in the rearing of their young, and parents tend to form pair-bonds for life. This means that a male's successful reproduction is limited to the number of offspring his mate can produce. A male who sneaks a mating with some other female, however, will increase his reproductive output. As the female's own mate may abandon her if he discovers that she has mated with another male, females resist these copulations with birds who are not their mates. This is why this mating outside of the pair-bond is classified as rape. In male nesting birds, it is a mating strategy, just as it is with scorpionflies. The precipitating factors are different, but the goal is the same. As human beings are historically also long-term pair-bonders with a high degree of investment in offspring by both parents, rape among our species may also serve the same kind of evolutionarily based purpose for us that it does for nesting birds. While we are not nesting birds, our shared strategies for mating and parenting suggest a shared rationale behind male rape in both species.

Barton, R. F. (1938) *Philippine Pagans: The Autobiographies of Three Ifugaos.*

Broude, Gwen J., and Sarah J. Greene. (1976) "Cross-Cultural Codes on Twenty Sexual Attitudes and Practices." *Ethnology* 15: 409–429.

Cagnolo, C. (1933) *The Akikuyu: Their Customs, Traditions, and Folklore.*

Chagnon, Napoleon A. (1968) *Yanomamo: The Fierce People.*

Cline, Walter. (1950) *The Teda of Tibesti, Borku, and Kawar in the Eastern Sahara.*

Daly, Martin, and Margo Wilson. (1983) *Sex, Evolution, and Behavior.*

Firth, Raymond. (1936) *We, the Tikopia: A Sociological Study of Kinship in Primitive Polynesia.*

Gladwin, Thomas, and Seymour B. Sarason. (1953) *Truk: Man in Paradise.*

Gorer, Geoffrey. (1938) *Himalayan Village: An Account of the Lepchas of Sikkim.*

Holmberg, Allan R. (1950) *Nomads of the Long Bow.* Washington, DC: Government Printing Office.

Leighton, Dorothea, and Clyde Kluckhohn. (1969) *Children of the People: The Navaho Individual and His Development.*

Lipkind, William. (1948) "The Caraja." In *Handbook of South American Indians,* vol. 3, edited by Julian H. Steward, 179–191.

Luzbetak, Louis J. (1951) *Marriage and the Family in Caucasia: A Contribution to the Study of North Caucasian Ethnology and Customary Law.*

Marshall, Donald S. (1950) "Cuna Folk: A Conceptual Scheme Involving the Dynamic Factors of Culture, as Applied to the Cuna Indians of Darien." Unpublished manuscript, Harvard University.

Matthews, W. (1877) *Ethnography and Philology of the Hidatsa Indians.*

Mead, Margaret. (1931) *Growing Up in New Guinea: A Comparative Study of Primitive Education.*

Murdock, George P. (1936) *Our Primitive Contemporaries.*

Murphy, Robert F. (1960) *Headhunter's Heritage: Social and Economic Change among the Mundurucu Indians.*

Murphy, Robert F., and Buell Quain. (1955) *The Trumai Indians of Central Brazil.*

Oliver, Douglas. (1955) *A Solomon Island Society: Kinship and Leadership among the Siuai of Bougainville.*

Opler, Morris E. (1941) *An Apache Life-Way: The Economic, Social and Religious Institutions of the Chiricahua Indians.*

Osgood, Cornelius. (1958) *Ingalik Social Culture.* Yale University Publications in Anthropology 55.

Palmer, Craig. (1989) "Is Rape a Cultural Universal? A Re-Examination of the Ethnographic Data." *Ethnology* 28: 1–16.

Parry, N. E. (1932) *The Lakhers.*

Pospisil, Leopold. (1958) *The Kapauku Papuans and Their Law.* Yale University Publications in Anthropology 54.

Powdermaker, Hortense. (1933) *Life in Lesu: The Study of a Melanesian Society in New Ireland.*

Raswan, Carl R. (1947) *Black Tents of Arabia.*

Rozée-Koker, Patricia. (1987) "Cross-Cultural Codes on Seven Types of Rape." *Behavior Science Research* 21: 101–117.

Saggs, H. W. F. (1962) *The Greatness That Was Babylon: A Survey of the Ancient Civilization of the Tigris Euphrates.*

Sanday, Peggy R. (1981) "The Socio-Cultural Context of Rape: A Cross-Cultural Study." *Journal of Social Issues* 37: 5–27.

Whiting, John W. M. (1941) *Becoming a Kwoma: Teaching and Learning in a New Guinea Tribe.*

Woodburn, J. (1964) "The Social Organization of the Hadza of North Tanzania." Unpublished dissertation, Cambridge University.

REPRODUCTIVE STRATEGIES According to Charles Darwin's theory of evolution by natural selection, the traits that are characteristic of a species today are the ones that proved to be advantageous in helping ancestral organisms to survive and to reproduce more successfully than other individuals who did not possess those traits. This means that organisms possess reproductive strategies, that is, strategies for producing more offspring than other individuals who did not have similar success in the past. Strategies for producing a maximum number of offspring, however, differ for males and females. This is because of the differences in the degree of investment that males and females make in offspring.

The discrepancy in investment in offspring made by males and females begins with the gametes. A sperm is minuscule in comparison with an egg. If a single sperm were blown up so that it was the size of a thumbnail, an equivalently enlarged egg would be the size of a living room. This means that it takes a tremendous amount of energy to make an egg compared to what it takes to make a sperm. Sperm, therefore, are "cheap" while eggs are "expensive," and this affects the number of gametes that each sex can produce. Thus, while a female can produce only a limited number of eggs in her lifetime, a male can produce what is, for practical purposes, an infinite number of sperm. If fertilization is internal, then the female is required to make further investments of time and energy in a pregnancy. And if the species is mammalian then the production of milk adds to the cost of the offspring. These investments on the part of a female are not trivial. Thus, for example, among red deer, the difference in mortality rate for nursing versus nonnursing females can be over 30 percent, with nonnursing females living longer than their nursing counterparts.

What are the consequences of the difference in male versus female investment in offspring for reproductive strategies? Because males spend so little on a single mating, it is worth their while to try to mate with as many females as possible. Even in species like our own where males participate in the rearing of young, a male will benefit from trying to mate with many females. If

the resulting offspring fails to survive, the male has invested almost nothing. And if the female manages to raise the infant without him, then his investment has paid off in a big way from the perspective of his reproductive success. For males, then, the best reproductive strategy entails competing with other males for access to females. The reproductive strategy of females, by contrast, reflects the greater investment that females make in the production of young. Female strategies also reflect the fact that females, unlike males, are limited in the number of offspring that they are able to produce in a lifetime. Thus, females tend to be conservative when it comes to mating in the sense that they are choosy about which males they will accept as mates. This is because a mistake is likely to be very expensive for the female, costing her the egg, a pregnancy, and whatever time and effort she has expended on nursing and caretaking. In particular, a female will prefer a male whose traits are most liable to contribute to survival and successful reproduction so that the offspring that she produces with him will inherit these traits. If the female belongs to a species for which two parents are optimal in the rearing of young, then she will also assess the degree to which potential mates are likely to be loyal and competent fathers.

Males across species compete with each other in a variety of ways for sexual access to females. Sometimes males will enter into physical combats. Elephant seals, a large species of mammal living off the California coast, provide a spectacular example of physical aggression as a mating strategy. Males arrive on the California beaches in early December and engage in sometimes bloody encounters until mid-March as they establish a dominance hierarchy. The victors then retain almost exclusive access to the female elephant seals, so that the reward for their ordeal can be a stunning superiority in reproductive success over the losers. For example, in one breeding season, 115 males were congregated on the beach, but 123 of the 144 matings that took place were performed by the top five males in the dominance hierarchy. Thus, 4 percent of the males in the group were responsible for 85 percent of the offspring born in the next season.

Human males also engage in physical aggression in pursuit of females. For instance, the Yanomamo of Brazil and Venezuela regularly raid neighboring villages, with the victors acquiring women, and the Yanomamo see this benefit as one of the principal goals of warring. Similarly, among Eskimo groups, men traditionally fought each other for wives, and one man sometimes killed another man in order to obtain his wife. More generally, in traditional societies much of the fighting between men is directly or indirectly over women. Male aggressive competition may also take the form of posturing in order to gain a reputation for being superior to other men. Among the Ilongot of the Philippines, young men tried to win over females by demonstrating their superior headhunting skills, and Ilongot men said that before "sitting with" a woman a youth should take a head.

Males across species also compete with each other by actively courting females. Males across many species are more noticeable than their female counterparts, and this greater degree of conspicuousness assists their courting activities. Sometimes males are more brightly colored, or they may have more elaborate plumage. Males also make more vocalizations than females in many species. Courtship may also involve the display of particular skills by males or the giving of gifts to the female. Some male insects present food items to females before mating with them, and females will refuse to mate with a male who does not bring a gift of food. Courtship is extremely common in human societies, and it is almost always the case that males court females. Further, males often offer gifts in an attempt to win the affections of a female, with the goal frequently being the attainment of sexual intercourse. In Mozambique, a Thonga boy brings along a gift when he visits a girl at night. In India, a Gond boy who wants to impress a girl favorably will give her a comb that he has carved himself.

Evolutionary theory explains gift-giving on the part of males in two ways. First, the presentation of some kind of valuable commodity is understood to be a payment for the sexual services of the female. The fact that gifts are often food items in both nonhuman species and in the case of human courtship suggests that the male is providing energy supplies to make up for the energy that she expends in the production of eggs, and so on. Gift-giving is also taken as a sign that the male is serious about his commitment to the rearing of offspring in species, like our own, where paternal care is important to the successful raising of offspring. The giving of an engagement ring has been interpreted as a signal that the courting man is in earnest about investing in a woman and her children. Gift presentations also serve as evidence that a male has resources that will be at the disposal of a female and her offspring should she be willing to mate with him.

Male competition also shows up in the treatment by males of a mate's offspring by another male. Langur monkeys live in what are known as harems. That is, a group of mature females remains and mates with a single adult male. A male, however, retains his position in a harem for a relatively brief period of time, after which he is ousted by another male. The new head of the harem then kills the infants of the females over whom he now has control. This wholesale infanticide has the consequence of decreasing the number of surviving offspring left by other langur males. Further, females remain infertile while they are nursing their infants. Thus, the females whose infants have been killed will become available as mates earlier than would have been the case otherwise. The male, then, advances his own reproductive success both by decreasing the success of his competitors and by insuring that the females in his harem will produce offspring for him as early as possible. Infanticide of an analogous sort is also practiced by human males. For example, an Amazonian Yanomamo man who marries a woman who has had a child with a former husband may kill the infant or require the woman to do so. Men explain this action by observing that the child would otherwise compete for his wife's time and milk with the infants that she will have with him. In many societies, a man who suspects his wife of having become pregnant by another man will either kill the infant or divorce the woman.

Males also increase their own reproductive success by blocking the access of other males to females. For instance, some nonhuman primate couples will mate exclusively with each other while the female is fertile. The male will entice the female away from the remaining members of the troop and keep her secluded, with the result that other males are denied matings with her. Many customs also appear across human societies that have the same effect of denying other males access to a female. Seclusion of women occurs in a number of societies around the world. In these cultures, a female lives almost exclusively in the company of other females so that a husband is virtually assured that his wife's offspring are his own. In some societies, the custom of infibulation, or sewing up the female genital opening, effectively bars access to a female by other males. The operation is performed when a girl is first likely to engage in sexual intercourse, and is undone when she marries. While she is nursing any children, she may be sewn up again until she is ready to resume sexual intercourse with her husband. Thus, it becomes less likely that other men will be able to fertilize the infibulated woman. In some societies, females undergo the procedure of clitoridectomy, or the removing of the clitoris. This operation is sometimes explained by its

practitioners as a way of diminishing sexual interest, and therefore the impulse to have affairs, on the part of wives.

Because sperm are so cheap to produce, it pays for males to try to mate whenever possible. This leads to a relatively low level of discrimination on the part of males regarding the objects of their mating efforts. Thus, males in nonhuman species will make sexual advances toward females of different species, body parts of stuffed female models, other males, and inanimate objects. None of these matings will result in offspring, but the tendency to mate indiscriminately is part of the overall male strategy of trying to obtain as many fertilizations as possible without wasting the time and energy of sizing up the partner. Human males are also more likely than females to direct sexual advances toward targets that will not net them a fertilization. Thus, homosexuality, fetishism, and sodomy are more frequent in males than in females.

What reproductive strategies are females likely to employ? As the investment that a female makes in an offspring is relatively costly, and as the number of offspring that she can produce is limited, females are predicted to be choosy about the partners with whom they are willing to mate. This shows up in a variety of ways across species, including our own. Females will not mate with just any male who solicits copulations. Male fruit flies, placed in a container with female flies, will try to mate with all of the females. The females, however, will refuse matings with some of the males. Females across species choose males who have characteristics that are likely to promote survival reproduction in themselves and, therefore, in their offspring and the offspring of a female who mates with them. Where size affects reproductive success, as in some insects, fish, and frogs, females will choose larger mates. Among birds, where males also caretake young, females will inspect the nests that courting males build before accepting them as mates, and males with inferior nests will be rejected. Pigeon females prefer older and more experienced males. Both of these qualities increase reproductive success.

This greater selectivity on the part of females is found in our own species. For instance, studies of computer dating have shown that females are more demanding regarding their requirements in a date and a mate than are males. This is true across qualities, such as education, intelligence, and economic status, although females are not fussier than males regarding the appearance of a potential partner. Girls are also less likely to respond enthusiastically to an actual date. Thus, males in the computer study were two and one-half times as likely to say that they were strongly attracted to their date than were females. And fewer girls considered their dates to be potentially acceptable marriage partners. In hunting societies, a man's success at gaining wives is often related to his success as a hunter. Among the Shavante of Brazil, the better a man is at hunting, the more wives he obtains. A Hadza man in Tanzania will have trouble marrying or keeping a wife if he cannot hunt big game. Among the Brazilian Mehinacu, a man who is having an extramarital affair is expected by his lover to bring gifts of meat. And Peruvian Sharanahua women urge men to go out and hunt, and reward successful men by having sexual intercourse with them.

While women themselves tend to be choosier about their sexual and marriage partners than are men, parents in many cultures still prefer to take the choice of a spouse out of the hands of their daughters. Thus, males choose their own wives in 50 percent of 157 cultures, whereas girls have autonomy in their choice of a spouse in only 36 percent of 161 cultures. In the remaining 64 percent of cultures, parents or other third parties select a girl's husband for her, and many explicitly observe that young girls cannot be trusted to make a wise choice. Thus, the parents of the girl are protecting their own reproductive success by choosing a son-in-law who is

more likely to produce surviving grandchildren for them.

The greater choosiness of females also shows up in their greater discrimination with regard to their sexual targets. Lesbianism is much less widely reported across cultures than is homosexuality. And females are less likely to direct sexual behavior at animals or inanimate objects. Females are also less easily aroused by the sight of a member of the opposite sex. The fact that pornography is almost exclusively directed at males reflects this difference. Thus, males begin to be ready to have sexual intercourse at the very sight of a female, while females require more extensive interaction with a member of the opposite sex before they become interested in sexual activity. Women the world over are made aware at an early age that they must cover their genitals in front of men, and modesty is more excessive for females than for males. Thus, cultural customs recognize that men respond to female nudity and attempt to minimize the chances that women will, in fact, arouse men by their very presence.

Finally, male-female differences regarding extramarital sexual behavior reflect the differences between the sexes in overall reproductive strategy. A survey of American middle-class couples revealed that 49 percent of men but only 5 percent of women claimed that they would like to have an extramarital affair. Similar results are reported for a number of other industrialized cultures. In Germany, 46 percent of unmarried working-class men involved in serious relationships said that they would have a casual sexual liaison if the opportunity presented itself, but the figure was only 6 percent for women. In Israel, where sexual egalitarianism is the stated philosophy of the nation, and contraception is readily available, more than 40 percent of adolescent boys and less than 10 percent of adolescent girls thought that it would be legitimate to engage in casual sexual contact. Thus, the extramarital sexual proclivities of men are consistent with a strategy of attempting to inseminate as many females as possible, while women are conservative in their extramarital behavior in line with their more general choosiness about mating.

See also ATTRACTIVENESS; COURTSHIP; DIFFERENTIAL REPRODUCTIVE SUCCESS; MARRIAGE PARTNERS, CRITERIA FOR CHOOSING; NATURAL SELECTION; SEX, EXTRAMARITAL.

Daly, Margo, and Martin Wilson. (1983) *Sex, Evolution and Behavior.*

Elwin, Verrier. (1947) *The Muria and Their Ghotul.*

Junod, Henri A. (1927) *The Life of a South African Tribe,* vol. 1.

Rosaldo, Michelle Z. (1980) *Knowledge and Passion: Ilongot Notions of Self and Social Life.*

Symons, Donald. (1979) *The Evolution of Human Sexuality.*

Trivers, Robert L. (1985) *Social Evolution.*

RESIDENCE RULES

When a couple are married, a decision about where they will live must be made. In Western societies, a bride and groom generally set up a household of their own away from their parents and kin. This way of establishing a home is known as neolocality because the couple go to live in a new place at some distance from the former residence of either spouse. Neolocal residence, however, is very uncommon across cultures. In only 5 percent of 565 societies do a newly married couple characteristically live by themselves. In the remaining cultures, a bride and groom will live with or near the parents or other relatives of one or the other spouse.

In 67 percent of 565 societies, marital residence is with the parents of the groom. This is called patrilocal postmarital residence. The couple may set up a household in close proximity to the husband's natal household or they may move into the husband's dwelling, thus forming an extended family. In Mexico, Mixtecan households are usually comprised of patrilocal extended families. A family lives in a compound consisting of a shared central patio, several sleeping rooms lining the periphery of the compound, and additional cooking huts. Married couples usually obtain a sleeping room within the compound of the husband's family or, if there is no room, they will find a house close by.

Another 15 percent of the sample of 565 societies is matrilocal. This means that a couple moves in with or lives very close to the parents of the wife. A Miskito boy of Middle America, who may have been betrothed in childhood, brings token gifts to his future bride and her family and occasionally comes to work for them. When the girl reaches puberty, the two are considered married and the boy comes to live with his bride and is considered a member of her family. As the household grows over the years, the husband sets up a new residence nearby.

In 4 percent of the 565 cultures, a bride and groom live with or near the husband's mother's brother. This is known as avunculocal residence, meaning the uncle's place. The Trobrianders of New Guinea exemplify this avunculocal residence pattern. When a Trobriand boy reaches adolescence, he goes to live in a bachelor's hut with other boys of his age in his mother's brother's village. When he is married, the man and his wife establish their own household in this same village.

Rules of residence that commit a couple to living with either the husband's or the wife's relatives result in unilocal living arrangements—that is to say, residence near only one of the couple's kin groups. In an additional 7 percent of the 565 societies, marital residence is bilocal, so that a couple may move in with or live near the parents of either spouse. Thus, couples can choose to reside in one of two places. The Hidatsa of the United States partition off a separate section of the mother's house for a daughter and her husband when the girl marries. When a household already contains a number of married sisters and their families, a younger sister will frequently move in with her husband's family instead of bringing her spouse to her mother's crowded lodge. A Javanese bride and groom move in with the relatives of either spouse unless there is already a vacant house on the land of one of their families. A couple living with in-laws will try to find a separate house by the time they have had a child or been married for a few years, but they will still be living near relatives. And Samoan newlyweds are given a mosquito net, bedding, and a bamboo pillow of their own and settle in the house of either set of parents.

Patterns of marital residence have profound effects upon the life of a husband or wife. When a newly married couple moves into the house or compound of the parents of one spouse, the entire membership of the new household tends to merge into a single, coherent unit. If residence is patrilocal, the new husband usually works under his father's supervision. In extended family settings, the bride and groom do not have substantial property of their own. The patrilocal rural Ukrainians say that a person owns nothing of his own except for his clothes. Everything else is common property. Similarly, among the bilocal Samoans, everything except for some personal possessions is the joint property of the descent group.

When a woman moves in with her husband, she may end up living very far away from her own family. By contrast, when it is the man who moves in with his spouse, his new household is usually close to home. In either case, the spouse who leaves home has to make what are often difficult adjustments. When a wife moves in with her spouse, she is likely to miss her family and feel like a stranger in her husband's home. An Alaskan Copper Eskimo bride sobs as she is led away from her familiar world to a strange new life. Among the Gusii of Kenya, the bride's ritualized behavior as she departs to her new home symbolizes the turmoil that patrilocality causes for a new wife. When it comes time for the couple to leave the bride's household, the girl will hide beneath the roof of a nearby house and her father may be forced to retrieve her. The relatives of the new husband drag her away as she tries to hold onto the house posts. They will then remain at her side to stop her from escaping. While the actions of the girl are partly a matter of custom, her anguish about leaving home is often sincere.

A bride who goes to live with her spouse's family also has to negotiate a new set of relationships with the members of her husband's household. For instance, a Hindu bride must wear a veil all day and obey all of the commands of the older women in her husband's household. She is not allowed to see her spouse except at night, as to do so would be regarded as shameful. A Turk woman also goes to live with her husband, which means that she becomes a member of his extended-family household. In the early years of her marriage, the new wife is treated more or less like a servant and is ordered about at the whim of her husband's relations. Her situation improves if a new bride is brought into the house or when she has given birth to a son. An inmarrying wife's domestic workload then becomes equivalent to that of her husband's sisters.

When a husband moves in with his wife's family, he is also likely to find his situation somewhat stressful. Typically, a man living matrilocally is expected to be loyal to his own family and also to that of his wife. This means that men who live with the families of their wives need to perform delicate balancing acts. Further, in some matrilocal households, a man is never master of the home in which he lives. Rather, it is the wife's brothers who are the authorities. A Navajo man of Arizona lives with his wife's family but is expected to attend the ceremonies and contribute to the economic support of his natal household. His wife's brother is the titular head of the household, but the senior female of the family has a good deal of real power and is consulted by the men in matters of importance. A man's wife is likely to take her own family's side against her husband. For his part, a husband's fondest attachment usually remains for life to his own mother. Whatever the strains associated with marital residence, a young couple will eventually settle into married life as they become the senior members of the household. The family will continue to incorporate new members as their sons or daughters marry and introduce their spouses into the family.

In some societies, couples may change their residence over the course of their marriage. In patri-matrilocal cultures, newlyweds first live with the groom's family and then with that of the bride. By contrast, in matri-patrilocal societies, the bride's family first receives the new couple, who then moves in with the relatives of the groom. In a number of cultures, a bride and groom will initially go to live with the parents of one or the other spouse but will then establish a household of their own after they have been married for a while or once a child or two have been born.

Causes of Residence Patterns

Neolocal residence tends to be found in societies with a monetary economy. This pattern may be a result of the fact that money is not perishable. Since a couple can save their money until they need to buy something, they are not forced to depend upon kin for whatever necessities they cannot provide for themselves. Neolocal residence may also make sense in cultures where people work for money because the job market may demand mobility on the part of workers. It is unrealistic for an individual who has to follow a job from one location to another to take a large extended family along.

Some experts have argued that patrilocality and matrilocality are caused by the relative contribution of men and women to the subsistence economy, so that residence rules will be patrilocal when men make the major contribution, while residence will be with the wife's family if women make the greater contribution. This pattern, however, is only true among indigenous North American cultures. Some theorists have also linked matrilocality and patrilocality to warfare. In particular, societies that wage war between distant groups tend to be matrilocal when the warfare interferes with a male-centered work force. This disruption of the work force means that women must take over the subsistence activities normally conducted by men. When women are largely responsible for doing the economic chores, women may wish to keep their daughters at home even after they are married. By contrast, societies that enter into wars with neighboring groups tend to be patrilocal. This may be because, where warfare is between close neighbors, families may want to keep their sons near home to help with defense since women do not typically engage in war. When war is with distant groups, the need for defense of the family may be less urgent, as the fighting will not be close to home.

In societies that allow a couple to live with either set of parents, this flexibility may be a product of necessity. Bilocal societies tend to have been recently depopulated by disease. Perhaps in these cultures a bride and groom are given latitude in their choice of residence because the parents of one of the partners may no longer be alive. The couple will then still be able to enjoy the benefits of living in an extended family, a necessity in many cultures with nonmonetary subsistence economies, in spite of the loss of some relatives.

Bohannan, Paul, and John Middleton, eds. (1968) *Marriage, Family, and Residence.*

Bowers, Alfred W. (1950) *Hidatsa Social and Ceremonial Organization.*

Conzemius, Edward. (1932) *Ethnographical Survey of the Miskito and Sumu Indians of Honduras and Nicaragua.*

Ember, Carol R., and Melvin Ember. (1988) *Anthropology.* 5th ed.

Ember, Melvin, and Carol R. Ember. (1983) *Marriage, Family, and Kinship: Comparative Studies of Social Organization.*

Fox, Robin. (1967) *Kinship and Marriage.*

Geertz, Hildred. (1961) *The Javanese Family.*

Leighton, Dorothea, and Clyde Kluckhohn. (1969) *Children of the People: The Navaho Individual and His Development.*

Pasternak, B. (1976) *Introduction to Kinship and Social Organization.*

Pierce, Joe E. (1964) *Life in a Turkish Village.*

Reichard, Gladys A. (1928) *Social Life of the Navaho Indians.*

Romney, Kimball, and Romaine Romney. (1966) *The Mixtecans of Juxtlahuaca, Mexico.*

Schusky, Ernest L. (1974) *Variation in Kinship.*

Service, Elman. (1971) "The Trobriand Islanders of Melanesia." In *Profiles of Ethnology,* edited by Elman Service.

Stephens, William N. (1963) *The Family in Cross-Cultural Perspective.*

RESPECT RELATIONSHIPS

In a number of cultures around the world, custom dictates that certain categories of individuals be shown respect by particular other categories of people. This respectful treatment is formally patterned and includes specific expectations regarding appropriate behavior and speech in the presence of the respected person. Respect relationships are especially common between relatives, but may also be extended to unrelated individuals.

In-laws are a common target of rules requiring respect. The Lepcha of Tibet demonstrate respect toward parents-in-law and social superiors by their extreme modesty in both speech and behavior when in their company. In Chile, a Mapuche husband refers to his wife's brother as "my comrade," and is called in turn "my big father." No joking, nudity, or references to sex or excretion are allowed between brothers-in-law or between their wives. Respect is also required between siblings in many cultures that exhibit patterned respect. Among the Khoi of southern Africa, a relationship of respect is expected between brothers and sisters, who are not permitted to speak directly to each other or to be at home alone together. In Brazil and Venezuela, Yanomamo brothers do not tend to get along well, especially if they are of roughly the same age. For them, mandated reserve and respect help to diffuse this conflict. Often, too, an individual must show respect to aunts and uncles. A south Asian Lakher niece and nephew regard their mother's brother with great reverence and respect. He, in turn, is obligated to assist his sister's children, who depend more on him than on their parents when they are in need of aid. So do grandparents receive respect in many cultures. A Mexican Tepoztlan child will kiss the hand of a grandparent in greeting as a sign of respect.

The father-child relationship is overwhelmingly characterized by respect of the father by the son or daughter. Signs of respect may include bowing, using respectful language, using restraint when the father is present, and according him certain prerogatives—for instance, the seat of honor or the most desirable food. This requirement that children respect their fathers often continues even when the son or daughter is married. In turn, the father is often quite restrained and formal with his child. A Silwa son is always expected to show deference to his father, especially as the boy becomes mature. He should not sit next to his father in a public gathering. If his father is sitting on a bench, the son should sit on the ground. A young man says very little in his father's presence, and retreats from an activity in which his father is participating as soon as he can. He must not smoke in his father's presence. A son should walk behind his father and should not sit while his father is standing. He must always seem to give his father his fullest attention. All of this is in the service of encouraging a son to respect and obey his father. In the Kenyan village of Nyansongo, a Gusii son owes his father obedience and respect, even when he is grown. A son is deferential to his father, and would never embarrass, contradict, or shout at him. Fathers, by contrast, may verbally abuse their sons for misbehavior. The deference relationship between father and son is not openly displayed on a regular basis because sons tend to avoid their fathers, but a man will never make any gestures toward his son that are inconsistent with the respect that is owed him. A father has the power to put a curse on a son who disobeys, and sons know of and fear this consequence and are careful to get permission before taking actions that might provoke disapproval.

More generally, there is a tendency across cultures for respect to be accorded to older men. Among the Nayar of India, a male is required to show respect and obedience to anyone who is older than he is. For example, males past puberty may never joke or chew betel nut in the company of an older real or classificatory brother. Nor may they touch a mother's brother, and a younger man should first remove his upper cloth when he approaches his maternal uncle.

Sometimes respectful behavior is directed toward nonrelatives. For instance, the *karanavan*, or head of the Nayar, is accorded respect by all members of the group. No male may touch the *karanavan*, and a man who wishes to speak to the *karanavan* must stand partially hidden behind a pillar with his hand covering his mouth to prevent his breath from reaching the headman.

There are also certain classes of individuals who are rarely accorded customary respect across cultures. For instance, the relationship of a male or female to older female relatives, including the mother, older sisters, aunts, and grandmothers, is not typically defined by requirements of respectful behavior. More generally, women receive less formally patterned respect than men do. And younger relatives of either sex are rarely treated respectfully by individuals who are their elders.

Societies that require respect toward one class of individuals often also demand respect for other classes of people. For example, if a person is expected to show respect toward his father, he will also display similar behavior toward other older relatives. By contrast, if a son is not expected to be respectful toward his father, he will not show respect toward other older male kin. Societies tend to be characterized by the presence or absence of generalized respect behavior. In the former, a number of kinds of people are customarily treated with respect. In the latter, there are no expectations of patterned respect behavior at all. The patterning of the relationship between father and child appears to define more general norms regarding respect. Thus, if a child is required to be respectful toward the father, then respectful behavior is also directed toward other individuals, especially other older relatives. Where the father and child relationship is not defined by respect, neither are any other interactions.

A society that requires respectful behavior toward categories of individuals is also extremely likely to have autocratic political organization. Such societies are characterized by coercive power over the populace. There is a single ruler—for instance, a king, lord, or sultan—as well as an army or police force that enforces rules. The population is segregated into castes or classes, one of which exercises control over the other. Thus, there is a fit between the form of government that a society embraces and norms of respect. Just as certain classes of people are more powerful and regarded with more respect in the society as a whole, so are certain people within the smaller sphere of the family and community treated with greater regard.

Chagnon, Napoleon A. (1968) *Yanomamo: The Fierce People.*

Faron, Louis C. (1961) *Mapuche Social Structure: Institutional Reintegration in a Patrilineal Society of Central Chile.*

Gorer, Geoffrey. (1938) *Himalayan Village: An Account of the Lepchas of Sikkim.*

LeVine, Robert A., and Barbara B. LeVine. (1966) *Nyansongo: A Gusii Community in Kenya.*

Parry, N. E. (1932) *The Lakhers.*

Schapera, Isaac. (1930) *The Khoisan Peoples of South Africa: Bushmen and Hottentots.*

Stephens, William N. (1963) *The Family in Cross-Cultural Perspective.*

Titiev, Mischa. (1951) *Araucanian Culture in Transition.*

ROMANTIC LOVE

Romantic love refers to an emotional state composed of idealization of another person in an erotic context and with the expectation that the feeling will last into the future. The loved person is seen as having extremely positive qualities and evokes both erotic and tender feelings in the partner. A survey of 166 cultures indicates that romantic love is experienced by persons in over 88 percent of these cultures. This means that romantic love is a near cultural universal, although it seems that the feeling is not felt or expressed at all in a few cultures. For instance, the Lepcha of Tibet are said to think of sex as a requirement, like food and drink. Sexual relations are pleasurable, but they are not experienced in a deeply personal or emotional way. Thus, partners need not and indeed are not expected to be greatly attached. One 14-year-old Lepcha boy said of a young woman with whom he had slept twice that he would happily sleep with her again, but that he did not want to marry her as he did not like her. The Papago of the southwestern United States are also said to show some suspicion of romantic love. Papago adults claim that when anyone feels too great an attachment to another person, even to a spouse, a snake will come to live with the love-sick individual in the place of the loved one. A young person who appears smitten will be asked what is bothering him. Is he married to a snake? In Indonesia, the Balinese word for love means "to desire, like, or want." The Manus of Oceania are said to have no word at all that translates as love.

While there are examples of cultures without romantic love, for many of the societies around the world the question is not whether people fall in love but with whom, when, and for how long. People in Western societies assume that men and women fall in love, marry, and stay in love with their spouses. Nothing about this pattern is inevitable, however, in human love relationships. The Kaska of Alaska say that love only begins to appear after two people have been married for some time. This attitude is also typical of relationships in Eastern cultures. David and Vera Mace (1959) relate the following observation from an Asian observer: "When marriage begins in the West, the fire is roaring and the kettle is boiling. From that time on the water gradually gets colder and colder. When our Eastern marriages begin, the fire is low and the kettle is cold. But as time goes on, the fire burns brighter, the water gets hotter, and the couple feel that their marriage is getting better and better every day!"

In some societies, romantic love is acknowledged as a powerful human emotion, but it is also believed to be a powerfully dangerous one. Sometimes the worry is that people who are in love will engage in sexual intercourse regardless of social norms or personal consequences. They may also want to choose mates in opposition to their own best interests and the interests of their kin. Or romantic love may be viewed as the cause of unstable family relations; where people are in love, favoritism, jealousy, and conflicting loyalties can follow. Societies that adopt such attitudes about romantic love are likely to try to diminish its influence by instituting arranged marriages, where third parties determine whom an individual will take as a spouse, for instance.

Where marriages are arranged, couples may still eventually come to love each other (the water gets hotter). Some cultures encourage the growth of affection between a couple who have not married for love by nurturing an idealized version of love in marriage for young people to anticipate. Raziyya Begam, a thirteenth-century Indian poetess, captures this sentiment: "Without seeing thy face I have given thee a place in my own eye, like a pupil. I have only heard thy name and I love thee. I have not seen thee, and yet I love thee as if I had seen and known thee" (Mace and Mace 1959).

In some cases, the marital relationship remains cool. The potentially disruptive forces of romantic love are too great to be tolerated. In traditional China, a man's primary attachment is expected to be to his parents for life. A wife remains subordinate in status and affection for many years into her marriage. Societies in which such cool marital relationships are the rule may provide men with a culturally accepted outlet for frustrated romantic longings. In China, prostitutes fulfill this function. They provide a romantic setting as a backdrop to an exciting sexual relationship. Men in traditional China did fall in love with courtesans and took these women into their households as concubines. The Japanese geisha plays an analogous role; she provides the romance that is missing at home in a dutiful but uneventful marital relationship.

Where romantic love is an accepted part of male-female relationships, it is not necessarily "'til death do us part." Trobriand adolescent boys of New Guinea are susceptible to puppy love and while under its spell will work tirelessly to win over the chosen girl, showing all the usual signs of despair when their love goes unrewarded. But the affect is only temporary, and youths expect to have a number of such relationships. Similarly, Samoan lovers declare their devotion to one another, but relationships do not last long and, indeed, an individual may be involved in a number of liaisons at once. To Samoans, lifelong faithfulness is difficult to contemplate. Marriages among the polygynous Rwala are based on love, but they soon cool. By the time his wife is some months pregnant, a husband is beginning to look about for a second spouse.

Cultures do differ regarding the importance placed on romantic love. These differences are associated with other features of society. First, romantic love is more likely to be found in cultures where spouses are not highly dependent upon each other for their subsistence. By contrast, where there is a high interdependence of spouses in subsistence activities, romantic love is less important. This pattern may highlight a practical function of romantic love. When a husband and wife are necessary to each other's economic well-being, the marriage has a better chance of being stable simply because the spouses need each other. Where this kind of economic dependence is absent, romantic love may serve as the alternative cement stabilizing the marriage. Romantic love also tends to be more common in societies where extended families live together than when married couples live on their own, perhaps because a strong emotional attachment between spouses helps to neutralize the tensions and conflicts that are likely to occur when many relatives are living under the same roof.

Even though some societies try to discourage romantic love, it is possible that most human beings thrive best when allowed to fall in love. In cultures where marriages are arranged, and therefore at least initially loveless, suicide rates are higher. The problem became so severe in Japan that plays showing love suicides were outlawed in 1722. In Korea, where marriages were also traditionally arranged, wives had been known to drown themselves, and Pokot of Kenya girls may hang themselves out of despair because their parents have arranged for them to be married.

See also MARRIAGE, ARRANGED.

Coppinger, Robert M., and Paul C. Rosenblatt. (1968) "Romantic Love and Subsistence Dependence of Spouses." *Southwestern Journal of Anthropology* 14: 310–319.

Covarrubias, Miguel. (1938) *Island of Bali.*

Fischer, Helen. (1992) *The Anatomy of Love.*

Gorer, Geoffrey. (1938) *Himalayan Village: An Account of the Lepchas of Sikkim.*

Honigmann, John J. (1946) *Culture and Ethos of Kaska Society.*

Jankowiak, William, and Edward Fischer. (1992) "Romantic Love: A Cross-Cultural Perspective." *Ethnology* 31: 149–156.

Mace, David, and Vera Mace. (1959) *Marriage: East and West.*

Malinowski, Bronislaw. (1929) *The Sexual Life of Savages in North-Western Melanesia: An Ethnographic Account of Courtship, Marriage and Family Life among the Natives of the Trobriand Islands, British New Guinea.*

Mead, Margaret. (1931) *Growing Up in New Guinea: A Comparative Study of Primitive Education.*

Murdock, George P. (1936) *Our Primitive Contemporaries.*

Naroll, Raoul. (1983) *The Moral Order.*

Rosenblatt, Paul C. (1967) "Marital Residence and the Functions of Romantic Love." *Ethnology* 6: 471–480.

Underhill, Ruth M. (1939) *Social Organization of the Papago Indians.*

When Nyakyusa boys of Tanzania reach the age of about ten or eleven, they move out of their parents' houses and into a village of their own. This settlement is built on the outskirts of the community in which their parents live. As the boys reach adulthood, their wives also come to live in the village and eventually this boys' town evolves into the new center of Nyakyusa society. Similarly, after his first initiation rites at puberty, an Australian Murngin boy leaves his parents' home and goes to live in the camp reserved for single males. Nyakyusa age-villages and Murngin bachelor camps are especially dramatic illustrations of a custom followed in less extreme form by a number of cultures around the world. This is the practice of spatially segregating parents and their offspring at some point during childhood or adolescence. Most commonly, parent-child separation focuses on the removal of the youngster from the parents' sleeping quarters. Thus, the young person sleeps apart from the parents but may come home to eat, do chores, or just hang around.

The segregation of parents and children at night is a common practice across cultures. But the separation is much more likely to apply to boys than to girls. Of 57 societies, 44 percent require boys to sleep in a different house; when he remains in the same house as his parents, a boy often sleeps in a separate part of the house by himself or with other men and away from his mother and other females. By contrast, it is uncommon for girls to sleep separately from both parents. In 61 percent of the same 57 cultures, unmarried girls sleep with their parents. The common pattern across cultures is for boys to be removed from the immediate vicinity of both parents or his mother but for a girl to remain with both parents or her mother. The Chinese reflect this pattern. A married couple sleeps in the same bed along with their young children. When a youngster turns seven or eight years old, he or she begins to sleep in another bed in the same room as the parents. Unmarried girls remain in the parents' room, but older unmarried boys begin to sleep in a front room apart from the rest of the family. Similarly, unmarried Ingalik males of Alaska sleep in the men's house, but women all sleep on the family bench, with a daughter between her mother and the wall. A Lakher bachelor of south Asia does not sleep at his parents' house; rather, two or three unmarried men go to sleep in a girl's house. But an unmarried daughter sleeps at home, often near the bed of her parents. And in New Ireland, Lesu boys are sleeping in the men's house by the time they are nine or ten years old, but girls stay at home until marriage.

Nevertheless, girls do sometimes sleep away from their parents' house just like their brothers. Unmarried females spend the night in a dwelling different from that of their parents in 12 percent of 57 societies. Bemba girls of Zambia generally go to the hut of an unmarried or

Children of the Chinese Dai ethnic minority training as monks. In many cultures children are segregated from their parents for specialized education.

widowed woman to sleep. Girls among the Fon of West Africa may sleep with their mothers but, more typically, they spend the night at their paternal grandmother's house. Ganda girls of Uganda stay with their married brothers. And by seven or eight years of age, southern African !Kung girls are likely to be sleeping with a grandmother or a widowed relative or friend.

The tendency for boys to be separated from their parents at night but girls to stay at home means that parents can supervise the activities of their daughters at night. Even when children of both sexes are separated from their parents, sleeping arrangements may allow parents some opportunity to keep an eye on a daughter. Among the Iban of Malaysia, boys and bachelors sleep on the veranda, while unmarried girls often sleep in the loft. The loft, however, is ac-

cessible to the sleeping quarters of the parents by a ladder. Thus, the activities of the daughters of the house are easily monitored by the mother and father. This tendency to be more vigilant about daughters than about sons is in keeping with the fact that parents around the world are often more concerned about the premarital sexual behavior of their daughters.

In a few societies, youngsters are sent to live away from their parents beginning at an early age. Thonga children of Mozambique usually go to live with their grandmothers when they are weaned. Bemba parents also send their children to live with their grandparents at around two or three years of age, and an elderly couple may have as many as five or six youngsters to tend.

The Nyakyusa say that they send their sons to live in age-villages so that the boys will not hear or see anything having to do with the sex lives of their parents. Indeed, the tendency for parent-child segregation to begin when a youngster reaches puberty suggests that the custom is associated with the emerging sexuality of the children. In particular, such separations may help household members obey the various incest prohibitions dictated by their culture. People are less likely to yield to temptation when they are physically separated from each other. The customs of the Igbo support the idea that parent-child segregation is related to sexual temptations and restrictions. While they are young, Igbo brothers and sisters sleep together in the same room apart from their parents. Eventually, an older unmarried son will move into a "single" house, while unmarried daughters continue to sleep in the house of their parents. However, a grown girl will not sleep at home if her father is there. Even while keeping their daughters at home, then, the Igbo prefer to keep sexually mature females and their fathers apart.

Fei, Hsiao-Tung. (1939) *Peasant Life in China: A Field Study of Country Life in the Yangtze Valley.*

Frayser, Suzanne G. (1985) *Varieties of Sexual Experience.*

Gomes, Edwin H. (1911) *Seventeen Years among the Sea Dyaks of Borneo: A Record of Intimate Association with the Natives of the Bornean Jungles.*

Herskovits, Melville J. (1938) *Dahomey: An Ancient West African Kingdom,* vol. 1.

Junod, Henri A. (1927) *The Life of a South African Tribe,* vol. 1.

Marshall, Lorna. (1959) "Marriage among the !Kung Bushmen." *Africa* 29: 335–364.

Osgood, Cornelius. (1958) *Ingalik Social Culture.* Yale University Publications in Anthropology 55.

Parry, N. E. (1932) *The Lakhers.*

Powdermaker, Hortense. (1933) *Life in Lesu: The Study of a Melanesian Society in New Ireland.*

Richards, Audrey I. (1940) *Bemba Marriage and Present Economic Conditions.* Rhodes-Livingstone Papers 4.

Roscoe, John. (1911) *The Baganda: An Account of Their Native Customs and Beliefs.*

Stephens, William N. (1963) *The Family in Cross-Cultural Perspective.*

Uchendu, Victor C. (1965) *The Igbo of Southeast Nigeria.*

Warner, W. Lloyd. (1937) *A Black Civilization: A Social Study of an Australian Tribe.*

Wilson, Godfrey. (1936) "An Introduction to Nyakyusa Society." *Bantu Studies* 10: 253–291.

SEGREGATION OF SEXES IN CHILDHOOD

The segregation of the sexes is often a by-product of living arrangements whose primary goal is to provide separate living quarters for parents and children. Because many households across cultures are comprised of multiple families, it is not only brothers and sisters who are housed separately. Opposite-sex cousins, aunts and nephews, uncles and nieces, and so on often are housed in separate sections of the same house or in different dwellings entirely. Brothers and sisters are segregated in 74 percent of 57 societies as a result of customs that require children to sleep apart from their parents. Usually, the separation occurs because a girl sleeps in the same house as her parents while a boy sleeps somewhere else.

Soon after she notes that her little son has begun to give up some of his infantile ways, a New Guinea Kwoma mother gives him a small bag that she has made especially for him and his father presents him with all of the apparatus a man needs for chewing betel. He is now a little man, his parents tell him. From this time on, the boy will spend his time with friends, playing games, wandering in the forest, and trying his hand at adult tasks. He will not play with girls; from now on, the sexes form their own peer groups and avoid having much to do with each other. The Kwoma illustrate this custom, practiced in some societies, of segregating boys and girls at or before puberty.

In some societies, adults consciously separate boys and girls in order to insure the good behavior of their unmarried girls. Angolan Mbundu parents tell their young daughters: "A girl does not play with boys, for boys are sharp ones. Don't play with them." The adult's goal in saying this is to minimize the likelihood of sexual activity. The Yahgan of Tierra del Fuego place a high value on premarital chastity and separate

boys and girls before puberty so that they will adapt to same-sex activities. Beginning at puberty, West African Fon girls are removed from the company of boys and warned about what will happen to them if they lose their virginity before marriage. However, many societies that disapprove of premarital sex find other ways to enforce chastity that do not require the sexes to live apart from each other.

Sometimes, the separation of the sexes is reserved for males and females who bear a specific relationship to each other. According to Samoan custom, brothers and sisters as well as cousins of the opposite sex must refrain from engaging in a wide variety of activities in each other's presence. They must not sit or eat together, or talk with each other in an informal manner. They may not touch each other, or use one another's possessions. They cannot dance on the same floor or be in the same place unless

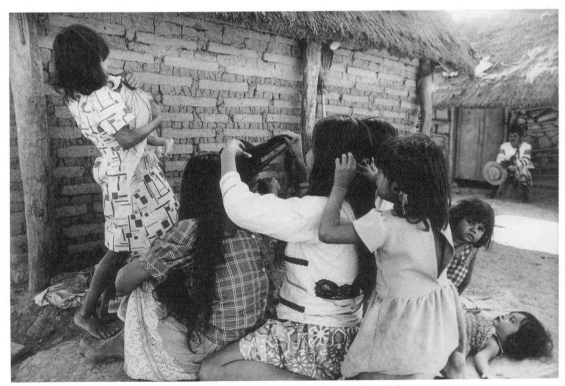

Huichol girls in Mexico grooming each other's hair.

they are at home or in a crowded setting. By the age of nine or ten, Samoan boys and girls are avoiding each other according to the prescribed rules. The avoidances also apply to the children of a brother or sister and to relationships resulting from marriage or adoption.

Childs, Gladwyn M. (1949) *Umbundu Kinship and Character.*

Gusinde, Martin. (1937) *The Yahgan: The Life and Thought of the Water Nomads of Cape Horn.*

Herskovits, Melville J. (1938) *Dahomey: An Ancient West African Kingdom,* vol. 1.

Murdock, George P. (1936) *Our Primitive Contemporaries.*

Whiting, John W. M. (1941) *Becoming a Kwoma: Teaching and Learning in a New Guinea Tribe.*

SEX, ATTITUDES TOWARD

Whereas most human beings the world over engage in sexual relations regularly during their adult lives, cultural attitudes about sex differ tremendously from place to place. Sex is variously viewed as a normal and natural impulse, a dangerous or magical activity, a dirty but necessary evil, or a sacred observance.

The idea that sex is simply a natural human function is characteristic of many societies. To the Lepcha in south Asia, sex is pleasant and fun, a necessity in the same way that food and drink are necessities. In Indonesia, the Javanese think of sex as an impulse which both the unmarried and married find hard to resist unless real constraints, such as the surveillance of a spouse, are applied. And halfway around the world in Panama, the Cuna believe that sex is a natural need requiring an outlet, especially in men.

In some other cultures, people hold the opposite view and believe that sex is potentially dangerous to those who engage in sexual activities and sometimes also to other individuals and to human pursuits more generally. The Konso of Ethiopia believe that coitus makes men weak and that they should, therefore, engage in intercourse only in moderation. According to one Konso man, "some girls' vaginas are so strong that they can snap off a man's penis." In Zaire, Azande men say that the sight of a woman's genitals or anus will have injurious effects. They, therefore, stay away from occasions such as the grain-pounding ritual associated with funeral feasts, where women sing lewd songs and dance obscene dances and are likely to expose their genitals.

In other cultures, attitudes about sex are mixed. The Kimam of New Guinea think that sperm has healing and energizing effects. But sex is seen as potentially dangerous for everyone, particularly for growing boys whose future as big, strong men can be jeopardized by sexual activity. Similarly, the Tallensi of Ghana view sex as pleasurable but enervating. Semen is thought to be the source of youth and vigor, and sexual intercourse represents the giving up of some of that vitality. The Siuai of Oceania believe that sexual intercourse interferes with the growth processes, affecting both crops and human infants. And among the Wogeo of New Guinea, sex is considered dangerous because it exposes each sex to the sexual "juices" of the opposite sex. Menstruation cleanses a woman and protects her from the hazards of intercourse, and from time to time a man must incise his penis, allowing the flow of blood to do the job of safeguarding him. Especially dangerous are a woman's sexual organs, and boys are warned to stay away from the opposite sex.

In some societies, the bodily fluids associated with sexual activity are viewed as dirty. Some rural Kurds believe that coitus is polluting, and asking a husband how many baths he has had is equivalent to asking him on how many occasions he has slept with his wife. To the Nyakyusa of Tanzania, menstrual, childbirth, and sexual excretions are all *ubunyali*, or filth. They are repulsive and dangerous, especially to an infant. Women, therefore, are always careful to clean themselves in the mornings after they have had sexual intercourse. If a woman touches the food that she prepares for her husband before washing, he will become ill.

For the traditional Kutenai of North America, sex was associated with magical properties. A man who was not moderate with respect to his sexual activities would find himself abandoned by the spirits, who would neither talk to him nor give him aid during military or economic crises. The Bemba of Zambia think of sex as pleasant, but sexual activity is also potentially dangerous and magical, even within marriage. A person who engages in sexual activity is "hot," so that purification is required after intercourse.

In some cultures, sex is associated with supernatural themes. The Bhil of India view sex as sacred, and believe that only married couples should engage in sexual intercourse. Even within the marital relationship a man and woman engage in sex, theoretically at least, in the service of a higher principle rather than for pleasure. The Bellacoola of the northwest coast of North America view sex as both natural and holy, and while too much sexual activity can cause a person to fail in his pursuits, sex in moderation can increase an individual's powers tremendously.

Attitudes toward sex are linked to some sexual behavior across cultures. In cultures where people believe that sex is dangerous, people less often engage in premarital sex than in cultures where sex is not seen as potentially harmful. And men are also less likely to engage in extramarital sexual relations when sex is perceived to be dangerous, and extramarital sex is condemned for wives in these cultures.

Evans-Pritchard, Edward Evan. (1929) "Some Collective Expressions of Obscenity in Africa." *Royal Anthropological Institute of Great Britain and Ireland* 59: 311–331.

———. (1934) "Social Character of Bride-Wealth, with Special Reference to Azande." *Man* 34: 172–175.

———. (1937) *Witchcraft, Oracles and Magic among the Azande*.

———. (1965) "A Final Contribution to the Study of Zande Culture." *Africa* 35: 1–7.

Fortes, Meyer. (1936) "Ritual Festivals and Social Cohesion in the Hinterland of the Gold Coast." *American Anthropologist* 38: 590–604.

———. (1938) *Social and Psychological Aspects of Education in Taleland*.

———. (1949) *The Web of Kinship among the Tallensi: The Second Part of an Analysis of the Social Structure of a Trans-Volta Tribe*.

Fuchs, Stephen. (1942) "The Marriage Rites of the Bhils in the Nimar District, C.P." *Man in India* 22: 105–139.

Geertz, Hildred. (1961) *The Javanese Family*.

Gorer, Geoffrey. (1938) *Himalayan Village: An Account of the Lepchas of Sikkim*.

Hallpike, C. R. (1972) *The Konso of Ethiopia*.

Leighton, Dorothea, and Clyde Kluckhohn. (1969) *Children of the People: The Navajo Individual and His Development*.

McIlwraith, Thomas F. (1948) *The Bella Coola Indians*.

Marshall, Donald S. (1950) "Cuna Folk: A Conceptual Scheme Involving the Dynamic Factors of Culture, as Applied to the Cuna Indians of Darien." Unpublished manuscript, Harvard University.

Masters, William M. (1954) *Rowanduz: A Kurdish Administrative and Mercantile Center.*

Messenger, John C. (1971) "Sex and Repression in an Irish Folk Community." In *Human Sexual Behavior,* edited by Donald S. Marshall and Robert C. Suggs, 3–37.

Nath, Y. V. S. (1960) *Bhils of Ratanmal: An Analysis of the Social Structure of a Western Indian Community.*

Oliver, Douglas. (1955) *A Solomon Island Society: Kinship and Leadership among the Siuai of Bougainville.*

Richards, Audrey I. (1939) *Land, Labor, and Diet in Northern Rhodesia.*

Serpenti, I. M. (1965) *Cultivators in the Swamps.*

Simpson, G. E. (1943) "Sexual and Familial Institutions in Northern Haiti." *American Anthropologist* 44: 655–674.

Whiteley, Wilfred. (1950) *Bemba and Related Peoples of Northern Rhodesia.*

Wilson, Godfrey. (1936) "An Introduction to Nyakyusa Society." *Bantu Studies* 10: 252–291.

SEX, EXTRAMARITAL

Rules regarding extramarital sex vary widely across cultures. In 56 percent of a sample of 112 societies, the extramarital sexual activities of husbands are not officially condemned. In these societies, a wife may accept or tolerate the adulterous behavior of her husband or she may respond with mild irritation. In the remaining 44 percent, extramarital sex for husbands is officially condemned and may be punished, sometimes severely. Extramarital sex on the part of wives is accepted or tolerated in 12 percent of 112 societies. It is condemned and may be punished harshly in the remaining 88 percent of these cultures. These numbers reflect the notable tendency for societies to take the marital infidelities of women more seriously than those of men, although cultures vary widely in the rules that have developed in regard to adultery.

For example, a North African Riffian husband who catches his wife in the act of adultery may have her slashed open from pubis to diaphragm or cut off her nose and let her go. If a Guatemalan Quiche man philanders, he is required to make a confession to his wife and her relatives or risk punishment by his ancestors. In Australia, an unfaithful Murngin husband will be verbally abused in public by his wife, who may also physically attack her husband's lover. By contrast, a Lesu husband and wife are allowed and, indeed, expected to conduct love affairs outside of marriage, and faithfulness to one's partner, particularly in the young, is viewed as abnormal. South Asian Lepcha spouses are each permitted to carry on affairs outside of marriage, a husband objecting only if his spouse actually has intercourse with another man in front of him.

Blame for adulterous affairs is not allocated in the same way across societies. In some cultures, the anger that an injured spouse feels or the punishment that society administers is directed toward the unfaithful husband or wife. But sometimes, the target is not the guilty spouse, but the lover. Among the Sherpa of Nepal and the Iban of Malaysia, the lover is required to pay a fine to the injured party in the case of the infidelity of either a husband or wife. A wronged Iban wife may thrash her husband's lover, but she then forfeits half of the fine that she would otherwise receive. An Igbo husband of Nigeria whose wife has committed adultery has a right to attack or demand compensation from her lover, or he might legitimately rape the lover's female kin. Adultery among the !Kung of southwest Africa provokes extreme anger in the husband, who is thought justified in killing a man with whom his wife has slept. It often happens that both lover and husband are killed with the poisoned arrows used by the !Kung in spite of the efforts of other band members to resolve the dispute more peaceably. Some societies hold responsible both parties to an extramarital affair. Among the Ifugao of the Philippines, the spouse and lover are equally guilty and equally likely to be punished. The wronged spouse may, and often does, forgive the spouse while still holding the lover accountable.

In some cultures, it is the woman who is held responsible, whether she is an adulterous wife or the lover of an adulterous husband. In South America, a Siriono husband blames his wife and not her lover for any episodes of infidelity. Wives, by contrast, direct their anger toward the other woman, consistent with the view among the Siriono that, in a sexual indiscretion, the woman is always to blame. The idea that sexual transgressions are always the fault of the woman is echoed in the Mataco husband's response to his wife's infidelity. He will not stop to consider the possible culpability of his spouse's lover. Rather, he always assumes that she must be to blame. Similarly, if an Argentinian Mataco husband commits adultery, his lover is often blamed for seducing him.

In many societies, public opinion virtually forces a husband to respond with force and drama to his wife's infidelity. Otherwise, he is seen as weak or cowardly and becomes a target of ridicule. A Chiricahua Apache husband who let his wife's infidelities go unnoticed was regarded as unmanly. While the community leaders attempted to avert any violence on the part of the wronged husband, his friends goaded him into action. Among the Ifugao, a wife caught in the act may be summarily killed by the injured husband. According to public opinion, pride requires this kind of extreme response, and a man

who let his wife's infidelity go unnoticed would be thought to lack self-respect.

In cultures where extramarital affairs are formally condoned for a husband or wife, the injured spouse is nevertheless likely to feel hurt and jealous. Among the Mbuti of central Africa, no legal or moral code prevents a married man from having an affair, but a husband tries to be discrete for fear of causing trouble at home. Oceanic Tikopian custom allows men to carry on affairs outside of marriage without incurring any penalties, but a husband will think twice about risking the jealous response of his wife, who will harangue him and attack him physically if she discovers that he has been sleeping with another woman.

In a number of cultures, extramarital affairs are condemned because they are seen as an infringement of the property rights of the injured spouse. Among the Wogeo of New Guinea, a man who is the lover of another man's wife is "the same as a thief" and a wife who has an affair is accused of giving away property that is not hers to bestow. According to this way of thinking, a woman who engages in sexual intercourse with a married man is no more than a "receiver of stolen goods." Similarly, among the Garo of India, adultery on the part of either spouse is an encroachment of the exclusive privileges of the other and the wronged husband or wife can demand that the spouse's lover pay him or her compensation.

In some societies, the normal restraints on extramarital sex are removed with respect to some categories of people. In India, Toda wives are permitted to conduct extramarital affairs with certain classes of males, including sacred dairymen. Husbands and wives among the North American Haida may carry on affairs with a clansman of the spouse, who may disapprove but has no legal recourse. Extramarital sex with any other individual is not permitted and serves as grounds for divorce. A Siriono husband may legally engage in sexual relations with his wife's real and classificatory sisters. Conversely, a woman may have intercourse with her husband's real and classificatory brothers and with the husbands and potential husbands of her own and her classificatory sisters. This means that any Siriono husband or wife may have sexual relations with as many as ten other individuals in addition to his or her actual spouse. In fact, however, while affairs between a man and his wife's sister or a woman and her husband's brother are common and accepted, spouses are likely to object to liaisons between mates and classificatory kin and tend to think of this kind of affair as adulterous. In India, Santal women may have sexual relations with the brothers of their husbands.

Prohibitions on extramarital sex may also be lifted on certain kinds of occasions. In Fiji, normal restrictions are lifted when men bring prisoners home in wartime. During the Fiesta of the Kid, the Goajiro of Colombia allow men and women to engage in sexual activities that are not permitted under normal circumstances. The Orokaiva permit extramarital sexual liaisons during initiation ceremonies that are not allowed at any other time. Sometimes special circumstances dictate relaxation of normal restrictions on extramarital sexual liaisons. For example, if a Tallensi husband proves to be sterile or impotent, he may permit his wife to have sexual relations with another man so that she may produce children. In this case, the wife's activities are not considered to be adulterous. Any other extramarital affair carried on by a wife is a crime against her husband's lineage ancestors.

Attitudes toward extramarital sex across cultures are not especially successful as brakes upon the actual behavior of either husbands or wives. Even where social conventions require the fidelity of a spouse, men and women are likely to carry on affairs outside of marriage. The Wogeo exemplify this pattern. Any Wogeo adult will insist that married people should be sexually faithful to each other. Nevertheless, virtually all spouses commit adultery at one time or another and are able to provide some justification for their actions. A husband might explain that his wife had driven him to adultery because of her constant suspicion, or the other woman had seduced him. The general sentiment is that, if two people have adultery in mind, they ought to be discreet in their activities so as not be found out.

Rules regarding extramarital sex for husbands and wives are associated with other sexual attitudes and behaviors across cultures. In societies that have restrictive rules regarding extramarital sex for wives, and in cultures where virtually no married men and women engage in extramarital affairs, attitudes toward premarital sex for females are also restrictive and few girls or boys actually engage in premarital sexual activity. In societies with permissive extramarital sex norms for wives and in cultures with high incidences of extramarital sex for men and women, premarital sexual behavior is allowed and pervasive. Infrequent extramarital sex for males is associated with modesty for women, punishment for but a relatively high incidence of rape, and wife beating, while the opposite pattern emerges where most husbands have affairs outside of marriage. Infrequent extramarital sex by women tends to occur in societies where males are aggressive and even hostile in their sexual overtures toward women. Where attitudes toward extramarital sex for men are restrictive, women tend to choose their own spouses, and sexual partners are likely to engage in foreplay. Where a wife's extramarital sexual behavior is condemned, talk about sex is inhibited, too much sexual activity is thought to be undesirable, sex is more generally seen as dangerous, homosexuality is condemned and punished, and men tend to boast about their sexual and other exploits. Thus, in some very real sense, cultures can be described as generally controlling and restrictive about sex, or free and easy.

See also DOUBLE STANDARD IN SEXUAL BEHAVIOR; JEALOUSY BETWEEN CO-WIVES; JEALOUSY BETWEEN MALES AND FEMALES.

Barton, R. F. (1938) *Philippine Pagans: The Autobiographies of Three Ifugaos.*

Bolinder, Gustaf. (1957) *Indians on Horseback.*

Broude, Gwen J. (1975) *A Cross-Cultural Study of Some Sexual Beliefs and Practices.* Unpublished dissertation, Harvard University.

Broude, Gwen J., and Sarah J. Greene. (1976) "Cross-Cultural Codes on Twenty Sexual Attitudes and Practices." *Ethnology* 15: 409–429.

Bunzel, Ruth. (1952) *Chichicastenango: A Guatemalan Village.*

Burling, Robbins. (1963) *Rengsanggri: Family and Kinship in a Garo Village.*

Coon, Carleton S. (1931) *The Tribes of the Rif.* Harvard African Studies 9.

Culshaw, W. J. (1949) *Tribal Heritage: A Study of the Santals.*

Firth, Raymond. (1936) *We, the Tikopia: A Sociological Study of Kinship in Primitive Polynesia.*

Fortes, Meyer. (1945) *The Dynamics of Clanship among the Tallensi: Being the First Part of an Analysis of the Social Structure of a Trans-Volta Tribe.*

———. (1949) *The Web of Kinship among the Tallensi: The Second Part of an Analysis of the Social Structure of a Trans-Volta Tribe.*

Frayser, Suzanne G. (1985) *Varieties of Sexual Experience.*

Fürer-Haimendorf, Christoph von. (1948) "The Raj Gonds of Adilabad." In *The Raj Gonds of Adilabad*, 1–21.

Gutierrez de Pineda, Virginia. (1950) *Social Organization in La Guajira.*

Hogbin, H. Ian. (1970) *The Island of Menstruating Men: Religion in Wogeo, New Guinea.*

Holmberg, Allan R. (1950) *Nomads of the Long Bow: The Siriono of Eastern Bolivia.* Washington, DC: Government Printing Office.

Marshall, Lorna. (1959) "Marriage among the !Kung Bushmen." *Africa* 29: 335–364.

Murdock, George P. (1936) *Our Primitive Contemporaries.*

Opler, Morris E. (1941) *An Apache Life-Way: The Economic, Social and Religious Institutions of the Chiricahua Indians.*

Powdermaker, Hortense. (1933) *Life in Lesu: The Study of a Melanesian Society in New Ireland.*

Roth, H. Ling. (1892) "The Natives of Borneo." *Anthropological Institute of Great Britain and Ireland* 21: 110–137; 22: 22–64.

Turnbull, Colin M. (1962) *The Forest People.*

———. (1965) *The Mbuti Pygmies: An Ethnographic Survey.* Anthropological Papers of the Museum of Natural History 50, pt. 3.

———. (1965) *Wayward Servants: The Two Worlds of the African Pygmies.*

Uchendu, Victor C. (1965) *The Igbo of Southeast Nigeria.*

Warner, W. Lloyd. (1937) *A Black Civilization: A Social Study of an Australian Tribe.*

Whiting, Beatrice B. (1950) *Paiute Sorcery.* Viking Fund Publications in Anthropology 15.

Williams, Francis E. (1930) *Orokaiva Society.*

SEX, FREQUENCY OF

While virtually all adults across cultures engage in sexual intercourse, the frequency with which individuals have sexual relations differs from one society to the next. Among the Keraki of New Guinea, intercourse is relatively infrequent, with adults engaging in sexual intercourse on an average of once a week. The Lepcha of Tibet provide an example of the opposite extreme, with couples claiming to copulate five or six, or even eight or nine, times each night when first married, although everyone admits that a person would in this case be tired the following day. Some Ifugao men of the Philippines say that they have intercourse eight to ten times per night. Between the two extremes are the !Kung of southern Africa. Some !Kung believe that intercourse once in five nights is the ideal, while others think that once in three nights is best. In most societies for which there is information, the average frequency of intercourse is reported to be once a day except for occasions on which coitus is prohibited by cultural rules.

Frequencies of sexual intercourse tend to go down as an individual becomes older or as a relationship becomes longer lasting. A Chiricahua man of the American Southwest remarked that he had coitus with his wife every night for the first few months of their marriage. After the first year, once a week or less was more typical. He continues, "Now after eleven years of married life, when I'm home, about once a week." Even the Lepcha say that, by the time they are 30 years old, sexual intercourse once a day is normal for married people.

Barton, R. F. (1938) *Philippine Pagans: The Autobiographies of Three Ifugaos.*

Ford, Clellan, and Frank A. Beach. (1951) *Patterns of Sexual Behavior.*

Gorer, Geoffrey. (1938) *Himalayan Village: An Account of the Lepchas of Sikkim.*

Marshall, Lorna. (1959) "Marriage among the !Kung Bushmen." *Africa* 29: 335–364.

Opler, Morris E. (1941) *An Apache Life-Way: The Economic, Social and Religious Institutions of the Chiricahua Indians.*

SEX, INITIATIVE IN

Regardless of how motivated human beings are to engage in sexual activity, if in fact such behavior is going to occur, someone has to take the first step. Societies around the world vary concerning their views on whether it should be the male or the female who makes the first sexual advances, and it is not always the case that actual behavior conforms to cultural etiquette.

The notion that it is the male who should initiate sexual relations is common but by no means universal around the world. In 50 percent of 34 societies, the boy is said always to take the initiative in attempting to persuade a girl to have sexual relations. Among the Marshallese of Oceania, a girl who directs sexual advances toward a boy will be assumed to be a prostitute or hopelessly in love. Tradition insists that a girl only agrees to intercourse because she has been seduced. The Ifugao of the Philippines believe that females naturally resist the advances of males and would be scandalized to hear that a girl had failed to resist the first solicitations of a boy. A south Asian Punjabi woman who is forward is regarded with disfavor and may be accused of instigating a seduction if some casual contact with a man leads to coitus. While these examples illustrate the culturally common tendency to prefer that males take the sexual initiative, these rules are not always honored in practice. For instance, although the Truk girl of Oceania is supposed to be retiring in her interactions with boys and careful not to submit to a boy's advances too freely, girls in this culture may be seen giggling, teasing, and peeping in a way that is sexually unambiguous. Similarly, the Lepcha of Tibet consistently claim that a woman will never make the first move in initiating a sexual encounter, but Lepcha men remember and report instances in their own courting days when girls made direct sexual advances to them.

In 32 percent of 34 cultures, both sexes are equally likely to try to initiate sexual encounters.

This is the case among the Balinese of Indonesia, where a boy may make his hopes clear to a girl by approaching her and asking: "Do you want?" Girls, however, are as likely to flirt with boys or to try to encourage a diffident suitor with a small gift. The Alorese of Indonesia say a woman will be certain to agree to have coitus if a man touches her breasts. Indeed, an Alorese phrase meaning sexual intercourse is "to pull a girl's breasts." One Alorese man describes this technique for seducing a woman: "Our hands move about at random and touch a girl's breast. That makes her spirit fly away, and she has to sleep with a man." But Alorese girls also initiate sexual relations, sometimes by tugging a man's hand. Less courageous boys will also use this strategy for approaching girls sexually. An Alaskan Ingalik boy may test the waters with a girl by slipping a hand into her trousers. The girl may acquiesce, or she may bite him on the shoulder in an attempt to get him to leave her alone. A girl may also ask a boy to sleep with her. Both boys and girls among the Kaska of Alaska are shy about making sexual advances and about receiving them, but each does attempt to engage the other sexually. Sexual invitations for both sexes may begin with winking and hand pressing, perhaps while a boy and girl are dancing. Returning the gesture signals consent, although some girls will become embarrassed at such proposals. A girl may also tease and rough-house with a boy and this, too, is a recognized strategy for suggesting sexual relations.

In 18 percent of 34 societies, girls usually or always take the initiative in inviting sexual relations. In Argentina, Mataco girls begin their active sexual lives after they are initiated, at which time they will have a series of brief affairs. At the evening dance, a girl will approach the boy of her choice and some time that night she will lead him away, perhaps to her parents' house. If a New Guinea Kwoma boy solicits sex from a girl, she may accuse him of rape if she is angry at him for some reason. Therefore, boys in this

culture avoid making the first sexual advances. Instead, a boy tries to attract a girl's attention by attending to his appearance and popping up in places where he is likely to meet up with her. The initial moves, however, are left to the female.

Sometimes the norms of a particular culture regarding who should properly initiate sexual relations vary according to whether the individual is unmarried or married. Among the Ingalik, unmarried boys and girls are equally likely to solicit sexual relations from one another, but it is considered inappropriate for a wife to make sexual advances to her husband, at least directly. Among the Lesu of New Ireland, a woman will suggest sexual intercourse with a man by showing her genitals. But it is shocking for a wife to go to her husband's bed, and Lesu women who are asked about the propriety of such behavior are likely to ask if the woman should be a man.

———

Barton, R. F. (1938) *Philippine Pagans: The Autobiographies of Three Ifugaos.*

Covarrubias, Miguel. (1938) *Island of Bali.*

DuBois, Cora. (1944) *The People of Alor: A Social Psychological Study of an East Indian Island.*

Erdland, August. (1914) *The Marshall Islanders: Life and Customs, Thought, and Religion of a South Seas People.*

Fock, Niels. (1963) "Mataco Marriage." *Folk* 5: 91–101.

Gladwin, Thomas and Seymour B. Sarason. (1953) *Truk: Man in Paradise.*

Gorer, Geoffrey. (1938) *Himalayan Village: An Account of the Lepchas of Sikkim.*

Honigmann, John J. (1949) *Culture and Ethos of Kaska Society.*

Osgood, Cornelius. (1958) *Ingalik Social Structure.* Yale University Publications in Anthropology 55.

Powdermaker, Hortense. (1933) *Life in Lesu: The Study of a Melanesian Society in New Ireland.*

Whiting, John W. M. (1941) *Becoming a Kwoma: Teaching and Learning in a New Guinea Tribe.*

Wilber, Donald N. (1964) *Pakistan: Its People, Its Society, Its Culture.*

SEX, PREMARITAL The interest in sex that emerges with puberty is universal; adolescents in all societies begin to be preoccupied with the opposite sex. But there is enormous variation in the societal rules that relate to the sexual impulses of adolescent boys and girls. Responses range from the enthusiastic endorsement of premarital sex to its unambiguous condemnation. Where cultures disapprove of sexual intercourse for the unmarried, the sexual behavior of girls is usually of more concern than are the activities of boys. The desire to control an adolescent girl's sexuality is itself related to other customs and beliefs characterizing the culture.

A number of cultures approve of premarital sex for unmarried females. Of 141 societies across the globe, 24.1 percent do not object if young single girls engage in sexual activity. The Tallensi of Ghana expect everyone past puberty to yield to his or her sexual impulses. Girls can engage in sexual relations without censure, and girlfriends enjoy frequenting the markets together to meet boys. During adolescence, Truk boys and girls of Oceania spend much of their time planning sexual intrigues. Adults take it for granted that the young people will be sexually active, and many people believe that a girl will not begin to menstruate unless she has had sexual intercourse. At the conclusion of her initiation ceremony, an Argentinian Mataco girl can take a man of her choosing home for the night and the two may sleep together. For the next few years, the girl will have a series of short affairs before she finds the man she wishes to marry. In the Philippines, Ifugao youngsters and adolescents sleep in their own houses, the males in a boys' dorm and the females in a dwelling that houses little girls, adolescent couples, and divorced and widowed women. The girls' dorm is the setting for a good deal of wholesale sexual experimentation. Wogeo boys and girls of New Guinea are allowed freedom in carrying on love affairs, as long as they are discreet.

Another 20.6 percent of the 141 societies tolerate premarital sexual activity for unmarried females. The Garo of India would prefer it if young people behaved themselves and refrained from experimenting with sex before marriage, but they expect both boys and girls to become somewhat undisciplined when they reach puberty. Boys at this age "cannot sit still"; they think of nothing but girls. Girls are more responsible, but they, too, become a bit unruly. The Garo philosophy is summed up by the typical refrain, "After all, they are young, so what can you do?"

Seventeen percent of the 141 societies mildly disapprove of premarital sex for females. They try to persuade girls to avoid having sexual relations, but they do not punish transgressors. Among the Kutenai of North America, virginity in a bride is valued, although it is not required. Adults attempt to keep a girl in line by warning her that if she has an affair with a boy she will turn into a frog when she dies and goes to live with her ancestors.

Premarital sex is condemned and punished in 34 percent of the 141 societies. Punishments may be mild or extreme. In the southwestern United States, a Chiricahua father may whip a daughter who has had sexual intercourse before marriage. If the whipping is executed in public, it reminds other girls of the consequences of losing their virginity. If a Javanese girl and boy are caught sleeping together, the furious neighbors summon officials or a band of young men to break into the house and compel the couple to be married on the spot. Kenuzi Nubians of Egypt insist upon virginity in brides. If a girl has sex before she is married, her nearest male relative will kill her. Death may seem a very harsh punishment for a girl who has violated the sexual prohibitions of her culture, but it is the most common penalty in societies that severely punish premarital sex.

In a number of societies, premarital sex is permitted as a test of fertility. In Malaysia, Iban couples are permitted to have sexual intercourse before marriage in order to make sure that the pair can produce children together, but if the girl becomes pregnant, the prospective father must marry her. A girl who was abandoned by her lover would commit suicide and the man would be blamed for her death and compelled to pay a large fine. Often, the couple must already be engaged before premarital sex is permitted for this purpose. Of the 141 societies, 4.3 percent exempt betrothed couples from bans against premarital sex.

Why do we see such a range of attitudes about premarital sex across cultures? And why do many cultures constrain adolescents from engaging in an activity that is so biologically compelling? In some cultures, premarital sex is prohibited for religious reasons. Egyptian religious beliefs require males and females to renounce the pleasures of heterosexual intimacy. Adolescent girls are discouraged from making themselves attractive to the opposite sex and any girl who tries to enhance her appearance will have trouble finding a husband or maintaining his good opinion of her.

Other societies disapprove of premarital sex because they wish to avoid premarital pregnancies. Indeed, in some cultures, sexual intercourse between unmarried girls and boys is accepted unless it leads to pregnancy. Illegitimate children present more difficulties for some cultures than for others. For instance, where descent is traced only through the father, the position of an illegitimate child is ambiguous, so premarital pregnancies create problems for the child, its parents and kin, and society at large. In cultures where a child belongs to its mother's lineage, the absence of a father is less disruptive. Rules about who lives where also affect attitudes toward illegitimate children. Where a wife and her children live with the father's family, an unwed mother and her child are a large inconvenience. Where families live with the mother's kin, an unmarried mother and her infant still have a place to live even though there is no one in the role of husband and father. Rules regarding premarital sex for girls are in fact related to descent and residence rules across cultures. Patrilineal and patrilocal societies tend to restrict the sexual behavior of single girls. By contrast, in matrilineal and matrilocal societies, where the child of an unwed mother is easily incorporated into the society, girls are permitted to engage in premarital sex.

Attitudes regarding the sexual behavior of unmarried girls are also affected by marriage customs. Parents want their daughters to make the most advantageous match possible and the sexual status of a girl influences her value as a prospective wife in many societies. A girl's sexual history is often taken as an indication of her future trustworthiness as a wife. Javanese parents worry that a daughter who begins to have affairs once she is sexually mature will send the message to a prospective husband that she is sexually promiscuous and will not be a faithful wife. Girls with reputations for being sexually experienced do not attract the most desirable suitors. Parents, therefore, arrange for daughters to be married at puberty and thus minimize the chances that a girl will be sexually active before she is married.

If the fact that a girl is not a virgin can materially affect her ability to attract a worthy husband, then premarital sex norms are usually restrictive. Virginity in a bride is valued in 36 percent of 134 cultures, and in three-fourths of these cultures it is actually required. The stakes become even larger in cultures where a prospective husband or his kin pay a bride price, or gift of money or goods, to his bride's family. In these cultures the value of the payment that the groom presents to the bride's kin is decreased or the bride price is forfeited altogether when the girl is not a virgin. A Kwoma girl of New Guinea tries to be discreet in her love affairs so that her relatives will not be made aware of her activities. The value of the bride price that a girl's family will receive at her marriage depends upon her sexual history, since the highest bride price is paid for a virgin. As brothers use their sister's bride price to pay for their own brides, they are eager to keep her from ruining her reputation. More generally, in societies with bride price, premarital sex for girls tends to be harshly condemned and severely punished. The connection between rules regarding premarital sex and bride price is highlighted by Kazak attitudes concerning the sexual behavior of unmarried girls. The Kazak expect brides to be virgins, and should a girl prove to have had sexual intercourse before marriage, her family will receive a smaller bride price. But once a girl is engaged and most of the bride price has been handed over to her relatives, she and her fiance may sleep together if they are discreet.

Rules regarding premarital sex for girls are also influenced by the way in which social status is allocated in a society. When class structure is fixed, so that an individual's status is determined at birth and fixed for life, people tend to marry within their own class. In these circumstances, a girl will marry a male whose status is equivalent to her own regardless of her sexual adventures before marriage. Premarital sex norms in such societies tend to be permissive. Where class structure is fluid, so that individuals can advance up the class hierarchy by their own efforts or through marriage, then a girl's sexual status may affect her chances of marrying a high-status man.

In such cultures, premarital sex norms for girls are more likely to be restrictive.

Premarital sex norms also vary with the size of the community. Rules tend to be permissive where communities are small, and restrictive where they are large. This pattern may be explained in part by the fact that many small communities are exogamous. That is, members of the group cannot marry one another. Rather, people seek spouses outside their own community. Where marriages are exogamous, it is often also the case that sexual intercourse between members of the same community is forbidden. Such relationships take on the character of incest. When young people are prohibited by other dictates from having sexual relations with other members of their own community, then opportunities to engage in premarital sex are minimized and rules prohibiting sex for unmarried people become redundant. Societies can also afford to relax their supervision of unmarried people in small communities because, in such settings, all members of the group are known to each other. Under these circumstances, if a premarital pregnancy occurs, it is relatively easy to identify the father and compel him to marry or otherwise compensate the girl. In large communities, by contrast, many people are strangers to each other and many others are only superficially acquainted. This makes it more difficult to identify the father of an illegitimate child or to force him to meet his responsibilities.

Societies that restrict the sexual behavior of unmarried adolescents are also very likely to restrict heterosexual and homosexual play and immodesty in childhood. The adults in these cultures may be attempting to rein in sexual behavior early in anticipation of adolescence. The association between severe sex training in childhood and strict premarital sex norms may also reflect conservative attitudes about sexual expression in general. This proposal is supported by a further set of relationships between rules regarding premarital sex and other cultural customs concerning love and sex. Where premarital sex norms are restrictive, talk about sex tends to be prohibited or at least circumscribed, homosexuality and extramarital sex for women tend to be condemned, wives tend not to engage in affairs outside of marriage, and love magic is likely to be present. Where rules regarding premarital sex are permissive, talk about sex is generally uninhibited, homosexuality and extramarital sex for wives is accepted or tolerated, women are likely to have extramarital affairs, and love magic is usually absent.

How many unmarried girls and boys engage in premarital sex? All or almost all single males have some premarital sexual experience in 59.8 percent of 107 societies. In an additional 17.8 percent, premarital sex is practiced by a moderate number of males. In 10.3 percent of the 107 cultures, some males engage in premarital sex but this is not typical adolescent behavior. Finally, it is rare to find an unmarried male who has had sexual relations in 12.1 percent of the 107 societies. In the case of single girls, the numbers look similar, but there are fewer places in which premarital sex is a universal practice for girls and more places where females almost never have sexual relations before marriage. Thus, virtually all girls engage in premarital sex in 49.1 percent of 114 societies. In 16.7 percent of these cultures, a moderate proportion of single girls have had sexual intercourse. In an additional 14 percent, an occasional girl will be sexually experienced before marriage. And premarital sex is rare in the remaining 20.2 percent of the 114 cultures.

Societal regulations regarding premarital sex are apparently effective in influencing the behavior of unmarried girls. In cultures that permit premarital sex, most single females are in fact experimenting with sex before marriage. In cultures that disapprove or prohibit premarital sex, most girls delay the onset of their sex lives until they are married women.

See also BRIDE PRICE; DOUBLE STANDARD IN SEXUAL BEHAVIOR; PREGNANCY, PREMARITAL; VIRGINITY.

Ammar, Hamed. (1954) *Growing Up in an Egyptian Village.*

Barton, R. F. (1938) *Philippine Pagans: The Autobiographies of Three Ifugaos.*

Broude, Gwen J. (1981) "Cultural Management of Sexuality." In *Handbook of Human Development,* edited by Robert Munroe, Ruth Munroe, and Beatrice B. Whiting.

Broude, Gwen J., and Sarah J. Greene. (1976) "Cross-Cultural Codes on Twenty Sexual Attitudes and Practices." *Ethnology* 15: 409–429.

Fortes, Meyer. (1938) *Social and Psychological Aspects of Education in Taleland.*

Frayser, Suzanne G. (1985) *Varieties of Sexual Experience.*

Geertz, Hildred. (1961) *The Javanese Family.*

Gutmann, Bruno. (1926) *Chagga Law.*

Herskovits, Melville J. (1938) *Dahomey: An Ancient West African Kingdom,* vol. 1.

Hogbin, H. Ian. (1945–1946) "Puberty to Marriage: A Study of the Sexual Life of the Native of Wogeo, New Guinea." *Oceania* 16: 185–209.

Hudson, Alfred E. (1938) *Kazak Social Structure.*

Linton, Ralph. (1933) *The Tanala: A Hill Tribe of Madagascar.*

Miner, H. (1965) *The Primitive City of Timbuctoo.*

Opler, Morris E. (1941) *An Apache Life-Way: The Economic, Social and Religious Institutions of the Chiricahua Indians.*

Osgood, Cornelius. (1958) *Ingalik Social Culture*. Yale University Publications in Anthropology 55.

Raum, O. F. (1940) *Chaga Childhood: A Description of Indigenous Education in an East African Tribe.*

Roth, H. Ling. (1892) "The Natives of Borneo." *Anthropological Institute of Great Britain and Ireland* 21: 110–137; 22: 22–64.

Spier, Leslie. (1928) *Havasupai Ethnography*. Anthropological Papers of the American Museum of Natural History 29.

Spoehr, Alexander. (1949) *Majuro: A Village in the Marshall Islands.*

Titiev, Mischa. (1951) *Araucanian Culture in Transition.*

Turney-High, Harry H. (1941) "Ethnography of the Kutenai." *American Anthropologist* 43(2) (Supplement).

Whiting, John W. M. (1941) *Becoming a Kwoma: Teaching and Learning in a New Guinea Tribe.*

SEX, TALK ABOUT

Sex figures importantly in the lives of most human beings. By adolescence, boys and girls the world over are preoccupied with thoughts of the opposite sex and many are already doing some experimenting. Most adults look forward to marriage to provide the context for a dependable sexual relationship. But whereas human beings are uniformly interested in having active sex lives, societal rules differ enormously regarding the degree to which sex is considered an appropriate topic of discussion. The Lepcha of Tibet pepper all of their conversation with explicit sexual allusions that include liberally sprinkled references to coitus and the primary sexual characteristics. Sexual commentary becomes epidemic in mixed company, with every allusion taking on a sexual meaning. Sexual innuendo and joking are considered appropriate even on the most serious occasions and a constant relay of obscene comments enlivens social events, especially when people have been drinking. By contrast, the Chiricahua of the American Southwest are extremely reserved when it comes to discussions of sex. Men even claim ignorance of the words that are used to describe female genital organs. A grown male who made mention of such things in company would be "no man at all." Among the Slave of Canada, young men are uncomfortable when sex becomes a topic of conversation and when asked the names for the male or female sexual organs will respond, "I don't know that word."

Whereas some cultures are characterized by a universal taboo against talk about sex, more typically such prohibitions are reserved for specific categories of people. The Nkundu of Zaire will employ sexual terms in front of their social equals, but discussions involving sexual references in the company of strangers, inferiors, or elderly people are unacceptable. Sometimes taboos on talk about sex target interactions between people of adjacent generations. The parent-child relationship is often singled out for special attention. Among the Gros Ventre of the United States, an individual would be extremely embarrassed if anything relating to sex occurred in the presence of a parent. Both fathers and sons would be mortified if one were to appear without clothing in the presence of the other and no daughter would make overt references to her condition if she were menstruating or pregnant. Any talk about sex between parents and children is avoided unless the discussion is of an entirely serious nature. This reserve about sexual matters in front of parents is extended to aunts and uncles and to brothers-in-law and sisters-in-law. The Nyakyusa of Tanzania chat about sex unselfconsciously with other people their own age, but they, too, remain reserved in front of their parents and, more generally, in the presence of any members of their parents' generation. Among the Saramaka of Suriname, no son or daughter would discuss sex with any parent, and talk about sex with parents-in-law is formally forbidden. In Kenya, Dorobo men do not discuss sex with their fathers, fathers' brothers, mothers, or mothers' sisters, although joking about sex is permitted between people of the same generation, including brothers and sisters.

The tendency for parents and children to be reticent in front of one another about sexual matters reflects a common theme across cultures. It is often the case that talk about sex is prohibited between people for whom sexual relations are also forbidden. The Ifugao of the Philippines do not permit any discussion of sex to occur between individuals who cannot marry one another. Among the Siuai of Oceania, a woman is prohibited from marrying her biological brother and any man classified as a sib brother, and any mention of sexual intercourse when a sister is present provokes intense shame on the part of these men. In the past, a brother would have killed anyone who talked about sex when his sister was present. Among the Marshallese of Oceania, the children of cross-cousins are classificatory siblings, who cannot marry each other or joke in front of one another about sexual matters.

Whereas talk about sex is often prohibited between children and their parents' generation, the same cultures are likely to permit sexual discussions and joking between grandchildren and grandparents. Among the Gros Ventre, grandparents can tell their grandchildren stories with sexual themes that would be entirely inappropriate in front of a son or daughter. And granddaughters will readily tease a grandmother about men. Similarly, any sexual matter may be discussed between a Saramakan grandparent and grandchild and such talk is often obscene.

Sometimes taboos against talk about sex apply only to mixed company. Konso males avoid sexual topics in public, but not in the men's sleeping houses. Koreans will not talk about sex in front of girls, but much of the conversation among boys themselves centers on sexual matters. Lebanese men will talk about sex among themselves, and so will women, but the subject is never thought appropriate when members of the opposite sex are present. Marshallese males enjoy telling each other obscene riddles that are forbidden in front of women. Sometimes one sex is more reticent about sexual topics than the other, even in same-sex groups. A Siuai man avoids using the term *ruru*, the word for coitus, and is uncomfortable discussing sexual intercourse even when euphemisms are employed. But Siuai women discuss sex among themselves without embarrassment or reserve, and often use terms referring to coitus or to the sexual organs when scolding or insulting someone. Among the Tallensi of Ghana, sex is discussed openly by men, women, and children, but females are more likely to use euphemisms than are men.

While many cultures forbid talk about sex between certain categories of people, in a number of societies people bearing some specific relationship to each other are expected to engage in sexual banter. Among the Navajo, custom dictates that cross-cousins tease each other about sex. And among the Gros Ventre, sexual teasing with brothers-in-law and sisters-in-law is expected. Some cultures encourage sexual joking between categories of people who are allowed or expected to marry each other. The Marshallese approve of both marriage and sexual joking between cross-cousins. The Tswana of Botswana say it is the culturally patterned sexual teasing between cross-cousins that leads to stable marriages because it promotes familiarity between a man and woman.

Cultural norms regarding talk about sex reflect other sexual attitudes held by a society. Where people restrict the premarital sexual behavior of girls, talk about sex tends to be inhibited. The Khmer of Indochina discourage talk about sex specifically because they assume that knowledge about sex increases sexual interest and eventually gets young people into trouble. Consequently, discussion of sex is avoided. Prohibitions against talk about sex are also associated across cultures with the disapproval of extramarital sex for wives. Where people are reserved in their discussion of sexual topics, impotence tends to be a problem for males. Cultures that disapprove of talk about sex also typically practice love magic. Finally, restrictive attitudes toward discussions of sex are found in societies that also expect women to display a high degree of modesty in their dress and toilet habits. Thus, cultures that restrict talk about sex in some or all circumstances also tend to be conservative regarding other aspects of their sex lives. They also tend to display traits that suggest some anxiety about sex.

Barton, Roy F. (1938) *Philippine Pagans: The Autobiographies of Three Ifugaos.*

Buchler, Ira. (1980) "The Organization of Social Life: The Perspective of Kinship Studies." In *People in Culture,* edited by Ino Rossi, 314–398.

Davenport, William. (1952) "Fourteen Marshallese Riddles." *Journal of American Folklore* 65: 265–266.

Flannery, Regina. (1953) *The Gros Ventre of Montana,* pt. 2.

Gorer, Geoffrey. (1938) *Himalayan Village: An Account of the Lepchas of Sikkim.*

Hallpike, C. R. (1972) *The Konso of Ethiopia.*

Honigmann, John J. (1946) *Ethnography and Acculturation of the Fort Nelson Slave.*

Hulstaert, Gustave. (1928) *Marriage among the Nkundu.*

Huntingford, G. W. B. (1951) "The Social Institutions of the Dorobo." *Anthropos* 46: 1–48.

Kahn, Morton C. (1931) *Djuka: The Bush Negroes of Dutch Guiana.*

Leighton, Dorothea, and Clyde Kluckhohn. (1969) *Children of the People: The Navaho Individual and His Development.*

Oliver, Douglas. (1955) *A Solomon Island Society: Kinship and Leadership among the Siuai of Bougainville.*

Opler, Morris E. (1941) *An Apache Life-Way: The Economic, Social and Religious Institutions of the Chiricahua Indians.*

Osgood, Cornelius. (1951) *The Koreans and Their Culture.*

Patai, R. (1956) *The Republic of Lebanon.*

Spoehr, Alexander. (1949) *Majuro: A Village in the Marshall Islands.*

Steinberg, David J. (1959) *Cambodia: Its People, Its Society, Its Culture.*

Wilson, Godfrey. (1936) "An Introduction to Nyakyusa Society." *Bantu Studies* 10: 253–291.

SEX, TECHNIQUES FOR INITIATING

Before they engage in sexual intercourse, human beings display a variety of patterns of interpersonal behavior as preambles to the main event of coitus. These preliminary interactions have a number of uses. They can serve as invitations to intercourse. They can aid an individual in testing the waters with a potential partner, helping each to assess the interest of the other in a sexual encounter. They can also play a role in preparing partners emotionally and physiologically for having sexual relations, acting as a kind of enlarged and sometimes symbolic foreplay.

The exploration of techniques for initiating sexual intercourse across societies is in essence the exploration of how one person asks another to engage in sex. Sometimes solicitations are indirect. For instance, in some societies today and in the past, invitations to have sexual relations begin with songs, letters, and other similar oblique appeals. In Assam, a Lhota man plays flute melodies that symbolize the name of the girl he is wooing. Among the Saulteaux of the United States and Canada, younger brothers serve as go-betweens for their older brothers, carrying letters back and forth between the hopeful sibling and the girl of his choice. In Oceania, a Trukese boy may arrange a meeting with a girl through letters carried by an emissary. The letter expresses the boy's great love for the girl and suggests a meeting. These notes are understood to be invitations to sexual relations. Girls are not supposed to respond immediately to such avowals, as this would imply that they were not appropriately conservative in their sexual behavior. When the girl does respond to such a letter, the couple meets, probably in the bush.

In some cultures, a boy or girl will try to attract a lover by giving gifts. When Thonga boys of Mozambique visit their girlfriends in their huts at night, they bring pieces of clothing or other gifts as a way of obtaining the girl's permission to have intercourse. The New Guinea Kapauku boy who has his eye on a particular girl will give her a bracelet, hairpin, or armlet. Kapauku girls, for their part, can suggest sexual intercourse to a boy by secretly giving him a sweet potato. In Indonesia, a Balinese girl may try to instill courage in a shy love by giving him some small token. An Australian Murngin woman sometimes attempts to persuade a man to have

sexual intercourse by sending him a present of food. If the man agrees, he will also give her a gift. Sometimes a smitten youth will indirectly signal his interest in a person. For example, a Kapauku youth will attempt to attract a girl's notice by staring at her and joking boisterously with his friends. A Comanche boy of the U.S. Plains who was interested in a specific girl would linger in a spot where she was likely to appear and would then walk toward her, hoping for some encouragement. If the girl was favorably disposed, the two would agree to a meeting, and the boy might even be invited to his sweetheart's tipi. If she was not interested, the girl would show this by her responses to the boy, who would slink away, humiliated.

Some societies have formalized customs by which potential lovers can pursue each other. Among the Thonga, a boy can practice the *gangisa,* a ritual for choosing lovers, after he has been initiated. It is the females who make the final choice of sexual partner, and the boys work at being chosen by running after the girls, flirting with them, and calling, "Choose me! Choose me!" During this time, boys also wear special printed material called *gangisa ntombi.* The term means "to make a girl choose," and a boy offers these prints to the girl to whom he is especially attracted in hopes of gaining her favor. For the Mataco of Argentina, the customary forum for allowing young people to find sexual partners is the dance. A girl will dance with the boy of her choice, holding him by the shoulder or about the body. She soon leads him away from the dance, perhaps to her parents' house. Sometimes cultures provide means by which boys or girls can advertise their interest in attracting a sexual partner. Mataco boys and girls wear distinctively applied face paint as a way of broadcasting their interest in finding a lover. When a girl likes a boy who has painted his face for this purpose, she will soon appear with the same pattern painted on her face. This means that the girl is willing to have sexual intercourse with the young man. The boy must now sleep with the girl or else run the risk of incurring her family's anger and of losing face.

In some societies, solicitations to engage in sexual relations are more direct, but still avoid physical contact. A Balinese boy may approach a girl with the straightforward question, "Do you want?" Some Kapauku boys will simply go up to a girl and ask her to engage in sexual relations. A Trukese boy sometimes slips into a girl's house and wakes her up in the middle of the night if he wishes to have sexual relations with her. Similarly, a particularly brave Comanche girl might creep into the tipi of a boy she likes.

Individuals may also communicate their sexual interest by more direct physical means. Kaska adolescents of Alaska are somewhat shy when it comes to overt sexual advances, but they manage to make their intentions known by resorting to roughhousing. A boy and girl may swipe at each with tree branches or push each other. Perhaps the girl will grab the boy's hat and run off. The boy follows and catches up with her, and they wrestle until someone is thrown down. Now the suitor may express his sexual interest more directly.

In some cultures, sexual invitations are more blatant from the start. In Alaska, an Ingalik boy may solicit sexual intercourse from a girl by trying to put his hand into her trousers. He might also follow her into the woods and wrestle her to the ground. Girls are not necessarily helpless in these situations. If she does not wish to encourage his advances, the girl may bite the boy on the shoulder, perhaps severely. Or she may seek the aid of a friend, with both girls ganging up on the aggressor. The Alorese of Indonesia say that if a man touches a woman's breasts she will not be able to resist him, and this is a common strategy for initiating sexual relations among these people.

Sometimes it is the female who makes the first overt solicitation. Lesu women of New Ireland may invite sexual intercourse by exposing their genitals to a man. In West Africa, a Dahomean woman may drop her short skirt if she is alone with a man in whom she is interested. Among the Kurtatchi villagers of the Solomon Islands a woman may lie down with her legs apart to attract a man with whom she wishes to have intercourse. This is in opposition to the normal modesty of Kurtatchi women, who are always careful to cover their genitals in the presence of others. Finally, among the Gond of India, a girl may try to persuade a boy to have intercourse by grabbing and playing with his penis.

See also SEX, INITIATIVE IN.

Covarrubias, Miguel. (1938) *Island of Bali.*

DuBois, Cora. (1944) *The People of Alor: A Social Psychological Study of an East Indian Island.*

Dunning, R. W. (1959) *Social and Economic Change among the Northern Ojibwa.*

Elwin, Verrier. (1947) *The Muria and Their Ghotul.*

Fock, Niels. (1963) "Mataco Marriage." *Folk* 5: 91–101.

Ford, Clellan S., and Frank A. Beach. (1951) *Patterns of Sexual Behavior.*

Gladwin, Thomas, and Seymour B. Sarason. (1953) *Truk: Man in Paradise.*

Honigmann, John J. (1949) *Culture and Ethos of Kaska Society.*

Junod, Henri A. (1927) *The Life of a South African Tribe*, vol. 1.

Osgood, Cornelius. (1958) *Ingalik Social Culture.* Yale University Publications in Anthropology 55.

Pospisil, Leopold. (1958) *The Kapauku Papuans and Their Law.* Yale University Publications in Anthropology 54.

———. (1959–1960) "The Kapauku Papuans and Their Kinship Organization." *Oceania* 30.

Powdermaker, Hortense. (1933) *Life in Lesu: The Study of a Melanesian Society in New Ireland.*

Wallace, Ernest, and Edward Adamson Hoebel. (1952) *The Comanches: Lords of the South Plains.*

Warner, W. Lloyd. (1937) *A Black Civilization: A Social Study of an Australian Tribe.*

SEX TABOO, POSTPARTUM

In a number of cultures around the world, cultural tradition prohibits a woman from engaging in sexual intercourse for a designated period of time after the birth of a baby. This prohibition is known as the postpartum sex taboo and occurs in 85 percent of a sample of 151 societies. The length of the postpartum taboo varies widely across cultures. Of the societies that have a taboo, 69 percent restrict a woman's sexual behavior for a year or less, 14 percent prohibit sexual intercourse for from one to two years, and the remaining 17 percent restrict sexual activity for more than two years. In one-third of the cultures that have no explicit postpartum sex taboo, a woman is expected to engage in sexual intercourse soon after the birth of her child.

The postpartum sex taboo is likely to lead to a considerable amount of frustration on the part of both the woman and her husband. However, the taboo only forbids sexual activity for the female. Thus, the postpartum sexual taboo only indirectly prevents a husband from engaging in sexual intercourse. In fact, across cultures, husbands who are affected by the taboo do tend to remain sexually active. This is reflected, in the first place, in attitudes toward and frequencies of extramarital sexual activity. Societies with a long postpartum sex taboo tend to have a double standard of extramarital sex, so that affairs on the part of husbands are treated as less serious than are those of females. And in societies with a postpartum sex taboo of one year or more, extramarital sex on the part of husbands is universal or almost universal. By contrast, few husbands have extramarital affairs where the taboo is short or absent. The long postpartum sex taboo is also associated with polygyny. In societies that prohibit wives from engaging in sexual intercourse for extended periods of time, a husband often still has access to legal and approved sex with his other wife or wives.

Extended prohibitions on sexual intercourse for women who have had a baby tend to be found in societies that depend upon root crops for their primary food source. This means that the diets of people in cultures with a long taboo are low in protein. One interpretation regarding the origins of the long taboo suggests that the prohibition allows women to provide a high-protein food supply for their babies. As a woman who abstains from sexual intercourse for an extended period of time will not have to nurse babies in rapid succession, her newest infant will have exclusive access to protein-rich milk for a few years. In this view, the long postpartum sex taboo may be a response to a society's ecological, and thus dietary, profile.

A number of social scientists have suggested that a long postpartum sex taboo results in a distancing between husbands and wives, leading to an especially close mother-child relationship and an absence of significant father-child contact, which leads to serious developmental consequences for boys raised in these households. But these proposed connections are not well supported by cross-cultural information. Indeed, although the long postpartum sex taboo clearly interferes with the sex lives of a husband and wife, this disruption of sexual activity has no predictable effect on the day-to-day nonsexual intimacy of a couple. Thus, spouses are just as likely to eat, sleep, and spend their leisure time together in cultures that have instituted a long taboo as they are in societies where the taboo is short or absent. Therefore, the idea that the taboo creates a climate for husband-wife aloofness is not in accord with the actual patterning of marital relationships across cultures.

Barry, Herbert, III, and Leonora M. Paxson. (1972) "Infancy and Early Childhood: Cross-Cultural Codes 2." *Ethnology* 10: 466–508.

Broude, Gwen J. (1975) *A Cross-Cultural Study of Some Sexual Beliefs and Practices.* Unpublished dissertation, Harvard University.

———. (1987) "The Relationship of Marital Infancy and Aloofness to Social Environment: A Hologeistic Study." *Behavior Science Research* 21: 50–69.

Levinson, David, and Martin J. Malone. (1980) *Toward Explaining Human Culture.*

SEX TABOOS

While all human societies condone sexual activity between married couples and a sizable number of societies also approve of or at least tolerate intercourse between unmarried partners, many cultures also constrain the sexual behavior of men and women in some way. Such constraints, or taboos, on sex play out differently in different cultures. Sex taboos can prohibit sexual intercourse in a specific place; at a specific time of day; before, during, or after particular events or activities; with particular categories of people; or at particular ages, stages, and crises in life.

Sex taboos restricting the places in which sexual activity can take place exist in a number of cultures. The Kikuyu of Kenya prohibit sexual intercourse from occurring anywhere but in a hut. Failure to abide by this rule brings bad luck. A Mende couple of West Africa should not engage in sex in the bush. Among the Bambara of West Africa, sexual activity outdoors affects all of the village land. The crops will fail and there will no longer be fruit on the trees. In Malaysia, if anyone in Semang society engages in sexual intercourse within the boundaries of the camp, the *Tapern*, or supernatural, will become angry. Semang couples, therefore, confine their sexual activity to the jungle.

Cultures can also regulate the time of day during which sexual activity can appropriately occur. The Cuna of Panama say that God wishes husbands to sleep with their spouses only at night. The Semang believe that sexual intercourse during the day causes thunderstorms that may result in deadly lightning or drowning, not only of the guilty couple but of others as well. In Nigeria, Igbo law also dictates that coitus should occur only at night, and a woman who is experiencing a long labor during the birth of a child may be suspected of having broken the "day coitus" taboo. Bambara custom also restricts coitus to the night. Albinos are believed to be the result of sexual intercourse that has taken place in the daylight.

Sex taboos associated with specific events or activities are common across cultures. Prohibitions against sexual intercourse while preparing for or engaging in combat are especially popular. Among the New Guinea Kapauku and the North American Kutenai, males abstain from sexual activity when at war. Ganda warriors of Uganda avoid sexual intercourse the night before the first battle when a prolonged conflict is anticipated. The Marshallese of Oceania impose a sex taboo upon men while they are being anointed to render them strong, attractive, and brave while in combat. The prohibition can then last as long as half a year.

Prohibitions against sexual activity associated with hunting are also common. Saami men are not permitted to sleep with their wives for three days after killing a bear; the leader of the hunt must abstain for five days. The Lepcha man of Tibet is continent for three months after he has set a bear trap. If the taboo is violated, the animal will not be caught. Among the Thonga of Mozambique, infringement of the sex taboo before and during a hunting foray is assumed to make the animals so wild that they cannot be overtaken. Indeed, the hunted creature will recognize and attack anyone who has broken the taboo. The Cuna of Panama avoid sexual relations when hunting for turtles, as do the Yapese of Oceania and Lesu of New Ireland when fishing.

Sex taboos are also associated with other activities across cultures. The Ganda refrain from engaging in sexual intercourse until the boards used for making a canoe have been cut, taken to the lake, and put in the water. A man also abstains from sexual activity when his future is being divined. Otherwise, his impending pursuits will not be successful. Gandan women also avoid sexual intercourse while mourning the dead. Since the Marshallese believe that women are unlucky and unclean, and that the spirits become displeased when men have any connection with females and the elements are robbed of their powers, Marshallese men abstain from sexual activity whenever they are taking care of important matters. The taboo also applies when canoes are being built. After a cult ceremony, a Kwoma man of New Guinea abstains from intercourse with his wife for from one to three nights, depending upon the importance of the ritual. But the taboo is invoked here for the protection of the woman, the fear being that the man's recent contact with the cult spirits might

be dangerous to a female with whom a man then cohabited. Men cleanse themselves well before coitus in order to eliminate the possibility that the spirit might infect the man's sexual partner. Among the Kikuyu of Kenya, sexual intercourse is prohibited while food is being prepared; otherwise, the food will be unclean and will need to be discarded. When travelling by sea, taking part in ceremonies, and mourning the dead, the Yapese respect a sex taboo.

Sometimes a society will prohibit sexual activity with or for certain categories of people. Among the Marshallese, when an ill individual is taking an herbal medicine, neither the patient nor the patient's spouse may engage in sex. If the taboo is broken, the sick person will become worse, and perhaps even die. Sexual intercourse is allowed only after the individual is completely well again. Similarly, Cuna medicine men remain continent when gathering medical materials in the forest or administering treatment to a sick person; otherwise, the female plant spirits will become jealous and the medicine will be rendered useless. After he has been initiated, a Kwoma man is prohibited from eating food prepared by a woman with whom he has had sex; his wife is the single exception to this taboo. Religious figures among the Yapese are expected to be continent for their entire lives.

Sexual activity is also forbidden for people at particular ages or stages in the life cycle, or for individuals at certain crisis points in their lives. In a number of societies, sexual intercourse is prohibited before a young person has attained puberty. In others, a youth must undergo the initiation ceremony traditional to his or her culture before the ban on sexual intercourse is lifted. Many societies insist upon abstinence during a woman's menstrual cycle or for some portion of a pregnancy. The postpartum sex taboo, which prohibits sexual intercourse between a husband and wife for some span of time after their infant has been born, is also common across cultures.

See also CONTINENCE AS A VIRTUE; MENSTRUAL TABOOS; SEX TABOO, POSTPARTUM.

Beaglehole, Ernest, and Pearl Beaglehole. (1938) *Ethnology of Pukapuka.*

———. (1941) "Personality and Development in Pukapukan Children." In *Language, Culture and Personality,* edited by Irving Hallowell and Stanley S. Newman, 282–292.

Collinder, Bjorn. (1949) *The Lapps.*

Erdland, August. (1938) *The Marshall Islanders: Life and Customs, Thought and Religion of a South Seas People.*

Evans, I. H. N. (1937) *The Negritos of Malaya.*

Gorer, Geoffrey. (1938) *Himalayan Village: An Account of the Lepchas of Sikkim.*

Hunt, E. E., David M. Schneider, Nathaniel R. Kidder, and William D. Stevens. (1949) *The Micronesians of Yap and Their Depopulation.*

Junod, Henri A. (1927) *The Life of a South African Tribe,* vol. 1.

Kagwa, Apolo. (1934) *The Customs of the Baganda.*

Kenyatta, Jomo. (1961) *Facing Mount Kenya: The Tribal Life of the Gikuyu.*

Little, K. L. (1951) *The Mende of Sierra Leone: A West African People in Transition.*

Murphy, Robert F., and Buell Quain. (1955) *The Trumai Indians of Central Brazil.*

Nordenskiold, Erland. (1938) *An Historical and Ethnological Survey of the Cuna.*

Paques, Viviana. (1954) *The Bambara.*

Pospisil, Leopold. (1958) *The Kapauku Papuans and Their Law.* Yale University Publications in Anthropology 54.

Powdermaker, Hortense. (1933) *Life in Lesu: The Study of a Melanesian Society in New Ireland.*

Roscoe, John. (1911) *The Baganda: An Account of Their Native Customs and Beliefs.*

Stout, David B. (1947) *San Blas Cuna Acculturation: An Introduction.*

Tobin, J. E. (1952) *Land Tenure in the Marshall Islands.*

Turney-High, Harry H. (1941) "Ethnography of the Kutenai." *American Anthropologist* 43(2) (Supplement).

Uchendu, Victor C. (1965) *The Igbo of Southeast Nigeria.*

Whiting, John W. M. (1941) *Becoming a Kwoma: Teaching and Learning in a New Guinea Tribe.*

SEX TRAINING IN CHILDHOOD

Human beings are incapable of engaging in full-blown sexual intercourse until they have attained sexual maturity. Still, children explore their own and other people's bodies, mimic the sexual activities of adults, and display other behaviors that anticipate adult sexual practices long before they reach puberty, and societal rules have developed in response to these behaviors. In some cultures, these childish activities are ignored or treated indulgently and even encouraged, while in others any suggestive behaviors on the part of a youngster are discouraged. Cultures also differ in the extent to which they provide the next generation with information about sex. Variations in these aspects of sex socialization are themselves predictably related to other attitudes and practices customarily displayed by a society in the domain of love and sex.

The rural Irish typify those societies in which sex socialization is severe. Adults condemn any behaviors in children that are even indirectly sexual in nature. Touching of one's own or another person's body is forbidden, nor is a child allowed to use any word that refers to a sexual organ or function. The Kwoma of New Guinea overlook it when a child explores his own body, and a small boy who handles his own genitals or looks at those of other males will not be scolded. But any child who displays an erection in public will be severely punished, and a female who sees a boy in this condition is supposed to beat his penis with a stick. It is often a sister's job to administer this punishment.

On the other hand, many societies view the sexual activity of children as natural, harmless, or even amusing, and adults in these cultures think nothing of playing with a youngster's genitals in the course of caring for the child. A Javanese mother will pat and stimulate her little son's penis while she is nursing or bathing him and an adult may pinch a small girl's genitals in fun while routinely taking care of her needs. No one minds if young children handle their own genitals. Chinese Manchu mothers tickle the genitals of their little daughters and suck the penis of a small son. In Arizona, Navajo adults regard sex as a natural function. They are not bothered when little boys and girls touch their own bodies and a mother may pat her infant's genitals while nursing the child. Among the Badjau of the Philippines, adults kiss and fondle a male infant's genitals as a means of quieting him. They say that this kind of attention makes the baby happy and demonstrates how proud the parent is to have a boy child. Pukapuka children of Oceania 12 years of age and younger can regularly be seen handling their genitals in public, and adults regard this behavior as a game that comes naturally to children. Brazilian Aweikoma youngsters grow up in a sexually open environment. Talk about sex remains unrestrained when youngsters are around, and adults will tease even very small children, claiming that this toddler has copulated with some old woman, or that a nine-year-old boy

has deflowered his adolescent cousin. The children themselves soon learn the art of sexual joking and one youngster will accuse another of having had a lover. A five- or six-year-old girl may be recruited to remove ticks from some man's genitals, and mothers regularly play with the genitals of their infant sons.

Childish attempts at imitating sexual intercourse are also regarded differently in different cultures. In the American Southwest, Hopi parents try to dissuade their children from engaging in sex play by telling them stories about the evil consequences of such activities. Children are led to believe that they can have babies and little girls are told that, if they give birth, everyone will die and the world will come to an end. Boys are warned that early sexual experience will cause them to stop growing and to become prematurely old. In Oceania, Trukese youngsters begin to engage in some sexual experimentation shortly before puberty. Parents disapprove of these activities, as it is thought that they may make a child sick. Adults, therefore, admonish children to wear clothes in the hope that this will prevent them from becoming sexually active. By contrast, Kenyan Kikuyu adults see no harm in the sexual experimentation of children, as no babies can be produced before puberty. When they play on the beach, Lesu boys and girls of New Ireland imitate the activities of their elders, and by the time they are around four years of age, they are mimicking sexual intercourse. Two children stand close together with their genitals touching. Adults regard these games as normal children's sport. The masturbatory activities and attempts at copulation displayed by Aweikoma children are also met by amusement and sometimes the gentle ridicule of their elders.

Cultures also differ regarding the extent to which they educate their children about sexual matters. Japanese parents avoid any discussion of sex with their children, whose primary sources of information about sexual matters are confused exchanges with other children and adolescents. Boys and girls sooner or later learn the lesson that sex is furtive and not to be approached openly and with candor. The Kaska of Alaska also dislike talking about sex and do not attempt to teach their children about sexual concerns, so young people simply pick up whatever information happens to come their way. Indochinese Khmer parents will not discuss sex in front of their children for fear that too much knowledge will motivate young people to become sexually active. Youngsters acquire most of their knowledge about sex from what they hear from friends, most of which is incorrect.

By contrast, children in other societies pick up a good deal of information about sex because of the unrestrained talk of the adults around them. In some cultures, there is a conscious attempt to transfer information about sex to young people. Lesu adults discuss sex, tell obscene stories, and exchange gossip in front of children, who come to have a good understanding of sexual matters as a result. Papago children in the southwestern United States are able to learn a good deal about sex from the constant chatter and joking about reproductive processes that buzzes around them. Navajo girls are explicitly instructed and advised about sex by older female relatives before puberty, and the father or mother's brother will talk to a boy.

Children in many cultures also acquire an education about sex from other children. In traditional Gond society youngsters of India learn about sexual techniques in the *ghotul,* the mixed-sex sleeping quarters where young people reside. Older boys teach younger boys and older girls teach younger girls, but sometimes a big girl will show a younger boy of whom she is fond the skills associated with sexual intercourse. Haitian children learn about sex by experimenting with one another, despite the disapproval of parents. Mbuti children of central Africa play house as soon as they can walk. They imitate the typical

household routine and, when their pretend chores are done, the playmates lie down and act out sexual intercourse. Among the Alor of Indonesia, groups of boys and girls sometimes play in the field houses together, copying the sexual activities of their parents.

Children also engage in sexual sport with other youngsters of their own sex. Among the games that Kwoma boys play together is one in which one youngster throws the other down and pretends to copulate with him. Another boy will then climb onto the original aggressor and simulate copulation, and more boys will line up and pile onto the heap, all the while laughing and screaming gleefully. One boy will call another his wife and say that he has made 'her' pregnant. Adolescents also like to join the game.

Patterns of sex socialization are related to other attitudes and beliefs about sex across cultures. Where adults discourage or punish sexual curiosity and activity in children, rules regarding premarital and extramarital sex also tend to be restrictive, but homosexual activities tend to be permitted. Love magic is likely to be present in such societies, and sexual abstinence may be recommended as a strategy for treating sickness. By contrast, societies that are indulgent regarding childhood sexual experimentation tend to permit premarital and extramarital sex but prohibit homosexuality. Love magic is not likely to be found in these cultures, nor is the idea that sexual abstinence can cure illness.

Beardsley, Richard K., John W. Hall, and Robert E. Ward. (1972) *Village Japan.*

DuBois, Cora. (1944) *The People of Alor: A Social Psychological Study of an East Indian Island.*

Elwin, Verrier. (1947) *The Muria and Their Ghotul.*

Geertz, Hildred. (1961) *The Javanese Family.*

Gladwin, Thomas, and Seymour B. Sarason. (1953) *Truk: Man in Paradise.*

Henry, Jules. (1941) *The Jungle People: A Kaingang Tribe of the Highlands of Brazil.*

Herskovits, Melville J. (1937) *Life in a Haitian Valley.*

Honigmann, John J. (1949) *Culture and Ethos in Kaska Society.*

Kenyatta, Jomo. (1961) *Facing Mount Kenya: The Tribal Life of the Gikuyu.*

Leighton, Dorothea, and Clyde Kluckhohn. (1969) *Children of the People: The Navaho Individual and His Development.*

Messenger, John C. (1971) "Sex and Repression in an Irish Folk Community." In *Human Sexual Behavior,* edited by Donald S. Marshall and Robert C. Suggs, 3–37.

Munroe, Robert L., and Ruth H. Munroe. (1975) *Cross-Cultural Human Development.*

Nimmo, H. A. (1964) "Nomads of the Sulu Sea." Unpublished dissertation, University of Hawaii.

Powdermaker, Hortense. (1933) *Life in Lesu: The Study of a Melanesian Society in New Ireland.*

Shirokogorov, Sergiei M. (1924) *Social Organization of the Manchus.*

Steinberg, David J. (1959) *Cambodia: Its People, Its Society, Its Culture.*

Textor, Robert B. (1967) *A Cross-Cultural Summary.*

Turnbull, Colin M. (1965) *Wayward Servants: The Two Worlds of the African Pygmies.*

Underhill, Ruth M. (1939) *Social Organization of the Papago Indians.*

Whiting, John W. M. (1941) *Becoming a Kwoma: Teaching and Learning in a New Guinea Tribe.*

Whiting, John W. M., and Irvin L. Child. (1953) *Child Training and Personality.*

SEXUAL BEHAVIOR, SAME-SEX

Sexual activity between members of the same sex is reported in a number of cultures around the world. The term *homosexuality* is conventionally reserved for male-male sexual relationships, with *lesbianism* used for female-female sexual relationships. Homosexual activities are relatively common in 41.4 percent of 70 cultures around the world and rare or absent in the remaining 58.6 percent of these societies. By contrast, lesbianism is rarely reported.

Male Homosexuality

Customary attitudes toward homosexuality range from positive acceptance to severe condemnation. In a sample of 42 cultures, 21.4 percent accept or ignore homosexual activities.

In another 14.3 percent of 42 cultures, homosexuality is ridiculed or scorned, but not punished. The Burmese refer to homosexuals as *mein ma sha,* or women-half. These men dress like women and wear face powder and jewelry. *Main ma sha* can also be distinguished from other men by their effeminate gestures. They are regarded with contempt but tolerated. The Trobrianders of New Guinea view homosexuality as well as other deviations from heterosexual activity as an inadequate and despicable substitute for sexual intercourse, and homosexuals are the target of verbal abuse and joking.

An additional 52.8 percent of the 42 societies disapprove of homosexual activity, some strongly enough to punish it severely. Homosexuality is seen by the Kwoma of New Guinea as unnatural and disgusting, and it is thought that anyone who would allow himself to be sodomized must be a ghost and not a man. The Goajiro of Colombia regard homosexuality with scorn and consider it to be the sort of activity that a man would force upon a slave as a way of humiliating him. The Chiricahua of the southwestern United States forbid homosexuality, and a man who engages in such practices is labeled a witch and put to death. Similarly, among the Rwala Bedouins, any man who engages in homosexuality will be killed.

Homosexuality is a foreign concept in the remaining 11.9 percent of the 42 cultures. To the Lepcha of Tibet, homosexuality is meaningless, and sodomy is a tremendously embarrassing topic that no one wishes to discuss. The Lesu of New Ireland have never heard of homosexuality and were surprised and horrified to hear that it is practiced by some men in other cultures. There is no term for homosexuality among the Pukapuka of Oceania nor any known instances of homosexuality. Most Haitian peasants are ignorant about homosexuality and do not understand why anyone would wish to engage in such practices when heterosexual relations are "so natural." Homosexuality is seen as a breach of God's law, a curse.

When homosexual activities are common in a society, they often occur when males, for one reason or another, are deprived of sexual contact with females. Marquesan boys of Oceania begin to engage in homosexual activities in childhood and will revert to these practices in adolescence and adulthood when heterosexual gratification is impossible. Because of the connection between homosexuality and heterosexual frustration, homosexual encounters are especially likely to be prevalent in adolescence, when males do not always have access to females. In Brazil, Nambicuara adolescents who are cross-cousins practice homosexuality, or "false love," because of the unavailability of girls as prospective wives. These relationships are carried out in the open and are regarded with amusement and greeted with joking on the part of onlookers. Adults do not take these encounters seriously, thinking of them as infantile. In some societies, older unmarried males recruit younger adolescent boys as sexual partners. For instance, among many groups of Australian aborigines, older males who do not yet have wives form homosexual relation-

ships with younger uninitiated boys. An Aranda bachelor of Australia often selects a ten- or twelve-year-old boy to be his "wife" for a number of years, and the two form a homosexual couple. During their puberty rites, New Guinea Keraki boys are introduced to homosexuality by older unmarried males; the custom is consistent with the Keraki belief that homosexual experience is necessary for the proper growth of boys. Homosexual activity is also part of the initiation rite for Kiwai boys of New Guinea and is thought to make boys stronger.

Societies that accept homosexual practices on the part of unmarried boys who have no other sexual outlet are likely to be much less tolerant of the same behavior on the part of a married male. Homosexuality is quite frequent among Nyakyusa boys of Tanzania when they are in their early teens and continues until marriage. People view these relationships as substitutes for heterosexual intercourse, and they are viewed as "a small wrong." A boy may be scolded or beaten by his own or classificatory father if his activities are found out, but older men are likely to regard these homosexual encounters more indulgently, dismissing them as a manifestation of adolescence. By contrast, a homosexual incident between grown men would be considered shameful, and adult males are forbidden to sleep together, sparing men the mortification that would be felt should one man ejaculate on another by accident while asleep. The sentiment is that an adult male would never have intercourse with another man and that such a thing is unheard of. Men "always want women; only when he cannot get a woman he does this, only in youth." Homosexual incidents are likely to occur among adolescent West African Fon boys once the girls have been withdrawn from their company, and these episodes are considered normal. Sometimes these relationships develop out of the mixed groups characteristic of childhood, where a number of boys and girls play together. When these groups break up, one of the remaining boys may take another "as a woman." Adolescent homosexual attachments sometimes form the basis for the "best friend" relationships between adult men, but homosexual activities themselves are disapproved of in grown men, and any male couple whose sexual relationship persists into adulthood works hard to conceal the attachment.

While male-male sexual contact occurs under some circumstances in many cultures, in no societies do all or most males engage in exclusive homosexuality. Indeed, such a pattern of sexual activity is logically impossible, as such a culture would soon die out for lack of new members. In a few cultures, homosexuality is practiced as a matter of course by most men, but in such cases males are also engaging in sex with women, and most are married. Among the Siwans of Egypt, for example, all men had homosexual relationships, and any man who did not form liaisons with other males was considered abnormal. Important men lent their sons to one another, and males discussed their homosexual liaisons openly. But all men were also expected to be involved in opposite-sex liaisons.

Physically demonstrative relationships between men in any given culture do not mean that homosexuality is also allowed in that society. For example, Mbuti boys of central Africa sometimes sleep together in one hut and, during these occasions, are likely to be in close physical contact, with legs entwined or thrown around one another's waist or hips. But no homosexual activity occurs, and the idea of something of the sort taking place horrifies the Mbuti, who only refer to homosexuality when they are extremely provoked and wish to level an enormous insult at a man.

Sometimes homosexual men also take on the dress and role of women. In Madagascar, some Tanala men practice both homosexuality and transvestism, and may also become co-wives. On the other hand, there is no inevitable relationship between the two customs. For instance,

many Tanala transvestites are not homosexual, and homosexuality is found in societies where transvestism is absent.

Attitudes toward homosexuality are predictably related to a variety of other customs and behaviors across cultures. Where homosexual practices are accepted or at least not disapproved, premarital sex for girls also tends to be accepted and frequent sexual activity is seen as desirable.

Restrictive attitudes toward homosexuality do not always result in the absence of homosexual practices. Of 19 societies in which men commonly form homosexual liaisons, 57.9 percent nevertheless condemn such practices. The motivation to engage in homosexuality seems in some societies to be sufficiently strong that men are willing to flaunt the norms of their communities.

Lesbianism

Lesbianism refers to any sexual activity in which the participating partners are women. Females engage in less same-sex sexual activity than do males, and descriptions of sexual behavior across cultures pay less attention to lesbian practices than they do to homosexual activity. Female-female sexual relationships are, nevertheless, reported in a small number of societies.

Where lesbian activities occur, they are often thought to be a response to conditions producing sexual frustration in women. For instance, young Mapuche girls of Chile commonly form lesbian attachments when the weather becomes warm. This is taken by the adults as an indication that a girl is ready to be married. Saulteaux women are known to form lesbian relationships, but this only occurs among unmarried girls. Same-sex sexual activity also occurs between girls at adolescence among the Kaska of Alaska, and people say that the cause is primarily the lack of opportunity for heterosexual relationships. The behavior is publicly disapproved, but nothing is done to a girl who is known to participate in homosexual activities. Nyakyusa women of Tanzania are also rumored to practice lesbianism. The relationships are far more likely to occur between older co-wives, who may be neglected sexually, than among young girls, for whom there is no shortage of men. Haitians say that a woman who does not have a satisfactory sexual relationship with her husband will turn to lesbianism.

In some cultures, lesbians are blamed for disasters befalling other individuals or the society more generally. In these and other societies, women who are sexually intimate may be severely punished. Among the Haitians, lesbian activity is regarded as the cause of a variety of misfortunes, including floods, droughts, epidemics, earthquakes, pests, and crop loss. The Azande of Zaire believe that female sexuality is potentially dangerous and that irregular sexual activities on the part of women are likely to bring bad luck. Therefore, lesbians are beaten by their husbands and are the target of scandal in the community as a whole. The Dahomey of West Africa believe that lesbianism causes frigidity in marriage. Among the Rwala, any woman engaging in lesbianism would be condemned to death.

In some cultures, lesbian couples employ devices as adjuncts to their sexual activities. For instance, artificial penises are used as props in lesbian interactions by the Chuckchee of Siberia, Mbundu of Angola, Nama of Nigeria, and Azande of Zaire.

Women may be physically affectionate with each other without graduating to genital intimacy. For instance, Cubeo girls of the Amazon will stroke one another's nipples, but only one case of true lesbianism has been discovered. The incidence of culturally accepted female-female nonsexual physical contact is far greater than is the reported incidence of lesbianism.

In the few cases where there are descriptions of both homosexuality and lesbianism in the same culture, same-sex sexual activity on the part of males is regarded with less disapproval than is that between females. Thus, for example, while the Manus of Oceania are amused by homosexuality in unmarried men, lesbian activities are disapproved and regarded as inappropriate. Both forms of same-sex sexual contact are rare. The Alorese of Indonesia are shocked by the idea of lesbianism and strongly condemn such behavior. By contrast, when little boys play in ways that mimic homosexual practices, adults only scold them, thinking that the behavior is not serious enough to earn more strict punishment.

Broude, Gwen J. (1981) "Cultural Management of Sexuality." In *Handbook of Human Development,* edited by Robert Munroe, Ruth Munroe, and Beatrice B. Whiting.

DuBois, Cora. (1944) *The People of Alor: A Social Psychological Study of the East Indian Island.*

Evans-Pritchard, Edward Evan. (1929) "Some Collective Expressions of Obscenity in Africa." *Royal Anthropological Institute of Great Britain and Ireland* 59: 311–331.

———. (1937) *Witchcraft, Oracles and Magic among the Azande.*

Ford, Clellan S., and Frank A. Beach. (1951) *Patterns of Sexual Behavior.*

Goldman, Irving. (1963) *The Cubeo: Indians of the Northwest Amazon.*

Gorer, Geoffrey. (1938) *Himalayan Village: An Account of the Lepchas of Sikkim.*

Gregerson, Edgar. (1983) *Sexual Practices.*

Gutierrez de Pineda, Virginia. (1950) *Social Organization in La Guajira.*

Hallowell, A. Irving. (1955) *Culture and Experience.*

Helm, June. (1961) *The Lynx Point People.* National Museum of Canada Bulletin 176.

Herskovits, Melville J. (1938) *Dahomey: An Ancient West African Kingdom,* vol. 1.

Linton, Ralph. (1933) *The Tanala: A Hill Tribe of Madagascar.*

Malinowski, Bronislaw. (1929) *The Sexual Life of Savages in North-Western Melanesia: An Ethnographic Account of Courtship, Marriage and Family Life among the Natives of the Trobriand Islands, British New Guinea.*

Masters, William M. (1953) *Rowanduz: A Kurdish Administrative and Mercantile Center.*

Mead, Margaret. (1931) *Growing Up in New Guinea: A Comparative Study of Primitive Education.*

Oberg, Kalervo. (1953) *Indian Tribes of Northern Mato Grosso, Brazil.*

Opler, Morris E. (1941) *An Apache Life-Way: The Economic, Social and Religious Institutions of the Chiricahua Indians.*

Orr, Kenneth Gordon. (1951) *Field Notes on the Burmese Standard of Living as Seen in the Case of a Fisherman-Refuge Family.*

Powdermaker, Hortense. (1933) *Life in Lesu: The Study of a Melanesian Society in New Ireland.*

Serpenti, I. M. (1965) *Cultivators in the Swamps.*

Suggs, Robert C. (1971) "Sex and Personality in the Marquesas." In *Human Sexual Behavior,* edited by Donald S. Marshall and Robert C. Suggs, 163–186.

Titiev, Mischa. (1951) *Araucanian Culture in Transition.*

Turnbull, Colin M. (1965) *Wayward Servants: The Two Worlds of the African Pygmies.*

Whiting, John W. M. (1941) *Becoming a Kwoma: Teaching and Learning in a New Guinea Tribe.*

Wilson, Monica. (1951) *Good Company.*

SEXUAL PARTNERS, FIRST

In many societies around the world, males and females remain virgins until they are married, or premarital sex may be permitted only between persons who are already betrothed to each other.

Under these circumstances, a person's first sexual partner is his or her spouse. But in many other societies, like the United States, many young people are already sexually experienced by the time they are married. In such cases, the first partner may be an age-mate, an older and more experienced individual, or a professional prostitute. Some societies specify that a virgin, especially a girl, should have her first sexual experience with a particular category of partner. This is one example of the more general custom of ritual defloration.

Among cultures that do not require virginity in their unmarried girls and boys, it is usual for young people to have their first sexual encounters with partners who are more or less their own age. Once he has been circumcised, an adolescent Kenyan Dorobo boy is permitted to have intercourse. Typically, he builds himself a small hut where he and a girl of his choosing can live together until she marries. After puberty, Trukese youngsters of Oceania begin to engage in sexual relations, and much of their time is taken up with negotiating one or another love affair with another adolescent.

In some cultures, a girl's first sexual encounter is likely to be with an older male. For instance, in Oceania, a Siuai girl is not supposed to engage in sexual intercourse until her breasts have grown; otherwise, it is said, her breasts will not become large and pendulous. But once she has matured sufficiently, a young or middle-aged man will abduct her while she is doing her chores and the girl will have her first sexual experience, usually without any objection on her part. In New Guinea, Wogeo girls typically become sexually active when they are around 16 years old. A girl's first partner is always an older man, and sometimes a married one. Many Wogeo males are tempted at the prospect of sleeping with a virgin, so sexually inexperienced girls are often pursued by a number of men at one time.

A boy may also be introduced to sexual intercourse by an older partner. Among the Tanala of Madagascar, girls are expected to remain virgins until marriage. Boys are not, and in fact premarital chastity in a male would be taken as a sign of impotence. Tanala boys, therefore, have their first sexual experiences with older, often married, women. Similarly, Javanese girls are married early to prevent them from becoming sexually active before they are wives. Otherwise, it would be hard for the girl to make a good match. Boys, as a result, generally have more sexual experience by the time they are married, and their early partners are often town prostitutes. Siuai boys are also usually initiated into sexual intercourse by an already experienced young woman. Less typically, an older sib-mate may allow a sexually naive boy to accompany him on a rendezvous with a girl. The younger boy may be allowed to watch the couple while they are engaging in coitus, or he may even be permitted to have intercourse with the girl himself.

Aweikoma adults of Brazil regularly talk and joke about sex in front of children, and youngsters are teased from infancy about their supposed sexual exploits. The first real sexual experience of both boys and girls often occurs at an early age with a much older person. In the case of a girl, this sexual initiation is likely to be violent.

Finally, in some societies a girl's first sexual partner is designated by custom. In Oceania, Marshallese girls lose their virginity to the chief during their initiation rites. In Australia, an Aranda girl's first sexual experience is with a number of her husband's male kin. As part of the marriage ceremony, the bride is taken to the bushes by some of her groom's relatives, all of whom have sexual intercourse with her before taking her back to her new husband.

See also DEFLORATION CUSTOMS; WEDDING NIGHT.

Erdland, August. (1914) *The Marshall Islanders: Life and Customs, Thought and Religion of a South Seas People.*

Geertz, Hildred. (1961) *The Javanese Family.*

Gladwin, Thomas, and Seymour B. Sarason (1953) *Truk: Man in Paradise.*

Henry, Jules. (1941) *The Jungle People: A Kaingang Tribe of the Highlands of Brazil.*

Hogbin, H. Ian. (1970) *The Island of Menstruating Men: Religion in Wogeo, New Guinea.*

Huntingford, G. W. B. (1953) *The Southern Nilo-Hamites.*

Linton, Ralph. (1933) *The Tanala: A Hill Tribe of Madagascar.*

Murdock, George P. (1936) *Our Primitive Contemporaries.*

Oliver, Douglas. (1955) *A Solomon Island Society: Kinship and Leadership among the Siuai of Bougainville.*

SEXUAL RECEPTIVITY

In most mammalian species, females are sexually receptive only when they are fertile. During this time of receptivity, the female is said to be in estrous. An estrous female will accept the sexual advances of males and may even seek out and solicit copulations. Estrous females also advertise their fertility by various physical signs. For example, the genitals of a female chimpanzee swell and change color when she is in estrus. Some females communicate their fertility by releasing pheromones, or chemicals, from the vagina. These are then sensed by nearby males, who interpret the odors as a sign of the female's sexual receptivity. Other females perfume their urine and spray it around to attract males. All female mammals employ some technique for communicating their fertility to the males of their species. They will then copulate with males who meet their standards for an appropriate mate. By contrast, when they are not in estrus, the same females will usually resist the sexual advances of males. Among female mammals there is an efficient and direct relationship between fertility and receptivity. The exception to this mammalian rule is the human female. Sexual receptivity in human females is not yoked to fertility. Further, fertility is masked in the human female. Neither the woman herself nor those around her can tell when she is able to conceive, and human females are more or less equally sexually receptive at all times of the menstrual cycle. No one knows why these traits have evolved in our species, but many hypotheses have been proposed.

A number of people have suggested that the loss of estrus in human females promotes stable long-term relationships between the sexes. In this view, natural selection has selected for continuous receptivity and masking of fertility so that a man will be more likely to remain with his mate and to help her in the rearing of offspring. Two reasons are offered for why a male would stay with a female under these circumstances. First, the promise of a regular sexual partner is seen as a magnet strong enough to persuade a male to make a long-term commitment to a woman. And second, it is predicted that a male who cannot be sure when his mate is fertile will remain with her permanently to increase the chances that he will sooner or later impregnate her. He may also be inclined to want to watch over her so that no other males can fertilize her, and this will also keep him by her side. This is advantageous for the woman, who gets a helpmate as a fringe benefit.

While these proposals seem persuasive to some individuals, others have pointed out weaknesses in the reasoning behind these theories. Males and females in species that do not exhibit continuous female receptivity nevertheless form long-term male-female pair-bonds. Male and female gibbons stay together in long-term relationships, but female gibbons have an estrous period, and copulations are infrequent among

mates. The proposal that continuous female receptivity is required for the formation of permanent relationships also tends to overemphasize the role of sex in human marriages. Across cultures, a person gets married for a variety of reasons. Marriage promises the attainment of adult status, economic security, exclusive sexual rights to another person, the production and legitimization of children, and a home of one's own. Human beings do not marry primarily for the purpose of obtaining a regular sexual partner.

Various people have suggested that the masking of fertility may advance a woman's reproductive success in one way or another. If a woman's fertile period is kept hidden, it becomes harder for her mate to prevent her from being impregnated by other males, as that would require his watching over her more or less all of the time. Some theories propose that this will make it easier for a woman to have sexual intercourse on the sly with a male who is in some way superior to her mate. If she is indeed fertilized by a superior male, then her reproductive success is increased. One problem with this hypothesis is that, if a woman's mate does not know when she is fertile, neither does the woman. This means that she does not know when to cheat on her mate with another male. Hidden fertility, then, seems to get in the way of this strategy of sneak fertilization as much as it advances it. Further, if females were regularly having sexual intercourse with other males on the sly, it is unclear why a male would want to take care of offspring of whose paternity he would be so unsure. A male living in a world where females were regular cheaters would do better to care for his sister's children. He could be assured of sharing at least some of their genes, as he knows that his sister and he share the same mother and therefore some genes, and that his sister's children share one-half of her genes. In fact, men in some human cultures follow exactly this strategy. These are cultures where sex norms are quite permissive and where a husband, therefore, is not sure that his wife's children are also his own.

Other theories propose that continuous receptivity in human females may serve as a strategy for extracting a steady stream of gifts from males in return for sex. In fact, males across societies do give females presents in an attempt to persuade them to have sexual intercourse. And among chimpanzees, males will share more meat with females who are in estrus and, therefore, sexually receptive, than those who are not. One theory of female sexuality proposes that continuous receptivity in human females, by promoting exclusive long-term male-female relationships, minimizes male competition for mates, allowing the high degree of male cooperation needed for successful human culture. Loss of estrus in human females has also raised the possibility that a woman who knew when she was fertile might avoid sexual intercourse during that period in an attempt to prevent the pain associated with labor and delivery of infants. But of course, a woman who is highly motivated not to have children can abstain from sexual intercourse entirely. Finally, it has been suggested that the loss of estrus simply followed upon a growing use of sex as a cultural tool. Cultures require couples to engage in sexual intercourse on their wedding night, before a hunt, after a hunt, and so on, thus dissociating sexual intercourse from fertilization. Once this occurred, the argument goes, estrus no longer performed a function and so it no longer had a selective advantage. Eventually, it just disappeared.

See also NATURAL SELECTION; REPRODUCTIVE STRATEGIES; SEXUAL SELECTION.

Daly, Margo, and Martin Wilson. (1983) *Sex, Evolution, and Behavior.*

Shaw, Evelyn, and John Darling. (1985) *Female Strategies.*

Symons, Donald. (1979) *The Evolution of Human Sexuality.*

SEXUAL RELATIONS, PATTERNS OF

When people in Western society speculate about human sexual behavior, they tend to assume that there is a high degree of regularity in the cultural patterning of sexual attitudes and practices. Thus, for example, we hear about the prudish Victorian era, where sex norms were said to be repressive and sexual activity itself inhibited. Juxtaposed against this profile of repression is, for instance, the sexual revolution of the 1960s, during which attitudes toward sex were thought to be greatly relaxed and sexual behavior free and easy. This presumption of consistency in sexual orientation, however, is an exaggeration. In fact, while certain sex norms and sexual activities do tend to co-occur across societies, cultures are not entirely consistent as regards their sexual orientation. It would be incorrect to assume that a culture was generally permissive or generally restrictive simply because it is tolerant or intolerant regarding some specific sexual behavior.

Some aspects of sexual orientation are predictably related across cultures. Attitudes toward and frequencies of premarital sex for boys and girls and frequencies of extramarital sex for husbands and wives tend to be related within a culture. Thus, a society is likely to have either permissive premarital sex norms and a high incidence of premarital and extramarital sex for both sexes or it is likely to have restrictive premarital sex norms and a low incidence of premarital and extramarital sex for males and females. Attitudes toward extramarital sex for either spouse, however, are not predictably related to this cluster of sex norms and practices. It seems, then, that people are consistent regarding their heterosexual activities before and while they are married and that cultural rules are either permissive or restrictive about premarital sexual activity in line with these trends.

Other attitudes and behaviors that tend to go together are frequency of homosexuality, concerns about and incidence of impotence, and male boasting. Thus, where homosexuality is present, men are not concerned about nor do they tend to experience impotence, and they do not boast. Alternatively, where homosexuality is absent, men are concerned about or tend to suffer from impotence and are also boastful. These behaviors all seem to be related to male sexual performance.

A final set of norms and practices also tends to co-vary within a culture. These have to do with attitudes toward extramarital sex. Where there is a single standard of extramarital sex, so that wives as well as husbands are permitted to engage in sexual intercourse outside of marriage, husbands are more likely to lend their wives to other men. Where there is a double standard, so that the extramarital affairs of wives are more harshly condemned than are those of husbands, men are not likely to share their wives. Thus, attitudes about extramarital sex are consistent.

Each cluster of sex norms and practices described here seems to reflect a particular theme having to do with sex. Since each cluster tends to be patterned independently of the others within a culture, the themes underlying these clusters must also be independent. Thus, the way in which people conduct their heterosexual premarital and extramarital sex lives is unrelated to male worries about sexual performance or to incidences of male-male sexual activity. Similarly, cultural attitudes toward extramarital sexual behavior for wives are independent of these other aspects of sexuality. For example, among the

Burmese, premarital sex is more or less universal for both sexes, homosexuality is ridiculed, and extramarital sex, while disapproved of for both spouses, is more harshly condemned in wives. The Badjau of the Philippines also scorn homosexuality, but premarital sex in this society is not common. Homosexuality is strongly disapproved by the Punjabi of South Asia, premarital sex is rare, and extramarital sex is allowed for both sexes. The Kwoma of New Guinea also condemn homosexuality and allow both partners to have extramarital affairs, but virtually everyone engages in premarital sex. Among the Truk of Oceania, homosexuality is unknown, premarital sex is nearly universal, and husbands but not wives may have extramarital sexual relations.

Broude, Gwen J. (1976) "Cross-Cultural Patterning of Some Sexual Attitudes and Practices." *Behavior Science Research* 2: 227–262.

———. (1983) "Male-Female Relationships in Cross-Cultural Perspective: A Study of Sex and Intimacy." *Behavior Science Research* 18: 154–181.

Broude, Gwen J., and Sarah J. Greene. (1976) "Cross-Cultural Codes on Twenty Sexual Attitudes and Practices." *Ethnology* 15: 409–429.

Levinson, David, and Martin J. Malone. (1980) *Toward Explaining Human Culture.*

SEXUAL RELATIONS, PRIVACY IN

How much value do human beings place on privacy when they are engaging in sexual activity? The tendency for a couple to try to practice discretion with regard to their sexual behavior is conspicuous across cultures, but how the quest for privacy is played out, and by whom, varies from one society to the next.

People in some cultures attempt to hide the fact that they are engaging in intimate activities while still, however, remaining in the presence of others. The !Kung of southern Africa sleep outside in a camp of perhaps 25 square feet. Each family, however, has its own sleeping place outside its own small hut, and couples who wish to engage in intercourse do so discreetly under cover of the woman's *kaross,* an all-purpose garment that she wears in daytime. Alor married couples of Indonesia also remain in a joint sleeping room when having sexual intercourse, but they try to wait until everyone else is asleep and, indeed, the idea of having sexual relations in public is deeply embarrassing to them. The Trumai of Brazil may also have sex at night in a room inhabited by other people, but, again, the couple waits until the others have fallen asleep. Couples in other cultures prefer to confine their sexual activity to secluded places where they are isolated from other people. The Siriono sleep in huts in which perhaps 50 hammocks may be hung in one unpartitioned space of some 500 square feet. Here, sex is most likely to take place in the bush so that some degree of privacy can be achieved. On the rare occasion, however, a couple will make do in their hammock. Siuai couples of Oceania take advantage of the fact that outsiders are fearful of intruding on a family garden plot lest they be accused of theft or sorcery. The gardens, as a consequence, serve as ideal sanctuaries for sexual intercourse and partners may camp in their garden for a night instead of remaining at home where many people sleep together in one room. Among the Jivaro of Ecuador, males and females sleep in different parts of a house. As a result, couples never engage in sexual relations inside a house. Rather, coitus occurs in the fields encircling the dwellings. The Semang of Malaysia confine their sexual activities to the jungle, as sexual relations

within the camp would anger the *tapern,* or supernatural. Among the Wogeo of New Guinea, privacy in sexual relations is sufficiently important that newly married couples will not even sleep in the same bed unless they are spending the night alone. While people in some cultures try to make the best of a crowded sleeping situation by being discreet, most people across cultures will engage in sexual relations in their houses only when afforded some degree of privacy in their sleeping arrangements. Otherwise, the tendency is to find some secluded spot away from the house when sexual activity is planned. In 80 percent of 15 societies where sleeping arrangements are relatively private, people remain indoors for sexual relations while in only 20 percent do couples still prefer outdoor locations. By contrast, people in 90 percent of 10 societies where sleeping arrangements are relatively public prefer to engage in sexual activity out-of-doors while in only 10 percent do couples have intercourse in their own beds.

In some societies, privacy is valued, but principally with respect to other adults. In other cultures, adults are also careful to shield their young children from opportunities to witness sexual intercourse. In Oceania, some Pukapuka parents refrain from engaging in sexual activity until they think that their children are asleep, or they may retire to the bush. But other parents are less concerned about preserving their privacy when their children might be witnesses to their behavior. By contrast, the Kwoma of New Guinea are careful about waiting until their youngsters are asleep before having intercourse. When their children "get sense"—that is, when they are around three or four years of age—the Hausa of Nigeria make arrangements for the youngsters to sleep in another house when a husband and wife plan intercourse. Among the Trobrianders of New Guinea, older children, especially boys, leave home in order to avoid constraining their parents' sexual lives by their potentially embarrassing presence.

The importance of privacy is also determined by the status of the couple. Young unmarried people appear to be less interested in being alone during sexual encounters than do married partners. Among the North American Saulteaux, an unmarried couple may have sexual intercourse in a bed roll in which the girl's younger sister is also sleeping. Groups of young Pukapuka boys and girls retire to the beach, where they entertain themselves and then form pairs for the purpose of engaging in coitus, all in the same place. The difference in attitudes about privacy between older people and young unmarried couples is highlighted by the Nuba of the Sudan. Beginning at puberty, girls sleep in a hut of their own, where they rendezvous with boyfriends. Five to eight girls may share a single hut, but the resulting absence of privacy is not worrisome to the young couples. The motivation for setting girls up in their own dwellings is to avoid the shame that would result from having a daughter entertain lovers under her parents' roof. Similarly, central African Mbuti adults have a lower tolerance for flamboyant sexual behavior than do their children. Parents regularly gripe about the noise that young people make while engaging in sexual intrigues, preferring that their children keep their adventures to themselves. It is not the sexual activity itself that bothers parents so much as the flagrant indiscretion of the young people, which deprives parents of the ability to feign ignorance of their children's activities. Married couples demonstrate a strong desire for maintaining privacy in their sexual activities in 75 percent of 16 societies. In 19 percent of those cultures, married partners are discreet in their sexual activity, but not excessively much. In the remaining 6 percent, representing only one society, married people are indifferent to matters of privacy regarding their sex lives. By contrast, four of the five most flagrantly immodest cultural descriptions of sexual relations refer to the behavior of young unmarried couples.

The legal status of a couple also sometimes makes a difference in where sexual activity is likely to take place and, therefore, how private the encounter is liable to be. The Lesu of New Ireland, Pukapukans of Oceania, and Trukese of Oceania typically engage in marital intercourse indoors. But extramarital affairs take place out-of-doors among the Lesu, and both extramarital and premarital sex happens outside in the other two cultures. Among the Lamba of Zambia and Lango of Uganda, legitimate sexual activity takes place only inside a house, again leaving unsanctioned liaisons to the out-of-doors. The consequence of this distinction between marital indoor sex and less respectable outdoor affairs means that extralegal sexual activities are likely to be carried out in private.

Finally, the likelihood that a couple will achieve privacy in their sexual activity can be affected by other beliefs about when or where coitus ought to take place. The sleeping arrangements of the Gond of India and Yurok of California would allow them a high degree of privacy if they chose to engage in sexual activity at home. But both societies believe that if sexual intercourse occurs inside a house, poverty will ensue. Thus, couples in these cultures sacrifice their best chance for seclusion during sexual intercourse because of a conflicting set of convictions about the consequences of engaging in certain kinds of sexual behavior.

While the desire for privacy in sexual activities is characteristic of human cultures, there are some societies that appear to view discretion in sexual intercourse as relatively or entirely unimportant. The Goajiro of Colombia engage in coitus at home or in the fields and are not concerned if other people, including young children, are present. The Mapuche of Chile try to remain discreet in their sexual encounters, but are not greatly disturbed by failures to achieve privacy. Similarly, while the Mbuti of central Africa practice some discretion in their sexual behavior, a couple will greet any individual who intrudes upon them without any great embarrassment. The Mbuti expect such a surprise visitor to continue on his way and let the couple be. The Nambicuara of Brazil can expect observers of their intimate activities to be less charitable. While Nambicuara couples are likely to leave camp and retire some way into the surrounding bush, other camp members, including children, may pursue the pair, laughing and teasing them as well as observing their behavior through breaks in the branches.

Cultural attitudes about the importance of privacy in sexual relations are related to some other kinds of behavior. Societies that value discretion in sexual activity also expect modesty in women, so that females are expected to undress, bathe, and eliminate in private. Where privacy in intercourse is not valued, women are more likely to perform these activities in front of other people, including sometimes people of the opposite sex. Finally, attitudes toward discretion in sexual activity are related to attitudes about homosexuality. Homosexuality is more likely to be accepted or tolerated where people also prefer to be private in their heterosexual behavior, while more public heterosexual activity is often found along with disapproval of homosexual behavior.

———

Beaglehole, Ernest, and Pearl Beaglehole. (1938) *Ethnology of Pukapuka.*

———. (1941) "Personality and Development in Pukapukan Children." In *Language, Culture and Personality,* edited by Irving Hallowell and Stanley S. Newman, 282–292.

DuBois, Cora. (1944) *The People of Alor: A Social Psychological Study of an East Indian Island.*

Dunning, R. W. (1959) *Social and Economic Change among the Northern Ojibwa.*

Evans, I. H. N. (1937) *The Negritos of Malaya.*

Ford, Clellan S., and Frank A. Beach. (1951) *Patterns of Sexual Behavior.*

Gutierrez de Pineda, Virginia. (1950) *Social Organization in La Guajira.*

Hogbin, H. Ian. (1934–1935) "Native Culture of Wogeo: Report of Field Work in New Guinea." *Oceania* 5: 308–337.

———. (1945–1946) "Puberty to Marriage: A Study of the Sexual Life of the Native of Wogeo, New Guinea." *Oceania* 16: 185–209.

Holmberg, Allan R. (1950) *Nomads of the Long Bow.* Washington, DC: Government Printing Office.

Karsten, Rafael. (1935) *The Head-Hunters of Western Amazonas: The Life and Culture of the Jibaro Indians of Eastern Ecuador and Peru.*

Levi-Strauss, Claude. (1948) *La Vie Familiale et Sociale des Indiens Nambikwara* [Family and social life of the Nambikwara Indians].

Malinowski, Bronislaw. (1929) *The Sexual Life of Savages in North-Western Melanesia: An Ethnographic Account of Courtship, Marriage and Family Life among the Natives of the Trobriand Islands, British New Guinea.*

Marshall, Lorna. (1959) "Marriage among the !Kung Bushmen." *Africa* 29: 335–364.

Murphy, Robert F., and Buell Quain. (1955) *The Trumai Indians of Central Brazil.*

Nadel, S. F. (1947) *The Nuba.*

Oliver, Douglas. (1955) *A Solomon Island Society: Kinship and Leadership among the Siuai of Bougainville.*

Smith, Mary. (1954) *Baba of Karo: A Woman of the Muslim Hausa.*

Titiev, Mischa. (1951) *Araucanian Culture in Transition.*

Turnbull, Colin M. (1965) *Wayward Servants: The Two Worlds of the African Pygmies.*

Whiting, John W. M. (1941) *Becoming a Kwoma: Teaching and Learning in a New Guinea Tribe.*

SEXUAL SELECTION

According to Charles Darwin's theory of evolution by natural selection, organisms belonging to the same species differ regarding the degree to which they possess genetically grounded traits that help them to survive and successfully reproduce relative to other members of their species. Traits that increase an organism's chances of survival and reproduction are said to be adaptive, while traits that are less effective at contributing to survival and reproduction are less adaptive, or maladaptive. Because they increase the chances of an organism's survival and reproduction, adaptive traits become better and better represented across future generations. In other words, these traits are selected for. Traits that do not contribute as effectively to survival and reproduction become less and less well represented across generations and are selected against. Darwin called the process of selecting for and against traits "natural selection."

While the term natural selection is used to refer to the selection of traits relevant to both survival and reproduction, Darwin also introduced a second term to indicate the process of selection of those characteristics of an organism that contribute specifically to reproduction. This is the process of sexual selection. If natural selection selects for and against traits having to do with both survival and reproduction, sexual selection selects for traits having to do with reproduction exclusively. Thus, traits that promote an organism's chances of successfully reproducing are selected for by sexual selection while traits that are inefficient in increasing an organism's reproductive success are selected against by the process of sexual selection. By employing a new term to talk about the selection of traits relevant to reproduction in particular, Darwin underscored the distinction between success at survival and success at reproducing. Thus, two organisms can be equally good at surviving, but

differentially successful at reproducing. Conversely, one organism can die long before another but still leave more surviving offspring. Thus, selection of traits relevant to survival and selection of traits relevant to reproduction deserve to be distinguished.

What sorts of traits promote or interfere with successful reproduction? That depends in the first place upon the sex of the organism. Across sexually reproducing species, different reproductive constraints operate on males and females, so the sexes are required to employ different kinds of strategies to achieve reproductive success. Thus, different traits will be selected for as promoting successful reproduction for males and females.

What are the differential constraints that lead to the need for different reproductive strategies for the sexes? In most sexually reproducing species, the male makes a far smaller investment in the production and nurturing of offspring than the female does. This begins as far back as the investment that it takes to produce a single sperm or a single egg. Eggs are much larger than sperm. If a sperm were the size of a fingernail, then an egg would be the size of an average living room. Because of the relative size of the sex gametes, females can produce far fewer eggs than males can produce sperm. Where fertilization is internal, the female then makes a further investment in the phase of pregnancy. If the organism is a mammal, then the female invests still more in nursing her offspring. Meanwhile, unless fathers are also required for the successful rearing of the young to reproductive maturity, the investment of the male is complete. While the female is still occupied with a particular infant, the male can occupy himself with trying to inseminate other females. Because of this enormous difference between the sexes in the investment that is made in a single offspring, males are limited in their potential reproductive capacity only by the number of females that they can inseminate. Females, by contrast, are limited by the number of eggs they can produce and the number of offspring that they can then successfully nurture. Those numbers are extremely small compared to the number of copulations that a male can theoretically manage. When males also participate in the rearing of offspring, as they typically do in the human species, then the difference in relative investment of the sexes in the reproductive effort becomes less extreme. But the balance is still in favor of males, especially as the initial minuscule investment in sperm makes it worthwhile for any male who has a pronounced paternal role to still try to inseminate additional females on the side.

Given the differences between the sexes in their investment in offspring, what strategies are most likely to increase reproductive success for males and females? And how will the strategies differ? In general, the optimal male strategy for gaining access to mates is to compete with other males for copulations. This means that sexual selection will select for traits that allow males to win in these within-sex competitions. The method of competition will depend upon the species doing the competing. Where females make the greater investment in offspring, by contrast, they do not need to compete with each other for males because there are more than enough males willing to mate with any female. Rather, the female mating strategy that promotes reproductive success consists of choosing the most desirable males, and sexual selection selects for traits that allow females to make this choice. Criteria for desirability will depend upon the species of animal doing the selecting.

Darwin's distinction between selection for traits that promote survival and selection for traits that promote reproduction allows us to entertain the possibility that the two selection processes may conflict. That is, traits that increase success in reproduction may interfere with

longevity. Indeed, this tends to be the case for males in many species where male competition for females is the optimal reproductive strategy. For instance, the intense fighting that often occurs between males who are competing for females injures and weakens not only the loser but the victor, shortening his life span. A male who opts for a long life and avoids confrontations with other males may live to old age, but he is unlikely to produce many offspring and so the traits that incline him to stay out of trouble will be selected against. In birds, males attract females by their bright color and songs. But these same traits also make the males more obvious to predators. So again, the very traits that promote reproductive success pose a threat to the animal's life. In fact, across species, females on an average outlive males, and sexual selection plays a major role in this differential longevity.

Human beings belong to a species for which male parental care assumes some importance. For this reason, the differential in male versus female investment in young is less extreme than it is in species where only the mother is responsible for the raising of offspring. Nevertheless, the strategy of winning females by competing with other males is characteristic of the human male. Competition tends to be in the form of striving for higher status and wealth than other males, thus attracting the attentions of girls and women. Similarly, human females give evidence of choosing between competing males. Girls and women across societies are attracted to men who will be good providers. Human males the world over also tend to adopt the strategy of trying to impregnate other women while directing the major portion of their time and resources to the children of their wives. This is reflected in the tendency of all or most men in a majority of human societies to engage in extramarital sex.

See also ATTRACTIVENESS; DIFFERENTIAL REPRODUCTIVE SUCCESS; EXTRAMARITAL SEX;

MARRIAGE PARTNERS, CRITERIA FOR CHOOSING;
NATURAL SELECTION; REPRODUCTIVE STRATEGIES.

Broude, Gwen J. (1980) "Extramarital Sex Norms in Cross-Cultural Perspective." *Behavior Science Research* 15: 409–429.

Daly, Martin, and Margo Wilson. (1983) *Sex, Evolution, and Behavior.*

Trivers, Robert L. (1985) *Social Evolution.*

SLEEP-CRAWLING Sleep-crawling refers to the custom whereby a man sneaks up on a woman while she is asleep and attempts to have sexual intercourse with her without her permission or knowledge. In no culture is sleep-crawling the usual way by which men solicit sexual relations from women. But in some societies, men will on occasion practice sleep-crawling as an alternative strategy for soliciting sex. Sometimes sleep-crawling is regarded as a bold and clever strategy for gaining sexual access to a woman. In other societies, it is regarded as unwholesome and even disgraceful.

Among the Lakher of south Asia, sleep-crawling is known as *aleuhno*. A man may attempt *aleuhno* if he is infatuated with a girl who has been slow to return his affection. He waits until the girl is asleep and then slinks over to her side and lies down beside her, being careful not to wake her up. Girls do not generally report incidents of sleep-crawling, and a man is unlikely to attempt *aleuhno* unless he has reason to believe that a girl will be somewhat sympathetic to his advances. There is no penalty for sleep-crawling; in fact, a man who has succeeded in his efforts to have sexual relations with a sleeping girl is admired by his peers. *Aleuhno* with a married woman is not acceptable, as it infringes upon the rights of the husband.

Navajo men of Arizona engage in the custom of "prowling." The man creeps up to the sleeping woman, lifts her skirt, and looks at and fondles her vulva. The trick is to avoid waking the woman, as any man who is found out at prowling will be the butt of an onslaught of jokes leveled at him by members of the girl's household. Should he be caught at prowling, he will also be required to give the girl some valuable present. A man who succeeds at prowling, by contrast, will have a great story to tell at the girl's expense. Navajo women see prowling as a real and unwelcome threat, and if a strange man happens to be staying at their hogan overnight they will sometimes stay up all night rather than risk becoming a victim of a prowler. A form of prowling is also practiced by women among the Navajo but, in these cases, the Navajo no longer consider the behavior an accepted custom; rather, prowling by a female is regarded as an idiosyncratic activity.

Among the Crow, sleep-crawling, if found out, was punished by the household of the victim. A man who wished to try his luck at sleep-crawling would creep under the tipi near where the desired girl slept and try to touch her genitals. If the inmates of the tipi caught the sleep-crawler, they would lash his arms to a long stick, tie him up in a blanket, and turn him out. The response to sleep-crawling among the Truk of Oceania is a combination of derision and sympathy. A Truk man will only resort to sleep-crawling if he wishes to have sexual relations with a woman he feels certain will not otherwise welcome him. For this reason it is especially important that the man avoid being caught in the act. Other people feel sorry for men who sleep-crawl because the Truk assume that no one would resort to this strategy if he were able to persuade any woman to engage in sex with him voluntarily. The Chiricahua of the American Southwest also disapprove of what they call night-crawling and the act is considered contemptible. If a man is caught night-crawling with a virgin, his horses will be killed; if the girl is not a virgin, he will be beaten.

In a number of cultures, the custom of slipping into a girl's house and sleeping with her on the sly is an accepted part of courtship. For instance, once a Mapuche couple of Chile has agreed to be married, the boy will sneak into the girl's bed at night, with the aid of a mediator familiar with the girl's household, and sleep with her. A Cayapa boy of Brazil who is planning to marry a particular girl will also try to pass part of each night with his fiancee under her mosquito net. Among the Sherpa of Nepal, a boy will sneak into the bed of a girl who is sympathetic to his advances. Sometimes, as in the case of the Cayapa, the parents of the girl would be angered if they caught a boy in bed with their daughter. By contrast, Sherpa parents are aware of the activities of their daughters, but pretend ignorance of these nighttime affairs. While in each of these instances a boy attempts to sleep with a girl without being caught by other members of her household, these are not genuine cases of sleep-crawling, as the boy's activities are expected and solicited by the girl. In sleep-crawling, by contrast, a male tries to take advantage of a woman who is ignorant of his activities while they are taking place.

Barrett, Samuel A. (1925) *The Cayapa Indians of Ecuador.*

Fürer-Haimendorf, Christoph von. (1964) *The Sherpas of Nepal: Buddhist Highlanders.*

Gladwin, Thomas, and Seymour B. Sarason. (1953) *Truk: Man in Paradise.*

Leighton, Dorothea, and Clyde Kluckhohn. (1969) *Children of the People: The Navaho Individual and His Development.*

Lowie, Robert. (1912) *Social Life of the Crow Indians.*

———. (1935) *The Crow Indians.*

Opler, Morris E. (1941) *An Apache Life-Way: The Economic, Social and Religious Institutions of the Chiricahua Indians.*

Parry, N. E. (1932) *The Lakhers.*

Titiev, Mischa. (1951) *Araucanian Culture in Transition.*

SORORATE

In a majority of societies around the world, when a man's wife dies, the widower is required or expected to marry a sister of his deceased spouse. This custom is known as the sororate. Of 159 cultures, 63 percent have institutionalized sororate marriage for surviving husbands. In Afghanistan, a Basseri widower is generally required to marry a sister of his deceased wife regardless of his personal preferences. Among the Kaska of Alaska, a young widower asks the permission of his late wife's parents to marry one of her sisters, and such marriages are welcomed. If a Kimam man in New Guinea should become a widower, his former wife's family has an obligation to provide him with a new wife. If she is widowed, the choice will be his deceased wife's sister. In Arizona, Navajo widowers generally marry a real or classificatory sister of the dead wife. In some societies, sororate remarriage is at the discretion of the dead wife's sister. In the southwestern United States, a Chiricahua widower is "bound" to his dead wife's sister and must marry her if she so wishes, but the woman is free to refuse. The man is then required to marry any cousin of his former spouse who wants him for a husband. If no woman claims him, however, he is free to marry as he desires. Remarriage to a sister of his dead wife can be economically advantageous for a man if it saves him from having to accumulate the customary payment to the bride's family that is required of men in many cultures when they get married. For example, In North Africa, Rif grooms must present bride-price gifts to their in-laws, but a widower marries one of his dead wife's sisters without paying another bride price.

See also LEVIRATE; WIDOW REMARRIAGE; WIDOWER REMARRIAGE.

Barth, Fredrik. (1961) *Nomads of South Persia.*

Coon, Carleton S. (1931) *The Tribes of the Rif.* Harvard African Studies 9.

Honigmann, John J. (1949) *Culture and Ethos of Kaska Society.*

Leighton, Dorothea, and Clyde Kluckhohn. (1969) *Children of the People: The Navaho Individual and His Development.*

Murdock, George P. (1949) *Social Structure.*

Opler, Morris E. (1941) *An Apache Life-Way: The Economic, Social and Religious Institutions of the Chiricahua Indians.*

Serpenti, I. M. (1965) *Cultivators in the Swamps.*

SPOUSE BEATING

Many women around the world can expect to be beaten at least occasionally by their husbands. In some societies, physical abuse of wives is persistent and severe enough to cause serious injury to the woman. Wife beating has a long history. In ancient Babylonia a husband could beat his wife, pull out her hair, and cause her permanent physical harm without censure. Similarly, Turkish husbands can strike their wives with impunity. The woman cannot complain and cannot always prevent beatings by behaving well, as her spouse may also abuse her for no apparent reason. In Tanzania, Hadza wives are sufficiently nervous about beatings from their husbands that no woman will stay alone in camp with her spouse. Among the Lesu of New Ireland, physical abuse of a wife is an accepted feature of married life, even when a couple is happy together. As one Lesu husband put it, "Beating one's wife is the custom of marriage." In 81.16 percent of 69 societies, men are known to beat their wives.

Wife beating is more frequently found in cultures where the status of women is inferior to that of men. Where men are in control of the products of economic activities and where men make the domestic decisions, wife beating is more likely to occur. In Oceania, a Manus husband will hit a wife who does not "hear his talk," that is, who fails to heed his commands. Also in Oceania, a Truk man has the right to beat a wife who fails to perform her household chores or to show the proper deference, and women often appear in public with large bruises. Physical abuse of wives is also more commonly found in cultures where divorce is more difficult for women than for men and where the husband's kin group has control over the remarriage of his widow. In cultures that lack all-female work groups, wife beating tends to be present. The connection between the status of a wife and wife abuse is illustrated by traditional Chinese practices. Chinese wives are required to show deference to their mothers-in-law, with whom they live, in all matters, and a wife who disobeys her husband's mother will be beaten by her spouse. By contrast, Semang wives of Malaysia, who enjoy a high overall status, are never beaten.

Wife beating can also be viewed as a particular example of a more general tendency toward aggressive behavior within a culture. The physical abuse of wives is associated with the torture and mutilation of enemies during war. In societies where wife beating is common, people are more likely to resort to physical force in an attempt to resolve disputes, and men also tend to become violent when they have been drinking. Child rearing techniques in wife-beating societies also tend to be neglectful or to emphasize physical punishment, and children are more liable to undergo ceremonial piercing, burning, and cutting in these cultures.

The custom of wife beating is also connected to certain attitudes and practices concerning sexual behavior. In societies where husbands strike their wives, rules regarding premarital sex for girls tend to be restrictive and female sexuality is more likely to be regarded as dangerous. Extramarital sexual affairs for husbands tend to be condemned and absent where wife beating occurs. Impotence also tends to be a problem for men in wife-beating cultures and homosexuality is rare or absent. Physical abuse of wives also occurs in cultures where love magic is present.

There is a relative absence of wife abuse in extended-family households across cultures. By contrast, a wife is more likely to be beaten by her spouse in cultures where the nuclear-family prevails. This connection between family form and wife abuse also shows up within cultures. For instance, the !Kung Bushmen of southern Africa live in nuclear-family households during the wet season and in more closely packed extended-family settings during the dry season. Wife beating is more common in the wet season, where the nuclear family prevails. Perhaps this association between household composition and wife abuse reflects the idea that there is safety in numbers. That is, a man may be less prone to mistreat his wife when other people are present. It is also possible that the isolation of the nuclear household setting leads to greater frustration and impatience on the part of household members, so that an angry spouse may be more likely to vent his emotions in the nuclear-family context.

In some societies, the physical abuse of wives is interpreted as a reflection of the husband's affection for his spouse. A Yanomamo woman of Brazil and Venezuela who fails to respond quickly to her husband's commands can expect to be beaten by her spouse, perhaps with his bare hand or perhaps with a stick of firewood. Some husbands, however, hit their wives with a machete or burn them with the hot end of some wood that has been thrust into the fire. Or a husband may shoot his wife with a barbed arrow. Some women are seriously injured and even killed as a result of these physical assaults by their husbands. Yanomamo women take it for granted that they will be abused in this way by their spouses, and many wives measure the devotion of their husbands by the magnitude of the wounds and scars that they have incurred during beatings.

Even where wife beating is condoned by the members of a culture, a woman may have some recourse if her treatment at the hands of her husband is considered to be too extreme. Among the Yanomamo, the brothers of a woman may intercede and arrange for their sister to become the wife of another man if her husband is judged to be too brutal in his treatment of his wife. Hadza women depend upon their female kin to act as buffers against a husband's violence. The mother of a beaten woman may threaten to take her daughter back, and a woman's female relatives may band together and beat the husband with their digging sticks if his abuse of his wife becomes too severe. Or a woman may come to her own defense when she is abused. In Tanzania, some Chagga husbands beat their wives often. The Chagga say that the proper strategy for persuading a man to stop abusing his spouse is for the woman to give him a sound thrashing back. Wives may attempt to avoid a beating by other means. In Kenya, a Masai woman who expects that her husband will strike her because she has committed some serious misdeed will try to win his forgiveness by giving him an ox that she has gotten from her father.

Public opinion can also serve to inhibit the level of violence that a husband is willing to visit upon his spouse. If a Masai wife has been beaten by her husband, she may escape to the house of one of her husband's age-mates. The husband will think twice about hitting her again for fear of being criticized by his peers. Among the Paiute of the southwestern United States, husbands are often violent toward their wives, and pregnant women have had miscarriages after having been punched in the stomach by a husband. Men who are known to behave this way begin to acquire a reputation in the community, and this acts to some extent as a brake on wife beating.

Chronic abuse on the part of a husband may be tolerated if the wife is thought to be in the wrong. In the Caribbean, if a Carib husband physically abuses his wife, she can complain to her relatives, and they will intercede for her. If he continues to misuse her, they will turn him out of the village. But a husband who beats a chronically lazy wife will not be criticized. Among the Paiute, if a husband's abuse is especially frequent, the woman's parents may counsel her to leave her husband, or a brother may assault him. But if her family believes that she is to blame for her treatment, they may scold her, perhaps in public, justifying the husband's behavior.

Even when a wife theoretically has the option of seeking protection from her husband, women may be fearful of exercising their rights. Belau wives are beaten by their spouses, sometimes with sticks. The wife's family can demand a payment from a husband who is abusive, but women are timid about informing relatives of the abuse for fear of being further mistreated in retaliation. When Rwala husbands beat their wives, the women try not to make any audible sounds while being hit, as this might cause the husband to extend the beating or attract the attention of other men who might then help her spouse.

Wife beating also exists in a number of cultures in which the practice is officially condemned. All Guatemalan Quiche husbands have beaten their wives, at least occasionally, even though to do so is regarded as a mortal sin car-

rying with it serious consequences. People say that a husband might lose a spouse he has beaten, or he and his children might become ill or suffer some other misfortune as a result of his physical abuse of his wife. When asked why they beat their wives, Quiche men typically say that they didn't know what they were doing. A Rwala husband would disgrace himself and his kin if he were seen beating or even quarreling with his wife, and both his and his wife's relatives would banish him from the camp and the tribe. But husbands do beat their wives often and severely with the stick they use to drive their camels, although they do this in private, when there are no witnesses.

In some cultures, sanctions against wife abuse successfully inhibit husbands from mistreating their spouses. If a Chinese Lolo husband mistreats his wife, she is likely to inform her parents, in which case the members of her clan would seek revenge. Among the Popoluca of Mexico, a man who beats his wife may be sent to prison and fined. In Panama, a Cuna husband who beats his wife will be punished on the road to heaven. Wife abuse is absent in these cultures.

The beating of a husband by a wife is not commonly reported across societies. Perhaps this is because the practice is condemned more strongly than is wife beating. Konso men of Ethiopia will sometimes beat their wives and this is thought to be an acceptable practice, within reason. Cases are also known of strong women who beat their spouses, but this is regarded as reprehensible. Sometimes a wife will physically abuse her husband in retaliation for a beating that she has received. While it is difficult to find descriptions of husband beating in cultures around the world, this does not mean that wives don't physically attack their spouses. Information about husband beating in the United States suggests that it is as common as wife beating, but underreported. It is possible, therefore, that husband beating simply does not get the attention that wife beating attracts. It may also be that women, who are in general less physically aggressive than men across cultures, simply do not display violence toward their husbands. The fact that men are everywhere larger and stronger than women also means that a woman who tries to abuse her husband runs the risk of being abused back, and more seriously.

Barnett, H. G. (1949) *Palauan Society: A Study of Contemporary Native Life in the Palau Islands.*

Broude, Gwen J. (1975) *A Cross-Cultural Study of Some Sexual Attitudes and Practices.* Unpublished dissertation, Harvard University.

Chagnon, Napoleon A. (1968) *Yanomamo: The Fierce People.*

Erchak, Gerald, and Richard Rosenfeld. (1992) "Wife Beating: Its Relationship to Societal Complexity, Violent Norms, and Women's Power." Paper presented at the meetings of the Society for Cross-Cultural Research, Santa Fe, NM.

Fei, Hsiao-Tung. (1939) *Peasant Life in China: A Field Study of Country Life in the Yangtze Valley.*

Foster, George M. (1942) *A Primitive Mexican Economy.*

Gillin, John. (1936) *The Barama River Caribs of British Guiana.* Papers of the Peabody Museum of American Archaeology and Ethnology, Harvard University, 14(2).

Gladwin, Thomas, and Seymour B. Sarason. (1953) *Truk: Man in Paradise.*

Gutmann, Bruno. (1926) *Chagga Law.*

———. (1932) *The Tribal Teachings of the Chagga,* vol. 1.

Hallpike, C. R. (1972) *The Konso of Ethiopia.*

Hollis, A. C. (1905) *The Masai: Their Language and Folklore.*

Lester, David. (1980) "A Cross-Cultural Study of Wife Abuse." *Aggressive Behavior* 6: 361–364.

Levinson, David. (1989) *Family Violence in Cross-Cultural Perspective.*

Makal, Mahmut. (1954) *A Village in Anatolia.*

Marshall, Donald S. (1950) "Cuna Folk: A Conceptual Scheme Involving the Dynamic Factors of Culture, as Applied to the Cuna Indians of Darien." Unpublished manuscript, Harvard University.

Mead, Margaret. (1931) *Growing Up in New Guinea: A Comparative Study of Primitive Education.*

Murdock, George P. (1936) *Our Primitive Contemporaries.*

Naroll, Raoul. (1983) *The Moral Order.*

Powdermaker, Hortense. (1933) *Life in Lesu: The Study of a Melanesian Society in New Ireland.*

Raswan, Carl R. (1947) *Black Tents of Arabia.*

Saggs, H. W. F. (1962) *The Greatness That Was Babylon: A Survey of the Ancient Civilization of the Tigris-Euphrates Valley.*

Stephens, William N. (1963) *The Family in Cross-Cultural Perspective.*

Whiting, Beatrice B. (1950) *Paiute Sorcery.* Viking Fund Publications in Anthropology 15.

Whiting, John W. M., and Beatrice B. Whiting. (1975) "Aloofness and Intimacy of Husbands and Wives: A Cross-Cultural Study." *Ethos* 3: 183–207.

Woodburn, J. (1964) *The Social Organization of the Hadza of North Tanzania.* Unpublished dissertation, Cambridge University.

Yueh-hua, Lin. (1961) *The Lolo of Liang Shan.*

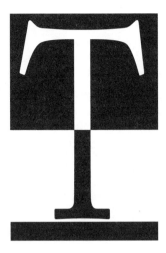

The attitude toward the transvestite varies widely in cultures in which the practice occurs. Among the Tanala of Madagascar, male transvestites wear women's clothing and do female chores. Some Tanala transvestites are also homosexual and take on the role of co-wife in polygynous households. The Tanala say that these men are feminine from birth and the society responds to them neutrally. The Amhara of Ethiopia assume that the desire of a man to dress and act like a woman must be the result of a biological mistake. They can appreciate why a woman might want to take on the more powerful role of a man, but why would a man wish to reduce himself to the status of a female unless there were something fundamentally abnormal? Thus, the transvestite is pitied. One case is reported of a Goajiro boy in Colombia who dressed in women's clothes and took on women's work. The females tolerated him but he was ridiculed by other males. In Oregon, a few Klamath men also lived as *berdaches*. Klamath transvestites were scorned and teased by other members of the community, but were allowed to live as they chose. Sometimes, an Eyak man of Alaska would live like a woman, doing women's work instead of hunting. These men were despised. Rarely, a woman will live as a man.

In some cultures, transvestites are permitted to marry. *Berdaches* were very uncommon among the Saulteaux, but some men did adopt the role, and they may have on occasion also taken husbands. Saulteaux folk wisdom claims that *berdaches* were always hermaphrodites, and the Saulteaux word for *berdache* means "split testicles." In the southwestern United States, Mojave transvestites were also allowed to marry as long as they had undergone an initiation ceremony. The Cheyenne Indians permitted married men to have a *berdache* as a second wife. Men who were impotent would also sometimes become transvestites. The status accorded them a place in society, and transvestite men outshone the women in their performance of daily pursuits.

TRANSVESTISM

The Mehinacu of Brazil tell the story of Tenejumine, whose father prayed for a daughter while having sexual relations. When he was grown, Tenejumine wore the belt characteristic of women's dress, painted his body in the style of females, and wore his hair in womanly fashion. He wove hammocks, ground manioc flour, and spun cotton, tasks reserved for the females in his culture. Women were fond of Tenejumine because he could fetch more water and carry more wood than any female. He was known to his community as Slightly a Woman.

Tenejumine is a classic example of a transvestite—that is, a male who dresses like a woman and takes on a woman's roles. Transvestites may, but need not, also engage in homosexual behavior. Among the traditional American Indians, transvestites are referred to as *berdaches*. In northern India, a special social category of men who dress and act like women are known as *hijras*. Transvestism tends to occur especially in societies that make minimal use of sex as a criterion for assigning roles.

A Zuni berdache—a man who dresses as and takes the social role of a woman.

In a number of cultures, a man who takes on the role of woman is regarded as especially powerful. Indeed, in some societies, a transvestite may also become a shaman. This is the case in Siberia with the Chuckchee transvestite, who, as shaman, has much power and status. The shaman dresses like a woman, affects female mannerisms and sometimes becomes another man's "wife." The two men engage in homosexual relations, but each is also likely to have a mate of the opposite sex with whom he has sexual intercourse. The Chuckchee attribute the characteristics of transvestites to the supernatural transformation of a conventional male, and other men are fearful that the same thing will happen to them. Some Alaskan Koniag boys are trained to take on a female role. They become proficient in women's work, dress in female clothing, and learn behaviors appropriate to the role of wife. When they are grown, they become the wives of important men. They are assumed to have special magical powers and are highly respected by other members of their community.

The *hijra* of north India exhibits many of the characteristics of transvestites in other cultures around the world. *Hijras* are considered to be neither men nor women; however, they dress and behave like women. The identifying characteristic of a *hijra* is his impotence, and *hijras* undergo the surgical removal of their genitals. They often earn a living by engaging in homosexual prostitution. *Hijras* form their own domestic units, headed by a guru, or teacher, who takes care of his charges much as any head of household cares for his dependents. The *hijra* is a quasi-religious figure, believed to be an instrument of Buhuchara Mata, the Indian mother goddess. *Hijras* perform rituals at important life-cycle transitions, such as at marriages or births. They are also thought to be able to curse people with sterility and other bad luck.

Birket-Smith, Kaj, and Frederica de Laguna. (1938) *The Eyak Indians of Copper River Delta, Alaska.*

Ember, Carol R., and Melvin Ember. (1988) *Anthropology,* 5th ed.

Ford, Clellan S., and Frank A. Beach. (1951) *Patterns of Sexual Behavior.*

Gregor, Thomas. (1985) *Anxious Pleasures.*

Linton, Ralph. (1933) *The Tanala: A Hill Tribe of Madagascar.*

Messing, Simon D. (1957) *The Highland-Plateau Amhara of Ethiopia.*

Munroe, Robert L., John W. M. Whiting, and David J. Hally. (1969) "Institutionalized Male Transvestism and Sex Distinctions." *American Anthropologist* 7: 87–91.

Nanda, Serena. (1990) *Neither Man nor Woman: The Hijras of India.*

Skinner, A. (1912) *Notes on the Eastern Cree and Northern Saulteaux.* Anthropological Papers of the American Museum of Natural History 9.

Spier, Leslie. (1930) *Klamath Ethnography.* University of California Publications in American Archaeology and Ethnology 30.

VIRGINITY Around the world, cultures vary widely regarding the value that they place on virginity in unmarried women. Of 134 societies, one-fourth are indifferent about whether or not girls remain virgins until marriage. Among the Marshallese of Oceania, for instance, every girl has already begun to be sexually active before puberty, and virginity in a bride is a foreign idea. The Tallensi of Ghana require the collaboration of a virgin boy or girl during the arrow medicine ritual, but a chosen child is only obliged to remain chaste until puberty, as no one would expect an adolescent to forego sexual relations. Instead, another youngster is recruited for the ceremony and the older one is released from the pledge of chastity. The Chuckchee of Siberia do not require virginity in a bride and, indeed, have no word for chastity.

While some societies place no value on virginity, 36 percent of the sample of 134 cultures think that virginity is important and 75 percent of these require brides to be virgins. In such cultures, tests of virginity are common. If a girl proves to be a virgin at marriage, the groom and his family may hold a celebration in her honor. If she fails to demonstrate that she is still a virgin, she and her family can often expect to pay a high price. Tests of virginity are common in societies that expect girls to be sexually inexperienced at marriage. All such tests require that the couple produce some blood-stained article of bedding or clothing as an indication that the girl's hymen was intact until the marriage was consummated. Among the Fon of West Africa, the groom sends the bride's father the mat on which the newly married couple have slept if the bride was indeed a virgin. If the couple had had coitus before the wedding night, the man gives the bride's father the cloth on which they first slept, which he had kept for this purpose. The girl's father is informed in the event that she was not a virgin, and the bride is required to disclose the name of the man with whom she has had sexual relations. She will be beaten until this information is divulged. On the first night of their marriage, the Basseri bride and groom of Afghanistan sleep in a tent that houses nothing but the girl's bedding and a white cloth on which the couple will lie. When the marriage has been consummated, a male relative of the groom shoots a gun. The women living in camp respond with a trilling sound. In the morning, the families of the couple check the cloth for signs of blood. The following narration of a conversation between Chinese Manchu brides and grooms captures the mood of the wedding night in a society that institutes tests of virginity in its unmarried girls. The groom opens the dialogue by inquiring of the bride whether she has had relations with anyone else before. The bride insists that she has not. "You are not telling me the truth," the groom returns. "I have heard that you have slept with someone before." "I will show you that it is not true if you think so," says the bride. She then places a bit of cloth beneath her body to absorb traces of the blood that will prove she is a virgin. Afterward, the cloth is buried behind the woman's house.

Public display of bloody cloth to prove bride's viginity following Bedouin wedding in Egypt.

Where virginity is valued and the bride proves to be sexually inexperienced, some kind of celebration may follow proofs of her virginity. If his bride proves to be a virgin, a Fur husband of the Sudan honors her with a feast. When a Tikopia groom of Oceania finds that his bride is a virgin, he is exultant. The happy groom wears a white *tiare* flower, whose petals are just beginning to unfold, in his hair. He will show off his adornment to the people outside his house and his reputation will be increased. If his wife was not a virgin, by contrast, then "there is no reputation for him." In the past, he might have smeared the blood produced by his virgin wife on his forehead. A north African Riffian couple consummate their marriage while the wedding guests are still congregated nearby. The appearance of the bloodstained marriage-bed cloth, which is passed among the crowd, evokes a celebration in response. In Suriname, if a Saramaka bride passes the virginity test, a feast and dances to all of the gods are attended by everybody in the village.

Where virginity is expected in a bride, the consequences can be very serious if a girl turns out to have been sexually experienced before marriage. In societies where the groom or his family transfer some kind of property to the bride or her family, the value of the bride price may be decreased substantially if the girl is not a virgin. Sometimes, the marriage is dissolved. A nonvirgin bride might also expect to be punished by her own family in some cultures. A Riffian groom who discovers that his wife has slept with someone before their marriage can send her back to her parents and have the bride price returned to him, or he can remain married to his bride but retrieve some part of the bride price. Among the Saramaka, a bride who was not a virgin could expect to receive fewer wedding presents from her new husband as well as some scolding or other punishment from her own family. A Goajiro husband of Colombia can request the return of half of the property that he gave to her

relatives if his bride was deflowered before her marriage. He can also take back the necklace that he gave to his bride when they were first betrothed. The bride-price payment for Zambian Lozi men is two beasts. One is the "beast of shame" and is given in return for the right of sexual intercourse with the wife. The other is the "beast of herding" and the payment for a virgin bride's fertility. If a bride is not a virgin, the payment is only the beast of shame. Among the Mao of Ethiopia, the father of a virgin bride receives a block of salt. For a nonvirgin daughter, he receives the salt in pieces; further, the salt has to be purified with goat's blood. The West Punjabi groom of south Asia can divorce a bride who is not a virgin. A Basseri man who unwittingly marries a nonvirgin can divorce her and keep the dowry.

Brides who are not virgins may also find themselves humiliated in front of other members of their community. Among the Saramaka, the other women talk about a girl who has not passed the virginity test and pull their lips at her the next morning. Her situation becomes the butt of gossip all over again whenever a quarrel breaks out. A Goajiro husband is deeply mortified to find himself married to a nonvirgin and wants his wife to feel the same shame that he does. He may nag at her about her prior sexual experience, repeatedly asking her why she was not a virgin when they were married. If he has been drinking, the husband may hound and ridicule his wife in public, singing insulting songs and rehearsing his grievances in front of his friends. Among the Fur, it is the wife's friends who contribute to her public humiliation by singing derisive songs. A Fon wife who was not a virgin at marriage can expect to have her husband and co-wives remind her of the fact whenever there is a quarrel. Sometimes, the repercussions for failing a virginity test take the most extreme of turns. Among the Rwala, the honor of the tribe hangs upon a girl's virginity. A girl who is discovered to have lost her virginity before marriage is liable to be killed by her father or brother and her body cut to pieces. Similarly, if a Kurd bride fails the virginity test, she is sent home; her kin are then expected to kill her.

If a groom is genuinely attached to his new wife, he may ignore the fact that she is not a virgin in spite of what custom requires. A Riffian husband who wishes to keep his bride's sexual status private might attempt to put off the formal virginity test until he can provide counterfeit evidence, although this is most likely to happen when the groom himself was responsible for her defloration. If he did not offer any proofs of his bride's virginity, the couple's status in the community would suffer. The Amhara husband of Ethiopia can annul a marriage to a nonvirgin, but a man who loves his bride may say nothing.

In some societies, virginity is only required of certain categories of women. For instance, in New Zealand, the Maori daughter of a high chief is required to remain a virgin if her parents wish to marry her to a high-ranking chief. In such cases, the girl is accompanied by female companions to prevent her from circumventing the prohibition.

More generally, societies that require virginity in their brides may take steps to increase the chances that girls do not have sexual relations before marriage. In some cultures, girls are chaperoned or otherwise segregated from the opposite sex. The Gros Ventre of the United States sent their prepubescent daughters to live with a female relative. Here, the girl was taught the various tasks traditionally performed by women in Gros Ventre society. But more importantly, she was isolated from men and closely watched by her guardian. The Somali insure virginity in their brides by practicing infibulation, a procedure that temporarily closes the vaginal opening.

Why is virginity valued in brides in some societies? The Goajiro male is attracted by the idea of having sexual relations with a virgin. In addition, there is the fringe benefit of the added prestige accruing to a man who has an untouched bride. In many societies, a husband is considered to have property rights over the woman for whom he has paid a bride price. If his wife has already slept with another man, the husband's claims have been infringed upon. Indeed, in some societies a husband can seek compensation from the former lover of his bride. The Igbo require virginity in their brides because they assume that a woman will not be untrue to the man who "breaks her virginity."

Barth, Fredrik. (1961) *Nomads of South Persia.*

Beaton, A. C. (1948) "The Fur." *Sudan Notes and Records* 29.

Bogoras, Waldemar. (1904–1909) *The Chukchee.*

———. (1929) "Siberian Cousins of the Eskimo." *Asia* 29: 316–322, 334–337.

Broude, Gwen J., and Sarah J. Greene. (1976) "Cross-Cultural Codes on Twenty Sexual Attitudes and Practices." *Ethnology* 15: 409–429.

Buck, Peter H. (1952) *The Coming of the Maori.*

Cerulli, Enrico. (1956) *Peoples of South-West Ethiopia and Its Borderland.*

Coon, Carleton S. (1931) *The Tribes of the Rif.* Harvard African Studies 9.

Erdland, August. (1914) *The Marshall Islanders: Life and Customs, Thought and Religion of a South Seas People.*

Flannery, Regina. (1953) *The Gros Ventre of Montana,* pt. 2.

Fortes, Meyer. (1936) "Ritual Festivals and Social Cohesion in the Hinterland of the Gold Coast." *American Anthropologist* 38: 590–604.

———. (1938) *Social and Psychological Aspects of Education in Taleland.*

———. (1949) *The Web of Kinship among the Tallensi: The Second Part of an Analysis of the Social Structure of a Trans-Volta Tribe.*

Gluckman, Max. (1959) "The Lozi of Barotseland in North-Western Rhodesia." In *Seven Tribes of British Central Africa*, edited by Elizabeth Colson and Max Gluckman, 1–93.

Herskovits, Melville J. (1938) *Dahomey: An Ancient West African Kingdom*, vol. 1.

Kahn, Morton C. (1931) *Djuka: The Bush Negroes of Dutch Guiana.*

Lewis, I. M. (1962) *Marriage and the Family in Northern Somaliland.*

Masters, William M. (1953) *Rowanduz: A Kurdish Administrative and Mercantile Center.*

Messing, Simon D. (1957) *The Highland-Plateau Amhara of Ethiopia.*

Oliver, Douglas. (1955) *A Solomon Island Society: Kinship and Leadership among the Siuai of Bougainville.*

Raswan, Carl R. (1947) *Black Tents of Arabia.*

Shirokogorov, Sergiei. (1924) *Social Organization of the Manchus.*

Uchendu, Victor C. (1965) *The Igbo of Southeast Nigeria.*

Wilber, Donald N. (1964) *Pakistan: Its People, Its Society, Its Culture.*

The experience of a newly married bride and groom on the night of their wedding varies widely from culture to culture. In some societies, a couple's first night together is their own business, while in others the relatives of the bride and groom, and also perhaps members of the larger community, intrude into the couple's privacy. The manner in which the wedding night is treated depends on the nature of the relationship of the couple before their marriage and on the degree of importance that the society places on the sexual status of the bride and groom. Where societies attach special significance to the wedding night, the focus of their interest tends to be on the consummation of the marriage or the sexual performance of the bride and groom. As a result, if the husband and wife are already well acquainted and have engaged in sexual relations before marriage, their first night together as man and wife is not likely to receive much formal attention. The Suiai of Oceania, for instance, take it for granted that a couple has already slept together before the ac-

tual wedding takes place; therefore, the wedding night does not have any special meaning for the society at large. Where a couple are sexually naive, by contrast, efforts might be made to counsel the pair on their first night together. Among the Khalka Mongols, a newly married bride and groom spend their wedding night in the company of the *bergen*. These are members of the wedding party who sleep in the tent with the new husband and wife and act as advisors and confidantes to the bride. The *bergen* persuade the girl to undress, offer helpful suggestions, and try to allay her fears by joking around with the girl.

The wedding night is especially likely to become a public affair if a society requires brides to be virgins. In these circumstances, proof of virginity is impatiently awaited by the couple's relatives or other members of the community. When a West African Fon couple gets married, the mothers of both the bride and groom keep watch on the night of the wedding. The next morning, the new groom presents the bride's father with the bloodstained mat on which the pair consummated their marriage. The new husband's sexual competence may also be tested on the wedding night. Among the Lebanese, the bloodstained sheet testifies not only to the bride's virginity but also to the groom's virility.

For a young and inexperienced girl, the wedding night can be anxiety-ridden. Ethiopian Amhara brides are often young and naive. While the first sexual experience on the night of their marriage is painful and embarrassing for these girls, the wedding night is a time of jubilation for the new husband. The morning after the marriage has been consummated, the young bride sits quietly with a serious look on her face. The groom, however, celebrates his victory by boasting to his friends as they stroll off, away from the house.

Sometimes, a bride and groom are unable to consummate their marriage on the wedding

327

night. A Riffian girl and boy of North Africa are often very shy with each other, with the result that the test for virginity may take place some time after the wedding itself. This is especially likely to be the case if the newlyweds are very young. Among the Kiribati, the expectation of shyness in a newly married couple is institutionalized. On the wedding night, the couple is urged by a gathering of spectators to overcome their modesty and consummate their marriage. But the relatives of the bride expect her to resist at first as an indication of her inexperience. Should she give in too quickly, they would be disgraced. When the groom finally does succeed in gaining sexual access to his bride, she utters a scream; this is taken as a signal for the groom's mother to inspect the sheets for the blood that is the evidence of virginity.

Some societies have instituted formal customs for deflowering a woman on her wedding night by someone other than the groom. The Australian Aranda bride is taken to the bush by some of her husband's relatives, where the men deflower her with a stone and then have intercourse with her. She is then taken back to her new husband.

While in most cultures the beginning of a marriage signals the start of a sexual relationship, for the south Asian Lakher bride and groom the opposite is true, at least in the first weeks after their wedding. In this culture, a newly married couple is expected to refrain from sleeping together for at least a month after their marriage, and some couples wait as long as a year. Otherwise, people would gossip about the unseemly haste with which the couple began to have intercourse. While they are honoring this custom, the bride sleeps in the house of her husband while he stays somewhere else. During this time, he courts her as if she were a stranger.

See also DEFLORATION CUSTOMS; SEX, PREMARITAL; VIRGINITY.

Coon, Carleton S. (1931) *The Tribes of the Rif.* Harvard African Studies 9.

Grimble, A. (1921) "From Birth to Death in the Gilbert Islands." *Royal Anthropological Institute of Great Britain and Ireland* 51: 25–54.

Herskovits, Melville J. (1938) *Dahomey: An Ancient West African Kingdom,* vol. 1.

Melikian, L. H., and E. T. Prothro. (1954) "Sexual Behavior of University Students in the Arab Near East." *Journal of Abnormal and Social Psychology* 49: 59–64.

Messing, Simon D. (1957) *The Highland-Plateau Amhara of Ethiopia.*

Murdock, George P. (1936) *Our Primitive Contemporaries.*

Oliver, Douglas. (1955) *A Solomon Island Society: Kinship and Leadership among the Siuai of Bougainville.*

Parry, N. E. (1932) *The Lakhers.*

Vreeland, Herbert H. (1953) *Mongol Community and Kinship Structure.*

WIDOW REMARRIAGE

When her husband dies, a Gheg Albanian widow could expect the brother, nephew, or cousin of her dead spouse to marry her. The male members of the deceased husband's family regard this as their responsibility, as a woman must remain in her husband's household to care for her children, and the Gheg find it unreasonable to expect her to remain celibate. As no strange men are permitted into the household, a resident of the house marries her himself. Among the Igbo of Nigeria, a widow is inherited by a son of one of her husband's other wives or, if no such sons exist, by one of her husband's brothers. Failing this, she can go home to her own parents. If she marries again, the bride price goes to her former husband's kin and not to her own family. Among the Garo of India, a widow may go to live with her daughter and son-in-law, and is referred to as the "wife" of her daughter's husband, although she does not typically have sexual relations with her son-in-law. The death of any individual is likely to be disruptive to the people who are left behind. When it is a husband and father who has died, the lives of the deceased man's wives and children are substantially affected, as are the financial arrangements between the families of the widow and her former spouse. Cultures often respond to the dislocations caused by the death of a husband by instituting strict guidelines for the proper disposal of widows. These include rules that determine whether and when a woman can remarry after her spouse has died, as well as who can and cannot become her new spouse.

In many cultures, it is considered unseemly for a widow to remarry until she has waited for some specified period of time after her husband has died, although what is considered an acceptable mourning period differs greatly from one society to the next. The waiting period is often viewed as a sign of respect to the dead man and his family, and when a woman marries before the mourning interval is over, her in-laws are likely to be resentful. Waiting periods also allow a widow to adjust to her new status and to take care of her young children without being distracted by a new husband and infant.

!Kung widows of southern Africa are expected to wait until one rainy season has passed before they remarry. The rain "washes the death away from the widow," who is then clean. An Ifugao widow of the Philippines who remarries before a year has passed since the death of her husband gravely insults her late spouse and his kin as well. A Khmer widow of Indochina may

remarry after three years spent in retreat. In Arizona, a Navajo widow was traditionally expected to wait two years before marrying or else she would be visited by the ghost of her dead husband. Among the Nicobarese of the Asiatic islands, a widow can remarry if she wishes, but she should wait until there have been several memorial feasts. This adds up to two or three years. In the past, a North American Omaha widow was expected to wait from four to seven years before remarrying to pay the respect due to her husband's memory. The waiting period also allowed a woman who was nursing to wean the child before she became pregnant by a new husband. If a woman did not wait for the allotted period, the relatives of her deceased husband could physically assault, but not kill, her.

In a few societies, widows are remarried almost immediately after the death of a husband. A Tiwi widow of Australia marries at the graveside of her former spouse. Siriono widows of South America may marry three days after the funeral of a husband. In both cases, the widow's next husband will be a brother of her dead spouse, making a quick remarriage easy to arrange. A Kapauku widow of New Guinea must wait ten days before remarrying, during which time she must display her grief by wailing as much as she can. If a woman remarries within three days of her husband's death, the sons or brother of her former husband will shoot her with an arrow and kill her. If a woman remarries after three but before ten days, people will gossip about her and call her immoral, and her late husband's kin will resent her bitterly. Kapauku widows who can still have children almost always remarry within six months after the death of a husband. One woman refused to take another spouse, moving in with her son instead. She was proclaimed a ghoul and accused of magically killing and cannibalizing children.

Many societies dictate which individuals are eligible to be the new mate of a widow. A majority of cultures have instituted the levirate, a custom requiring or recommending marriage between a woman and a brother of her deceased spouse. Among the Chiricahua of the United States Southwest, for instance, if a brother of a deceased man wishes to marry the widow, she is required to agree to the arrangement. But if she remains unmarried for a few years, she is no longer obligated to her brother-in-law and can marry any man who asks her. In many other societies, a marriage is arranged between the widow and some other relative of her dead spouse. Often, these customs reflect the feeling of members of the culture that it is the duty of the deceased husband's family to provide for his widow. A Gheg Albanian widow may marry a younger brother or other relative of her dead husband. If the dead man's family cannot find a new partner for the widowed individual, then the surviving spouse is owed a compensatory payment, unless the families of the widow and her former husband agree to end all marital obligations to each other. In this case, the widowed person is "set free" and can marry anyone. The relatives of a deceased person do not like to make such an arrangement, as it implies that they were not able to meet their responsibilities, and widowed women themselves prefer to have a new spouse provided for them. Where widows are expected to remarry a husband's kinsman, a woman may end up serially marrying a number of her male relatives. A Nyakyusa woman of Tanzania may be ten years younger than her husband if she is a senior wife and as much as 40 or 50 years younger if she is a junior wife. As a result, a woman may be widowed and inherited by the relative of a dead husband several times during her lifetime.

In cultures where widow remarriage to a relative of the deceased husband is the norm, a woman may be permitted to circumvent custom and marry another man of her own choosing. For instance, Banen widows of Cameroon are inherited by the sons of their former husbands, but they may go back to their own families if they desire. In Oregon, Klamath widows are officially required to marry a brother of the deceased husband or his nephew or other relative, but the woman has to agree to the arrangement, and circumstances might make marriage to her husband's relation unappealing. For instance, she might not wish to take on the role of secondary wife to a man who is already married. A widow who wishes to marry a man of her own choice does so without informing her husband's family, who might, if they knew of her plans, kill her intended new husband.

Where widows are expected to marry a relation of the dead spouse but do not, some kind of material compensation often must be paid to the husband's family. Or, if a bride price was paid to the widow's family when she first married her now dead husband, some or all of the payment might be returned to her in-laws. Among the Ifugao of the Philippines, a widowed person must pay the relatives of the dead spouse the *gibu* of the dead before a remarriage can properly take place. The *gibu* ends the obligation that exists between the still-living husband or wife and the soul of the dead spouse and also between the couple's two families. If a Gheg widow marries someone of her own choosing, then a payment is made to the family of the deceased spouse. A New Guinea Kwoma widow is expected to marry the oldest man belonging to her husband's lineage and generation. Should she marry someone else, however, the new husband must pay a bride price to the man who should properly have inherited her.

Even where a widow is theoretically free to marry someone other than a kinsman of her former husband, it may be difficult for the woman to do so. Chilean Mapuche widows can technically remarry within or outside of the husband's clan. However, if a woman marries outside the clan, she must relinquish any claims to her husband's land. Since a woman will have trouble arranging a marriage unless she has land of her own, especially if she is older or has many children, marriage outside the clan is, in practice, unlikely. Among the Cayapa of Brazil, the family of a deceased husband commonly responds to the remarriage of his widow with anger, and suspicions that the surviving wife may have caused her spouse's death are liable to surface among the dead man's kin. Thus, while a Cayapa woman is not prevented from remarrying (as long as the man has not been married before), most widows do not take a new husband. Cubeo widows of the Amazon are free to remarry after a waiting period of one year, but men are a bit afraid to marry a woman whose husband has died, so widows have trouble finding another spouse even though there are fewer marriageable women than men who want a wife.

Sometimes an eligible kinsman will try to pressure the widow into marriage because the arrangement is convenient for him. A south Asian Lakher widow may marry any man any time she pleases after the death of a former spouse. But a surviving brother of a deceased man may try to persuade the widow to marry him, as he will be saved the trouble of paying a bride price for a wife.

The degree of choice that a woman has in obtaining a new husband may depend upon whether she has dependent children. Among the Nuba of the Sudan, widows are required to marry a real or classificatory brother or other clan relative of the deceased husband, and women who do not wish to make such a match sometimes commit suicide. A woman who can no longer have children does not typically remarry but, rather, lives in her husband's house or moves in with a brother or son. Among the Tanala of Madagascar, a widow without children must get the permission of her in-laws before she remarries, but this is more or less a matter of politeness and a demonstration of respect for her dead spouse. If a widow has children, her former husband's parents can oppose her remarriage if they do not believe that her prospective new husband will make a good father, and they may pressure her to leave the children behind or to bring her new spouse to live with them.

Customs regarding the remarriage of widows may also depend upon the age of the woman. Among the Tanala, the marriage ceremony for a young widow is the same as it is for a first marriage. An older widow may move in with a man without benefit of a ceremony. The sentiment among the Tanala is that such women know what they want and should be left to do what they please, and relatives are in any event happy not to have to take care of the woman.

While it is the deceased husband's family that most often inherits the responsibility for taking care of a widow, sometimes the woman's own family shoulders the burden. The future of a Pakistani widow depends upon her current circumstances, including whether or not she has children (particularly sons), how well she gets on with her husband's relatives, and whether her own family can take her in. Her own brothers will want to provide for her if they can because of the *izzet*, or prestige, that is reflected upon them as a result.

In some societies the remarriage of a widow is unusual. A young Indian Burusho widow will eventually remarry, taking her nursing child with her but leaving her older children with her dead spouse's family. But an older widow is likely to "guard her husband's grave," living in the house that she shared with her husband or in a nearby home of her own with her single daughters and remaining a respected member of her husband's family. Remarriage is also infrequent among Tikopia widows of Oceania, even if the woman herself wishes to marry. This is especially true if she has young children. The broken earlobe of the woman indicates her decision to remain single. A widow's in-laws and her society at large think that the proper place for a mother is with her children in the household of her deceased husband. A woman who does remarry will leave her children with their father's relatives and make no subsequent formal visits to them in order to avoid the harsh words and blows of her angry in-laws. Inca widows were subsidized by the community in which they lived and only rarely married again.

In other cultures, there is no remarriage of widows at all, and sometimes the widow is expected to take her own life. A Korean woman whose husband has died may throw herself at her husband's grave as if to join him, although no woman in reality kills herself in this way. Widows are expected to avoid sexual relationships for the remainder of their lives, and remarriage is rare except among poorer people. In the past, a Maori widow of New Zealand was likely to kill herself when her husband died. A Fijian widow might have been strangled to death upon the death of her husband. Women were thought to sometimes prefer this fate, as a wife was believed to be reunited with her first husband at her death if she survived him, and a husband would be angry with a spouse who remained alive so long after him. A widow who was not strangled to death would often kill herself. Women who did not die with their spouses lived in shame, and were regarded as loose even if their behavior was in fact exemplary. A new mother, however, was not required to follow her dead husband to the grave, and was allowed, instead, to raise her infant without any discredit to her character. A Chinese Manchu widow cannot remarry if she has a son over 12 years of age.

By contrast, some cultures require a widow to remarry. In Suriname, a Saramaka widow marries her husband's brother or other kinsman, at least temporarily, after the mourning period. If there are no available relatives from her husband's line, a suitable husband must be found for her by the family of the head man. Otherwise, she cannot come out of mourning.

In some places around the world, widows are highly esteemed, as the status of a woman may actually be raised after her husband has died. Among the Khmer, a widowed woman becomes the head of her household and has the legal right to superintend any family matters. Such women are very powerful.

See also LEVIRATE; SORORATE; WIDOWER REMARRIAGE.

Altschuler, Milton. (1971) "Cayapa Personality and Sexual Motivation." In *Human Sexual Behavior: Variations in the Ethnographic Spectrum* edited by Donald S. Marshall and Robert C. Suggs, 38–58.

Barrett, Samuel A. (1925) *The Cayapa Indians of Ecuador.*

Barth, Fredrik. (1961) *Nomads of South Persia.*

Burling, Robbins. (1963) *Rengsanggri: Family and Kinship in a Garo Village.*

Coon, Carleton S. (1931) *The Tribes of the Rif.* Harvard African Studies 9.

Deane, W. (1921) *Fijian Society.*

Dorsey, J. Owen. (1884) *Omaha Sociology.* Third Annual Report of the Bureau of American Ethnology, 1881–1882.

Dugast, I. (1954) "Banen, Bafia, and Balom." In *Peoples of the Central Cameroons: Tikar,* edited by M. McCulloch, M. Littlewood, and I. Dugast, 134–153.

Dupire, Marguerite. (1963) "The Position of Women in a Pastoral Society." In *Women of Tropical Africa,* edited by Denise Paulme, 47–92.

Durham, Mary E. (1928) *Some Tribal Origins, Laws and Customs of the Balkans.*

Eglar, Zekiye. (1960) *A Punjabi Village in Pakistan.*

Firth, Raymond. (1936) *We, the Tikopia: A Sociological Study of Kinship in Primitive Polynesia.*

Fürer-Haimendorf, Christoph von. (1964) *The Sherpas of Nepal: Buddhist Highlanders.*

Gillin, John. (1936) *The Barama River Caribs of British Guiana.* Papers of the Peabody Museum of American Archaeology and Ethnology, Harvard University, 14(2).

Goldman, Irving. (1963) *The Cubeo: Indians of the Northwest Amazon.*

Green, M. M. (1947) *Ibo Village Affairs.*

Hart, C. W. M., and Arnold R. Pilling. (1960) *The Tiwi of North Australia.*

Hewes, Gordon W., and Chin Hong Kim. (1950) "Korean Kinship Behavior and Structure." Unpublished manuscript, Human Relations Area Files (New Haven, CT).

Hiroa, Te Rangi. (1949) *The Coming of the Maori.*

Holmberg, Allan R. (1950) *Nomads of the Long Bow.* Washington, DC: Government Printing Office.

Honigmann, John J. (1949) *Culture and Ethos of Kaska Society.*

Izikowitz, Karl. (1951) *Lamet: Hill Peasants in French Indochina.*

Kahn, Morton C. (1931) *Djuka: The Bush Negroes of Dutch Guiana.*

Kenyatta, Jomo. (1961) *Facing Mount Kenya: The Tribal Life of the Gikuyu.*

Leighton, Dorothea, and Clyde Kluckhohn. (1969) *Children of the People: The Navaho Individual and His Development.*

Linton, Ralph. (1933) *The Tanala: A Hill Tribe of Madagascar.*

Lorimer, Emily O. (1939) *Language and Hunting in the Karakoram.*

Marshall, Lorna. (1959) "Marriage among the !Kung Bushmen." *Africa* 29: 335–364.

Nadel, S. F. (1947) *The Nuba.*

Opler, Morris E. (1941) *An Apache Life-Way: The Economic, Social and Religious Institutions of the Chiricahua Indians.*

Parry, N. E. (1932) *The Lakhers.*

Potash, B., ed.(1986) *Widows in African Societies: Choices and Constraints.*

Shirokogorov, Sergiei M. (1924) *Social Organization of the Manchus.*

Spier, Leslie. (1930) *Klamath Ethnography.* University of California Publications in American Archaeology and Ethnology 30.

Steinberg, David J. (1959) *Cambodia: Its People, Its Society, Its Culture.*

Titiev, Mischa. (1951) *Araucanian Culture in Transition.*

Turney-High, Harry H. (1941) "Ethnography of the Kutenai." *American Anthropologist* 43(2) (Supplement).

Wilson, Monica. (1951) *Good Company.*

WIDOWER REMARRIAGE

In Western cultures a man is free to remarry whomever he pleases whenever he pleases after the death of his wife, or he may choose not to remarry at all. But in many cultures around the world, a widower's behavior is constrained by customs dictating who shall be his new wife and for how long he should mourn his dead wife before he can fittingly remarry.

Cultures typically require a man to wait for a specified period of time before taking a new wife. A Haitian widower officially mourns his spouse for a year. If he remarries before the mourning period is over, it is thought that his new mate will die. A Korean husband mourns for one and one-half years and may then remarry. In the southwestern United States, a Havasupai widower is expected to wait a decent period of time as a sign of respect for the dead before acquiring a new spouse, and the kin of the dead partner are likely to resent too quick a remarriage. The parents of the wife can request gifts from the new spouse if a son-in-law marries too quickly. In Arizona, a Navajo widower who does not wait for a decent period of time before remarrying is liable to be haunted by the ghost of his former wife. In the past, North American Omaha widowers were required to wait four to seven years before remarrying, a period equivalent to the mourning period for widows. His dead wife's relatives were justified in taking away a man's ponies if he did not respect this custom.

In the majority of cultures around the world, widows are required or expected to marry a sister of the deceased wife. In other societies, a widower can marry a woman of his own choosing, as long as she is a widow. This is the case, for example, with older Kaska men of Alaska whose wives have died. After the mourning period is over, a Korean husband may take a concubine for a mate. And Brazilian Cayapa widowers are permitted to take any woman as a new wife, as long as the woman has never been married before, although most Cayapa men do not remarry.

See also LEVIRATE; SORORATE; WIDOW REMARRIAGE.

Altschuler, Milton. (1971) "Cayapa Personality and Sexual Motivation." In *Human Sexual Behavior: Variations in the Ethnographic Spectrum,* edited by Donald S. Marshall and Robert C. Suggs, 38–58.

Barth, Fredrik. (1961) *Nomads of South Persia.*

Coon, Carleton S. (1931) *The Tribes of the Rif.* Harvard African Studies 9.

Dorsey, J. Owen. (1884) *Omaha Sociology.* Third Annual Report of the Bureau of American Ethnology, 1881–1882.

Herskovits, Melville J. (1937) *Life in a Haitian Valley.*

Hewes, Gordon W., and Chin Hong Kim. (1950) "Korean Kinship Behavior and Structure." Unpublished manuscript, Human Relations Area Files (New Haven, CT).

Honigmann, John J. (1949) *Culture and Ethos of Kaska Society.*

Leighton, Dorothea, and Clyde Kluckhohn. (1969) *Children of the People: The Navaho Individual and His Development.*

Opler, Morris E. (1941) *An Apache Life-Way: The Economic, Social and Religious Institutions of the Chiricahua Indians.*

Serpenti, I. M. (1965) *Cultivators in the Swamps.*

WIFE SHARING

In a number of societies around the world, a husband is permitted to lend his wife to a specific other man or to a particular category of men. Sometimes two men may exchange wives for a night. When a husband lends or exchanges his wife, he is practicing the custom of wife sharing. Wife lending or exchange appears in 34 percent of 101 cultures.

Where wife sharing occurs, the man who is granted sexual privileges to a woman is often a real or classificatory relative of the husband. Among the Banen of Cameroon, any male relative of a husband can have sexual intercourse with his wife if she is willing. Her spouse cannot prevent her from having sexual intercourse with these men. West African Mende husbands may share or lend a wife to a relative from time to time. A son is sometimes allowed to sleep with one of his father's wives, as long as it is not the boy's own mother. In some societies, two brothers who are especially close may share wives. A Truk man of Oceania might allow a sexually inexperienced real or classificatory brother to practice with his wife. Brothers may also receive permission to sleep with a sister-in-law as long as she is willing, and a husband may ask his wife to stay with one of his brothers when he is away on a trip. A wife's sisters are also supposed to be available to the husband, but such liaisons are in fact less frequent than are sexual encounters between wives and the husband's brothers. When he is old, a Nigerian Tiv man may allow his sons sexual access to his wife.

Sometimes wife sharing occurs between men who have a personal relationship. Two married Alaskan Kaska men who are good friends may sometimes exchange wives. A woman whose spouse has made such arrangements cannot say no; her husband is the "boss." On the other hand, the wife may herself be attracted to the man to whom she is being lent and, therefore, welcome the chance to be with him. These sorts of exchanges are often made when people have been drinking. In some cultures, men of the same age-grade are sometimes granted access to each other's spouses. In Zaire, Nkundo wives are lent to their husbands' age-mates when they come to visit while on a trip. The husband will say to the guest, "Here is your house; here are your wives." Husbands in this society, however, are not compelled to share their wives, but do so as a sign of friendship. Sometimes it is the wife herself who initiates a wife-lending arrangement. For example, when members of her husband's age-group or another special guest comes to visit, a Kenyan Kikuyu wife may invite a man of her choosing to stay with her for the night.

Wife-sharing customs often serve some function beyond the companionship and sexual satisfaction that the arrangement affords the recipient. Sometimes wife lending or exchange creates bonds of obligation between two men in other areas of life. Among the Khoi of southern Africa, two men from distant groups can form a bond of brotherhood. They kill a sheep and eat or drink from the same utensil. Men united in such a relationship have rights to each other's property and wives as well as duties to protect and show hospitality to one another. In the past, a Kimam man of New Guinea might request that a friend lend him his wife for a few hours.

The favor could not be refused. A wife was officially required to do her husband's bidding, but in fact the woman had to agree. Often, the friends exchanged wives. The lending of a wife bound the two men to each other so that either was expected to help the other whenever asked.

In some cases, a man will lend his wife in return for some favor. A Mende man of West Africa who has several wives may allow one or more to have a lover in anticipation of some reward to himself. The wife's lover may, for instance, help the husband to complete his work. A Kiribati man's paternal uncles are permitted sexual access to their nephew's wife, and the husband will encourage such arrangements, in part out of respect for his relatives but in part because he will receive additional land in the bargain.

Sometimes wife sharing helps to cement relationships between pairs or groups of men whose connection is otherwise uneasy or uncertain. Among the Aranda of Australia, when there is potential conflict between two communities, the men from one group will offer some of their wives to the enemy group as a way of attempting to diffuse hostilities. The success of the effort is measured by whether the women are accepted or rejected. In southern Africa, the infrequent !Kung custom of /kamheri permits men to exchange wives for a while, as long as the women agree. The remark of one !Kung husband highlights the peacekeeping nature of the custom, "If you want to sleep with someone's wife, you get him to sleep with yours, then neither of you goes after the other with poisoned arrows." Among the Tiv of Nigeria, the village head may lend his wife to a man who is visiting in the village as a demonstration of goodwill.

A society that approves of wife lending does not necessarily permit women other kinds of extramarital license. For instance, Australian Aranda husbands will lend wives to other men on their own initiative, but the same woman will be severely punished for any affairs that she may invite on her own. Indeed, the customs of wife lending or exchange are at first puzzling, as men across cultures typically place great value on the fidelity of their spouses. Darwin's theory of natural selection proposes that husbands ought to be especially sensitive to and intolerant of any extramarital sexual liaisons in which their wives might engage. This is because an unfaithful wife might become pregnant by her lover without her husband's knowledge. Her spouse would, as a consequence, be investing in a child that was not his. The fact that many instances of wife sharing include a concrete return to the husband helps to solve the puzzle of why one man would lend his wife to another man. Such arrangements net the lender some kind of gain in property or aid that helps him to support himself and his family.

Further, the tendency of some cultures to restrict wife sharing to related men is consistent with kin selection theory, which claims that related individuals ought to help each other. As relatives share genes in common, any act of one individual that benefits a relation also helps to increase the representation of the helper's genes in the gene pool. Further, if a woman becomes pregnant by a relative of her spouse, her husband will be investing in a child to whom he is genetically related and will be contributing to his own fitness as well as to that of his kin. Finally, the tendency for some cultures to permit wife lending between friends is consistent with natural selection theory. If the arrangement solidifies ties of loyalty and obligation, then men who have shared wives are contributing to their own future welfare by increasing the chances that they will be helped by their friends in times of need.

See also KIN SELECTION; NATURAL SELECTION; REPRODUCTIVE STRATEGIES; SEX, EXTRAMARITAL.

Abraham, Roy C. (1933) *The Tiv People.*

Broude, Gwen J., and Sarah J. Greene. (1976) "Cross-Cultural Codes on Twenty Sexual Attitudes and Practices." *Ethnology* 15: 409–429.

Dugast, I. (1954) "Banen, Bafia, and Balom." In *People of the Central Cameroons: Tikar*, edited by M. McCulloch, M. Littlewood, and I. Dugast, 134–153.

Gladwin, Thomas, and Seymour B. Sarason. (1953) *Truk: Man in Paradise.*

Grimble, A. (1921) "From Birth to Death in the Gilbert Islands." *Royal Anthropological Institute of Great Britain and Ireland* 51: 25–54.

Honigmann, John J. (1949) *Culture and Ethos of Kaska Society.*

Hulstaert, Gustave. (1928) *Marriage among the Nkundu.*

Kenyatta, Jomo. (1961) *Facing Mount Kenya: The Tribal Life of the Gikuyu.*

Little, Kenneth L. (1951) *The Mende of Sierra Leone: A West African People in Transition.*

Marshall, Lorna. (1959) "Marriage among the !Kung Bushmen." *Africa* 29: 335–364.

Murdock, George P. (1936) *Our Primitive Contemporaries.*

Nimendaju, Curt. (1946) "The Eastern Timbira." *University of California Publications in American Archaeology and Ethnology* 41.

WOMAN EXCHANGE

When a Mbuti boy of central Africa wishes to marry a particular girl, he is required to supply a sister or other female relative as a wife for one of the men belonging to the family of his prospective bride. A girl who is married without being exchanged in this way loses both status and security in her community. If either girl is unable to work diligently or to bear children, or if one of the wives decides that she wishes a divorce, both marriages are terminated unless a substitute wife can be found to replace the departing girl. Because of a shortage of potential spouses, Nigerian Tiv men also obtain wives by exchanging sisters with other men from different lineages. If a man has no available sister, he may substitute a mother's brother's daughter, although this is less preferred as a method for acquiring a spouse. The Mbuti and Tiv exemplify the custom of woman exchange whereby two women are swapped between the families or communities of two men who are looking for wives. Usually, each woman is the sister or real or classificatory relative of the man who exchanges her. Woman exchange is quite uncommon as a mode of obtaining a wife. It is found in only 3 percent of 542 societies around the world. Class stratification, individual property rights, and inheritance rules tend to be absent in societies that practice woman exchange. In most societies around the world, marriages are accompanied by the transfer of tangible property from the family of one prospective spouse to the relatives of the other. Where there are status differences between individuals in a culture, a person of superior power, privilege, or wealth can also barter these less tangible commodities for a desirable spouse. Since individuals in societies that practice woman exchange lack personal property or differential status, female relatives may serve as the substitute for other kinds of "goods" to be transferred at marriage. The threat that one wife will be removed from her husband and returned home should the other wife be abused or prove inadequate may make marriage arrangements less of a gamble, as each family will be less likely to try to cheat or offend the other. Woman exchange may also lend some stability to marriage, as the dissolution of one union usually means that the other marriage must also be dissolved.

Levinson, David, and Martin J. Malone. (1980) *Toward Explaining Human Culture.*

Murdock, George P. (1949) *Social Structure.*

Textor, Robert B. (1967) *A Cross-Cultural Summary.*

Turnbull, Colin M. (1965) *The Mbuti Pygmies: An Ethnographic Survey.* Anthropological Papers of the Museum of Natural History 50, pt. 3.

BIBLIOGRAPHY

Abraham, Roy C. (1933) *The Tiv People.*

Ackerman, Charles. (1963) "Affiliations: Structural Determinants of Differential Divorce Rates." *American Journal of Sociology* 69: 13–20.

Albert, Ethel. (1963) "Women of Burundi: A Study of Social Values." In *Women of Tropical Africa,* edited by Denise Paulme, 179–216.

Alford, Richard D. (1988) *Naming and Identity: A Cross-Cultural Study of Personal Naming Practices.*

Altschuler, Milton. (1964) *The Cayapa: A Study in Legal Behavior.*

———. (1971) "Cayapa Personality and Sexual Motivation." In *Human Sexual Behavior: Variations in the Ethnographic Spectrum,* edited by Donald S. Marshall and Robert C. Suggs, 38–58.

Ames, David. (1953) *Plural Marriage among the Wolof in the Gambia.*

Ammar, Hamed. (1954) *Growing Up in an Egyptian Village.*

Amoo, J. W. A. (1946) "The Effect of Western Influence on Akan Marriage." *Africa* 16: 228–237.

Arensberg, Conrad M., and Solon T. Kimball. (1940) *Family and Community in Ireland.*

Ayres, Barbara. (1974) "Bride Theft and Raiding for Wives in Cross-Cultural Perspective." *Anthropological Quarterly* 71: 138–252.

Bandelier, Adolph F. (1876–1879) *On the Social Organization and Mode of Government of the Ancient Mexicans.*

Barnett, H. G. (1949) *Palauan Society: A Study of Contemporary Native Life in the Palau Islands.*

———. (1960) *Being a Palauan.*

Barrett, Samuel A. (1916) "Pomo Buildings." In *Holmes Anniversary Volume, Anthropological Essays,* 1–17.

———. (1917) *Ceremonies of the Pomo Indians.*

———. (1925) *The Cayapa Indians of Ecuador.*

———. (1926) *Pomo Folkways.*

Barry, Herbert, III, and Leonora M. Paxson. (1972) "Infancy and Early Childhood: Cross-Cultural Codes 2." *Ethnology* 10: 466–508.

Barth, Fredrik. (1961) *Nomads of South Persia.*

Barton, Roy F. (1919) *Ifugao Law.*

———. (1938) *Philippine Pagans: The Autobiographies of Three Ifugaos.*

———. (1946) "The Religion of the Ifugaos." *American Anthropologist* 48.

Basedow, Herbert. (1925) *The Australian Aboriginal.*

Batchelor, John. (1927) *Ainu Life and Lore: Echoes of a Departing Race.*

Baxter, P. T. W., and Audrey Butt. (1953) *The Azande, and Related Peoples of the Anglo-Egyptian Sudan and Belgian Congo.*

Beaglehole, Ernest, and Pearl Beaglehole. (1938) *Ethnology of Pukapuka.*

———. (1941) "Pangai: Village in Tonga." *Polynesian Society* 2(4): 3–145.

———. (1941) "Personality and Development in Pukapukan Children." In *Language, Culture and Personality,* edited by Irving Hallowell and Stanley S. Newman, 282–292.

Beardsley, Richard K., John W. Hall, and Robert E. Ward. (1972) *Village Japan.*

Beaton, A. C. (1948) "The Fur." *Sudan Notes and Records* 29.

Belo, Jane. (1935) "A Study of Customs Pertaining to Twins in Bali." *Tijdschrift voor Indische Taal- Land- en Volkenkunde* 75: 484–549.

———. (1936) "The Balinese Temper." *Character and Personality* 4: 120–146.

———. (1936) "Study of a Balinese Family." *American Anthropologist* 38: 12–31.

———. (1949) *Bali: Rangda and Barong.*

———. (1953) *Bali: Temple Festival.*

Benedict, Ruth. (1934) *Patterns of Culture.*

———. (1952) *Thai Culture and Behavior.*

Bennett, Wendell C., and Robert M. Zingg. (1935) *The Tarahumara: An Indian Tribe of Northern Mexico.*

Bergman, Sten. (1938) *In Korean Wilds and Villages.*

Best, Elsdon. (1924) *The Maori.*

Birket-Smith, Kaj, and Frederica De Laguna. (1938) *The Eyak Indians of Copper River Delta, Alaska.*

Blanguernon, Claude. (1955) *The Hoggar.*

Bogoras, Waldemar. (1904–1909) *The Chukchee.*

———. (1929) "Siberian Cousins of the Eskimo." *Asia* 29: 316–322, 334—337.

Bohannan, Paul. (1963) *Social Anthropology.*

Bohannan, Paul, and John Middleton, eds. (1968) *Marriage, Family, and Residence.*

Bolinder, Gustaf. (1957) *Indians on Horseback.*

Bowers, Alfred W. (1950) *Mandan Social and Ceremonial Organization.*

———. (1965) *Hidatsa Social and Ceremonial Organization.*

Brant, Charles. (1951) "Burmese Kinship and the Lifecycle: An Outline." *Southwestern Journal of Anthropology* 7: 437–454.

———. (1954) *Tadagale: A Burmese Village in 1950.*

Briggs, L. L. (1958) *The Living Races of the Saraha Desert.* Papers of the Peabody Museum, Harvard University, 28.

Broude, Gwen J. (1975) "A Cross-Cultural Study of Some Sexual Beliefs and Practices." Unpublished dissertation, Harvard University.

———. (1976) "Cross-Cultural Patterning of Some Sexual Attitudes and Practices." *Behavior Science Research* 2: 227–262.

———. (1980) "Extramarital Sex Norms in Cross-Cultural Perspective." *Behavior Science Research* 13: 181–218; 15: 409–429.

———. (1981) *Cross-Cultural Study of Sex and Intimacy.* Paper presented at the 10th annual meetings of the Society for Cross-Cultural Research, Washington, DC.

———. (1981) "Cultural Management of Sexuality." In *Handbook of Human Development,* edited by Robert Munroe, Ruth Munroe, and Beatrice B. Whiting.

———. (1983) "Male-Female Relationships in Cross-Cultural Perspective: A Study of Sex and Intimacy." *Behavior Science Research* 18: 154–181.

———. (1983) "Roots: Some Correlates of Marital Intimacy and Aloofness." Paper presented at the 12th Annual Meetings of the Society for Cross-Cultural Research, Washington, DC.

———. (1986) "The Relationship between Male-Female Roles and Marital Intimacy and Aloofness." Paper presented at the 15th Annual Meetings of the Society for Cross-Cultural Research, San Diego.

———. (1987) "The Relationship of Marital Infancy and Aloofness to Social Environment: A Hologeistic Study." *Behavior Science Research* 21: 50–69.

———. (1990) "The Division of Labor by Sex and other Gender-Related Variables: An Exploratory Study." *Behavior Science Research* 24: 29–50.

———. (1990) "Protest Masculinity: A Further Look at the Causes and the Concept." *Ethos* 18: 103–122.

Broude, Gwen J., and Sarah J. Greene. (1976) "Cross-Cultural Codes on Twenty Sexual Attitudes and Practices." *Ethnology* 15: 409–429.

———. (1983) "Cross-Cultural Codes on Husband-Wife Relationships." *Ethnology* 22: 263–280.

Buchler, Ira. (1980) "The Organization of Social Life: The Perspective of Kinship Studies." In *People in Culture*, edited by Ino Rossi, 314–398.

Buchler, Ira R., and Henry A. Selby. (1968) *Kinship and Social Organization: An Introduction to Theory and Method.*

Buck, Peter H. (1952) *The Coming of the Maori.*

Bunzel, Ruth. (1952) *Chichicastenango: A Guatemalan Village.*

Burling, Robbins. (1963) *Rengsanggri: Family and Kinship in a Garo Village.*

Cagnolo, C. (1933) *The Akikuyu: Their Customs, Traditions, and Folklore.*

Carcopino, Jerome. (1940) *Daily Life in Ancient Rome: The People and the City at the Height of the Empire.*

Cerulli, Enrico. (1956) *Peoples of South-West Ethiopia and Its Borderland.*

Chagnon, Napoleon A. (1968) *Yanomamo: The Fierce People.*

Childs, Gladwyn M. (1949) *Umbundu Kinship and Character.*

Christensen, James. (1954) *Double Descent among the Fanti.*

Cipriani, Lidio. (1961) "Hygiene and Medical Practices among the Onge (Little Andaman)." *Anthropos* 56: 481–500.

———. (1966) *The Andaman Islanders.*

Cline, Walter. (1950) *The Teda of Tibesti, Borku, and Kawar in the Eastern Sahara.*

Collier, J. F., ed. (1988) *Marriage and Inequality in Classless Societies.*

Collinder, Bjorn. (1949) *The Lapps.*

Comaroff, J., ed. (1980) *The Meaning of Marriage Payments.*

Conzemius, Eduard. (1932) *Ethnographical Survey of the Miskito and Sumu Indians of Honduras and Nicaragua.*

Coon, Carleton S. (1931) *The Tribes of the Rif.* Harvard African Studies 9.

———. (1950) *The Mountains of Giants: A Racial and Cultural Study of the North Albanian Mountain Ghegs.*

Coppinger, Robert M., and Paul C. Posenblatt. (1968) "Romantic Love and Subsistence Dependence of Spouses." *Southwestern Journal of Anthropology* 14: 310–319.

Coughlin, Richard. (1965) "Pregnancy and Childbirth in Vietnam." In *Southeast Asian Customs,* edited by Donn V. Hart.

Covarrubias, Miguel. (1938) *Island of Bali.*

Culshaw, W. J. (1949) *Tribal Heritage: A Study of the Santals.*

Dallet, Charles. (1874) *A History of the Church in Korea.*

Daly, Margo, and Martin Wilson. (1983) *Sex, Evolution, and Behavior.*

Daly, Margo, M. Wilson, and S. J. Weghorst. (1982) "Male Sexual Jealousy." *Ethnology and Sociobiology* 3: 11–27.

Datta-Majumder, Nabendu. (1956) *The Santal: A Study in Culture Change.*

Davenport, William. (1952) "Fourteen Marshallese Riddles." *Journal of American Folklore* 65: 265–266.

Deane, W. (1921) *Fijian Society.*

De Smidt, Leon Sylvester. (1948) *Among the San Blas Indians of Panama, Giving a Description of Their Manners, Customs and Beliefs.*

Dickemann, Mildred. (1981) "Paternal Confidence and Dowry Competition: A Biocultural Analysis of Purdah." In *Natural Selection and Social Behavior,* edited by Richard D. Alexander and Donald W. Tinkle.

Dieterlen, Germaine. (1951) *An Essay on the Religion Bambara.*

Donner, Kai. (1926) *Among the Samoyed in Siberia.*

Dorsey, George A., and James R. Murie. (1940) *Notes on Skidi Pawnee Society.*

Dorsey, J. Owen. (1884) *Omaha Sociology.* Third Annual Report of the Bureau of American Ethnology, 1881–1882.

DuBois, Cora. (1944) *The People of Alor: A Social Psychological Study of an East Indian Island.*

Dugast, I. (1954) "Banen, Bafia, and Balom." In *Peoples of the Central Cameroons: Tikar,* by Merran McCulloch, M. Littlewood, and I. Dugast, 134–153.

Dundas, Charles. (1924) *Kilimanjaro and Its People: A History of the Wachagga, Their Laws, Customs, and Legends, Together with Some Account of the Highest Mountain in Africa.*

Dunning, R. W. (1959) *Social and Economic Change among the Northern Ojibwa.*

Dupire, Marguerite. (1963) "The Position of Women in a Pastoral Society." In *Women of Tropical Africa,* edited by Denise Paulme, 47–92.

Durham, Mary E. (1928) *Some Tribal Origins, Laws and Customs of the Balkans.*

Durham, William H. (1991) *Coevolution, Genes, Culture, and Human Diversity.*

Dyk, Walter. (1951) "Notes and Illustrations of Navaho Sexual Behavior." In *Psychoanalysis and Culture,* edited by George B. Wilbur and Warner Muensterberger.

Dyott, George M. (1926) *On the Trail of the Unknown in the Wilds of Ecuador and the Amazon.*

East, Rupert. (1939) *Akiga's Story: The Tiv Tribe as Seen by One of Its Members.*

Eglar, Zekiye S. (1960) *A Punjabi Village in Pakistan.*

Elmendorf, W. W. (1960) "The Structure of Twana Culture." *Washington State University Research Studies, Monograph Supplement 2.*

Elwin, Verrier. (1947) *Muria Murder and Suicide.*

———. (1947) *The Muria and Their Ghotul.*

Ember, Carol R., and Melvin Ember. (1988) *Anthropology.* 5th ed.

Ember, Carol R., and David Levinson. (1991) "The Substantive Contributions of Worldwide Cross-Cultural Studies Using Secondary Data." *Behavior Science Research* 25: 79–140.

Ember, Melvin. (1975) "On the Origin and Extension of the Incest Taboo." *Behavior Science Research* 10: 249–281.

Ember, Melvin, and Carol R. Ember. (1983) *Marriage, Family, and Kinship: Comparative Studies of Social Organization.*

Erchak, Gerald, and Richard Rosenfeld. (1992) "Wife Beating: Its Relationship to Societal Complexity, Violent Norms, and Women's Power." Paper presented at the meetings of the Society for Cross-Cultural Research, Santa Fe, NM.

Erdland, August. (1914) *The Marshall Islanders: Life and Customs, Thought and Religion of a South Seas People.*

Evans, I. H. N. (1937) *The Negritos of Mayala.*

Evans-Pritchard, Edward Evan. (1929) "Some Collective Expressions of Obscenity in Africa." *Royal Anthropological Institute of Great Britain and Ireland* 59: 311–331.

———. (1934) "Social Character of Bride-Wealth, with Special Reference to Azande." *Man* 34: 172–175.

———. (1937) *Witchcraft, Oracles and Magic among the Azande.*

———. (1965) "A Final Contribution to the Study of Zande Culture." *Africa* 35: 1–7.

———. (1971) *The Azande: History and Political Institutions.*

Faron, Louis C. (1956) "Araucanian Patri-Organization and the Omaha System." American Anthropologist 58: 435–456.

———. (1961) *Mapuche Social Structure: Institutional Reintegration in a Patrilineal Society of Central Chile.*

———. (1964) *Hawks of the Sun: Mapuche Morality and Its Ritual Attributes.*

Fei, Hsiao-tung. (1939) *Peasant Life in China: A Field Study of Country Life in the Yangtze Valley.*

Ffoulkes, Arthur. (1908) "The Fanti Family System." *African Society Journal* 7: 394–409.

Firth, Raymond W. (1936) *We, the Tikopia: A Sociological Study of Kinship in Primitive Polynesia.*

Fischer, Helen. (1992) *The Anatomy of Love.*

Flannery, Regina. (1953) *The Gros Ventre of Montana,* pt. 1.

———. (1953) *The Gros Ventre of Montana,* pt. 2.

Fletcher, Alice C., and Francis La Flesche. (1911) *The Omaha Tribe.* Twenty-seventh Annual Report of the Bureau of American Ethnology, 1905–1906.

Fock, Niels. (1963) "Mataco Marriage." *Folk* 5: 91–101.

Foner, Nancy. (1984) *Ages in Conflict.*

Ford, Clellan S., and Frank A. Beach. (1951) *Patterns of Sexual Behavior.*

Fortes, Meyer. (1936) "Ritual Festivals and Social Cohesion in the Hinterland of the Gold Coast." *American Anthropologist* 38: 590–604.

———. (1938) *Social and Psychological Aspects of Education in Taleland.*

———. (1945) *The Dynamics of Clanship among the Tallensi: Being the First Part of an Analysis of the Social Structure of a Trans-Volta Tribe.*

———. (1947) "Ashanti Survey, 1945–46: An Experiment in Social Research." *Geographical Journal* 110: 149–179.

———. (1949) "Time and Social Structure: An Ashanti Case Study." In *Social Structure: Studies Presented to A. R. Radcliffe-Brown,* edited by Meyer Fortes.

———. (1949) *The Web of Kinship among the Tallensi: The Second Part of an Analysis of the Social Structure of a Trans-Volta Tribe.*

———. (1950) "Kinship and Marriage among the Ashanti." In *African Systems of Kinship and Marriage,* edited by A. R. Radcliffe-Brown and Daryll Forde, 252–284.

Foster, George M. (1942) *A Primitive Mexican Community.*

———. (1942) *A Primitive Mexican Economy.*

———. (1959) "The Coyotepec Molde and Some Associated Problems of the Potter's Wheel." *Southwestern Journal of Anthropology* 15: 53–63.

Fox, Robin. (1967) *Kinship and Marriage: An Anthropological Perspective.*

Frayser, Suzanne G. (1985) *Varieties of Sexual Experience.*

Freeman, John D. (1958) "The Family System of the Iban of Borneo." In *The Developmental Cycle in Domestic Groups,* edited by Jack Goody, 15–52.

Freud, Sigmund. (1950) *Totem and Taboo*. Originally published 1910.

Fuchs, Stephen. (1942) "The Marriage Rites of the Bhils in the Nimar District, C.P." *Man in India* 22: 105–139.

Fürer-Haimendorf, Christoph von. (1948) "The Raj Gonds of Adilabad." In *The Raj Gonds of Adilabad*, 1–21.

———. (1964) *The Sherpas of Nepal: Buddhist Highlanders*.

Gabb, William. (1876) *On the Indian Tribes and Languages of Costa Rica*. American Philosophical Society Proceedings 14.

Gamble, David P. (1949) *Contributions to a Socioeconomic Survey of the Gambia*.

———. (1957) *The Wolof of Senegambia, Together with Notes on the Lebu and the Serer*.

Gaulin, Steven, and James Boster. (1990) "Dowry as Female Competition." *American Anthropologist* 92(4): 994–1005.

Gayton, Anna. (1948) *Yokuts and Western Mono Ethnography*.

Geertz, Clifford. (1959) "Form and Variation in Balinese Village Structure." *American Anthropologist* 61: 991–1012.

Geertz, Hildred. (1961) *The Javanese Family*.

Gessain, Monique. (1960) "Coniagui Women." In *Women of Tropical Africa*, edited by Denise Paulme.

Gillin, John. (1936) *The Barama River Caribs of British Guiana*. Papers of the Peabody Museum of American Archaeology and Ethnology, Harvard University, 14(2).

Gladwin, Thomas. (1948) "Comanche Kin Behavior." *American Anthropologist* 50: 73–94.

Gladwin, Thomas and Seymour B. Sarason. (1953) *Truk: Man in Paradise*.

Glascock, Anthony. (1984) "Decrepitude and Death-Hastening: The Nature of Old Age in Third World Societies." *Studies in Third World Societies* 22: 43–67.

Gluckman, Max. (1959) "The Lozi of Barotseland in North-Western Rhodesia." In *Seven Tribes of British Central Africa*, edited by Elizabeth Colson and Max Gluckman, 1–93.

Goldman, Irving. (1963) *The Cubeo: Indians of the Northwest Amazon*.

Goldschmidt, Walter. (1966) *The Culture and Behavior of the Sebei*.

Gomes, Edwin H. (1911) *Seventeen Years among the Sea Dyaks of Borneo: A Record of Intimate Association with the Natives of the Bornean Jungles*.

Goody, J., and S. T. Tambiah. (1973) *Bridewealth and Dowry*.

Gorer, Geoffrey. (1938) *Himalayan Village: An Account of the Lepchas of Sikkim*.

Graham, Walter. (1924) *Siam*, Volumes 1–2.

Gray, Robert F., and P. H. Gulliver. (1964) *The Family Estate in Africa*.

Green, M. M. (1947) *Ibo Village Affairs*.

Gregerson, Edgar. (1983) *Sexual Practices*.

Gregor, Thomas. (1985) *Anxious Pleasures*.

Griffis, William. (1882) *Corea: The Hermit Nation*.

Grigson, Wilfrid. (1949) *The Maria Gonds of Bastar*.

Grimble, A. (1921) "From Birth to Death in the Gilbert Islands." *Journal of the Royal Anthropological Institute of Great Britain and Ireland* 51: 25–54.

Gunn, Harold D. (1956) *Pagan Peoples of the Central Area of Northern Nigeria*.

Gusinde, Martin. (1937) *The Yahgan: The Life and Thought of the Water Nomads of Cape Horn*.

Gutierrez de Pineda, Virginia. (1950) *Social Organization in La Guajira*.

Gutmann, Bruno. (1926) *Das Recht der Dschagga* [Chagga law].

———. (1932) *Die Stammeslehren der Dschagga* [The tribal teachings of the Chagga], vol. 1.

Hallowell, A. Irving. (1955) *Culture and Experience.*

Hallpike, C. R. (1972) *The Konso of Ethiopia.*

Handy, Edward Smith Craighill. (1923) *The Native Culture of the Marquesas.*

Hart, C. W. M., and Arnold R. Pilling. (1960) *The Tiwi of North Australia.*

Haviland, William A. (1987) *Cultural Anthropology,* 5th ed.

Helm, June. (1961) *The Lynx Point People.* National Museum of Canada Bulletin 176.

Henry, Joseph. (1910) *The Soul of an African People. The Bambara, Their Psychic, Ethical, Religious and Social Life.*

Henry, Jules. (1941) *The Jungle People: A Kaingang Tribe of the Highlands of Brazil.*

Herskovits, Melville J. (1937) *Life in a Haitian Valley.*

———. (1938) *Dahomey: An Ancient West African Kingdom,* vol.1.

Hewes, Gordon W., and Chin Hong Kim. (1950) "Korean Kinship Behavior and Structure." Unpublished manuscript, Human Relations Area Files (New Haven, CT).

Hickey, Gerald C. (1964) *Village in Vietnam.*

Hiebert, Paul G. (1976) *Cultural Anthropology.*

Hilger, M. Inez. (1957) *Araucanian Child Life and Its Cultural Background.*

Hiroa, Te Rangi. (1949) *The Coming of the Maori.*

Hofer, Myron A. (1987) "Early Social Relationships: A Psychologist's View." *Child Development* 58: 633–647.

Hogbin, H. Ian. (1934–1935) "The Father Chooses His Heir." *Oceania* 11: 1–39.

———. (1934–1935) "Native Culture of Wogeo: Report of Field Work in New Guinea." *Oceania* 5: 308–337.

———. (1942–1943) "A New Guinea Infancy, from Conception to Weaning in Wogeo." *Oceania* 13: 285–309; 15: 324–352; 16: 185–209, 275–296.

———. (1944–1945) "Marriage in Wogeo, New Guinea." *Oceania* 15: 324–352.

———. (1945–1946) "Puberty to Marriage: A Study of the Sexual Life of the Native of Wogeo, New Guinea." *Oceania* 16: 185–209.

———. (1970) *The Island of Menstruating Men: Religion in Wogeo, New Guinea.*

Hollis, A. C. (1905) *The Masai: Their Language and Folklore.*

Holmberg, Allan R. (1950) *Nomads of the Long Bow.* Washington, DC: Government Printing Office.

Honigmann, John J. (1946) *Ethnography and Acculturation of the Fort Nelson Slave.*

———. (1949) *Culture and Ethos of Kaska Society.*

Howell, William. (1908–1910) "A Collection of Articles on the Sea Dyak." *Sarawak Gazette* 38–40.

Hudson, Alfred E. (1938) *Kazak Social Structure.*

Hulstaert, Gustave. (1928) *Marriage among the Nkundu.*

Hunt, E. E., David M. Schneider, Nathaniel R. Kidder, and William D. Stevens. (1949) *The Micronesians of Yap and Their Depopulation.*

Huntingford, G. W. B. (1951) "The Social Organization of the Dorobo." *African Studies* 1: 183–200.

———. (1951) "The Social Institutions of the Dorobo." *Anthropos* 46: 1–48.

———. (1953) *The Southern Nilo-Hamites.*

Hupka, Ralph B., and James M. Ryan. (1990) "The Cultural Contribution to Jealousy: Cross-Cultural Aggression in Sexual Jealousy Situations." *Behavior Science Research* 24: 51–72.

Huxley, M., and C. Capa. (1964) *Farewell to Eden.*

Izikowitz, Karl Gustav. (1951) *Lamet: Hill Peasants in French Indochina.*

Jankowiak, William, and Edward Fischer. (1992) "Romantic Love: A Cross-Cultural Perspective." *Ethnology* 31: 149–156.

Jenness, Diamond. (1922) *The Life of the Copper Eskimos.*

Jochelson, W. (1926) *The Yukaghir and Yukaghirized Tungus.* Memoirs of the American Museum of Natural History 13.

Junod, Henri A. (1927) *The Life of a South African Tribe,* vol. 1.

Kagwa, Apolo. (1934) *The Customs of the Baganda.*

Kahn, Morton C. (1931) *Djuka: The Bush Negroes of Dutch Guiana.*

Karsten, Rafael. (1935) *The Head-Hunters of Western Amazonas: The Life and Culture of the Jibaro Indians of Eastern Ecuador and Peru.*

———. (1967) *The Toba Indians of the Bolivian Gran Chaco.*

Kenyatta, Jomo. (1961) *Facing Mount Kenya: The Tribal Life of the Gikuyu.*

Kluckhohn, Clyde, and Dorthea Cross Leighton. (1947) *Children of the People.*

Kramer, Augustin, and Hans Nevermann. (1938) *Ralik-Ratak (Marshall Islands).*

Kroeber, Alfred L. (1908) *Ethnology of the Gros Ventre.* Anthropological Papers of the American Museum of Natural History 1.

———. (1909) "Classificatory Systems of Relationship." *Journal of the Royal Anthropological Institute of Great Britain and Ireland* 39: 77–84.

———. (1925) *Handbook of the Indians of California.*

Lane, R. B. (1965) "The Melanesians of South Pentecost." In *Gods, Ghosts, and Men in Melanesia,* edited by P. Lawrence and M. J. Meggitt, 250–279.

Larken, P. M. (1930) "Impressions of the Azande." *Sudan Notes and Records* 13: 99–115.

Leavitt, Gregory C. (1989) "Disappearance of the Incest Taboo: A Cross-Cultural Test of General Evolutionary Hypotheses." *American Anthropologist* 91: 116–131.

Lebeuf, Annie M. D. (1963) "The Role of Women in the Political Organization of African Societies." In *Women of Tropical Africa,* edited by Denise Paulme.

Lehman, F. Rudolf. (1951) "Notes on the Daily Life of the Nyakyusa." *Sociologus* 1: 138–148.

Leighton, Dorothea, and Clyde Kluckhohn. (1969) *Children of the People: The Navaho Individual and His Development.*

Leith-Ross, Sylvia. (1939) *African Women.*

Lester, David. (1980) "A Cross-Cultural Study of Wife Abuse." *Aggressive Behavior* 6: 361–364.

Levine, Nancy. (1988) *The Dynamics of Polyandry: Kinship, Domesticity, and Population in the Tibetan Border.*

LeVine, Robert A., and Barbara B. LeVine. (1966) *Nyansongo: A Gusii Community in Kenya.*

Levinson, David. (1989) *Family Violence in Cross-Cultural Perspective.*

Levinson, David, and Martin J. Malone. (1980) *Toward Explaining Human Culture.*

Levi-Strauss, Claude. (1945) "The Social and Psychological Aspect of Chieftainship in a Primitive Tribe: The Nambikuara of Northwestern Mato Grosso." New York Academy of Sciences *Transactions,* series 2, 7: 16–32.

———. (1948) *La Vie Familiale et Sociale des Indiens Nambikwara* [Family and social life of the Nambikwara Indians].

———. (1948) "The Nambicuara." In *Handbook of South American Indians,* vol. 3, edited by Julian H. Steward, 361–369.

Lewis, I. M. (1962) *Marriage and the Family in Northern Somaliland.*

Lewis, Oscar. (1960) *Tepoztlán: Village in Mexico.*

Lhote, Henri. (1944) *The Hoggar Tuareg.*

Lin, Yueh-hwa. (1961) *The Lolo of Liang Shan.*

Linton, Ralph. (1923) *Annual Ceremony of the Pawnee Medicine Men.*

———. (1933) *The Tanala: A Hill Tribe of Madagascar.*

———. (1939) "Marquesan Culture." In *The Individual and His Society,* edited by Abram Kardiner, 138–196.

Lipkind, William. (1948) "The Caraja." In *Handbook of South American Indians,* vol. 3, edited by Julian H. Steward, 179–191.

Lips, Julius E. (1947) "Naskapi Law: Law and Order in a Hunting Society." *American Philosophical Society* 379(4): 379–492.

Little, Kenneth L. (1951) *The Mende of Sierra Leone: A West African People in Transition.*

Loeb, Edwin M. (1926) *Pomo Folkways.*

Lorimer, Emily O. (1939) *Language Hunting in the Karakoram.*

Lowie, Robert. (1912) *Social Life of the Crow Indians.*

———. (1935) *The Crow Indians.*

Lumholtz, Carl. (1902) *Unknown Mexico: A Record of Five Years' Exploration of the Western Sierra Madre: In the Tierra Caliente of Tepic and Jalisco; and among the Tarascos of Michoacan.*

———. (1912) *New Trails in Mexico.*

Luzbetak, Louis J. (1951) *Marriage and the Family in Caucasia: A Contribution to the Study of North Caucasian Ethnology and Customary Law.*

Mace, David, and Vera Mace. (1959) *Marriage: East and West.*

McIlwraith, Thomas F. (1948) *The Bella Coola Indians.*

Mair, Lucy P. (1965) *An African People in the Twentieth Century.*

Makal, Mahmut. (1954) *A Village in Anatolia.*

Malinowski, Bronislaw. (1922) *Argonauts of the Western Pacific: An Account of Native Enterprise and Adventure in Archipelagoes of Melanesian New Guinea.*

———. (1929) *The Sexual Life of Savages in North-Western Melanesia: An Ethnographic Account of Courtship, Marriage and Family Life among the Natives of the Trobriand Islands, British New Guinea.*

Manoukian, Madeline. (1950) *Akan and Ga-Adange Peoples of the Gold Coast.*

Maretzki, Thomas W., and Hatsumi Maretzki. (1966) *Taira: An Okinawan Village.*

Marshall, Donald S. (1950) "Cuna Folk: A Conceptual Scheme Involving the Dynamic Factors of Culture, as Applied to the Cuna Indians of Darien." Unpublished manuscript, Harvard University.

Marshall, Lorna. (1959) "Marriage among the !Kung Bushmen." *Africa* 29: 335–364.

Marshall, William E. (1873) *A Phrenologist among the Todas.*

Masters, William M. (1953) *Rowanduz: A Kurdish Administrative and Mercantile Center.*

Materi, Irma. (1949) *Irma and the Hermit: My Life in Korea.*

Matthews, W. (1877) *Ethnography and Philology of the Hidatsa Indians.*

Maybury-Lewis, David. (1967) *Akwe-Shavante Society.*

Mead, Margaret. (1928) *Coming of Age in Samoa: A Psychological Study of Primitive Youth for Western Civilization.*

———. (1931) *Growing Up in New Guinea: A Comparative Study of Primitive Education.*

Meggitt, M. J. (1964) "Male-Female Relationships in the Highlands of Australian New Guinea." *American Anthropologist* 66: 204–224.

Melikian, L. H., and E. T. Prothro. (1954) "Sexual Behavior of University Students in the Arab Near East." *Journal of Abnormal and Social Psychology* 49: 59–64.

Messenger, John C. (1971) "Sex and Repression in an Irish Folk Community." In *Human Sexual Behavior,* edited by Donald S. Marshall and Robert C. Suggs, 3–37.

Simon D. Messing. (1956) "Ethiopian Folktales Ascribed to the Late Nineteenth Century Amhara Wit." *Journal of American Folklore* 70: 69–72.

———. (1957) *The Highland-Plateau Amhara of Ethiopia.*

Middleton, John. (1953) *The Central Tribes of the Northeastern Bantu: The Kikuyu, Including Embu, Meru, Mbere, Chuka, Mbiwi, Tharaka, and the Kamba of Kenya.*

———. (1965) *The Lugbara of Uganda.*

Miner, H. (1965) *The Primitive City of Timbuctoo.*

Minturn, Leigh, and John T. Hitchcock. (1966) *The Rajputs of Khalapur, India.*

Monteil, Charles V. (1924) *The Bambara of Segou and Kaarta: An Historical, Ethnographical and Literary Study of a People of the French Sudan.*

Morris, John. (1938) *Living with Lepchas: A Book about the Sikkim Himalayas.*

Mukhopadhyay, Carol C., and Patricia J. Higgins. (1988) "Anthropological Studies of Women's Status Revisited: 1977–1987." *Annual Review of Anthropology* 17: 461–495.

Munroe, Robert L., and Ruth H. Munroe. (1975) *Cross-Cultural Human Development.*

Munroe, Robert L., John W. M. Whiting, and David J. Hally. (1969) "Institutionalized Male Transvestism and Sex Distinctions." *American Anthropologist* 7: 87–91.

Murdock, George P. (1936) *Our Primitive Contemporaries.*

———. (1949) *Social Structure.*

———. (1971) "Cross-Sex Patterns of Kin Behavior." *Ethnology* 10: 359–368.

Murdock, George P., and Suzanne F. Wilson. (1970) "Settlement Patterns and Community Organization: Cross-Cultural Codes 3." *Ethnology* 9: 302–330.

Murphy, Robert F. (1960) *Headhunter's Heritage: Social and Economic Change among the Mundurucu Indians.*

Murphy, Robert F., and Buell Quain. (1955) *The Trumai Indians of Central Brazil.*

Murphy, Yolanda, and Robert F. Murphy. (1985) *Women of the Forest.* 2d ed.

Musil, Alois. (1928) *The Manner and Customs of the Rwala Bedouins.*

Nadel, S. F. (1947) *The Nuba.*

Naik, T. B. (1956) *The Bhils: A Study.*

Nanda, Serena. (1990) *Neither Man nor Woman: The Hijras of India.*

Naroll, Raoul. (1983) *The Moral Order.*

Nash, M. (1965) *The Golden Road to Modernity.*

Nath, Y. V. S. (1960) *Bhils of Ratanmal: An Analysis of the Social Structure of a Western Indian Community.*

Netting, R. M. C., E. R. Wilk, and E. J. Arnould, eds. (1984) *Households: Comparative and Historical Studies of the Domestic Group.*

Newman, Philip L. (1965) *Knowing the Gururumba.*

Niblack, Albert F. (1890) *The Coast Indians of Southern Alaska and Northern British Columbia.* Annual Reports of the Board of Regents, Smithsonian Institute.

Nicolaisen, Johannes. (1963) *Ecology and Culture of the Pastoral Tuareg.*

Nimmo, H. A. (1964) "Nomads of the Sulu Sea." Unpublished dissertation, University of Hawaii.

Nimuendaju, Curt. (1946) "The Eastern Timbira." University of California Publications in *American Archaeology and Ethnology* 41.

Nordenskiold, Erland. (1938) *An Historical and Ethnological Survey of the Cuna.*

Nydegger, William F., and Corinne Nydegger. (1966) *Tarong: An Ilocos Barrio in the Philippines.*

Oberg, Kalervo. (1953) *Indian Tribes of Northern Mato Grosso, Brazil.*

Oliver, Douglas. (1955) *A Solomon Island Society: Kinship and Leadership among the Siuai of Bougainville.*

Opler, Morris E. (1941) *An Apache Life-Way: The Economic, Social and Religious Institutions of the Chiricahua Indians.*

———. (1946) "Chiricahua Apache Material Relating to Sorcery." *Primitive Man.*

Orr, Kenneth Gordon. (1951) *Field Notes on the Burmese Standard of Living as Seen in the Case of a Fisherman-Refuge Family.*

Osgood, Cornelius. (1951) *The Koreans and Their Culture.*

———. (1958) *Ingalik Social Culture.* Yale University Publications in Anthropology 55.

Palmer, Craig. (1989) "Is Rape a Cultural Universal? A Re-Examination of the Ethnographic Data." *Ethnology* 28: 1–16.

Paques, Viviana. (1954) *The Bambara.*

Parker, Hilda, and Seymour Parker. (1986) "Father-Daughter Sexual Abuse: An Emerging Perspective." *American Journal of Orthopsychiatry* 56: 531–549.

Parry, N. E. (1932) *The Lakhers.*

Pasternak, B. (1976) *Introduction to Kinship and Social Organization.*

Patai, R. (1956) *The Republic of Lebanon.*

Paulme, Denise. (1960) "Introduction." In *Women of Tropical Africa,* edited by Denise Paulme.

Pierce, Joe E. (1964) *Life in a Turkish Village.*

Porter, Richard H. (1987) "Kin Recognition: Functions and Mediating Mechanisms." In *Sociobiology and Psychology,* edited by Charles Crawford, Martin Smith, and Dennis Krebs, 175–204.

Pospisil, Leopold J. (1958) *The Kapauku Papuans and Their Law.* Yale University Publications in Anthropology 54.

———. (1959–1960) "The Kapauku Papuans and Their Kinship Organization." *Oceania* 30.

———. (1963) *Kapauku Papuan Economy.*

———. (1964) *The Kapauku Papuans of West New Guinea.*

Potash, B., ed. (1986) *Widows in African Societies: Choices and Constraints.*

Powdermaker, Hortense. (1933) *Life in Lesu: The Study of a Melanesian Society in New Ireland.*

Putnam, Patrick. (1948) "The Pygmies of the Ituri Forest." In *A Reader in General Anthropology,* edited by Carleton S. Coon, 322–342.

Radcliffe-Brown, Alfred R. (1922) *The Andaman Islanders: A Study in Social Anthropology.*

Raswan, Carl R. (1947) *Black Tents of Arabia.*

Raum, O. F. (1940) *Chaga Childhood: A Description of Indigenous Education in an East African Tribe.*

Reay, Marie. (1953–54) "Social Control amongst the Orokaiva." *Oceania* 24: 110–118.

Reichard, Gladys A. (1928) *Social Life of the Navaho Indians.*

Rey, C. F. (1935) *The Real Abyssinia.*

Richards, Audrey I. (1939) *Land, Labor, and Diet in Northern Rhodesia.*

———. (1940) *Bemba Marriage and Present Economic Conditions.* Rhodes-Livingstone Papers 4.

Rivers, W. H. R. (1906) *The Todas.*

Romney, Kimball, and Romaine Romney. (1966) *The Mixtecans of Juxtlahuaca, Mexico.*

Rosaldo, Michelle Z. (1980) *Knowledge and Passion: Ilongot Notions of Self and Social Life.*

Roscoe, John. (1911) *The Baganda: An Account of Their Native Customs and Beliefs.*

Rosenblatt, Paul C. (1967) "Marital Residence and the Functions of Romantic Love." *Ethnology* 6: 471–480.

Rosenblatt, P., and D. Unangst (1974) "Marriage Ceremonies: An Exploratory Cross-Cultural Study." *Journal of Comparative Family Studies* 5: 41–56.

Roth, H. Ling. (1892) "The Natives of Borneo." *Anthropological Institute of Great Britain and Ireland* 21: 110–137; 22: 22–64.

Rozée-Koker, Patricia. (1987) "Cross-Cultural Codes on Seven Types of Rape." *Behavior Science Research* 21: 101–117.

Saggs, H. W. F. (1962) *The Greatness That Was Babylon: A Survey of the Ancient Civilization of the Tigris-Euphrates Valley.*

Sanday, Peggy R. (1981) *Female Power and Male Dominance.*

———. (1981) "The Socio-Cultural Context of Rape: A Cross-Cultural Study." *Journal of Social Issues* 37: 5–27.

Schapera, Isaac. (1930) *The Khoisan Peoples of South Africa: Bushmen and Hottentots*

Schlegel, Alice. (1991) "Status, Property, and the Value on Virginity." *American Ethnologist* 18(4): 719–734.

Schlegel, Alice, and Rohn Eloul. (1987) "A New Coding of Marriage Transactions." *Behavior Science Research* 21: 118–140.

Schlippe, Pierre de. (1956) *Shifting Cultivation in Africa: The Zande System of Agriculture.*

Schulze, Louis. (1891) "The Aborigines of the Upper and Middle Finke River." *Royal Society of South Australia, Transactions and Proceedings and Report* 14: 210–246.

Schusky, Ernest L. (1974) *Variation in Kinship.*

Scott, James George. (1910) *The Burman, His Life and Notions.*

Seligman, C. G., and B. Z. Seligman. (1932) *Pagan Tribes of the Nilotic Sudan.*

Serpenti, I. M. (1965) *Cultivators in the Swamps.*

Service, Elman. (1971) "The Trobriand Islanders of Melanesia." In *Profiles of Ethnology,* edited by Elman Service.

Sharp, R. L., et al. (1954) *Siamese Village.* Bangkok.

Shaw, Evelyn, and John Darling. (1985) *Female Strategies.*

Shirley, Robert W., and A. Kimball Romney. (1962) "Love Magic and Socialization Anxiety: A Cross-Cultural Study." *American Anthropologist* 64: 1028–1031.

Shirokogorov, Sergiei. M. (1924) *Social Organization of the Manchus.*

Shostak, Marjorie. (1981) *Nisa: The Life and Words of a !Kung Woman.*

Simmons, Leo W. (1945) *The Role of the Aged in Primitive Society.*

Simpson, G. E. (1943) "Sexual and Familial Institutions in Northern Haiti." *American Anthropologist* 44: 655–674.

Skinner, A. (1912) *Notes on the Eastern Cree and Northern Saulteaux.* Anthropological Papers of the American Museum of Natural History 9.

Slair, John B. (1897) *Old Samoa.*

Smith, Mary F. (1954) *Baba of Karo: A Woman of the Muslim Hausa.*

Smith, Michael G. (1955) *The Economy of Hausa Communities of Zaria.*

———. (1957) "Cooperation in Hausa Society." *Information* 11: 1–20.

Smithson, Carma Lee. (1959) *The Havasupai Woman.*

———. (1964) *Havasupai Religion and Mythology.*

Sokolovsky, Jay, ed. (1990) *Culture, Aging, and Society.*

Spier, Leslie. (1928) *Havasupai Ethnography.* Anthropological Papers of the American Museum of Natural History 29.

———. (1930) *Klamath Ethnography.* University of California Publications in American Archaeology and Ethnology 30.

Spoehr, Alexander. (1949) *Majuro: A Village in the Marshall Islands.*

Steinberg, David J. (1959) *Cambodia: Its People, Its Society, Its Culture.*

Stephens, William, and Roy G. D'Andrade. (1962) "Kin-Avoidance." In *The Oedipus Complex: Cross-Cultural Evidence,* by William Stephens, 124–150.

Stephens, William N. (1962) *The Oedipal Complex: Cross-Cultural Evidence.*

———. (1963) *The Family in Cross-Cultural Perspective.*

Stevenson, Matilda Cox. (1901–1902) *The Zuni Indians.* Twenty-third Annual Report of the Bureau of American Ethnology, Smithsonian Institute.

Stirling, A. Paul. (1957) "Land, Marriage, and the Law in Turkish Villages." *International Social Science Bulletin* 9: 21–33.

———. (1965) *Turkish Village.*

Stirling, Matthew. (1938) *Historical and Ethnographical Material on the Jivaro Indians.*

Stone, D. (1962) *The Talamancan Tribes of Costa Rica.* Papers of the Peabody Museum, Harvard University, 43.

Stout, David B. (1947) *San Blas Cuna Acculturation: An Introduction.*

———. (1948) "The Cuna." In *Handbook of South American Indians,* Volume 4, edited by Julian H. Steward: 257–68.

Suggs, Robert C. (1971) "Sex and Personality in the Marquesas." In *Human Sexual Behavior,* edited by Donald S. Marshall and Robert C. Suggs, 163–186.

Swanton, John. (1924–1925) *Social Organization and Social Usages of the Indians of the Creek Confederacy.* U.S. Bureau of American Ethnology, Annual Report 42.

Swift, M. G. (1965) *Malay Peasant Society in Jeleb.*

Symanski, Richard. (1981) *The Immoral Landscape: Female Prostitution in Western Societies.*

Symons, Donald. (1979) *The Evolution of Human Sexuality.*

Tanner, Nancy M. (1981) *On Becoming Human.*

Taylor, Douglas M. (1938) *The Caribs of Dominica.*

———. (1946) "Kinship and Social Structure of the Island Carib." *Southwestern Journal of Anthropology* 2: 180–212.

Textor, Robert B. (1967) *A Cross-Cultural Summary.*

Titiev, Mischa. (1951) *Araucanian Culture in Transition.*

Tobin, J. E. (1952) *Land Tenure in the Marshall Islands.*

Tooby, John, and Leda Comides. (1992) "The Psychological Foundations of Culture." In *The Adapted Mind,* edited by Jerome Barkow, Leda Comides, and John Tooby, 19–36.

Trigger, Bruce G. (1969) *The Huron: Farmers of the North.*

Trivers, Robert L. (1985) *Social Evolution.*

Tschopik, Harry, Jr. (1946) "The Aymara." In *Handbook of South American Indians,* edited by Julian H. Steward.

———. (1951) *The Aymara of Chucuito, Peru.*

Turnbull, Colin M. (1962) *The Forest People.*

———. (1965) *The Mbuti Pygmies: An Ethnographic Survey.* Anthropological Papers of the Museum of Natural History 50, pt. 3.

———. (1965) *Wayward Servants: The Two Worlds of the African Pygmies.*

Turney-High, Harry H. (1941) "Ethnography of the Kutenai." *American Anthropologist* 43(2) (Supplement).

Uchendu, Victor C. (1965) *The Igbo of Southeast Nigeria.*

Underhill, Ruth M. (1936) *The Autobiography of Papago Woman.*

———. (1939) *Social Organization of the Papago Indians.*

van den Berghe, Pierre L. (1979) *Human Family Systems.*

Venieminov, Ivan Evsieevich Popov. (1840) *Zapiski ob Ostravakh Unalashkinskago Otdiela* [Notes on the islands of the Unalaska district], vols. 2–3.

Vreeland, Herbert H. (1953) *Mongol Community and Kinship Structure.*

Wallace, Ernest, and Edward Adamson Hoebel. (1952) *The Comanches: Lords of the South Plains.*

Warner, W. Lloyd. (1937) *A Black Civilization: A Social Study of an Australian Tribe.*

Waterman, Thomas T., and Alfred Kroeber. (1934) *Yurok Marriages.*

Westermarck, Edward. (1922) *The History of Human Marriage.* Originally published 1897.

Whiteley, Wilfred. (1950) *Bemba and Related Peoples of Northern Rhodesia.*

Whiting, Beatrice B. (1950) *Paiute Sorcery.* Viking Fund Publications in Anthropology 15.

———, ed. (1963) *Six Cultures: Studies of Child Rearing.*

Whiting, John W. M. (1941) *Becoming a Kwoma: Teaching and Learning in a New Guinea Tribe.*

———. (1970) *Kwoma Journal.*

Whiting, John W. M., and Beatrice B. Whiting. (1975) "Aloofness and Intimacy of Husbands and Wives: A Cross-Cultural Study. *Ethos* 3: 183–207.

Whiting, John W. M., and Irvin L. Child. (1953) *Child Training and Personality.*

Whyte, Martin K. (1978) "Cross-Cultural Codes Dealing with Relative Status of Women." *Ethnology* 17: 211–237.

———. (1978) *The Status of Women in Preindustrial Society.*

Wilber, Donald N. (1964) *Pakistan: Its People, Its Society, Its Culture.*

Williams, Francis E. (1930) *Orokaiva Society.*

Wilson, Godfrey. (1936) "An Introduction to Nyakyusa Society." *Bantu Studies* 10: 253–291.

Wilson, Monica. (1951) *Good Company.*

———. (1957) *Rituals of Kinship among the Nyakyusa.*

———. (1959) *Communal Rituals of the Nyakyusa.*

Wolf, Arthur P. (1970) "Childhood Association and Sexual Attraction: A Further Test of the Westermarck Hypothesis." *American Anthropologist* 72: 503–515.

———. (1994) *Sexual Attraction and Childhood Association: A Chinese Brief for Edward Westermarck.*

Woodburn, J. (1964) "The Social Organization of the Hadza of North Tanzania." Unpublished dissertation, Cambridge University.

Young, Ernest. (1898) *The Kingdom of the Yellow Robe: Being Sketches of the Domestic and Religious Rites and Ceremonies of the Siamese.*

Yueh-hua, Lin. (1961) *The Lolo of Liang Shan.*

Zingg, R. M. (1938) *The Huichols.* University of Denver Contributions to Anthropology.

ILLUSTRATION CREDITS

7	Lila AbuLughod/Anthro-Photo
10	Stuart Smucker/Anthro-Photo
22	New China Pictures/Eastfoto
25	ITAR-TASS/Sovfoto
30	ITAR-TASS/Sovfoto
41	Irven DeVore/Anthro-Photo
66	Henry Bagish/Anthro-Photo
92	ITAR-TASS/Sovfoto
103	Irven DeVore/Anthro-Photo
106	Hank Meals
112	Lila AbuLughod/Anthro-Photo
118	Hank Meals
125	American Museum of Natural History
134	CTK/Eastfoto
136	Eastfoto
140	American Museum of Natural History
184	Library of Congress
194	ITAR-TASS/Sovfoto
202	ITAR-TASS/Sovfoto
203	Eastfoto
204	ITAR-TASS/Sovfoto
207	Irven DeVore/Anthro-Photo
210	Lila AbuLughod/Anthro-Photo
212	Sid Schuler/Anthro-Photo
225	Mark Jenike/Anthro-Photo
233	The Bettmann Archive
270	New China Pictures/Eastfoto
272	Hank Meals
318	Courtesy of the Southwest Museum, Los Angeles. Photo #LS.430.
322	Lila AbuLughod/Anthro-Photo

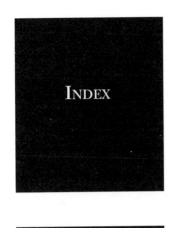

INDEX

Abkhaz (Eastern Europe)
  bride price, 41
  divorce, 75, 76
  extramarital sex, 83
  ideal spouse, 215
  marriages, 78, 219, 237
  rape, 252
Adolescents
  age-grade profile, 8
  heterosexual behavior, 3–4, 306
  homosexual behavior, 297–298
  See also Children; Females; Males
Affection
  in marriage, 4, 217
  public display of, 4–5
  same-sex, 6–7, 117–118
  See also Attachments
Affinal relationships, defined, 165. *See also* Marriage
Age
  bride price and, 41
  at marriage, 199–201, 220
  modesty requirements by, 229–230
  of remarried widows, 331
Age-grades
  associations based on, 19–20
  cultural expectations by, 8–10
  defined, 8
  elderly, 89
  wife sharing within, 335

Age-sets
  defined, 10
  initiation into, 10–11, 19–20
  retirement of, 13
  work responsibilities of, 12
Agricultural societies, 70, 126. *See also* Hunter-gatherer societies
Ainu (Japan), 49, 75, 93, 217
Aleut (Alaska), 48
Alor (Indonesia)
  attractiveness criteria, 31
  divorce, 77
  ideal spouse, 215, 216–217
  lesbianism, 299
  primary attachment, 28
  sexual attitudes, 280, 289, 295, 305
  work activities, 136
Altruism
  evolutionary perspective on, 13–14, 15
  between kin, 15–16, 161
  reciprocal, 14–15, 16–18
Amahuaca (Peru), 48
American (U.S. contemporary) culture
  age distinctions in, 8, 9–10
  elderly in, 89
  extramarital affairs in, 259
  families of, 102
  husband beating in, 314–315
  ideal spouse in, 217
  kin terminologies of, 168, 169, 170
  romantic love in, 265
Amhara (Ethiopia)
  bride theft, 39
  ideal spouse, 215, 217
  impotence, 147
  marital age, 200, 220
  prostitution, 247, 248
  sleeping arrangements, 108
  transvestism, 317
  wedding night, 324, 327
Andaman Islanders
  elderly, 90
  marriages, 17, 121, 201–202
  menstrual taboos, 224
Animal species
  alarm calling by, 164
  courtship by, 55
  kin identification by, 163
  reproductive strategies of, 256–259, 301–303
Anlo Ewe (Ghana), 94

Apache. *See* Kiowa Apache; Western Apache.
Aranda aboriginals (Australia)
  defloration customs, 64, 328
  divorce, 78–79
  marriages, 96, 207
  nudity, 228
  prostitution, 247
  sexual behavior, 297, 301
  wife sharing, 335–336
Arapesh (New Guinea), 41
Arawak (British Guiana), 90
Arunta (Australia), 90
Ashanti (Ghana)
  bride price, 42
  divorce, 75, 76
  incest taboo, 149–150
  marriages, 17, 98, 219–220
  sibling attachments, 27
Associations
  age-grade basis of, 19–20
  guilds, 21–22
  military, 22–23
  same-sex, 20, 21
  secret, 23
  voluntary membership in, 19, 21–23
Attachments
  friendship, 28, 117–119, 140
  kin-group, 27–28, 103, 104
  marital, 4, 24, 103, 217
  nonmarital, 5, 24–26
  primary, 24–28, 266
  of romantic love, 265–267
  same-sex, 6–7, 117–118
  sibling, 26–27, 140–141
Attractiveness
  cleanliness as criterion for, 216–217
  cultural variances of, 29
  as spouse criterion, 215–216
  universal indices of, 31–32
Avoidance relationships, 32–35. *See also* Parents-in-law
Aweikoma (Brazil)
  divorce, 78
  marriages, 153, 211
  sexual behavior, 6, 294, 301
Aymara (Peru), 175
Azande (Zaire)
  attractiveness criteria, 31
  bride price, 41–42
  impotence, 147
  incest, 148

  lesbianism, 299
  marriages, 177, 190, 207, 208, 209, 219, 220–221
  sexual behavior, 82, 273
  sleeping arrangements, 109
Aztecs (Mexico), 75, 190–191, 195

Babylonians, 50, 252, 312
Badjau (Philippines)
  divorce, 76, 77
  fathers-to-be, 110–111
  public display of affection, 4
  sexual behavior, 116, 294, 304
Baiga (India), 153–154
Balinese (Indonesia)
  chaperonage, 47
  leisure activities, 181
  love magic, 175
  marriages, 39–40, 42, 48–49, 144, 191, 199
  public display of affection, 5, 6
  sexual initiation, 280, 288–289
  sleeping arrangements, 108
  status of women, 185
Bambara (West Africa)
  ideal spouse, 215–216
  impotence, 148
  marriages, 190, 193, 208–209
  sex taboos, 291
Banen (Cameroon), 330, 334
Basseri (Afghanistan), 311, 321
Bedouin (Middle East), 147, 196
Belauans, 133, 183, 248
Bellacoola (northwest North America), 193
Bemba (Zambia)
  household arrangements, 125, 269–270
  primary attachment, 24–25
  prostitution, 247
  sexual attitudes, 274
Betrothal, 37, 48–49
Bhil (India)
  kin group attachments, 27–28
  marriages, 40, 214
  sexual attitudes, 274
  work activities, 133, 135
Bipedalism, 127–128, 129, 130
Birth control, 3
Boasting, sexual, 38–39
Body painting, 55
Bontoc Igorot (Philippines), 90
Bororo (Brazil), 242, 247

Boys. *See* Males
Bribri (Central America), 181, 203
Bride capture, 39–40
Bride price
    versus bride service, 44
    as divorce issue, 42–43, 77
    versus dowry, 87
    function of, 40
    in half-marriage, 206
    levirate custom and, 174, 330
    for nonvirgins, 323
    obligations of, 42, 94
    offspring and, 17
    as premarital pregnancy issue, 244, 283
    sororate custom and, 312
    types and value of, 41–42
Bride service, 43–44
Brno (Czechoslovakia), 62
Burmese
    chaperonage, 47
    divorce, 75, 76–77
    elopement, 96
    ideal spouse, 217
    marriages, 62, 156
    sexual attitudes, 296, 304
Burundi (Zaire), 242
Burusho (India)
    fathers-to-be, 111
    ideal spouse, 215
    marriages, 192, 235
    sleeping arrangements, 108–109
    widowhood, 331

Callinago (Caribbean), 215, 245
Canoe building, 292
Caraja (Brazil), 253
Caribs, 3, 314
Castes, marriages within, 48–49
Castration anxiety, menstrual taboos and, 226
Cayapa (Brazil)
    affection bonds, 6–7
    barren wives, 74–75
    courtship, 54
    divorce, 79
    ideal spouse, 214
    marriages, 193–194
    sleep-crawling, 311
    widowhood, 331, 334
Chagga (Tanzania)
    avoidance relationships, 33

    bride price, 42
    courtship, 55–56
    divorce, 75, 76
    joking relationships, 159
    kin attachments, 24–25, 118
    marriages, 209
    sexual behavior, 4
    wife beating, 313
Chaperons, 47
Cheyenne (U.S. Plains), 22–23, 41, 317
Childbirth
    fathers present at, 110–111
    postpartum taboo, 290–291
Childhood familiarity theory, 150–151
Children
    age-set initiation of, 11
    betrothal of, 48–49, 190
    bride price and, 17
    courtship by, 54–55, 56
    of divorce, 76
    of extramarital relationships, 57, 58, 157, 246
    fathers' relationship with, 263–264
    household arrangements for, 108–109, 123–125, 143, 269–270, 271
    physical affection between, 6–7
    of polygynous marriages, 211, 213
    of premarital pregnancies, 84–85, 244–245, 282
    of rape victims, 252
    sex segregation of, 271–273
    sex training of, 293–295
    status conferred by, 190, 242
    of widows, 331
    See also Adolescents; Females; Males
Chimpanzees, 127, 129
Chinese
    concubinage, 50, 266
    divorce, 76
    in-law relationships, 241
    levirate custom of, 174
    marriages, 48, 192, 195
    same-sex affection, 6
    sleeping arrangements, 108, 269
    wife beating, 312
Chiricahua (southwestern United States)
    attractiveness criteria, 31, 217
    avoidance customs, 33
    chaperonage, 47
    homosexuality, 296–297
    marriages, 78, 155, 311–312
    modesty, 227, 229–230

Chiricahua *(continued)*
  mother-son attachment of, 26
  public display of affection, 4
  rape, 252
  sexual behavior, 52, 276, 279, 281, 288
  sexual conversations, 285
  sexual double standard, 58, 84
  sleep-crawling, 310–311
  spouse selection, 220
  widowhood, 330
Chuckchee (Siberia)
  attractiveness criteria, 31, 32
  bride service, 44
  child betrothal, 48, 49
  divorce, 76
  elderly, 90, 93
  lesbianism, 299
  marriages, 193, 204, 212
  spouse selection, 216, 321
  status of women, 61
  transvestism, 318
Circumcision, as age-set initiation, 11
Clan, 69–70
  defined, 66–67
  See also Descent groups
Clitoridectomy
  as age-set initiation, 11–12
  as reproductive strategy, 258
Clothing, and modesty, 228, 229–230
Comanche (U.S. Plains)
  courtship, 56
  kin attachments, 27
  leisure activities, 180
  marriages, 200, 221
  sexual initiation, 288, 289
Complementary filiation principle, 65
Compromise group, defined, 67. *See also* Descent
  groups
Concubinage, 49–50
Coniagui (New Guinea), 177
Conjugal violence, 312–315
Consanguineal relationships
  defined, 165
  two types of, 167
  See also Kin
Contraception, 3
Copper Eskimo. *See* Eskimo groups
Courtship
  gifts during, 55, 121, 201, 205, 249, 257
  male-female interpretation of, 56

  participants' ages, 54–55
  sleep-crawling during, 311
  timing of, 53–54
Credit unions, 22
Creek (North America), 26, 93, 248
Crow (U.S. Plains)
  elderly, 38, 93, 94
  kinship terminology, 171
  marriages, 208
  sexual attitudes, 38, 288
  sleep-crawling, 310
Cubeo (Amazon)
  defloration customs, 63
  ideal spouse, 215, 216
  lesbianism, 299
  marriages, 196, 197, 219
  sexual attitudes, 5, 188
  widowhood, 331
Cuckoldry, 56–58
Cuna (Panama)
  divorce, 74
  love magic, 175
  modesty, 229
  rape, 251
  sexual attitudes, 273, 291, 292
  unmarried pregnancy, 244

Dahomey (West Africa), 289, 299
Darwin, Charles
  on adaptive traits, 161
  on differential reproductive success, 85
  evolution by natural selection theory of, 71, 231
  fitness concept of, 57, 58, 115–116, 231
  See also Evolution by natural selection
Defloration customs, 63–64, 300, 328
Descent groups
  ambilineal, 65–66, 68
  bilateral, 67–69, 172
  matrilineal, 25, 67, 68, 70, 171, 186
  patrilineal, 65, 67, 68, 70, 170–171
  unilineal, 65–66, 67, 171
  various functions of, 69–70
  See also Kin
Differential reproductive success, 71–73, 85, 231, 336
Division of labor, 130, 133, 135–137, 178
Divorce
  children of, 76
  culturally permitted, 73–74
  grounds for, 74–76, 78–79, 155
  property distribution in, 76–77

Dorobo (Kenya), 109, 286, 300
Dowry, 87
    See also Bride price
Dragaletvsy (Hungary), 62

East Africa, age-grades in, 10
Eastern cultures, romantic love in, 265–266
East Pomo (California), 236
Eating arrangements
    husband-wife, 132–133, 140, 223
    menstrual taboos and, 225
Egyptians, 62, 78, 282
Elderly
    age-grade profile of, 8, 9, 20
    age-set responsibilities of, 12
    as co-wives, 95
    determinants of, 89
    economic contribution by, 91, 93
    food exemptions for, 93–94
    as property owners, 90, 94
    respect for, 90–91, 264
Elephant seals, reproduction strategies of, 256–257
Elopement, 95–97
Endogamy, 97–98
Eskimo groups
    bride service among, 44
    elderly, 90–91, 93–94
    ideal spouse, 215, 216
    kinship terminology of, 172
    male sexual aggression of, 257
    marriages, 207, 261
Evolution by natural selection
    of adaptive traits, 161, 308
    based on differential reproductive success, 71–73, 85, 231, 336
    of bipedalism, 127–128, 129–130
    as environment-driven, 231–232, 234–235
    versus kin selection, 161–164
    versus sexual selection, 308, 309
    See also Reproduction
Exogamy, 99, 283
Extended family, 101, 126
Eyak (Alaska), 108, 317

Families
    as ambiguous term, 102
    definition and types of, 101
    nuclear, 101, 102–103, 126, 313
    of orientation or procreation, 165, 167

residences of, 104–105, 107
    See also Households
Fang (Cameroon), 248
Fathers
    bilateral descent from, 67
    at childbirth, 110–111
    of illegitimate children, 244, 282
    patrilineal descent from, 65, 67, 70
    respect relationship with, 94, 263–264
Fathers-in-law. *See* Parents-in-law
Females
    adolescent sexual behavior, 3–4
    age-grade profiles of, 9
    in arranged marriages, 192–195, 219–220, 259, 267, 282
    attractiveness criteria for, 31
    chaperons of, 47
    as concubines, 49–50
    courtship, 53–56
    defloration customs, 63–64
    and differential reproductive success, 73, 131
    elderly, 91
    in female-based societies, 20–21
    fertility, 301–303
    first sexual partner, 300–301
    friendships, 118, 119
    lesbian relationships, 298–299
    marital age, 199–200
    marriage partner selection, 219, 220, 221
    in men's houses, 223
    and menstrual taboos, 224–226
    and modesty, 227–230
    and physical affection, 6–7
    and premarital sex, 243–245, 281–282
    prostitution, 246–249
    rape, 252–254
    seclusion of, 111, 113–114, 178, 180, 181, 258
    and sexual double standard, 82–83
    as sexual initiator, 279, 280
    status of, 177–178, 183–186, 264, 312
    work activities, 130, 133, 135–137
    See also Children; Wives
Fertility, sexual receptivity and, 301–303
Fictive kin, 114–115
Fiji widows, 332
Fitness concept (Darwin), 15, 57, 58, 115, 231
    versus inclusive fitness, 116
    See also Evolution by natural selection
Fon (West Africa)
    divorce, 79

Fon *(continued)*
   homosexuality, 297–298
   impotence, 148
   joking relationships, 159
   sleeping arrangements, 270
   virginity, 83, 272, 321, 327
Food-gathering societies. *See* Hunter-gatherer
   societies
Food sharing, 15
Food taboos, 93–94
Foreplay, 116–117
Fox (Iowa), 167
Freud, Sigmund, 149
Friendships, 28, 117–119, 140
   See also Attachments
Fulani (Sudan), 242
Fur (Sudan), 321, 323

Ganda (Uganda)
   avoidance customs, 32–33
   divorce, 79
   extramarital sex, 83
   male-female relative status, 61, 62, 184, 185
   marriages, 192
   sex taboos, 291, 292
   sleeping arrangements, 143, 270
Garo (India)
   divorce, 73, 79
   family residences, 104, 126
   marriages, 139, 193
   sexual attitudes, 83, 276, 281
   widowhood, 329
Genealogies
   consanguineal and affinal relationships in, 165,
      167, 169
   See also Kin
Generation-sets, defined, 13
Genetic traits
   as adaptive, 161, 308
   bipedalism, 127–128
   and Darwinian fitness, 57
   environmental impact on, 231–232, 234–235
   reproductive success of, 71–72
   sexual selection of, 308–309
   See also Evolution by natural selection
Gere (Ivory Coast), 21
Germany, 259
Gheg (Albania), 58, 199, 328, 330
Gifts
   during courtship, 55, 121, 201, 205, 257
   food sharing as, 15
   on formal occasions, 14
   as payment for sex, 55, 249, 257, 288
   reciprocal exchange of, 16, 17–18, 121
Girls. *See* Females
Goajiro (Colombia)
   attractiveness criteria, 31, 32
   divorce, 75
   homosexuality, 296
   ideal spouse, 215, 216
   love magic, 175
   marital spying, 57, 58, 156
   prostitution, 248
   sexual behavior, 277, 306
   transvestism, 317
   virginity, 323, 324
Godparenthood, 115
Gond (India)
   childhood sex training, 295
   impotence, 148
   sexual behavior, 249, 289, 306
   sleeping arrangements, 143
Gros Ventre (United States)
   avoidance customs, 32, 33
   divorce, 79
   female seclusion, 114
   marital age, 200
   sexual conversations, 285, 286
   sexual double standard, 62, 83
   virginity, 324
Guilds, 21–22, 23
Gururumba (New Guinea), 14, 133
Gusii (Kenya)
   age-set initiation, 11–12
   attractiveness criteria, 31
   bride price, 17
   family residences, 107, 261
   in-law relationships, 241, 242
   marriages, 104, 154, 178–179
   respect relationships, 264
   sexual boasting, 38

Hadza (Tanzania)
   divorce, 76
   kin attachments, 24–25
   living arrangements, 125, 181–182
   marriages, 202, 259
   rape, 252
   wife beating, 312, 313

Haida (United States)
  descent groups, 69–70
  household composition, 123
  infidelity, 276–277
  as newlyweds, 236
Haitians
  childhood sex training, 295
  female seclusion, 114
  illegitimate children, 245
  marriages, 205
  prostitution, 248
  sexual orientation, 297, 299
  widowers, 333
Hamilton, W. D., 116
  kin selection theory of, 161–164
Hausa (Nigeria)
  avoidance customs, 33
  family residences, 105
  female seclusion, 113
  fictive kin, 114
  impotence, 147–148
  kin group attachments, 28
  newlyweds, 237
  sexual privacy, 305
Havasupai (southwestern United States)
  adolescent social behavior, 3
  chaperonage, 47
  male dominance, 62, 183
  marriages, 96, 220, 237–238
  public display of affection, 4, 5
  sexual double standard, 82
  unmarried pregnancy, 244
  widowers, 333–334
Hawaiians, 172
Hidatsa (United States), 5, 25, 251, 261
Hijras, 317, 318–319
Hindu (India)
  bride theft, 40
  female seclusion, 113
  marriages, 98, 204, 206
  residences, 261
Homosexuality
  cultural attitudes toward, 85, 296, 304, 307
  and lesbianism, 259, 298–299
  as premarital behavior, 297–298
  sexual continence and, 52
  of transvestites, 317, 318
Hopi (southwestern United States)
  attractiveness criteria, 31
  childhood sex training, 294

  descent groups, 69
  elderly, 90, 91, 93
  joking relationships, 158
  marriage ceremonies, 203, 204
  sexual initiation, 288
Households
  avunculocal, 260
  children in, 269–271
  cultural determinants of, 126
  extended family, 101, 123, 313
  matrifocal, 101, 124
  matrilocal, 260, 261–262
  men's houses, 222–224
  neolocal, 260, 262
  of newlyweds, 237–238
  nuclear, 101, 102–103, 126, 313
  patrilocal, 260, 261
  polygynous, 101, 123, 125, 143
  residential layout of, 104–105, 107
  segregation of sexes in, 4, 271
  sleeping arrangements in, 108–109, 142–143, 305
Huichol (Mexico), 5, 236
Human relationships
  characteristic features of, 128–129
  See also Attachments; Marriage; Sexual
    relationships
Human species
  bipedalism of, 127–128
  differential reproduction of, 71–73
  female sexual receptivity of, 302–303
  friendship dependence of, 117–118
  as hunter-gatherer adaptation, 128, 132, 232, 234
  See also Evolution by natural selection
Hunter-gatherer societies
  bride service in, 44
  descent rules in, 70
  family households of, 126, 130
  as human profile, 128, 132, 232, 234
Hunting, sexual continence and, 51, 292
Huron (Ontario), 77, 192, 249
Husbands
  in arranged marriages, 219–220, 259
  bride price rights of, 42
  bride service by, 43–44
  concubines for, 49–50
  as cuckolds, 56–58
  divorce from, 74, 75–76, 77, 78–79
  dowry for, 87
  extramarital relationships of, 83–84, 85, 275, 290
  household arrangements for, 223, 261–262

Husbands *(continued)*
  impotence, 75
  jealousy of, 155–157
  marital reciprocity of, 17
  as newlyweds, 321, 323–324, 327–328
  in polyandrous marriages, 210–211
  premarital relationships of, 82
  sleeping arrangements, 108, 109
  as widowers, 311–312, 333–334
  wife beating, 312–314
  wife sharing, 334–336
  wives' deference to, 61–63
  work activities, 133, 135–137
  See also Males
Husband-wife relationships. *See* Marriage
Hymen, and defloration customs, 63–64
Hypergamy, 144–145

Iban (Malaysia)
  courtship, 53
  divorce, 77, 79–80
  elopement, 97
  marriages, 24, 190, 192–193, 204
  sexual attitudes, 275, 282
  sleeping arrangements, 270
  spouse selection, 220
Ifaluk (Micronesia), 135–136
Ifugao (Philippines)
  fathers-to-be of, 110
  kin group attachments, 27
  marriages, 156–157, 190, 198–199, 205
  rape, 252, 253
  sexual behavior, 187, 276, 279, 281
  in sexual conversations, 286
  sexual double standard, 84
  widowhood, 329, 330
Igbo (Nigeria)
  age-set responsibilities, 12
  in associations, 21, 22
  eating arrangements, 132
  ideal spouse, 214
  sexual attitudes, 275–276, 291
  sleeping arrangements, 108, 271, 324
  widowhood, 328–329
Ijaw (Nigeria), 20–21
Ilocano (Philippines), 105
Ilongot (Philippines), 15, 257
Inca (South America), 93, 148, 248, 332

Incest taboo
  childhood segregation and, 271
  versus exogamy, 99
  explanations for, 148, 149–150
  inbreeding hypothesis on, 150–151
India, betrothals in, 37
Industrial societies, 16, 259. *See also* American (U.S. contemporary) culture
Infants
  birth of, 110–111, 290–291
  of divorce, 76
  killing of, 211, 257–258
  maternal bond with, 128, 129, 131, 143
  See also Children
Infertility, bride price and, 42
Infibulation, 258
Ingalik (Alaska)
  household arrangements, 124–125, 269
  male houses, 223
  rape, 251
  sexual behavior, 187, 280, 289
  sexual double standard, 82
Inis Beag (Ireland), 200
In-laws. *See* Parents-in-law
Inuit (North America), 114–115
Irish
  childhood sex training, 293–294
  in-law relationships, 242–243
  modesty, 227
Iroquois (New York), 91, 171
Islamic cultures, 113, 227–228
Israelis
  child rearing, 102–103
  nonmarriage, 150–151
  sexual behavior, 259

Japanese
  childhood sex training, 294–295
  concubinage, 266
  ideal spouse, 214
  marriages, 195, 267
Javanese
  childhood sex training, 294
  divorce, 73–74, 79
  ideal spouse, 215
  marriages, 192, 236, 261
  sexual behavior, 84, 273, 281–282, 301
  status of women, 61

Jealousy, 58, 153–154, 155–157
Jivaro (Ecuador)
    child betrothal, 48
    family residences, 105, 108
    ideal spouse, 216
    sexual behavior, 51, 305
Joking relationships, 158–159, 167, 285, 286

Kapauku (New Guinea)
    bride price, 41, 42–43
    divorce, 77, 79
    family units, 101
    friendships, 118, 140
    marriages, 69, 139–140, 194–195
    sexual behavior, 38, 246, 288, 291
    unmarried pregnancy, 244
Karimojong (East Africa), 13
Kaska (Alaska)
    avoidance customs, 33
    bride service, 44
    childhood sex training, 295
    divorce, 76
    friendships, 117, 119
    lesbianism, 298
    modesty, 228
    public display of affection, 6
    romantic love, 265
    sexual behavior, 52, 187, 280, 289
    sexual boasting, 38
    sororate custom, 311
    widowers, 334
    wife sharing, 335
Katab (Nigeria), 132
Kazak (central Asia)
    bride price, 43, 283
    child betrothal, 49
    marriages, 144
    sexual negotiation, 249
    sleeping arrangements, 109
Kenuzi Nubians (Egypt), 281–282
Keraki (New Guinea), 278–279, 297
Khalka Mongols, 24, 235, 327
Khmer (Indochina)
    childhood sex training, 295
    divorce, 77
    in sexual conversations, 286
    widowhood, 329, 332
Khoi (southern Africa)
    elderly, 93

    household arrangements, 124
    male-female relative status, 185
    respect relationships, 263
    wife sharing, 335
Kikuyu (Kenya)
    age-set commonality, 12
    childhood sex training, 294
    divorce, 75, 77
    family residences, 105
    female sexual relationships, 50, 247, 335
    impotence, 147
    leisure activities, 138
    modesty, 229
    rape, 252
    sex taboos, 291, 292
Kimam (New Guinea)
    avoidance customs, 33
    child betrothal, 48
    levirate custom, 173
    as newlyweds, 237
    sexual attitudes, 51, 273
    sororate custom, 311
    wife sharing, 335
Kin
    altruism between, 15, 16–17, 161
    based on genetic and marital relationships,
        164–165
    behavioral expectations of, 167–168
    descent rules governing, 64–67
    fictive, 114–115
    food sharing by, 15
    functional limitations of, 19
    joking relationships of, 158, 159, 167–168
    marriages between, 48, 49, 99, 168, 189–190, 193
    as priority relationship, 103, 104
    selection theory regarding, 161–164, 336
    sexual taboos regarding, 148–150, 151, 167
    of spouse groups, 27–28
    wife sharing between, 334–335
Kin selection theory, 161–164
Kinship terminologies
    classificatory, 168, 169, 170
    six systems of, 170–172
Kiowa-Apache (west central United States), 167
Kiribati (Pacific Islands)
    divorce, 78
    female seclusion, 114
    joking relationships, 158
    marriages, 328, 335

Kiwai Papuan (New Guinea)
elderly, 91, 93
homosexuality, 297
work activities, 135–136
Klamath (Oregon), 317, 330
Koniag (Alaska), 318
Konso (Ethiopia)
modesty, 229
sexual attitudes, 51, 273, 286
wife beating, 314
Koreans
concubinage, 50
female seclusion, 111, 113
marriages, 62, 237, 267
nudity, 228
in sexual conversations, 286
widowed, 332, 333, 334
Kpelle (Liberia), 16, 23, 94
!Kung (southern Africa)
avoidance customs, 34
fictive kin, 114–115
gift-giving, 16
household arrangements, 270
ideal spouse, 215
leisure activities, 138
modesty, 228–229
sexual behavior, 51, 58, 276, 279, 305
widowhood, 329
wife sharing, 335
Kurds, 274, 324
Kurtatchi (Solomon Islands), 289
Kutenai (North America) 216, 274, 281, 291
Kwakiutl (United States), 31, 91, 201
Kwoma (New Guinea)
adolescent social behavior, 3, 7
attractiveness criteria, 31
betrothal, 37
childhood sexual behavior, 271–272, 294, 295
divorce, 79
elopement, 96
gift exchange by, 121
homosexuality, 296
kinship reciprocity, 16, 168
modesty, 228, 229
rape, 252, 253
sex taboos, 292
sexual behavior, 188, 280, 283, 304, 305
sexual boasting, 38
sleeping arrangements, 143

unmarried pregnancy, 244
widowhood, 330

Lakher (south Asia)
concubinage, 50
courtship, 53
cuckolded husbands, 58
impotence, 147
marriages, 144–145, 236, 328
rape, 253
respect relationships, 263
sexual behavior, 188, 288, 310
sleeping arrangements, 109, 269
widowhood, 331
Lamba (Zambia), 306
Lamet (Southeast Asia), 53, 174, 222, 223
Lango (Uganda), 147, 306
Lebanese, 286, 327
Leisure activities, 137–138, 180–182
Lenge (Mozambique), 31
Lengua, 93
Lepcha (Tibet)
bride service, 44
homosexuality, 297
marriages, 156, 195, 199, 211, 238
modesty, 229
rape, 251
romantic love, 265
sex taboos, 292
sexual behavior, 44, 83, 116, 273, 275, 279
sexual conversations, 285
unmarried pregnancy, 245
Lesbianism, 259, 298–299
Lesu (New Ireland)
childhood sex training, 294, 295
children's segregation, 269
homosexuality, 297
leisure activities, 181
marriages, 210, 211, 235
rape, 251
same-sex affection, 6
sex taboos, 292
sexual behavior, 83, 249, 275, 280, 289, 306
wife beating, 312
Letter writing, 54
Levirate custom, 173–174, 200, 328, 330
Lhota (Assam), 288
Lineage
defined, 66

as political determinant, 69
Lolo (China), 78, 314
Love, romantic, 265–267. *See also* Affection
Love magic, 175–176, 295
Lozi (Zambia), 79, 96, 156, 323
Lugbara (Uganda), 159, 241
Lunda (Africa), 9

Mace, David, 265
Mace, Vera, 265
Madrid aristocracy, 62
Mae Enga (New Guinea), 179
Males
  adolescent behavior of, 3–4
  age-grade profile of, 8–9
  age-set initiation of, 10–11
  in arranged marriages, 219–220, 259
  in associations, 20, 22–23
  boasting by, 38–39
  castration anxiety of, 226
  concubines for, 49–50
  elderly, 91, 264
  exclusive houses for, 222–224
  first sexual partner of, 300–301
  friendships of, 117–119
  high status of, 183–185
  in homosexual relationships, 296–298
  as hunters and protectors, 127–128, 129–130, 131
  marital age, 199–200
  marriage partner selection by, 220, 221
  modesty, 227–230
  physical affection between, 6
  as rapists, 251, 252
  reproductive strategies of, 73, 256–258
  sleep-crawling, 310–311
  transvestism, 298, 317–319
  work activities, 133, 135–137
  See also Children; Husbands
Manchu (China)
  childhood sex training, 294
  menstrual taboo, 225–226
  virginity, 321
  widowhood, 332
Manus (Oceania)
  avoidance customs, 33, 242
  bride price, 41
  household arrangements, 132, 143
  in joking relationships, 158
  lesbianism, 299

marriages, 177
menstrual taboo, 226
modesty, 227, 229–230
rape, 251
romantic love, 265
wife beating, 312
Mao Enga (New Guinea), 223
Mao (Ethiopia), 323
Maori (New Zealand)
  levirate custom, 173
  marriages, 144, 203
  virginity, 324
  widowhood, 332
Mapuche (Chile)
  courtship, 54, 56
  fathers-to-be, 111
  in-law relationships, 263
  marriages, 4, 62
  sexual behavior, 306, 311
  widowhood, 330–331
Marquesa (Oceania)
  homosexuality, 297
  ideal spouse, 215
  marriages, 190, 210, 211, 212
Marriage
  age at, 199–201, 220
  arranged, 192–195
  attachment in, 4, 24, 103, 217
  betrothal in, 37, 48–49
  ceremonies, 201–204
  courtship before, 52–56
  cuckoldry in, 56–58
  descent groups regulating, 69, 70
  eating arrangements in, 132–133, 140, 223
  economic arrangements before, 40–44, 87, 121
  endogamous, 97–98
  exogamous, 99, 283
  forms of, 205–206
  group, 211–212
  hostility characterizing, 177–179
  household arrangements in, 108–109, 142–143, 260–262, 305
  hypergamy in, 144–145
  intimate versus aloof, 139–142
  jealousy in, 58, 153–154, 155–157
  joking in, 159
  between kin, 48, 49, 168, 189–190, 193, 196–197
  versus kin attachments, 27–28
  leisure activities, 137–138, 180–182

Marriage *(continued)*
    levirate custom of, 173–174, 200, 328, 330
    male-female relative status in, 61–63, 83–84
    monogamous, 206
    of newlyweds, 235–238, 260, 327–328
    polyandrous, 206, 209–211, 212–213
    polygynous, 73, 101, 105, 153–154, 206–207, 208–209, 212–213, 290
    public display of affection, 4–5
    reasons for, 189–191, 302
    and remarriage, 78, 329–334
    romantic love and, 266
    sororate custom of, 311–312
    surrogate, 115
    through woman exchange, 336–337
    of transvestites, 317
    trial, 98–99, 205
    work activities in, 133, 135–137
Marshallese (Oceania)
    defloration customs, 64
    divorce, 80
    ideal spouse, 215
    in joking relationships, 159, 286
    marital jealousy, 155
    prostitution, 247
    sex taboos, 291–292
    sexual behavior, 3, 82, 279, 286, 321
    virginity, 301
Masai (Kenya), 156, 313–314
Mataco (Argentina)
    courtship, 55
    marriages, 4, 155, 198, 218
    sexual behavior, 276, 280, 281, 288–289
Matrilineal descent, 25, 67, 70, 171, 186
Mbundu (Angola)
    childhood segregation, 272
    courtship, 54
    fathers-to-be, 111
    ideal spouse, 217
    leisure activities, 137–138
    lesbianism, 299
    marriages, 198
    unmarried pregnancy, 244
Mbuti (central Africa)
    childhood sex training, 295
    defloration customs, 63–64
    homosexual behavior, 297–298
    marriages, 202, 221, 336–337
    menstrual practices of, 226
    sexual behavior, 188, 249, 276, 306–307

Mehinacu (Brazil), 259, 317
Mende (West Africa)
    associations, 21, 23
    marriages, 190
    sexual behavior, 249, 291
    status of women, 61–62
    wife sharing, 334, 335
Menomini (east central United States), 288
Menstrual taboos, 224–226, 273
Miskito (Central America), 33, 260
Mixtecan (Mexico)
    family residences of, 105, 107, 260
    work activities, 133
Modesty, 227–230
Moiety, 66, 69. *See also* Descent groups
Mojave (southwestern United States), 317
Mongols, 78, 90
Montagnais (Canada), 80
Mossi (West Africa), 241
Mothers
    bilateral descent from, 67
    infants' bond with, 128, 129, 131
    infants sleeping with, 143
    primary attachments to, 24–26, 266
    as seductive/hostile, 141
    See also Parents
Mothers-in-law. *See* Parents-in-law
Mundugumor (New Guinea), 158
Mundurucu (Brazil)
    elderly, 91
    kin group attachments, 15, 27
    male-female relative status, 178, 186–187
    male houses, 223
    rape, 253
Muria Gond (India)
    bride service, 44
    divorce, 44
    elopement, 96
    ideal spouse, 215
    marriages, 191, 194, 203, 204
    sleeping arrangements, 108
Murngin (Australia)
    household arrangements, 125
    kin group attachments, 27
    marriages, 154, 199
    sexual behavior, 188, 275, 288
Muslim cultures, 50

Nama Hottentot (southern Africa), 237, 252
Nama (Nigeria), 299

Nambicuara (Brazil)
  child betrothal by, 48
  leisure activities, 138
  marriages, 62, 196, 235
  public display of affection, 4–5
  sexual behavior, 297, 307
Namesakes
  as kin equivalents, 114–115
Natural selection. *See* Evolution by natural selection
Navajo (Arizona)
  childhood sex training, 294, 295
  divorce, 78
  elderly, 90, 93, 94
  household arrangements, 262
  ideal spouse, 216, 217
  in joking relationships, 158, 159, 286
  kin attachments, 26
  male-female relative status, 185
  marriages, 155, 237
  modesty, 227
  rape, 251
  sexual behavior, 38, 310
  sororate custom, 311
  widowhood, 329, 334
  work activities, 133, 135
Nayar (South India), 103, 210, 264
Negri Sembilan (Pacific Islands), 237
Neo-Darwinism, 161
Newlyweds, 235–238, 260, 327–328. *See also* Marriage
Nicobarese (Asiatic Islands), 54, 185, 329
Nkundo (Zaire)
  defloration customs, 64
  household arrangements, 124
  marriages, 155, 207, 238
  in sexual conversations, 285
  wife sharing, 335
Nuba (Sudan), 4, 306, 331
Nudity, 228
Nuer (Sudan), 10–11, 115
Nyakyusa (Tanzania)
  child betrothal by, 48, 49
  children's segregation by, 269, 270–271
  friendships, 117
  household arrangements, 109, 123–124
  impotence, 148
  marriages, 190, 205–206, 236
  menstrual taboo, 224
  sexual attitudes, 274, 297, 298–299
  sexual conversations, 286
  widowhood, 330

Oedipal complex, 149
Omaha (North America)
  elderly, 90, 91
  friendships, 118
  kinship terminology, 170–171
  levirate custom, 173
  marriages, 24
  secret societies, 23
  widowhood, 329, 334
Orokaiva (New Guinea)
  friendships, 28
  marriages, 190, 236
  sexual attitudes, 277, 288
Otoro Nuba (Sudan), 54–55, 123, 188
Oto (west central), 288

Paiute (southwestern United States)
  courtship, 53–54
  marriages, 156, 238
  wife beating, 313–314
Pakistani widows, 331
Palauan (Pacific Islands), 20, 26, 64
Papago (southwestern United States), 132, 180, 265, 295
Parents
  children segregated from, 269–271
  children's sexual reservation with, 285–286
  courtship role of, 53–54
  elopement reaction of, 96–97
  and godparenthood, 115
  marriages arranged by, 192–195, 199–200, 219–220, 221, 259, 282
  newlyweds living with, 260–262
Parents-in-law
  avoidance relationships with, 32–33, 34, 95, 241–242, 261
  bride-price payments to, 40–42, 94
  bride service for, 43–44
  and divorce grounds, 75–76
  newlyweds living with, 260–262
  respect relationships with, 263
Patrilineal descent, 65, 67, 70, 170–171
Pawnee (U.S. Plains)
  friendships, 118
  household arrangements, 124
  marriages, 210
  nudity, 228
  prostitution, 247
Pentecost (Oceania), 118
Poison oracle, 177

Pokot (Kenya), 267
Politics
  lineage determinants in, 69
  male-female relative status in, 183
  respect patterns and, 264–265
Pomo (California)
  elderly, 93, 94
  male houses, 222–223
  newlyweds, 238
  secret societies, 23
Popoluca (Mexico), 44, 123, 314
Poro secret society, 23
Pregnancies
  premarital, 84–85, 243–245
Promiscuity, 246, 247, 282–283
  versus sexual diversity, 245
Property
  elderly ownership of, 90, 94
  and male-female relative status, 183, 185
  marital consolidation of, 196
  sexual exclusivity as, 276
  of widows, 330–331
  versus woman exchange, 337
Prostitution, 246–249
Pukapuka (Oceania)
  attractiveness criteria, 31
  childhood sex training, 294
  defloration customs, 64
  marriages, 203
  sexual behavior, 297, 305, 306
  sleeping arrangements, 143
Punjabi (South Asia), 199–200, 279, 304
Purdah. See Females, seclusion of

Quiche (Guatemala)
  concubinage, 50, 220
  divorce, 79, 220
  infidelity, 275
  marriages, 78, 235–236
  wife beating, 314

Rajput (India)
  dowry, 87
  female seclusion, 57–58
  marriages, 139
  status of women, 61, 113, 184
Rakshasa (marriage by capture), 40
Rape, 251–254
Raziyya Begam, 266

Religion, male-female status in, 183, 185
Reproduction
  environmental impact on, 72
  female strategies for, 87, 249, 256, 258–259
  lack of, 74–75
  male strategies for, 72–73, 254, 256–258
  male versus female investment in, 308–309
  to maximize fitness, 57, 71–72, 115–116, 161
  in polygynous marriages, 213
  and sexual double standard, 85
  See also Evolution by natural selection
Residences. *See* Households
Respect relationships, 263–265
Riffian (North Africa)
  infidelity, 275
  levirate custom, 173
  sororate custom, 312
  virginity, 321, 324, 328
Romantic love, 265–267
Rwala
  courtship, 53
  marriages, 235, 266
  rape, 252
  sexual behavior, 297, 299
  unmarried pregnancy, 244
  virginity, 323–324
  wife beating, 314

Saami, 244, 292
Samoans
  in associations, 20
  avoidance customs, 33
  descent rules, 65
  elderly, 91
  family residences, 107, 261, 272–273
  gift exchange, 121
  kin reciprocity, 16
  rape, 253
  sexual behavior, 266, 288
Sanpoil (northwestern United States), 288
Santal (India)
  bride theft, 40
  male-female relative status, 184, 185
  marriages, 144
Saramaka (Suriname)
  household arrangements, 124
  impotence, 147
  modesty, 229
  as newlyweds, 235

sexual conversations, 286
virginity, 321, 323
widowed, 173, 332
Saulteaux (North America)
joking relationships, 158
lesbianism, 298
sexual behavior, 116, 187, 288, 306
transvestism, 317
Sebei (Uganda), 178
Semang (Malaysia)
elderly, 93
as newlyweds, 236
sexual behavior, 291, 305
status of women, 312
Sex, extramarital
and cuckoldry, 56–58
cultural attitudes toward, 117, 303–304
as divorce grounds, 75
double standard for, 58, 83–84, 85–86
jealousy over, 155–157, 276
postpartum sex taboo and, 290
prohibitions lifted on, 277
versus promiscuity, 245
punishment for, 275–276
as reproductive strategy, 73, 85, 246, 259–260
Sex, premarital
cultural attitudes toward, 303, 304
double standard for, 82–83
as fertility test, 282
and marital expectations, 282–283
percentage engaging in, 284
pregnancies from, 84–85, 282
punishment for, 281–282
Sexual relations
abstinence from, 51–52, 54
avoidance, 34–35
boasting about, 38–39
chaperons' restriction of, 47
with concubines, 49–50
conversations about, 285–287
during courtship, 54, 311
cultural attitudes toward, 273–274
and defloration, 63–64
double standard in, 82–86
evolutionary changes in, 131
exogamy rules and, 99
first partner in, 300–301
foreplay in, 116–117
frequency of, 278–279

gift exchange for, 55, 249, 257, 288
and impotence, 147–148
initiation of, 187–188, 279–280
and joking, 159, 167
love magic in, 175–176
marriage type reflected in, 141–142
and modesty, 227, 228–229
of newlyweds, 235–236, 327–328
privacy in, 304–307
promiscuity in, 245–246
by rape, 253–254
by sleep-crawling, 310–311
taboos on, 148–151, 167, 225, 271, 290–292
See also Homosexuality; Sex, extramarital;
Sex, premarital
Sexual selection, of reproduction traits, 308, 309.
See also Evolution by natural selection
Sharanahua (Peru), 259
Shavante (Brazil)
age-grade segregation, 12, 13
divorce, 76, 78
female reproductive strategy, 259
friendships, 118
leisure activities, 180
male houses, 223
modesty, 228
polygyny, 73
Sherpa (Nepal)
household arrangements, 123
levirate custom, 173
sexual behavior, 84, 156, 275
sleep-crawling, 311
unmarried pregnancy, 245
Shilluk (Sudan), 109, 247
Silwa, 264
Siriono (South America)
attractiveness criteria, 31
bride service, 44
kin attachments, 27
leisure activities, 180
marriages, 153, 154, 196, 202, 211–212
modesty, 228
rape, 251
sexual behavior, 276, 277, 305
widowhood, 329
Siuai (Oceania)
attractiveness criteria, 31
first sexual partner, 300, 301
friendships, 117

Siuai *(continued)*
    household arrangements, 104–105, 124, 126
    ideal spouse, 217
    illegitimate children, 244–245
    leisure activities, 180
    male houses, 223
    marriages, 153, 196–197, 207–208
    menstruation practices, 226
    rape, 251–252, 253
    sexual behavior, 187–188, 246, 273, 305, 327
    sexual conversations, 286
Siwan (Egypt), 297–298
Slave (Canada), 5, 285
Sleep-crawling, 310–311
Somali
    bride price, 41
    kin group attachments, 27
    marriages, 61, 236
    virginity, 324
Songhai (North Africa), 132
Songs, as sexual initiation technique, 288
Sororate custom, 311–312
Spouse beating, 312–315
Sri Lanka, 37
Stem family, 101
Subanum (Philippines), 40–41, 200, 204
Sudanese, 4, 171
Suku (Zaire), 27, 237
Swazi (East Africa), 41

Taboos
    food, 93–94
    incest, 99, 148, 149–151, 271
    menstrual, 224–226
    postpartum sex, 290–291
    on sexual activity, 291–292
    on sexual conversation, 285–286
Taira (British Guiana), 107, 133, 135
Taiwanese, 150
Tallensi (Ghana)
    descent group influence, 69
    divorce, 74
    incest taboo, 149
    marriages, 57, 156, 191
    sexual behavior, 188, 273, 277, 281, 321
    in sexual conversations, 286
    sleeping arrangements, 109
    status of women, 184
Tanala (Madagascar)
    eating arrangements, 76, 77, 132

first sexual partner, 300–301
    homosexual behavior, 297–298
    ideal spouse, 217
    impotence, 147
    marriages, 154, 196, 197, 209
    modesty, 229–230
    sexual behavior, 82, 245–246
    transvestism, 317
    widowhood, 331
Tarahumara (Mexico), 158, 167
Teda (Sudan), 132, 252
Temne (West Africa), 23
Tenejumine story, 317
Tepoztlán (southern Mexico)
    bride service, 44
    courtship, 54
    respect relationships, 115, 263
    work activities, 135
Thai
    divorce, 76
    household arrangements, 124
    modesty, 229
    newlyweds, 238
    sexual behavior, 76
Thonga (Mozambique)
    courtship, 55, 257
    incest, 148
    segregation of children, 270
    sex taboos, 292
    sexual behavior, 246, 249, 288
Tibetans, 210, 211
Tikopia (Oceania)
    kinship relationships, 165
    nudity, 228
    rape, 252
    sexual behavior, 155, 276
    virginity, 323
    widowhood, 331–332
Timbira (Brazil), 25–26, 246
Tiriki (Kenya), 8–9, 20
Tiv (Nigeria)
    age-set protection, 12
    female role, 58, 335, 337
    political allegiances, 69
Tiwi (Australia), 48, 95, 329
Toda (India)
    defloration customs, 63
    infidelity, 276
    marriages, 210, 211, 212
    status of women, 184

Tongan (western Polynesia), 31, 209
Transvestism, 147, 298, 317–319
Trobriand (New Guinea)
    elopement of, 96–97
    household arrangements, 125, 260
    marriages, 96, 139, 221, 235–236
    prostitution, 248
    romantic love, 266
    same-sex relationships, 6, 117–118
    sexual behavior, 116, 296, 305
    status of women, 184
Truk (Oceania)
    avoidance customs, 34
    childhood sex training, 294
    courtship, 54
    on homosexuality, 304
    kin attachments, 24–25
    marriage ceremonies, 202–203
    prosmiscuity view, 246
    same-sex friendships, 118
    sexual behavior, 38, 116, 281, 300, 306
    sexual initiation, 279, 288, 289
    sleep-crawling, 310
    sleeping arrangements, 109
    wife beating, 312
    wife sharing, 334
Trumai (Brazil)
    child betrothal, 49
    leisure activities, 180–181
    marriages, 4
    nudity, 228
    rape, 251
    sexual behavior, 38, 188, 305
Tswana (Botswana), 80, 286
Tuareg (Sahara)
    courtship, 187
    in-law relationships, 241
    marriages, 197
    status of women, 62
Turks
    impotence, 147
    in-law relationships, 242, 261
    leisure activities, 181
    wife beating, 312
Twana (Puget Sound), 143

Ube (Ivory Coast), 21
Ukrainians, 61, 184–185, 261
Ulad-Nail (Algeria), 248
Uwougu, 102

Victorian England, 20
Vietnamese, 38, 216, 246
Virginity
    cultural attitudes toward, 52, 245–246, 321
    and defloration, 63–64, 300, 328
    double standard enforcing, 82–83
    as marital value, 282–283
    proof of, 321
    wedding night, 321, 323–324, 327–328

Wallace, Alfred Russell, 231
War
    rape during, 251–252
    and residence patterns, 262
    sex taboos during, 291–292
Warriors
    age-grade profile of, 8–9, 20
Wedding night, 321, 323–324, 327–328
West Punjabi (south Asia)
    kin attachments, 26–27
    leisure activities, 180
    male status of, 62, 222
    virginity, 323
Western Apache (southwestern United States), 288
Widowers
    remarriage rules for, 333–334
    sororate custom of, 311–312
Widows
    as concubines, 50
    levirate custom of, 173–174, 200, 328, 330
    as prostitutes, 247
    remarriage rules for, 329–332
Witchcraft, 75, 147
Witoto (Amazon), 94
Wives
    barren, 74–75, 115
    beating of, 312–314
    as co-wives, 95
    divorce from, 17, 74, 75, 76, 77, 78–79
    exchange of, 17, 336–337
    extramarital relationships of, 51–52, 56–57,
      83–84, 85, 275, 276
    household arrangements, 108, 109, 123–124,
      260–261
    illegitimate children of, 85
    in-law relationships, 241–243
    jealousy of, 155, 156–157
    in lesbian relationships, 299
    marital attachment of, 24
    as newlyweds, 321, 323–324, 327–328

Wives *(continued)*
    as nonvirgins, 321, 323–324
    in polygynous marriages, 153–154, 207–209
    premarital relationships of, 82–83, 85
    prostitution, 248
    qualities desired in, 214–217
    rape of, 252
    sharing of, 334–336
    work activities, 130, 133, 135–137
    See also Females
Wobe (Ivory Coast), 21
Wogeo (New Guinea)
    bride theft, 39
    first sexual partner, 300
    household arrangements, 123
    ideal spouse, 216
    marriages, 190, 191, 193, 236
    menstrual taboos, 224, 226
    sexual behavior, 273, 276, 277, 281, 305
    sexual double standard, 84

Wolof (Senegal), 147, 197

!Xhosa (South Africa), 93

Yahgan (Tierra del Fuego), 58, 77, 272
Yako (Nigeria), 65–66
Yanomamo (Brazil and Venezuela)
    elderly, 91
    reproductive strategies, 73, 257, 258
    respect relationships, 263
    wife beating, 313
Yapese (Oceania), 51, 292
Yokuts (California), 90, 222, 223
Yoruba (West Africa), 21–22, 23
Yukaghir (Siberia), 220
Yurok (California), 206, 306

Zulu (South Africa), 12
Zuni (New Mexico), 143, 224–226